The Law
Relating to Banking

The Law

Relating to Banking

By

T. G. REEDAY

LL.B.(Hons.)(Lond.), F.C.I.S., A.I.B.
of Lincoln's Inn, Barrister;
First Place, Final Examination, Institute of Bankers,
Beckett, Whitehead and Charles Reeve Prizeman;
a Head of Department, School of Law,
Polytechnic of Central London

FOURTH EDITION

LONDON
BUTTERWORTHS
1980

ENGLAND:	BUTTERWORTH & CO. (PUBLISHERS) LTD. LONDON: 88 Kingsway, WC2B 6AB
AUSTRALIA:	BUTTERWORTHS PTY. LTD. SYDNEY: 586 Pacific Highway, Chatswood, NSW 2067 Also at Melbourne, Brisbane, Adelaide and Perth
CANADA:	BUTTERWORTH & CO. (CANADA) LTD. TORONTO: 2265 Midland Avenue, Scarborough M1P 4S1
NEW ZEALAND:	BUTTERWORTHS OF NEW ZEALAND LTD. WELLINGTON: 77–85 Custom House Quay
SOUTH AFRICA:	BUTTERWORTH & CO. (SOUTH AFRICA) (PTY.) LTD. DURBAN: 152–154 Gale Street
U.S.A.:	BUTTERWORTH & CO. (PUBLISHERS) INC. BOSTON: 10 Tower Office Park, Woburn, Mass. 01801

©

Butterworth & Co. (Publishers) Ltd.

1980

ISBN Casebound 0 406 64766 6

Limp 0 406 64767 4

Printed in Great Britain
by W & J Mackay Limited, Chatham

CITATION OF CASES

SCOTTISH CASES

THE older Scottish cases are reported in Morison's *Dictionary*, consisting of 22 volumes. These cases are cited by their year and the page on which they appear: thus, (1703) Mor. 1062. There are five supplementary volumes, known as Brown's *Supplement*. In addition, there are other collections of cases, such as Elchies' *Decisions* (2 vols., 1733-54), Hume's *Decisions* (1 vol., 1781-1822), and Bell's octavo and folio *Cases* (2 vols., 1790-5).

The Faculty Collection contains cases from 1738 to 1841. The volumes most frequently referred to are those covering the years between 1808 and 1825. These reports are cited by the date of the decision: thus, 10th January 1812, F.C.

The Session cases were in the hands of private reporters until 1907, when they were acquired by the Faculty of Advocates. From 1907 onwards they are cited thus: 1907 S.C. 15. The earlier Session Cases consist of five series, which, strictly speaking, should be referred to by the year (in brackets) and the initial letter of the editor's, or a reporter's, name, although in practice the date or the bracketing is frequently omitted.

The citation is as follows:—

- (1831) 10 S. 82 refers to the first series (16 volumes, from 1821 to 1838), edited by Shaw.
- (1847) 10 D 82, to the second series (24 volumes, from 1838 to 1862), edited by Dunlop.
- (1871) 10 M. 82, to the third series (11 volumes, from 1862 to 1873), edited by Macpherson.
- (1882) 10 R. 82, to the fourth series (25 volumes, from 1873 to 1898), edited by Rettie.
- (1903) 5 F. 82, to the fifth series (8 volumes, 1898 to 1906), referred to as Fraser.

There are also other contemporaneous reports, viz., the *Scottish Jurist* (45 volumes running from 1829 to 1865), referred to as Sc. Jur.; the *Scottish Law Reporter* (61 volumes, from 1865 and ending in 1924), referred to as S.L.R.; and the *Scots Law Times* (beginning in 1893, and referred to as S.L.T.). The *Session Notes*, a series of short reports of cases not yet reported at length elsewhere, began in 1925 and ended in 1948; these reports are referred to by the year with S.N. added. A similar series of short reports has appeared since 1949 in the *Scots Law Times*, referred to as S.L.T. (Notes). A series of reports of cases decided in the Land Court was begun in 1912; the mode of reference is 1953 S.L.C.R. 40. Land Court decisions have also been reported, since 1964, in the *Scots Law Times*, referred to as, e.g., 1964 S.L.T. (Land Court) 4.

Decisions in the Sheriff Court are reported in the *Scots Law Times* (e.g. 1955 S.L.T. (Sh. Ct.) 100) and also in the *Scottish Law Review* (e.g. (1885) 1 Sh. Ct. Rep. 6).

The reports of decisions of the House of Lords in Scottish cases appear at the beginning of the Session Cases, and are cited thus: 10 M. (H.L.) 4; 1907 S.C. (H.L.) 4. The older cases are to be found in private reports.

These are:—

Robertson's Reports (1 vol.), 1707-1727.
Paton's Reports (6 vols.), 1726-1821.
Dow's Reports (6 vols.), 1813-1818.
Bligh's Reports (6 vols.), 1819-1821.
Shaw's Reports (2 vols.), 1821-1824.
Wilson and Shaw's Reports (7 vols.), 1825-1835.
Shaw and M'Lean's Reports (3 vols.), 1835-1838.
M'Lean and Robinson's Reports (1 vol.), 1839.
Robinson's Reports (2 vols.), 1840-1841.
Bell's Reports (7 vols.), 1842-1850.
Macqueen's Reports (4 vols.), 1851-1865.

Criminal (Justiciary) Cases are reported in the Justiciary reports, viz.:— Shaw, 1819-1831 (1 vol.); Syme, 1826-1830 (1 vol.); Swinton, 1835-1841 (2 vols.); Broun, 1842-1845 (2 vols); Arkley, 1846-1848 (1 vol.); J. Shaw, 1848-1851 (1 vol.); Irvine, 1851-1868 (5 vols.); Couper, 1868-1885 (5 vols.); White, 1885-1893 (3 vols.); and Adam, 1893-1916 (7 vols.). From 1874 to 1917 Justiciary Cases are also included in the volumes of Session Cases, and the reference to these reports is, e.g., (1892) 10 R. (J.) 1, 1916 S.C. (J.) 1. From 1917 onwards the criminal reports are referred to as, e.g., 1917 J.C. 100, and are usually bound with Session Cases.

ENGLISH CASES

The earlier English cases appear in private reports. These are generally cited by the initials of the reporters' names, but there are a few in which this is not so. Thus: Q.B. stands for Adolphus and Ellis's Reports (1841-52, 18 vols.); H.L.C. for Clark's Reports (1846-66, 12 vols.); Exch. for Welsby, Hurlston and Gordon's Reports (1848-56, 11 vols.).

In 1865 the Council of Law Reporting undertook the issuing of reports, and their publications are called "Law Reports" (L.R.). The Courts were separate until the Judicature Act, when they became Divisions of the High Court. Hence the Court of Queen's Bench (or Q.B.) in 1875 became Queen's Bench Division (or Q.B.D.). From 1865 to 1875 the letters L.R. are therefore prefixed in the citation of these Reports, followed by the number of the volume and the name of the court: thus, L.R. 3 H.L.; L.R. 5 Q.B.; L.R. 5 Ch.; L.R. 5 C.P. (i.e., Common Pleas); L.R. 3 Ex. (i.e., Exchequer); L.R. 3 Eq. (i.e. Equity); L.R. 3 P. & D. (i.e., Probate and Divorce).

From 1876 to 1890 L.R. is omitted and D. added for the Divisions, and the volumes are cited consecutively according to the courts; thus 2 App. Cas.; 2 Q.B.D.; 2 Ch.D.; 3 C.P.D.; 2 Ex.D.; 2 P.D. In 1881 the Queen's

Bench, Common Pleas, and Exchequer Divisions were consolidated into the Queen's Bench Division—hence C.P.D. and Ex.D. appear only between 1875 and 1881.

After 1890 the year is inserted in square brackets and D. omitted: thus, [1891] A.C., or Q.B., or Ch., or P. In 1953, the series known as the *Weekly Law Reports* began, replacing the *Weekly Notes*. It is cited thus: [1955] 1 W.L.R. 100; cases reported in volumes 2 or 3 of the *Weekly Law Reports* are intended for publication in the " Law Reports " series in due course.

In addition to the Law Reports, there are other series of English reports of considerable importance. Those of a general nature are the *All England Reports* (cited thus, for example: [1952] 2 All E.R. 100), the *Times Law Reports* (ended 1953, and cited latterly thus, for example: [1952] 1 T.L.R. 100), the *Justice of the Peace Reports* (cited thus, for example: 50 J.P. 100). There are, in addition, several series of specialised reports such as the *Tax Cases* (50 Tax Cas. or T.C. 100) and *Lloyd's List Reports* ([1952] 1 Lloyd's Rep. 100). The important series of the *Law Times Reports* ran from 1859 to 1947 and the *Law Journal Reports* from 1832 to 1949.

To my friends and acquaintances now or formerly in the business of banking, and especially to the late Owain W. Jones, LL.B., A.I.B., Barrister.

Preface to the Fourth Edition

Any book which endeavours to deal with a wide-ranging spectrum of law is particularly susceptible to changes in the law. The past four years have seen an especially heavy flow of statutes, statutory instruments and cases, which have been incorporated in the text where appropriate. I am obliged to the publishers and the printers for their co-operation in fitting in at the proof stage some amendments which occurred in December 1979 so that this edition is as up-to-date as it is possible to be. The new Government's Companies Bill 1979 is noted at the end of Chapter 4, but as it had not become law by the end of 1979, it should emerge as the Companies Act 1980. Despite its compendious title the Banking Act 1979 has changed little in this book, as the Act is largely concerned with the control of banks as organisations. The Consumer Credit Act 1974 continues to make slow and laborious progress towards full implementation: no doubt it will get there someday, for as the poet Swinburne puts it:

> . . . even the weariest river
> Winds somewhere safe to sea.

It made another move forward on 27 January 1980 when the repeal of the Moneylenders Act 1927, mentioned on page 30, came largely into force.

On a happier note, the Institute of Bankers celebrated its centenary in 1979; and unless something drastic happens, the Bills of Exchange Act should do likewise in two years' time.

As with the two preceding editions I must express my appreciation and thanks to Mr. R. McC. M. Adams, Resident Solicitor of the National Westminster Bank Limited, for his helpful comments on current developments; to Butterworth's editorial staff for their general guidance and the revision of the index and of the tables of statutes and cases; and to my one-time banking colleague in Leeds, Mrs. Angela E. Powell, for her assistance in proof-reading.

January, 1980   T. G. REEDAY.

Preface to the First Edition

"A prudent man shuns hyaenas;
No banker is imprudent.
No banker fails to shun hyaenas."

Lewis Carroll

This syllogism, or flawed logic, first caught my attention long before I commenced a career destined to fluctuate between banking and the law. The falsity of the second line is shown by the number of cases which have been decided adversely to banks, though they must be set against many millions of banking transactions which are happily and successfully concluded. The justification for this book as a new assortment of familiar topics is that it is designed to meet the tri-composite syllabus of the Institute of Bankers in its subject, Law Relating to Banking. It is hoped that the book will be of assistance to present and future bankers, as well as perhaps to other students who may be particularly interested in this aspect of the commercial scene.

The pattern of the book is based on the three Sections of the Institute syllabus, starting with a resumé of the law of contract, the bedrock of the whole subject, followed by chapters on Agency, Partnership, Companies and Bankruptcy to complete Section A. Then come four chapters covering the securities most commonly taken by banks—land, life policies, stocks and shares, and guarantees—which comprise Section B. The last five chapters deal with Section C, together with promissory notes which have been added for the sake of completeness, and include the full text of the Bills of Exchange Act 1882 and the Cheques Act 1957.

For bibliography, readers seeking the larger air on individual topics are recommended to turn to the following other Butterworth publications: Stevens' *Mercantile Law*; Cheshire and Fifoot's *Law of Contract*; Fridman's *Law of Agency*; Underhill's *Law of Partnership*; Magnus and Estrin's *Companies: Law and Practice*; Cheshire's *Modern Real Property*; and finally Paget's *Law of Banking*, to which all students of banking in the last resort are debtors.

I would like to thank Butterworth's editorial staff for their valuable help, particularly in providing the index and the tables of cases and statutes.

T. G. REEDAY.

April, 1968

Contents

CHAPTER 4—COMPANIES

CHAPTER 5—BANKRUPTCY

CHAPTER 10—BILLS OF EXCHANGE—INTERPRETATION, PARTIES, CONSIDERATION AND NEGOTIATION

CHAPTER 11—BILLS OF EXCHANGE—DUTIES OF THE HOLDER

CHAPTER 12—BILLS OF EXCHANGE—LIABILITY OF PARTIES, DISCHARGE OF BILLS, ETC.

CHAPTER 13—CHEQUES

CHAPTER 14—PROMISSORY NOTES AND SUPPLEMENTARY MATTERS

Table of Statutes

References in this Table to *"Statutes"* are to Halsbury's Statutes of England (Third Edition) showing the volume and page at which the annotated text of the Act will be found. Page references printed in bold type indicate where the Act is set out in part or in full.

Table of Cases

Chapter 1

Contract

INTRODUCTION

This opening chapter is a resumé of the law of contract, because
although the circle of the law relating to banking includes segments of
other branches of the law such as tort, the area within its circumfer-
ence is largely that of contract, for the relationship of banker and
customer is a contractual one, being usually that of debtor and
creditor or, less frequently, when the customer has loan or overdraft
facilities, creditor and debtor. Lingering ideas that the relationship
was a fiduciary one (i.e. that the bank held the money in trust for the
customer) or simply one of safe custody of the money were rejected by
the House of Lords in *Foley* v. *Hill* (1848), where it was held that the
relationship was the ordinary one of debtor and creditor; money paid
in became the banker's money to make what profit for himself that he
could, subject to his contractual liability to repay the money when
demanded.

The law of contract is particularly interesting as being the branch
of law most often encountered by everyone in daily life, not merely by
students in examinations. From childhood days when they buy their
first packet of sweets from the local shop many persons operate the
law of contract daily, whether they appreciate that fact or not, for
contracts cover a vast range of human activities from buying a newspaper or travelling on public transport to business deals involving
enormous sums.

TYPES OF CONTRACTS

A contract is an agreement to do or refrain from doing some act which
will be enforced by the law. Contracts fall into three classes:

(1) Contracts of record, which are obligations imposed by a court,
e.g. a judgment debt. They derive their binding force from the authority of the Court and must normally be executed immediately. In so far

as these obligations are imposed from above independently of consent, they are not contracts in the general sense, and for that reason will not be considered further.

(2) Specialty contracts (i.e. contracts under seal, or deeds), which must be written, sealed and delivered. By s. 73 of the Law of Property Act 1925 a person who executes a deed must also sign it or place his mark on it, and by s. 74 a deed is executed by a company through the affixing of its seal. The writing may be done with any instrument, and on paper or parchment, and the seal may be a wafer, or a bit of sealing wax, or the printed letters "L.S." in a circle ("Locus Sigilli"—the place of the seal). This last method, which is now common, was upheld by the Court of Appeal in *First National Securities, Ltd.* v. *Jones* (1978), where a mortgagor of land challenged the validity of his legal charge on the basis that it was not executed as a deed. The document began "Now This Deed Witnesseth", and ended with "Signed Sealed and Delivered by the above-named Mortgagor in the presence of . . .". Across the printed circle was the mortgagor's signature. Held, the legal charge was validly executed as a deed; in modern times the encircled "L.S." was a familiar feature of documents intended to serve the purpose of the seal if the signatory intended to deliver the document as his deed; the mortgagor had placed his signature across the circle and this was sufficient evidence that the document had been executed as the mortgagor's deed. One of the judges thought that it would still have been valid, even if the signature was not over the circle but opposite the words "Signed Sealed and Delivered".

Delivery may be actual, i.e the handing over of the deed, or constructive, i.e. inferred, as by words importing an intention to deliver. If a conditional delivery is made to someone not a party to the deed, the document is called an "escrow", and takes effect only when the condition is fulfilled. In *Glessing* v. *Green* (1975) the Court of Appeal held that where in a sale of land a conveyance is executed in escrow there must be a time limit within which the implied condition of the escrow is to be performed and that the purchaser cannot insist on the right to perform the condition free from any such limit. Specialty contracts derive their binding force from the form in which they are made, and, except for contracts in restraint of trade, do not require consideration.

(3) Simple contracts, i.e. all contracts outside the previous categories, which derive their binding force from mutual agreement and must be supported by consideration. Simple contracts may be made either orally or in writing or by conduct, or they may be partly written and partly verbal. In a simple contract a statement is presumptive evidence only, and not conclusive evidence of its truth,

whereas a party to a deed is "estopped" (prevented by law) from denying the truth of statements made therein.

In general, contracting parties may make their contract in any way they choose, but there are occasions when the law prescribes a particular mode of contracting, viz:

(a) Contracts which must be under seal. These include (i) gratuitous promises, or contracts made without consideration, such as gifts to be handed over in the future; (ii) leases of land for more than 3 years; (iii) conditional bills of sale, and (iv) transfers of British ships or shares therein.

(b) Contracts which must be in writing. These include (i) bills of exchange and promissory notes; (ii) contracts of marine insurance; (iii) consumer credit agreements; and (iv) consumer hire agreements. The last two are now regulated by the Consumer Credit Act 1974 which sets up a system of licensing by the Director General of Fair Trading (an office created by the Fair Trading Act 1973) with new terminology and comprehensive documentation. Broadly speaking, the Act applies to credit extended to individuals, not corporations, with an upper limit of £5,000. However, by s. 38 (1) of the Banking Act 1979 the Director General of Fair Trading is obliged to exempt banks from the burdensome documentation in relation to overdrafts required by Part V of the 1974 Act unless he considers it would be against the public interest to do so. Under s. 185 of the 1974 Act there is exemption from supplying to all parties to a joint overdraft the periodic statements of account required by s. 78 (4) where one of the joint debtors has signed a dispensing notice, and s. 38 (3) of the Banking Act 1979 makes it clear that such a dispensing notice is operative also in relation to any subsequent agreement which modifies the original agreement.

(c) Contracts which are unenforceable by action unless evidenced by some memorandum in writing signed by the party to be charged or his agent. These consist of (i) a promise to answer for the debt, default, or miscarriage of another person (a guarantee): s. 4 of the Statute of Frauds 1677; and (ii) any contract for the sale or other disposition of land or any interest in land: s. 40 of the Law of Property Act 1925. The memorandum required need not be on one piece of paper; it may extend over several, provided one at least is signed and all are sufficiently connected to each other and are consistent so that they can be read together. If there is no memorandum the contract is unenforceable, except that in certain cases for the sale and leasing of land part performance of the agreement by one party with the other's consent will be admitted in lieu of writing, e.g. where a person who has orally agreed to buy a house is allowed to decorate it or make alterations to it.

In *Steadman* v. *Steadman* (1974) the House of Lords reviewed the doctrine of part performance and held that in order to establish facts amounting to part performance it was necessary for a plaintiff to show that he had acted to his detriment and that the acts in question were such as to indicate on a balance of probabilities that they had been performed in reliance on a contract with the defendant which was consistent with the contract alleged; there was no general rule that payment of a sum of money could never constitute part performance.

ELEMENTS OF CONTRACT

To constitute a valid contract the following elements must be present:
  1 Offer and Acceptance.
  2 An Intention that the agreement shall result in contractual relations.
  3 Form or Consideration.
  4 Capacity of the parties to contract.
  5 Reality of Consent.
  6 Legality of Object.

If any one or more of these constituent elements is missing, the contract will be, according to the circumstances, void, voidable or unenforceable.

Void means destitute of all legal effect, the whole transaction is a nullity. The expression "void contract" is really a contradiction in terms because there has never been a contract.

Voidable means capable of affirmation or rejection at the option of one of the parties, the other party having no such option. In other words, the contract contains some flaw, of which one of the parties may, if he chooses, take advantage and repudiate the contract. This option will, however, be lost if there is unreasonable delay, if benefits have been received, if *restitutio in integrum* is impossible (i.e. the parties cannot be restored to their original positions), or if third parties have acquired rights for value under the contract.

Unenforceable means that the contract is valid but cannot be enforced by action owing to some technical defect, i.e. failure to comply with statutory requirements, either by reason of lapse of time, or want of written form, or absence of a stamp. Such a contract may become enforceable in the future if the particular defect is cured. A new type of unenforceable contract has arisen under s. 40 of the

Consumer Credit Act 1974, which provides that the consequence of failure to obtain a licence where required by the Act is that any regulated agreement made by the creditor or owner while unlicensed (other than a non-commercial agreement) is unenforceable against the debtor or hirer. The Director General of Fair Trading is empowered in certain circumstances to make an order that regulated agreements made by a trader during that period are to be treated as if he had been licensed.

The essentials of a contract will now be discussed in more detail.

OFFER AND ACCEPTANCE

There must be mutual assent by the parties to the terms of the contract, and this consists of a definite offer or proposal by one party and its unqualified acceptance by the other party. The offer and/or acceptance may be by words spoken or written (i.e. express), or by acts or conduct (i.e. implied). The offer may be specific, that is, made to a definite person or persons; or it may be general, that is, made to the general public or the world at large. A specific offer can be accepted only by the party to whom it is addressed.

The classic case of a general offer which any member of the public who learns of it may turn into an agreement by accepting it is: *Carlill* v. *Carbolic Smoke Ball Co.* (1893). The defendants advertised that they would pay £100 to any person who succumbed to influenza after using one of their smoke balls, a medical preparation. The plaintiff read the advertisement, bought and used the ball as directed but, nevertheless, caught influenza. She sued for the £100. *Held* by the Court of Appeal: the advertisement was an offer to contract which the plaintiff had accepted by performing the conditions and she was entitled to the £100. In this case the commendation of goods was sufficiently explicit for the law to be able to enforce it, but often trade puffs or boasts (such as "the best value on the market") are too nebulous to become part of the terms of a contract.

An offer lapses: (i) if not accepted within a reasonable time or within the time specified, if any: *Ramsgate Victoria Hotel Co.* v. *Montefiore* (1866), where an offer to buy shares made on June 8th was accepted on November 23rd, the acceptance was held to be invalid as an unreasonable length of time had elapsed before it was made; or (ii) if either party dies before the offer is accepted.

An offer may be revoked, either expressly or impliedly, at any time before acceptance but not after: *In Re National Savings Bank Association* (1867). A revocation is not complete until it actually reaches the offeree: *Byrne* v. *Van Tienhoven* (1880). To be effective it must have come to the knowledge of the offeree, and not merely that he was in a position to learn of the revocation. Provided that the offeror can show that the offeree knows of the revocation, from whatever source (e.g. a third party), the offer is revoked: *Dickinson* v. *Dodds* (1876). Even though an offeror has agreed to keep the offer open for a specified period he may still revoke it before that time has expired, unless (i) it has been accepted before notice of revocation has reached the offeree; or (ii) there was consideration for keeping the offer open.

If the parties use the post, then the first of the negotiating parties to use the post constitutes it as his agent, and so if an offer is made by post, unless the offer otherwise directs, the offeree may accept by post. Such acceptance is complete as soon as the letter of acceptance is posted, prepaid and properly addressed, whether it reaches the offeror or not: *Household Fire Insurance Co.* v. *Grant* (1879). The same applies to an acceptance by telegram or cable. But with instantaneous communication, e.g. by telex, or by telephone, an acceptance is complete only when received by the offeror: *Entores, Ltd.* v. *Miles Far East Corporation* (1955). In *The Brimnes* (1974) where a telex message was sent during business hours it was treated by the Court of Appeal as having been received when it was received by the plaintiff's telex machine at some time before 18.00 hrs even though it was not seen by a member of their staff until the following morning.

This was regarded as a special case, justified on its particular facts, by the House of Lords in *Mardorf, Peach & Co., Ltd.* v. *Attica Sea Carriers Corporation of Liberia* (1977), which concerned a payment order issued under the London Currency Clearing Scheme by one bank to another; as between banks a payment order is the equivalent of cash but a customer cannot draw on it. The respondent charterers' bank delivered at about 15.00 hours on a Monday a payment order to the appellant owners' bank. The receiving bank began to process it in the usual way; in normal circumstances the processing could take up to 24 hours before the owners' account would be credited with the sum. The bank informed the owners that the payment had been received, but the owners at once instructed the bank to refuse the money and return it to the charterers' bank. It was held that since the owners' bank had no authority to accept late payment, its acceptance of the payment order was provisional only, depending on the owners' decision whether to accept or reject it. The subsequent processing of the order by the bank was no more than an internal ministerial act which was provisional and reversible. The owners had rejected the payment as soon as circumstances permitted, and the receipt and processing of the payment order did not therefore constitute a waiver of the owners' right to withdraw the ship for non-payment of hire due on the preceding Sunday.

As regards auction sales, the bid itself constitutes the offer, which the auctioneer is free to accept or reject. A bid may be retracted at any time before the auctioneer announces the completion of the sale by the fall of the hammer or other customary method; once the hammer has fallen the offer made by the bidder has thereby been accepted, and the offer cannot be revoked—s. 57 of the Sale of Goods Act 1979.

An offer must be communicated, for otherwise the offeree has no opportunity of accepting or rejecting the offer: *Taylor* v. *Laird* (1856). However, an offer may be communicated although the offeree does not know all the terms or conditions attached to the offer. This situation often arises in respect of tickets issued by railways, omnibus and shipping companies, airlines, cloak room proprietors and the like. The ticket or slip often refers to time-tables or bye-laws or conditions of which the offeree is ignorant, and whether or not the offeree is bound thereby depends on the test laid down in *Parker* v. *S. E. Railway* (1877). Did the defendant do what was reasonably sufficient to give notice of the conditions to the class of persons to which the plaintiff belonged? If so, the plaintiff is bound by the conditions whether he has read them or not. Thus, in *Alderslade* v. *Hendon Laundry, Ltd.* (1945) it was held that a limitation of liability clause printed on the inside of a laundry book was sufficiently drawn to the attention of customers, so that the plaintiff was bound by it.

On the other hand, in *Chapelton* v. *Barry Urban District Council* (1940) it was held that the plaintiff, who was injured when a deckchair he had hired from the defendants collapsed, was not bound by a clause excluding liability printed on the back of the ticket because no reasonable man would have assumed that the ticket was anything more than a mere receipt. An automatic car park ticket which referred to conditions displayed on the premises was considered by the Court of Appeal in *Thornton* v. *Shoe Lane Parking, Ltd.* (1971). It was held that the act of the customer in causing the ticket to be issued by machine on driving his car into the car park was an irrevocable step, and so conditions could not thereafter be incorporated into the contract; accordingly, the terms of the offer were those contained in the notice placed at or near the ticket machine and the customer was bound by them if they were sufficiently brought to his notice beforehand. On the facts, adequate notice had not been given and so the defendants' attempt to rely on an exemption clause failed. As will be discussed later, the efficacy of clauses excepting or restricting liability is now considerably curtailed by the Unfair Contract Terms Act 1977.

An offer must be distinguished from (i) a mere declaration of intention; (ii) an invitation to treat, i.e. to make an offer; (iii) an option; and (iv) an agreement to negotiate. Examples of (ii) are goods in a shop window, and a prospectus issued by a company. The exhibition of an article with a price tag in a shop window is not an offer—the offer occurs when a potential customer enters the shop, tenders the price and asks for the article. The shopkeeper is not bound to accept this offer, he may accept or reject it as he pleases. The same applies to a self-service system—picking up an article does not constitute acceptance of an offer to sell, but is an offer by the customer to buy, which is accepted or rejected when he reaches the cash desk with the article: *Pharmaceutical Society of Great Britain* v. *Boots Cash Chemists (Southern), Ltd.* (1953). In like manner, a company prospectus is not an offer, but an invitation to make an offer, so that a person makes an offer to the company by applying for shares (or debentures etc.) and the company's acceptance is its allotment of the shares etc. if made. In *Gibson* v. *Manchester City Council* (1979) the City Treasurer wrote to the tenant of a council house that the council "may be prepared to sell the house" to him and invited him "to make a formal application to buy". The tenant completed and returned the application to purchase, but before contracts were exchanged, the Council refused to proceed due to a change of political control. The House of Lords held that the parties had not concluded a binding contract, because the Council had never made an offer capable of acceptance but only an invitation to treat. As regards (iv), in *Courtney and Fairbairn, Ltd.* v. *Tolaini Brothers (Hotels), Ltd.* (1975) the Court of Appeal decided that a building contract which did not contain a price or any method of ascertaining the price was no more than an agreement to negotiate fair and reasonable contract terms and was too uncertain to have any binding force, as no court could estimate the damages in the event of breach.

A tender is an offer to perform a contract for a certain price. For example, a company may invite tenders for the supply of 2,000 specified articles over the next two years. If X offers to supply them at £5 each and his tender is accepted by the company, there is a valid contract whereby X is obliged to supply, and the company is bound to accept, 2,000 articles, and the actual amounts supplied from time to time over the period are immaterial. A tender must be distinguished from the offer of the price, known as "legal tender" (to be discussed later); and also from a standing offer, which is an arrangement whereby one person stands ready to supply articles up to an agreed number at an agreed price whenever the other party requests a precise quantity. Thus, with a standing offer there is not one contract only, but a series of contracts made each time the other party accepts the standing offer by ordering a quantity of the articles, so that a person may revoke his standing offer at any time, and cannot be made liable for further deliveries, though he is bound by requisitions already made.

Acceptance is the assent made by the offeree to the offer either in writing or by words or conduct, but it must be signified by some extraneous act—a mere mental determination to accept is of no effect. An acceptance must be communicated to the offeror, and, as already stated, an acceptance by post is complete at the moment when the letter is posted, even if it never reaches its destination. However, where an agreement contained an option to purchase "exercisable by notice in writing to the [defendant] at any time within six months from the date hereof" and the notice was lost in the post, it was held that as the agreement prescribed the mode in which the option was to be exercised, it could only be exercised in the prescribed way and so the mere posting of the notice did not constitute a valid exercise of the option: *Holwell Securities, Ltd.* v. *Hughes* (1973). If a letter of acceptance from the offeree and a letter of revocation from the offeror cross in the post, there is a valid contract, for the acceptance takes effect before the revocation does, as revocation, like an offer, only operates from the time when it reaches the offeree: *Henthorn* v. *Fraser* (1892).

An acceptance cannot be revoked, nor can it be dispensed with by the offeror, though he may prescribe a particular method of acceptance. In *Felthouse* v. *Bindley* (1862), where the plaintiff wrote to his nephew offering to buy a horse and adding: "If I hear no more about him, I consider the horse mine at £30 15s 0d." it was held that there was no contract as the acceptance had not been communicated.

An acceptance must be an absolute and unqualified assent to all the terms of the offer—in *Neale* v. *Merrett* (1930) the defendant offered land to the plaintiff at £280, the plaintiff replied accepting, and enclosed £80 with a promise to pay the balance by monthly instalments of £50 each: it was held that there was no contract because the acceptance was not an unqualified one. It must be made while the offer is in force and before it has lapsed or been revoked. An offer becomes irrevocable by acceptance.

If the acceptance is made "subject to contract" or some similar wording, which makes it a tentative acceptance only, then there is no contract, until such time as a proper or formal contract is signed by the parties. This situation is often part of the negotiations for a purchase of a house; if the prospective purchaser accepts "subject to contract" then until the formal contract is completed either party may withdraw without liability, e.g. the vendor may sell to someone else at a higher price, or, as in *Chillingworth* v. *Esche* (1924), the purchaser may decide not to proceed. In *Law* v. *Jones* (1973) a majority of the Court of Appeal held that an oral agreement to sell land which was later set out in a solicitor's letter expressed to be "subject to contract" was a sufficient writing to satisfy s. 40 of the Law of Property Act 1925 (see page 3). This case "sounded an alarm bell in the offices of every solicitor in the land", but fortunately in *Tiverton Estates, Ltd.* v. *Wearwell, Ltd.* (1974) a strong Court of Appeal unanimously held that *Law* v. *Jones* was wrongly decided because it conflicted with earlier decisions of equal authority and refused to follow it, holding that a document expressed to be "subject to contract" did not constitute a sufficient memorandum to satisfy s. 40.

An offer is rejected (i) if the offeree communicates his rejection to the offeror; (ii) if the offeree makes a counter-offer; or (iii) if the offeree accepts subject to conditions. An illustration of a counter-offer is the case of *Hyde* v. *Wrench* (1840), where the defendant offered to sell his farm for £1,000 to the plaintiff, who in turn offered £950, which was refused. The plaintiff later increased his offer to £1,000, but this was also declined by the defendant; the plaintiff's action failed because the original offer was terminated by his counter-offer and could not therefore be accepted later. This case was applied by the Court of Appeal in *Butler Machine Tool Co., Ltd.* v. *Ex-Cell-O Corporation, Ltd.* (1979), a "battle of forms" in which the plaintiffs, sellers, made a quotation for the sale of a machine tool subject to certain terms and conditions (including a "price variation clause") which "shall prevail over any terms and conditions in the Buyer's order". The defendants, buyers, ordered the machine on different terms and conditions including a fixed price, with a tear-off acknowledgement and receipt stating "we accept your order on the Terms and Conditions stated thereon". The sellers completed and returned this acknowledgement. HELD, the buyers' order was a counter-offer which destroyed the sellers' offer, and the sellers by completing and returning the acknowledgement had accepted the counter-offer on the buyers' terms and conditions, and could not claim to increase the price under the price variation clause contained in their own offer.

INTENTION TO CREATE CONTRACTUAL RELATIONS

The parties to the offer and acceptance must intend that their relationship shall create legal obligations, i.e. they must intend their agreement to be a legally binding contract, enforceable in the courts. Some agreements may be made subject to a condition expressly excluding legal liability. Such a condition ousting the jurisdiction of the courts is commonly found in football pool rules, and is not contrary to public policy, but is binding. Thus, in *Appleson* v. *Littlewood, Ltd.* (1939) such a clause defeated the plaintiff's action to obtain £4,335 which he claimed he had won on a football pool.

Similarly, agreements of a social or domestic nature do not contemplate legal relations and so are not enforceable as contracts, e.g. arrangements between friends to play golf or dine together. On the other hand, arrangements made between husband and wife when they are not living in amity but are separated or about to separate may be shown by the circumstances to be intended to create legal relations: *Merritt* v. *Merritt* (1970).

In *Albert* v. *Motor Insurers' Bureau* (1971) the House of Lords considered the familiar practice whereby workmen go to their place of employment in the motor vehicle of a fellow workman upon the terms of making a contribution to the costs of the transport, and held that in determining whether it was a carriage for hire or reward the test to be applied was whether there had been a systematic carrying of passengers which went beyond the bounds of mere social kindness, i.e. whether the carrying had become a predominantly "business" arrangement rather than a predominantly social one; if the carrying of passengers had acquired such a "business" character, it was immaterial that neither the driver nor the passenger intended any contractual relationship to result.

Under the Law Reform (Miscellaneous Provisions) Act 1970 an agreement between two persons to marry one another no longer has effect as a contract, so that breach of promise of marriage (which has figured in novels, plays and Gilbert and Sullivan's "Trial by Jury") has ceased to be legally actionable. The Act provides that gifts between engaged couples may be recovered where made on condition, express or implied, that they are to be returned, if the agreement to marry is terminated; an engagement ring is presumed to be an absolute gift, though the presumption may be rebutted by proving that it was given conditionally.

FORM OR CONSIDERATION

As already stated, a specialty contract, or deed, depends for its validity on its form alone and does not require consideration except where it is a contract in restraint of trade, though in most cases there is consideration as well.

A simple contract must have consideration, of which the standard definition is that from *Currie* v. *Misa* (1875): "Some right, interest, profit or benefit accruing to one party, or some forbearance, detriment, loss or responsibility given, suffered or undertaken by the other". In other words, it is the element of exchange which is the root of every simple contract, e.g. when a person enters a shop and purchases an article, that person hands over cash and receives the article, whilst the shopkeeper parts with the article and receives cash therefor. In such a situation, where the act constituting the consideration is completely performed, the consideration is said to be "executed". When the consideration takes the form of promises to be performed in the future the consideration is said to be "executory".

The general rules as to consideration are:

1. It is necessary to the validity of every contract not under seal and of a contract in restraint of trade even if under seal. In the case of bills of exchange, consideration is presumed, i.e. in contrast to the general onus of proof a plaintiff suing on a bill of exchange has not to prove consideration—it is up to the defendant to prove the absence of it.

2. It need not be adequate or equivalent to the promise, but it must have some value. What sort of a bargain the contracting parties make—good, bad or indifferent—is their own concern, and the Court will not intervene so long as the consideration is real, i.e. it has some value in the eye of the law. A moral obligation does not amount to consideration, nor does a promise to do what the promisee can legally demand already. However, where the promisor is already under an obligation to some one other than the promisee, there will be consideration: *Shadwell* v. *Shadwell* (1860), where an uncle promised an annuity to a nephew if the latter would marry the lady to whom he was already engaged, and the fulfilment of this engagement was held to be sufficient consideration to support the uncle's promise.

It was held as long ago as *Pinnel's Case* (1602) that payment of a smaller sum of money is not a satisfaction of an agreement to pay a larger sum, even though the creditor agrees to take it in full discharge. However, if the creditor agrees to take a smaller sum before the larger sum is actually due, then the debtor gets a good discharge, e.g. if £50 is due and payable on January 1st, the obligation will be legally discharged by the creditor's agreement to take £45 in full satisfaction on the preceding December 1st (this is a form of "accord and satisfaction" to be discussed later under "Discharge of Contract").

An agreement without consideration intended to have legal consequences and to be acted on, which, to the knowledge of the promisor, has been so acted on, although it cannot be enforced, is binding on the promisor in that he will not be allowed to act inconsistently with his promise. This innovation was made by DENNING, J. (as he then was) in *Central London Property Trust, Ltd.* v. *High Trees House, Ltd.* (1947).

3. It must be legal. An illegal consideration vitiates the whole contract, a point to be dealt with later under "Legality of Object".

4. It must not be past, i.e. wholly done and finished before the promise is made. Past consideration must be distinguished from "executed" consideration, which is present or contemporaneous. In *Roscorla* v. *Thomas* (1842) a warranty in respect of a horse was given after the sale of the horse had been concluded; it was held that the warranty was not binding, because it was unsupported by fresh consideration, the sale price being past consideration. There are two exceptions to this rule as to the inadequacy of past consideration:

(i) Where there is a precedent request and the subsequent promise to pay is merely the fixing of the price: *Lampleigh* v. *Braithwait* (1615). For example, if X asks Y to carry out some task for him, and Y reasonably assumes that his remuneration will be fixed later, then a subsequent agreement as to how much Y is to receive will be binding.

(ii) In the case of a bill of exchange an antecedent debt or liability is sufficient consideration: s. 27 of the Bills of Exchange Act 1882.

5. Consideration must move from the promisee, i.e. the person to whom the promise is made must furnish the consideration. In other words, only the parties to a contract can acquire rights and obligations under it, and a third party (or stranger) cannot claim under the contract. For example, if X promises Y and Z in a joint agreement to pay £100 to Z in return for services to be rendered to X by Y, then although Z is a party to the contract he cannot enforce it because no consideration moved from him, but Y can do so because he gave consideration for X's promise.

6. Forbearance to sue or take other action, unaccompanied by any express or implied promise to forbear, is not consideration.

CAPACITY TO CONTRACT

That the parties to a contract should have contractual capacity to enter into that contract is a self-evident requirement, but certain special categories of persons fall to be considered:

(i) Aliens

This category includes all persons who are neither British citizens, nor British protected persons. Normally, such persons are called "alien friends", except when a state of war exists between their own country and the United Kingdom, when they are termed "alien enemies". An alien friend may enter into a contract in the same way as a British citizen, save that he cannot own any share in a British ship (Merchant Shipping Act 1894). Contracts with an alien enemy are void, unless he is permitted to be at liberty in England by licence of the Crown. His power to sue or exercise rights in relation to property in the United Kingdom is suspended in time of war, but he may be sued in respect of any contract valid when entered into, and if sued, he may defend himself. The term "alien enemy" includes not only a subject of an enemy state, but also a British subject or a subject of a neutral power who is resident in enemy territory: *Porter* v. *Freudenberg* (1915). It does not include a British soldier detained as a prisoner of war on enemy soil: *Vandyke* v. *Adams* (1942). The general rule is that an alien enemy's rights of action are suspended during wartime, but will revive on the cessation of hostilities.

(ii)   Minors (or Infants)

From 1st January 1970 attainment of majority takes place at the age of 18: s. 1 of the Family Law Reform Act 1969. Section 9 of the Act defines "attainment" as the commencement of the anniversary of date of birth; this amends the common law rule that infancy ceased at the first instant of the day preceding the 21st birthday (because the law does not recognise fractions of a day) but the section applies only in relation to any enactment, deed, will or other instrument, subject to any provision therein. Section 12 provides that "minor" may be used instead of "infant". Contracts entered into by infants are governed by the Infants Relief Act 1874 and a considerable amount of case law from the days when persons came of age at 21, which is still relevant apart from the reduction to 18. These contracts may be classified as follows:

(a) *Binding during infancy.*— Under the Act, an infant is bound by contracts for the supplying to him (or her) of goods which are "necessaries". These include food, drink, medicine and clothes, but whether particular articles are or are not "necessaries" is a question of fact to be decided by the Court, having regard to the infant's station in life and the degree to which he was already in possession of similar articles. As in all instances of incapacity, the infant claiming the benefit of it must prove his incapacity, but it is for the plaintiff to prove that the infant was not sufficiently provided with similar necessaries at the times in question. Thus, in *Nash* v. *Inman* (1908) the plaintiff, a Savile Row tailor, supplied a Cambridge undergraduate with clothing, including 11 fancy waistcoats, to the value of £145 at a time when he was adequately provided with clothes; his claim failed because the Court of Appeal held that, though clothes in reasonable quantities are necessaries, the defendant's purchases were sheer extravagance, and so could not be necessaries.

The test of the standard or condition in life of the infant means that the son of a rich man can be held liable to pay for, say, a gold watch, whereas the same article would not be deemed a necessary for a far less favoured infant. Goods supplied to an infant for gifts to his fiancee may be considered necessaries: *Elkington & Co., Ltd.* v. *Amery* (1936). By s. 3 of the Sale of Goods Act 1979 an infant is bound to pay a reasonable price for necessaries sold and delivered to him. This will not necessarily be the agreed price, and liability does not arise until delivery.

At Common Law an infant is bound by contracts of apprenticeship and service, provided they are clearly for his benefit. Liability for such contracts arises as soon as they are made. In these contracts for necessary services no unreasonable burdens must be placed on the infant, nor will the Court enforce any contract which attempts to exploit the infant: *De Francesco* v. *Barnum* (1890). Two examples of contracts upheld by the Court are: *Clements* v. *L. N. W. Railway Co.* (1894), where an infant porter had to join a railway sick pay scheme as part of the conditions of his employment (the scheme was reasonable and beneficial to the infant); and *International Correspondence Schools Ltd* v. *Ayres* (1912), where the infant had to pay for tuition supplied by the plaintiffs, for education, like earning a living, is beneficial to infants.

It should be noted, however, that if an infant carries on business, he is not liable on contracts made by him in the course of trade: *Mercantile Union Guarantee Corporation Ltd* v. *Ball* (1937). For example, an infant trader would not be liable for stock-in-trade which he bought on credit, or for a motor lorry obtained on hire-purchase.

(b) *Voidable.*—Certain contracts entered into by infants will be binding on them unless repudiated within a reasonable time of attaining full age. What is a reasonable time is a question of fact to be decided in the particular circumstances. The contracts falling within this category are those of a continuing nature, viz: leases, partnerships, marriage settlements, shares etc. in companies, and similar investments in permanent property. Thus, in *Davies* v. *Beynon-Harris* (1931) an infant took a lease of a flat shortly before he attained his majority, and three years later he was sued for the rent then in arrears: he was held liable as the lease was binding on him unless he had repudiated it within a reasonable time of attaining his majority.

In *Steinberg* v. *Scala* (*Leeds*), *Ltd.* (1923) the plaintiff infant took shares in the defendant company, paid the amount due on allotment and the first call, but later, whilst still an infant, she repudiated the contract and claimed her money back. No dividend had been paid, and the shares appeared always to have been at a discount. It was held that she could repudiate and have her name removed from the share register, so that she would not be liable for future calls, but her right to recover the money paid was lost, as there had not been a total failure of consideration (i.e. the shares had some value)— the test as to this being the same in the case of an infant as in that of a person of full age.

(c) *Void.*—Section 1 of the Infants Relief Act 1874 provides that all contracts entered into by infants for the repayment of money lent or to be lent, or for goods supplied or to be supplied (other than necessaries), and all accounts stated with infants, shall be absolutely void.

An infant cannot give any valid security for his debts, nor can he give a guarantee; and as loans to infants are void, any guarantee in respect of them is equally ineffective: *Coutts & Co.* v. *Browne-Lecky* (1947), an aspect to be discussed more fully in Chapter 9 on Guarantees. An infant cannot be sued on a negotiable instrument even if given for necessaries: *Re Soltykoff* (1891). If, however, a loan for the purchase of necessaries is so spent, the lender is subrogated to the rights of the seller, and is allowed in equity the same right of recovery that an unpaid seller of necessaries would have had: *Lewis* v. *Alleyne* (1888).

In *R. Leslie, Ltd.* v. *Sheill* (1914) an infant managed to borrow £400 from moneylenders by fraudulently misrepresenting himself to be of full age, but although an infant is in general answerable for his torts, the Court of Appeal held that he could not be liable either in contract or for the tort of deceit, because to allow the injured party to sue for a tort that is directly connected with a void contract would be tantamount to enforcing a void contract. However, by the equitable doctrine of restitution, if an infant has obtained goods by fraud, then the Court will order the return of such goods as are in his possession and unpaid for: *Stocks* v. *Wilson* (1913). As restitution stops at the goods, where these have been sold by the infant, he is not accountable for the proceeds of sale.

If an infant buys and pays for goods that are not necessaries, he cannot retain the goods and recover his money. Recovery is possible only where there has been a total failure of consideration. Thus, in *Valentini* v. *Canali* (1890) an infant obtained furniture to the value of £102 against a payment of £68 and a promissory note for the balance.

After using the furniture for some months he sought to recover his £68 on the grounds that the contract was void under the Act of 1874: the Court held he was entitled to have the contract set aside and he could not be sued on the promissory note, but he could not recover the £68 as it represented the use he had had out of the furniture.

(d) *Unenforceable.* — All contracts to which an infant is a party and which do not fall within the preceding three categories are unenforceable against the infant, either during or after infancy. As the infant can enforce them, they are not void. Section 2 of the Act of 1874 provides that even if an infant ratifies after coming of age a contract made during infancy the contract is unenforceable, notwithstanding there is any new consideration for the ratification.

(iii) Married Women

As a result of considerable legislation from 1870 onwards married women now have the same full proprietary rights and contractual capacity as single women.

(iv) Mentally Disordered Persons and Drunken Persons

Although still used in popular speech, the words "lunacy" and "insanity" are now replaced since the Mental Health Act 1959 as regards the law by the phrase "unsoundness of mind", and persons suffering therefrom are now described as mentally disordered persons.

Contracts with mentally disordered persons are voidable, not void, but in order to repudiate the contract the mentally disordered person must show that the other party took advantage of his disability, or knew of it at the time the contract was made: *Imperial Loan Co.* v. *Stone* (1892). A mentally disordered person must pay a reasonable price for necessaries: *Re Rhodes* (1890). A contract entered into by a person suffering from unsoundness of mind may be subsequently ratified during a lucid interval.

Similar considerations have been applied to contracts made by elderly people whose powers are failing. Such an example of senility occurred in *Manches* v. *Trimborn* (1946), where the defendant, an elderly woman, drew a cheque in favour of the plaintiff. The defendant was capable of understanding that she was signing a cheque, but not of understanding the transaction to which the cheque related, and the plaintiff knew this. It was held that the defendant was not liable on the cheque.

Contracts made with a drunken person are voidable at the option of that person, provided he can prove (and the onus of proof lies with him) that he was so drunk at the time as not to know what he was doing, that the other party knew of this and took advantage of it. When this is the case, the drunken person may repudiate the contract when sober, or ratify it so that it becomes binding: *Matthews* v. *Baxter* (1873). Whether or not a person is in a complete state of drunkenness may be a difficult question of fact, because many drunken persons are quite capable of transacting business. In any case, a contract for the supply of necessaries at a reasonable price and in the absence of unfair dealing will be binding: *Gore* v. *Gibson* (1845).

(v) Corporations

The contractual capacity of a corporation is governed by (i) natural possibility—i.e. being an artificial and not a natural person it has to contract through an agent; and (ii) legal possibility, i.e. restrictions on its powers imposed by law at the time of its formation or subsequently.

Thus, as an artificial person a corporation is unable to enter into contracts of a personal nature—it cannot be the treasurer of a friendly society, nor can it act as a doctor, solicitor or accountant, though it can act as secretary of a company. (It must be added that some corporations, known as "corporations sole" consist of one person only, e.g. a Bishop. We are not concerned with these, but with the great majority of corporations, known as "corporations aggregate", being groups of individuals on whom the law confers a separate legal personality.)

The extent of legal possibility depends on the type of corporation, for there are three ways in which corporations may be created:

(a) by Royal Charter, e.g. the Bank of England, and the Institute of Chartered Secretaries and Administrators.

(b) by special Act of Parliament, e.g. most waterworks undertakings, and nationalised industrial concerns such as the National Coal Board.

(c) under the provisions of a general Act of Parliament, viz: the various Companies Acts, of which the current one is the Companies Act 1948. Of all corporations, companies are by far the most numerous and important, and Chapter 4 will be devoted to them.

A corporation created by Royal Charter may contract to the same extent as a private individual, subject to any limits imposed in the Charter. If such a corporation makes a contract in excess of its powers, the contract is valid, but the corporation may be liable to forfeit its Charter.

All other corporations are subject to the *ultra vires* doctrine, i.e. anything done "beyond their powers" is void. If incorporation was effected by a special Act of Parliament, then that Act will contain the restrictions. As regards companies incorporated under the various Companies Acts, each company must have a Memorandum of Association, setting forth the objects of the company and the extent of its powers, and anything outside the scope of the Memorandum is *ultra vires* the company and void, even though all the members of the company ratify the contract. However, this doctrine has been restricted by s. 9 (1) of the European Communities Act 1972 which now provides that, in favour of a person dealing with a company in good faith, any contract decided on by the directors is deemed to be one within the capacity of the company. The Act does not change the reverse position, i.e. the company cannot enforce an *ultra vires* contract against the third party.

With reference to the mode of contracting by corporations, companies are empowered by s. 32 of the Companies Act 1948 to contract in the same manner as a private individual—depending on the nature of the contract it may be given under the common seal of the company, or be in writing signed on behalf of the company, or be made verbally by any person acting under the authority of the company. The contracts of other corporations have now been put on a similar basis by the Corporate Bodies' Contracts Act 1960.

(vi) Miscellaneous

Due to their status certain persons have limited contractual capacity for particular contracts or for periods of time. These include:

(a) *Foreign sovereigns and states, and their diplomatic staffs.*—Foreign sovereigns and states may contract, but the contract cannot be enforced against them unless they voluntarily submit to the jurisdiction of the English Courts. This immunity applies even if the foreign sovereign lives in England under a false name as a private citizen: *Mighell* v. *Sultan of Johore* (1894).

Under the Diplomatic Privileges Act 1964 (which has replaced earlier provisions) diplomatic representatives of foreign and commonwealth countries are privileged in varying degrees from being sued in the English Courts. The diplomats and their staffs are allocated to three categories, the highest category carrying the highest degree of immunity and so on. These representatives may submit voluntarily to the jurisdiction, but only with the express consent of their sovereign, or the head of the mission. In any event, their diplomatic immunity ceases after a reasonable time has elapsed from the ending of their mission or employment.

(b) *Professional.*—A barrister cannot sue for his fees. Fellows of a College of Physicians may also be prohibited by byelaw from suing for their expenses, charges or fees.

(c) *Undischarged Bankrupts.*—Whilst undischarged bankrupts, i.e. persons who have been adjudicated bankrupt and have not yet received their order of discharge, may contract, they are subject to certain restrictions (to be discussed in Chapter 5).

(d) *Credit-Unions.*—Long a feature in America and Ireland, these thrift and loan societies have now been recognised by the Credit Unions Act 1979, which permits their registration, with certain prescribed objects, under the Industrial and Provident Societies Act 1965. Membership is limited to persons of a particular occupation, or who reside in a particular locality, or who are employed in a particular locality or by a particular employer or who are members of another bona fide organisation. Members (minimum number 21, maximum 5,000) are restricted as to the amount of shares of £1 denomination in the society which they may hold to 2,000 each, and a loan to a member of full age shall not be more than £2,000 in excess of his total paid-up shareholding in the credit union at that time.

(e) *Trade Unions.*—These enjoy a privileged position in our law. Their exact legal status was not clear, though in *Bonsor* v. *Musicians' Union* (1955) the House of Lords held that a registered trade union could be sued in its own name for breach of contract by one of its members whom it had wrongfully expelled. The Trade Union and Labour Relations Act 1974 now provides that a trade union is not a body corporate, but it is capable of making contracts and of suing and being sued in its own name.

REALITY OF CONSENT

There must be a genuine and complete agreement between the parties to the contract, and various factors may operate to prevent such true consent. The nature and the consequences of these factors will now be considered under the four headings of (1) Mistake, (2) Fraud, (3) Misrepresentation, and (4) Duress and Undue Influence.

1. MISTAKE

Mistake is an intricate topic because of variations in the quality and range of the mistake, for it may be of a serious or insignificant nature and it may be made by both parties (mutual) or by one party (unilateral); these factors will determine the effect of the mistake on the contract. The mistake may be of fact, or of law, but the latter does not invalidate the contract, for the general principle is that ignorance of the law is no excuse: *ignorantia juris haud excusat.*

The following mistakes of fact will make the contract void, because they go to the very root of the contract, and prevent any true agreement, or "*consensus ad idem*", being arrived at between the parties. In short, there is no "meeting of minds":

(a) Mistake as to the nature of the contract itself. The plea here is "*non est factum*" (it is not his deed), so that where a person signs a contract in the mistaken belief that it is a totally different document and without carelessness on his part, he can escape liability. The position was considered at length by the House of Lords in *Saunders* v. *Anglia Building Society* (1970) (reported in the Courts below *sub nom. Gallie* v. *Lee*). The appellant was the executrix of an elderly widow who had signed a deed of assignment of a lease to L without reading it because her spectacles were broken and she had been induced to think it was a deed of gift to her nephew P. The building society lent £2,000 in good faith on the document. In holding that the document was binding, the House of Lords laid down that the plea of *non est factum* can only rarely be established by a person of full capacity and although it is not confined to the blind and illiterate any extension of the scope of the plea would be kept within narrow limits. In particular, it is unlikely that the plea would be available to a person who signed a document without informing himself of its meaning. The burden of establishing the plea falls on the party seeking to disown the document and that party must show that in signing the document he acted with reasonable care. *Foster* v. *Mackinnon* (1869)—see Chapter 14—was approved; and *Carlisle and Cumberland Banking Co.* v. *Bragg* (1911) was overruled. The distinction formerly drawn [in *Howatson* v. *Webb* (1907)] between the character and the contents of the document was disapproved as unsatisfactory; it has now to be shown in a more general sense that there is a fundamental or radical or total difference between the document as it is and the document as it was believed to be. LORD HODSON added that where there was an error of personality, it may or may not be fundamental; "the question cannot be answered in isolation . . . in the case of deeds error of personality is not necessarily so vital as in the case of contracts." In *United Dominions Trust, Ltd.* v. *Western* (1975) the Court of Appeal, applying the above doctrine, held that a person who signed a form in blank leaving the details to be filled in by a third party was bound by the form as completed.

(b) Mistake as to the identity of the person contracted with, whenever his identity is a material element.

This question of identity is important where goods have been acquired and then passed on to an innocent third party, for if the first contract is void, no title to the goods can be acquired by an innocent third party. On the other hand, if the first contract is voidable, but not void, then an innocent third party who acquires the goods before avoidance of the first contract gets an indefeasible title by s. 23 of the Sale of Goods Act 1979. Illustrations are:

In *Cundy* v. *Lindsay* (1878) one Blenkarn, by writing from "37, Wood St., Cheapside" and fraudulently misrepresenting himself to be the respectable firm of Blenkiron & Co., who carried on business in the same street, obtained goods on credit from Lindsay & Co. and sold them to Cundy. The House of Lords held that there was no contract, because the sellers thought they were dealing with one party, whereas in fact they were dealing with someone else, and as the contract was void, Cundy, the innocent purchaser of the goods from Blenkarn, could acquire no title to the goods and was liable for their value.

In *Phillips* v. *Brooks, Ltd.* (1919) a man entered the shop of the plaintiff, a jeweller, and posing as Sir George Bullough, obtained a valuable ring against a cheque, subsequently dishonoured; he pawned the ring with the defendants, who had no notice of the fraud. Held, the plaintiff intended to contract with the man in the shop, whether or not he was Sir George Bullough, and intended to pass the title to the ring to him though he would not have formed this intention but for the fraudulent impersonation. As the contract was voidable, not void, the defendants had a good title. This case was followed by the Court of Appeal in *Lewis* v. *Averay* (1971) another face-to-face transaction, where the rogue posed as a well-known film actor.

A voidable contract can be rescinded without actual communication to, or re-possession from, the person whose title is being avoided, where this cannot be done because that person has absconded: *Car and Universal Finance Co., Ltd.* v. *Caldwell* (1964) in which the seller of a car, on finding that the cheque he received had been dishonoured, immediately informed the police and the Automobile Association of the fraudulent transaction: his action was held by the Court of Appeal to be sufficient to avoid the contract.

(c) Mutual mistake as to the identity of the subject-matter of the contract. For example, in *Raffles* v. *Wichelhaus* (1864) A agreed to buy from B a cargo of cotton to arrive "ex 'Peerless' from Bombay". There were two ships named "Peerless" coming from Bombay, one sailing in October, the other in December; A meant the earlier one, whereas B meant the later one: it was held there was no contract. However, if the parties had both meant the same ship, but described it by a wrong name, there would have been a contract, for the misdescription would not have been vital.

(d) Mutual mistake as to the existence of the subject-matter of the contract. For example, in *Strickland* v. *Turner* (1852) the plaintiff purchased an annuity in respect of a person who, unknown to both parties to the contract, was already dead. It was held that there was no contract. As regards goods (which may, for instance, have been lost at sea before the contract is entered into), the same position arises by virtue of s. 6 of the Sale of Goods Act 1979 which provides that: "Where there is a contract for the sale of specific goods, and the goods without the knowledge of the seller have perished at the time when the contract is made, the contract is void".

(e) Mutual mistake as to the intention of the other party. Here, the contract actually made is fundamentally different from the contract the parties intended to make. An example is *Scriven Bros. & Co.* v. *Hindley & Co.* (1913), where an auctioneer intended to sell tow and the buyer intended to buy hemp. Both tow and hemp were amongst the lots to be sold, and due to an ambiguity in the auction particulars the buyer bid an excessive price for an item of tow, thinking it was hemp, and from the price bid the auctioneer must have realised there was a mistake. It was held that there was no contract.

(f) Mutual mistake as to the existence of a state of facts forming the basis of the contract. Thus, in *Cooper* v. *Phibbs* (1867) Cooper, having obtained a three-year lease of a salmon fishery from persons believing themselves to be entitled to it, subsequently found that he himself was the owner of the fishery. The House of Lords drew a distinction between mistake caused by ignorance of a general rule of law, where the maxim "Ignorance of the law is no excuse" applies, and mistake caused by ignorance of a particular or private right, to which the maxim has no application, and held that Cooper was entitled to avoid the lease.

In contrast to the foregoing the following types of mistake have no effect on the contract:

(i) Mistake as to the expression of the contract. Where the parties have reduced their contract to a writing which does not express their real intention, the contract is not void, though if the error is mutual, rectification of the document can be obtained. In *W. Higgins, Ltd.* v. *Northampton Corporation* (1927) a builder in working out his prices for a tender to the corporation for the erection of houses made an over-deduction, so that the subsequent contract did not correctly represent his intention because of the error, but it did correctly represent the corporation's intention: the Court refused to rectify the contract.

(ii) Mistaken motive or error of judgment. The general maxim here is *"caveat emptor"* (let the buyer beware). In the absence of any misrepresentation as to the goods by the other party, a person who makes a bad bargain has only himself to blame, and must bear the loss, for it is caused by his own ignorance, e.g. where he over-estimates the quality of the goods. Thus, in *Smith* v. *Hughes* (1871) the buyer bought oats from the seller, the oats were new but he thought he was buying them as old oats; the contract was held to be valid, for the seller had done nothing to induce the mistake on the part of the buyer.

(iii) Mistake by one party as to his power of performance. If a party undertakes to perform a certain task, e.g. the construction of a ship, by a specified date, and due to circumstances such as shortages of labour or materials, or strikes, the target date cannot be attained, the delay is not excused, unless the contract's provisions cover the point, for such events can be foreseen and guarded against, e.g. by a strike clause, in the contract. Thus, in *Davis Contractors Ltd.* v. *Fareham Urban District Council* (1956) the contractors undertook to build seventy-eight houses for the council for a fixed sum within a period of eight months; due to inadequate supplies of labour and without fault on either side the work took twenty-two months to complete. The contractors' claim to be paid a sum in excess of the contract price failed, for the House of Lords held that the contract was not frustrated and the unexpected turn of events was not a ground for relieving the contractors of their obligation and allowing them to recover on the basis of a *quantum meruit.*

2. FRAUD, OR FRAUDULENT MISREPRESENTATION

During the course of negotiations culminating in a contract, various statements will have been made by one party to the other. Where these induce the contract, but form no part of it, then if they turn out to be false, they are known as fraudulent or innocent misrepresentations according to whether they were made deliberately or honestly. If the statements are incorporated in the contract, they become either conditions or warranties, which will be discussed later.

Fraud covers a wide range of deceitful activities, so long as the following elements are present:

(a) A false representation of a material fact;

(b) Made knowing of its falsehood or without belief in its truth, or recklessly not caring whether it was true or false;

(c) With the intention that it should be acted upon by the party misled;

(d) Actually misleading that party; and

(e) Damage must have been suffered.

These elements may be elaborated as follows:

The false representation must be in in respect of a material fact, so that a mere expression of opinion (as when a salesman praises his goods) is no fraud, nor usually is a declaration of intention. Mere non-disclosure does not amount to fraud, though it may do so when a partial or fragmentary statement of fact is rendered untrue by what is not stated, as happened in *R* v. *Kylsant* (1932). The plaintiff must be within the class of persons at whom the fraudulent statement was aimed, and he must actually be deceived, for if he does not rely on the fraudulent misrepresentations, but relies on his own skill and judgment or on his own inquiries and investigations, his claim will fail.

The injured party's remedies for fraud are:

    (1) He may affirm the contract and bring an action for damages for deceit.

    (2) He may repudiate the contract and (a) set up the fraud as a defence to an action brought on the contract; (b) bring an action or counterclaim for damages or for rescission or both.

The circumstances in which the right to rescind a voidable contract will be lost have already been noted. Finally, it must be added that by s. 6 of the Statute of Frauds Amendment Act 1828 (commonly called Lord Tenterden's Act) no action will lie on a representation as to character, conduct, credit, ability, trade or dealings of any other person unless the representation is in writing signed by the party to be charged therewith. Despite this general wording it was held by the House of Lords in *Banbury* v. *Bank of Montreal* (1918) that the Act applies only to actions in tort for fraudulent misrepresentations and not to actions for breach of contract or for the breach of some other duty of care in making representations. As the signature of an agent is not sufficient under the Act, it is generally considered that a corporate body would only be liable if its seal were affixed to the representation. In practice, this is never done, and indeed, because of the Act, most bank references are not signed in any way.

In the case of false or misleading descriptions in relation to goods criminal sanctions are provided by the Trade Descriptions Acts 1968 and 1972.

3. MISREPRESENTATION

Misrepresentation may be made quite innocently, in that although there is a false representation of a material fact, it is made by a person who honestly believes it to be true. Innocent misrepresentation renders the contract voidable in the usual way, but formerly the right to rescind was lost if the contract had been carried out and except in certain cases the party misled could not claim damages. Now, however, s. 1 of the Misrepresentation Act 1967 provides that the right to rescind for innocent misrepresentation will be available even though the misrepresentation has become a term of the contract; and/or the contract has been performed. Furthermore, s. 2 of this Act gives the Court a discretionary power to award damages in lieu of rescission for innocent misrepresentation, and provides that the party misled by such a misrepresentation and suffering loss thereby will be entitled to damages unless the maker of the statement can show that he had reasonable grounds to believe, and did believe up to the time the contract was made, that the facts represented were true. By s. 3 provisions in agreements excluding or restricting liability for misrepresentations made before the contract was made are of no effect except in so far as the Court considers reliance thereon to be fair and reasonable in the circumstances.

Conditions and Warranties

A false statement which becomes incorporated in a contract so as to be a term of the contract may be either a condition or a warranty. A condition goes to the root of the contract, and breach of it entitles the injured party to rescind the contract and claim for any damage suffered; alternatively, he may affirm the contract and treat the breach of condition as a breach of warranty, which is not a vital term of the contract but merely collateral to its main purpose and gives only a claim in damages.

Whether a term of an ordinary contract amounts to a condition or to a warranty depends on the facts of each case. For example, in *Bettini* v. *Gye* (1876) B was engaged by G, the director of the Italian opera in England, to sing on certain dates and to arrive in England for rehearsals six days before the first date. He arrived only two days before, and G repudiated the contract for alleged breach of condition. It was held that the term as to rehearsals did not go to the root of the contract, and so was not a condition but only a warranty: therefore, the contract could not be repudiated. Had B arrived some days after the first engagement date the matter would then have been more serious, and would have been a breach of condition.

In insurance law, however, the word "warranty" has not the same meaning as it has in general contract law but is equivalent to a condition, so that on a breach of warranty a contract of insurance can be repudiated.

Although there is a presumption that if the word "condition" is used in a contract, it indicates a term breach of which, however small, will give rise to a right to repudiate, the word will not be given that meaning if such a construction produces a result so unreasonable that the parties could not have intended it and if there is some other possible and reasonable construction: *L Schuler AG* v. *Wickman Machine Tool Sales, Ltd.* (1973), where the House of Lords held that a "condition" that once one of Wickman's representatives failed to make one visit out of thousands contracted for, Schuler thereby acquired an immediate right to repudiate the agreement was unreasonable and therefore a breach of it did not entitle Schuler to repudiate.

Conditions and warranties loom large in the sale of goods; over the years documents of sale came almost always to contain clauses excluding the rights which the Sale of Goods Act 1893 would otherwise have conferred on the buyer, but exemption clauses have been radically curtailed by the Supply of Goods (Implied Terms) Act 1973 and the Unfair Contract Terms Act 1977. The implied terms relating to title etc. in contracts of sale and hire purchase cannot in any contract be excluded or restricted by a term of the contract. As against a person dealing as consumer the implied conditions in contracts of sale and hire purchase relating to correspondence with description, merchantable quality, fitness for purpose and correspondence with sample cannot be excluded or restricted by a contract term. As regards a person dealing otherwise than as consumer such liability can only be excluded or restricted by a term of the contract in so far as it satisfies the requirement of reasonableness. Section 11 of the 1977 Act provides that the requirement of reasonableness "is that the term shall have been a fair and reasonable one to be included having regard to the circumstances which were, or ought reasonably to have been, known to or in the contemplation of the parties when the contract was made", and that in determining "reasonableness" regard shall be had to the guidelines set out in Schedule 2 to the Act; it also provides that it is for those claiming that a contract term or notice is reasonable to show that it is. These powers are now consolidated in the Sale of Goods Act 1979.

Conditions and warranties are less prominent in the banker and customer relationship, though this has some implied terms and conditions of its own, which were mainly defined in *Joachimson* v. *Swiss Bank Corporation* (1921). An example is the banker's duty of secrecy, further elaborated in *Tournier* v. *National Provincial and Union Bank of England Ltd.* (1924), where qualifications to the duty were set out; namely, that disclosure by the bank is justified (a) under compulsion by law (e.g. under the Bankers' Books Evidence Act 1879); (b) under a public duty; (c) where required by the interests of the bank (e.g. the issuing of a writ against a customer claiming payment of his overdraft and stating the amount thereof); and (d) where made with the customer's express or implied consent. Nowadays, banks include advising on investments as part of their services to customers and consequently, as an implied term of the contract between them, a bank will be liable if it fails to exercise reasonable care and skill in advising a customer on investments: *Woods* v. *Martins Bank Ltd.* (1958).

Non-disclosure

In contrast to active or positive misrepresentation, there is a passive or negative side, i.e. silence, or non-disclosure by a party of facts within his knowledge. With most contracts there is no duty on a contracting party to disclose to the other material facts which he knows will influence him in coming to a decision, and this applies even when he knows the other party is ignorant of the facts or labouring under a misapprehension concerning them. However, there are certain contracts known as contracts *uberrimae fidei* (of the utmost good faith), in which there is a duty to enlighten the other party as to all material facts, and failure to do so makes the contract voidable at the option of the party to whom all was not revealed. These contracts form an exception to the general rule because in them by their very nature one of the parties alone possesses full knowledge of all the material facts, and so non-disclosure would unduly prejudice the other party. There are five categories of contracts *uberrimae fidei:*

(1) Contracts of insurance. The proposer must disclose to the insurer every circumstance which would influence the insurer's judgment.

(2) Contracts to subscribe for shares in companies. Under the Companies Act 1948 a company's prospectus must disclose all relevant information, so that would-be investors can properly make up their own minds.

(3) Contracts of Family Arrangements. When members of a family make arrangements for the settlement of the family property, each member must reveal his relevant personal affairs.

(4) Contracts for the sale of land, to a limited extent, in that the vendor must disclose all facts which might influence the purchaser and are not apparent from a reasonably careful inspection of the property, e.g. restrictive covenants.

(5) Contracts of Suretyship and Partnership, to a limited extent, in that although there is no duty to disclose before the contracts are made, once they are in existence a certain degree of disclosure becomes necessary.

4. DURESS AND UNDUE INFLUENCE

These derive from the Common Law and Equity respectively, and have the effect of making the contract voidable. Duress consists of

- (i) Actual or threatened physical violence or imprisonment,
- (ii) Threatened criminal proceedings,
- (iii) Implied threat of criminal proceedings.

Duress must be of the person, not of goods. Physical violence conjures up lurid pictures of the "protection rackets" beloved of gangsters. Threats of criminal proceedings against a person have sometimes been used to coerce that person (or some relative) into making a contract.

More likely to arise in practice is undue influence, which is both subtle and pervading. It occurs when one party to a contract is in a superior or dominating position over the other party, and therefore can influence the other to enter into a transaction which, had the parties been at arm's length, might not take place. In the following relationships undue influence is presumed on the part of the first-mentioned person, who has the onus of disproving it:

- (i) parent and child,
- (ii) guardian and ward,
- (iii) trustee and *cestui que trust* (beneficiary),
- (iv) solicitor and client,
- (v) doctor or hospital authorities and patient,
- (vi) religious adviser or superior and member of the congregation or disciple.

As between husband and wife there is no such presumption: *Howes* v. *Bishop* (1909). As between fiance and fiancee, since *Zamet* v. *Hyman* (1961), there is probably no such presumption unless the transaction is manifestly unfavourable. However, in these relationships, and in any other situation where there is no presumption, undue influence may be proved as a fact, but here the burden of proof is on the person alleging the influence. In *Re Brocklehurst* (1978) a strong-minded, autocratic and eccentric old baronet leased the shooting rights over his estate for 99 years as a gift to the proprietor of a small garage who had kept him company and performed personal services for him; the donor insisted that the lease be drawn up by the donee's solicitor and refused to take independent advice. This very valuable gift was attacked on the grounds of undue influence, but was upheld by a majority of the Court of Appeal.

An example of the wide-ranging nature of undue influence is *Lloyds Bank Ltd.* v. *Bundy* (1974) which will be discussed in Chapter 9 on Guarantees. Another illustration of inequality of bargaining power is *Clifford Davis Management, Ltd.* v. *W.E.A. Records, Ltd.* (1975) where members of a "pop group" had entered into a manifestly unfair contract with the plaintiff without any independent legal advice (the documents were long and had been professionally drafted). An interim injunction restraining the defendants from publishing works infringing the contract was discharged by the Court of Appeal.

Finally, moneylending contracts contain an element of undue influence, because a necessitous borrower usually has to take such terms as the moneylender decrees. The business of moneylending has been regulated by the Moneylenders Acts 1900–1927, but as these became increasingly out-of-touch with the modern commercial scene, with effect from a date still to be appointed they are repealed and replaced by the Consumer Credit Act 1974, of which ss. 137–140 provide for the Court's power to re-open extortionate credit bargains and agreements on similar, but more extensive, lines to those in the Moneylenders Acts 1900–1927. Canvassing a personal debtor/ creditor agreement (but not an overdraft) off trade premises is already prohibited by s. 49.

LEGALITY OF OBJECT

Clearly, no system of law will condone agreements between individuals that the law itself prohibits or regards as contrary to public policy. Contracts tainted with illegality are void, though if a contract is partly legal and partly illegal, if the former can be severed from the latter, it can be enforced. The various categories of illegal contracts can be set out as follows:

(a) Contracts tending to injure the public service, e.g. agreements for sale of public offices, or for procuring a title of honour.

(b) Contracts tending to impede the administration of justice, e.g. an agreement to stifle a criminal prosecution.

(c) Contracts of maintenance or champerty. Maintenance is officiously intermeddling in another's lawsuit, and champerty is assisting a person to bring a lawsuit in return for a share in the proceeds.

(d) Contracts of trading with the enemy.

(e) Contracts to commit a crime or a civil wrong.

(f) Immoral contracts. So far the cases on this aspect have centred round sexual immorality, and the test is whether the party seeking to enforce the contract has participated in the furtherance of the illegal intention.

(g) Contracts affecting the freedom and sanctity of marriage. An agreement in total restraint of marriage is void as being contrary to public policy, but one containing a partial restraint, e.g. not to marry a particular person or class of persons will be upheld. Marriage brokerage contracts, whereby a person undertakes to introduce someone to a member of the opposite sex with a view to matrimony, are void.

(h) Sundry contracts deemed contrary to public policy, e.g. an agreement by a newspaper not to comment on the conduct of a particular person.

(i) Contracts in restraint of trade. These have been the source of much litigation. They comprise two main categories: (i) those which restrict a person wholly or partially from following his trade, profession or calling; and (ii) those intended to protect a proprietary interest, as where the vendor of a business agrees to restrictions in whole or in part on his right to compete in business with the purchaser. The Courts are more willing to enforce contracts of the second type than those of the first type, and their approach to any contract in restraint of trade is governed by the rules laid down by the House of Lords in *Nordenfelt* v. *Maxim-Nordenfelt Guns and Ammunition Co., Ltd.* (1894). These are: (a) all contracts in restraint of trade are prima facie invalid, (b) no distinction is to be made between general and partial restraints, and (c) a contract imposing a restraint will be upheld where the restriction is reasonable as between the parties concerned and also with reference to the public interest.

Similarly, any condition which an employer imposes on an employee in a contract of service that after the termination of the employment the employee will not compete against the former employer is invalid, unless it is necessary to protect the employer against improper use by the ex-employee of trade secrets, trade connections or confidential information, and is no wider as to time and space than is reasonably necessary to effect that purpose. Various occupations have been examined by the Courts to see whether they gave rise to a confidential relationship that could justify a restraint imposed on the employee. For example, it has been held that there is no confidential relationship calling for any protection of the employer as between a reporter and a newspaper proprietor: *Leng* v. *Andrews* (1909); as between a canvasser and a clothing company: *Mason* v. *Provident Clothing and Supply Co., Ltd.* (1913); and a motor salesman and a firm of car dealers: *Vincents of Reading* v. *Fogden* (1932). On the other hand, a dairyman may be protected against his former milk roundsman: *Home*

Counties Dairies, Ltd. v. *Skilton* (1970); a ladies' hairdresser against a former assistant: *Marion White, Ltd.* v. *Francis* (1972); and a mail order company against a former compilor of its catalogue: *The Littlewoods Organisation, Ltd.* v. *Harris* (1978).

In *Scorer* v. *Seymour Johns* (1966), where there was a covenant by an employee not to engage as an estate agent within five miles of Kingsbridge and Dartmouth, the Court of Appeal enforced the covenant as to the Kingsbridge area (where he had been employed) but not in respect of Dartmouth, the more important town, because he had never been employed there. This case was applied by the Court of Appeal in *T. Lucas & Co., Ltd.* v. *Mitchell* (1972), where a sales representative had covenanted not to deal in his allocated district (Greater Manchester) in similar goods for one year after the termination of his employment by the plaintiffs and not to solicit orders or supply goods to any of their customers in the district supplied by them during the last twelve months of his employment. HELD, although the restraint on dealing in the Manchester area was invalid as being too wide, the covenants were severable and an injunction was granted against soliciting or supplying by the defendant in that area. In *A. Schroeder Music Publishing Co., Ltd.* v. *Macaulay* (1974) the House of Lords set aside a contract whereby a young and unknown song-writer entered into an exclusive contract for five years with the appellants, who were not obliged to publish any of his compositions, so that his work would be sterilised and he could earn nothing if they chose not to publish, on the ground that it was an unreasonable restraint of trade.

Whilst on the subject of trade, mention can be made of a different type of restriction—retail price maintenance. Under this system a manufacturer imposes conditions when selling his goods as to the price at which a retailer may in turn sell those goods to the public. At common law the manufacturer could not enforce the conditions against a retailer with whom he had no contractual relationship (there being some intermediary between them) because of the basic rule that a stranger to a contract cannot sue on it. The position is now governed by the Resale Prices Act 1976 (replacing earlier legislation) which prohibits collective and individual minimum resale price maintenance agreements but application for exemption may be made to the Restrictive Practices Court by the Director General of Fair Trading, or any supplier of the goods of the class in question, or any trade association whose members consist of or include such suppliers. Under the sister statute, the Restrictive Trade Practices Act 1976 (which consolidated earlier legislation) the Director General has two main duties: (1) to keep the register of agreements subject to registration (these are restrictive agreements as to production or supply of goods or as to services, or information agreements as to goods or services); and (2) to bring the registered agreements before the Restrictive Practices Court to declare whether or not they are contrary to the public interest. Finally, it may be noted that the Fair Trading Act 1973 contains a re-enactment, with some changes as to substance and detail, of the monopoly and merger provisions of earlier legislation, and also confers certain consumer protection functions upon the Director General.

There are certain contracts which, although not illegal, are void, i.e. they cannot be sued upon. Of these, the main category declared void by statute is:

Contracts by way of gaming or wagering, which are made null and void by the Gaming Act 1845. This is why gambling debts are called "debts of honour". A gaming contract is a wager upon the outcome of any game, e.g. a football match. A wager is more comprehensive, being an agreement between two parties that upon the happening of some uncertain event one party shall pay a sum of money to the other, neither having any other interest in the contract than the sum to be won or lost. What distinguishes a contract of insurance from a wagering contract is that in the former insurable interest must exist (see Chapter 7).

Effect of Illegality on the Consideration

One other aspect of illegality that warrants attention is the effect which it has on money paid or property transferred by one party to the other. In general, the plaintiff has no right of recovery, the legal maxim being *ex turpe causa non oritur actio* (no action arises out of a base cause). Once the Court discovers the illegality, it will not lend its aid to the plaintiff. In *Spector* v. *Ageda* (1971) it was held that where a loan was knowingly made in order to discharge an existing loan which was wholly or partially illegal, the loan was itself tainted with illegality.

However, to this general rule of irrecoverability, there are the following exceptions:

(1) Where the parties are not in *pari delicto* (in equal fault), e.g. when the plaintiff has been the victim of fraud or duress. So, in *Hughes* v. *Liverpool Victoria Legal Friendly Society* (1916) the plaintiff, who had entered into an illegal contract of assurance (there being no insurable interest) because of the fraud of the Society's agent, recovered the premiums paid.

(2) Where the parties genuinely repent before the contract has been performed in any way. Thus, if the illegal purpose has not been carried out, either party may recover money paid or goods delivered under the contract: *Taylor* v. *Bowers* (1876).

(3) Money paid under marriage brokerage contracts is recoverable, even though there has been part performance by the defendant: *Hermann* v. *Charlesworth* (1905).

(4) Where money has been deposited with a stakeholder under an illegal contract, it may be recovered at any time before it has been paid over to the winner: *Barclay* v. *Pearson* (1893).

EXCEPTION CLAUSES

Before discharge of contract is considered, discussion is needed of clauses in contracts which exempt, exclude, disclaim or restrict the liability of a contracting party (already mentioned under "Conditions and Warranties"). There has tended to be a tug-of-war between the general principle of English law that parties are free to contract as they think fit, and the reluctance of the Courts to uphold such clauses.

Consequently, the idea developed that an exception clause was nullified by a fundamental breach of contract, or a breach of a fundamental term. However, in a case concerning exception provisions in a charterparty, *Suisse Atlantique Société D'Armement Maritime S.A.* v. *N. V. Rotterdamsche Kolen Centrale* (1966), the House of Lords rejected this idea, laying down that in each case the question is one of the construction of the contract whether the exception clause was intended to give exemption from the consequences of a fundamental breach; if a breach occurs, entitling the other party to repudiate the contract, but he elects to affirm it, the exception clause continues unless on the true construction of the contract it is not intended to apply to and to continue after such a breach, in which case the party in breach is unable to rely on the exception clause.

The following are three examples of subsequent cases in which the Court of Appeal held that the respective defendants were guilty of such fundamental breach of contract that their exclusion or limitation clause ceased to have any effect: (1) *Harbutt's Plasticine, Ltd.* v. *Wayne Tank and Pump Co., Ltd.* (1970), where the defendants agreed to install certain equipment in the plaintiff's factory and because wholly unsuitable material was used, the factory was destroyed by fire; (2) *Levison* v. *Patent Steam Carpet Cleaning Co., Ltd.* (1977), where the defendants collected from the plaintiff's home a valuable Chinese carpet to be cleaned by them, and it was never returned; (3) *Photo Production, Ltd.* v. *Securicor Transport, Ltd.* (1978), where the defendants had contracted with the plaintiff company to guard its factory, but while carrying out a night patrol there an employee of the defendants deliberately lit a small fire, which got out of control and destroyed the factory.

Some of the methods used by the Courts to mitigate the hardship caused by exception clauses are now incorporated in the Unfair Contract Terms Act 1977. With the exception of liability for breach of implied obligations in sale of goods and hire purchase contracts (see p. 27), the Act regulates only "business liability", i.e. liability arising from things done or to be done in the course of a business or from the occupation of business premises. Liability for death or personal injury resulting from negligence cannot be excluded or restricted by a contractual term or notice, and similar exclusions or restrictions for other loss or damage are subject to the test of reasonableness. The Act also subjects to this test any attempt to exclude or restrict liability where one of the parties deals as a consumer, or on the other's written standard terms of business.

The common law doctrine of fundamental breach is modified by s. 9 of the 1977 Act whereby, notwithstanding that a contract has been terminated by breach or by a party electing to treat it as repudiated, a term of a contract which is required to meet the requirement of reasonableness may nevertheless be found to be so, and be given effect to. In contracts outside the Act, e.g. where two private individuals contract, the common law doctrine of fundamental breach may still be invoked.

Finally, although this is a slight digression in that it concerned the effect of an exception clause solely in tort, the case of *Hedley Byrne & Co., Ltd.* v. *Heller & Partners, Ltd.* (1963) must be considered. The facts were that the plaintiff company, advertising agents, lost money through the liquidation of a client about whom they had received via their own bank two status reports from the defendant merchant bank, and sued in respect of these references for the tort of negligence (which requires a legal duty of care on the part of the defendant, a breach by the defendant of that duty, and non-remote damage arising from that breach). Reversing previous decisions of the Court of Appeal that there was no legal liability in tort for negligent misstatements causing financial loss, the House of Lords held that the situation (which was not a contractual or a fiduciary relationship) was a "special relationship", justifying the imposition of a duty of care in these circumstances, unless expressly excluded, which it was by the disclaimer incorporated in the replies. Thus, in the absence of a clear "without responsibility" clause, a bank replying to a status inquiry emanating from the customer of another bank now owes a legal duty of care to that inquirer, and will therefore be liable if the reply is given negligently. Moreover, despite its title, the Unfair Contract Terms Act

1977 also applies to tort as regards negligence and so the "without responsibility" clause will now only be effective if it satisfies the requirement of reasonableness, the test being that it should be fair and reasonable to allow reliance on it, having regard to all the circumstances. Thus, the Act prescribes a different test of reasonableness in tort to that in contract, already set out on p. 27. When replying to status inquiries banks have used printed forms which incorporate a disclaimer clause over a very long period of time, and this would be one point to be taken into account when assessing whether the clause is "reasonable".

In an appeal from Australia, *Mutual Life and Citizens' Assurance Co., Ltd.* v. *Evatt* (1971), the Judicial Committee of the Privy Council looked more closely at the supplier of the information. The appellant company gave the respondent, without any disclaimer, advice as to the financial stability of its co-subsidiary company, as a result of which he suffered loss, but it was held (by a majority of 3 to 2) that there was no liability because *Hedley Byrne* should be understood as restricted to advisers who carried on the business or profession of giving advice of the kind sought in the course of their business. However, in *Esso Petroleum Co., Ltd.* v. *Mardon* (1976) the Court of Appeal preferred the view of *Hedley Byrne* by the minority in the *Mutual Life Case*, ORMROD, L.J., commenting: "If the majority view were to be accepted the effect of *Hedley Byrne* would be so radically curtailed as to be virtually eliminated."

As the same facts may create alternative liability in contract or in tort (usually for the tort of negligence), though damages cannot be recovered twice over, where a bank supplies a reference on one customer to another customer, then there is a contractual relationship as well, and if the reply is given negligently, any disclaimer clause will have to be construed by the Court as sufficiently precise to exclude liability both in contract and in tort, as well as satisfying the different tests of "reasonableness" in contract and in tort prescribed by the Unfair Contract Terms Act 1977.

It may be added that in the rare event of fraud (which constitutes the tort of deceit) a disclaimer of liability clause, however widely drawn, will be ineffective whatever the relationship of the parties may or may not be, for it is part of the fraud, and a person cannot by such a clause licence himself to commit fraud. This view received support in the Australian case of *Commercial Banking Co. of Sydney, Ltd.* v. *R. H. Brown & Co.* (1972) in which it was held that where a reply to a status enquiry was so recklessly and unjustifiably given as to amount to a fraudulent representation, the disclaimer clause in it had no effect.

DISCHARGE OF CONTRACT

There are various ways in which a contract may come to an end, and these are:

1. Performance

The vast majority of contracts are duly performed by both parties carrying out their appropriate obligations. Performance must be in the exact manner prescribed by the contract and within any agreed time limit, or, if no time has been fixed, within a reasonable time. Tender is an offer of performance and may consist of money or goods. To constitute a valid legal tender of money, the party must offer the exact amount, as change cannot be demanded, in the following ways—Bank of England notes up to any amount; and, under s. 2 of the Coinage Act 1971, (a) gold coins up to any amount; (b) cupro-nickel or silver coins of denominations of more than 10p, up to £10; (c) those of not more than 10p, up to £5; (d) bronze coins up to 20p; (e) other coins if made current by proclamation made under the Act up to such amount as may be specified in the proclamation. If a valid tender is refused, the obligation to pay the debt remains, but if sued, the debtor merely pays the money into Court, whereupon the other party must bear the whole costs of the action. If the subject-matter of the tender is goods, then a correct tender of the goods, which is refused, operates as a complete discharge, and entitles the party tendering to recover damages for breach of contract.

Apart from legal tender, payment may, with the consent of the creditor, be made by cheque or other instrument, this being known as conditional payment. The creditor's right of action is suspended until the cheque etc. is presented for payment, but if it is then dishonoured the creditor may sue either on the original debt, or on the cheque or other instrument. Payment by post will only discharge the debtor where the creditor has requested payment in this manner and the debtor has acted in a reasonable manner and in accordance with business practice. In *Zim Israel Navigation Co., Ltd.* v. *Effy Shipping Corporation* (1972), where a charterparty required payment in cash and the method of payment used was a transfer of funds between banks A and B ending in the crediting of the payee's account with bank B, it was held that payment was not effected until the payee was in a position to draw on that account for the amount of the funds transferred.

If the debtor owes more than one debt and pays to the creditor a sum which is insufficient to satisfy the whole of the debts, the payment must be *appropriated*, viz:

(a) *To whichever debt the debtor indicates.*—Illustrations of this from banking (a field in which the appropriation of payments is particularly important) are where a customer, whose account is overdrawn, pays in a credit which he stipulates is to cover certain cheque(s) which he has issued, or, alternatively, which he earmarks as covering debit interest charged by the bank so that he may obtain for tax purposes a Form R. 62 (Bank Interest Certificate). The customer's instructions to apply the credit to meet, say, cheque A and return cheques B and C unpaid, must be observed, quite apart from the state of the account, unless the bank has given previous notice, which has expired, that the account is to be closed.

(b) *If the debtor does not appropriate, then the creditor may do so.*—The creditor does not have to appropriate at once, but may do so at any time before bringing an action. He may even appropriate to a statute-barred debt. Having once exercised his own option as to appropriation, he cannot thereafter retract or alter it. To use again the banking example set out above, if the customer did not specify which cheque was to be paid by the credit lodged, the bank, as creditor, could decide whether to use it to pay cheque A or B or C, assuming it was sufficient to cover any one of the three but no more.

(c) *If neither the debtor nor the creditor appropriates.*—The operation of the law laid down in *Devaynes* v. *Noble* (1816), commonly known as the Rule in *Clayton's Case*, constitutes the appropriation.

The Rule is as follows: Where there is a continuous, unbroken, running account with payments in and out, in the absence of appropriation by the person paying in, or, failing him, the person receiving payment, the earlier payments in are, in the absence of special circumstances, attributed to the earlier payments out, and so on in regular sequence.

In other words, the first item on the credit side of a current account discharges or reduces the first item on the debit side, and so on. This rule is of great significance in banking, because although it occasionally operates in a bank's favour, it more often operates to the bank's detriment and to prevent it doing so, a current account must be broken and subsequent transactions passed through a new account. When this course is necessary will be examined in later Chapters.

As regards trust accounts, the Rule does not apply to a mixed fund of trust money and the trustee's own money, in that the trustee is deemed to have drawn out his own money first so long as any remains in the mixed fund (i.e. there is a presumption against a breach of trust by the trustee): *Re Hallett's Estate* (1880). However, if the trust moneys of several beneficiaries are mixed and there is not sufficient left to satisfy all, then the Rule in *Clayton's Case* applies as between the beneficiaries.

2. Agreement

Just as a contract is entered into by mutual agreement of the parties, it may likewise be terminated by mutual agreement. If both parties still have obligations to perform, a bilateral discharge can be effected whereby each party agrees to release his rights under the contract in consideration of a similar release by the other. In this way the old contract can be dissolved without any replacement, or an entirely new agreement can be substituted for it, or it may continue with modified or varied terms. No particular formalities are necessary for complete rescission—it may be done orally even though the contract is one which must be evidenced in writing, but if such a contract is altered (not extinguished) there must be written evidence of the alteration as there was of the original contract. If one party has performed all his obligations, but the other has not, then a unilateral discharge is necessary, whereby the former party releases the latter from his obligations, and as there is no consideration to support this variety of release it must be under seal to be effective.

Two other ways in which a contract may be discharged by agreement are accord and satisfaction, and merger. Accord and satisfaction is where, after a breach of the contract has occurred, the parties agree that one of them shall give and the other shall accept something different in kind (the agreement is the accord, the actual carrying out of it is the satisfaction). An example would be where one party is due to pay money but owing to his lack of funds the parties agree that he should hand over specified goods instead, and this is actually done. It was formerly considered that taking a cheque for a smaller sum instead of cash for a larger sum amounted to accord and satisfaction, but this was rejected by the Court of Appeal in *D. and C. Builders, Ltd.* v. *Rees* (1966) who held that payment by a debtor whether in cash or by cheque of a lesser sum than the amount of the debt was not a settlement of the debt which was binding at law on the creditor (i.e. he can still sue for the balance).

Merger occurs when a contract of lower degree (e.g. a simple contract) is merged into one of higher degree (e.g. a deed) between the same parties and relating to the same subject-matter. It also takes place when a breach of contract case is heard and determined by the Court, for the Court's decision is a contract of record, which supersedes the original contract made by the parties whether it was a simple contract or a deed.

Finally, the contract itself may contain provisions for discharge, e.g. a term (a) providing for termination on the non-fulfilment of a condition, or (b) releasing the parties from liability on the happening of a specified event, or (c) giving either party power to terminate the contract, as in a lease, or in a contract of employment, by giving the appropriate notice. Where one of the parties to a contract of service gave notice determining the contract, that party could not thereafter unilaterally withdraw the notice: *Harris and Russell, Ltd.* v. *Slingsby* (1973) (although it was always open to the other party to agree to the withdrawal of the notice). Contracts of employment have received considerable statutory intervention, and are now subject to the Equal Pay Act 1970, the Race Relations Act 1976, the Sex Discrimination Act 1975, and the Employment Protection (Consolidation) Act 1978. In *Mount* v. *Oldham Corporation* (1973) the Court of Appeal recognised the well-established usage in the educational world that, if a parent wished to withdraw a child from school, he was bound to give a term's notice, or to pay a term's fees in lieu of notice.

The absence of a power of termination was considered by the Court of Appeal in *Staffordshire Area Health Authority* v. *South Staffordshire Waterworks Co.* (1978). The parties had agreed in 1929 that the company would supply 5000 gallons of water per day free and such further water as required at 7d per 1000 gallons (2.9 new pence since decimalisation). In 1976 the company gave 6 month's notice of termination, indicating that it was prepared to continue the free 5000 gallons but would charge for any excess at 45p per 1000 gallons. HELD, during a period of inflation this agreement had become unfair and because inflation was a circumstance which the parties never had in mind the contract would cease to bind the parties for ever and could be determined on reasonable notice.

As regards the closing of a bank account, the customer may do so by withdrawing the balance (subject to any agreed period of notice in the case of a deposit or savings account), or by paying off all indebtedness. On the other hand, if the bank wishes to close an unsatisfactory account (not being a debit one repayable on demand), it must give the customer reasonable notice in writing to enable him to make arrangements to meet outstanding cheques, bills etc. What is reasonable depends on all the circumstances; in *Prosperity, Ltd.* v. *Lloyds Bank Ltd.* (1923), it was held that a month's notice was insufficient for a company whose business had widespread ramifications.

3. Acceptance of Breach

One party may commit a breach of contract either by repudiating his liability, or by disabling himself by his own act from carrying out the contract, or by failing or refusing to meet all his obligations under the contract: such conduct gives the other party the option of treating the contract as still in existence, or as discharged by breach so that he can then sue for damages.

Repudiation arises where, before the time for performance has arrived, a party declares his intention of not performing the contract. This is known as anticipatory breach, of which an illustration is *Hochster* v. *De La Tour* (1853), where a courier who had been engaged as from a fixed future date was told before that date that his services would not be required. It was held that he could sue for damages forthwith and need not wait until the time for performance. Of course, he may decide to wait until that time in case the other party changes his mind and goes ahead with the contract, but there is a risk here—the contract may be discharged by other circumstances during that period, in which event the plaintiff's right of action will be lost. This is shown by *Avery* v. *Bowden* (1856), where the defendant refused to load the plaintiff's ship with a cargo of wheat. The plaintiff did not take proceedings immediately and before the time for performance had expired, the outbreak of the Crimean War ended the contract; it was held that the plaintiff had no cause of action.

An example of self-induced disability is *Synge* v. *Synge* (1894), where a man who promised before marriage to settle a particular house on his wife after marriage conveyed that house to a third party; it was held that his wife could sue for breach of contract.

Impossibility of performance is also relevant to the question of breach of contract. A contract which is clearly impossible is void because of the absence of any real consideration—an old example used to be to fly to the moon, but scientific progress has now achieved this—however, a contract to drain the Atlantic ocean would seem to be still quite impossible. Apart from this variety, impossibility does not in general discharge a contract, subject to the following exceptions:

(a) *Statutory interference.*—Where the contract was originally lawful, but due to a subsequent change in the law, it becomes legally impossible to perform, it will be discharged. Thus, the seller of a quantity of wheat was excused from performance when the wheat was requisitioned by the Government before the property in it had passed to the buyer: *Re Shipton, Anderson & Co. and Harrison Bros. & Co.'s Arbitration* (1915). In contrast, where the statutory powers are already in existence at the time the contract is made, then a contracting party cannot shelter behind their subsequent exercise and will be liable for breach of contract caused thereby: *Walton Harvey, Ltd.* v. *Walker and Homfrays, Ltd.* (1931).

(b) *Accidental destruction of subject-matter.*—An illustration of this is *Taylor* v. *Caldwell* (1863), where a music-hall was hired for a series of concerts, but it was destroyed by fire before the date of the first concert: it was held that performance of the contract was excused.

(c) *The cessation of circumstances, the continued existence of which formed the basis of the contract.*—A number of cases on this point arose out of the postponement of the Coronation of Edward VII due to the King's sudden illness. For example, in *Krell* v. *Henry* (1903) the defendant agreed to hire a room from the plaintiff for two days, in order (as both parties knew) to watch the Coronation procession. When it was cancelled, the defendent declined to pay the balance of the rent, and the plaintiff's claim for it failed, because it was held that the basis of the contract must be assumed to have been the existence of the procession.

(d) *Personal incapacity.*—In contracts for personal services, i.e. where personal qualifications are important, illness or death may incapacitate that person.

For example, in *Robinson* v. *Davison* (1871) the defendant, a pianist, had agreed to play at a concert to be given on a specified day. The contract contained no reference to illness. She was unable to appear, due to illness. It was held that she was not liable for breach of contract, as the contract was conditional upon her being well enough to perform.

(e) *A fundamental change of circumstances.*—This may frustrate the adventure or the commercial or practical object of the contract.

Thus, the contract may be ended by frustration due to the occurrence of an event which the parties did not contemplate or for which neither party was responsible. Similarly, in *Metropolitan Water Board* v. *Dick, Kerr & Co., Ltd.* (1918) the company having agreed in July 1914 to construct some reservoirs for the Board, on the outbreak of the Great War the work was stopped by the Ministry of Munitions; the House of Lords held that this put an end to the contract, because the character and duration of the interruption would make it, if resumed, a very different contract based on changed conditions.

But a change in circumstances which is not fundamental does not terminate the contract. In *Tsakiroglou & Co., Ltd.* v. *Noblee Thorl G.m.b.H* (1962) a shipment of groundnuts which would normally have been sent through the Suez Canal was not despatched since it would have had to go round the Cape of Good Hope at great expense and delay because the Suez incident in 1956 had unexpectedly blocked the Canal; the House of Lords held that the contract was not frustrated.

As regards the financial aspect of frustration, the Law Reform (Frustrated Contracts) Act 1943 provides that upon frustration, except in so far as is expressly provided for by the contract, all sums paid to any party in pursuance of the contract before discharge are recoverable, and sums payable cease to be payable. At the discretion of the Court a payee who has incurred expenses may retain or recover from the payer whatever is considered just, and where one party has obtained a valuable benefit (other than the payment of money), the other party may recover from him such sum as is considered just. Finally, if part of a contract is frustrated and the contract is severable, the Act will apply only to the frustrated part.

REMEDIES FOR BREACH OF CONTRACT

When a breach of contract has occurred, the injured party has the following courses of action open to him:

(i) Refusal of Further Performance

The injured party may regard the total breach as a discharge of the contract and refuse to do anything under it himself; and at the same time he may sue for damages for breach of contract.

(ii) Damages

He may continue to act upon the contract and sue for damages for breach of contract. A successful plaintiff is always entitled as of right to the common law remedy of damages, but where he has sustained no loss, nominal damages only will be awarded. Real or substantial damages are those intended as compensation for the actual loss suffered. Thus, in a contract for the sale of goods the measure of damages is the difference between the market price at the time of the breach and the contract price. In *Jarvis* v. *Swan Tours, Ltd.* (1973) the Court of Appeal held that damages could be awarded for mental distress or inconvenience in an action for breach of contract, and a proper case for such damages was a failure to provide a holiday or entertainment and enjoyment for which the plaintiff had paid. It applied this principle in another "spoilt holiday" case, *Jackson* v. *Horizon Holidays, Ltd.* (1975), where it was also held that where a person had entered into a contract for the benefit of himself and others who were not parties to the contract, he could sue for damages not only for himself but also for the others even though he was not a trustee for them, i.e. the plaintiff could additionally claim for the discomfort, vexation and disappointment suffered by his wife and children. It also applied it in *Heywood* v. *Wellers* (1976), where the plaintiff had suffered mental distress due to her solicitor's negligent failure to enforce an injunction protecting her from molestation by a man. Since the abolition of the action for breach of promise of marriage, exemplary or vindictive damages (i.e. made very heavy by way of punishment) can no longer be awarded in contract. A plaintiff is under a duty to mitigate his loss, i.e. he must do the best he can to minimise the damage he has suffered, e.g. a person wrongfully dismissed from his employment must take all reasonable steps to obtain suitable employment elsewhere.

When no sum is named in the contract as the amount to be paid by a defaulting party, the damages are "unliquidated", i.e. the Court will award such damages as it thinks appropriate. When the sum payable in the event of breach is fixed or ascertained by the parties in the contract, that sum can be recovered where it is liquidated damages (a genuine pre-estimate of the probable loss or damage), but not where it is a penalty (an extravagant sum by way of deterrent) in which event only the actual damage suffered can be claimed.

Any loss or damage which is too remote cannot be recovered. The test for determining remoteness of damage is that laid down in *Hadley* v. *Baxendale* (1854); "The damages should be such as may fairly and reasonably be considered either arising naturally, i.e. according to the usual course of things, from such breach of contract itself, or such as may reasonably be supposed to have been in the contemplation of both parties at the time they made the contract, as the probable result of the breach of it". In the case itself, the crankshaft of the steam engine at the plaintiff's mill had broken and it was delivered to the defendant, a carrier, to be taken to a foundry for use as a pattern for a new one. The carrier delayed delivery of the crankshaft beyond a reasonable time causing the mill to be idle, but he had not been informed that delay would result in the plaintiff losing a particularly valuable contract. It was held that the defendant was not liable for loss of profits during the period of delay. *Hadley* v. *Baxendale* was applied by the House of Lords in *The Heron II* (1967), where a ship had been chartered to carry a cargo of white sugar from Constanza to Basrah. The normal length of the voyage was 20 days, but the shipowner deviated in his own interest and thereby prolonged the voyage by 9 days. At Basrah there was, as the shipowner knew, a market for white sugar. During the 9 days the market fell and the charterers lost more than £4,000. The House of Lords held that the loss of profit was recoverable as damages for breach of contract because on the knowledge available to the shipowner at the time the contract was made he must have realised it was not unlikely that the sugar would be sold in Basrah market on arrival and that prices were apt to fluctuate daily.

A final point relating to damages of concern to plaintiffs, especially banks, is whether or not interest can be included in the claim. The answer is that interest can be recovered; where agreed, either expressly by the parties, or impliedly from trade usage or the course of dealing; in respect of overdue bills of exchange and promissory notes—s. 57 of the Bills of Exchange Act 1882; and by s. 3 of the Law Reform (Miscellaneous Provisions) Act 1934 the Court may allow interest at such rate as it thinks fit on all claims for debt or damages from the date when the claim arose to judgment.

(iii) Quantum Meruit

Where a person performs any part of a contract which is severable he may bring an action for the value of the work he has done, instead of one for damages. This remedy is known as suing on a *quantum meruit* ("as much as he has deserved"). For instance, in *Planchè* v. *Colburn* (1831) the plaintiff was engaged by the defendant to write a book to be published by instalments in a weekly magazine. After a few numbers had appeared, the magazine was abandoned. It was held that the plaintiff could recover on a *quantum meruit* an amount equivalent to the work he had done.

Similarly, where the work provided for in a lump sum contract is completely performed, but is done badly, the person who has done the work can recover the agreed lump sum, less an appropriate deduction for the bad workmanship: *Dakin & Co., Ltd.* v. *Lee* (1916). This type of situation is likely to occur when a builder, decorator or electrician etc. does the work agreed, but with defects, so that the law makes a suitable allowance with which they may be put right. In considering whether this doctrine of substantial performance applies, it is relevant to take into account both the nature of the defects and the proportion between the cost of rectifying them and the contract price: *Bolton* v. *Mahadeva* (1972).

(iv) Specific Performance

Instead of or in addition to claiming damages, the injured party may ask the Court for a decree of specific performance, which orders the parties to carry out the actual contract. This remedy is an equitable one, and therefore is available only at the Court's discretion, being normally granted in contracts for the sale of land or of unique or valuable objects, e.g. a particular painting by a famous artist. Here, the intending purchaser would much rather have the painting, because damages would be a poor substitute for it. On the other hand, specific performance is not available in the following circumstances:

(a) Where damages would be an adequate remedy. Thus, a contract will not be specifically enforced where it is for the sale of an article generally available, e.g. a car of the ordinary, mass-produced variety so that there are thousands like it.

(b) In moneylending contracts.

(c) Where there is a want of mutuality. It must be clear that at the time when the contract was made the remedy would be available to either party in the event of a breach. Thus, specific performance would not be granted to an infant plaintiff, as it could not be awarded against him if he was the defendant.

(d) Where the execution of the contract would require the supervision of the Court, e.g. in building contracts, or in contracts of personal service.

(e) Where the plaintiff has been responsible for fraud, mistake or accident in relation to the contract.

(f) Where in general it would be inequitable, e.g. if the plaintiff's loss is trivial or he has unduly delayed his claim for this remedy; or if granting it would cause undue hardship to the defendant.

In a case concerning the sale of land, *Johnson* v. *Agnew* (1979), the House of Lords held that where a vendor obtained an order for specific performance and it became impossible to enforce it, he then had the right to ask the Court to discharge the order and terminate the contract. On such an application he could be awarded damages at common law for breach of contract since the contract was not rescinded *ab initio* but remained in existence until terminated by the Court, but the Court would not make an order discharging the decree of specific performance and terminating the contract if to do so would be unjust, in the circumstances then existing, to the other party.

(v)   Injunction

The type of injunction appropriate to actions for breach of contract is the prohibitive injunction—an order of the Court restraining a person from doing some act. This remedy also is discretionary, having been devised by Equity to cover situations in which the Common Law remedy of damages was inadequate or unsuitable. Thus, where a contract in restraint of trade is valid and the party subject to the restrictions has not observed them, the other party will ask for an injunction ordering him to refrain from those contravening acts.

An injunction may be used as an indirect method of obtaining specific performance, and this extends to contracts for personal services when they contain express negative covenants. Thus, in *Lumley* v. *Wagner* (1852) the defendant agreed to sing at the plaintiff's theatre for a certain period and nowhere else; it was held that though specific performance could not be granted an injunction would be granted to prevent her singing for a third party.

LAPSE OF TIME

The passage of time does not generally terminate contracts, but in order to prevent legal actions being brought on very old claims the law prescribes periods after which no action can be brought for breach of contract, though as the contract itself remains good the creditor can obtain payment in any other way where possible. The Limitation Act 1939 provides the following periods of limitation—simple contracts, the right of action is barred after six years from the date on which the cause of action accrued; specialty contracts and judgment debts, twelve years from date of accrual (s. 2). If, however, a breach of contract gives rise to a claim for damages for personal injuries, the period is reduced to three years by the Law Reform (Limitation of Actions, &c.) Act 1954; but by the Limitation Act 1963, as amended by the Law Reform (Miscellaneous Provisions) Act 1971, the Court can allow an action to be brought outside this period where the delay is due to the plaintiff's lack of knowledge of material facts.

Section 22 of the Act of 1939 provides that if the plaintiff, when the cause of action arises, is an infant and is not in the custody of a parent, time does not begin to run until the person ceased to be under the disability or died, and the period is six years whether the contract be a simple or a specialty one. Similar provisions are laid down by s. 31 in the case of unsoundness of mind of the plaintiff. As regards fraud, s. 26 provides that when:

(a) the action is based upon the fraud of the defendant or his agent; or

(b) the right of action is concealed by the fraud of the defendant or his agent; or

(c) the action is for relief from the consequences of a mistake, time does not begin to run until the plaintiff has or by the exercise of reasonable diligence could have discovered the fraud or mistake.

A statute-barred right of action can be revived by an acknowledgement in writing signed by the party liable or his agent or by part payment. Thereafter, time begins to run afresh. Payment of interest revives the right of action in respect of the principal but not in respect of other instalments of interest which have become barred: s. 23.

The Common Law rule that the debtor must seek out his creditor does not apply in banking as regards credit accounts. The bank is not liable to repay until demand has been made by the customer: *Joachimson* v. *Swiss Bank Corporation* (1921). Thus, the Limitation Act 1939 does not commence to run against the customer until such demand has been made. The important case just cited did not deal with overdrawn accounts, and in the absence of express agreement as to demand or date of repayment it would appear that time runs from the date of each advance. Mere debiting of interest by the bank will not revive the debt, and it will therefore become statute-barred six years after the last transaction on it by the customer or the last acknowledgment by him of the debt.

THE OPERATION OF CONTRACT

As an agreement made between contracting parties, a contract cannot confer either rights or liabilities on one who is not a party to it. The fundamental principle that a stranger to a contract cannot enforce it has been affirmed by the House of Lords on three occasions:

(1) *Dunlop Pneumatic Tyre Co., Ltd.* v. *Selfridge & Co., Ltd.* (1915) which concerned a price maintenance agreement (statutory intervention on this point has already been noted).

(2) *Scruttons, Ltd.* v. *Midland Silicones, Ltd.* (1962), where it was held that S. Ltd., as strangers to a contract of carriage, could not rely on a clause in it limiting liability.

(3) *Beswick* v. *Beswick* (1967), where an elderly coal merchant had agreed with his nephew, the appellant, to transfer to him his business assets in consideration of the nephew paying him £6 10s. 0d. a week, and after his death £5 a week for life to his wife (who was not a party to the agreement). The nephew took over the business, but after his uncle's death he paid only one sum of £5 to the widow, the respondent. HELD, (1) the widow as administratrix of a party to the contract was entitled to specific performance of the promise by the nephew and was not limited to recovering merely nominal damages on the basis of the loss to the estate; (2) but she could not enforce the obligation in her personal capacity as she was not a party to the contract.

ASSIGNMENT OF CONTRACTS

Whether rights or liabilities under a contract can be transferred or assigned during its currency to a third party depends initially on the particular contract, because those involving personal credit, ability or qualifications, e.g. contracts to sing, or to paint a picture, or contracts of employment, cannot be assigned either at law or in equity. In the case of other contracts assignment may take place either:

(1) By operation of law.

This type of devolution of contractual rights and liabilities occurs on the death or bankruptcy of either party. In the event of death, all rights and liabilities pass to the deceased's personal representatives; in bankruptcy, they pass to the bankrupt's trustee in bankruptcy.

(2) By act of the parties.

(a) Rights

Rights under contracts come within that category of personal property, or personalty, known as "choses (=things) in action", defined in *Torkington* v. *Magee* (1902) as: "Chose in action is a known legal expression used to describe all personal rights of property, which can only be claimed or enforced by action and not by taking physical possession". Thus, debts, stocks and shares, goodwill, patents, trademarks and copyright are in this class, in contrast to those things which have a material or tangible physical form and are called "choses in possession", e.g. a book, or piece of furniture. Choses in action may be either legal or equitable. A legal chose in action is one enforceable by a common law action, e.g. a debt, whereas an equitable chose in action is one which, prior to the Judicature Act 1873, was only enforceable in the Court of Chancery, e.g. a reversionary interest under a will or settlement, but which is now enforceable in any Division of the High Court.

Certain rights cannot be assigned on the grounds of public policy, e.g. pensions payable to public servants, and sometimes a contract may provide that rights under it cannot be assigned, or that the other party must consent to any assignment. Apart from these special features, either party may make a legal or an equitable assignment of his rights under the contract to a third party. Some contracts are assigned in accordance with statutes that govern them, independently of the general methods (e.g. bills of exchange, stocks and shares, and life policies which will be discussed in later Chapters;

there are also bills of lading under the Bills of Lading Act 1855, and marine policies under the Marine Insurance Act 1906).

The general method of effecting a legal assignment is set out in s. 136 of the Law of Property Act 1925, which provides that all debts and other legal choses in action may be assigned, but the assignment must be:

(i) In writing, signed by the assignor;

(ii) Absolute, and not by way of charge only;

(iii) Followed by express notice in writing given to the debtor, trustee or other person who holds the funds assigned.

It was held in *Re Pain* (1919), in respect of similar wording in a section of the Judicature Act 1873 now replaced by s. 136, that even an equitable chose in action may be legally assigned. Thus, a mortgage taken by a bank on a customer's reversionary interest under a will or settlement is in the form of a legal assignment. In any event, if the assignment for any reason fails to take effect as a legal one, it will still constitute an equitable assignment provided the intention to assign is clear.

It would appear that for the purposes of s. 136 "signed" means, in the case of a company or other corporation, that the assignment is executed under its common seal. Under s. 136 the legal assignment must be absolute and never for part only of a debt, for otherwise the debtor will be inconvenienced by having to seek out two creditors. The assignment is absolute where the assignor retains no interest in the property, even though it is by way of mortgage or by way of trust: this is really a question of wording. If the assignor (creditor) assigns the debt due to him from his debtor absolutely to the bank, subject to a proviso for re-assignment in the event of the assignor himself ceasing to be indebted to the bank, this is by way of charge but it is absolute and therefore a legal assignment; but if the assignor merely charges the debt in general terms as security to the bank, then it will be only an equitable assignment. Of course, if the assignor wishes to assign part of a debt, or a future debt, then the assignment is necessarily an equitable one. However, it was held at first instance in *Siebe Gorman & Co., Ltd.* v. *Barclays Bank Ltd.* (1978) that there could be a fixed charge over future book debts in a debenture, and this innovation will be looked at again in Chapter 4. An assignment of part of a debt, to be effective, must be an assignment of part of a specified fund; a mere order by a creditor to his debtor to pay money to a third party where no fund is specified out of which payment is to be made does not constitute an equitable assignment: *Percival* v. *Dunn* (1885). The usual instance of a future debt is where the money will only become due and payable as and when work is done under a contract; it is not a debt that already exists.

Express notice in writing must be given to the debtor, because otherwise if he pays the original creditor (the assignor) in ignorance of the assignment, he obtains a good discharge. Alternatively, the debtor can be made a party to the assignment, in which event he will covenant that the sum assigned is still due and owing and that he will pay it to the assignee. A legal assignment does not require consideration: *Re Westerton* (1919), so there can be a valid legal assignment by way of gift. If the notice gives the wrong date of the assignment the notice is bad, for it is a notice of a non-existing document: *W. F. Harrison & Co., Ltd.* v. *Burke* (1956). On the other hand, if the notice gives no date at all it is a valid notice of assignment under s. 136 so long as the notice makes it plain that there has been an assignment and the debtor knows to whom he has to pay the debt in the future: *Van Lynn Developments, Ltd.* v. *Pelias Construction Co., Ltd.* (1968).

Provided s. 136 is compiled with, the assignee obtains a legal right to the chose in action, and can sue on it in his name or give a good discharge for it without the concurrence of the assignor.

If the requirements of s. 136 are not complied with, there may still be a valid equitable assignment, for no particular formalities are necessary for an equitable assignment, provided the intention to assign is clear. It need not be in writing. Notice, verbal or in writing, to the debtor is not essential, though it is highly desirable in order to ensure that the debtor does not pay the assignor in ignorance of the assignment, and to obtain priority over any subsequent assignee. Where the equitable assignment is in respect of a future debt or property, consideration must be present or the assignment will not be enforced: *Glegg* v. *Bromley* (1912).

An equitable assignee of a legal chose in action cannot enforce the right assigned by action without joining the legal owner: *Performing Right Society, Ltd.* v. *London Theatre of Varieties, Ltd.* (1924). Nor has he the power to give a good discharge without the concurrence of the legal owner. An equitable assignee of an equitable chose in action can bring an action in his own name, except where the assignment is conditional or is for part only of the debt, when the assignor must be joined in the action.

Both a legal and an equitable assignee take subject to equities (i.e. defences available against the assignor). Thus, if the debtor has a valid right of set-off against the assignor, he can exercise it against the assignee. Similarly, any defect in title is perpetuated, as an assignee gets no better title than his assignor had at the time of the assignment.

(b) Liabilities

These can only be assigned with the consent of the other party to the contract, a procedure known as Novation, i.e. a tripartite agreement which is really a new contract, substituting a new party for an existing one. Assignment of liabilities under a contract must be distinguished from vicarious performance of them, or delegation when personal performance is not essential, e.g. the builder of a house usually sub-contracts specialist tasks such as plumbing and electrical wiring.

DEVELOPMENT OF NEGOTIABILITY

Within the general framework of assignability there is a special area of negotiability, a concept of the Law Merchant (*Lex Mercatoria*), which developed from the customs of the merchants. Historically, the commercial community found the mediaeval common law cumbersome and unsatisfactory for purposes of trade and so the merchants, drawing on their international background, developed a practice of transferring documents representing rights. Ultimately, some documents were recognised as being transferable free from equities and came to be called negotiable instruments. In mediaeval times there were special courts for the settlement of disputes between merchants, as they had their own customary law, and amongst them were the Courts of the Staple set up by Edward III, which recognised the mercantile instrument known as a bill of exchange as early as the 14th century, though the first reported case in which the Common Law Courts did so is *Martin* v. *Boure* (1603).

Bills of exchange originated in Italy, and the words "of exchange" show the value received or exchange element behind the documents and distinguish them from other types of bills. To the man-in-the-street "bills" are merely unpaid invoices. From the ordinary bills of exchange there later developed the best known and most frequently used variety of bill, the cheque, so called as a variation of the word "check" (still the transatlantic spelling) because of the counterfoils attached to them for checking purposes, other bills of exchange and promissory notes not having counterfoils.

By the beginning of the 17th century the Common Law Courts had gradually assimilated the various commercial courts, and the long and difficult process of incorporating the law merchant into the common law was successfully consumated by Lord Mansfield, Chief Justice of the Court of King's Bench from 1756 to 1788, who has been aptly described as the founder of the commercial law of this country.

The categories of negotiable instruments are not closed, for this process of incorporation still takes place very occasionally. If at any time it can be proved that a certain mercantile custom fulfils the conditions of universal recognition by the business community of this country (not the usage of any foreign country in which the instrument was issued) and of reasonableness, the Courts will recognise it as law. Thus, in *Goodwin* v. *Robarts* (1875) it was held that scrip issued in England by the agents of foreign governments was rendered negotiable by the usage of the English money market; and in *Bechuanaland Exploration Co.* v. *London Trading Bank* (1898) bearer debentures were recognised as negotiable instruments, evidence having been given that they were so treated by general mercantile custom. Recently, negotiable certificates of deposit, issued in sterling, dollars and Eurodollars, have appeared upon the commercial scene; they are bearer certificates and are accepted by the usage of the London market as negotiable instruments.

Whether a particular document is a negotiable instrument or not depends on if it is accorded all the characteristics of negotiability by mercantile custom, or by statute, or by recognition by the Courts. Hence, transferability and negotiability are not the same; negotiable instruments must be transferable, but transferable instruments are not necessarily negotiable—some are given this additional status, but the rest are not, for negotiability is a special attribute relating to title. Statute law may also take away negotiability, as will be seen when ss. 36 and 81 of the Bills of Exchange Act 1882 are discussed in Chapters 10 and 13 respectively.

CHARACTERISTICS OF A NEGOTIABLE INSTRUMENT

All the following features must be present if the document is to pass the negotiability test:

1. The document must be transferable by delivery, or by indorsement and delivery. The negotiable instrument is itself a written document, and when payable to bearer it is simply handed over to the transferee; if payable to order, it requires indorsement and then delivery.

This distinguishes it from such documents as a fire insurance policy or a bill of sale. A legal assignment, as already noted, must be in writing.

2. The legal title passes to the person who takes it in good faith and for value and without notice of any defect in the title of the transferor

(such a person being known in the case of a bill of exchange as a "holder in due course"). Thus, the transferee can acquire a better title to the instrument than that of his transferor. This runs counter to the general rule in contract of *Nemo dat quod non habet* (no one can give what he has not got), and is the essence of negotiability. For example, in *Miller* v. *Race* (1758) the plaintiff acquired in good faith and for value a bank note which had previously been stolen in a mail robbery. When he presented it to the bank for payment, the bank refused to pay, and it was held that the bank was liable to him on the note.

On the other hand, in an ordinary assignment the assignee can only acquire the same title as his assignor had.

3. The holder for the time being can sue in his own name.

A legal assignee can do this, but generally speaking an equitable assignee cannot do so.

4. The title passes free from equities of which the transferee has no notice. Thus, the existence of some defect, such as a counter-claim, set-off or right which the debtor may exercise against the transferor cannot be used against the transferee of a negotiable instrument when he is not aware of it. Suppose A buys goods from B and gives him in settlement a negotiable instrument, which B passes to C, who takes it as holder in due course; if it transpires that the goods are defective, so that A has a claim in this respect against B, this does not affect the title acquired by C, because he takes free from equities.

In an ordinary assignment, the assignee takes subject to equities.

5. Notice of the transfer need not be given to the party liable on the instrument. It would, for instance, be an impossible situation if every time a £1 note changed hands notice of this fact had to be given to the Bank of England. Payment will be made to the person presenting the negotiable instrument at the appropriate time whoever he may be.

In a legal assignment, notice is an essential element under s. 136; and in an equitable assignment it is highly desirable in order to ensure payment to the assignee and to establish the priority of the assignment as between competing assignees.

To sum up, the basic questions for determining the negotiability of any instrument are: Is the transferee able to sue in his own name without notice to the party liable? and Does the transferee who takes in good faith and for value acquire a good title to the instrument, despite any defect or flaw in the transferor's title? Where the answers are "Yes", the instrument is negotiable, and so has the attributes of cash in that it can pass easily from owner to owner throughout the community. Thus, bills of exchange, promissory notes (including bank notes), cheques, treasury bills, dividend warrants, bearer debentures, bearer shares and certain scrip are negotiable. On the other hand, by their origin money orders and postal orders are "not negotiable"—these words which appear on them do not change the position, as they do when placed on a cheque, because they are merely pointing out a fact which already exists (as an emergency measure postal orders were statutorily made legal tender during wartime). Registered stock, share or debenture certificates, stock transfers, bills of sale, dock warrants, I.O.U.s., and insurance policies are not negotiable. Bills of lading (being both contracts of carriage of and receipt for goods and also documents of title to those goods) are sometimes called "quasi-negotiable", because they are transferable and by s. 1 of the Bills of Lading Act 1855 a transferee can sue and be sued in his own name; but, apart from certain other statutory exceptions in favour of pledgees, a transferee of a bill of lading cannot get a better title to it than that of his transferor.

Chapter 2

Agency

INTRODUCTION

In modern, highly-organised countries, people are less able to cope directly with all their activities, and often have to delegate tasks to other persons known by the general name of agents. The extent of this devolution is shown by the wide variety of agencies in operation, such as employment, estate and travel agencies. Sometimes a person described commercially as an agent (e.g. sole agent, or concessionaire, for some article or commodity) is legally not an agent but a principal because he buys and re-sells on his own account. In the realm of hire-purchase, difficulties have arisen as to the exact relationship of dealers and finance companies: a majority of the House of Lords held in *Branwhite* v. *Worcester Works Finance, Ltd.* (1968) that the dealer is not normally the agent in law of the finance company in relation to a hire-purchase transaction.

In law, then, the term "agent" has a rather narrower meaning, namely a person who is employed by a principal for the purpose of bringing that principal into contractual relations with third parties. Thus, in *Towle & Co.* v. *White* (1873) an agent was defined as "a person invested with a legal power to alter his principal's legal relations with third parties". The maxim underlying that branch of the law of contract relating to agency is *Qui facit per alium facit per se* (he who does a thing through another does it himself). Consequently, provided the principal has full contractual capacity, he can employ as agent a person lacking contractual capacity, such as an infant, and in the normal way he will be bound by what that agent does, even though if the agent entered into the contract on his own behalf it might be void because of his infancy, e.g. the borrowing of money. This situation does not apply where the positions are reversed, for a principal lacking contractual capacity cannot overcome his disability by employing an agent who has full contractual capacity; any purported authority would be of no effect in these circumstances. Whether or not a principal can delegate a particular task is, of course, determined by the general law. Thus, s. 136 of the Companies Act 1948 provides that any member of a company is entitled to appoint a proxy to attend and vote for him at meetings of the company. On the other hand, the carrying out of a promise of marriage is non-delegable, the parties to the marriage must be personally present at, and take part in, the ceremony, because English law (unlike some foreign systems of law) does not permit marriage by proxy.

Agency is particularly important in banking, because banks act as agents on behalf of their customers, and often on behalf of other banks, in a variety of matters, such as the collection of cheques and bills of exchange; the payment of money by means of cheques, bills of exchange or other instruments; foreign transactions; dealings with securities and so on. Again, banks have to deal with a large number of agents in the course of daily banking business such as directors of companies, partners of firms, and persons to whom a power of attorney has been granted, or who have been appointed under some form of mandate to act on behalf of customers. The legal principles of agency in general, and its particular reference to banking, will now be considered in detail.

TYPES OF AGENTS

Agents may be divided into various classifications, which can be set out as follows:

(a) *Special.*— those with authority to act only on a particular occasion or for a specific purpose, e.g. to sign cheques on the principal's account or to buy a particular article for him. To make the principal liable for the acts of a special agent the other contracting party will usually have to prove that the agent had actual authority to do what he did.

(b) *General.*— those with authority to do anything coming within certain limits, e.g. a partner is a general agent of the firm and his other partners for the purpose of the business of the partnership. The acts of a general partner within the ordinary course of the duties assigned to him, i.e. within his "ostensible authority", will be binding on his principal.

(c) *Universal.*— those with unlimited authority to act for the principal in any capacity.

(d) *Del credere.*— those who, for an extra commission, undertake responsibility for the due performance of their contracts by persons whom they introduce to their principals. For example, factors may enter into *del credere* agreements to guard their principals against loss from sales on credit, and advertising agents may do so in respect of forward advertising orders which they place with television companies and newspapers. An agreement to be a *del credere* agent is not a guarantee, but an indemnity to the principal against the agent's own misfortune in introducing defaulting debtors, and therefore need not be evidenced in writing. A *del credere* agent only undertakes that the buyers will pay, and does not make himself liable to his principal if a buyer refuses to take delivery: *Gabriel & Sons* v. *Churchill and Sim* (1914).

(e) *Mercantile.*— s. 1 (1) of the Factors Act 1889 defines a mercantile agent as one "having in the customary course of his business as such agent authority either to sell goods, or to consign goods for the purpose of sale, or to buy goods, or to raise money on the security of goods."

METHODS OF APPOINTMENT

An agent, who may or may not be a servant of the principal, can be appointed in any of the following ways:

(i)   By deed

If the agent is to have authority to contract under seal, then his own appointment must also be under seal (and stamped as a deed, i.e. 50p impressed), when it is known as a power of attorney. The absence of a deed will not, however, be a defence to a principal who is present and allows the agent to enter into the contract for him: *Ball* v. *Dunsterville* (1791).

A power of attorney is the actual authority or instrument embodying an authorisation to one person, the attorney (grantee or donee), or to two or more persons either jointly, or jointly and severally, to act on behalf of the principal (grantor or donor). Unless the contrary is provided, there is a presumption in favour of joint authority in which event the attorneys must all act together and if one dies the agency does not remain in the survivor. Traditionally a power of attorney begins: "Know all men by these Presents that I . . . do hereby appoint . . .", and sets out a series of clauses elaborating the position of the attorney, usually concluding with a "general" or "omnibus" clause which authorises the attorney to do any act the principal himself could do, but this refers only to acts incidental to those specifically authorised. The principal's signature is attested, preferably by two witnesses. Thus, the attorney has no authority to do any acts outside the scope of the powers specifically given, e.g. authority to operate on a bank account does not include power to overdraw or give security: these powers must be specifically conferred (an "omnibus" clause alone not being sufficient for this purpose). However, important changes have been made by the Powers of Attorney Act 1971 whereby a General Power of Attorney in the form prescribed in the Schedule, viz.

"THIS GENERAL POWER OF ATTORNEY is made this day of 19

by AB of

I appoint CD of   [or CD of   and EF of

jointly, *or* jointly and severally] to be my attorney [s] in accordance with section 10 of the Powers of Attorney Act 1971.

IN WITNESS etc.,   "

or in a form to like effect but expressed to be made under the Act will operate to confer on the donee[s] of the power authority to do on behalf of the donor anything which he can lawfully do by an attorney (s. 10). This Act of 1971 largely amends s. 25 of the Trustee Act 1925 and repeals ss. 123–125 (1) and 126–129 of the Law of Property Act 1925. By s. 1 a power of attorney shall be signed and sealed by, or by direction and in the presence of, the donor; if another person so executes it on behalf of the donor then two other persons must be present as witnesses and attest it (thus, physically incapable persons can now grant a power of attorney).

Filing of a power of attorney at the Central Office of the Supreme Court or at the Land Registry has been abolished by s. 2, though the right to search for, inspect or copy those already filed is preserved. By s. 3 a photocopy of a power of attorney, certified by the donor or by a solicitor or stockbroker, and any copy of a photocopy similarly certified shall be sufficient proof of the existence and contents of the power.

Sections 4 and 5 deal with revocation. By s. 4 a power of attorney whenever created which is given to secure (a) a proprietary interest of the donee; or (b) the performance of an obligation owed to the donee, shall not be revoked, so long as the donee has that interest or the obligation remains undischarged, either by the donor without the donee's consent, or by reason of the death, incapacity or bankruptcy of the donor or, if the donor is a body corporate, by reason of its dissolution. Illustrations of this point occur in bank security forms which sometimes empower the bank to complete on behalf of the mortgagor instruments to transfer title, e.g. in the case of land, an equitable mortgage under seal (see Chapter 6). The gist of s. 5 is that where the donee of a power of attorney acts in pursuance of the power at a time when it has been revoked he shall not incur any liability (either to the donor or to any other person) if at that time he did not know of the revocation; and where a person, without knowledge of the revocation, deals with the donee the transaction shall be as valid as if the power has then been in existence. In practice, a power of attorney often provides that it shall be irrevocable for a specified period, usually one year but as regards normal banking transactions, if the principal revokes the power during that period and revocation has either directly or indirectly (e.g. knowledge of the execution of a later power in favour of a different attorney) been communicated to the bank, then the bank must act upon that revocation.

Section 7 provides that the donee of a power of attorney may (a) execute any instrument with his own signature and, where sealing is required, with his own seal, and (b) do any other thing in his own name, by the authority of the donor of the power; any document so executed or thing so done has the same effect as if executed or done by the donee with the signature or seal, or in the name of the donor.

By s. 9, as an amendment to s. 25 of the Trustee Act 1925, of which sub-sections (1) to (8) and (11) are replaced by these new provisions, powers of attorney delegating all or any of the trusts, powers and discretions vested in trustees may be granted for periods up to 12 months in the absence of contrary provisions in the trust instrument and provided notices are given as required by s. 9 (2) (4), but a sole co-trustee may not be granted such a power of attorney unless that co-trustee is a trust corporation. A power given under this section has to be attested by at least one witness.

It may be added here that if a joint account holder gives a power of attorney to an outside party, the power does not enable the attorney to operate on the joint account in place of his principal unless the other party, or parties, to the joint account agree; but where the account is a trust account, the concurrence of the other trustee(s) is not necessary when the power is conferred under s. 25 of the Trustee Act 1925, as amended.

(ii)   In writing

If the agent is not required to contract under seal, then his appointment may be in writing, but even this is unnecessary except where written form is required by statute, e.g. a lease (unlike an agreement for a lease) cannot be made by an agent unless he has been appointed in writing, but this does not apply to leases at the best rent for three years or less where the lessee takes possession: ss. 53 and 54 of the Law of Property Act 1925. Again, the copy of any prospectus that a company has to deliver to the registrar of companies for registration must be signed by every person named therein as a director or proposed director or by his agent authorised in writing: s. 41 (1) of the Companies Act 1948. On the other hand, no formality is required for the appointment of an agent to sign a memorandum of a contract which is unenforceable unless evidenced in writing, e.g. a guarantee.

Needless to say, a bank always asks for written evidence in the shape of a mandate to put the matter beyond doubt and argument. A mandate, which must be distinguished from a power of attorney (described above), does not generally of itself delegate powers (though this depends on its precise wording): it is an advice or confirmation that power has been delegated coupled with a request to accept the instructions of the agent for the purpose indicated. Even if the mandate form is in its phraseology an authority, e.g. when it commences "I hereby authorise . . .", it is an authority addressed to one party alone, and not to the world at large as is a power of attorney. Each bank has various mandate forms covering authorities to draw cheques etc. on the principal's account, whether in credit or overdrawn, to make periodical payments (standing orders), to buy or sell stock exchange securities and the like. Customers holding stocks and shares often complete mandate forms addressed to the company concerned, or other body, authorising the payment of dividends or interest direct to their bank. Mandate forms are not subject to stamp duty. The bank or other party to whom the mandate is addressed must ensure that the agent, being a special one, acts only within the scope of his actual authority, for there can be no implied authority, e.g. an authority to sign cheques *per procurationem* (abbreviated as "per pro." or "p.p.") does not connote power to overdraw the relative account(s) unless so provided by the mandate.

(iii)   Orally

Except in cases where a written appointment of an agent is required by law (see (ii) above), an agent may be appointed by word of mouth and this will suffice for simple contracts. Indeed, the great majority of agencies are created in this way. A homely example that frequently happens is when a parent sends out a child on an errand to the local shop.

(iv) By implication or estoppel

Agency may be implied from the relationship of principal to agent, without an express authority. Examples of situations where agency is implied are:

(a) A wife can pledge her husband's credit for necessaries;

(b) A son can drive the motor car owned by his mother: *Smith* v. *Moss* (1940):

(c) A partner can order goods required for the firm's business;

(d) A bank becomes the customer's agent for collection of cheques lodged by the customer for the credit of his account (there is no express contract here).

Estoppel is a rule of evidence whereby a party is estopped (i.e. precluded or prevented) from denying the existence of some state of facts which he has previously asserted. Circumstances, called agency by estoppel, may therefore arise because a person may have so acted that he cannot afterwards deny that some-one else was his agent. A familiar banking example would be that if a customer regularly sent one of his clerks to collect his bank statement, he could not subsequently challenge the bank's action on a particular occasion, since he would be estopped from denying that the clerk was his agent for that special purpose.

(v)   Ratification

This is a procedure whereby a non-existent agency at the time of the contract being made can arise and be made retrospective by ratification. In other words, the principal subsequently confirms and adopts the contract as made. The legal maxim here is: *omnia ratihabitio retrotrahitur et mandato priori aequiparatur* (a ratification has a retrospective effect and is equivalent to a prior command). Thus, ratification is thrown back to the time when the act was done, but to be effective any ratification must comply with the following conditions:

(a) That the agent contracts as agent. If he contracts in his own name with an undeclared intention to act on behalf of another for whom he then had no authority to act, that undisclosed principal cannot ratify: *Keighley, Maxsted & Co.* v. *Durant* (1901). Notwithstanding this House of Lords ruling, however, the Court of Appeal held in *Spiro* v. *Lintern* (1973) that the defendant husband was under a duty to the plaintiff to disclose that his wife had acted without his authority in selling his house; his failure to do so amounted to a representation by conduct that she had that authority, and so the plaintiff was entitled to specific performance of the contract of sale between him and the husband by virtue of the wife's agency by estoppel.

(b) That the principal was in existence and had contractual capacity at the time of the contract. Two cases illustrate these aspects:

Kelner v. *Baxter* (1866), where it was held that a company which had not been incorporated when the contract was entered into on its behalf by the promoters could not subsequently ratify that contract (though it may make a new contract to the same effect, provided the contract is not ultra vires); and

Boston Deep Sea Fishing and Ice Co., Ltd. v. *Farnham* (1957) where it was held that a principal who was an enemy alien when the contract was made (and therefore had no contractual capacity by English law) could not ratify the contract after he ceased to be an enemy alien.

(c) That the whole (and not merely a part) of the contract is ratified. Thus, the principal cannot take over the benefits of the contract, whilst rejecting the burdens.

(d) That it takes place within any period fixed for ratification, or, if none has been fixed, then within a reasonable time.

(e) That the principal had full knowledge of the material facts or intended to adopt the acts of his supposed agent whatever their nature or culpability: *Marsh* v. *Joseph* (1897).

As regards banks in particular it may be noted that if a bank has inadvertently paid a company's cheque bearing an unauthorised signature, the transaction can be ratified or confirmed by the company.

(vi) By necessity

Where circumstances amount to an emergency the agent may bind his principal without prior authority or subsequent ratification. These special circumstances are where the agent, lawfully in possession of another's property, is compelled to incur expense in order to preserve the property. It must be practically impossible to communicate with the owner and obtain his instructions: *Springer* v. *Great Western Railway Co.* (1921). Also, the action taken must be reasonably necessary and done in good faith to preserve the property. For example, a master of a ship may borrow money on the owner's credit to purchase necessaries in the course of a voyage if communication with the owner is impossible (this is not very likely to arise nowadays in view of the worldwide cable, wireless and telephone systems).

Another example is *Great Northern Railway Co.* v. *Swaffield* (1874), where a horse was consigned to Swaffield who failed to meet it at Sandy station. As there was no accommodation at the station the horse was left at a livery stable, and it was held that the railway company was entitled to claim reimbursement from Swaffield as an agent of necessity.

For agency by necessity to arise there must almost certainly be already some existing contractual relationship between the parties; it was said in *Jebara* v. *Ottoman Bank* (1927) that it is extremely doubtful whether a person can be bound in this way by the act of a complete stranger.

At common law a deserted wife could pledge her husband's credit for household expenses or borrow money on his credit, but this agency of necessity was abolished by s. 41 of the Matrimonial Proceedings and Property Act 1970.

AUTHORITY, DUTIES AND RIGHTS OF AGENTS

The overall authority possessed by an agent may be expressly provided in the terms of his appointment, or may be implied by the circumstances of the case, e.g. a partner in a trading firm has implied authority to borrow money on behalf of the firm. In the case of a special agent the third party must make himself acquainted with the extent of the agent's authority; in the case of a general agent, his acts bind the principal if they are within the scope of his ostensible authority, even though they may be in excess of his actual authority, provided the third party is unaware of the limitation on that apparent authority. The agent's authority will in general be strictly construed by the Courts, but incidental powers necessary to carry it out will be implied, especially in the case of mercantile contracts.

The actual duties and rights of an agent as against his principal (to which the principal for his part has corresponding rights and duties) may be summarised as follows:

(a) The agent has a duty to carry out his appointed tasks with reasonable skill and diligence.

Reasonable here means appropriate to the circumstances—an agent must normally show no less diligence than he would have shown had he been dealing with his own affairs, and if he professes any special skill which is requisite to the function he has been appointed to perform, then he must display this skill, or he will be liable to indemnify his principal for any resultant damage even though he has done his best. In this respect there is a difference between a gratuitous agent and a paid agent. A gratuitous, or unpaid, agent is liable only for gross negligence—he is expected to use "such care and diligence as persons ordinarily use in their own affairs, and such skill as he has", whereas a paid agent is expected to use "care and diligence such as are exercised in the ordinary and proper course of similar business, and such skill as he ought to have, viz the skill usual and requisite in the business for which he receives payment" *per* CROMPTON, J., in *Beal* v. *South Devon Railway Co.* (1864).

(b) The agent must not delegate his authority.

The legal maxim here is *delegatus non potest delegare* (an agent may not delegate his authority), for the agent himself has a delegated authority from his principal, who intends the agent to use it himself, and not to delegate it still further to some other person who may not be known to, or approved by, the principal. Thus, if A authorises B to sign on his bank account, B cannot himself sub-delegate this power to C. To this general rule that an agent's duty is non-delegable, there are the following exceptions, set out in *De Bussche* v. *Alt* (1878), viz, where

(i) Custom sanctions delegation.

(ii) Delegation is necessary to proper performance. For example, if a customer gives his bank instructions to buy or sell quoted stocks and shares on his behalf, then the bank will have to employ a stockbroker to effect the transactions because the bank cannot itself deal on a stock exchange.

(iii) There is statutory, express or implied authority to delegate. Thus, when a client employs a solicitor, there is implied authority to allow some of the work to be delegated to clerks.

(iv) Where unforeseen emergencies arise which impose upon the agent the necessity of employing a substitute.

In *John McCann & Co.* v. *Pow* (1975) the Court of Appeal held that an estate agent, in particular one who claimed to be a sole agent, did not have implied authority to appoint a sub-agent, since he held a position of discretion and trust, and was bound to discharge his functions and duties personally in the absence of express authorisation to delegate them.

(c) The agent must not misuse or disclose confidential material and information acquired in the course of his agency.

Except in his principal's interest, an agent may not use material and information which he has obtained or been supplied with only for his principal and in the course of his agency. He also owes a duty not to disclose secret or confidential information or documents entrusted to him in the course of his agency: *Weld-Blundell* v. *Stephens* (1920) where the House of Lords awarded nominal damages against a chartered accountant whose partner negligently lost a confidential letter written to the accountant by a client: the letter contained libels on third parties, who recovered damages from the client when they learnt of the libels.

(d) The agent must act in good faith for the benefit of his principal, and must not make any secret profit or take any bribe, in the course of his agency.

This is why bank advices to customers for whom the bank has acted in stock and share transactions disclose that the stockbrokers' commission is divisible with the bank.

"If and so long as the agent is the agent of one party, he cannot engage to become the agent of another principal without the leave of the first principal with whom he has originally established his agency": LORD HANWORTH, M.R., in *Fullwood* v. *Hurley* (1927). This was applied in *North and South Trust Co.* v. *Berkeley* (1971), where it was held that the long-standing practice at Lloyd's whereby brokers acted as dual agents, viz as agents of the assured generally and as agents of the insurer (particularly for the purposes of passing instructions to assessors and solicitors acting on behalf of the insurers) was wholly unreasonable and therefore incapable of being a legal usage.

If an agent allows his duty and his interest to conflict, so that he lets his personal interests be advanced by accepting a secret profit or illicit commission, then the principal can claim that profit or commission, and can also refuse to pay the agent the commission due to him on account of the transaction in respect of which the profit or commission was taken. The mere agreement by the agent to accept such profit or commission is sufficient, and if the money is paid over to him, his principal may recover it as money received to his use. It is not necessary that the principal should have suffered any loss through the transaction, or even that the agent should be acting directly in his principal's business. In *Reading* v. *Attorney-General* (1951) an Army sergeant had received some £20,000 from smugglers in Cairo during the Second World War because he rode on their civilian lorries in uniform so that his presence ensured that the lorries and their illicit loads got past the police without interference: the Crown recovered the money, for the sergeant, as their servant, had used his employment as the means of obtaining a secret profit for himself.

The principal may claim any bribe received by the agent from a third party during the agency. Furthermore, an agent who receives a bribe can be dismissed without notice: *Boston Deep Sea Fishing Co.* v. *Ansell* (1888); nor may he claim his commission in respect of that transaction.

If the principal has suffered loss on the contract, he may sue either the agent or the party who offered the bribe for damages; or he may refuse to be bound by the contract, irrespective of any effect the bribe may have had on the agent's mind. It may be added that both parties to the bribe are guilty of a criminal offence under the Prevention of Corruption Act 1906.

(e) The agent has a right to the remuneration agreed by the principal, or if none has been fixed, to reasonable remuneration which is customary in the particular business or appropriate to the particular circumstances.

If the terms on which commission is to be paid are clearly stated in the contract, there is no room for implied terms: *Luxor (Eastbourne), Ltd.* v. *Cooper* (1941). As regards banking, a bank has an implied right to charge commission (and interest on debit balances) on current accounts in the absence of special arrangements made with particular customers. The interest rate will be agreed when the borrowing is arranged, and is normally a certain percentage above base rate to keep pace with fluctuations therein. Commission is normally fixed on an ad hoc, or rule-of-thumb, basis depending on the average balance on the account, the number of entries and any other facilities utilised, except in the case of important or active accounts where it is usually a percentage on turnover. As regards estate agents, their commission has given rise to much litigation, particularly over whether they can claim commission only in respect of the first transaction arising from an introduction, or on subsequent transactions, or on transactions only completed after the agency has been terminated. No general principle can be formulated on this point, it all depends on the precise wording of the agreement made between the parties.

(f) The agent is entitled to be indemnified against losses and liabilities properly incurred in the execution of his agency.

In *Hichens, Harrison, Woolston & Co.* v. *Jackson & Sons* (1943) stockbrokers were instructed through a firm of solicitors to sell shares, but subsequently the solicitors' client repudiated the contract, and the stockbrokers under the rules of the Stock Exchange had to purchase the shares elsewhere to fulfil their bargain: it was held that the stockbrokers were entitled to be indemnified by the solicitors. It will be appreciated that a similar situation could arise as regards banks who frequently accept instructions from their customers for the purchase or sale of securities quoted on stock exchanges and pass on these orders to stockbrokers. As stock transfer forms are not now signed by the transferee (the purchaser), difficulties of the purchaser's refusal to sign will not arise in respect of these, but they will still arise if the customer refuses to sign the form as transferor (the vendor) because the stockbrokers will have to buy in to replace the stocks or shares not delivered and will claim indemnity from the bank which has instructed them for any loss incurred in the replacement, the bank in turn claiming indemnity from its own principal, the customer.

(g) The agent has a right to a lien, the exact extent of which will vary with the particular class of agent concerned.

Thus, factors, bankers, stockbrokers and solicitors, for example, have a general lien, or the right to retain the property of another until all moneys owing to them by that person are paid, but a banker's lien goes further than the others in that it allows a bank to realise negotiable securities after reasonable notice, and recoup itself from the proceeds.

RELATIONS WITH THIRD PARTIES

Whilst the basis of agency is to bring the principal into contractual relations with a third party so that the principal alone is liable on the contract and entitled to its benefits, the agent himself having no rights or liabilities vis-à-vis the third party, this situation may be varied in certain cases. Thus, an agent may be liable:

(a) if he agrees to be so;

(b) where the principal does not exist, or does not have contractual capacity. As already mentioned, ratification is not possible here, but whether or not the agent is liable depends on the exact way he has made the contract. In *Kelner* v. *Baxter* (1866) the proposed directors, who contracted in their own names for the purchase of wine on behalf of an hotel company not yet formed and took delivery of the wine, were held personally liable. This is now supported by s. 9 (2) of the European Communities Act 1972 which provides that a contract purporting to be made by a non-existent company will take effect (subject to any agreement to the contrary) as a contract entered into by the person purporting to act for the company or as agent for it and he shall be personally liable on the contract accordingly. Consequently, it overrules *Newborne* v. *Sensolid (Great Britain), Ltd.* (1954) where it had been held that a contract made in the name of a company not yet formed and authenticated by the signature of a "director" was a complete nullity, and neither the company nor the actual signatory had any rights or liabilities thereunder;

(c) where the contract is by deed, and the agent executes it in his own name;

(d) where he becomes a party to a bill of exchange in his own name;

(e) where trade custom makes him liable—for example, in the London fruit trade.

It was formerly considered that if an English agent contracted on behalf of a foreign principal, then there was a presumption that the agent and not the principal was liable, unless a contrary intention plainly appeared from the contract itself or the surrounding circumstances. However, decisions in the present century have taken the opposite view, and in *Teheran-Europe Co., Ltd.* v. *S. T. Belton (Tractors), Ltd.* (1968) the Court of Appeal held that no such presumption exists; the foreign nationality of the principal being merely one factor to be taken into account in determining whether the contract in the circumstances excluded enforcement by or against the foreign principal.

Where a third party, who knows who the real principal is, nevertheless elects to give credit to the agent personally in circumstances which enable him to hold the agent liable, then his right of action against the principal is lost, for he has waived it by his own conduct.

The basic situation as regards relations with third parties is also affected by two factors, (i) when the agent exceeds his authority, and (ii) when the name of the principal is not disclosed, both of which call for fuller treatment:

(i) Agent exceeding his authority

In order to assess whether a particular transaction does exceed the agent's actual authority, it is necessary to establish the limits of that authority as laid down by the principal. If the authority is in writing, its extent is a question of construction; if it is oral, its extent is a question of fact. Incidental powers necessary to carry out the authority will normally be implied, though where the terms of the authority are clearly defined, there is no room for implied terms. Thus, the manager of a shop has implied authority to order goods for the purposes of the trade carried on, to receive payments from customers, and to give receipts therefor. In *Re Wallace* (1884) a solicitor who was authorised to conduct legal proceedings was held to be justified in presenting a bankruptcy petition. If the authority given by the principal is ambiguous or equivocal, and the agent interprets it one way and acts upon it, the principal cannot repudiate it on the basis that he intended the authority to be interpreted in another way: *Ireland* v. *Livingston* (1872).

If the third party knows the agent is exceeding his actual authority, then he cannot make the principal liable, unless the latter chooses to ratify the contract. Such knowledge by the third party may be actual, or constructive, as where the circumstances should have put him on inquiry. Two cases which illustrate this aspect are:

(a) *Colonial Bank* v. *Cady and Williams* (1890), of which the facts were: Executors of the registered owner of shares in a New York company signed as executors the transfers on the back of each certificate without filling up the blanks and sent the certificates to their London stockbrokers, who fraudulently deposited the certificates (admitted to be not negotiable) with the bank, which took them *bona fide* and without notice as security for advances, but took no steps to obtain registration. The House of Lords upheld the executors' title to the shares as against the bank on the ground that the documents were ambiguous, being consistent either with an intention of the executors to sell or pledge the shares or to have themselves registered as owners, and so were sufficient notice to cast on the bank the duty of inquiring into the extent of the stockbrokers' authority.

(b) *Reckitt* v. *Barnett, Pembroke and Slater, Ltd.* (1929), where a fraudulent attorney of Sir Harold Reckitt drew a cheque on his grantor's account to settle a debt of his own which he had incurred to the respondents by buying a Daimler motor-car. The House of Lords held that the transaction was not within the terms of the power of attorney, and in the absence of actual authority, the respondents, having notice that the appellant's money was being applied for the attorney's private purposes, were not entitled to the proceeds of the cheque.

So much for the agent's actual authority. The third party, however, is not so much concerned with this, as with the agent's apparent or ostensible authority.

Usually the situation is that the third party deals with an agent who appears to be clothed with a certain authority, and in this event where the contract is within the apparent authority of the agent, the third party is not affected by any secret limitations on that authority of which he is not aware. It sometimes happens, for example, that junior partners in a firm may be restricted as to the amount for which they can pledge the firm's credit, but if they contract for more than that amount in the usual course of the firm's business with an innocent third party, the latter will not be bound by the internal restriction and the firm will be liable, its only remedy being to sue the agent for breach of contract of agency. Similar difficulties over internal regulations arise in respect of companies and will be dealt with under the Rule in *Turquand's Case* in Chapter 4 on Companies.

If an agent exceeds his authority or represents himself as having authority which he does not possess he may be sued by the third party for breach of warranty of authority, so long as the third party did not know of the want of authority: *Collen* v. *Wright* (1856). This is so even though the agent's authority has been terminated without his knowledge by the death or mental disorder of the principal: *Yonge* v. *Toynbee* (1910).

Whether he is a party to it or not, the principal is liable for the fraud or other wrongful acts of his agent committed in the course of the agency and within the scope of the agent's authority or implied authority, even if the fraud is committed by the agent for his own benefit. However, in *Sorrell* v. *Finch* (1976) the House of Lords held that the engagement of an estate agent by a prospective vendor did not confer on the estate agent any implied or ostensible authority to receive as agent of the vendor a pre-contract deposit from a would-be purchaser. The purchaser was at all times until contract the only person with any claim or right to the deposit moneys, and in the absence of any express authority (by the vendor), the vendor was not liable for the deposit when the agent misappropriated it.

It will be recalled (from Chapter 1 on Contract) that s. 6 of the Statute of Frauds Amendment Act 1828 (Lord Tenterden's Act) provides that no action will lie on a representation as to the credit etc. of a person unless the representation is in writing signed by the party to be charged therewith (i.e. the signature of an agent will not bind his principal). This Act, however, applies only to fraudulent misrepresentation: *Banbury* v. *Bank of Montreal* (1918). An incorporated bank would not, therefore, be liable on a fraudulent representation as to credit unless it was issued under the common seal of the company (which is never done in practice). Although in *Barwick* v. *English Joint Stock Banking Co., Ltd.* (1867) the bank was held liable for a fraudulent representation in a letter signed by its manager that a cheque issued in favour of the plaintiff by a third party would be paid "in priority to any other payment, except to this bank", on the ground that this was within the scope of the manager's duty, the defence of Lord Tenterden's Act was not pleaded. In a case where it was raised, *Hirst* v. *West Riding Union Banking Co., Ltd.* (1901) the bank avoided liability for a fraudulent representation made by one of its branch managers.

If the agent makes a statement which he believes to be true, when expressly authorised to make it by his principal who knows it to be false, the agent is not liable, but the principal is. If both principal and agent know the statement is false, both are liable as joint tortfeasors for deceit. If, however, the agent makes a statement which he believes to be true, whereas the principal knows it to be false but has not expressly authorised the agent to make it and has not been guilty of deliberate fraudulent conduct, such as purposely employing an agent known to be ignorant of the facts so as to avoid disclosure, then neither principal nor agent is liable for fraud: *Armstrong* v. *Strain* (1952), where it was said: "There is no way of combining an innocent principal and agent so as to produce dishonesty." If the agent's fraudulent conduct is not authorised by the principal and is not within the scope of the agent's implied authority, then the agent alone is liable, even though he acted solely for the principal's benefit.

The principal cannot retain a profit made by the fraud of his agent whether he authorised that fraud or not; and money paid by the third party in reliance on a fraudulent misrepresentation can be recovered.

(ii)   The undisclosed principal

The doctrine of the undisclosed principal has two aspects: (a) where the agency is known—this frequently occurs e.g. a hotel doorman who hails a taxi for a guest, and (b) where the agency is not known—this is less frequent and more complicated. Where the agency is known and it is clear on the face of the contract that it is expressly made on behalf of a principal, though he is not named, then the agent is not liable. If this fact is not clear, then the third party may proceed against either the agent or the principal when his name becomes known; both are liable, but liability being alternative not joint, the third party, once he has made his choice, cannot subsequently sue the other: *Scarf* v. *Jardine* (1882). The commencement of proceedings against either is *prima facie* evidence of the third party's choice, but if that evidence is rebutted this does not bar subsequent proceedings against the other: *Clarkson Booker, Ltd.* v. *Andjel* (1964). On the other hand, a judgment obtained against the party he chose to sue is conclusive evidence of his choice and even if unsatisfied (i.e. not paid, or fulfilled) bars proceedings against the other.

Where the agency is not known, then the rules just mentioned will apply, once the third party becomes aware of the existence and identity of the undisclosed principal. The alternative remedy against the principal may be lost, however, to the extent that the principal has in the meantime honestly settled with his agent. Conversely, if the principal sues on the contract, he must do so subject to any right of set-off that the third party may have acquired against the agent before he knew that he was acting for a principal. If in the contract the agent describes himself as a principal in such a way as to exclude the possibility of an undisclosed principal, the agent alone can sue or be sued.

CLASSES OF AGENTS

The main classes of agents will now be considered, with the particular features relating to them.

(a) *Auctioneers.*—An auctioneer is one who conducts auctions, which are public sales where articles are sold to the highest of successive bidders. He is an agent of the vendor and when the goods have been knocked down, he has power to sign the memorandum of sale as agent for the buyer also, at the time of the sale or as soon as practicable thereafter so it forms part of the transaction. His signature is then sufficient to satisfy the requirements of s. 40 of the Law of Property Act 1925 that a contract for the sale or other disposition of land or any interest in land is unenforceable unless evidenced by some memorandum in writing signed by the party to be charged or his agent.

He should sell at the best price and only for cash, unless it is customary to accept a cheque and he acts without negligence in doing so. He has power to receive the purchase money when the sale is for cash, but only a deposit (usually ten per cent) on a sale of land, as settlement will take place later. This deposit is held by the auctioneer as stakeholder for the two parties to the contract and pending completion he must not pay it over to the vendor without the purchaser's consent. If the sale is completed, or the purchaser defaults, the auctioneer will pay the deposit to the vendor after deducting his commission. As the auctioneer has a lien on the goods for the whole price until it has been paid, if the purchaser defaults, he is entitled to sue for the price in his own name, even though he has received a deposit which covers his commission: *Chelmsford Auctions, Ltd.* v. *Poole* (1973). If the vendor defaults, the auctioneer will return the deposit to the purchaser. The auctioneer can retain any interest earned by the deposit while in his hands.

The vendor may place a reserve price on the goods and may reserve a right for himself or his agent to bid, but such right must be expressly notified: s. 57 of the Sale of Goods Act 1979.

If an auctioneer innocently and in good faith sells and delivers goods on behalf of a principal who has not title to them, the auctioneer is liable to the true owner for their value in an action for conversion, even though he has already paid the proceeds to his principal: *Consolidated Co.* v. *Curtis & Son* (1892). It is said that this encourages the business community to be circumspect, i.e. to deal with the right person, not merely to have some perfectly good reason for having dealt with the wrong person. Thus, the tort of conversion (any unauthorised dealing with the goods of another which has the effect of depriving the true owner of his property) is one of the occupational hazards of auctioneers, as it is of bankers and brokers.

(b) *Bankers.*— In view of the detailed treatment required the particular facets of agency that concern banks are dealt with under the next heading of this Chapter.

(c) *Brokers.*— A broker is an intermediary or middleman in mercantile transactions, who arranges bargains and contracts between other parties in return for a commission or brokerage. The mode of dealing used by brokers is to send a "bought note" to the buyer and a "sold note" to the seller, the two notes constituting the contract between the parties. Brokers must be distinguished from factors, because unlike the latter brokers do not have possession of the goods, they cannot sue and act in their own name, nor (apart from special custom) can they buy and sell in their own name. As far as conversion is concerned, brokers, like auctioneers, deal with the goods of others at their peril: thus, in *Hollins* v. *Fowler* (1875) a cotton broker innocently purchased cotton from someone who had no title to it and later sold it to a manufacturer, receiving only the usual commission; the House of Lords held that the broker was liable to refund to the true owner the full value of the cotton.

(d) *Confirming Houses.*— In transactions between an English exporter and a foreign buyer, or between a foreign exporter and an English buyer, the exporter often knows nothing about the importer. The international nature of the trade increases the exporter's reluctance to rely solely on the buyer, so a confirming house may intervene for a commission on behalf of the buyer, by lending its name to him, in that it confirms the contract and assumes responsibility for the payment of the price. Thus, its function appears to be wider than that of a bank under an irrevocable credit which pays against delivery in accordance with the terms of the credit but incurs no liability on the contract. The legal position of a confirming house was considered in *Rusholme and Bolton and Roberts Hadfield, Ltd.* v. *S. G. Read & Co. (London), Ltd.* (1955), where the Court took the view that the liability of a confirming house went beyond that of a del credere agent, and on the documents in question the confirming house had assumed towards the plaintiffs the financial liability of a principal buyer, and accordingly were liable in damages for breach of contract when the Australian company for whom they acted cancelled the orders.

(e) *Estate Agents.*— An estate agent acts as a go-between in sales of land and houses. The growth in home ownership greatly expanded estate agency work and led to calls for statutory controls, which are now contained in the Estate Agents Act 1979. Indeed, the Act applies not only to estate agents as normally understood but also to all who carry on "estate agency work", which is widely defined as covering anything done by a person in the course of a business (including a business in which he is employed) pursuant to instructions from a client who wishes to dispose of or acquire an interest in land:

(a) for the purpose of or with a view to effecting the introduction to the client of a third person who wishes to acquire or dispose of such an interest; and

(b) after such an introduction has been effected in the course of that business, for the purpose of securing the disposal or acquisition.

However, the Act does not apply to things done in the course of his profession by a practising solicitor or a person employed by him. Under the Act agents who take deposits without being insured to cover any subsequent loss commit a criminal offence. Agents must also notify charges to sellers before acting for them and must disclose to prospective purchasers any interest they have in the property being sold.

(f) *Factors.*—A factor is an agent employed to buy, sell or deal in goods or merchandise, and is sometimes called a consignee and sometimes a commission agent. Factors have possession of the goods, they may buy and sell in their own name, and also sue and act in their own name, give warranties, receive payments, give receipts and even pledge the goods of their principals. They have an insurable interest in goods, and if instructed to do so are bound to insure, if possible (i) when having in their hands the property of their principals; (ii) when they have insured on previous occasions and have given no notice of a contrary intention; and (iii) when they accept bills of lading with directions to insure. They have a lien for the general balance of their charges on goods which have come to them as factors and on the proceeds of sale thereof. In turn they must keep and render proper accounts, and pay over to their principals all moneys received on the principals' account, less commission and expenses only. The general law on factors and mercantile agents is laid down in the Factors Act 1889, of which s. 2 (1) is of particular interest because it protects *bona fide* purchasers and pledgees from mercantile agents in possession of the goods or documents of title with the consent of the owner who were not in fact authorised to make the dispositions they did make. Section 1 (1) of the Act defines a mercantile agent as one "having in the customary course of his business as such agent authority either to sell goods, or to consign goods for the purpose of sale, or to buy goods, or to raise money on the security of goods." The following, however, are excluded from the operation of the Act: (1) agents who have the control or management of goods only as clerks, servants, cashiers, caretakers; (2) agents with whom goods are deposited for safe custody, as bailees, wharfingers and warehousemen; and (3) agents who are employed in the service of goods, as carriers or forwarding agents. On the other hand it has been held that a person who has no general occupation as an agent may be a mercantile agent even though he acts for one principal only and on one occasion only, provided he acts in a business capacity. The term "Goods" means corporeal, movable property, and does not include shares, stocks, scrip, bills, notes, cheques, title deeds, choses in action, or other incorporeal rights and property.

An example of s. 2 operating to a bank's detriment occurred in *Lloyds Bank Ltd.* v. *Bank of America National Trust and Savings Association* (1938), where documents of title pledged with the plaintiff bank were re-delivered to the pledgor under a trust receipt, but the pledgor, who was a mercantile agent, then fraudulently pledged them with the defendant bank which acted in good faith. The plaintiffs' claim failed because the Court of Appeal held: where rights of ownership are divided between different persons (the pledgor and the plaintiffs) and one of them is given possession with the consent of the other, those persons are the "owner" and the one in possession acting as mercantile agent can sell or pledge the goods so as to bind all interests, and thus pass a good title to the third party.

(g) *Insurance Brokers*.— An insurance broker is an agent employed to arrange insurance policies, the name being particularly applied to one who negotiates a policy of marine insurance. He is an intermediary between the insured and the underwriter, but his position is special in that he is also a principal for the purpose of receiving the premium from the insured and paying it over to the underwriter from whom he receives the policy. Thus, he is a creditor of the insured for the premium, and a debtor to the underwriter, from whom he receives the policy. The underwriter cannot sue the insured for the premium; but in the event of loss the insured may sue the underwriter direct. An insurance broker is an exception to the general rule that brokers have no lien, because by s. 53 (2) of the Marine Insurance Act 1906, he has a lien over the policy as against the insured for the premium and charges. The case of *Woolcott* v. *Excess Insurance Co., Ltd.* (1978) concerned the non-disclosure by insurance brokers of the plaintiff's criminal record, notwithstanding the fact that the brokers, as agents for the defendant insurance company, knew something of the plaintiff's past: it was held that though on these facts the company was not entitled to avoid the policies, it was entitled to be indemnified by the brokers, since the brokers, as the company's agents, were under a duty to disclose their knowledge of the plaintiff's criminal past to their principal. The Insurance Brokers (Registration) Act 1977 now provides for the registration of insurance brokers, for the regulation of their professional standards and for connected purposes.

(h) *Managing Owner, or Ship's Husband.*—Such a person is one of a number of co-owners of a ship who is appointed as agent by the others to see that the ship is well managed in all respects and to do what is necessary to make her a profitable speculation.

(i) *Partners.*—A partner is an agent of the firm and his other partner(s) for the purpose of the business of the partnership, with implied authority to bind the firm in the ordinary course of its business. His exact position, and partnership in general, form the subject of the next Chapter.

(j) *Shipbrokers.*—A shipbroker is an agent employed to arrange the chartering of ships. If a charter-party (a contract for the hiring of a ship or part of a ship on a voyage or time basis) is signed, he normally receives commission from the shipowner. His role as an agent may also extend to buying, selling and insuring ships.

(k) *Shipmasters.*—A master or captain of ship is an agent for the owner, with considerable powers and duties, for the managing and navigating of the ship for the purpose of bringing each voyage to the best possible termination.

(l) *Shop stewards.*—The position of shop stewards as agents of their trade union was considered by the House of Lords in *Heatons Transport (St. Helens), Ltd.* v. *Transport and General Workers Union* (1973). It was held that the original source of shop stewards' authority was the agreement, entered into by each member by joining the union, whereby the members authorised specified persons or classes of persons to do particular kinds of acts on behalf of all members, i.e. the union. The basic terms of that agreement were to be found in the union's rule book, but there could also be discretion conferred by members on committees or officials to act in a particular way; if the authority of certain members to take a particular type of action was not excluded by the rules, and if such authority was reasonably to be implied from custom and practice, such authority would exist and continue to exist until unequivocally withdrawn.

(m) *Stockbrokers.*—A stockbroker is an agent for his client on a commission basis in the buying and selling of stocks and shares. His commission must be shown on the contract note. Normally he does business with a stockjobber or dealer, who is a principal, though he may buy and sell on his own account, but not without the knowledge or consent of his client. If, instead of contracting for his client in the normal way with a stockjobber, the stockbroker secretly sells his own securities to the client, the latter may repudiate the contract altogether: *Armstrong* v. *Jackson* (1917).

(n) *Wives.*— A husband is bound to maintain his wife according to his estate and condition, and so the wife has implied authority to pledge his credit for household expenses, unless he has forbidden her to do so and provides them himself or has supplied her with a suitable allowance. Separate and special notice must be given to each tradesman, so the sort of notice which often appears in the local press is unnecessary or ineffective. If the wife habitually contracts on behalf of her husband as his agent, he will be liable whether for necessaries or not. The abolition of the deserted wife's agency of necessity has already been noted on p. 64.

SPECIAL FEATURES OF AGENCY RELATING TO BANKING

Four aspects will be considered under this heading: (i) bills of exchange; (ii) borrowing of money; (iii) cheques; and (iv) bailment.

(i)   Agency and Bills of Exchange

As regards the signing of bills of exchange (including cheques, and also promissory notes), the principal's signature may be written by the hand of an agent, as where a partner signs the firm's name. More commonly he may sign "p.p." or "per pro." (short for "*per procurationem*") the principal, or in the case of a company "For" (or "For and on behalf of") the Company, followed by his capacity. A "per pro." signature operates as notice that the agent has merely a limited authority to sign and the principal is only bound by such signature if the agent in so signing was acting within the limits of his authority. An agent who signs a bill for his principal in excess of his authority is not liable on the instrument personally, though he may be sued by the holder for breach of warranty of authority. If an agent signs for, or for and on behalf of his principal, he is not personally liable; but merely adding after his signature such words describing himself as agent, manager and the like does not exempt him from liability; i.e. whatever formula is used, the words must give notice that the signature is given in the capacity of an agent. If an agent signs his own name, he alone is liable, because in the case of bills of exchange the doctrine of the undisclosed principal cannot be invoked.

An agent for collection must exercise due care in presenting for acceptance and/or payment. If a bill is dishonoured while in the hands of an agent, the agent is allowed the prescribed time to advise his principal, and the principal in turn has a similar allowance as regards other parties, though the agent may give notice direct to those parties. Where a bill is held by a person as agent, he holds it subject to any defences against his principal.

(ii)   Borrowing of Money

Banks are naturally concerned to impose liability on a principal for money borrowed by his agent without or in excess of authority. A lender acting in good faith has an equitable right of subrogation, that is, he is allowed to recover against the principal to the extent to which the money borrowed has been applied in paying the legal debts of the principal. This right to stand in the shoes of the creditor is available even when the agent is known to have no authority to borrow. It does not prejudice the principal, for it merely means that he has exchanged creditors. Subrogation may assist a bank which has advanced money to a company where that borrowing is *ultra vires* the company and where s. 9 of the European Communities Act 1972 cannot be relied on: it may also be possible to sue the directors for breach of implied warranty of authority. Subrogation may also be used where the advance is *ultra vires* the directors, but *intra vires* the company, when the company is not prepared to ratify its directors' action.

(iii)   Cheques

As regards the payment of cheques, subrogation here assists an agent who has paid his principal's debts without authority. Thus, in *B. Liggett* (*Liverpool*), *Ltd.* v. *Barclays Bank Ltd.* (1928) the bank, contrary to instructions, honoured the company's cheques on the signature of one director only, the cheques having been drawn in favour of and the proceeds received by trade creditors. The bank, on being sued by the company for the amount of the cheques, was held to be entitled to take credit for such payments. The liabilities of the company had not been increased by the payments, and if the bank was refused equitable relief, the company would have unjustly enriched itself at the expense of the bank.

Such a situation periodically arises, particularly as regards companies; where a signature is missing and cannot be easily obtained, but the customer is a good and valued one, and the cheque is for a normal trade debt, the bank usually pays it, relying on the customer to ratify its action, either by signing the cheque correctly or by an appropriate letter. If the customer is unobliging, the bank may claim subrogation. Of course, in the case of a financially doubtful customer, the bank may be glad of the opportunity to return the cheque marked "Another signature required", and so on, but this is another matter.

When a bank collects cheques for a customer, deviation from traditional methods, custom or usage can be dangerous. In *Forman* v. *Bank of England* (1902), the plaintiff paid into his account at the defendant's Law Courts Branch a cheque payable alternatively at Barclay & Co., Ltd., Norwich or 54, Lombard St., London. It was a recognised and general custom amongst London banks that cheques in that form be treated as London cheques, but the defendant bank sent it to Norwich via the Country Clearing, with the result that a cheque drawn by the plaintiff and presented two days later was dishonoured for lack of funds. The plaintiff was awarded £75 damages. On the other hand, in *Schioler* v. *Westminster Bank Ltd.* (1970), where the defendant's Guernsey Branch forwarded a dividend warrant in Malayan currency for realisation in sterling in London, with consequent deduction of £995 U.K. income tax, for which the plaintiff sued, the bank avoided liability, because in the absence of express instructions from the plaintiff (who was domiciled in Denmark but resident in England) it was not doing anything unusual and there was no alternative method available to it for collecting the warrant for the credit of the customer's account.

An agent can receive cash on behalf of his principal, but difficulties can arise when he handles cheques payable to his principal. In *Australia and New Zealand Bank, Ltd.* v. *Ateliers de Constructions Electriques de Charleroi* (1966) a Belgian company had appointed one H. as its representative in Australia for the sale of its heavy electrical equipment to various bodies, including the Snowy Mountains Hydro-Electric Authority. Fifteen cheques drawn by the Authority in favour of the company, care of H, were delivered to H as the company's agent. H endorsed the cheques for the company (which had no bank account in Australia) paid them into his own account, and periodically remitted sums to Belgium. His bank did not ask for any confirmation of the irregular endorsement or his authority to endorse the cheques; nor had his Belgian principal given him any instructions as to payment or inquired or complained about the procedure re remittances. When H became insolvent the company sued his bank for shortfall of £55,540 due to them from H. Allowing the bank's appeal, the Judicial Committee of the Privy Council held that normally it would be quite wrong for any agent without specific authority to endorse his principal's cheques and pay them into his own account, but taking a practical, commercial view of the whole of the facts, the proper inference in law was that there was an implied actual authority from the principal to the agent to deal with the cheques as he did, and therefore the bank was not liable in conversion.

(iv) Bailment

A bailment arises where personal property is delivered by one party (the bailor) to another party (the bailee) on a condition express or implied that the property shall be returned to the bailor or disposed of in accordance with his directions as soon as the purpose for which the bailment arose has been fulfilled. Bailment can exist independently of contract, though there is often a contract to set out the terms and conditions. Examples of bailment are hire-purchase, pledge, carriage of goods, delivery of goods for repair, etc. and—the point at which banks become involved—safe custody. Warehousemen, of course, are bailees, but they are more concerned with the preservation of merchandise, than the safety of valuables, which is the banks' special concern.

It is generally considered (though opinions to the contrary have been expressed) that bailment is not implied in the ordinary banker and customer relationship, i.e. there is no obligation on a bank to accept property from a customer for safe custody. Such facilities might be expressly agreed when the account is opened, but this would be exceptional, and normally safe custody items are accepted at the bank's discretion, so that they would be declined if they were too bulky, or undesirable for some other reason.

Another unresolved difficulty is whether banks are gratuitous bailees, or bailees for hire or reward, because, apart from the special case of safe deposit facilities for which banks charge a periodical rental and which are available to the general public, banks do not make a special charge for safe custody services. It is argued that in so far as this may be borne in mind when assessing the commission to be debited to a customer's account, the bank may be deemed to be a paid bailee. On the other hand, some customers who utilise the safe custody service may not be charged any commission because of a substantial average credit balance on their account or the value of their connections. However, the difference has little practical effect, since banks take the same care of the items in their strong-rooms whatever sort of bailee they may actually be. Legally, a gratuitous bailee is bound to take the same care of the property as a reasonably prudent man with the same facilities at his command would take in respect of similar goods of his own; whereas a paid bailee is expected to have the best possible safeguards and to exercise the same degree of care and skill as may reasonably be expected in the ordinary and proper course of a similar business to that for which he is paid. To counter modern criminals' scientific progress in safe breaking, banks are constantly improving their strongrooms at great expense, and so their standard of care of customers' property entrusted to them for safe custody does not fall below that expected of a paid bailee. In *Moynihan* v. *National Bank Ltd.* (1969) Lady Moynihan sued for the loss of her jewels which were kept in a deed box at the bank and were stolen in a weekend raid on the bank's strongroom. The bank denied negligence; however, during the hearing the case was settled for an undisclosed sum.

Thus, the bank will not be liable if property held in safe custody is destroyed by fire or otherwise, lost or stolen unless there is negligence on the part of the bank, and the degree of negligence required to establish liability will depend on the relevant circumstances of the case, including what type of bailee the bank is held to be. Customers should therefore be advised to insure the items they deposit; in fact, they will be quoted a lower premium by the insurers than would be the case if the items were kept on their own premises. If the bank seeks to exclude or limit its liability as bailee in any way, then by the Unfair Contract Terms Act 1977 (discussed in Chapter 1) the term or notice to that effect must satisfy the test of reasonableness.

Difficulties over theft arise when the thief is a servant of the bailee. Whilst it is true that theft (or any other crime) by a servant or agent is outside the scope of his employment in that he is not paid to do that sort of act, nevertheless a bailee for reward will be liable if the goods are stolen by the very servant deputed by the bailee to handle or look after the goods. In *Morris* v. *C. W. Martin & Sons, Ltd.* (1965), where a mink stole left for cleaning was purloined by the servant of the defendants who was given the task of cleaning it, the defendants were held liable by the Court of Appeal. On the other hand, the mere fact that the master by employing a rogue gives him an opportunity to steal or defraud does not make the master liable; a theft by any servant who is not employed to do anything in relation to the goods bailed is entirely outside the scope of his employment and cannot make his employer liable, unless he knew or ought to have known that this servant was dishonest because then the master could be liable in negligence for employing him. Thus, a bank as employer would not normally be liable for the theft of safe custody items by a clerk other than those entrusted with the items though as bailees have to disprove negligence, the bank could be in difficulties here if there had been clear breaches of its internal security regulations, e.g. permitting both keys to a dual-lock safe to be held by the same member of its staff, or negligence by the key-holders themselves.

A more likely source of trouble to a bank is the release of safe custody items, which must only be given up to the depositor against his receipt or to the correct third party duly authorised by the depositor. If the property is released in good faith to the wrong person, whether because of a forged instruction, a fraudulent impersonation, or pure mistake the bank will be liable to the true owner in conversion; thus, in *Langtry* v. *Union Bank of London* (1896) the bank handed over Mrs. Langtry's property to the bearer of a skilfully forged authority on her notepaper and settled her claim out of court for £10,000. Sometimes the bank may be able to avoid liability by pleading estoppel, in that the customer by his own conduct has facilitated the fraud, or is estopped from denying that someone is his agent (see Methods of Appointment, *ante*).

As regards the wide-spread practice of night safe facilities, where wallets are deposited from the street after banking hours in special safes, the relative agreement entered into between the customer and the bank normally provides that until the wallet is opened and the contents deposited the relationship between the parties is that of bailor and gratuitous bailee.

As a bailee can have no better title than his bailor, if the property does not belong to the bailor, a bank as bailee may be faced with a claim by the true owner. If at the time the true owner intervenes, the bank has already properly returned the property to the bailor, the bank has no liability, for re-delivery to the bailor is not a conversion (all the bank has done is to restore the *status quo* as it was before the bailment occurred). If the bank has possession of the property, then it must deliver to the true owner to avoid liability in conversion, but where the position as to ownership is not clear, because, for instance, a third party has lodged a claim to it, the bank's best course is to interplead, i.e. it holds itself out as ready and willing to hand the property to whichever of the rival contestants the Court declares to be entitled to the property.

If a bank refuses to hand over the property bailed to the depositor when he demands it, then if the refusal is absolute and unqualified the bank would have been liable, before the coming into force of the Torts (Interference with Goods) Act 1977, for the tort of detinue (wrongful detention of the goods of another). It is now liable in conversion as the Act abolished detinue, but extended conversion to include what would otherwise have been detinue. However, if a bank has reasonable doubt as to the authenticity of instructions from a customer, the bank can delay delivery for a reasonable period to make enquiries without incurring liability, for its refusal is not an absolute one: *Clayton* v. *Le Roy* (1911).

Any authority to deliver the property bailed to a third party is cancelled by the death of the depositor; only the legal personal representative(s) can deal with the property. Similar considerations apply if the depositor becomes mentally unsound, or bankrupt, when a Receiver or the Court of Protection takes over in the first case, and the Trustee in Bankruptcy in the second case.

Where a bank holds safe custody items in the joint names of two or more depositors, the items must be delivered up against a joint receipt or on joint instructions, unless a mandate is revoked by the death, unsoundness of mind or bankruptcy of one of the parties. Joint account mandates usually include a clause to the effect that, on the death of any party to the account, money standing to the credit of the joint account, and in addition any items held by way of security or safe custody, for collection or for any purpose whatsoever, may be held to the order of the survivor(s). Without such a clause, which is only there basically to ensure that the bank gets a good receipt from the survivor(s), it would be unsafe, in the event of one of the joint depositors dying, for the bank to deliver the property to the survivor(s) in reliance on the right of survivorship (the *jus accrescendi*) which applies to the balance of a joint account, for the property may not be joint but common, when the right of survivorship does not apply and to be safe, the bank would have to get the legal personal representative(s) of the deceased to join in the receipt or instructions. Similar considerations apply if one of the joint depositors becomes mentally unsound, or bankrupt, when a Receiver or the Court of Protection must join in the discharge in the first eventuality, and the Trustee in Bankruptcy in the second.

TERMINATION OF AGENCY

The agency may be ended by act of the parties, by operation of law or by effluxion of time etc.:

(1) By act of the parties

This may be:

    (a) Renunciation, if the agent gives up his agency.

    (b) Revocation, if the principal withdraws the agency.

Here, third parties must be advised if the revocation is to be effective, or there should be a reasonable inference that the authority has been cancelled. Otherwise, the principal will be bound where third parties have acted in good faith on the strength of the previous authority. In like manner, a retiring partner who remains ostensibly a member of the firm is liable for debts incurred after his retirement. Where a bank learns of a dispute between the parties to a joint account with mandate for either (or any one) to sign, it may have to regard the mandate as cancelled.

(2) By operation of law

This may be:
   (a) On the death, mental unsoundness, or bankruptcy of the principal.
   (b) On the death or mental unsoundness of the agent.
If the agent is adjudicated bankrupt, this does not necessarily affect his agency, for as long as the principal has full contractual capacity, his agent may be under a contractual disability. However, in some cases a bank may need to exercise care, as when it has a wife's account, on which the husband has power to sign "per pro." and the husband becomes bankrupt, for there then becomes a possibility of abuse by the agent of his agency.
   (c) By the relationship becoming illegal: for example, where either principal or agent becomes an alien enemy due to the outbreak of war, or resides in another state against which economic sanctions have been imposed by the United Kingdom government.

(3) By effluxion of time, or fulfilment or frustration of purpose

   (a) An agent may be employed for a fixed term, so that the agency will end when that period has expired. If during the currency of the agency, the principal sells his business or ceases to trade so that the agent can no longer earn his commission, it is a question of fact whether the principal has agreed to carry on his business for the whole of the term: only if this is the case will the principal be liable for breach of contract. The time element often appears in powers of attorney, which may be for a fixed period, or may be operative only whilst the principal is out of the United Kingdom.
   (b) An agency may be fulfilled by complete performance, e.g. when an estate agent engaged to sell a house finds a buyer who is accepted.
   (c) It may occasionally happen that the agency is frustrated by the destruction of the subject-matter, e.g. when an estate agent is engaged to sell a house, but before he does so the house is burnt to the ground.

Chapter 3

Partnership

DEFINITION AND NATURE

The principal statute governing partnerships is the Partnership Act 1890 and references in this Chapter to sections mean sections of that Act unless the contrary is stated. The Act commences with the following definition in s. 1 (1): "Partnership is the relation which subsists between persons carrying on a business in common with a view of profit". Given two or more persons acting together, the points to be considered are: (a) is it a business? (for not every occupation can be called a business); and (b) is it being carried on with a view of profit? Before looking at these points in detail, one must note that s. 1 (2) provides that companies registered under the Companies Acts, or formed or incorporated by any other Act of Parliament or letters patent or Royal Charter, or engaged in working mines within the Stannaries (i.e. Devon and Cornwall), are not partnerships.

Partners are called collectively a firm, and the name under which the business is carried on is called the firm name: s. 4. A partnership is not a separate legal entity as is a company, and the firm name is merely a convenient expression for the collective names of the individual partners. Hence, solicitors describing themselves as "Tom, Dick, Harry & Co." are a firm, notwithstanding the "and Company" at the end. The present partners' names may be totally different from the original founders' names; this does not matter, for persons may carry on business under any name they please, provided they do not infringe the general law by fraudulently implying that their business is the same as that conducted by a trade competitor, or fail to comply with the Registration of Business Names Act 1916. Section 1 of this Act requires registration of the name, when either the firm name does not consist of the true surnames of all the partners, or a member of the firm has changed his name. The Registrar can refuse registration if he considers the firm name to be "undesirable". Section 18 of the same Act requires that the true names of all partners shall appear on all trade catalogues, trade circulars, show cards and business letters. By

s. 439 of the Companies Act 1948 no person or persons can trade or carry on business under any name or title of which the word "limited", or any contraction or abbreviation of it, is the last word without being duly incorporated with limited liability.

The confusion between companies and firms is not helped by the newspapers, which often call a company, even a very well-known one such as Imperial Chemical Industries Limited, "a firm". To the man in the street this misdescription may be of little or no consequence, but it is not one to which students of the law should be a party. A company is an incorporated body, with a separate legal personality, even though the word "company" is often not included in its name; sometimes it is, as in F. W. Woolworth & Co., Limited. A partnership is a firm whether its name ends with "Co." or "& Co." or not, for it must not end with the word "limited"; a partnership is not, in English law, a distinct legal person, though it is in Scots law. A further source of confusion arises over insolvency, in which event individuals and firms are made bankrupt, whereas companies are wound up: Chapters 4 and 5 will elaborate on this, but it must be noted that although the Act of 1890 sometimes speaks of "winding up" the affairs of a partnership, this is merely the ordinary usage of the words (i.e. "concluding") and not the special legal method of dissolution applicable to companies.

RULES FOR DETERMINING THE EXISTENCE OF PARTNERSHIP

Section 2 of the Act of 1890 provides that the following do not of themselves constitute partnership:

(1) Joint tenancy, tenancy in common, joint property, common property or part ownership, whether the tenants or owners do or do not share any profits made by the use thereof. (Co-ownership does not necessarily result from agreement or involve working for a profit, and a joint owner has a right to free disposal of his property: in short, partnership is a special category of the wider concept of co-ownership.)

(2) The sharing of gross returns.

(3) The receipt by a person of a share of the profits, or of a payment contingent on or varying with the profits. However, the section declares that such receipt is prima facie evidence that he is a partner (i.e. although partnership is implied by profit-sharing the latter is

only one aspect, and consideration of the full facts may dispel any appearance of partnership), and it then specifies five instances in which profit-sharing does not of itself create a partnership:

(a) The receipt of instalments of a debt out of accruing profits:

(b) Remuneration of servants or agents by a share of profits:

(c) Payment of an annuity to a widow or child of a deceased partner out of profits:

(d) Payment to lenders of money either of a rate of interest which varies with profits or of a share of the profits:

(e) Payment of a portion of the profits in consideration of the goodwill of a business which has been bought.

In these last two instances the next section (s. 3) provides that the lender of the loan or the seller of the goodwill shall rank after other creditors in the event of the bankruptcy of the borrower or buyer.

As regards the meaning of the word "business" in s. 1, the section of the Act giving definitions (s. 45) merely states that business includes every trade, occupation or profession. But this must be read in conjunction with the general background of professional and commercial life; though normally there is no restriction on the nature of partnership business except that it must be legal (a partnership of bank-robbers or any other partnership in crime would obviously receive no recognition or assistance from the Courts), there are a few idiosyncrasies. Thus, by their own rules of etiquette barristers are forbidden to practice in partnership; and in medical partnerships and firms of solicitors all the partners must have the requisite professional qualifications. The common sense approach is that "business" really connotes those recognised callings in which people hold themselves out as offering to the public professional assistance or the supply of goods or services. That co-ownership does not imply a business can be illustrated by the position of the trustees of a marriage settlement—they may be joint owners of real property and of a portfolio of stocks and shares, but they are not partners because they do not carry on a business (a buying and selling of property with a view of profit).

In *Keith Spicer, Ltd.* v. *Mansell* (1970), where the defendant and B were merely working together to form a company without any intention to trade as partners before incorporation, it was held that they were not partners.

The phrase in s. 1 "with a view of profit" gives the object of the partnership—it is a joint operation for the sake of gain, so that an association for charitable or religious purposes is not a partnership. "Profit" in this context means "net profit", i.e. the difference between the gross returns and the outgoings of the business.

FORMATION OF PARTNERSHIP

Partnership is created by agreement, which may be oral, implied by conduct, written (i.e. Articles of Partnership), or under seal (i.e. a formal Deed of Partnership). A partnership may be constituted forthwith or from an agreed date. It may be for a definite period of time, or to carry out a single venture (when it is often called a "syndicate"), otherwise it is a partnership at will, i.e. any partner may determine the partnership at any time on giving notice of his intention so to do to all the other partners. The general provisions of the Partnership Act 1890 apply, save in so far as it is possible to modify them by express agreement between the partners.

As regards the contractual capacity needed to be a partner, everyone except alien enemies and convicts may be a partner. An existing partnership between a British citizen and a foreigner is dissolved if war breaks out between the United Kingdom and the foreigner's own country. However, although both infants and mentally disordered persons may be partners, they are to some extent exceptions to the general rule that each partner is liable for the debts of the firm. Thus, an infant partner is not personally liable for the firm's debts, but unless he repudiates the partnership either during infancy or when he attains his majority he will become equally liable with his co-partners for debts incurred after he attained his majority. Failure to repudiate will not, however, make him liable for partnership debts incurred whilst he was an infant: *Goode* v. *Harrison* (1821). If a person is mentally disordered when he enters into the contract of partnership, the general rules of contract (see p. 17, *ante*) apply, so that unsoundness of mind is not in itself a bar to entry into partnership. In an existing partnership, if one of the partners becomes mentally disordered, this does not in itself automatically dissolve the partnership, although application may be made to the Court for a decree of dissolution of the partnership. In appropriate circumstances the Court will grant an interim injunction, i.e. until the hearing of the action, to restrain the mentally disordered partner from interfering in the firm's business, otherwise he might run up enormous liabilities binding on his co-partners where such debts were incurred within his ostensible authority and the other contracting parties were unaware of his mental disorder.

A limited company can be a partner, but this does not increase the liability of the members of that company. This practice is sometimes followed by merchant banking or financial partnerships, which include as a partner a company controlled by the other partners and often called ". . . Continuation Limited", thereby ensuring that the firm has one partner who never dies or retires.

Finally, when forming a partnership, regard must be had to statutory provisions as to the number of partners there may be in a partnership. Section 434 of the Companies Act 1948 (which, as amended by the Banking Act 1979, now applies to all partnerships) imposes a maximum limit of twenty partners in a partnership, but this limit has been removed by s. 120 of the Companies Act 1967 so far as partnerships of solicitors, or of accountants, or of members of a recognised stock exchange are concerned, and the Department [formerly Board] of Trade is also empowered to make regulations by statutory instrument that s. 434 shall not apply to the formation of partnerships for other purposes specified in the regulations. It has made such regulations in respect of firms of patent agents, surveyors, auctioneers, valuers, estate agents, land agents, actuaries, consulting engineers and building designers, provided that at least three-quarters of the partners hold an appropriate professional qualification (S.I. 1968 No. 1222; S.I. 1970 Nos. 835, 992 and 1319).

TYPES OF PARTNERS

A general partner is one who is personally liable for all debts and obligations of the firm and who takes part in its management. Hence, he is also called an active partner.

A dormant or sleeping partner is one who contributes capital, shares in the profits and has personal liability for the firm's debts and obligations, but takes no part in the management.

A salaried partner is one held out to the world as being a partner, with his name appearing as a partner on the firm's notepaper and so on, but he receives as remuneration a salary (paid as an outgoing of the firm before net profits are calculated) rather than a share of the profits, though he may, in addition to his salary, receive some bonus or other sum of money dependent on the profits. It was held in *Stekel* v. *Ellice* (1973) that describing a person as a salaried partner was not conclusive one way or the other of the question whether he was a partner in the true sense; the question whether there was a partnership depended on the nature of the relationship and not on the label attached to it.

A limited partner is a special type of partner under the provisions of the Limited Partnerships Act 1907. His liability is limited to the amount of capital he actually contributes and he cannot take part in the management of the firm. He takes a "back seat" because of the statute, whereas a dormant or sleeping partner does so by inclination. Limited partnerships will be dealt with separately at the end of this Chapter.

An incoming partner is one admitted into an existing firm. Section 17 (1) provides that such a person does not become liable to the creditors of the firm for anything done before he became a partner. He may, however, make himself so liable by special agreement, i.e. by the general legal process of novation, whereby the firm's creditors expressly or impliedly agree to accept the liability of the new firm and to discharge the old firm, though in practice this is more likely to occur when he joins the firm in place of a partner who is retiring.

An outgoing partner is one retiring from a continuing firm, and s. 17 (2) provides that such a person does not cease to be liable for partnership debts or obligations incurred before his retirement, though under s. 17 (3) he may be discharged by an agreement between himself, the new firm and the creditors, and this agreement may be either express or inferred as a fact from the course of dealing between the creditors and the new firm. In the absence of express novation the Court is very shy of inferring it from the course of dealing, and mere adoption by the creditors of the new firm as their debtor does not of itself discharge a retiring partner. Where the creditor knows of the change in the constitution of the firm, making no claim on the retiring partner for a long period, then a novation will be inferred. Similar principles apply where a partner dies, in so far as his continuing liability falls on his personal representatives. As regards debts created after his retirement, an outgoing partner is not liable, because his retirement cancels his agency, provided that notice of his retirement has been given both publicly in the Gazette and privately by circular or notice to all persons who have had dealings with the firm. From the retiring individual's point of view it is most important that these notices be given, because by s. 36 (1) a creditor who has had dealings with the firm is entitled to treat all apparent members of the old firm as still being members until he has notice of the change; however, by s. 36 (2) notice in the Gazette is sufficient for persons who had no dealings with the firm before the date of the dissolution or change. Even if no notice was given or advertisement published a retiring partner will not be liable to persons who had no previous dealings with the firm and did not know him to be a partner: *Tower Cabinet Co., Ltd.* v. *Ingram* (1949), where, after a partnership between C and the defendant had been dissolved, C ordered goods from the plaintiff on the partnership's old stationery which showed the defendant as a partner. If a retiring partner consents to be held out as connected with the firm, as where he allows his former partners to retain his name as part of the firm name, or allows his name to remain over the shop or premises or to be used in advertisements or invoices of the firm, he will continue to be liable for the firm's subsequent debts.

A quasi or nominal partner is not strictly a partner, and does not share in the profits, but under the doctrine of "holding out" (stated in s. 14) he is estopped by his conduct from denying that he is a partner. Hence, he is sometimes called a partner by estoppel. The effect of s. 14 (1) is that every one who by words spoken or written or by conduct misleads others into believing he is a partner, so that on the faith of such representations they give credit to the firm, is liable to them as a partner. It is not necessary that the holding out be communicated directly by the party holding out to the creditor; the news can be communicated to the creditor through a third party: *Martyn* v. *Gray* (1863). (It is on this ground of "holding out" that, as mentioned in the last paragraph, a retiring partner who fails to give notice of his retirement is liable for future debts.) However, where after a partner's death the partnership business is continued in the old firm's name, the continued use of that name or of the deceased partner's name as part of it does not of itself make his estate liable for any partnership debts contracted after his death: s. 14 (2).

RELATION OF PARTNERS TO THIRD PARTIES

Section 5 provides that every general partner is an agent of the firm and of his other partners for the purpose of the business of the partnership; and the acts of any partner within the usual course of the firm's business bind the firm and his partners unless the person with whom he dealt knew that in fact the partner so acting had no authority or did not know or believe him to be a partner.

A general or ordinary partner (as distinct from a limited partner) has the following implied powers:

    (a) To sell and buy goods for the purpose of the partnership business;

    (b) To give discharges for money received from debtors;

    (c) To engage servants for the partnership business;

    (d) To draw cheques, unless this is not in the usual course of the partnership business: *Backhouse* v. *Charlton* (1878).

In addition to the foregoing, in a commercial or trading partnership (which was defined in *Higgins* v. *Beauchamp* (1914) as one in which the principal operations are buying and selling), a partner may bind the firm:

    (e) By contracting debts and paying debts on its account, and

drawing, making, signing, indorsing, accepting, transferring, negotiating and discounting negotiable instruments;
(f) By borrowing money on the credit of the firm;
(g) By pledging partnership goods or securities for the purpose
of its business.

In a non-trading partnership, e.g. one of medical doctors, solicitors,
or accountants, as well as auctioneers, farmers or miners, these
additional powers may be given to a partner by express agreement.

The implied authority of a partner in any partnership, whether
trading or non-trading, does not extend to the following acts:

(i) The execution of deeds, for an agent cannot bind his
principal by deed unless he himself is expressly authorised by deed;

(ii) The giving of a guarantee in the firm name, unless trade
custom is shown;

(iii) The acceptance of property in lieu of money in satisfaction
of a partnership debt;

(vi) Authorising a third party to use the firm name in legal or
other proceedings;

(v) Submitting disputes to arbitration.

Additional powers may, of course, be given to any partner by express
agreement.

A partner cannot as a rule bind his co-partners by accepting a bill of
exchange in blank or an accommodation bill. A bill accepted in blank
by one partner in the name of the firm is not binding on it except in
favour of a *bona fide* holder for value without notice of the way in which
the bill was accepted: *Hogarth* v. *Latham & Co.* (1878). The same
applies to an accommodation bill except where such holder for value
took it without notice that the firm was an accommodation party.

In order to bind the firm by the doctrine of apparent or ostensible
authority, the act must be done in relation to the partnership business; it must be an act for carrying on business in the usual way, and
be done as a partner and not as an individual. For example, if a
partner in a firm of butchers signed a contract in the firm name to buy
a boat, this would not be binding on his other partners, being beyond
the scope of his ostensible authority in that it is an act foreign to the
firm's business, unless the other partners have expressly authorised
him to make the purchase, or subsequently ratify his action in doing
so. A partner who exceeds his authority is personally liable.

In the event of there being a limitation or restriction on the power of
one or more partners to bind the firm, this will bind a party having
notice of the limited authority, but it does not affect those who have no
actual knowledge of it provided the act done in contravention of the

limit is still within the ostensible authority of the partner. Thus, the Articles or Deed of Partnership may impose a limit on the amount for which junior partners may pledge the firm's credit, but as the Articles or Deed are private documents, the limit is unavailing against an innocent third party relying on the usual scope of a partner's authority.

A firm, and each of its members, is liable for the wrongful acts or omissions (torts) on the part of one of the partners acting in the ordinary course of the business of the firm, or with the authority of his co-partners. This point is covered by s. 10 as regards ordinary torts, and by s. 11 as regards specific torts in the nature of fraudulent misappropriations of property. For example, a firm of consulting engineers would be liable for negligence by a partner in constructional work, and a firm of solicitors would be liable for professional negligence by one of its partners. In contrast, a firm will not be liable for a tort committed by a partner outside his ostensible authority, e.g. where he commenced a malicious prosecution for an alleged theft of partnership property: *Arbuckle* v. *Taylor* (1815). It may be mentioned here that the same principle applies to the vicarious liability of a master or employer for his servants' torts; thus, in *Bank of New South Wales* v. *Owston* (1879) the bank was held not liable for a malicious prosecution instigated by one of its managers because the arrest and prosecution of offenders is not within the ordinary scope of a bank manager's authority.

Lord Tenterden's Act has already been mentioned in the two preceding Chapters, and in so far as partnerships are concerned it was held in *Williams* v. *Mason* (1873) that if one of two partners signs a representation as to credit etc. to which the Act relates, the signature does not render the other partner liable but only the signatory.

A surviving partner has power to mortgage the partnership property, both real and personal, to secure a debt in the name of the firm (e.g. a bank overdraft) in so far as it is necessary for the purpose of winding up the partnership. Persons dealing with a surviving partner in this way are, in the absence of evidence to the contrary, entitled to assume that the mortgage is made in the proper course of winding up: *Re Bourne* (1906). Such a mortgage obtains priority over the lien on the surplus assets of a deceased partner's personal representatives for his share in the partnership.

LIABILITY TO THIRD PARTIES

Section 9 provides that every partner in a firm is liable jointly with the other partners for all the debts and obligations of the firm incurred while he is a partner, and after his death his estate is also severally liable for such debts and obligations, subject to prior payment of his separate debts.

Thus, liability so far as contracts are concerned is joint (i.e. single or solid); though by special agreement it may be made joint and several (or separate). With joint liability, each partner is liable jointly with all the others and not by himself, so the plaintiff, before the coming into force of the Civil Liability (Contribution) Act 1978, could bring only one action, not several actions, against the members of the firm. The Act now provides that judgment obtained against one person jointly liable shall be no bar to an action against others jointly liable "in respect of the same debt or damage". It overrules *Kendall* v. *Hamilton* (1879), where it was held that judgment obtained against the ostensible partners which was unsatisfied barred fresh proceedings against a subsequently discovered wealthy sleeping partner in the firm. The plaintiff should sue the partners by their firm name, not individually; though he need not sue all the members, but if he does not choose to do so, he may find it necessary to bring subsequent proceedings against the other(s), although the Court may, on an application by any defendant, order the omitted member(s) to be added as co-defendant(s).

If the creditor proceeds against the firm and gets judgment, he may issue execution against the property of the members, and where the joint property of the firm is not sufficient to satisfy his judgment, he can proceed against the separate or private property of each partner, for each is individually liable to his last penny for the whole of the debts and liabilities of the firm. After the death of a partner, his estate is similarly liable, subject to prior payment of his separate or private debts.

Section 12 provides that liability for wrongs done by a partner is joint and several; so that a judgment against one partner has never been a bar to a subsequent action against the other(s). Hence, a plaintiff suing in tort may proceed against each partner separately, either contemporaneously or one after the other.

RELATION OF PARTNERS TO EACH OTHER

Within the general framework of the law the partners may make what arrangements they like between themselves; this is why, although a partnership agreement may be verbal, it is preferable to reduce it to writing (either articles or a deed) so that all aspects of the partners' relations between themselves can be provided for, thus eliminating uncertainty, misunderstandings and disputes. These can otherwise occur over quite simple matters such as what holidays each partner shall have and when he can take them, let alone such vital questions as remuneration, sharing of profits, interest on capital, drawings and so on. The situation can be looked at under two heads: (A) partnership property; and (B) the basic rights of partners *inter se*.

(A) Partnership property is that owned by the firm. It may have been originally brought into the partnership stock or acquired, whether by purchase or otherwise, on account of the firm, or for the purposes and in the course of the partnership business: s. 20. By s. 21 property bought with partnership money is deemed to have been bought on account of the firm, unless a contrary intention appears. Partnership property must be distinguished from property owned by an individual partner but used for the purposes of the partnership business, e.g. where one partner owns the shop premises in which the firm trades and receives rent from the firm in respect thereof; or where he owns equipment which the firm uses gratuitously. It is often a difficult question of fact into which category particular property is to be placed, the answer depending on the exact circumstances and on any express or implied agreement between the partners as to that item. It is important to know the true position for the following reasons:

   (i) Any increase in the value of partnership property accrues to the firm, whereas if the property belongs to an individual partner the enhanced value is his alone: *Robinson* v. *Ashton* (1875).

   (ii) In the event of bankruptcy, partnership property is joint estate, whereas the property of an individual partner is his separate estate—a distinction to be considered later under the heading "Distribution of assets in bankruptcy".

   (iii) By s. 22 a partner's interest in partnership land or any heritable interest therein is to be treated as personalty, and not realty, unless the contrary intention appears. On the other hand, a partner's own land is realty.

(B) In the absence of any special provisions, the following are the basic rights of a partner as regards his co-partners:

(1) He is entitled to the utmost fairness and good faith from his co-partners in all partnership matters (and he in turn must act similarly towards them). Thus, s. 29 provides that every partner must account to the firm for any benefit derived by him without the consent of the other partners through a partnership transaction or connexion, and this accountability for private profits extends to the personal

representatives of a deceased partner whilst the partnership is being wound up because of the death. It was held in *Thompson's Trustee in Bankruptcy* v. *Heaton* (1974) that when the assets of a partnership included a leasehold interest a partner who acquired the freehold reversion was under a fiduciary duty to the other partners to account for the benefit derived from the transaction; the same principle applied when the property of a dissolved partnership included a leasehold interest—each of the former partners owed the same obligation to the other former partners in respect of that interest as he did whilst it remained partnership property. As regards the duty of a partner not to compete with his firm, s. 30 provides that a partner who carries on any business of the same nature as and competing with that of the firm without the consent of the other partners must account for and pay over to the firm all profits made by him in that business.

(2) He is entitled to take part in the management of the partnership business: s. 24 (5); but he is not entitled to any remuneration: s. 24 (6).

(3) He can prevent the introduction of a new partner—this requires the unanimous consent of all existing partners: s. 24 (7).

(4) The nature of the partnership business cannot be changed without the unanimous consent of all the partners, though differences in ordinary matters connected with the business may be decided by a majority of the partners: s. 24 (8).

(5) The partnership books are to be kept at the principal place of business of the partnership, and every partner may, when he thinks fit, have access to and inspect and copy any of them: s. 24 (9). This right to examine the books may be delegated by the partner to an agent to whom the other partners can have no reasonable objection: *Bevan* v. *Webb* (1901).

(6) He cannot be expelled by a majority of his co-partners unless a power to do so has been conferred by express agreement between the partners: s. 25.

(7) He is entitled to indemnity by the firm in respect of payments made and personal liabilities incurred by him in the ordinary and proper conduct of the business of the firm; or in or about anything necessarily done for the preservation of its business or property: s. 24 (2).

(8) He is entitled to interest at five per cent. per annum on any actual payment or advance to the firm which he makes beyond the amount he had agreed to subscribe, from the date of such payment or advance: s. 24 (3). Apart from agreement, express or implied, a partner is not entitled to receive interest on the capital subscribed by him: s. 24 (4).

(9) In the absence of any special agreement, all the partners are entitled to share equally in the capital and profits of the business and must contribute equally towards the losses: s. 24 (1). Partners are joint owners of all property brought into, or acquired by, the firm, but on the death of any partner his interest in the property passes to his personal representative(s): s. 20.

(10) He can assign, either absolutely or by way of charge, his share in the assets and profits of the partnership, and the assignee has the right to receive, in whole or in part, the share of the profits and, on dissolution, the share of the property to which the assigning partner would otherwise be entitled, but the assignee cannot during the continuance of the partnership inspect the firm's books or interfere in the management or administration of the business: s. 31. For example, a partner can mortgage his share in the partnership as security for his personal bank borrowing, though in practice this is rarely done.

DISSOLUTION OF PARTNERSHIP

This may be effected without the intervention of the Court in some circumstances, or by order of the Court in other circumstances. As regards dissolution without reference to the Court, s. 32 provides that, subject to any agreement between the partners, a partnership is dissolved:

(a) If entered into for a fixed term, by the expiration of that term:

(b) If entered into for a single adventure or undertaking, by the termination of that adventure or undertaking:

(c) If entered into for an undefined time, by any partner giving notice to the other or others of his intention to dissolve the partnership, in which case the partnership is dissolved as from the date mentioned in the notice as the date of dissolution, or, if no date is so mentioned, as from the date of the communication of the notice. In *Moss* v. *Elphick* (1910), where the articles provided that the partnership should be terminated "by mutual agreement only", it was held that one partner could not determine the partnership by notice against the will of the other.

Later sections of the Act add to the above the following further circumstances for dissolution outside the Court:

(d) By the death or bankruptcy of any partner, unless otherwise agreed: s. 33 (1).

(e) At the option of the other partners, if any partner suffers his share of the partnership property to be charged under the Act for his separate debt: s. 33 (2). This does not refer to a voluntary assignment or charge, e.g. as security to a bank, but means an involuntary alienation under s. 23 (2) which empowers the court, on application of a judgment creditor of a partner, to make an order charging his interest in the assets and profits with payment of the judgment debt and interest and to appoint a receiver of that partner's share of profits.

(f) The happening of any event which makes the partnership unlawful: s. 34. An example would be where an alien is in partnership with a British citizen and war breaks out between his country and the United Kingdom.

In addition to these statutory provisions, dissolution outside the Court may arise from fraud making the original contract of partnership voidable at the option of the party deceived, or it may be that the partnership articles or deed make other circumstances a ground for dissolution. For example, the partnership agreement may make mental disorder, physical incapacity, incompatibility of temperament, or criminal conduct a ground for dissolution without the intervention of the Court, which would otherwise be necessary. Thus, in *Carmichael* v. *Evans* (1904) partnership articles provided that if a partner was "addicted to scandalous conduct detrimental to the partnership" or guilty of "any flagrant breach of the duties of a partner", he could be expelled: it was held that a conviction for dishonesty (defrauding a railway company by travelling without a ticket) was a sufficient ground for dissolution.

If dissolution is desired in circumstances not covered by ss. 32–34 already outlined, or by the terms of the partnership agreement, then recourse must be had to the Chancery Division of the High Court. By s. 35, on application by a partner, the Court may decree a dissolution of the partnership in any of the following cases:

(a) (Repealed by the Mental Health Act 1959, discussed below.)

(b) When a partner, other than the partner suing, becomes permanently incapable of performing his part of the partnership contract:

(c) When a partner, other than the partner suing, has been guilty of conduct prejudicial to the firm's business:

(d) When a partner, other than the partner suing, wilfully or persistently breaks the partnership agreement so that it is not reasonably practicable for the other members to continue in partnership with him:

    (e) When the business of the partnership can only be carried on at a loss:

    (f) Whenever the Court considers it just and equitable to decree dissolution.

Mental disorder of a partner does not automatically dissolve the partnership, but is a ground for dissolution in that by ss. 101 and 103 of the Mental Health Act 1959 a judge of the Court of Protection may order the dissolution of the partnership when, after considering medical evidence, he is satisfied that, by reason of mental disorder, a partner is incapable of managing his property and affairs.

If the articles in *Carmichael* v. *Evans* (1904), discussed above, had not provided grounds for dissolution, it might be that the Court would have held that a conviction for dishonesty fell within category (c)—conduct prejudicial to the firm's business. Whether particular conduct is so or not is a question of fact: thus, a conviction for a motoring offence, say, dangerous driving, would not normally appear to be within category (c), unless driving was an integral part of the firm's business, as in taxi, car-hire, and funeral undertaking partnerships. Category (f) gives the Court a wide discretion, which is similar to that conferred on the Court by category (f) of s. 222 of the Companies Act 1948 as regards ordering the winding up of a company.

After dissolution the authority of each partner to bind the firm continues so far as may be necessary to wind up the affairs of the partnership and to complete transactions begun but unfinished at the time of dissolution: s. 38. Unless modified by agreement, losses, including losses of capital, are paid first out of profits, next out of capital, and then by the partners individually in the proportion in which they were entitled to share profits: s. 44, which further provides that the assets of the firm, including the sums, if any, contributed by the partners to make up losses or deficiencies of capital, shall then be applied:

    (i) In paying debts and liabilities to third persons:

    (ii) In repaying advances made to the firm by any partner:

    (iii) In repaying capital contributed by the partners:

    (iv) The ultimate residue, if any, shall be divided among the partners in the proportion in which profits are divisible. (This will be equally unless the articles or deed of partnership provide otherwise.)

A complication may arise in connection with contribution towards losses, and that is the insolvency of a partner. In this event, where partners have contributed unequal capital and agree to share profits and losses equally, then the solvent partners are not liable to contribute the insolvent one's equal share of lost capital, but the amount available after the solvent partners have made their proper contribution is divided rateably according to the amount of capital standing to the credit of each solvent partner: *Garner* v. *Murray* (1904). In short, the insolvent partner's share of the deficiency is borne by the other partners in proportion to their capital, and not in the proportion that ordinary losses are borne.

Sometimes a partner pays a premium on entering a partnership for a fixed term. If the partnership is dissolved before the expiration of that term, then the Court may order the repayment of the premium or a proportion thereof, unless the dissolution is due to the misconduct of the partner who paid the premium or is effected by an agreement containing no provision for a return of any part of the premium: s. 40.

On the dissolution of a firm the assets must be realised for the purpose of winding up, and included amongst them is the intangible, sometimes valuable but always difficult to define, asset known as goodwill, which is in a sense the popularity, approbation or reputation of a business however achieved. Considered as a marketable asset (for, in the absence of agreement, goodwill must be sold on dissolution), goodwill is the privilege of trading as the recognised successor of the old firm with the probability that the customers or clients thereof will continue to resort to the successor. Pending the sale of goodwill, a partner may restrain any other partner from doing anything likely to decrease its value, e.g. using the firm's name. Goodwill may be sold when a partner dies, for the right to it does not vest in the survivors.

On a sale of the goodwill, the purchaser alone may represent himself as continuing or succeeding to the business, but unless the vendor has expressly agreed not to compete with the purchaser, he can do so, though not under a name which would amount to a representation that he was carrying on the old business, and he must not solicit any customers of the old firm: *Trego* v. *Hunt* (1896). This rule against canvassing old customers does not apply to a sale by the trustee in bankruptcy, or by the trustee under a deed of assignment for the benefit of creditors.

If no sale of goodwill can take place, then each partner may not only canvass old customers, but may also use the firm name, as long as he does not hold out the other partners as still being in partnership with him, inconvenient though this course can be.

BANK ACCOUNTS OF PARTNERSHIPS

(i) Opening the account

When requested to open a partnership account, a bank should first verify that the relationship between the parties concerned is that of partners, i.e. are they carrying on a business in common with a view of profit? In most cases this will be clear from the facts, which may already be known to the bank, or the parties may produce articles of partnership, or a deed of partnership, but if there is any doubt in the matter the bank should treat the account as a joint account.

The bank is under no obligation to obtain a copy of the articles or deed of partnership, when there is one, but if the bank does obtain such a copy, then it is deemed to have knowledge of its terms, and must conduct the account accordingly. Where, as is often the case, the firm's name does not consist of the true surnames of all the partners, the bank can usefully ask for production of the relevant certificate under the Registration of Business Names Act 1916, though it is not legally obliged to do so. Since 8th April 1969 the certificate no longer gives the name of the proprietor but only certifies that the business has been registered, so that if a bank requires full information as to a registration after that date (e.g. where the circumstances are suspicious) it must arrange a search of the Register (fee 5p). Production of the certificate or a search made may enable the bank to defeat any argument that, when collecting cheques and the like, the bank has lost its statutory protection under s. 4 of the Cheques Act 1957 because of its negligence: this situation occurred in *Smith and Baldwin* v. *Barclays Bank Ltd.* (1944) in relation to s. 4's now repealed predecessor, s. 82 of the Bills of Exchange Act 1882. The Act of 1916, however, is often disregarded, probably from ignorance of its existence, so that no certificate may be forthcoming, but in this event the bank can draw the partners' attention to the Act and point out that, apart from the penalty incurred by non-compliance, it is in the partnership's own interest to protect its name in this way.

The bank will, of course, take up the appropriate references where the partners are not already well-known to the bank. Once satisfied as to the existence of the partnership and the reputation of the individual partners the bank will have its usual form of mandate for partnerships accounts completed and signed by all partners. This will show how and by whom the account is to be conducted, including the withdrawal of securities held for safe custody, and in it the partners will undertake to be jointly and severally liable to the bank for all debts and liabilities. In the absence of such agreement their liability would be joint only (Partnership Act 1890, s. 9) though it has already been noted that the basic drawback of joint liability has been abolished by the Civil Liability (Contribution) Act 1978, so that any accidental omission by a bank to obtain contractual several liability from two or more joint borrowers does not now inhibit separate proceedings against each of the borrowers. In any event, it is important to the bank to establish joint and several liability, because it can then:

    (a) set-off the balances on private accounts of the partners against a debit balance on the partnership account (there is no right of set-off in the reverse direction without a special arrangement); and

    (b) rank equally with private creditors (instead of being subordinated to them) when claiming against the private estates of the partners in the event of bankruptcy or death of a partner.

Any delegation of authority to outside parties must be signed by all the partners.

In *Alliance Bank Ltd.* v. *Kearsley* (1871) one of two partners opened an account with the plaintiff bank in Manchester, saying that as he was the only resident partner in Manchester the account had better be opened in his name. This was done, and later when the account was overdrawn, the bank sought recovery from the other partner, but the bank's claim failed, because it was held that it was not in the ordinary course of business to open a bank account for a firm in a name other than that of the firm.

(ii) Operating the account

As regards revocation of mandates, this can be done by any one partner, so that he can stop any cheque whether he signed it or not, and also stop all withdrawals whether all partners sign or not. All mandates must be regarded as cancelled by a dissolution of the firm.

As regards advances to partnerships, this aspect is to be considered according to whether the partnership is a trading or a non-trading one. It has already been observed that in a trading partnership a partner has implied power to borrow, so that if the bank relies on this, it must be sure that the advance is for the ordinary business of the firm, i.e. not to finance some transaction foreign to the ostensible object of the firm. In practice, the bank obtains an undertaking signed by all the partners to be liable for any overdraft—this usually being incorporated in the mandate when the account is opened.

From the financial angle, the bank will consider the resources of the individual partners (except limited ones, if any) after making due allowance for their private liabilities. Security, if taken, may be either partnership property or the separate property of an individual partner, or possibly a guarantee or other third party security. In a trading partnership, a partner has implied power to pledge partnership securities for the purpose of its business, but again the bank will normally get all partners to join in the charge, and this will in any event be necessary where the property, such as land or stocks and shares, is in the joint names of the partners.

In a non-trading partnership no partner has implied authority to borrow on the firm's behalf or to pledge its securities, so that these points must be covered by the bank obtaining an express request for an advance signed by all the partners, with any security similarly created, or their express authority for one or more partners to overdraw the account and, where required and possible, to give security.

A continuing guarantee or other third party security given in respect of the firm's indebtedness should contain a clause that it is to remain operative notwithstanding any change in the constitution of the firm, otherwise such a change would determine the security. Where a partner pledges his separate property to secure future advances to his firm, any advance made after his death cannot be charged against that property. In partnerships which contain any infant partners, the bank can look only to the partners of full age and capacity for the repayment of any indebtedness, an infant partner not being liable, though he has power to bind the firm.

Sometimes a partnership will insure the lives of the individual partners, the premiums being paid from the firm's account. In this event although the policy is *prima facie* the property of the individual partner, a form of trust is set up and if such a policy in the name of an individual partner is offered as security for the firm's indebtedness it must be charged as a partnership security by all the partners joining in the charge.

(iii) Effect of the death, bankruptcy, mental disorder or retirement of a partner

(a) *Death of a partner.*—Section 33 (1) provides: "Subject to any agreement between the partners, every partnership is dissolved as regards all the partners by the death or bankruptcy of any partner".

Thus, if there is no agreement to the contrary, the partnership is dissolved by the death of any partner, and the surviving partner(s)' duty is to wind up the affairs of the firm, for which purpose they may continue the bank account, though new mandates should be taken signed by all of them, unless they are all obliged to sign already. Usually, to avoid upsetting the continuity of the business, the partnership agreement will provide that notwithstanding the death of one or more partners, the business shall not be wound up, but that instead the surviving partner(s) shall carry on the business, provisions being included for the method of ascertaining the share of the deceased and payment of it to his personal representatives. Without such an agreement a firm with a large number of partners would be liable to periodic disturbance.

The deceased's personal representatives cannot claim to take part in the management of the firm in any event, though their interests are safeguarded by such an agreement. On the death of one partner in a firm having a bank account, the surviving partner has a right to draw cheques upon the account: *Backhouse* v. *Charlton* (1878). It was also held in this case that where a bank has no notice of the state of accounts between the deceased partner and the survivors, it is under no duty to enquire. Where surviving partners continue the business they constitute a fresh partnership and the bank will require new mandates, and also new security forms unless those held remain effective notwithstanding changes in the constitution of the firm.

Some banks, in the absence of objection to it, continue to pay cheques signed by the partner before, and presented after, his death. Others require the confirmation of the surviving partners before paying such cheques. If the partnership account is overdrawn and liability for it is joint and several (which is customary with bank mandate forms), and the deceased partner's estate is being relied on, then the account must be broken to prevent the operation of the Rule in *Clayton's Case* (1816) to the bank's detriment, any subsequent transactions being passed through a new account. This is because the estate of the deceased partner is liable only for debts incurred before his death: s. 36 (3), which makes a similar provision as regards the bankruptcy of a partner, or his retirement (where there is no "holding out"). It has already been noted that the surviving partners can pledge partnership property for winding up purposes and that such a charge has priority over the lien of the deceased partner's personal representatives.

(b) *Bankruptcy of a partner.*— As s. 33 (1) also applies in the event of bankruptcy of a partner, the partnership will be dissolved thereby, unless the partnership agreement provides otherwise. As regards cheques signed by the bankrupt partner, it is advisable to obtain the other partners' confirmation of cheques dated before his bankruptcy and essential to do so in respect of cheques dated afterwards, for the bankrupt partner's authority to bind the firm ceases on his bankruptcy. The firm's account will be dealt with in a similar manner to that described in the preceding paragraph. A credit account can be continued, for cheques signed by the other partners can be paid and the balance of the account can be safely released to them. It is the responsibility of the other partners to account for the bankrupt partner's share of the assets, and neither the bankrupt partner nor his trustee has any power to deal with partnership affairs. An overdrawn account must be broken to forestall the Rule in *Clayton's Case*, assuming that joint and several liability has been undertaken by the partners and that the bank wishes to prove against the bankrupt's estate.

(c) *Bankruptcy of the partnership.*—The bankruptcy of a partner, which does not involve the bankruptcy of the partnership so long as at least one of the other partners has sufficient assets to ensure the firm's solvency, must be distinguished from a bankruptcy of the partnership, which necessarily involves the bankruptcy of all the partners. If this happens, then the firm's account and the private accounts of any of the partners with the bank must be stopped, whether they are in credit or debit. A receiving order made against the firm operates as an order against each partner and if adjudication eventually follows, this will be made against each partner by name and not against the firm.

(d) *Mental disorder of a partner.*—The mental disorder of a partner does not automatically dissolve the partnership, unless the partnership articles or deed so provide, but an application for dissolution may be made to the Court, either by another partner or by a person acting for the mentally disordered partner. It is clearly in the interests of all concerned to have the matter legally determined. Where the partnership account is in credit, new mandates should be taken from the other partners. If the account is overdrawn, with joint and several liability, and the bank is relying on the mentally disordered partner, then it should be broken to avoid the operation of the Rule in *Clayton's Case*. In any event, the confirmation of the other partners should be obtained before paying any cheques signed by the mentally disordered partner.

(e) *Retirement of a partner*—On the retirement of a partner, new mandates will be required from the remaining partners, plus any new partner who may then be introduced. If there is a debt of the old firm which has not been paid off, e.g. by a secured loan to the new firm, then the agreement of the new partner to the pledge of partnership assets to secure the old debt should be obtained.

DISTRIBUTION OF ASSETS IN BANKRUPTCY

Where all the partners are bankrupt, the method of distributing the joint and separate estates is laid down by s. 33 (6) of the Bankruptcy Act 1914 as follows:

"In the case of partners the joint estate shall be applicable in the first instance in payment of their joint debts, and the separate estate of each partner shall be applicable in the first instance in payment of his separate debts. If there is a surplus of the separate estates, it shall be dealt with as part of the joint estate. If there is a surplus of the joint estate, it shall be dealt with as part of the respective separate estates in proportion to the right and interest of each partner in the joint estate."

(This rule also applies to the administration of the assets of deceased partners, i.e. where the deceased leave more debts than assets.)

As an arithmetical example of the method's operation, suppose X, Y and Z are in a partnership which becomes bankrupt, liabilities and assets being as follows: the firm owes £5,000 and has assets of £3,000; X owes his separate creditors £1,000 and his separate estate is £500; Y owes his separate creditors £750 and his separate estate is £1,000; Z's separate creditors and his separate estate both total £500. The separate creditors of X and Z take all their respective separate estates, those creditors of X having to be content with 50p in the £. The separate creditors of Y take their full repayment of £750 out of his separate estate, leaving a balance of £250 which goes to augment the firm's assets to be distributed among the joint creditors. Where the situation is that one partner is insolvent, but another partner is solvent, with sufficient separate estate to pay off the joint creditors in full, then the solvent partner having done so may prove against the insolvent partner's estate for the amount which he has paid beyond his proportion.

However, to this general rule there are the following exceptions:

1. Where there is no joint estate, the joint creditors may prove against the separate estates on an equal footing with the separate creditors.

2. If a joint creditor is the petitioning creditor in the separate bankruptcy of one of the partners, he is allowed to prove for his joint debt in competition with the separate creditors: s. 114 of the Bankruptcy Act 1914.

3. Where a partner has fraudulently, and without the consent of his co-partners, converted partnership property to his own use, the joint estate may prove for the value of that property against that partner's separate estate in competition with his separate creditors.

4. Where a creditor has been defrauded by the partners, or by any of them so as to make the firm liable, he may prove, at his election, against either the joint estate or the separate estate of the fraudulent partners, but not both.

5. Where one or more partners carry on a separate trade, with a distinct capital, and debts have arisen between them and their firm in the ordinary course of business, each estate may prove against the other(s).

6. Where a creditor of the firm has also a distinct contract for the same debt against one or more of the individual partners, he may prove against both the joint estate and the separate estate(s), so long as he does not get more than 100p in the £. This right is now contained in Article 19 of Schedule II to the Bankruptcy Act 1914. An earlier illustration of it occurred in *Ex parte Honey, Re Jeffery* (1871), where a joint and several promissory note had been signed by (a) two members of a firm; (b) the firm itself; and (c) several other persons. When the firm became bankrupt, the holder of the note proved against the joint estate and also against the separate estate of the two partners who had signed the note, and the Court upheld his right to do so and to receive dividends from all three estates.

Partners may not compete in an administration with the firm's creditors either against the joint or against any of the separate estates. Thus, if the firm is bankrupt, the partners' claims against the firm are postponed to the claims of the firm's creditors, and any claim by the firm against individual partners is postponed to the claims of each partner's separate creditors. On the other hand, if there are no joint creditors because they have been paid by a solvent partner, or where there is no possibility of a surplus being available to joint creditors from the separate estate of a partner because he is clearly insolvent, the solvent partner is allowed to prove as a creditor in respect of his separate debt against the separate estate of the insolvent partner.

If a partner has pledged his separate property to secure advances to his firm, the creditor holding that security may first prove on the joint estate and then realise the security on the separate estate, so long as he does not get more than 100p in the £, because to surrender the security would not augment the joint estate. A corresponding rule applies to the reverse situation, i.e. where a separate creditor holds a security on the joint property. Thus, security deposited by a partner to secure the firm's bank account is collateral security, and the bank may prove for the full amount of the debt against the firm, making up any deficiency from the security. Should there be any surplus this must be paid over to the trustee of the partner who deposited the security.

LIMITED PARTNERSHIPS

These are a special type of partnership created by the Limited Partnerships Act 1907, with the idea of allowing some partners to enjoy the advantage of limited liability, as possessed by members of a limited company. In practice, little use has been made of the Act—in the first five years of its existence only 492 limited partnerships were registered—because at the same time private companies were afforded statutory recognition by s. 37 of the Companies Act 1907, such companies being now governed by s. 28 of the Companies Act 1948. The superior advantages of the private company led to a great increase in their number, which stole the thunder from limited partnerships, whose name is rather misleading because, although certain partners in such a firm have limited liability, yet the firm has not. Companies form a logical development in the commercial scene and will be dealt with in the next Chapter.

Except in so far as the Limited Partnerships Act 1907 provides otherwise, the Partnership Act 1890 and the rules of equity and common law applicable to partnerships shall apply to limited partnerships: s. 7 of the Act of 1907. The constitution of a limited partnership is governed by s. 4 of the Act of 1907 (as amended by the Banking Act 1979), which, in effect, provides as follows:—

(1) Such a partnership must not consist of more than twenty persons, but s. 121 of the Companies Act 1967 removed this maximum limit in the case of solicitors, accountants and members of a recognised stock exchange; it also empowers the Department of Trade to make regulations by statutory instrument that the limit of twenty persons shall not apply to limited partnerships specified in the regulations. The regulations which have been made are set out in S.I. 1971 No. 782 and exempt from that prohibition limited partnerships carrying on one or more of the following activities—surveying, auctioneering, valuing, estate agency, land agency and estate management.

(2) It must always include one or more general partners as well as one or more limited partners, i.e. there cannot be a partnership which consists solely of limited partners.

(3) A general partner is any partner who is not a limited partner, and is liable for all the debts and obligations of the firm.

(4) A limited partner is one who contributes on entering the partnership a stated amount of capital in cash or in property valued at a stated amount, and whose liability for the debts and obligations of the firm is limited to the amount so contributed.

(5) If a limited partner withdraws directly or indirectly any part of the capital he has contributed, he is liable for the firm's debts and obligations up to the amount so withdrawn.

(6) A corporation may be a limited partner.

Section 5 provides that every limited partnership must be registered, otherwise it will be treated as a general partnership and every limited partner shall be deemed to be a general partner. Section 15 provides that the Registrar of Companies will act as registrar for limited partnerships at [Cardiff] or Edinburgh, according to whether the principal place of business is in England and Wales or Scotland. The manner and particulars of registration are laid down in s. 8 which provides that registration is effected by posting or delivering to the appropriate registrar a statement signed by the partners containing particulars as to the firm's name, the general nature of the business, the principal place of business, the full name of each partner, the date of commencement and term of the partnership, a statement that it is limited and the description of each limited partner as such, and the amount contributed by him and whether in cash or otherwise. Section 9 provides that if any change occurs in any of the above particulars, or if a general partner becomes a limited partner or *vice versa*, notice of the change must be given to the registrar within seven days, otherwise the general partners are liable to a default fine.

The fees and forms for registration are prescribed by the Limited Partnership Rules 1907 (S.R. & O. 1907 No. 1020) as amended by S.I. 1974 No. 560. For preliminary registration the current Form LP5 requires in addition to the particulars set out in s. 8 a statement of the amounts contributed by the limited partner and the capital due thereon; the registration fee is now £2 plus the appropriate capital duty. For changes, Form LP6 requires in addition to the particulars set out in s. 9 any increase in the amount contributed and in the capital due to be shown.

If a general partner becomes a limited partner, or an assignment is made of a limited partner's share in the firm, notice of the fact must be forthwith advertised in the Gazette: s. 10.

The statements filed with the registrar in respect of limited partnerships may be inspected by the public, who may also obtain certified copies of or extracts from any registered statement: s. 16. The fee for inspection is 5p.

The particular role of a limited partner is prescribed by s. 6, namely, that he must not take any part in the management of the partnership business, and he cannot bind the firm, but he may by himself or his agent inspect the books, examine into the state and prospects of the business, and advise with the partners thereon. If a limited partner takes part in the management of the business, he will be liable as a general partner for all the debts and obligations of the firm incurred while he so takes part in the management. A limited partner cannot bar the entry of a new partner. The death or bankruptcy of a limited partner does not dissolve the partnership, and his mental disorder is only a ground for dissolution if his share cannot be otherwise ascertained and realised. On dissolution the right to wind up the affairs of the partnership is vested in the general partners, unless the Court otherwise orders.

By s. 6 (4) of the Act of 1907, coupled with s. 399 (9) of the Companies Act 1948, a limited partnership may be wound up by the Court in accordance with winding up procedure for unregistered companies, but this method is not used in practice because, by s. 127 of the Bankruptcy Act 1914, subject to certain modifications, limited partnerships may be made bankrupt in the same way as ordinary partnerships, and if all the general partners are adjudged bankrupt, the assets of the limited partnership shall vest in the trustee.

The position of a limited partner can be seen to have some resemblance to that of a shareholder in a private limited company. Both have limited liability and can take no part in the management, though the limited partner may inspect the books and examine into the state and prospects of the business and advise thereon, and to this extent he is better off than a shareholder. Neither their personal fate, as regards death, bankruptcy or mental disorder, nor their charging of their shares or interest affects the association to which they respectively belong. Finally, the only way in which a limited partner can withdraw is by assigning his share in the partnership with the consent of the general partners (his assignee then becoming, by s. 6 (5), a limited partner with all the rights of the assignor). The parallel course for a shareholder in a private company is, subject to the restrictions on transfer which must necessarily be imposed by the articles of the company, to transfer his shares.

CONCLUSION

At this half-way stage—that is, after considering partnerships but before passing on to companies in the next chapter—it may be helpful to summarise the main differences (alluded to from time to time in both chapters) between these two types of business associations. Apart from divergencies as regards the permitted numbers of their respective members, and the obvious fact that they are regulated by different statutes, the two differ as follows:—

1. A partnership is not, in England and Wales, a separate legal entity, whereas a company is. One consequence of this is that partnership property is jointly owned by the partners, but property owned by a company belongs solely to the company, and no member of the company in such capacity has any personal interest in it. Again, partners can conduct any business they agree upon, but the *ultra vires* doctrine restricts a company to the objects clause of its Memorandum of Association.

2. A partnership does not have perpetual succession, whereas a company has. Consequently, a partnership may be dissolved by various circumstances, but a company continues, despite changes in its members, until it is wound up in the manner prescribed by the Companies Act 1948.

3. A partnership has no common seal of its own as evidence of its formal acts, whereas a company has.

4. In an ordinary partnership all the partners have unlimited liability for the debts of the firm, whereas except in the very rare case of unlimited companies, the liability of a member of a company is limited.

5. In an ordinary partnership all the partners can take part in the management of the firm, but in companies the members cannot do so, except where they are also directors or senior executives of the company.

6. In the event of insolvency, a partnership is subject to the bankruptcy machinery, whereas a company is wound up in the manner prescribed by the Act of 1948.

7. Partnership affairs are private, whereas company procedures (e.g. meetings and accounts) are the subject of considerable statutory provisions, and the documents relating to companies, including their accounts, are filed with the Registrar of Companies and are available for inspection by the general public.

8. The difficulties of partners and members of private companies in transferring their respective interests have already been mentioned, but in contrast to this a member of a public company can dispose of his shares or stock at any time with a minimum of formalities and, where the company has a stock exchange quotation, finding a purchaser presents no difficulty.

9. A partnership cannot create a floating charge over its assets, whereas a company can, and in practice often does give a floating charge as security for an advance.

10. Partners are assessable to income tax on the firm's profits, whether withdrawn by them or not, whereas a company has to pay corporation tax on its profits and its members are only liable for income tax on the profits distributed as dividends, but part of the corporation tax paid in advance by the company when the dividend is paid is credited against the income tax liability of the members.

Chapter 4

Companies

NATURE

As the most common type of corporation, companies have already been briefly mentioned in Chapter 1 as regards their capacity to contract, and this chapter will now deal with their formation, operation and termination.

Like any other corporation, a company is an artificial legal person, with a separate existence quite distinct from that of its directors and members. It has a distinctive name in which it can sue and be sued, and the use of a common seal. Finally, it has perpetual succession inasmuch as it never dies, but continues in being notwithstanding changes in its members unless and until it is dissolved by the prescribed legal means. It is like a river that flows on, though at any given point the water constituting it is always changing. This fundamental principle of the separate identity of a company, even a so-called "one-man company", was established in *Salomon* v. *Salomon & Co., Ltd.* (1897), of which the facts were:

Aron Salomon incorporated his business as a limited company, in which he himself held 20,001 shares, and his wife, four sons and a daughter held one share each. The company borrowed money from Salomon in his private capacity and issued debentures to him giving him a first charge upon the company's assets. Subsequently, the company became insolvent and went into liquidation; as against the liquidator, Salomon claimed to be a "secured" creditor and as such entitled to be paid in priority to the company's ordinary creditors. His claim was upheld by the House of Lords, on the ground that Salomon was a different person from Salomon and Co., Ltd., the company he formed, and therefore he could deal with the company as a private individual.

Thus, no director or member, however large his shareholding, owns any of the company's property; nor has he any insurable interest in it—*Macaura* v. *Northern Assurance Co.* (1925).

Paradoxically, a business describing itself as, say, "The Loamshire

113

Meat Company", is almost certainly not a company in the legal sense, but a partnership, or even a sole trader, carrying on business under that name. All registered companies must end their name with the word "limited" unless permitted to dispense with it by the Department of Trade where the company has been formed for religious, charitable or similar purposes, or unless it is that rare bird, an unlimited company. In the reverse situation, a person or persons who carry on business under a name ending with "limited" or any contraction of that word, without being duly incorporated with limited liability, are liable to a fine not exceeding £5 for every day upon which that name has been used: s. 439 of the Companies Act 1948.

Companies are formed by compliance with the provisions of the Companies Act for the time being in force. The magic formula of limited liability was thrown open to all by the Companies Act 1862, followed by the Acts of 1908, 1929 and 1948, with various amending Acts in between these principal ones. Thus, the Companies Act 1929 was substantially amended by the Companies Act 1947 and the two of them were then repealed and replaced by the Companies Act 1948, except for a few sections of the 1947 Act on bankruptcy and other points which still remain in force. In its turn, the 1948 Act has been amended by the Companies Acts 1967 and 1976. About half of the 1976 Act dealt with accounts, accounting records and auditors. More company legislation will be forthcoming in the future in order to give effect to the successive directives issued by the Council of Ministers of the European Communities to harmonise company legislation. A Companies Bill 1979 has been introduced to meet the requirements of the Second Directive by making fundamental changes in the classification of public and private companies and an outline of this Bill is given at the end of this Chapter.

Each company when formed is given a number, so that the size of a number gives a rough indication of the company's age. It will be spoken of as registered under the Companies Act 1862 or 1908 or 1929 or 1948, as the case may be; but for disciplinary control all companies are currently governed by the Companies Acts 1948 to 1976. References in this chapter to sections will be to sections of the 1948 Act, unless the contrary is stated. The duty of supervising companies rests on the Board [now Department] of Trade, which, by s. 424, is empowered to appoint Registrars of Companies and their staffs. Various sections which require action to be done by companies, usually the filing of returns with the Registrar of Companies, carry a fine imposable for non-compliance on the company and every officer who is in default. Fees are governed by the Companies (Fees) Regulations 1975 (S.I. 1975 No. 596).

The mechanics of forming a company are comparatively easy and the procedure will now be examined in detail.

FORMATION OF A COMPANY

By s. 1 any seven or more persons, or two in the case of a private company, associated for a lawful purpose may form an incorporated company in the manner prescribed by the Act. Three types of companies are possible:—

(a) A company having the liability of its members limited by the amount, if any, unpaid on their shares (known as "a company limited by shares"—and forming the vast majority of all companies).

(b) A company having the liability of its members limited by the amount that they have undertaken to contribute to the assets in a winding up (known as "a company limited by guarantee"—these companies may or may not have a share capital: there are a modest number of them, usually of a non-profit making character and concerned with charitable, educational and similar purposes).

(c) A company not having any limit on the liability of its members (known as "an unlimited company"). These are comparatively rare—they have the advantages of incorporation, viz. a separate legal personality, perpetual succession and the use of a common seal, but their members have unlimited liability for the company's debts. One or two banks come within this category, e.g. Coutts & Co., and also various unlimited land, estate or consultancy companies, where the primary function is to hold land or assets or to provide a specialised service rather than commercial trading. There has been some increase in their number since 1967 because they are now the only companies whose financial affairs remain secret.

The two principal documents to be completed before applying for registration of a company are the Memorandum of Association, and the Articles of Association. There is an important distinction between the purpose and content of these, which can be elaborated thus:

The Memorandum of Association

This is the mainspring of the company. It is a deed which states and defines the constitution and the powers of the company, and at common law any act beyond these powers is *ultra vires* the company and void: *Ashbury Railway Carriage and Iron Co.* v. *Riche* (1875). This rule, however, is now restricted by s. 9 (1) of the European Communities Act 1972 (see page 131).

By s. 2. as amended by s. 30 of the 1976 Act the Memorandum of Association must state:

(a) The name of the company, ending with the word "limited" (or "cyfyngedig" in the case of a company whose registered office is situate in Wales), in the case of companies limited by shares or by guarantee, unless that word is dispensed with, which the Department of Trade can sanction under s. 19 where it is proved to its satisfaction that the company is formed for promoting commerce, art, science, religion, charity or any other useful object. A company which has obtained such a dispensation is now required by s. 9 (7) (c) of the European Communities Act 1972 to state in all business letters and order forms of the company that it is, in fact, a limited company. Section 17 provides that no company shall be registered by a name which in the opinion of the Department of Trade is undesirable. In practice, the ever-increasing number of companies makes it difficult to choose a name clearly dissimilar from existing companies, and certain words in a name, e.g. "Royal" and "Bank", will now hardly ever be permitted.

(b) Whether the registered office of the company is situate in England or Wales or Scotland. This is to locate the company for disciplinary purposes—in the first two cases the company comes under the Registrar of Companies, Crown Way, Maindy, Cardiff CF4 3UZ, and in the last case it comes under the Registrar of Companies for Scotland, 102 George Street, Edinburgh EH2 3DJ. There are certain inherent differences between the law of England and the law of Scotland as regards companies, due to each country having its own distinct system of law. For example, not until the Companies (Floating Charges) (Scotland) Act 1961 could a Scottish company create a floating charge, and not until the Companies (Floating Charges and Receivers) (Scotland) Act 1972 could a receiver be appointed in respect of such a charge (the usual remedy in England and Wales). Prior to the coming into force of s. 30 of the Companies Act 1976 the choice of situation lay between England and Scotland, as "England" included Wales: Wales and Berwick Act 1746, but s. 30 now allows a company's memorandum to state that its registered office is to be situate in Wales, and a company whose registered office was already situate in Wales was permitted during the ensuing 12 months to change its memorandum by special resolution so as to provide that its registered office be situate in Wales. Such a company may also state its name with "cyfyngedig" as the last word of that name. New companies whose registered office is to be situate in Wales may deliver for registration memorandum and articles in Welsh, accompanied by a certified translation into English, and an existing company which changed the situation of its registered office to Wales within the 12 months' period was authorised to file with the Registrar a certified translation into Welsh of its memorandum and articles. Subsequent documents delivered to the Registrar by any company whose registered office is situate in Wales may be in Welsh, accompanied by a certified translation into English.

The actual address of the registered office is not stated in the Memorandum, but is filed separately with the Registrar when making the application for registration: s. 23 of the 1976 Act, and any subsequent changes have to be notified to the Registrar within 14 days. Under s. 9 (7) of the European Communities Act 1972 companies now have to show on business letters and order forms their place of registration, registered number and the address of their registered office.

(c) The objects of the company. These are the purposes which the company is to pursue. The objects clause should define and delimit the whole field of industry or commerce within which the corporate activities of the company are to operate. The idea of the objects is that a person will know what business a company is carrying on when investing his money in it, and so will not be surprised later to find that the company has switched to a totally different business. In practice, however, the objects clause often runs to twenty or more paragraphs of which only the first few really deal with objects, and then in as far-reaching a manner as possible. The remaining clauses really enumerate the powers of the company, e.g. to borrow and lend money, to mortgage, charge, guarantee and so on.

Occasionally a company (or more likely its liquidator) has sought to avoid liability by pleading that a transaction is *ultra vires* the objects of the company, as in *Re Introductions, Ltd*. (1969) where the company, formed in 1951 in connection with the Festival of Britain, later switched to the sole activity of pig-breeding, which was *ultra vires* the company. Large sums were borrowed from a bank against debentures on the company's assets. The Court of Appeal held that the debentures were void. Under s. 9 (1) of the European Communities Act 1972, a third party dealing with a company in good faith would be protected in these circumstances. However, the third party would not be acting in good faith if he had actual notice (as the bank had in the case from its copy of the Memorandum and Articles) that the transaction was *ultra vires* the company.

(d) That the liability of the members is limited (in the case of companies limited by shares, or by guarantee, and if the latter it must also state the amount of liability undertaken by each member).

(e) Where a company has a share capital (and is not an unlimited company), a statement of the share capital showing the amount and division thereof. For example, "The share capital of the company is £100, divided into 400 Ordinary Shares of 25p each".

The Memorandum must be signed by at least seven persons in the case of a public company, or by at least two persons in the case of a private company, and each signatory must take at least one share and write opposite his name the number of shares he takes. By s. 3 each subscriber's signature must be witnessed. Section 4 provides that the company can only alter its Memorandum in accordance with the express provisions of the Act. In fact, it is possible to change the various clauses, except (b)—the country, England (or Wales) or Scotland, in which the registered office is situated: this is the domicile of the company and cannot be changed, though the actual address within England (or Wales) or Scotland can be changed by the company at will. With regard to the other clauses of the Memorandum, changes can be effected as follows:—

(i) The name: by s. 18 a company may change its name by special resolution and with the consent of the Department of Trade, which will then issue an official certificate recording the change. The fee payable to the Department is £40. The rights and liabilities of the company are not affected by such a change—it is still the same legal entity, but now bearing a different name. Thus, a company may have its name changed when there is a change of ownership of the company, or a change in its business. As regards both the original and any subsequent name the Department of Trade may order a change of name where it is too like that of an existing company. Furthermore, s. 46 of the Act of 1967 empowers the Department of Trade to direct a change of name by a company whose registered name is considered to give so misleading an indication of the nature of its activities as to be likely to cause harm to the public.

It may be mentioned here that by s. 141 both special and extra-ordinary resolutions must be passed by a majority of not less than three-fourths of such members as, being entitled to do so, vote in person or by proxy at a general meeting of which due notice of the resolution has been given. Basically, a meeting to pass a special resolution requires twenty-one days' notice, whereas fourteen days will suffice for the latter type. However, s. 133 allows a meeting to be called at shorter notice than the foregoing, provided 95 per cent. in nominal value of the shareholders so authorise, except where it is the annual general meeting, when 100 per cent. must agree.

The Registration of Business Names Act 1916 extends to companies, so that if a company carries on business in a name which is not its corporate name without any addition, it must register under the Act.

(ii) The objects clause may be altered by special resolution for seven purposes specified in s. 5 (1), namely, to enable the company:

(a) to carry on its business more economically or more efficiently; or

(b) to attain its main purpose by new or improved means; or

(c) to enlarge or change the local area of its operations; or

(d) to carry on some business which under existing circumstances may conveniently or advantageously be combined with the business of the company; or

(e) to restrict or abandon any of the objects specified in the memorandum; or

(f) to sell or dispose of the whole or any part of the undertaking of the company; or

(g) to amalgamate with any other company or body of persons; and the consent of the Court is not necessary unless an objection is made to the alteration. By s. 5 (2) such an objection must be made by at least 15 per cent. of the shareholders (or of the members if the company is not limited by shares), or 15 per cent. of any debentureholders whose debentures entitle them to object to alterations of the company's objects, provided none of the objectors consented to or voted in favour of the alteration. By s. 5 (3) the objection must be made within twenty-one days after the date on which the resolution was passed. However, s. 5 (9) provides that the validity of an alteration is not challengeable after expiry of twenty-one days after the date of the resolution on the grounds that it was not authorised by s. 5 (1), so that the list of seven authorised alterations stated therein is largely nullified.

(iii) The limited liability clause may be deleted by re-registering the company as unlimited under the procedure set out in s. 43 of the Companies Act 1967; conversely, an existing unlimited company may be re-registered under s. 44 as a limited company. These new provisions are stated by s. 45 to replace the earlier provisions on re-registration contained in s. 16 of the 1948 Act.

(iv) As regards share capital, s. 61 provides that a company limited by shares may in general meeting alter its share capital by increasing it, consolidating and dividing shares (e.g. making five 5p shares into one 25p share; or dividing each £1 share into four 25p shares), converting shares into stock, or reconverting stock into shares, and cancelling shares not taken up. A notice of increase of capital must be filed with the Registrar of Companies within fifteen days (s. 63), and any other change must be notified to him within one month (s. 62). By s. 66 a company may reduce its share capital by special resolution to extinguish or reduce unpaid liability, or cancel capital lost or unrepresented by assets, or return share capital in excess of the company's needs, but by s. 67 any such reduction must be confirmed by the Court.

In *Re Harris and Sheldon Group, Ltd.* (1971) it was held that a change in the description of a share from 5/- to 25p is not a change in the fixed amount of a share and it is not therefore an alteration of a condition in the memorandum so that it requires no formalities by virtue of the Companies Act 1948.

The Articles of Association

These are the internal rules and regulations as to the persons by whom and the manner in which the company's business is to be conducted. Articles are of inferior status compared with the Memorandum, for they supplement the Memorandum but cannot increase the area of the company's powers (or contravene express provisions of the Companies Acts). Nevertheless, they are of considerable importance because they show the practical day-to-day machinery whereby the government of the company will be carried on—hence, they fix the powers of the directors, and how they may be exercised, and also such features as the transfer and transmission of shares, voting rights of members, and regulations for the affixing of the company's seal.

Articles may make such provisions as the members of the company decide, and as far as the initial registration of the company is concerned, s. 6 provides that Articles of Association may, in the case of a company limited by shares, and shall in the case of companies limited by guarantee or unlimited companies, be registered. By s. 8, if a company limited by shares and registered after July 1st, 1948 does not register Articles, its Articles will be the regulations contained in Table A, the First Schedule to the Companies Act 1948. Part I of Table A is a model set of Articles for a public company. A private company may adopt Table A as its Articles provided that Part II of that Table is incorporated. Some companies adopt a complete set of their own articles, but in practice the majority adopt a shortened set of Articles, i.e. incorporating the regulations of Table A by reference except where excluded or modified. The Articles must be printed, divided into paragraphs numbered consecutively, signed by each subscriber, and witnessed: s. 9.

Within the sphere permitted to them, Articles may be altered by special resolutions at any time: s. 10. Any such alteration must be for the benefit of the company as a whole, and can be made retrospectively: *Allen* v. *Gold Reefs of West Africa, Ltd.* (1900).

A completed copy of both Memorandum and Articles of Association (now unstamped: Finance Act 1970) is filed with the Registrar of Companies when incorporation is requested, and any alterations to them must be filed with the Registrar, and copies subsequently issued must include all current alterations. Under ss. 47–49 of the Finance Act 1973 the former stamp duties on authorised capital and issues of loan capital have ceased; instead, duty is charged in accordance with EEC Directive 69/335 at the rate of 1 per cent. on issues of share capital, including any premium that is paid, and credit will be given for duty that has already been paid on earlier increases in authorised capital. The fee payable to the Registrar for incorporation is £50.

Each company is given its own file at the registry. This file starts with the documents lodged on incorporation, and is added to as and when further documents, including details of charges and annual returns, are lodged, so that there is a more-or-less up-to-date case history of every company available for personal inspection by anyone on payment of a fee, at present 5p per company. Whilst s. 5 (7) of the 1948 Act provides that when the objects clause of the memorandum has been altered, a reprinted memorandum including the alterations has to be filed with the Registrar, s. 9 (5) of the European Communities Act 1972 further provides that when notice of any other alteration in the memorandum or any alteration in the articles is given to the Registrar, "the company shall send with it a printed copy of the memorandum or articles as altered." This was done to ensure that the public had available for easy inspection the latest version of the company's constitution in one document. Photostat copies of any document on the file may be obtained on paying additional fees. Thus, the documents on the file are public documents and ignorance of their contents cannot be pleaded. There are still search facilities in London, at Companies House, 55–71, City Road, London EC1Y 1BB, although the Registry has moved to Cardiff, where searches can also be carried out.

When the appropriate formalities of applying for registration of a company have been complied with, the Registrar of Companies will issue a Certificate of Incorporation in respect of the new company as from the date stated therein: s. 13. This certificate will also give the registered number allotted to the company and state, in the case of a limited company, that the company is limited. On receipt of this certificate a private company may commence activities forthwith, but a public company requires a further certificate, a Certificate to

Commence Business, which is issued after the provisions of s. 109 as to allotment and so on have been satisfied.

PRIVATE COMPANIES

Unless and until the Companies Bill 1979 becomes law, a private company is defined by s. 28 as one which by its articles (a) restricts the right to transfer its shares; (b) limits the number of its members to fifty (not including employees, or former employees who remain members); and (c) prohibits any invitation to the public to subscribe for any shares or debentures in the company. The vast majority of companies are private companies. Compared with a public company, a private company has certain advantages, e.g. it need have only two members, instead of seven; by s. 176 it need have only one director, instead of the minimum of two necessary for a public company; and it does not have to hold a statutory meeting under s. 130. Its main advantage—secrecy of its financial affairs—was abolished by s. 2 of the Act of 1967, since when all private companies have to file a copy of their balance sheet and accounts with their annual return (the requirements for which are set out in ss. 124–128 and the Sixth Schedule of the 1948 Act as amended by the 1967 Act). Sole traders and partnerships when considering whether or not to turn their businesses into companies have to weigh the disadvantage of publication of their financial affairs against the advantages of limited liability and perpetual succession.

Private companies can transform themselves into public companies, and *vice versa*, though the former course is more usual than the latter, for a private company which grows in size and importance often "goes public" in order to get an official quotation for its shares and to raise funds on a stock exchange. A public company need not have its shares etc. quoted on a stock exchange but usually most of them do. All that a private company need do to become a public company is to delete from its articles the restrictions necessary under s. 28, making certain it has at least seven members and two directors. By s. 30 it must deliver to the Registrar a statement in lieu of prospectus in the form prescribed in the Third Schedule of the Act (or else deliver a prospectus under s. 41) within fourteen days of such change in its articles. A public company wishing to become a private company must alter its articles to include the appropriate restrictions under s. 28, and must reduce the number of its members where necessary below fifty. By s. 31 members are severally liable for the whole debts of the company, where business is carried on for more than six months with less than seven members in the case of a public company, or two in the case of a private company, if they are cognisant of this fact.

THE OPERATION OF COMPANIES

Although a company is a separate legal entity, its personality is artificial and it can only act through physical persons, principally its directors, s. 455 defining the word "director" as including "any person occupying the position of director by whatever name called". The directors act collectively as a board, headed by a chairman, though there is usually at least one managing director to whom the day-to-day running of the business is delegated. Directors have been described as "commercial men managing a trading concern for the benefit of themselves and all other shareholders in it". In some respects directors are trustees, and in other respects they are agents or managers, their duties being spelt out of the law in general and the Companies Acts in particular. They are trustees for the company, and not for an individual shareholder or for third parties who have contracted with the company. Approving transfers, issuing and allotting shares and making calls are instances of directors acting as trustees for the company. Similarly, directors act as agents of the company, making contracts on its behalf, and as such they are subject to the general requirements of the law of agency, discussed in Chapter 2. Thus, the company as principal is liable on the contracts which they make and not the directors unless they contract in their own names (and in this event the other contracting party can sue them or the company at his option), or, by s. 108 (4), contract for the company without legibly stating its name, e.g. failing to use the word "limited" in the case of a limited company, of which an illustration occurred in *British Airways Board* v. *Parish* (1979) where the managing director who had so signed a company cheque was held to be personally liable to the payee when the cheque was not met. Section 9 (7) of the European Communities Act 1972 now requires a company to state particulars relating to the registered office and other matters on "all business letters and order forms of the company."

In *Durham Fancy Goods, Ltd.* v. *Michael Jackson (Fancy Goods), Ltd.* (1968), where the plaintiff company drew a bill on the defendant company but incorrectly described it as M. Jackson (Fancy Goods) Ltd., and a director of the drawee company signed the acceptance without correcting the name of the company, it was held that although he had contravened s. 108 the plaintiff company was estopped from enforcing personal liability against him since they themselves were responsible for the wrong description; the liability could, however, have been enforced by any other holder not affected by estoppel.

In *Hendon* v. *Adelman* (1973), a cheque had been signed by three defendants on behalf of "L.R. Agencies Ltd." printed in error for the correct name "L. & R. Agencies Ltd." because the bank had not copied the company's name properly: held, the signatories were personally liable to the holder of the cheque which had been returned marked "Orders not to pay".

In *Maxform Spa* v. *B. Mariani and Goodville, Ltd.* (1979), G. Ltd. had registered the name "Italdesign" as a business name and in that name was the drawee of a bill of exchange which was accepted by the sole director. When the bill was dishonoured, the director was held personally liable on the ground that it was not possible to take the view that the word "name" in s. 108 meant other than the registered name of the company.

By s. 21 of the 1976 Act a statement of the first director(s) and secretary must be delivered with the memorandum on application for registration. This statement must be signed by the subscribers to the memorandum and contain a consent to act signed by the director(s) and secretary. The persons so named in the statement are deemed to be the first director(s) or secretary on incorporation. If the articles name the first director(s) or secretary, such appointments are void until the above-mentioned statement has been delivered. In the case of public companies, by s. 181 a person cannot be named as a director or proposed director in a prospectus or statement in lieu of prospectus unless he or his agent has signed and filed with the Registrar of Companies a written consent to act and signed either the memorandum for his qualification shares (if any) or an undertaking to take such shares and pay for them. The Act does not make it obligatory for directors to hold any shares in their company, this matter being left to articles, but where articles do require a director to hold a stated number of qualification shares then if he fails to have such shares registered in his name within two months of his appointment, or within such shorter time as may be fixed by the articles, he will cease to be a director: s. 182. The articles usually set out the minimum and maximum numbers of directors and provide for the appointment of future directors, the disqualification of directors, and—though private companies often omit this—for their periodical retirement and re-election, generally on the basis that one-third of the Board retires by rotation each year. By s. 184 directors may be removed by the company by ordinary resolution, but special notice (i.e. not less than twenty-eight days' notice of intention to move the resolution: s. 142) has to be given to the company and the director(s) in question may make representations on the matter for circulation to members. Under s. 28 of the 1976 Act a person persistently in default in relation to the delivery of any return, account or other document or the giving of notice to the Registrar may be subject to a Court order disqualifying him from being a director or in any way concerned with the management of a company for a specified period not exceeding 5 years. The Secretary of State is required by s. 29 to maintain a Register of Disqualification Orders, open to inspection on payment of a fee (fixed at 5p by S.I. 1977 No. 776). The orders to be registered are those made under s. 188 of the 1948 Act, under s. 9 of the Insolvency Act 1976, and under s. 28 itself.

Section 177 provides that every company must have a secretary, and by s. 178 no person can be appointed as secretary of the company who is the sole director of the company, or who is a corporation, the sole director of which is the sole director of the company. The appointment of a secretary and his removal is done by the directors, except that sometimes the articles of a company being formed will name the first secretary of the company. Legally, the 19th century view was that the secretary was a mere servant who had to do what he was told by directors, but a modern, realistic view of his status was taken by the Court of Appeal in *Panorama Development (Guildford), Ltd.* v. *Fidelis Furnishing Fabrics, Ltd.* (1971), namely, that the secretary was ostensibly the company's chief administrative officer and could be held out as having authority to sign contracts within quite a considerable part of the company's administration; the company was therefore liable on car-hire contracts entered into by its secretary on its behalf. Practically, the secretary's importance varies with the size of his company and the functions entrusted to him, so that he is often highly placed in the executive echelon.

Ultimately, the control of the company rests in the hands of its members through their votes at general meetings, but it must be remembered that many private and some public companies are "family" or director-controlled companies (i.e. the directors, their relatives and friends command a majority of the votes) and in other companies with a large capital widely held it is difficult for members to exert their power to full advantage.

CAPITAL

The capital of a company comprises the funds subscribed by the members. The statement contained in the last clause of the memorandum is the nominal or authorised capital, being the amount deemed sufficient for the company's activities. The whole of the authorised capital may or may not actually be issued; that which has been issued being known as issued or subscribed capital. For example, if a company with a capital of £10,000 in £1 shares has issued 6,000 shares, it may at any time issue all or any of the remaining shares; once all 10,000 shares have been issued, the capital must first be increased before the company can issue any more shares. Furthermore, only part of the issued or subscribed capital may be actually paid up, i.e. the shares may be partly paid, say, £1 shares 50p paid. In such a case the amount represented by the uncalled proportion of each share is known in the aggregate as the uncalled capital, and this may be called up by the company as and when required. Partly paid shares are seldom encountered nowadays. The creation of reserve liability by a limited company is allowed by s. 60, which provides that any portion of the uncalled capital may by special resolution be designated as not capable of being called up except in the event and for the purposes of the company being wound up. Such capital is known as reserve capital, its idea being to enhance the financial repute of the company, though the procedure is now rarely used.

Companies often issue shares at a premium, i.e. at a higher price than the nominal value of the shares, determined by the attractiveness the company has for investors, and sometimes the premium is substantial, e.g. £1 shares issued at 300p. By s. 56 the premium must be transferred to an account to be called "the share premium account" which, generally speaking, is considered as part of the paid up share capital of the company.

The converse situation, the issuing of shares at a discount, e.g. £1 shares issued at 80p is *ultra vires* (being a reduction of share capital) except as allowed by s. 57, whereby a company may issue at a discount shares in the company of a class already issued, provided:

(a) the issue is authorised by a resolution passed at a general meeting, and is sanctioned by the Court;

(b) the resolution must specify the maximum rate of discount at which the shares are to be issued;

(c) the company must have commenced business at least one year prior to the date of issue;

(d) the shares must be issued within one month of the Court order, unless the Court allows an extension.

The capital may consist of one or more classes or types of shares; details of these and of their transfer will appear in Chapter 8 on Stocks and Shares.

BANK ACCOUNTS OF COMPANIES

Whilst an ordinary trade creditor of a company has hardly ever bothered to look at its memorandum and articles, banks, before opening an account for a company, normally obtain, peruse and retain a copy of the company's memorandum and articles of association, and also request a sight of its certificate of incorporation. Unless reliance is to be placed on s. 9 (1) of the European Communities Act 1972 (which has unresolved difficulties in the absence of judicial interpretation) banks will probably continue this practice. In the case of a public company the certificate to commence business should also be produced for inspection and return, though even before this is granted to the company the bank can open an account solely for the receipt of money subscribed by the public under any initial offer of shares. Points to note in the memorandum include the borrowing powers of the company, its power to deal with negotiable instruments, to give security, and guarantees of the normal banking variety, what powers are given to invest or lend the company's money and its authorised capital, and, notwithstanding the above-mentioned s. 9 (1), the bank ought to satisfy itself that the company is trading in accordance with its objects. Points to note in the articles include any special provisions as to the operation of bank accounts, signature of negotiable instruments, etc. and generally how the affairs of the company are to be conducted, whether any power is given to directors to delegate their authority, whether all acts of directors must be done at a board meeting or not, what is the quorum for directors' meetings, whether "interested" directors can vote, the extent of the directors' borrowing powers, and how the company's seal is to be affixed. It is also relevant to ascertain whether the articles give the company a first and paramount lien on its own shares, and the provisions for convening general meetings of the company and the voting rights thereat.

If express provisions as to signature of negotiable instruments etc. are contained in the articles, the bank must see that the mandate it receives complies with the articles. Normally, this question is not covered specifically, and therefore it is a matter for the board of directors to decide by whom negotiable instruments etc. are to be signed. Bank mandate forms for companies embody a series of resolutions to be passed by a board meeting of the company, covering the opening of the account, details of signatories in respect of cheques, bills of exchange, promissory notes and the like whether the account be in credit or in debit, the withdrawal of safe custody items and analogous matters, so that when completed and returned to the bank

they are certified, usually by the Chairman and the Secretary, to be a
true extract of the minutes of a board meeting held at a particular
place and date at which the resolutions set out therein were duly
passed. The mandate normally contains spaces for specimen signatures of the designated signatories, otherwise these will have to be
obtained separately.

The bank should, of course, satisfy itself as to the appointment of
the directors. If the company has just been incorporated, then, as
already mentioned, a statement of the first director(s) and secretary
with their signed consent to act must have been delivered on application for registration of the company: the details to be given are those
prescribed in s. 200, viz. each director's full name (including any
former names), usual residential address, business occupation and
other directorships; and in respect of the secretary, or joint secretaries, names and addresses only. These details can be checked by
searching the company's file at the Companies Registry. By s. 200 as
amended by s. 22 of the 1976 Act a company must file with the
Register within 14 days details of any change among its directors or in
its secretary or any changes in their particulars, together with a
signed consent to act by a new director or secretary.

Needless to say, the bank must keep to the terms of the mandate,
the points to watch being that cheques etc. bear the requisite number
of signatures, that any alterations are initialled by all the signatories,
and that the signatures are in a form appropriate to bind the company, given that the company has power to contract by bill of
exchange or promissory note. On this last point s. 33 provides that:
"A bill of exchange or promissory note shall be deemed to have been
made, accepted or endorsed on behalf of a company if made, accepted
or endorsed in the name of, or by or on behalf or on account of, the
company by any person acting under its authority". Thus, the bill or
note could be executed under the seal of the company (though this is
not done in practice), or the name of the company if written on it by an
authorised person would suffice. However, to obviate the difficulty of
ascertaining whether such a signature was attached by a person
having authority to do so, the usual form is to have "per pro." or
"p.p." followed by the correct name of the company and underneath
the personal signature(s), or such phrases as "For" or "For and on
behalf of" (the company) followed by signatories who state their
capacity, e.g. Director, or Secretary. The basic test with any document is whether the words used sufficiently indicate that the signature
was affixed in the capacity of agent for the company, or whether they
are words of description only, so as to impose liability on the agent
personally instead of on the company.

BORROWING POWERS OF COMPANIES

The aggregate amount of borrowing by companies, whether from the banks or other institutions or from the general public is enormous. It is important, therefore, that banks and other lenders ascertain the borrowing powers of companies; the general public will rely on the details in the prospectus which must necessarily be issued in connection with a public loan.

A trading company has implied power to borrow and give security, provided such power is not expressly prohibited in the memorandum of association, i.e. no express power to borrow and give security need be conferred by the memorandum. A non-trading company cannot borrow unless expressly so authorised by its memorandum, in which event it may raise money, with or without giving security, as the directors think fit, subject to any particular restrictions in the memorandum. A limit on the company's borrowing powers may be imposed by the memorandum, but this is seldom done. Where there is any limit in the memorandum, any borrowing that contravenes that limit is *ultra vires* the company and void, unless reliance can be placed on s. 9 (1) of the European Communities Act 1972 (see page 131). A practice often followed is to have the company's borrowing powers unlimited, but to impose a restriction in the articles on the directors' borrowing powers, though, on the other hand, many companies allow their directors to have the same unlimited borrowing powers as the company has.

However, in the case of companies whose shares or debentures are quoted on a stock exchange the rules of the stock exchange require a reasonable limit on directors' borrowing powers—this may be liberal, e.g. six times the amount of the issued capital—but the existence of a limit does give some protection to shareholders, for if the directors wish to exceed their powers they must obtain the sanction of the company in general meeting. Furthermore, various companies incorporated under the Act of 1929 may still have articles which include Clause 69 of Table A of the Act of 1929, and numerous companies incorporated under the Act of 1948 may have articles which include Clause 79 of Table A of the Act of 1948. Both these Clauses impose limits on directors' borrowing powers as follows:

By Clause 69 the amount for the time being remaining undischarged of money borrowed or raised by the directors for the purposes of the company (otherwise than by the issue of share capital) shall not at any time exceed the issued share capital of the company without the sanction of the shareholders in general meeting. It should be noted that the barrier is the issued, not the nominal nor the paid up, share capital. The bank which advances money to a company whose directors' borrowing powers are limited in this way must ascertain the existing total borrowing from all sources, e.g. debentures, loans from directors or building societies or other parties (but not trade creditors), and to the extent that any proposed bank advance would, if added to this total, exceed the company's issued share capital, the bank must ask for and obtain a certified copy of the resolution of a general meeting sanctioning such excess. Alternatively, the general meeting could pass a special resolution altering the articles with, if necessary, retrospective effect to increase the limit in Clause 69, e.g. to twice the issued share capital, or to exclude the Clause altogether and substitute therefor some other higher limit or no limit at all.

By Clause 79, which will apply unless excluded or modified by the articles of a company formed since July 1st, 1948, the same ceiling on the directors' borrowing powers is imposed as in Clause 69 of the 1929 Act, but there is a further restriction in that for the purposes of Clause 79 the term "borrowing" includes any securities given by the company to cover its liabilities (which may not necessarily be debts) or to cover the debts or liabilities of third parties. This factor will have to be taken into account by a bank when assessing the directors' borrowing powers in the manner just described, whether the proposed bank advance is to be made to the company itself, or to an individual against security provided by the company. However, Clause 79 also differs from its predecessor in that:

(a) Clause 79 excludes from the calculation of the amount borrowed or secured by the directors "temporary loans obtained from the company's bankers in the ordinary course of business". As bank advances are theoretically intended to be temporary, being repayable on demand, it would appear that banks can disregard Clause 79, but it all depends on what is meant by temporary, and in the absence of judicial interpretation banks are not too keen to rely on this phrase unless the borrowing has clearly been arranged for a very short period only.

(b) Clause 79 further provides that no lender or other person dealing with the company shall be concerned to see or inquire whether the limit (on the directors' borrowing powers) is observed, but the debt incurred or security given will be invalid where the lender or the recipient of the security has express notice that the limit is being exceeded.

Thus, although there is no obligation on the banks or other lenders to question the directors as to the existing borrowing of the company, nevertheless banks do normally make inquiries by perusing balance sheets and so on—they do not lend completely in the dark—and having done so and become aware that the directors' borrowing powers have been or will be exceeded, they cannot disregard their findings, for they have obtained express notice of the limit being exceeded. Similar considerations relate to the purpose for which the money is intended to be applied; where there is a general power to borrow money for the purposes of the company the lender is not bound to enquire into those purposes and misapplication of the money by the company without the lender's knowledge does not avoid the loan: *Re David Payne & Co., Ltd.* (1904). The loan will be avoided where the lender knows that the money was intended to be misapplied: *Re Introductions, Ltd.* (1969), discussed at p. 117, *ante*.

If *ultra vires* borrowing has taken place, a bank, or any other lender, will wish to know the legal position, and what may be done to rectify matters. The answer will depend on the nature of the excess, which may be *ultra vires* the company or *ultra vires* the directors, and the position must now be examined in the light of the substantial restriction on the *ultra vires* doctrine made by s. 9 (1) of the European Communities Act 1972, which may or may not apply depending on the circumstances.

(1) Contracts ultra vires the company

(i) Where the European Communities Act 1972 applies.

Section 9 (1) of this Act provides that "in favour of a person dealing with a company in good faith, any transaction decided on by the directors shall be deemed to be one which it is within the capacity of the company to enter into, and the power of the directors to bind the company shall be deemed to be free of any limitation under the memorandum or articles of association; and a party to a transaction so decided on shall not be bound to enquire as to the capacity of the company to enter into it or as to any such limitation on the powers of the directors, and shall be presumed to have acted in good faith unless the contrary is proved".

There is no definition of "good faith" in the Act or in the Companies Acts, though a third party would not act in good faith if he has actual notice that the transaction is *ultra vires*, but it is not certain to what extent constructive notice or failure to make inquiries in suspicious circumstances is enough to negative good faith. What is meant by "decided on by the directors" is not clear, probably it means decided on by a resolution at a board meeting or, as articles sometimes provide, by all the directors agreeing to a resolution which has the same effect as though passed at a board meeting.

(ii)　Where the Act of 1972 does not apply.

Where the Act does not apply, because, say, the other party did not deal in good faith, the contract is void and neither can enforce it against the other. Thus, in relation to borrowing any advance made to a company beyond a limit expressed in its memorandum of association, or any advance at all made to a non-trading company whose memorandum confers no power to borrow, is *ultra vires* the company and void. The position is incapable of ratification, and any security given by the company in respect of the loan is also void. The lender has, however, the following rights:

(a)　*Subrogation.*—By which he stands as a creditor of the company in the shoes of such creditors as have been paid out of the moneys he has advanced, unless his loan has been misapplied: *Neath Building Society* v. *Luce* (1899). But even where subrogation is available he does not get the benefit of any securities the former creditors may have held or of any priority they may have enjoyed: *Re Wrexham, Mold and Connah's Quay Railway* (1899).

(b)　*Injunction.*—He may obtain an injunction restraining the company from parting with the loan, or with specific assets purchased with it.

(c)　*An action for breach of implied warranty of authority.*—This lies against the directors, if he can show that, although aware of the authorised limit, he was not aware that the company had already borrowed to an extent which would make his loan *"ultra vires"*: *Weeks* v. *Propert* (1873). From this angle it is advantageous to obtain from the directors a statement of the total of the existing borrowing when making the advance.

(2)　Contracts ultra vires the directors

When a company enters into a contract within its powers but *ultra vires* the directors, the position now depends as follows:—

(i)　Where the European Communities Act 1972 applies.

Section 9 (1) of this Act provides in favour of a person dealing with the company in good faith that "the power of the directors to bind the company shall be deemed to be free of any limitation under the memorandum or articles of association; and a party to a transaction [decided on by the directors] shall not be bound to enquire as to . . . any such limitation on the powers of the directors and shall be presumed to have acted in good faith unless the contrary is proved".

"Good faith" and "decided on by the directors" have been discussed in (1) (i) above.

(ii) Where the Act of 1972 does not apply.

Where the Act does not apply, because, say, the matter was not decided on by the directors, then the third party will have to rely, if he can, on the Rule in *Turquand's Case*, should the company decline to ratify the position.

For example, if an advance is beyond the limit of the directors' borrowing powers expressed in the articles, so long as it is within the company's powers, the excess can be regularised by:

(a) *Ratification.*— The company in general meeting can, if it wishes, ratify the directors' actions.

(b) *Alteration of articles.*— The company in general meeting can, if it wishes, alter its articles by special resolution with retrospective effect to increase, or abolish, the limit on the directors' borrowing powers.

(c) *Reliance on the Rule in Turquand's Case* (discussed below).— Where the lender was unaware through no fault of his own that the directors had already borrowed up to their limit, and has consequently relied on the ostensible authority of the directors.

If the company refuses either to ratify the excess borrowing or to alter its articles to cover it, and if in the circumstances the Rule in *Turquand's Case* cannot be successfully pleaded, the lender must fall back on the remedies in the event of borrowing *ultra vires* the company, set out in (i) above.

THE RULE IN TURQUAND'S CASE

This remains an important principle of company law, and where it operates it affords protection to outside parties dealing with companies, though there is now less need for it, in view of the protection given by s. 9 (1) of the European Communities Act 1972. It was formulated in the case of *Royal British Bank* v. *Turquand* (1856), where articles gave the directors power to borrow with the sanction of a general meeting and the bank lent without inquiring if such a meeting had taken place. It was held that the bank was not obliged so to inquire, and as it lent *bona fide*, it stood in as good a position as if the sanction of a general meeting had in fact been obtained. The principle of law (the Rule) expressed in the decision is that where a company is regulated by an Act of Parliament, general or special, or by a deed of settlement or memorandum and articles registered in some public office, persons dealing with the company are bound to read the Act and registered documents and to see that the proposed dealing is not inconsistent therewith; but they are not bound to do more; they need not inquire into the regularity of the internal proceedings, they are entitled to assume that all is being done regularly. An instance of the application of the Rule occurred in *Dey* v. *Pullinger Engineering Co.* (1921), where a managing director, who drew a bill of exchange on behalf of a company without any authority was held to bind the company.

The Rule in *Turquand's Case* is, however, subject to the following limitations:

(1) If a person has notice that the proposed dealing is not consistent with the company's registered documents then he is affected by it: *Howard* v. *Patent Ivory Manufacturing Co.* (1888).

(2) A director cannot rely on the Rule so as to obtain its protection: *Morris* v. *Kanssen* (1946), a complicated case as regards the facts which went to the House of Lords and in which, very briefly, Mr. Morris thought he was a director of a company when he was not, and acted as a director in the allotment and issue of shares to himself and others. (It will be recalled that under s. 9 (1) the onus of disproving good faith falls on the company, and it would seem that where a director deals with his company as a third party the company will have much less difficulty in disproving his good faith than that of an outside third party.)

(3) It does not apply where the requisite signatures are forged: *Ruben* v. *Great Fingall Consolidated* (1906).

(4) If a servant of the company, e.g. director, secretary or branch manager, purports to make a contract on the company's behalf which is not within the ordinary ambit of his powers, nor within the powers which the company has held him out as possessing, the company is not liable merely because, under the articles, power to make such a contract may have been delegated to him, especially where the other contracting party did not know of the power of delegation. Three cases which illustrate this aspect and in which each contracting party failed to bind the respective company are:

Houghton & Co. v. *Nothard, Lowe and Wills, Ltd.* (1927), where a director purported to make on behalf of his company an agreement with the plaintiffs whereby the plaintiffs were to sell on commission goods imported by the defendant company, on terms that the plaintiffs should retain the proceeds of sale as security for a debt due from another company;

Kreditbank Cassel G.m.b.H. v. *Schenkers, Ltd.* (1927), where the manager of the Manchester branch of a company carrying on business as forwarding agents purported to draw bills of exchange on behalf of his company which he subsequently indorsed on their behalf, and which eventually were discounted by the bank;

Rama Corporation, Ltd. v. *Proved Tin and General Investments, Ltd.*

(1952), where a director of the defendant company purported to make an agreement with a director of the plaintiff company whereby the two companies were to join in subscribing to a fund to be used for financing the sale of goods produced by a third company, the defendant company being responsible for administering the fund and accounting to the plaintiff company.

Thus, in each of these three cases there was a most unusual transaction which could not be within the ostensible authority of the official of the company concerned, so that each plaintiff had nothing to go on beyond the fact that power to do the act in question might have been delegated under the articles to the official who did it, but none of the plaintiffs had any knowledge of the articles. This explanation of the three cases was given by the Court of Appeal in *Freeman and Lockyer* v. *Buckhurst Part Properties (Mangal), Ltd.* (1964), where a director of the defendant company had instructed the plaintiffs, a firm of architects, to do work in connection with the company's estate; the company's articles contained power to appoint a managing director but none had been appointed. The Court of Appeal found that the director had no actual authority to employ the plaintiffs but had ostensible authority as he had acted throughout as managing director, and, distinguishing the three cases for the reasons discussed above, held the company liable, because the director's act in engaging the plaintiffs was within the ordinary ambit of the authority of a managing director and the plaintiffs did not have to inquire whether he was properly appointed: it was sufficient for them that under the articles there was in fact power to appoint him as such.

This last case was applied in *Hely-Hutchinson* v. *Brayhead, Ltd.* (1967), where the chairman of the company, though not appointed as managing director, acted in that capacity with the acquiescence of the board of directors. The Court of Appeal held that on the facts the chairman had implied authority from his board to enter into contracts with the plaintiff.

SECURITIES GIVEN BY COMPANIES

Subject to any special restrictions in its memorandum, a company may charge its property of whatever nature as security for advances, e.g. it can mortgage its freehold or leasehold property, or stocks and shares which it holds, just as a private person can. There are, however, two distinguishing features as regards charges created by companies, and these are, firstly, that most charges must be registered with the Registrar of Companies, and, secondly, there is a particular type of charge known as a floating charge which has long been a distinctive feature of English company law.

By s. 95 the following charges created by a company incorporated in England must be registered with the Registrar of Companies within twenty-one days of their creation, otherwise they are void as against a liquidator or creditor of the company, though the advance itself is not affected and the moneys secured immediately become payable:

(a) a charge for the purpose of securing any issue of debentures;
(b) a charge on uncalled share capital of the company;
(c) a charge created or evidenced by an instrument which, if executed by an individual, would require registration as a bill of sale;
(d) a charge on land, wherever situate, or any interest therein, but not including a charge for any rent or other periodical sum issuing out of land;
(e) a charge on book debts of the company;
(f) a floating charge on the undertaking or property of the company;
(g) a charge on calls made but not paid;
(h) a charge on a ship [or aircraft] or any share in a ship;
(i) a charge on goodwill, on a patent or a licence under patent, on a trade mark or on a copyright or a licence under a copyright.

By a process of elimination, it will be seen that all mortgages and charges by a company must be registered with the exception of specific charges on stocks and shares, on life policies or on produce, and bills deposited to secure an advance.

An unregistered mortgage is avoided as against a subseqent registered incumbrancer even though he had express notice of the prior mortgage when he took his own security: *Re Monolithic Building Co.* (1915).

Some elaboration is needed as regards the charges specified in s. 95. The point about (c) is that every mortgage or charge within the meaning of the Bills of Sale Acts must be registered if a power is reserved under the terms of the instrument for seizure or possession of the chattels.

As regards (d), any charge on land, whether by legal or equitable mortgage (in the latter case, however informally, e.g. a letter undertaking to deposit title deeds as security) must be registered. If the charge (not being a floating charge) is one that is unsupported by a deposit of title deeds, then registration under s. 95 is not sufficient to dispense with registration under the Land Charges Act 1972 as a puisne mortgage or a general equitable charge (see Chapter 6). In *Re*

Molton Finance, Ltd. (1967), where title deeds and documents had been deposited by the company as security for a loan made to it but no charge had been registered, the lenders argued that they had a valid common law lien on them, but this was rejected by the Court of Appeal, which held that the deposit of the deeds and documents was merely ancillary to the equitable charge created and that the contractual right to their retention was lost when the charge was avoided by non-registration under s. 95. The same applies where title deeds are deposited to secure a debt owed by a third party: *Re Wallis and Simmonds (Builders), Ltd.* (1974). On the other hand, since an unpaid vendor's lien arises by operation of law and not by reason of a contract between the parties, it is not "a charge created . . . by a company" within s. 95 and so is not void for non-registration: *London and Cheshire Insurance Co., Ltd.* v. *Laplagrene Property Co., Ltd.* (1971).

So far as (e) is concerned, book debts are not defined in the Act, but in *Dawson* v. *Isle* (1906) they were defined as debts accruing in the ordinary course of trade and entered in the books. In *Re Kent and Sussex Sawmills, Ltd.* (1964) it was held that where a bank took as security an irrevocable authority by a company to pay moneys due under a contract direct to its bank, that was a charge on book debts which required registration under s. 95, and so the bank lost its security for want of registration. Section 95 will also apply where a company deposits hire purchase agreements as security: *Independent Automatic Sales, Ltd.* v. *Knowles and Foster* (1962). An absolute assignment, on a sale of book debts to a third party or to a collecting organisation (this latter is the American method of financing known as factoring, which has also been operated in England for some years now) is outside the provisions of s. 95 because it is not an assignment by way of charge. In *Paul and Frank, Ltd.* v. *Discount Bank (Overseas), Ltd. and the Board of Trade* (1966) the plaintiff company and its liquidator claimed that the standard letter of authority whereby the benefits of a bad-debt policy issued by the Export Credits Guarantee Department of the Board of Trade were assigned to the bank was void for non-registration under s. 95. The Court rejected the claim, holding that although the letter of authority was a charge, "book debts" in s. 95 meant debts which in the ordinary course of business would be entered in the well-kept books of a company, and that as the E.C.G.D. policy would not be so entered at the date of the letter of authority before liability was established or the amount ascertained, the charge was not registrable. Thus, although a future debt, in the sense of debts under a future contract for goods to be sold or work to be done can be charged, in this instance the debt was a hypothetical one and would so remain unless and until a valid claim arose under the policy.

Item (f), floating charges, will be considered later under the heading of "Debentures", the word "debenture" being defined in s. 455 as including debenture stock, bonds and any other securities of a company whether consisting a charge on the assets of the company or not.

Registration of the charge is effected by lodging the actual instrument of charge, accompanied by Companies Form 47 giving the prescribed details of the charge, with the Registrar of Companies within twenty-one days of the date of its creation. This is primarily the company's responsibility, but any interested party may take this action and recover the fees from the company, which is why banks normally attend to the registration themselves instead of leaving it to the customer. The instrument will be stamped with a small rubber stamp by the Registrar and returned to the party lodging it, together with the certificate of registration of a charge which the Registrar is required to issue by s. 98 (2). The Form 47 is inserted by the Registrar in his file relating to the company, and details of the charge are entered on a separate register of charges kept by the Registrar in accordance with s. 98 (1), and located at the back of the file.

By s. 101 the twenty-one day period for registration may be extended by the Court when satisfied that the failure to register was accidental, or due to inadvertence or some other sufficient cause: an example of this was *Re Kris Cruisers, Ltd*. (1949), where the secretary thought the company's solicitor had registered the charges, and the solicitor thought the secretary had done so; the Court allowed registration out-of-time. In *Watson* v. *Duff Morgan and Vermont (Holdings), Ltd*. (1974) where an order had been made under s. 101 for registration of a first debenture out-of-time "without prejudice to the rights of any parties acquired prior to the time when the said debenture is to be actually registered", it was held that this proviso related only to rights acquired during the period when the first debenture was void, and so it had not made the plaintiff's first debenture subject to the rights of the defendants' second debenture, for this had been created on the same day as the first debenture to which it was expressly made subject, and the mere expiration of the 21 day period had not conferred any rights on the defendants.

Not unnaturally, some companies are reluctant to create registrable charges because of consequent adverse publicity in trade papers and so on, and both this point and other circumstances can cause difficulties over the time factor in registration. In *Esberger and Son, Ltd*. v. *Capital and Counties Bank* (1913) the bank took an undated but otherwise completed memorandum of deposit of title deeds from the company in September, 1910, held it unregistered until June 14th, 1911 when the manager dated it that day and registered it on July 3rd,

1911, i.e. within twenty-one days of the date. SARGANT, J., set aside the charge on the ground that the time when the charge was actually executed was the operative date, not the date it bore, and so the registration was well out-of-time. It would appear, however, that there is nothing to prevent a mortgagee taking a succession of charges on the same property every twenty-one days and not registering them, so that there would always be a current charge available for registration within the twenty-one day period, but this sort of activity is not likely to commend itself to a bank.

In any event, there is another feature which was not raised in *Esberger's* Case, and this is the conclusiveness of the Registrar's certificate. This point now appears in s. 98 (2), which provides that the Registrar's certificate of registration of the mortgage or charge shall be conclusive evidence that the requirements of the Act as to registration have been complied with. In *National Provincial and Union Bank of England* v. *Charnley* (1924) the Court of Appeal, on the basis of a similar provision in the Act of 1908, refused to go behind the Registrar's certificate and upheld the validity of the charge even though the particulars submitted for registration incorrectly described the subject matter of the charge. This case was followed in *Re Mechanisations (Eaglescliffe), Ltd.* (1964), where the particulars registered incorrectly described the amount secured by the charge, and also in *Re Eric Holmes (Property), Ltd.* (1965), where a charge in which the date had been incorrectly inserted was upheld. The point reached the Court of Appeal again in *Re C. L. Nye, Ltd.* (1970), where a solicitor acting for the mortgagee of premises (a bank) took a charge (undated) on the 28th February 1964; the charge was put in a safe and lost sight of until 18th June 1964 when the solicitor dated it that day and registered it on 3rd July 1964. Following its own decision in *Charnley's* Case, the Court of Appeal held that the charge was valid and effective, and there being no evidence that any other person had given credit to the company between the dates when the charge should have been and when it was registered, the maxim that no one can take advantage of his own wrong had no application. It would seem, therefore, that banks can now avoid the pitfall of *Esberger's* Case, although it must be remembered that the House of Lords may someday take a different view of the matter than that of the Court of Appeal.

By s. 97, where the company acquires property already subject to a charge of a kind registrable under s. 95 the company shall register the charge with the Registrar of Companies within 21 days after the date on which the acquisition is completed. There is a default fine for failure to register, but no adverse consequences to the security. It was held in *Capital Finance Co., Ltd.* v. *Stokes* (1968) that where a company purchased land, and part of the purchase price was left on mortgage by the vendor, the charge was created after the acquisition of the land and thus fell within s. 95, not s. 97, so that as it had not been registered under s. 95 it was void.

By s. 103 each company must keep at its registered office a copy of every instrument creating a registrable charge, and by s. 104 also keep there a register of charges and enter therein all charges specifically affecting property of the company and all floating charges. Failure by the company to record these charges in its own register does not invalidate the charges. Under s. 105 the copies of these instruments and the company's own register of charges must be open for inspection by any creditor or member of the company free of charge, and by the general public on payment of a fee not exceeding 1s (5p).

Finally, by s. 100, if the debt for which the charge was given has been paid or satisfied in whole or in part, or part of the property or undertaking has been released from the charge or has ceased to form part of the company's property or undertaking, the Registrar may enter on the register a memorandum of satisfaction in whole or in part, or of the fact that some of the property or undertaking has been released, as the case may be. This memorandum is set out on Companies Form 49, or 49A or 49B as appropriate, which is executed under the common seal of the company and verified by a statutory declaration by a director and the secretary. Registration of any discharge or release of security is permissive, whereas registration of the charge itself is obligatory in that failure to register renders the company and every officer in default liable to a fine of £50: s. 96 (3); and also deprives the chargee of his security: s. 95 (1).

DEBENTURES

The normal way in which a company raises loans is by the issue of debentures, which are documents issued by a company, usually under its seal, as evidence of a loan and of any charge securing it. It is possible to issue "naked" or unsecured debentures (often called "unsecured loan stock") and this is done at time by companies of high repute; occasionally the debentures or loan stock may be expressed to be convertible, i.e. capable of being converted into shares of the company at some future date(s) and at a stated price(s). In practice, most debentures issued to the public, and all those taken by banks as security, are supported by a charge, or a combination of charges, on the assets of the company.

Debentures or debenture stock issued to the public, and usually quoted on a stock exchange, are normally of the fixed sum variety, providing for repayment at a specified date and interest at a specified rate until repayment; they are issued in a series, all ranking equally with each other, e.g. a company may issue 50,000 six per cent. Debentures of £10 each, or £500,000 six per cent. Debenture Stock transferable in multiples of £1. With large public issues there is often also a trust deed whereby the assets charged as security are transferred by the company to trustees (generally, a trust corporation, such as a bank or insurance company) to hold on behalf of the debenture-holders. Debentures are normally in registered form, transferable by duly stamped instruments of transfer, but, subject to exchange control regulations, they may be payable to bearer. Those which are backed by a first charge on the property of the company are known as First Mortgage Debentures. There are no legal obstacles to issuing debentures at a discount. Possible variations in the pattern of debentures are that they can have no date fixed for repayment, when they are known as perpetual or irredeemable debentures (s. 89), and repayment may be effected by periodical drawings e.g. one-tenth of the debentures, to be decided by annual drawings (i.e. a lottery), are to be repaid each year for ten specified years. Redeemed debentures can be re-issued under the terms of s. 90 unless articles provide to the contrary or the company has resolved or otherwise manifested its intention to cancel the debentures; the person to whom the debentures are re-issued has the same priorities as if the debentures had never been redeemed. By s. 99 a copy of the Registrar of Companies' certificate of registration must be endorsed on every debenture or certificate of debenture stock issued by the company the payment of which is secured by the charge registered.

When taken as security by a bank in respect of advances made to a company, debentures may similarly be the registered or bearer type, but usually the debenture is in the standard "all moneys" form drawn up by the bank. A registered or "fixed sum" debenture can be deposited with the bank under a memorandum of deposit with a blank transfer, or it can be transferred—or issued direct—to the bank or its nominee company. The memorandum of deposit (sometimes known as a "*Buckley*" agreement) is necessary to link the debenture with the bank advance, i.e. to show it is held as security by the bank and not merely as an investment, and to provide for interest being paid on the fluctuating debit balance(s) of the company, instead of as a percentage on the face value of the debenture. Bearer debentures may be taken by a simple deposit, though it is customary and preferable also to take the memorandum of deposit already mentioned. In practice, that procedure is seldom used, as banks generally require debentures to be given in their standard, printed forms, securing "all moneys" by a combination of fixed and floating charges.

The advantage of the "all-moneys" debenture is that it secures all moneys at any time and from time to time owing by the company to the bank on any account whatever, so that the debenture always keeps pace with the advance, whereas if the bank held a fixed sum debenture any excess would be unsecured thereby and another debenture would have to be taken. The usual clauses will appear in the bank form of debenture—covenant to repay on demand, effect as a continuing security, obligation to keep the property insured and so on, and also the clauses special to debentures—the fixed and floating charges, restrictions on the company's power to mortgage or charge in priority to, or equally with, the debenture, the appointment of a receiver and manager in the event of the company defaulting, and the provision by the company to the bank of periodical statements of its current assets and liabilities.

With effect from 1st August 1971 *ad valorem* stamp duty on legal and equitable mortgages and charges was abolished by the Finance Act 1971 in respect of instruments executed on or after that date or in the case of unlimited securities in respect of further monies advanced after that date.

FIXED AND FLOATING CHARGES

Secured debentures may be supported by either a fixed charge on the fixed assets of the company, or a floating charge on all or some of the assets, or by a combination of the two. This last is the course normally adopted by bank debentures, as follows:

A fixed charge is given on the goodwill and on the uncalled capital of the company, and a fixed first charge by way of legal mortgage is given on the freehold and leasehold property of the company and on the fixed plant and machinery (so that the company is prevented from dealing with or disposing of such property without the concurrence of the debenture-holder). A first floating charge is then created on all the other property and assets of the company.

A floating charge is a charge given on the assets of a company but it does not prevent the company from dealing with any of its assets in the ordinary course of business. It floats like a cloud over the assets, but does not settle on them unless and until the undertaking charged ceases to be a going concern, or the chargee intervenes, when the charge is said to "crystallise" or become fixed. The characteristics of a floating charge were stated in *Re Yorkshire Woolcombers Association* (1903) to be:

> (1) a charge on both present and future assets;
>
> (2) the assets are constantly changing from time to time in the ordinary course of business;
>
> (3) until the holder takes some steps to enforce the security, the company can carry on its business in the usual way.

Thus, a floating charge is more widespread than a fixed charge, though as a security it provides its holder with a light rein in contrast to the rigid harness of a fixed charge. For example, it is possible to take a fixed charge on stock or book debts as at a certain date, but as the stock-in-trade is sold or the debts paid the fixed charge is gradually reduced and will eventually cease. On the other hand, a floating charge on stock or book debts covers them as they are at any time and from time to time, so that although the stock sold and the debts paid will cease to be subject to the charge, after-acquired stock and book debts will be caught by the charge, which continues on this revolving basis until it is determined, when it will change to a fixed charge.

The nature of a charge over future book debts was considered in *Siebe Gorman & Co., Ltd.* v. *Barclays Bank Ltd.* (1978). The bank's debenture contained a first fixed charge on all book debts and other debts now and from time to time owing to the company (and a floating charge over all other assets); it also provided: "During the continuance of this security the company shall pay into its account with the bank all moneys which it may receive in respect of book debts and other debts hereby charged and shall not without the prior consent of the bank in writing purport to charge or assign the same." SLADE J., held, *inter alia*, that it was possible in law for a mortgagor, by way of continuing security for further advances to grant to a mortgagee a charge on future book debts in a form which created in equity a specific charge on the proceeds of debts as soon as they were received and consequently prevented the mortgagor from disposing of an unencumbered title to the subject matter of such charge without the mortgagee's consent even before the mortgagee had taken steps to enforce the security, and there was no reason why the Court ought not to give effect to the intention of the parties as stated that the charge ought to be a fixed first charge on book debts. Thus, the debenture on its true construction conferred on the bank a specific charge in equity on all future debts to the company.

The following two cases illustrate respectively implications of set-off and lien in relation to a floating charge. In *Rother Iron Works, Ltd.* v. *Canterbury Precision Engineers, Ltd.* (1973) the plaintiffs owed the defendants £124 and thereafter ordered goods value £159 from the defendants but before this contract was carried out a bank holding a debenture containing a floating charge on the plaintiffs' assets appointed a receiver and manager. The Court of Appeal held that the defendants were only liable to pay £35 to the receiver, being entitled to set off the £124 already due to them; the crystallisation of the floating charge on the appointment of the receiver operated to charge by way of equitable assignment the plaintiffs' rights under the existing contract for the purchase by the defendants of goods from the plaintiffs; those rights were always subject to the defendants' right to assert its set-off of £124 and settle the account with a payment of £35, and the debenture-holder as equitable assignee could not be in a different or better position than the plaintiff company. This was applied in another Court of Appeal case, *George Barker (Transport), Ltd.* v. *Eynon* (1974), where the plaintiffs claimed a general lien over goods collected for a company from a dockside for delivery to consignees in respect of all outstanding transport charges due to them from that company. Although the plaintiffs had collected the goods some days after a bank had appointed the defendant as receiver of the company under its debenture, it was held that their right of lien had come into existence at the time the contract was made, i.e. before the appointment, and so the plaintiffs could exercise their rights despite the appointment of the receiver.

A debenture secured by a floating charge only is not a very good security, because there are the following defects in floating charges:

(1) Section 322 provides that if a company goes into liquidation within twelve months of the creation of a floating charge on its undertaking or property, unless it is proved that the company immediately after the creation of that charge was solvent, the charge is invalid except to the amount of any cash paid at the time or subsequent to its creation with interest at five per cent. per annum or such other rate as the Treasury may prescribe.

In other words, unless the company was solvent when the floating charge was created, the charge will not cover past advances. However, the Rule in *Clayton's Case* (1816) here assists the bank because where the account is continued in the normal way and is sufficiently active, the credits paid in will, under the Rule, be appropriated to the repayment of the debt existing at the time when the charge was taken and subsequent withdrawals will be fresh advances covered by the charge. In this way the "hardening period" under s. 322 may be reduced by the turnover on an overdrawn account, even without any increase in the total indebtedness. The application of the Rule in this way occurred in *Re Thomas Mortimer, Ltd.*, decided in 1925 but not reported until 1965, which was approved by the Court of Appeal in *Re Yeovil Glove Co., Ltd.* (1965).

(2) As the company is free to deal with and dispose of the assets covered by the charge, which remains dormant until it crystallises, by the time the debenture-holder does intervene, there may be few assets left, for they may have been dissipated by several years of unprofitable trading. A bank tries to watch the position by requiring periodical certificates from the company of its liquid assets and liabilities, e.g. quarterly, or monthly, or even more frequently if the company is in really low water, so that if the position drastically deteriorates the bank can call in the advance, appoint a receiver or possibly pursue some other remedy, and thereby crystallise the charge. But even with this procedure, losses by the company may be sudden and unexpected, and at the risk of emphasising the obvious, it is not the amount which the charge is stated (or was stamped) to cover that is financially material, but the amount the assets will yield on realisation.

The freedom of a company to handle its assets covered by a floating charge is so great that it can, where its memorandum of association so authorises, dispose of all its assets in exchange for shares in another company: *In Re Borax Company* (1901). Of course, the shares received in such an exchange would be picked up by the floating charge, but the debenture-holder would normally prefer to have more disposable assets such as land, plant and machinery, stock-in-trade and so on, rather than shares in another company, which, if unquoted, would be difficult to realise.

Another drawback for the debenture-holder is the increasing practice of large suppliers of providing in their contracts that the goods remain their property until payment and if the goods are sub-sold before payment then the sale proceeds must be held in trust for the supplier. In *Aluminium Industrie Vaasen B.V.* v. *Romalpa Aluminium, Ltd.* (1976) the Dutch plaintiff had such a clause in its contract for the supply of aluminium foil to the English defendant, the bankers of which subsequently appointed a receiver under the terms of a debenture held by them. The Court of Appeal held that the Dutch company was entitled to trace the proceeds of sale and recover them in priority to the secured and unsecured creditors of the English company. It was also held at first instance that the arrangement was not registrable as a charge on book debts under s. 95 since the English company had not created a charge over the re-sale proceeds, but the Court of Appeal did not comment on this aspect. However, whilst the plaintiffs succeeded in the *Romalpa Case* because of their elaborate contractual stipulation, it all depends on the exact circumstances, particularly the wording of the reservation of title clause, and two subsequent cases in which attempts to acquire rights over the finished products failed for different reasons are described below.

In *Re Bond Worth, Ltd.* (1979), on the wording of the clause the supplier of raw fibre to the company purported to retain until payment in full the equitable and beneficial ownership of the fibre and also of other products produced from it or the respective proceeds of sale thereof, but there was no question of bailment since it was provided that the property in the fibre passed to the company upon delivery. SLADE, J., dismissed the supplier's claim on the ground that, as the legal title passed on delivery, the clause could only operate as an equitable floating charge over the goods; it was never intended to be invoked by the supplier unless and until the company proved to be in financial difficulties: such a charge was registrable under s. 95 and as it had not been registered it was void against creditors of the company.

In *Borden (UK), Ltd.* v. *Scottish Timber Products, Ltd.* (1979) the plaintiff supplier's contract with the defendant purchaser provided that the property in the goods (resin used in the manufacture of chipboard) would "pass to the customer when (a) the goods, the subject of the contract, and (b) all other goods, the subject of any other contract between the company and the customer . . . had been paid for in full". The Court of Appeal refused to grant to the plaintiff a tracing order in respect of the proceeds of sale of chipboard for there was no bailment as a different object would have been returned to that bailed; once the resin was used in the manufacturing process it ceased to exist and title to it was likewise extinguished: the question of s. 95 consequently did not arise.

(3) If the company is wound up, by s. 319 preferential creditors must be paid first. On the other hand, in respect of assets covered by a fixed charge preferential creditors have no priority. Section 94 confers the same priority as regards preferential creditors where a receiver is appointed, but the company is not at the time in course of winding up.

(4) A floating charge is only an equitable charge, and so it does not prevent the company from making specific charges on its property unless otherwise agreed. Thus, a person who takes a legal mortgage, or even an equitable mortgage by deposit of title deeds or other documents, for value and without notice of any prohibition or restriction on the company's power to mortgage or charge, will obtain priority over the holder of the floating charge: *English and Scottish Mercantile Investment Co., Ltd.* v. *Brunton* (1892).

For this reason, bank debenture forms include a clause on the following lines: "The Company shall not be at liberty without the consent in writing of the Bank to create any Mortgage or Charge upon and so that no lien shall in any case or in any manner arise on or affect any part of the property and assets ranking either in priority to or pari passu with the floating charge hereby created". This restriction is often extended to the assignment by the company of all or any part of its book debts present or future for valuable consideration or otherwise (i.e. to prevent the company from selling its book debts as distinct from charging them). Another clause will provide that the company will deposit with the bank during the continuance of the debenture all deeds and documents of title relating to freehold and leasehold property for the time being belonging to the company.

The restriction imposed, as in the above example, on the company's power to mortgage or charge is not in itself sufficient to protect the holder of the floating charge; a further step is needed for this purpose, namely, the holder must ensure that details of the restriction appear on Companies Form 47 to be filed with the Registrar of Companies when observing s. 95. When this is done, anyone searching the company's file at Companies House will discover not only the existence of the floating charge but also the restriction on the company's power to mortgage or charge, and even if he overlooks it he will be deemed to have become aware of it.

TRANSFER AND DISCHARGE OF DEBENTURES

Debentures or debenture stock of the fixed sum variety issued to the general public can be transferred in the same way as stocks and shares, i.e. by an ordinary instrument of transfer stamped at the rate of £2 per cent. on the consideration in the case of registered debentures, or by mere delivery in the case of bearer ones.

The standard form of debenture taken by a bank is also transferable in that the form usually provides that "the Bank" shall include the Bank's successors and assigns (or persons deriving title under the Bank). When debentures carried stamp duty a bank would sometimes accept a transfer of a debenture granted to another bank when the company concerned changed its bank, but nowadays each bank prefers to take its own form of debenture and have the original debenture discharged.

Discharge of debentures or debenture stock of the fixed sum variety issued to the general public will consist of repayment at maturity in accordance with the terms of the issue, or otherwise by agreement. In the case of the standard form of debenture given to a bank as security, when the indebtedness is repaid and assuming that borrowing by the company is not likely to recur in the near future, the debenture will be discharged by the bank completing under its common seal the form of receipt indorsed thereon (usually already printed, for use when required). The company should thereafter file a memorandum of satisfaction with the Registrar of Companies in accordance with s. 100; or one of partial satisfaction where, for example, some but not all of a series of debentures have been redeemed. The great majority of debentures run their course in the ordinary way and the indebtedness they represent or secure is duly repaid, but in the remaining cases where the company gets into financial difficulties, the holder must look to his remedies.

REMEDIES OF A DEBENTURE-HOLDER

On default by the company in its obligations under the debenture, the holder may intervene to enforce his security, thereby crystallising any floating charge. The remedies which may be employed by a debenture-holder to recover his money are:

(1) A receiver may be appointed, if the debenture authorises this; if not, then the debenture-holder(s) may apply to the Court for one to be appointed. Bank debenture forms normally provide that the bank may appoint by writing any person to be a receiver, who is, so far as the law allows, the agent of the company, and there will also be power to change the receiver if occasion demands. This is the remedy generally employed by banks.

In *Cripps (Pharmaceuticals), Ltd.* v. *Wickenden* (1973) the appointment of a receiver by a bank which held a debenture was challenged on the grounds that it had been done too precipitately. However, the validity of the appointment was upheld because (i) the appointment of a receiver by a debenture holder took effect when the document of appointment was handed to him by a person having the necessary authority in circumstances from which it might fairly be said that he was appointing a receiver, and the receiver accepted the proffered appointment, although the acceptance might be tacit. The date of the instrument was irrelevant except as a piece of evidence if the actual date of handing over was not known; (ii) where money was repayable on demand, all a creditor had to do was to give the debtor time to get the money from some convenient place; he was not obliged to give the debtor time to negotiate a deal which might produce the money.

(2) Where trustees of the company's property have been appointed under a trust deed, e.g. in the case of a public issue of debentures quoted on a stock exchange, then provided the trust deed

includes, as is customary, a power of sale, the trustees may realise the property without the aid of the Court.

(3) The debenture-holders (or any one of them on behalf of all) may sue for the debt or for an order of the Court for sale of the security, or foreclosure of it.

(4) A winding up petition may be presented (in practice, liquidation often follows on a receivership). The effect of a subsequent winding up on a receiver's powers was considered in *Sowman* v. *David Samuel Trust, Ltd.* (1978), and it was held that although the winding up deprived the receiver of power to bind the company personally by acting as its agent, it did not affect his power to hold and dispose of the company's property comprised in the debenture, including the power to use the company's name for that purpose; and also the power of attorney given to the debenture-holders in the debenture had not been revoked by the winding up. The contract to sell the property made by the receiver was therefore an effective exercise of the power of sale, and the subsequent conveyance under the power of attorney to complete the sale was effective to transfer the legal estate in the land.

The alternative courses open to a secured creditor as regards proving in the winding up of an insolvent company are the same as those available in bankruptcy, set out in Chapter 5 at page 191.

As to the role of the receiver, he is the agent of the debenture-holders who appoint him, unless the debenture expressly provides that he is to be the agent of the company, which will then be responsible for his acts, defaults and remuneration. A body corporate cannot act as receiver: s. 366. An undischarged bankrupt can only act as receiver with the consent of the Court: s. 367. If the receiver is appointed by the Court, he is personally liable (as the Court cannot be liable), but he is entitled to be indemnified out of the assets of the company in priority to the debenture-holders. He is called a receiver and manager when his duties entail carrying on the business of the company, provided that such business is included in the charge, i.e. the goodwill of the company must be charged under the debenture either expressly or by implication. For example, it may be advisable to continue the business so that a more beneficial realisation of assets may be achieved, as by completing contracts or turning work-in-progress into finished products and so on. Where the company is not a going concern, he is purely a receiver.

The receiver will realise the assets charged by the debenture, pay out the preferential creditors (which he is required to do by s. 94) and any secured creditors who have priority over the debenture, and thereafter apply the residue: (i) in payment of the costs of the receivership; (ii) in or towards the discharge of the debt owing to the debenture-holders; and (iii) to the company, where there are any surplus proceeds. The receiver can then bow out, and if what is left of the company is financially viable, the company can resume normal activities. However, it often happens that the company's financial position is irremediable and so some creditor will present a winding up petition, resulting in the appointment of a liquidator, who will take over any surplus from the receiver. In *Re Emmadart, Ltd.* (1979) it was held that the receiver had no power to present a winding up petition in the company's name as the company's agent, but that he could do so where a winding up order was needed to protect the company's assets.

By s. 369 a receiver or manager appointed out of Court may apply to the Court for directions; and is personally liable on contracts which he makes in the performance of his functions, unless he specifically contracts out of that liability. Sometimes a receiver may apply to the Court for power to raise money for the preservation or salvage of the company's property in priority to the debenture-holders; for example, this course was authorised in *Greenwood* v. *Algeciras Railway* (1894).

When a receiver or manager is appointed, the person making the appointment must notify the Registrar of Companies within seven days: s. 102. Notice is also required when he ceases to act. By s. 307, when there is a receiver or manager acting, the company's invoices, orders for goods and business letters must contain a statement of this fact.

Section 7 of the Administration of Justice Act 1977 enables a receiver or manager of a company appointed in one part of the United Kingdom to exercise his powers in relation to property situated in any other part of the United Kingdom, so far as their exercise is not inconsistent with the law applicable there.

Where a company had invited the bank to appoint a receiver in the belief that a guarantee supported by the floating charge was valid and effective, but the guarantee was later held to be invalid on challenge by the liquidator, the House of Lords held that until the invitation was withdrawn, the receiver was not a trespasser, but the service of proceedings by the liquidator cancelled the invitation, and from that moment the receiver became a trespasser and, as such, liable in damages for his subsequent conduct: *Ford and Carter, Ltd.* v. *Midland Bank Ltd.* (1979).

LOANS AND GUARANTEES BY COMPANIES

Where so empowered by its memorandum of association, a company may lend money and give guarantees, but s. 190 imposes restrictions on this right where the persons benefiting are directors. It provides that a company may not make loans to a director or to a director of its holding company, nor may it provide a guarantee or other security to cover an advance made to such a director by any other person, but these restrictions do not apply:

[(a) This allowed the loan or guarantee where the company was an exempt private company, but it was repealed by s. 2 of the Act of 1967.]

(b) To a subsidiary company where the director is its holding company. (Thus, an inter-company loan by a subsidiary to its holding company, or a subsidiary's guarantee of a bank advance to its holding company is permissible, even though the latter is a director of the former.)

(c) To loans made by a company, or guarantees given, when the ordinary course of business of the company includes the lending of money or the giving of guarantees. (Thus, a bank can allow an overdraft to its directors in the normal course of business.)

(d) To loans or to guarantees covering directors where the object of the loan is to provide funds to meet expenditure incurred by the directors for the purposes of the company or to enable them properly to perform their duties. In this exception, the approval beforehand of the company in general meeting must be obtained, or else its subsequent confirmation.

A further restriction on the purpose of the loan or guarantee is imposed by s. 54 on all companies. It provides that a company may not provide direct or indirect assistance to any person to purchase or subscribe for its own shares, or the shares of its holding company. There are the following exceptions:

(a) A company whose normal business is the lending of money. (Thus, a bank may make an advance to a customer to enable him to buy the bank's own shares.)

(b) A company may do so for the purposes of any trust for the benefit of its employees, including any director holding a salaried employment.

(c) A company may do so to enable employees, other than directors, to acquire fully paid shares in the company.

However, in *Victor Battery Co., Ltd.* v. *Curry's, Ltd.* (1946) it was held that a debenture issued by a company in connection with a purchase of its shares to a party who took it in good faith and without knowledge that its purpose was forbidden by statute, was valid. Some learned authors have doubted this first-instance case on the grounds that, if correct, it appears to render the section (now s. 54 of the Act of 1948) of little value, and that it is difficult to see why a security rendered unlawful by the section should not be void. It was not followed in another first-instance case, *Heald* v. *O'Connor* (1971), where it was held that a debenture issued by a company to provide assistance for the purchase of its own shares was void under s. 54, and therefore the defendant's personal guarantee indorsed on the debenture was also void— this followed from the well-known case of *Coutts & Co.* v. *Browne-Lecky* (1947) (discussed in Chapter 9 on Guarantees).

QUORUMS AND INTERESTED DIRECTORS

In making advances to companies, and particularly when taking securities from companies, banks normally require a certified copy of the relevant minute(s) of the board meeting authorising the borrowing and / or the creation of the security, and this involves an examination of the aspects of quorums and interested directors. The proceedings of directors are transacted at board meetings and the minimum number of directors necessary under the articles to constitute a valid meeting is the quorum. The relevant regulations of Table A of the 1948 Act, if adopted, are: Clause 99, which provides that the quorum necessary for the transaction of the business of the directors may be fixed by the directors, and unless so fixed shall be two; and clause 106, which provides that a resolution in writing, signed by all the directors, shall be as valid and effectual as though passed at a meeting of the directors duly convened and held. These clauses may, of course, be excluded or varied as a company decides, e.g. in the case of a private company with a sole director the quorum will have to be fixed at one. Clause 106 is very useful where the number of directors is small and they live a long distance apart, so that formal board meetings may be few and far between.

If the quorum is clearly stated in the articles, e.g three, then a bank could not rely on any security created at a board meeting at which apparently only two directors were present, because the other directors could repudiate it or, if the company eventually went into liquidation, its liquidator would certainly do so. The bank would have been put on notice as to non-compliance with the articles, the quorum thus acting as a bar to independent action by a director or directors insufficient in number to form a quorum against the wishes of the other directors, though it is always possible for the latter to ratify the unauthorised action so as to bind the company thereby. If the articles allow the directors to fix the quorum, and the bank receives with its security a copy of the minute(s) with the usual certificate that the board meeting was properly convened and held, then the bank can rely on the Rule in *Turquand's Case* (already discussed), if it subsequently transpires that a quorum as fixed internally by the directors was not present.

The other point which arises whenever a company gives a debenture, guarantee, indemnity or, indeed, any type of security, is whether the effect of its action is to relieve all or some of its directors of their own personal liabilities. For example, if a company gives a debenture to its bank to secure an overdraft already guaranteed by the directors personally, then those directors are "interested" in the creation of the debenture: *Victors, Ltd.* v. *Lingard* (1927), and the question then is whether by the articles directors can be counted in the quorum and vote on the matter, notwithstanding their interest, or whether they have to be excluded in calculating the quorum and from participating in the transaction. On the other hand, no difficulties arise where the company's security has been given first and the directors' personal guarantee is taken later, for now the directors are incurring liability for the company, not shifting their own liabilities on or back to the company; or where the company's security and the directors' personal guarantee are taken contemporaneously as part and parcel of the same transaction with the bank.

Section 199 imposes a duty on a director to disclose the nature of his interest at a meeting of the directors of the company where he is in any way directly or indirectly interested in a contract or a proposed contract with the company; this can be done by a general disclosure, e.g. that the director is also a director of various other companies. This important duty is based on the equitable principle that a trustee must not make a profit out of his trust. Clause 84 of Table A of the 1948 Act, if adopted, excludes interested directors from voting or forming part of the quorum, but there are certain exceptions to this prohibition.

If articles allow interested directors to vote, then the matter can be dealt with in the usual way, though the bank should check that the certified copy of the board minute(s) relating to the creation of the security shows that disclosure of interest has been duly made. If articles do not allow interested directors to vote or be counted in the quorum, then the security must be authorised by an independent quorum, i.e. one consisting of directors who have no personal interest in the subject-matter. In the last resort, if interested directors cannot participate and it is not possible to obtain an independent quorum, the creation of the security or other transaction must be authorised by the company in general meeting, at which the quorum fixed under the articles for a general meeting must be present. Alternatively, the company in general meeting could pass a special resolution altering the articles so that they allow interested directors to vote, and this would avoid any recurrence of the problem in the future. Where the directors are also members of the company, then they can vote as members at a general meeting upon a matter in which they are personally interested, unless the articles expressly disqualify directors from voting as members in these circumstances.

WINDING UP OF COMPANIES

Although a company has perpetual succession, in that it is not affected by changes in its members but carries on indefinitely, its existence can be terminated by the method prescribed in the Act of 1948 and known as winding up, or liquidation. This applies whether or not the company is solvent, because the process of bankruptcy (discussed in the next Chapter) does not apply to companies, though if a company cannot pay its debts the winding up procedure to be used has many analogies with bankruptcy. In particular, s. 306 provides that in every winding up (subject, in the case of insolvent companies, to the application of the law of bankruptcy) all claims against the company, present or future, certain or contingent, ascertained or sounding only in damages, are provable; s. 317 provides that the respective rights of secured and unsecured creditors, provable debts and kindred matters are to prevail in the winding up of an insolvent company as in a bankruptcy; s. 319 makes the rights of preferential creditors similar; and s. 320 extends the doctrine of fraudulent preference to winding up proceedings.

Section 211 sets out the three possible methods of winding up: (1) by the Court; or (2) voluntary; or (3) subject to the supervision of the Court. These will now be examined in more detail.

1. Compulsory winding up by the Court

By s. 222 a company may be wound up by the Court if:

(a) the company has by special resolution resolved that the company be wound up by the Court;

(b) default is made in filing the statutory report or in holding the statutory meeting;

(c) the company does not commence its business within a year from its incorporation or suspends its business for a whole year;

(d) the number of members is reduced, in the case of a private company, below two, or, in the case of any other company, below seven;

(e) the company is unable to pay its debts;

(f) the Court is of opinion that it is just and equitable that the company should be wound up.

The ground most frequently used is (e), inability to pay debts. By s. 223 as amended by the Insolvency Act 1976 this is deemed to occur: (i) when a creditor to whom at least £200 is owed leaves at the registered office of the company a demand under his hand requiring the company to pay the sum due and the company has for three weeks thereafter neglected to pay the sum or to secure or compound for it to the reasonable satisfaction of the creditor; (ii) if execution or other process issued on a judgment, decree or order of any Court in favour of a creditor of the company is returned unsatisfied in whole or in part; (iii) (applies only in Scotland); or (iv) if it is proved to the satisfaction of the Court (which shall take into account the contingent and prospective liabilities of the company) that the company is unable to pay its debts. As regards (i), the debt must be an undisputed one, and a winding up order will not be made if the company *bona fide* disputes the debt: *Re London and Paris Banking Corporation* (1874). In computing periods of time, unless there is an indication to the contrary, fractions of a day are ignored and the day on which the initial event occurs is excluded. Thus, in *Re Lympne Investments, Ltd.* (1972), where the demand was made on 4 November 1971 and the petition presented on 25 November 1971, the petition was dismissed because it had been presented one day too soon. As regards (iv), the Court may be satisfied by any evidence that it deems to be sufficient; in *Re Patrick and Lyon, Ltd.* (1933) it was held that a company is not solvent unless it can pay its debts as they fall due and the fact that assets exceed liabilities is not of itself sufficient to prove solvency. However, the fact that for the time being a company had insufficient liquid assets to pay its present debts where repayment of those debts had not been demanded did not prove inability to pay its debts; the company might have other assets which could be realised in a few days and would suffice for the discharge of all its immediate accrued liabilities: *Re Capital Annuities, Ltd.* (1978).

Ground (b) in s. 222 does not apply to a private company, and in any event the Court, instead of making a winding up order, will normally order that the statutory report be filed, or the statutory meeting be held. The petition to the Court must be presented by a shareholder, at least fourteen days after the last day on which the meeting should have been held: s. 224.

In the case of (d) it is also possible under s. 224 for a contributory to present the petition, a contributory being defined in s. 213 as every person liable to contribute to the assets of a company in the event of its being wound up (this includes every holder of fully paid shares, since every member is primarily liable to contribute subject to the limit he can be called upon to pay). The actual extent of a contributory's liability is laid down in s. 212 and will be discussed later. This right of a contributory to petition is, however, restricted by s. 224 to cases where (i) the number of members has fallen below the statutory minimum or (ii) he has been a registered member for six out of the eighteen months before the commencement of the winding up, or the shares have devolved on him through the death of a former holder. The word "contributory" was construed in *Re Bayswater Trading Co., Ltd.* (1970) as including the personal representative of a deceased member. In practice, the Court does not normally make an order on this ground of insufficient members, but leaves the company to wind up voluntarily.

The residuary power of the Court under (f) is rarely used, but it has been successfully invoked where the company's affairs were deadlocked because of complete disagreement between the two directors: *Re Yenidje Tobacco Co., Ltd.* (1916); and also where there was an unjustifiable exclusion of a director from participation in the company's affairs: *Re Lundie Brothers, Ltd.* (1965). These cases were approved by the House of Lords in *Ebrahimi* v. *Westbourne Galleries, Ltd.* (1973) where the appellant had been removed from office as a director of the company. In restoring the winding up order made by the trial judge, their Lordships held that provision (f) enabled the court to subject the exercise of legal rights to equitable considerations; thus, a director member might be able to prove some underlying obligation of his fellow member(s) in good faith, or confidence, that so long as the business continued he should be entitled to management participation, and that the obligation was so basic that, if broken, the conclusion must be that the association should be dissolved.

Power of the Department of Trade and the Bank of England to Present a Petition

In addition to the foregoing, there is power to present a winding up petition given the following circumstances:

(1) To the Department of Trade, by s. 35 of the Companies Act 1967 if it appears expedient in the public interest as a result of investigations by inspectors appointed by the Department or of information or documents obtained under its statutory powers conferred by the Acts of 1948 to 1967.

(2) To the Bank of England, by s. 18 of the Banking Act 1979 in respect of a recognised bank or licensed institution under the Act if

(a) the institution is unable to pay sums due and payable to its depositors, or is able to pay such sums only by defaulting in its obligations to its other creditors or (b) the value of the institution's assets is less than the amount of its liabilities.

Presentation of a Petition—the Aftermath

When the winding up petition is presented, the Court may make a winding up order, or dismiss the petition, or order the petition to stand over to a future date whilst further information etc. is sought. If a majority of creditors oppose a winding up, the Court may refuse to make a winding up order. It is not to be refused on the ground that the company has no assets: s. 225. By s. 229 a winding up by the Court commences at the date of the presentation of the petition except where, before the presentation of the petition, a resolution has been passed for voluntary winding up, in which event the winding up commences at the time of the passing of the resolution.

The date when the winding up commences is important for various reasons, principally because by s. 227 dispositions of property, transfers of shares and so on made after that date are void unless the Court otherwise orders; by s. 228 executions, attachments etc. made thereafter are void to all intents; and generally the business of the company is terminated as a going concern.

A case in which the Court exercised its discretion under s. 227 is *Re T. W. Construction, Ltd.* (1954), where a bank allowed a company a temporary overdraft after exhibition of certain documentary credits, the moneys under which were eventually paid direct to the bank. The liquidator subsequently appointed sought to reclaim these moneys but it was held that the transaction was for the benefit of and in the interests of the company to enable it to carry on its business and the bank was allowed to retain the moneys paid in to reduce the overdraft.

Section 237 gives the Court power to appoint a liquidator or liquidators, and s. 238 further authorises the Court to appoint a liquidator provisionally at any time after the presentation of a winding up petition, and in England he may be either the official receiver or any other fit person. Almost invariably it will appoint the official receiver as provisional liquidator. Thereafter, meetings of creditors and contributories take place at which there may be appointed another liquidator and/or a committee of inspection, which consists of creditors and contributories. In a compulsory winding up all the powers of the directors cease when the winding up order is made: *Fowler* v. *Broad's Patent Night Light Co.* (1893). Detailed rules of procedure in winding up are laid down in the Companies (Winding Up)

Rules 1949 (S.I. 1949 No. 330), as amended by various statutory
instruments up to S.I. 1979 No. 209. Fees in relation to winding up are
prescribed in the Companies (Department of Trade) Fees Order 1975
(S.I. 1975 No. 1351) as amended by various statutory instruments up
to S.I. 1979 No. 779.

When a bank learns that a winding up petition has been presented
against a company customer but has not yet been heard by the Court,
it should pay only cheques presented by the company for cash over
the counter, e.g. wages cheques, any other cheques being returned
marked "Winding up petition presented". Practice, however, varies
between banks and some take the view that the company's account,
whether in credit or overdrawn, can be continued, reliance being
placed on the liquidator not challenging the payment of cheques
apparently drawn in the ordinary course of business, or if he does,
that the Court will uphold them under s. 227. Support for this view
has come from *Re Operator Control Cabs, Ltd.* (1970), where the bank
stopped the company's account when the petition was presented; on
an application by the company to the vacation court it was held that
as, on the evidence, it was to the advantage of the petitioner, the
creditors and the company that it should continue trading, payments
made out of the company's bank account in the ordinary course of
business and dispositions of its property similarly made to its customers at the full market price should not be avoided by s. 227.

If a winding up order is made, the account will be stopped completely; any credit balance will be claimed by the liquidator. Where
the company is indebted to the bank, the latter will look to its security,
if any, or else prove as an unsecured creditor, and possibly as a
preferential creditor (which will be discussed later). If the petition is
eventually dismissed, the account can again be operated in the ordinary way, though where the account is overdrawn, it is extremely
likely that the bank will already have called in the debt.

List of Contributories, and their Liability

Section 257 provides that as soon as may be after making a winding
up order, the Court shall settle a list of contributories and shall cause
the assets of the company to be collected and applied in discharge of
its liabilities. Under s. 273 this duty of settling the list of contributories may be delegated to the liquidator, and it is so delegated
by the Companies (Winding Up) Rules 1949. Sometimes the list is
divided into two:—

(1) The A List which lists the members of the company at the date
of the commencement of the winding up; and

(2) The B List which can only be settled on the direction of the Court and which gives the names of persons who have ceased to be members, but who were members within one year of the commencement of the winding up.

As regards the contributories' liability, the effect of s. 212 is that no contribution is required from those persons on either list whose shares are fully paid. If the shares are not fully paid, the liquidator first makes a call for the unpaid portion on the members on the A List, and if they cannot pay, he has recourse to those on the B list, though such persons cannot be required to contribute in respect of debts incurred by the company after they ceased to be members.

2. Voluntary winding up

By s. 278 (1) a company may be wound up voluntarily:

(a) when the period, if any, fixed for the duration of the company by the articles expires, or the event, if any, occurs on the occurrence of which the articles provide that the company is to be dissolved, and the company in general meeting has passed a resolution requiring the company to be wound up voluntarily;

(b) if the company resolves by special resolution that the company be wound up voluntarily;

(c) if the company resolves by extraordinary resolution to the effect that it cannot by reason of its liabilities continue its business, and that it is advisable to wind up.

Within fourteen days of a resolution for voluntary winding up being passed, it must be advertised in the Gazette: s. 279. A voluntary winding up commences at the time of the passing of the resolution to do so: s. 280; and its effect is, by s. 281, that the company thereupon ceases to carry on business except so far as may be required for the beneficial winding up thereof. When a bank learns that a meeting to consider a winding up resolution has been called by a company customer, it need take no action in relation to the account pending the meeting (except where the account is overdrawn and the bank decides to call in the debt) because the winding up will commence only if and when the appropriate resolution is passed.

There are two types of voluntary winding up: (i) a members' voluntary winding up, and (ii) a creditors' voluntary winding up, and whether a winding up is the former or the latter will be determined by whether or not the company files a statutory declaration of solvency. By s. 283 this declaration is to be made by the directors or a majority of them to the effect that they have made a full inquiry into the affairs of the company and that, having done so, they have formed the opinion that the company will be able to pay its debts in full within such period not exceeding twelve months from the commencement of the winding up as may be specified in the declaration. It further provides that the declaration must be made within five weeks immediately preceding the date of the passing of the resolution for winding up the company and be delivered to the Registrar of Companies for registration before that date, and it must embody a statement of the company's assets and liabilites as at the latest practicable date before the making of the declaration.

For example, a company may be highly solvent but the directors and principal shareholders may wish to retire, and if they cannot sell the company as a going concern, by transferring their shares to a purchaser, they can file a statutory declaration of solvency and then during the period of its availability pass the appropriate resolution to wind up, so that this will be a members' voluntary winding up. If the declaration cannot be filed, because the directors have no reasonable grounds for believing that the company can pay its debts in full within a year, then the company is insolvent and it will be a creditors' voluntary winding up, whether it is commenced correctly under s. 278 (1) (c), or initially under s. 278 (1) (a) or (b) but then it is found that the declaration of solvency cannot be made, or if made cannot be implemented, e.g. because assets such as stocks and shares have unexpectedly collapsed in value. In this latter event, once the liquidator becomes aware of the company's insolvent state, he must summon a meeting of creditors under s. 288.

Thus, in the case of a members' voluntary winding up, the creditors will be paid in full and so the company controls its own liquidation, e.g. it has the choice of liquidator, on whose appointment the directors' powers cease except so far as the company in general meeting or the liquidator sanctions their continuance: s. 285. Further sections of the Act dealing with detailed matters are ss. 286–291. On the other hand, a creditors' voluntary winding up is under the control of the creditors, for they will lose at least a part of their claim, and the relevant provisions are ss. 293–300. For example, s. 293 provides for a meeting of creditors, which has to be advertised in the Gazette and in two local newspapers circulating in the area; s. 294 provides for the appointment of a liquidator by the creditors; s. 295 provides for the appointment of a committee of inspection; and by s. 296 (2) on the appointment of a liquidator, all the powers of the directors cease, except so far as the committee of inspection, or if there is no such committee, the creditors, sanction their continuance. Sundry provisions applicable to every voluntary winding up are contained in ss. 301–310.

3. Winding up subject to the supervision of the Court

This is a voluntary winding up which subsequently, either by order of the Court or on a petition by a creditor, becomes subject to the supervision of the Court. The making of a supervision order is in the discretion of the Court, which will have regard to the wishes of creditors and contributories. An order will not be made on a contributory's petition unless a case of fraud or improper or corrupt influence is made out: *Re Bank of Gibraltar and Malta* (1865). Sometimes, during the course of a voluntary winding up a dissatisfied creditor may file a petition for a compulsory winding up by the Court; this may be granted, or, in lieu of a compulsory order, the Court may make a supervisory order: *Re West Hartlepool Ironworks Co.* (1875). Winding up subject to supervision is dealt with in ss. 311–315, but in practice it is very rarely used, and the Jenkins Committee Report on Company Law published in 1962 recommended, *inter alia*, that it be abolished, but so far this has not been implemented by legislation.

PREFERENTIAL CREDITORS AND WAGES ACCOUNTS

Various creditors are given preference under s. 319 for their claims during certain periods and, in two instances, up to a stated amount, in the event of the company being wound up. By s. 94 they are given the same priority if a receiver of the company is appointed, but the company is not at the time in course of being wound up. If the receiver exhausts the assets in carrying on the business of the company on behalf of the debenture-holders without providing for preferential debts, he is liable in damages to those preferential creditors: *Woods* v. *Winskill* (1913). Similarly, in *Inland Revenue Commissioners* v. *Goldblatt* (1972) it was held that the receiver was under a positive statutory duty to pay the preferential creditors in priority to the debenture holder and that, having broken that duty when he knew or ought to have known of the existence of preferential creditors, he (and also the debenture holder) were liable in damages to them.

Preferential creditors have priority over creditors holding a floating charge and over unsecured creditors, but not over creditors who hold a fixed charge on the company's property, e.g. a legal mortgage on land, and not over the costs of liquidation. Where the charge is partly fixed and partly floating (as in the usual bank debenture form), the priority of the preferential payments applies only to assets covered by the floating charge: *Re Lewis Merthyr Consolidated Collieries, Ltd.* (1929).

Priority will only be conferred to the extent that at the time of winding up there is still a floating charge; subsequent preferential creditors having no priority in respect of assets on which the floating charge has crystallised: *Re Griffin Hotel Co., Ltd.* (1941). Thus, if, before the commencement of a winding up, a bank holding a floating charge calls in the debt without obtaining repayment in full and appoints a receiver, its charge will have crystallised by the step taken to enforce it, and so will rank before subsequent preferential creditors (but not before those existing at the date of crystallisation). If a winding up petition is presented by another creditor or a resolution to wind up is passed before the floating charge has crystallised, then preferential creditors at that date have priority over it—though the fact of winding up will itself crystallise the floating charge, as at the commencement of winding up the charge was still floating. Whilst it remains to be seen what view a higher court would take of the matter, the advantage of establishing a fixed charge over future book debts as a genuine fixed or specific charge (done in *Siebe Gorman & Co., Ltd.* v. *Barclays Bank Ltd.* (1978), see p. 143) is that it would rank ahead of preferential creditors, whereas if it was regarded as a floating charge in disguise, it would be postponed to them.

The list of preferential creditors set out in s. 319 (1) is similar to that in s. 33 of the Bankruptcy Act 1914 in the case of bankruptcy, and includes rates, taxes, wages and salaries of employees, all their accrued holiday remuneration, and various national insurance contributions. Certain of these taxes are not currently chargeable, e.g. profits tax, excess profits tax and purchase tax. Value added tax is now part of the preferential claims: s. 41 of the Finance Act 1972. The claims of the state and local authorities are limited to a twelve month period, though the Inland Revenue are not restricted to any particular year and may prefer any one year's assessment. Claims for wages and salaries are limited to the previous four months, i.e. before the winding up or the appointment of a receiver as the case may be, as well as, by s. 319 (2) as amended by the Insolvency Act 1976 to a maximum of £800 per person. Under s. 121 of the Employment Protection (Consolidation) Act 1978 certain other payments are to be treated as wages.

Section 319 (4) allows anyone who has advanced money to the company to pay wages and salaries and accrued holiday remuneration to have priority for his advance to the extent to which those preferential claims have been satisfied from that advance. There is no parallel in bankruptcy to this right of subrogation. A bank when lending money to a company whose financial survival is in doubt will, therefore, normally require that company to operate a separate

Wages Account (which will include salaries). There is no legal necessity for such a separate account: *Re Primrose (Builders), Ltd.* (1950), but
having one makes it easier for the bank to keep the position under
review, and also prevents the operation of the Rule in *Clayton's Case*,
which in a large and active account can result in credits lodged wiping
out the wages debits before the four month period has expired. Thus,
in *Re Rampgill Mill, Ltd.* (1967) the wages cheques, which were cashed
under an open credit arrangement at another bank, were debited to
the ordinary current account, not to a separate wages account. It was
held that the moneys paid out under the open credit arrangement
were advances for purpose of paying wages and therefore preferential,
though the bank had to reduce its claim in that some of the earlier
items had been wiped out by the operation of the Rule in *Clayton's
Case*.

Only wages, salaries and accrued holiday remuneration are
covered, so that where a cheque is for "Wages and petty cash", the
latter element obtains no preference. Furthermore, the money must
actually have been used to pay wages etc., hence banks require
certificates from those companies operating wages accounts stating
the names of the employees, their respective amounts of wages etc.,
and confirming that they were actually paid. The relationship between the company paying the money and the recipients must be that
of employer and employee, not that of employer and sub-contractor
for labour only: *Re C. W. and A. L. Hughes, Ltd.* (1966) where it was held
that moneys advanced by a bank on a wages account for the payment
of the subcontractors were not given priority by s. 319.

It must be remembered that the maximum as regards priority for
wages and salaries is £800 per person, spread over the permitted
period of the previous four months. Thus, in the case of employees
taking home £80 per week, only ten weeks' wages will carry priority.
In using a wages account, cheques for wages, salaries and holiday
remuneration (and nothing else) are debited to the account regularly
up to the maximum period of four months, and thereafter as each new
debit is passed to the account, the earliest debit, which will then have
lost its priority by being out of time, is cleared by transfer to the
ordinary current account, so that at any given time the balance of the
wages account represents the available preferential items.

Even where a bank holds a debenture secured by the usual fixed
and floating charges, it is always advantageous to insist on a separate
wages account when circumstances appear to justify one, because the
bank can then claim if necessary as a preferential creditor for the
wages etc. in priority to its own floating charge. Often there are other
preferential creditors for large amounts, particularly the Inland

Revenue or Customs and Excise, and as all preferential creditors rank equally, the bank will wish to be numbered amongst them, for after they have been paid there may be little or nothing left on which a floating charge can fasten, and unsecured creditors are sometimes left without any dividend at all.

Finally, an interesting case in which a bank succeeded in getting paid in full because it was able to spread its claim over both preferential and secured debts is *Re William Hall (Contractors), Ltd.* (1967). The bank held four legal mortgages on land by the company, which owed the bank £7,921, of which £2,274 was a preferential debt for wages' advances. The properties were sold by the bank for £5,779, and the bank appropriated these proceeds of sale in discharge of all the non-preferential debt and claimed as a preferential creditor for the balance. The mortgages empowered the bank to appropriate as it wished, but quite apart from this, the Court held that as a general principle of law a secured creditor was entitled to apply his security in discharge of whatever liability of his debtor he might think fit, and therefore the bank was entitled to take the course it did.

FRAUDULENT TRADING

Section 332 provides that if in the course of winding up it appears that the business of the company has been carried on with intent to defraud creditors or for any fraudulent purpose, the Court may declare any culpable persons to be personally responsible without limitation of liability for all or any of the debts of the company: there are also criminal penalties.

Continuing to trade when there is no reasonable prospect of paying debts amounts to fraudulent trading: *Re William C. Leitch Brothers, Ltd.* (1932). It was held in *Re Gerald Cooper Chemicals, Ltd.* (1978) that it did not matter that only one creditor was defrauded and that he was defrauded by one transaction. Money recovered from culpable persons must be treated as general assets available for all creditors and defrauded creditors are given no preferential rights: *Re William C. Leitch Brothers, Ltd.* (*No. 2*) (1933).

The position of a company secretary (in fact, a partner in the auditors to the company) was considered in relation to s. 332 in *Re Maidstone Buildings Provisions, Ltd.* (1971). It was held that the secretary in performing the duties appropriate to his office was not concerned in carrying on the business of the company: furthermore, to be liable under s. 332 a person must have taken some positive steps to carry on business, mere inertia was not enough and accordingly failure in his other capacity as financial adviser to the company to advise the directors that trading should cease was not sufficient to render him a party to the carrying on of the company's business.

Another case in which a fraudulent trading claim failed is *Re Sarflax, Ltd.* (1979), where a company stopped trading and transferred most of its assets to its parent company, the purchase price being set against sums which it owed to the parent company. HELD, although closing down the business could constitute carrying it on for the purposes of s. 332, merely giving preference to one creditor over the others does not amount to an "intention to defraud" within s. 332.

It may be added as a postscript that under s. 9 of the Insolvency Act 1976 the Court has power to order that a director of an insolvent company whose conduct makes him unfit to be concerned with the management of a company shall not, without leave of the Court, be a director of or in any way, whether directly or indirectly, be concerned or take part in the management of a company for a specified period not exceeding 5 years.

CESSATION OF COMPANIES

The final end of a company's existence comes in the following ways:

In the case of a compulsory winding up by the Court, s. 274 provides that when the affairs of the company have been completely wound up, the Court, on application by the liquidator in that behalf, shall make an order that the company be dissolved from the date of the order.

In the case of a members' voluntary winding up, by s. 290 as soon as the affairs of the company are fully wound up, the liquidator has to make an account and submit it to the final general meeting of the company called for that purpose. Within one week of that meeting the liquidator must file a copy of the account with the Registrar of Companies, and three months after such registration the company shall be deemed to be dissolved. Section 300 provides the same procedure as regards a creditors' voluntary winding up, save that in addition to the general meeting of the company there must also be a meeting of creditors for the same purpose.

Even after any type of winding up has culminated in the dissolution of the company, the Court has power under s. 352 (1) within two years of the date of dissolution to declare that dissolution void, on application being made by the liquidator or other interested party, e.g. a person having an unsatisfied claim against the company. In *Foster Yates and Thom, Ltd.* v. *H. W. Edgehill Equipment, Ltd* (1978) the Court of

Appeal held that a pending action by a company ceased absolutely and for all time on the company's dissolution and was not revived by a subsequent order under s. 352 declaring the dissolution void.

Section 353 empowers the Registrar of Companies, after prescribed formalities as to inquiries and notice, to strike the name of a defunct company off the register and dissolve the company. This may be used after or in place of winding up when the company is not carrying on business or in operation, as where all the directors and members have disappeared, but striking off in this way does not affect the liability of any director, managing officer or member, or the power of the Court to wind up a company whose name has been struck off the register. Within a period of twenty years after the striking off has been advertised in the Gazette, the company or any member or creditor thereof may apply to the Court for an order that the name of the company be restored to the register, and where such an order is made and an office copy thereof delivered to the Registrar, the company shall be deemed to have continued in existence as if its name had not been struck off. Each year a considerable number of companies are struck off under this section.

It was held in *Re Test Holdings (Clifton), Ltd.* (1969) that where a company has been struck off under s. 353, the Court has power under s. 352 (1) to declare the dissolution void.

It is unlikely that any company struck off under s. 353 will have a bank account other than a dormant one, but if it should happen that a bank sees the name of a company customer in the list of struck-off companies and subsequently a cheque is presented drawn by that company, then as the company has formally ceased to exist, the cheque should be returned with the answer "Refer to Drawer" or possibly "Company Dissolved".

COMPANIES BILL 1979

This would completely alter the classification of public and private companies as it has existed since 1908, whereby the private company is defined and any other company is a public company, by repealing s. 28 of the 1948 Act and providing that in future the expression "private company" means a company that is not a public company, the latter being defined in clause 1 as a company limited by shares or limited by guarantee and having a share capital the memorandum of which states that the company is to be a public company and in relation to which the provisions of the Bill as to the registration or re-registration of a public company have been complied with.

Both a private company and a public company will be allowed a minimum membership of two and no maximum membership, and companies limited by guarantee without a share capital and unlimited companies will become private companies. A public company will be required to have and to maintain at all times a minimum issued share capital of £50,000, but no minimum or maximum capital is prescribed for a private company. A public company, in addition to stating in its memorandum that it is to be such a company, must have as the last part of its name in the memorandum instead of the word "limited" the words "public limited company" or its abbreviation "p.l.c." (or the equivalent in Welsh, for which the abbreviation is "c.c.c.").

Provisions are contained in the Bill for the initial registration of both public and private companies, the re-registration of a private company as a public company, and vice versa, and the re-registration of an unlimited company as a public company. The time scale allowed will permit a gradual changeover. If an old public company cannot comply with the capital requirement mentioned above or for some other reason does not wish to re-register as a public company, it may pass a special resolution to acquire the status of a private company; and if it fails to take any action within 18 months from the date the Act comes into force, the Secretary of State may present a petition for the winding up of the company.

It also repeals, *inter alia*, ss. 109 and 130 of the 1948 Act (see p. 122, *ante*).

Chapter 5

Bankruptcy

INTRODUCTION

One of the tasks of a legal system is to provide a method whereby the estate of a person who becomes unable to pay his debts is administered so as to ensure its equitable distribution among his creditors while the debtor himself is freed from the burden of his debts so that he can make a fresh start. In English law this procedure is known as bankruptcy in the case of individuals, there being a more or less parallel procedure in the case of companies, known as winding up, which was considered in the preceding Chapter. Several thousand persons are made bankrupt each year, and it was estimated that there were upwards of 60,000 undischarged bankrupts by the time that the Insolvency Act 1976 initiated a continuing system of automatic discharge. The principal Statute relating to bankruptcy is the Bankruptcy Act 1914 and references in this Chapter to sections mean sections of that Act, unless the contrary is stated. The Act of 1914 is supplemented by the Bankruptcy (Amendment) Act 1926 and the Bankruptcy Rules 1952 (S.I. 1952 No. 2113/L.14, as amended by various statutory instruments up to S.I. 1977 No. 1394). Some useful amendments to the Act were made by the Insolvency Act 1976, which also provides that the Secretary of State may by regulations increase or reduce monetary limits relating to bankruptcy and winding up. Fees are now regulated by the Bankruptcy Fees Order 1975 (S.I. 1975 No. 1350), as amended by S.I. 1976 No. 687 and S.I. 1979 No. 780.

Before looking at the actual mechanics of the bankruptcy process, one may note that any person who has capacity to contract may be made bankrupt, but certain categories need some elaboration, as follows:

(1) An alien may be made bankrupt, provided he:
    (a) is domiciled in England;
    or within a year previous to the presentation of the petition, he
    (b) has ordinarily resided or had a dwelling-house in England;
      or

(c) has carried on business in England, personally, or by means of an agent or manager; or

(d) has been a member of a firm or partnership which has carried on business in England: s. 4 (1).

Section 4 was considered by the Court of Appeal in *Re Brauch* (*A Debtor*) (1978), where the debtor, who promoted and controlled property development companies incorporated in the Channel Islands, worked partly from an office in the Channel Islands and partly from an office in London. It was held: (i) in order to show that a debtor had "carried on business in England" it was not sufficient to show that he had been running his company's business in England, even if he was the sole beneficial shareholder and in complete control. This did not, however, preclude the Court from finding that he had been carrying on personally a business of his own in England independent of that of the companies, and the totality of the evidence was that he had been carrying on such a business; (ii) in order to establish "ordinary residence" it was not essential for the petitioning creditors to specify the place or places at which the debtor had resided in England within the relevant period or to show that he had been there for a commercial purpose. The fact that the debtor had not been a casual visitor to England, had spent nights there, had come to England on business and had so spent a material proportion of his time was sufficient to establish that he had "ordinarily resided . . . in England". It followed that there was jurisdiction to make the receiving order under either (i) or (ii).

(2) A company cannot be made bankrupt, but if it cannot pay its debts it may be dealt with under the analogous process of winding up, laid down in the Companies Act 1948.

(3) A deceased person cannot be made bankrupt, but where he dies leaving more debts than assets his estate may be administered in bankruptcy, for a creditor whose debt would have been sufficient to found a bankruptcy petition may petition the Court for an Order for the Administration of the Estate according to the law of bankruptcy. If satisfied, the Court will, on prescribed notice having been given to the personal representatives of the deceased, make the Order, which operates in a similar way to an Order of Adjudication, and will override a grant of Probate or Letters of Administration. By s. 33 (5) the date of death is substituted for the date of the receiving order, but the priority over all other debts given by s. 130 (6) to the payment of funeral and testamentary expenses is not affected. An innovation made by the Criminal Justice Act 1972 (see the next paragraph) is that the estate of a deceased offender may be administered in bankruptcy.

(4) An imprisoned person can be made bankrupt in the usual way. The Criminal Justice Act 1972 now provides that the Crown Court may make a criminal bankruptcy order in respect of an offender where it appears that he has caused loss or damage to property exceeding £15,000.

(5) An infant is not likely to be made bankrupt, because of his large degree of inability to incur binding debts (see Chapter 1 on Contract). However, he may be made bankrupt in respect of unpaid debts for necessaries, or an unsatisfied judgment against him in tort (e.g. for libel, conversion or negligence) or for unpaid taxes.

(6) A married woman may, since the Law Reform (Married Women and Tortfeasors) Act 1935, be made bankrupt so far as concerns her separate property just as if she were a single woman.

(7) A mentally disordered person can be made bankrupt for debts incurred whilst of sound mind, or if the Court consents.

(8) A partnership may be made bankrupt and this necessarily involves the bankruptcy of all the partners. On the other hand, a creditor may present a petition against any one or more partners of the firm without including the others (s. 114); and if this is carried to its normal conclusion one or more partners will be made bankrupt, but not the others. The special complications as regards proving against the joint estate of the firm and the separate estates of the individual partners have already been considered in Chapter 3 on Partnership.

Bankruptcy proceedings in their full progression from act of bankruptcy to discharge consist of the following steps:

    (i) The commission of an available act of bankruptcy.
    (ii) The presentation of a petition.
    (iii) The making of a receiving order.
    (iv) The meeting of creditors.
    (v) The public examination.
    (vi) The order of adjudication.
    (vii) The order of discharge.

and these steps will now be examined in detail.

ACTS OF BANKRUPTCY

To set the bankruptcy machinery in motion there must first of all be an act of bankruptcy on the part of the debtor, and s. 1 (1) provides that a debtor commits an act of bankruptcy in each of the following cases:

    (a) If in England or elsewhere he makes a conveyance or assignment of his property to a trustee or trustees for the benefit of his creditors generally.

This assignment must therefore comprise the whole of the debtor's property and must be for the benefit of all the creditors.

(b) If in England or elsewhere he makes a fraudulent conveyance, gift, delivery, or transfer of his property, or any part thereof.

In bankruptcy law "fraudulent" has a special or technical meaning, beyond its normal meaning of criminal or dishonest. If the effect of the conveyance, etc. is to delay or defeat creditors, then it will be deemed to be a "fraudulent conveyance" etc., even though it has been made in good faith by the debtor. An instance of a conveyance made with no deliberate intention to defraud creditors, but which had the effect of delaying creditors and was therefore upset as a fraudulent conveyance, occurred in the case of *Re Simms* (1930). Simms was a builder, with creditors of £28,000 and a bank overdraft of £6,500. He incorporated a private limited company to which he transferred his business assets of £17,000 in exchange for shares issued by the company, and the company took over his liabilities. The company then arranged bank accommodation against a debenture on the company's assets and paid off Simms' overdraft. An unsatisfied creditor petitioned against the debtor in his private capacity alleging that the conveyance of his business assets to the company was a fraudulent conveyance, and his contention was upheld by the Court, for the substitution of shares for substantial business assets had the effect of delaying creditors, so the conveyance to the company was void and in consequence the bank's debenture was worthless.

A conveyance may also be fraudulent under s. 172 of the Law of Property Act 1925, where the actual intention to defraud creditors must be proved, whether the conveyance is voluntary or for valuable consideration. In *Lloyds Bank Ltd.* v. *Marcan* (1973) M had given a legal charge on land to the bank. On his failing to comply with a demand for repayment, the bank commenced proceedings against M claiming possession of the property. In order to enable his wife, his children and himself to remain in the property, M leased the property to his wife for a term of 20 years "at the best rent that can reasonably be obtained at the date hereof" (it was subsequently fixed at £375 p.a.). M appreciated that the effect would be to prevent the bank obtaining possession but neither he nor his wife appreciated that the grant of a lease, even at a rack rent, would reduce the value of the lessor's interest in the property. The Court of Appeal held that in granting the lease expressly to deprive the bank of its ability to obtain vacant possession and to do so when he knew the bank was seeking possession was, in the context of the relationship of debtor and creditor, less than honest. It therefore followed that M had acted with "intent to defraud" within s. 172 (1) of the Law of Property Act 1925 so that the lease was voidable at the instance of the bank. Section 172 was again considered in *Cadogan* v. *Cadogan* (1977), where the plaintiff's attack upon a voluntary conveyance of a house made by her husband to their son failed, because it was held that s. 172 had been enacted to protect creditors whose debts subsisted at the date of the order setting aside the conveyance and did not empower the Court to create a debt where none existed; the phrase "thereby prejudiced" in s. 172 meant prejudiced by the conveyance at the date it was avoided.

(c) If in England or elsewhere he makes any conveyance or transfer of his property or any part thereof, or creates any charge thereon which would be void as a fraudulent preference if he were adjudged bankrupt.

Fraudulent preference is a complex topic, with particular hazards to banks, and will be dealt with later under a separate heading.

(d) If with intent to defeat or delay his creditors he does any of the following things, namely, departs out of England, or being out of England remains out of England, or departs from his dwelling-house or otherwise absents himself, or begins to keep house.

In short, this is any deliberate avoidance or dodging of creditors. To keep house is to avoid attending at one's place of work (if any) and to stay indoors, usually in a distant part of the house, so as to be out of sight of one's creditors and silent to their calls.

(e) If execution against him has been levied by seizure of his goods under process in an action in any court, or in any civil proceedings in the High Court, and the goods have been either sold or held by the sheriff for twenty-one days.

This is self-explanatory.

(f) If he files in the court a declaration of his inability to pay his debts or presents a bankruptcy petition against himself.

Here, the debtor himself institutes bankruptcy proceedings to get himself relieved of the burden of his debts.

(g) If a creditor has obtained a final judgment, or order against him for any amount, and execution thereon not having been stayed, has served on him in England, or, by leave of the Court, elsewhere, a bankruptcy notice under this Act, and he does not, within ten days after service of the notice where effected in England (or within the prescribed time where service is effected elsewhere) either comply with the notice or satisfy the Court that he has a counter-claim set off or cross-demand equal to or exceeding the judgment debt, which could not have been set up in the action in which judgment was obtained. (The original period of seven days was increased to ten by the Insolvency Act 1976.)

Non-compliance with a bankruptcy notice is the most frequently used Act of Bankruptcy on which a creditor founds his petition. Having obtained judgment, the creditor serves a bankruptcy notice on the debtor requiring him to pay the judgment debt or sum ordered to be paid, or to secure or compound for it to the satisfaction of the creditor or the Court. The notice indicates the consequences of non-compliance. A bankruptcy notice served in England by a creditor abroad must comply with Exchange Control Regulations where applicable. Occasionally, this act of bankruptcy is committed by a wealthy person who obstinately refuses to satisfy a judgment debt after service of a bankruptcy notice, even though he can easily do so.

(h) If the debtor gives notice to any of his creditors that he has suspended, or that he is about to suspend, payment of his debts.

This notice need not be in writing, and it is sufficient if the language used is such as to lead any reasonable person to suppose that the debtor intends to suspend payment: *Crook* v. *Morley* (1891).

In addition to these eight acts of bankruptcy set out in s. 1 (1) of the Act of 1914, there are under later legislation:—

A ninth act—in that the Criminal Justice Act 1972 provides that a person against whom a criminal bankruptcy order is made is to be treated as a debtor who has committed an act of bankruptcy on the date on which the order is made. Similar provisions are contained in the Powers of Criminal Courts Act 1973.

A tenth act—under s. 11 of the Insolvency Act 1976, where a person fails to make any payment which he is required to make by virtue of an administration order (under the County Courts Act 1959) the Court may, if it thinks fit, revoke the administration order and make a receiving order against that person, whereupon he shall be deemed to have committed an act of bankruptcy at the time when the order is made.

An act of bankruptcy ceases to be available three months after it has occurred: s. 4 (1). At any time whilst it is available, a petition founded on that act may be presented by one or more creditors.

Where necessary, a bank should seek verification of information about the commission of an act of bankruptcy, for if information came to the bank in a roundabout way and without verifying it the bank acted upon it and returned unpaid cheques drawn by the customer in favour of third parties the bank would be liable to him in damages if the returns were unjustified. On the other hand, if the bank simply dismissed the information without checking it, and bankruptcy followed within three months, then it could be liable to the Trustee for any moneys paid out, subject to the provisions of s. 46, discussed later under "Protected Transactions".

PRESENTATION OF A PETITION

A petition for the making of a receiving order against the debtor may be presented either by the debtor himself, or by one or more creditors, and once presented cannot be withdrawn except by leave of the Court.

If the petition is that of the debtor himself, he must allege in it his inability to pay his debts (s. 6). Its presentation amounts to an act of bankruptcy under s. 1 (1) (f) and the Court will at once make a receiving order (s. 6). In the case of debts payable by instalments, there is no inability to pay debts if the debtor can meet the instalments as and when they fall due. This was decided in *Re A Debtor* (1967), of which the facts were as follows: an infant plaintiff had been awarded £2,400 damages for personal injuries against the infant debtor, the damages to be paid by weekly instalments of 25s. The debtor was able to pay all his debts presently payable on the footing that only 25s. weekly was payable for the judgment debt. He presented his own petition in bankruptcy and was subsequently adjudicated bankrupt, but the adjudication was annulled by the Chancery Divisional Court on the application of the infant plaintiff because, since only debts presently payable had to be considered in determining whether there was inability to pay debts for the purposes of s. 6 of the Bankruptcy Act 1914, the debtor had not shown inability to pay his debts.

A creditor's petition, based on an available act of bankruptcy, may be presented by one creditor, or by several jointly, to whom an amount of £200 or more is owing, after deducting security. A secured creditor (i.e. one who holds a mortgage, charge or lien on any of the debtor's property as security for the debt; not one who holds "third party" security) must in his petition either state that he is willing to give up his security for the benefit of creditors, or give an estimate of its value. A creditor's petition must be accompanied by an affidavit verifying the facts stated in the petition (s. 4). An alien can present a bankruptcy petition if a debt is owing to him for which he can maintain an action: *Re Myer, Ex parte Pascal* (1876). The Criminal Justice Act 1972 provides that a person specified in a criminal bankruptcy order as having suffered loss or damage of any amount is to be treated as a creditor for that amount and can present a criminal bankruptcy petition to the High Court, as also can the Official Petitioner (the Director of Public Prosecutions).

Where possible a copy of the creditor's petition must be personally served on the debtor, but the Court may order substituted service to be made if the debtor conceals himself. The petition will be heard after an interval of eight days at least from the date of service. If the nature of the case requires it, the official receiver may be appointed interim receiver before the making of a receiving order: s. 8.

At the hearing of the creditor's petition, the Court may dismiss it, if not satisfied with the proof of the matters required to be shown, or if there is other "sufficient cause": s. 5 (3). Illustrations of the latter are where the debtor has no assets and no reasonable probability of any, for then the proceedings will be a mere waste of money (though as MEGARRY, V-C expressed it in *Re Field (A Debtor)* (1978): "A man may indeed be too poor to be made bankrupt; but the burden of proof is heavy"); or where the petition is of an oppressive character, being brought for some collateral end or to extort more than is due. If satisfied, the Court will make a receiving order.

RECEIVING ORDER

The effect of this order, which dates from the first moment of the day on which it is made, is to constitute the Official Receiver of the district—an official appointed by the Department of Trade—as the receiver of the debtor's property. It gives him power to receive all moneys due to the debtor, but does not give him power to dispose of any of the debtor's property, e.g. if a life policy of the debtor then matures the official receiver can give a valid discharge for the policy moneys, but he cannot surrender or sell the policy. The receiving order is served on the debtor and is advertised in the Gazette. It does not make the debtor bankrupt, but merely takes the disposition of his property out of his hands and also prevents his creditors from proceeding against him. In any event, s. 108 gives the Court a general discretion to rescind its orders, though in *Re a Debtor (No. 12 of 1970)* (1971) the Court of Appeal laid down that this discretion should only be exercised to rescind a receiving order in circumstances equivalent or closely analogous to those expressly recognised by the Act as enabling a bankruptcy to be halted or annulled, e.g. where the Court approves a scheme of arrangement or composition, or considers that the debtor ought not to have been adjudged bankrupt, or where it is proved that the debts have been paid in full. In *Re Field (A Debtor)* (1978) it was suggested that if after investigation the Official Receiver were to be satisfied that the debtor had no assets and no prospects of ever having any, he could and should support an application by the debtor to have the receiving order rescinded.

Where the estate is under £4,000 and a receiving order is made, the Court can order a "summary administration", a simplified procedure laid down in s. 129. This allows the estate to be administered by the official receiver as trustee without a committee of inspection, but by special resolution the creditors may select a trustee and have the estate administered in the ordinary way.

MEETING OF CREDITORS

After the making of the receiving order, the debtor will attend a private interview with the Official Receiver, at which he will receive instructions on the preparation of a Statement of Affairs to be submitted to the first meeting of the creditors. He is given seven days in which to prepare this statement.

The first meeting of the creditors (who may be represented by a proxy) must be held within 14 days of the making of the receiving order, unless the Court orders otherwise; it is generally the most important, and often proves to be the only meeting. The debtor may submit a composition or a scheme of arrangement to this meeting; such a scheme is not to be confused with a deed of arrangement, to be discussed later. The distinction between a scheme and a composition is that where a debtor makes over his assets to be administered by a trustee, that is a scheme; but where a debtor keeps his assets and undertakes to pay over to the creditors a certain sum, that is a composition: *Re Griffith* (1886). Any composition or scheme of arrangement must normally offer at least 25p in the £, and must be approved by a majority in number and three-fourths in value of the creditors. Where this is done, the composition or scheme will be considered by the Court and if it provides for the payment of the preferential creditors and is one which the Court considers reasonable, and calculated to benefit the general body of creditors, the Court will sanction it and rescind the receiving order.

If the creditors are not offered a composition or scheme of arrangement, or if any which is offered is rejected, they will resolve to have the debtor adjudicated bankrupt and normally elect a Trustee in Bankruptcy (often a chartered accountant, though the official receiver may be appointed), and in some cases a committee of inspection as well, which supervises the Trustee. After this, or if no creditors' meeting takes place, then a public examination of the debtor will be arranged by the official receiver.

PUBLIC EXAMINATION OF THE DEBTOR

Notice of this is given to the creditors and the debtor, and it will be published in the Gazette and in a local paper. This public examination takes place in open court, for the purpose of ascertaining the cause of the debtor's failure, both for the protection of the public as well as in the interests of the creditors. The debtor will be examined on oath as to his conduct, dealings and property by the Court, the official receiver, the trustee, or by any creditor who has tendered a proof or his representative authorised in writing. The examination may commence before the meeting of creditors, but it must not be declared closed until after the time fixed for that meeting. The Court may adjourn the examination if it sees fit and if the debtor fails to attend, a warrant may be issued for his arrest. At the close of the public examination, the Court makes the Adjudication Order. Section 6 of the Insolvency Act 1976 confers a general discretion on the Court to dispense with public examinations on the application of the official receiver.

ORDER OF ADJUDICATION

This is the order which actually declares the debtor bankrupt and vests his property in the trustee for the time being. Whilst it normally follows the public examination, the debtor may, at his own request, be adjudged bankrupt at the time of the receiving order. In any event, the debtor is always adjudicated unless the creditors adopt a scheme or accept a composition approved by the Court and which is actually carried into effect so that the receiving order is rescinded. However, adjudication is not final in that it may be annulled:

(i) If the Court thinks that the debtor ought not to have been made bankrupt; or

(ii) If the debts are paid in full or, in the case of disputed debts, secured to the satisfaction of the Court; or

(iii) If subsequent to adjudication a scheme of arrangement is submitted, accepted and sanctioned by the Court.

The trustee takes the property without any conveyance; the certificate of his appointment is sufficient evidence of ownership (s. 53). He has power to sell or otherwise dispose of the assets for the benefit of the creditors as a whole. Normally, he will have been appointed by the creditors at their first meeting, or by their committee of inspection; failing these, the Department of Trade will appoint, the official receiver acting in the meantime. The complexities of the collection, realisation and distribution of the debtor's property will be dealt with a little later. As regards the debtor himself, from the time of his adjudication he becomes an undischarged bankrupt and so remains until he receives his discharge. As such he is subject to certain legal disabilities, e.g. he cannot act as director of a company without leave of the Court by which he was adjudged bankrupt: s. 187 of the Companies Act 1948; and s. 367 of the same Act provides that he may not act as receiver or manager of the property of a company on behalf of debenture holders, except where he is appointed by the Court. It is a punishable offence for an undischarged bankrupt (1) to obtain credit to the extent of £50 or more without disclosing his bankruptcy; or (2) to trade under an assumed name without disclosing his other name: s. 155 of the Bankruptcy Act 1914, as amended by the Insolvency Act 1976.

The bankruptcy of a husband does not affect his continuing common law obligation to maintain his wife and children and to provide accommodation for them; even though a bankrupt, he can properly be regarded as in rateable occupation of premises, and so the right of the rating authority to issue a distress warrant in respect of unpaid rates was not affected by his bankruptcy: *London Borough of Hounslow* v. *Peake* (1974).

ORDER OF DISCHARGE

This is the order of the Court granting the bankrupt a release, and terminating his status as an undischarged bankrupt. Henceforth, he is no longer liable for debts incurred before his bankruptcy. Section 26 of the Act of 1914, as amended by s. 1 of the Bankruptcy (Amendment) Act 1926, provides that a bankrupt may at any time after being adjudged bankrupt, apply to the Court for an order of discharge. The application is heard in open court after fourteen days' notice to the creditors; and the trustee, the creditors and the official receiver may all object. Various factors, including the official receiver's report on the debtor's conduct and affairs, are taken into consideration at the hearing, at the end of which the Court will grant or refuse a discharge. Where granted, the order of discharge will be one of four alternatives, viz:

(1) An unconditional order, which releases the bankrupt immediately.

(2) A conditional order, which has the same effect but subject to conditions binding the bankrupt's after-acquired property,

e.g. that he set aside for the benefit of his creditors a specified sum each month from his earnings or income.

(3) A suspensive order, which has a delayed effect, in that it does not operate until the expiration of a specified time, e.g. two years, or until a certain dividend has been paid.

(4) A conditional and suspensive order (being a combination of these two preceding types of order).

Under s. 7 of the Insolvency Act 1976 (which was brought into force on 1 October 1977 by S.I. 1977 No. 1375) the Court may, if it thinks fit, make an order for the automatic discharge of the bankrupt after 5 years, and an automatic discharge was given on 1 October 1977 for all those made bankrupt before 1 October 1967, whilst those made bankrupt between 1 October 1967 and 1 October 1972 will also receive an automatic discharge on the tenth anniversary of their adjudication. Where such an order has not been made and the debtor has not applied under s. 26 of the Act of 1914, s. 8 provides for an automatic review by the Court after 5 years on the application of the official receiver.

By the Bankruptcy Acts 1883 and 1890 certain public disqualifications, as to sitting or voting in the House of Lords, being elected to or sitting or voting in the House of Commons, being a member of a local authority or a justice of the peace remain in force for five years from the date of discharge unless the bankrupt obtains from the court with his discharge a certificate to the effect that his bankruptcy was caused by misfortune without any misconduct on his part. Such a certificate of misfortune will be withheld where bankruptcy was due to the way in which the debtor conducted his affairs, e.g. by obtaining short-term finance to buy large amounts of shares, which fell sharply when the Council of the Stock Exchange suspended dealings in them: *Re a Debtor* (1964).

Finally, one must add that it is possible for a person to be made bankrupt more than once in a lifetime, and this sombre state of affairs does occasionally befall. By s. 39 (1), as amended by s. 3 of the Bankruptcy (Amendment) Act 1926, where a second or subsequent receiving order is made against a bankrupt or where an order is made for the administration in bankruptcy of the estate of a deceased bankrupt, then for the purposes of any proceedings consequent upon such order, the trustee in the last preceding bankruptcy is deemed to be a creditor in respect of any unsatisfied balance of the debts provable against the property of the bankrupt in that bankruptcy.

If a receiving order is made against a trustee in bankruptcy, by s. 94 he thereby vacates his office of trustee.

THE DEBTOR'S PROPERTY

Whilst the word property covers all assets of the debtor of whatever nature, the law of bankruptcy draws a distinction between property which is divisible amongst creditors, and property which is not so divisible. The latter category is a meagre one but at least it prevents the bankrupt from being wholly destitute.

Section 38 (as amended by the Insolvency Act 1976) provides that the following property is not divisible amongst the creditors:

(1) Property held by the bankrupt on trust for any other person;

(2) The tools of his trade, and the necessary wearing apparel and bedding of himself, his wife and children, not exceeding the value of £250 in all. (However, so far as seizure of property by legal process is concerned, by the Protection from Execution (Prescribed Value) Order 1963 (S.I. No. 1297 of 1963), made under s. 37 (2) of the Administration of Justice Act 1956, the value of the wearing apparel, bedding and tools of trade of a judgment debtor or his family protected from execution in the Courts is £50).

Other exceptions not mentioned in the Act are:

(3) Such part of the bankrupt's personal earnings as is necessary for the support of himself and his family, *Re Roberts* (1900).

(4) Rights of action by the bankrupt to recover damages for personal injuries.

(5) The benefit of contracts requiring the personal skill of the bankrupt (e.g. to sing). If the bankrupt elects to perform such a contract, his trustee may enforce it as against the other contracting party. On the other hand, by s. 38 divisible property includes:

(a) All the property belonging to the bankrupt at the commencement of his bankruptcy, or that may be acquired by him before discharge.

(b) All goods which at the commencement of the bankruptcy, were in the possession, order or disposition of the bankrupt, in his trade or business, by consent and permission of the true owner, i.e. goods of which the bankrupt is the reputed owner.

The purpose of this doctrine of reputed ownership is to protect creditors from the consequences of the false creditworthiness which a debtor might acquire from apparently owning property which was not in fact his: for example, a van hired from a car-hire firm by the bankrupt for business purposes might fall within s. 38 and so be claimed by the bankrupt's trustee. Household goods in the possession of the bankrupt at his home under a hire-purchase agreement are not within s. 38 because they are in his possession for private purposes, not "in his trade or business." Property held by the bankrupt as trustee and goods and chattels in the hands of an executor or factor are not normally within the reputed ownership aspect, and the presumption of ownership may be rebutted by trade custom, e.g. cattle taken in for grazing. Another example of a general trade custom which defeated reputed ownership occurred in *Re Parker* (1885) where it was held that hotel furniture is not in the reputed ownership of the bankrupt, since it is well known that such furniture is frequently hired. Where reputed ownership applies, the only remedy of the true owner, whose goods have been swept into the bankrupt's estate, is to prove for the value of the goods, i.e. he can only get whatever dividend is paid, not the return of his goods.

Possession by a bank of a warehousekeeper's certificate and a delivery order will not take the goods out of the order and disposition of the bankrupt, unless the goods have been transferred into the name of the bank. If the true owner of the goods demands possession of them before the bankruptcy and fails to obtain them through no fault of his own, they are not caught by the reputed ownership clause because they are not in the bankrupt's possession with the owner's consent. Where the owner retrieves the goods before a receiving order is made and without notice of an act of bankruptcy, his title to the goods is superior to that of the trustee.

A trade debt which has been assigned by a person who becomes bankrupt remains within his order and disposition until notice of the assignment has been given to the debtor, and, in the case of a general assignment of book debts, it so remains until the assignment is registered as an Absolute Bill of Sale.

(There is no parallel to the reputed ownership doctrine as regards companies' winding up.)

Where any part of the property of the bankrupt is of an onerous nature, such as land burdened with onerous covenants, partly paid shares, unprofitable contracts or unsaleable property, s. 54 empowers the trustee, within certain limits and with permission where requisite, to disclaim such onerous property; but any person injured by a disclaimer has a right to prove against the estate to the extent of his injury.

Where husband and wife were joint tenants of the matrimonial home on the normal statutory trust for sale, and the husband was adjudicated bankrupt with no other realisable asset, it was held that the Court had a discretion whether or not to order that the trust for sale should be carried into effect and was not bound to exercise that discretion in the trustee's favour: the question was whose voice in equity should prevail: *Re Turner* (*a Bankrupt*) *Ex parte Trustee of the*

Bankrupt (1975). In the circumstances the Court did in fact make the order for sale sought by the trustee because his claim, based on his statutory duty, was the stronger in equity.

Under s. 55 the trustee can, without further permission:

(1) sell the bankrupt's property by public auction or private contract, with power to transfer it to any person or company (the word "sell" includes the transfer of a thing in action by assignment and the words "any person" include the bankrupt himself: *Ramsey* v. *Hartley* (1977) where the Court of Appeal upheld an assignment by the trustee to the bankrupt of a right of action in tort for negligence);

(2) give receipts which will effectually discharge the person making a payment to him;

(3) prove, rank, claim and draw a dividend in respect of any debt due to the bankrupt.

With the permission of the committee of inspection (not a general permission, but only a permission to do a particular thing) the trustee has various further powers specified in ss. 56, 57 and 58.

RELATION BACK

We have seen that the divisible property which passes to the trustee is that at the commencement of the bankruptcy (s. 38), but in order that the trustee is not in practice left empty-handed as he probably would be if the commencement of the bankruptcy was, for this purpose, the date of the order of adjudication, s. 37 provides that the bankruptcy shall be deemed to relate back to, and to commence at, the first provable act of bankruptcy within three months preceding the presentation of the petition. Thus, the title of the trustee to the bankrupt's property is not limited by the date of his appointment, or of the adjudication order, or of the receiving order, but it relates back up to a maximum of three months before the presentation of the petition, whether this is presented by a creditor or the debtor himself, to the first available act of bankruptcy within that period. This act may be the one on which the petition was founded, but where the debtor has committed a series of acts of bankruptcy (some of which may not be discovered until the trustee investigates the bankrupt's affairs) then the trustee must ascertain the first available act of bankruptcy during the three months period, and the date of that act will be the commencement of his title.

For example, if a debtor who has been in financial difficulties for some time commits acts of bankruptcy on January 1st, February 10th and March 15th, and a petition is presented on April 20th based on the act committed on March 15th, the trustee's title can relate back for three months from April 20th (i.e. to January 20th) and it will commence with the earliest provable act within this period, so that in fact it commences on February 10th. The act on January 1st although the first in time cannot be used because it has ceased to be available.

RECOVERY OF PROPERTY

In addition to the doctrine of relation back, there are certain transactions by a person who is subsequently adjudicated bankrupt which are void against the trustee, so that he can claim restoration of the property. These are:

(1) A voluntary settlement made within two years of the bankruptcy.

This type of settlement is a conveyance or transfer of property without valuable consideration (it does not include settlements made in consideration of marriage). Furthermore, a voluntary settlement made within ten years of the bankruptcy is also void unless it can be proved that the settlor was solvent at the time of making the settlement, apart from the property comprised in the settlement: s. 42 (1). Where the property comprised in a voluntary settlement has been dealt with in good faith and for valuable consideration before the trustee attempts to recover it, the trustee cannot reclaim either the property or the proceeds received: *Re Macadam Ex parte Guillaume* (1950).

(2) A general assignment of book debts, as regards any book debts which have not been paid at the commencement of the bankruptcy, unless it has been registered as a bill of sale under the Bills of Sale Act 1878: s. 43 (1).

(3) Rights of execution creditors which have not been exercised. If a creditor has issued execution against the goods or lands of a debtor, or has attached any debt due to the debtor, he must give up the property so taken if a receiving order is made, or if he has notice of a bankruptcy petition or an act of bankruptcy before the execution or attachment has been completed: s. 40 (1). Whilst the goods taken in execution, or the money produced from the sale thereof, are still in the sheriff's hands, they may be taken by the official receiver or trustee, though the costs of the execution shall be the first charge on the goods or money so taken: s. 41 (1).

(4) A fraudulent preference (discussed under the next heading).

(5) A spouse's charge in respect of rights of occupation on the estate or interest of the other spouse.

Such a charge, notwithstanding it is registered, is void against the trustee in bankruptcy of the other spouse, the trustees under a conveyance or assignment of property by the other spouse for the benefit of his or her creditors generally or the personal representatives of the deceased, insolvent other spouse: s. 2 (5) of the Matrimonial Homes Act 1967.

FRAUDULENT PREFERENCE

Any conveyance or transfer of property or charge thereon made by a debtor when insolvent in favour of a creditor or of any person in trust for any creditor with a view of giving such creditor or any surety or guarantor for the debt to such creditor an advantage over other creditors shall be deemed fraudulent and void as against the trustee in bankruptcy: s. 44 (1). The fraudulent preference must have been made within six months of the presentation of the petition on which the debtor was adjudged bankrupt: s. 44 (1) as amended by s. 115 (3) of the Companies Act 1947 (which doubled the original period of three months).

The necessary elements which must be proved by the trustee in order to establish a transaction as a fraudulent preference can be analysed as follows:

(1) That the transfer or payment etc. was made voluntarily with the intention of giving preference to a creditor, or to any surety or guarantor for the debt due to such creditor. The word "preference" implies an act of free will, so that if the preference is not made voluntarily it will not be fraudulent. Hence, pressure by the creditor on the debtor (which often occurs where a bank is pressing strongly for reductions on a deteriorating debit account) may defeat a subsequent claim of fraudulent preference, but to do so the pressure must be real, so that the debtor is under some genuine apprehension, which is operative on his mind and is the dominant influence affecting it. The state of the debtor's mind when he enters into the transaction being attacked is the all important factor. The pressure need not include the threat of legal proceedings, civil or criminal, though in practice it often does. Where the debtor's action is to prevent an undisputed debt from becoming statute-barred, or to meet trade acceptances as they fall due in order to be able to continue trading, then it will not amount to a fraudulent preference. Where a solicitor made over property on the eve of his bankruptcy to repair a breach of trust committed by him—and to shield himself against possible criminal proceedings, it was held not to be a fraudulent preference: *Sharp* v. *Jackson* (1899).

Thus, the mere fact that a creditor is preferred is not sufficient, for there must be intention to prefer, and this essential quality of a fraudulent preference was explained by LORD TOMLIN in *Peat* v. *Gresham Trust, Ltd.* (1934) as follows:

"The onus is on those who claim to avoid the transaction to establish what the debtor really intended, and that the real intention was to prefer. The onus is only discharged when the Court, upon a review of all the circumstances, is satisfied that the dominant intent to prefer was present. That may be a matter of direct evidence, or of inference, but where there is not direct evidence and there is room for more than one explanation it is not enough to say there being no direct evidence the intention to prefer must be inferred."

In *Re William Hall (Contractors), Ltd.* (1967) where a bank held four memoranda of deposit of title deeds (which included the usual undertaking to create a legal mortgage upon request by the bank) for some 13 years and then took the legal mortgages shortly before the company went into liquidation, a challenge of the legal mortgages as a fraudulent preference failed, for it was held that the company's intention in executing the legal mortgages was simply to carry out its pre-existing obligation under the memoranda of deposit.

In *Re F. L. E. Holdings, Ltd.* (1967) it was held that the execution of a legal charge in favour of a bank was not a fraudulent preference because on the evidence the dominant intention at that time was to keep on good terms with the bank in the hope of future banking facilities, not to confer an advantage on the bank.

(2) That the preference occurred within the requisite period, i.e. six months preceding the presentation of the petition (see above).

(3) That the debtor was insolvent at the time the preference was made.

(Fraudulent preference also applies in companies' winding up: s. 320 of the Companies Act 1948).

Banks are particularly prone to be involved in a fraudulent preference, even though the debtor intends to prefer someone else and is not amiably disposed towards the bank, because fraudulent preference extends to payments with the intention of preferring a surety or guarantor, and the trustee is entitled to recover from the person (e.g. a bank) to whom the payment is made, even though this is not the person preferred. In an unreported case, *Re T. N. Barling & Co., Ltd.* (1932), where there was a fraudulent preference of a guarantor of the company's bank account by lodging credits to the account, it was held that the bank and not the guarantor was liable to refund to the liquidator the amount of the credits paid in. The same course was adopted by the trial judge in the case of *Re Lyons* (1934), where a trader had a bank overdraft limit of £2,000 guaranteed by his father and having known for some months that he was insolvent, he had by the end of August ceased to pay anything to the general body of his creditors, but continued to pay moneys received from his debtors into the account so that by October, when a bankruptcy petition was presented, the overdraft had been reduced from about £2,000 on September 12th to £1,300. The judgment against the bank was reversed by the Court of Appeal on the facts, namely, that after September 12th the bankrupt operated his account in exactly the same way as before when there was admittedly no intention to prefer anyone, but the principle of the decision was not questioned.

Similarly, in *Re Conley* (1938) the Court of Appeal held that, if on the facts fraudulent preference was established, the two banks concerned would have to refund to the trustee payments made to them which had placed the bankrupt's account in credit, so that third party securities lodged by his wife and mother to secure his overdraft had been given up at their request.

Another example of a bank being innocently involved in a fraudulent preference is *Re M. Kushler, Ltd.* (1943) where the company had an overdraft at a bank guaranteed by its director, Mr. Kushler, and secured by the deposit of certain policies belonging to him. Having been advised that it was insolvent, he delayed payments to creditors so that the normal flow of payments into the company's account put it in credit. The fact that the overdraft was guaranteed by the director was concealed at a meeting of creditors. The Court of Appeal held that the payments into the bank were made with a view of giving the bank preference over the other creditors and so discharging the guarantor, and the bank had to refund to the liquidator the credits received.

The potentiality of a fraudulent preference could also arise in respect of bills of exchange. If an insolvent person paid funds to his bank to meet a bill accepted for his accommodation, which the bank had discounted for him, with the intention of preferring the acceptor, then if the person was subsequently adjudged bankrupt within the fraudulent preference period, his trustee could recover the funds from the bank. Here again, the person making the payment is not intending to prefer the bank as a creditor, but the surety of that creditor (i.e. the acceptor of the accommodation bill discounted by the bank); nevertheless the loss falls initially on the bank. Prior to the Companies Act 1947 it usually remained with the bank, because if the security given up by the bank in reliance on the fraudulent preference payment was deposited by a third party, as in *Re Conley* (1938), then as such a party does not normally assume personal responsibility but only charges the security he deposits, the bank, having given up that security, had no recourse against the depositor for the sums it had had to refund to the trustee; and even if the security was a guarantee, i.e. carrying personal responsibility on the part of the third party, this would often have already been given up or cancelled, leaving the bank remediless against the one time guarantor. For this reason, some bank guarantees contain a clause empowering the bank to retain the guarantee for at least six months after it has apparently ceased to operate (see Chapter 9).

In any event, this particular hardship of innocent third parties caught in a fraudulent preference not intended for their benefit was mitigated by an amendment to s. 44 of the Bankruptcy Act 1914 made by the combined effect of s. 92 and s. 115 of the Companies Act 1947, which now provide:

(1) That the person actually preferred (the surety) shall be subject to the same liabilities as though he had undertaken personal liability for the debt to the extent of the charge or the value of the property charged, whichever is the less.

(2) That the Court has power to order repayment by the surety to the extent of his liability; in these circumstances the person to whom the payment was made can bring in the surety as a third party in any action for the recovery of the sum paid.

These provisions also apply in the winding up of companies, being now for that purpose reproduced in s. 321 of the Companies Act 1948.

Thus, although the bank (or other party who has received the actual payments constituting the fraudulent preference) remains liable to refund them to the trustee, or the liquidator in the case of a company winding up, it is given a right of recourse against the person actually preferred and is not obliged to bring a separate action against him, but although his personal liability is revived, any security previously surrendered to him is not revived.

PROTECTED TRANSACTIONS

In order to protect innocent persons who have dealt with the debtor in good faith, not knowing of the bankruptcy proceedings against him, the Act of 1914 contains two sections (45 and 46) which mitigate the rigours of "relation back" in particular circumstances. Section 45 provides that, subject to the provisions of the Act as to the effect of bankruptcy on certain settlements, assignments and preferences, any payment by or to the bankrupt, and any conveyance by or any contract, dealing or transaction by or with him for valuable consideration will hold good, provided it takes place before the date of the receiving order, and before any notice to the person dealing with the bankrupt of any available act of bankruptcy. (The exceptions to the section have already been discussed under "Recovery of Property".) Thus, from the point of view of banks, until a bank receives notice of an act of bankruptcy (which does not include notice of an intention to commit an act of bankruptcy) by a customer it may safely make and receive payments on that customer's account, so long as a receiving order has not been made. The operation of s. 45 is illustrated in *Re Green* (1979), where an order under the Attachment of Earnings Act 1971 had been made against the debtor requiring his employer to make specified deductions from his earnings and pay them into Court monthly. Moneys received by the Court had not been distributed when a receiving order was made. It was held that since the judgment creditors had no notice of an act of bankruptcy, the transactions before the date of the receiving order were protected by s. 45 and belonged to the judgment creditors, but the last payment in belonged to the Official Receiver because it was not made before the date of the receiving order.

Section 45 was considered in *Re Keever* (1966) where a customer whose bank balances were: Private a/c DR £352; Loan a/c DR £1,000, paid into the credit of her private a/c a cheque for £3,000, the proceeds of which were received the next day by the bank, which was unaware that a receiving order had that day been made against the customer, or that there had been a petition presented or an act of bankruptcy committed. The trustee claimed the £3,000 on the ground that s. 45 did not protect the bank because the proceeds of the £3,000 cheque were received by the bank on the day on which the receiving order was made. It was held that the handing of a cheque to a bank for collection in circumstances creating a lien was a "contract, dealing or transaction" for valuable consideration within the meaning of s. 45, and so the bank was entitled to set-off the two debit balances against the £3,000; alternatively, the bank became, when the cheque was paid in, not only an agent for collection, but also a holder in due course within s. 29 of the Bills of Exchange Act 1882, and so could rely on s. 38 (2) of that Act.

Section 46 provides that any payment or delivery of property to a bankrupt, or to a person claiming by assignment from him, will hold good provided the payment or delivery takes place before the date of the receiving order, and without notice of the presentation of a bankruptcy petition, and is either in the ordinary course of business, or otherwise *bona fide*. Thus, a bank is protected by this section even though it has notice of an act of bankruptcy, so long as the payments or deliveries of property are made to the debtor or his assignee, and they take place before a receiving order is made, or notice of the presentation of a petition is received. Judicial interpretation of s. 46 is provided by *Re Dalton* (1962) in which it was held that payments made by a solicitor to creditors at the debtor's direction out of money in the solicitor's hands were payments "to" the bankrupt, and although not in the ordinary course of business they were *bona fide*, and therefore were a good discharge to the solicitor. Although the question of a bank paying cheques in favour of third parties was not considered, it would seem by analogy that s. 46 ought to protect such payments by a bank; some banks take this view and will pay such third party cheques, but others continue to pay only those cheques payable to the customer himself, pending clarification of the legal position of banks under s. 46.

It will be observed that these sections refer to notice of an act of bankruptcy, and notice of the presentation of a petition, but to the "date" of the receiving order. Thus, the making of a receiving order terminates the protection of ss. 45 and 46, whether or not the person dealing with the bankrupt had notice of the receiving order, subject only to the limited protection of s. 4 of the Bankruptcy (Amendment) Act 1926 which was designed to mitigate the hardship that occurred in *Re Wigzell* (1921). In this case, a bankruptcy petition was contested and, pending appeal, advertisement of the receiving order was stayed. The appeal was subsequently dismissed and the receiving order was advertised and back-dated to the day on which it was originally made. In the meantime, the debtor's bank had continued his account, and it was held that the bank must account to the trustee for transactions after the date of the receiving order, even though it had no knowledge of the receiving order and could not by any reasonable means have ascertained that it had been made. This situation has to some extent been alleviated by s. 4 of the Act of 1926 which provides that where a person has paid or transferred money or property of the bankrupt to another person on or after the date of the receiving order without knowledge that it has been made and before it has been gazetted, then, if the transaction is void, the trustee's right to recover from the innocent payer or transferor cannot be enforced except where and so far as the Court is satisfied that it is not reasonably practicable to recover from the person to whom the money or property was paid or transferred. Thus, from a banking point of view, if a bank makes payments from the bankrupt's account after a receiving order has been made, of which the bank is not aware, but before it has been advertised in the Gazette, the trustee must make every effort to obtain repayment from the persons to whom the payments were made and only if his efforts fail can he resort to the bank. The limited protection of s. 4 will cease when the receiving order has been advertised in the Gazette as this advertisement constitutes notice to the world.

The next section of the Act of 1914, s. 47, gives protection to persons dealing directly with an undischarged bankrupt in respect of after-acquired property. All property, whether real or personal, acquired between the commencement of the bankruptcy and discharge vests in the trustee (s. 38); but s. 47 provides that dealings *bona fide* and for value between the bankrupt and any person in respect of property acquired after adjudication shall, if completed before any intervention by the trustee, be valid against the trustee. This protection afforded to people dealing with the bankrupt in certain transactions does not prevent the trustee from claiming at any time money or property from the bankrupt himself. The receipt of any money, security or negotiable instrument from, or by the order or direction of, a bankrupt by his banker and any payment and any delivery of any security or negotiable instrument made to, or by the order of, a bankrupt by his banker are declared to be a dealing with the bankrupt for value so that the banker comes within the ambit of the protection. As the section makes no provision as to the effect of knowledge of the bankruptcy, it would appear that such knowledge is immaterial.

Although by s. 38 the title to any after-acquired property vests immediately in the trustee, the bankrupt has a right to possession until the trustee intervenes, for so long as the property remains in the hands of the bankrupt, the trustee's title is subject to qualification to the extent required to protect transactions under s. 47: *In Re Pascoe* (1944).

RIGHTS OF CREDITORS

These depend on the type of creditor, of which there are four:

(a) *Preferential Creditors.*— It has already been noted in the previous Chapter that by s. 319 of the Companies Act 1948, certain debts must be paid in priority to all others in the winding up of a company. A similar priority in the bankruptcy of an individual is conferred by s. 33 of the Bankruptcy Act 1914, as amended by various Acts, on the following debts:

(i) Local rates due and payable within twelve months prior to the date of the receiving order;

(ii) Income tax and other assessed taxes assessed on the bankrupt up to April 5th before the date of the receiving order, not exceeding one year's assessment (the Inland Revenue can select the year);

(iii) Value added tax due within twelve months prior to the date of the receiving order;

(iv) Employer's liability for P.A.Y.E. tax due within a similar period.

 (v) Wages and salaries of clerks or servants of the bankrupt during the four months prior to the date of receiving order, with a maximum of £800 per claimant. Under s. 121 of the Employment Protection (Consolidation) Act 1978 certain other payments are to be treated as wages.

(vi) Contributions payable under social insurance legislation by the bankrupt as an employer within twelve months prior to the date of the receiving order.

Section 33 also applies in the case of a deceased person dying insolvent, the date of his death being substituted for the date of the receiving order, but the priority given by s. 130 (6) to the payment of funeral and testamentary expenses is not affected.

Priority is also given by s. 72 of the Trustee Savings Bank Act 1969 to a trustee savings bank in respect of its money or property held or possessed by its bank officer; and by s. 59 of the Friendly Societies Act 1974 as regards money or property of a registered society or branch in the possession of any officer.

(b) *Secured Creditors.*—A secured creditor is a creditor who holds a mortgage, charge or lien on any of the debtor's property as security for a debt due to him from the debtor. The holder of a bill of exchange or promissory note is not as such a secured creditor, though he may hold collateral documents as security, e.g. bills of lading, which will make him a secured creditor. Guarantees and third party mortgages, charges or liens can be disregarded when submitting a proof (a claim on the bankrupt's estate for the sum, which may be actual or contingent, due to a creditor, verified by affidavit). The test is would the security if given up augment the estate against which proof is made: if not, the creditor can prove for the whole debt without deducting the value of the security: *Re Turner, Ex Parte West Riding Union Banking Co.* (1881). Where property was jointly owned by the bankrupt and another and jointly charged by them to a bank (whose realisation of the security was insufficient to cover the debt), it was held that the bank was not entitled to prove for the full amount of the balance, but for half the balance only, since it must give credit for the other half as secured: *Re Rushton (a bankrupt)* (1971).

There are four courses available to a secured creditor—he may:

(i) Give up his security and prove for his entire debt; or

   (ii) Realise his security and prove for any deficit after deducting the net amount realised; or

  (iii) Value his security and prove for any deficit, but in this case the trustee may redeem the security at the assessed value if the proof is for purposes of dividend, and at the assessed value + twenty per cent, if it has been used for the purposes of voting at creditors' meetings; or

  (iv) Rely entirely on his security and not prove at all.

By s. 5 of the Insolvency Act 1976 the requirement in the 1914 Act that the debt be proved by an affidavit delivered or posted to the trustee is now modified to the extent that an affidavit may be required by the official receiver or trustee, but if not then an unsworn claim suffices. A creditor who has submitted a proof may subsequently, with the leave of the Court, amend that proof if he can show that he made a *bona fide* mistake or that the security has altered in value since he lodged his proof.

If a creditor omits to state in his proof that he is secured, when this omission is discovered the security must be surrendered to the trustee for the general benefit of creditors, unless the Court is satisfied that the omission was inadvertent, when it may allow the proof to be amended upon such terms as it considers just: s. 11 of the Bankruptcy (Amendment) Act 1926.

Where the security has been valued, the creditor may at any time by notice in writing, require the trustee to elect whether he will or will not redeem the security, and the trustee must then, if he wishes to redeem, do so within six months otherwise his right to do so is lost. If the trustee is dissatisfied with the valuation, he may require the property to be sold, on such terms as he and the creditor may agree or the Court may fix. In the case of a petitioning creditor who is also secured, the trustee is not entitled to redeem his security at the value assessed in the petition, his right to redeem only arising where the value has been assessed for the purpose of proving: *Re Vautin* (1899).

Where the security consists of goods which have been pledged, the official receiver or trustee may serve written notice of his intention to inspect the goods, and after such notice the pledge must not realise his security until he has given the trustee a reasonable opportunity of inspecting the goods and of exercising his right of redemption if he thinks fit to do so: s. 59.

Of the foregoing alternatives as regards proof, a bank will usually choose either (ii) realisation, or (iii) valuation, according to the nature of the security, e.g. quoted stocks and shares, and life policies, can be easily realised, but there will often not be time to realise other securities such as land. If a bank holds ample security it may decide on (iv) waiver of proof, but it will never, or hardly ever, choose (i) surrender of security in exchange for the hazards of proof.

(c) *Unsecured Creditors.*—These are the ordinary creditors, who do not hold any security on the debtor's property. Their only remedy is to prove for their debt and receive such dividend, if any, as is available for distribution from the estate after payment of the expenses and the preferential debts. It may be added that a landlord is in a special position as regards his rent in that he can distrain, i.e. seize his tenant's chattels in payment of the rent, but he has no priority over the other creditors unless he distrains. If he distrains after commencement of the bankruptcy, he can only do so for six months' rent accrued prior to adjudication, not including any rent payable for the period after the date when distress was levied, and for any deficit remaining after the distress, he may prove as an ordinary creditor: s. 35 (1).

(d) *Deferred Creditors.*—Certain debts are not payable until all other creditors have been paid in full. These deferred debts are an exception to the general rule that all debts other than preferential debts rank equally, and comprise:

(i) If there is a claim by a person for agreed interest exceeding five per cent. per annum, the claim is deferred so far as it relates to interest in excess of five per cent. per annum: s. 66.

(ii) Certain debts within s. 3 of the Partnership Act 1890, e.g. loans for business purposes where the rate of interest varies with profits.

(iii) Loans by a wife to a husband, or by a husband to a wife for purposes of his or her trade or business: s. 36 of the Act of 1914.

(iv) The claim of a joint creditor against the separate estate of a bankrupt partner is postponed to the claims of the separate creditors: s. 63 (see also Chapter 3).

(v) The trustees of a settlement which has been avoided have a deferred right to claim a dividend: s. 42.

It may be added as a postscript that in *Miliangos* v. *George Frank (Textiles), Ltd.* (1975) two of the Law Lords were of opinion that where a foreign money obligation is the subject of a proof in bankruptcy or companies liquidation, the date for conversion into sterling should be the date of the admission of the proof. However, their dicta were not followed at first instance in *Re Dynamics Corporation of America* (1976) where it was held that the relevant date was the date of the winding up order when all other claims fell to be ascertained.

Contingent claims

Section 30 provides that a creditor may prove for all debts and liabilities, present or future, certain or contingent, to which the debtor is subject at the date of the receiving order, or to which he may become subject before his discharge by reason of any obligation incurred before the date of the receiving order; the following debts are not provable:

(1) Demands in the nature of unliquidated damages not arising from a contract, promise or breach of trust;

(2) Debts contracted by the debtor after the creditor has notice of an available act of bankruptcy.

(3) Debts the value of which cannot be fairly estimated, in which event the Court may on application declare the debt not provable.

Mutual dealings

Section 31 provides that where there have been mutual credits, mutual debts or other mutual dealings between a debtor and his creditor, an account shall be taken of what is due from one to the other, and the balance of the account, and no more, shall be claimed or paid. This prevents a creditor from having to pay in full any sum he owes to the bankrupt, whilst receiving only a dividend in respect of the debts owed to him by the bankrupt. In *National Westminster Bank Ltd* v. *Halesowen Presswork and Assemblies, Ltd.* (1972) the company's accounts with the bank were, at the time a winding up resolution was passed, No. 1 frozen (by agreement) at £11,879 DR and No. 2 £8,634 CR. The House of Lords held that the bank was entitled to set off the credit balance on the 2 account against the debit on the 1 account because the agreement to keep the accounts separate was ended by the winding up resolution, and even if the bank was not otherwise entitled to combine the accounts, it could do so under s. 31 (as applied by s. 317 of the Companies Act 1948) since the parties could not contract out of s. 31 as its provisions were mandatory, prescribing the course to be followed in the administration of the bankrupt's property.

Re D. H. Curtis (Builders), Ltd. (1978) has shown that s. 31 is not limited to mutual contractual claims, the judge holding that the Crown was entitled to set off the money which it was owed by the company against the input tax repayment owed to the company by the Commissioners of Customs and Excise.

Statute-barred debts

No proof can be submitted in respect of a statute-barred debt: *Re Art Reproduction Co., Ltd.* (1951).

BANKRUPTCY AND EVERYDAY BANKING

Leaving aside the complications of bankruptcy on the bank accounts of partnerships, which were considered in Chapter 3 on Partnership, this heading will comprise (i) bankruptcy of customers; (ii) accounts with undischarged bankrupts; (iii) bills of exchange; and (iv) bankrupt payee of a cheque.

(i) Bankruptcy of customer

Though there may be ominous signs preceding it, the first clear indication of trouble is an act of bankruptcy by a customer. Notice of this may be actual formal notice or knowledge of facts which may constitute an act of bankruptcy. An intention to commit an act of bankruptcy is not sufficient and may be ignored or preferably treated with caution until the act itself is committed. Thus, the mere statement by a customer, or the comments of others, that the customer is insolvent do not amount to notice. However, in any doubtful circumstances, the bank should make prudent enquiries as to the accuracy of the information it has received. The mere calling together of his creditors by a debtor and his offer to them of a composition do not in themselves amount to an act of bankruptcy, though the outcome may be a deed of arrangement, which is an act of bankruptcy.

Once the bank learns of an available act of bankruptcy by a customer, it will take action as follows:

(a) *With a credit account.*—payments should be made only to the customer, who should be advised accordingly, against the existing balance. In England cheques do not amount to an assignment of funds in the hands of the bank, so cheques in favour of third parties should not be paid. This applies even if the customer pays in funds with instructions to utilise it for the payment of a specified cheque, since the appropriation is revoked by notice of an act of bankruptcy. However, in the case of a deed of arrangement (as this is an assignment) the bank can claim the protection of s. 46 if it pays over the balance to the trustee named in the deed. Credits subsequently paid in should be placed to a suspense account for three months, and the customer advised accordingly, in case they are claimed by the trustee.

If bankruptcy proceedings did follow, then the credits would be the property of the trustee, who could sue the bank in conversion if it had allowed the customer to handle them (s. 46 would not apply because the credits are not payments or deliveries to the bankrupt).

(b) *With an overdrawn account.* — the bank will not pay any cheques at all, because they cannot be included in the proof, and even if there is surplus security for the overdraft this cannot be relied on, for if bankruptcy proceedings follow the surplus security may be claimed by the trustee under "relation back". Credits will be placed to a suspense account for three months, as stated in (a) above.

In either case, where securities are held in safe custody, they may be delivered to the customer himself, but not to third parties at his request. If there is a deed of arrangement, then the securities may be given up to the trustee named in the deed.

Whether the account is in credit or in debit, the above restrictions imposed by notice of an act of bankruptcy will last for three months (after which time that act will cease to be available) unless the bank has notice of a second or subsequent act of bankruptcy, which will continue the situation, or receives notice of the presentation of a petition, the next step in the bankruptcy process. Once notice of the presentation of a petition is received, no transactions must be permitted on the account, nor must any securities be released unless and until the petition is dismissed. If the bank has already incurred obligations on behalf of the customer, e.g. where it has bought stocks and shares on his instructions but settlement day has not yet arrived—when it does, the customer's account may be debited but the securities themselves should be accounted for to the trustee. It may be that the bank receives notice of the making of a receiving order without any prior intimation of the presentation of a petition, or even of an act of bankruptcy, and as soon as this notice is received, the account must be stopped completely, for only the official receiver or the trustee can now give a good discharge to the bank.

The foregoing will also apply to a joint account one party to which is the subject of bankruptcy proceedings. On notice of the presentation of a petition or the making of a receiving order the account, when in credit, should be stopped, and the balance will have to be apportioned between the solvent party or parties and the trustee. Care should be taken that the answer on any cheques which have to be returned does not damage the credit of the solvent party or parties. Where the joint account is in debit, it will again be stopped and any cheques presented will be returned. If liability on the account is joint only, then the bankruptcy of one party will discharge his estate; if the normal mandate making liability joint and several has been taken, and the bankrupt's estate is being relied on, then the bank can prove against the bankrupt's estate for the debit balance without prejudice to his rights against the solvent party or parties—the stopping of the account will also prevent the operation adversely to the bank of the Rule in *Clayton's Case*.

As a postscript, it may be mentioned that a trustee in bankruptcy must not pay any money received by him as trustee into his private bank account: s. 88. Under s. 89 (as amended by the Insolvency Act 1976) he must pay it into the Insolvency Services Account at the Bank of England unless the Department of Trade authorises payment into a local bank on application of the committee of inspection, or the trustee where there is no such committee. However, in *Re Walker (a Bankrupt)* (1974) the Court of Appeal refused to intervene when the Department of Trade declined permission on the ground that it had no power under s. 89 to give the necessary authorisation where the sole purpose of having an account with a local bank was to earn interest.

(ii) Accounts with undischarged bankrupts

One of the reasons for the care exercised by banks when opening accounts, with their insistence on references, is to obviate as far as possible the subsequent discovery that the customer is an undischarged bankrupt. However, occasionally one slips through the net, and when a bank ascertains that a customer is an undischarged bankrupt, by s. 47 it must forthwith inform the trustee or the Department of Trade of the existence of the account, and thereafter must not make any payments out of it except under an order of the Court or in accordance with the instructions of the trustee, unless by the expiration of one month from the date of giving the information no instructions have been received from the trustee. Failure to do so will mean the bank will be liable to the trustee for all the money paid out of the account.

If the bank can find out from the customer who his trustee is, then the bank will advise the trustee, but if this is not immediately possible, then the bank will advise the Department of Trade (Bankruptcy and Companies Liquidation Headquarters) in London which can check its records and advise the trustee in question. Where the customer, on being informed by the bank of its action, alleges he has obtained his discharge, he should be asked to produce a copy of the order of discharge. Alternatively, if no directions have been received from the trustee after one month from the time of giving the notice, the account may be resumed.

Although s. 47 is silent on the point, it would appear prudent also to apply this procedure to an account where it is clear that the account-holder is acting as a mere nominee of the undischarged bankrupt, e.g. his wife, because the section only protects people dealing direct with the undischarged bankrupt. But if a scrutiny of the account shows that it is the wife's own purely personal account (fed, for example, by her own salary), as she is fully entitled to such an account, no action need be taken by the bank, except to keep the account under surveillance for any possible abuse of it by the husband. In these circumstances, however, the bank may prefer to take steps to close the account.

In any case where a bank has suspicions about a customer being a bankrupt, it is possible to check up on the point (independently of asking the customer) by making a personal search, at a fee of 25p per search, in the Bankruptcy Register in London, kept by the Chief Bankruptcy Registrar in the High Court under the Bankruptcy Rules 1952. By r. 360 this register is open to the public for inspection, though the registrar may, however, refuse to allow a person to search if he is not satisfied as to propriety of the object for which the search is required. There is no provision for official searches. The brief information available to the general public is limited to the salient points of each bankruptcy, e.g. the act of bankruptcy on which the petition was presented, the date of the receiving order and so on. If the person was made bankrupt under some other name than that which he uses at present, a search against the latter only will not reveal anything.

(iii) Bills of Exchange

So far as the bankruptcy of a customer concerns bills of exchange, the bank may be involved because those bills are domiciled at the bank, or because they have been discounted by the bank. With bills accepted payable at the bank, once the bank learns of an act of bankruptcy by the acceptor, or of any later stage in his bankruptcy proceedings, then bills will be returned unpaid when presented.

If the bank has discounted bills for a customer who becomes bankrupt during their currency, it may set off the contingent liability of the bankrupt on the bills (such liability being a provable debt) against any credit balance it may hold, paying over to the trustee any surplus only; s. 31. It may prove for any deficiency, subject to a rebate of interest at five per cent. per annum from the time when the dividend is declared to that at which the bill would have matured. Normally, the bank will seek to enforce payment from the other parties to the bill, but if they are also insolvent, the bank can prove for the full amount of the bill against all parties to it, so long as it does not get more than 100p in the £, except that once a dividend has been declared out of the estate of any one of the parties, it can only prove for the balance against the estate of any other party.

Where the bank has discounted a bill for a customer and during the currency of the bill its acceptor becomes bankrupt, the bank cannot compel the customer to take up the bill, nor can it retain against the contingent liability on the bill any credit balance he may have. The bank can seek payment at maturity from the other parties to the bill. If, before the bill matures, the bank proves against the acceptor's estate for the full amount of the bill, subject to a rebate of interest at five per cent. per annum from the time when the dividend is declared to that at which the bill would have matured, and a dividend is declared, then the bank can recover the balance from the other parties to the bill at its maturity.

Finally, it must be noted that when a bill of exchange is on the face of it expressed to be drawn against specific goods or securities the holder does not obtain thereby any charge upon the goods or securities except in the case of double insolvency. Thus, if both drawer and acceptor of the bill of exchange become bankrupt the holder is entitled to have any goods or securities held by the acceptor for it applied in taking it up: this is the Rule in *Ex Parte Waring* (1815). If the proceeds of the goods or securities fall short of the amount of the bill, the holder can prove for the deficiency. It is not necessary that the insolvent estates are actually administered in bankruptcy, as it is sufficient that they are both administered for the benefit of creditors under the control of a court of justice.

(iv) Bankrupt payee of cheque

It may occasionally happen that a bank is presented with an open cheque over the counter in favour of a person known to be an undischarged bankrupt. This cheque should not be paid because it may belong to the trustee, in which case the payee's title will be defective, so that the cheque will not be discharged by payment to the payee, and the customer will still be liable on it to the trustee. The bank should safeguard its customer by returning the cheque marked "payee bankrupt", i.e. the answer must not damage the credit of the drawer, who should be advised that the cheque has been dishonoured and the reason for this course.

If the cheque was paid and it transpired that the money belonged to the trustee and was not after-acquired, the bank would be account-able for it to the trustee in an action for conversion and would have no recourse against the customer. However, if the bank did not know the payee was bankrupt and it paid the cheque in good faith and in the ordinary course of business the bank would be protected by s. 60 of the Bills of Exchange Act 1882 against an action by the trustee for conversion.

DEEDS OF ARRANGEMENT

A debtor is sometimes able to make a private arrangement with his creditors outside the provisions of the Bankruptcy Act 1914, the normal method being to use a type of contract known as a deed of arrangement (or assignment) as prescribed by the Deeds of Arrangement Act 1914. By such a deed a debtor assigns his property to a trustee as representative of the creditors, and this deed must be distinguished from a scheme of arrangement, which is a feature of bankruptcy and has already been discussed.

A deed of arrangement is any instrument, whether under seal or not, made for the benefit of creditors generally or made by an insol-vent debtor for the benefit of three or more creditors. It may be

(1) An assignment of property;

(2) A deed or agreement for a composition; and in cases where the creditors obtain control over the debtor's property,

(3) A letter of licence;

(4) An agreement for the carrying on or winding up of the debtor's business.

(Section 1 of the Deeds of Arrangement Act 1914).

By s. 2 (as amended by s. 22 (1) of the Administration of Justice Act 1925) a deed of arrangement will be void unless it is registered at the Department of Trade within seven days after first execution and is properly stamped. Fees are now regulated by the Deeds of Arrange-ment Fees Order 1973 (S.I. 1973 No. 1993). A deed for the benefit of creditors generally is also void unless assented to by a majority in number and value of the creditors before or within twenty-one days of registration, and within twenty-eight days of registration a statutory declaration must be filed confirming that the assents have been obtained: s. 3. Within a further seven days the trustee under the deed must give security unless the creditors dispense with it, and in default the Court may declare the deed void or appoint a new trustee: s. 11.

Although deeds of arrangement as such are voluntary transactions and no part of the machinery of bankruptcy, a deed of arrangement for the benefit of creditors generally is an act of bankruptcy as regards any creditor who has not assented to the deed, or recognised it, e.g. by trading with the trustee. Thus, any dissenting creditor may present a bankruptcy petition against the debtor during the three-month period that the deed is an available act of bankruptcy. However, s. 24 of the Deeds of Arrangement Act 1914 provides that if the trustee serves the appropriate notice on any creditor the period during which that creditor can petition is cut to one month. Should the deed become void under s. 2 for lack of adequate assents then any creditor may found a bankruptcy petition on it.

As far as banks are concerned, where the deed of arrangement is an act of bankruptcy, then the bank will treat it as such and deal accordingly with the account(s) of the customer who has created the deed. However, if the deed covers the property of the customer generally, or refers specially to his bank account, then no transactions can be allowed on that account at all. If the trustee named in the deed requests the bank to pay over any credit balances to him, the bank can validly do so because, as the deed is an assignment, the bank will be protected by s. 46 of the Bankruptcy Act 1914 provided it makes the payment before the date of a receiving order and without notice of the presentation of a bankruptcy petition.

If a bank is asked by the trustee named in the deed to open an account for this trusteeship, the bank can do so, but the account must be in the name of the debtor's estate: s. 11 (iv) of the Deeds of Arrangement Act 1914. No withdrawals, however, should be permitted for three months from the date of the deed, in case bankruptcy proceedings based on the deed are put in motion by a dissenting creditor. In other words, until the deed ceases to be an available act of bankruptcy, the account is purely a paying-in account fed by the collection of debts and the realisation of other assets, but once the danger of bankruptcy proceedings is past the account can be a normal current one.

Where a bank's customer, who is overdrawn, gets into financial difficulties and approaches his bank with a request that it assents as a creditor to a proposed deed of arrangement, the bank should consider the deed carefully and estimate whether it is to the bank's advantage or not, compared with bankruptcy proceedings. For example, the deed may provide that all security, including third party security, must be taken into account, and if the bank held any third party security it might be worse off under the deed than it would be in bankruptcy proceedings, where such security need not be included in the proof.

CONCLUSION

The advantages of the ordinary bankruptcy proceedings are publicity; the supervision of the Court, which means matters are summarily enforceable, and the debtor can be punished if he conceals assets; statutory provisions protecting the estate; and the creditors through their committee of inspection can take a hand in the administration of the estate. The disadvantages are those common to legal procedure—slowness and expensiveness, but from the practical point of view bankruptcy proceedings frequently result in forced sales at low prices so that the dividend is correspondingly reduced.

These disadvantages can be largely overcome by resorting to the deed of arrangement system: and, furthermore, such a composiíion is not so much of a stigma on the debtor as being adjudged bankrupt. Yet there are numerous other drawbacks to a deed of arrangement: it is usually, as already elaborated, an act of bankruptcy which creates uncertainty; moreover, as it is not an official document (i.e. it is not sealed by the Court, or embodied in an order of the Court), it is not summarily enforceable; and as the trustee under a deed of arrangement gets only what is assigned to him, and cannot avail himself of relation back or set aside voluntary conveyances and fraudulent preferences, there may be fewer assets yielded than would be the case if bankruptcy proceedings were instituted.

Chapter 6

Land

INTRODUCTION

Land is the basic form of property because of its indestructibility and is known in legal language as realty or real property to distinguish it from personalty, or personal property. Technically, only freeholds are real property, for leaseholds are classified as personal property but at an early stage in our history they were sub-classified as chattels real (in contrast to chattels personal) and as such have become included in real property law. Consequently, landholding in England and Wales must be viewed briefly against an historical background, before the present-day position is considered. In the Middle Ages land was the chief source of wealth, and therefore a feudal system was developed, based on the doctrine of tenure (which must not be confused with the landlord and tenant relationship). The characteristics of this doctrine are that all land was owned by the King and that apparent owners of it really held it, mediately or immediately, as his tenants. A few tenants, known as tenants in chief, held land directly of the King, and they in turn made grants to the actual possessors in return for services rendered in accordance with the particular type of tenure.

There were four main types of free tenure, i.e. free from all servile conditions: (1) knight service (involving military service by the tenant); (2) frankalmoin (religious service); (3) serjeanty (some form of personal service); and (4) socage (payment of a rent). The Statute of Tenures 1660 converted military tenures into socage; and over the years frankalmoin and serjeanty fell into disuse. There was also a non-free tenure, known at first as villeinage and subsequently as copyhold, whereby the tenant had to perform agricultural services of an uncertain nature, which were in time superseded by an annual cash payment. The Real Property Legislation of 1925 converted all tenure to common socage, which is now identical with freehold, a much more familiar expression. This mass of legislation, which came into force on January 1st, 1926, consisted of seven Acts of Parliament dealing with various aspects of land law and was an heroic attempt to bring some sort of order and as much simplicity as possible into a branch of our law once described by Oliver Cromwell as "an ungodly jumble".

To this end, s. 1 of the Law of Property Act 1925 provides that the only legal estates in land which may now be created are:

(i) in the case of freeholds, the fee simple absolute in possession;
(ii) in the case of leaseholds, the term of years absolute.

The person or persons in whom the legal estate is vested is called the "estate owner", and must be of full age.

There are also five legal interests which bind a purchaser for value without notice: (a) an easement or profit held in perpetuity or for a term of years absolute; (b) a rent charge in possession held as in (a); (c) a charge by way of legal mortgage; (d) land tax, tithe rent charge etc.; and (e) rights of entry respecting legal leases or legal rent charges. All other estates, interests, and charges in or over land take effect as equitable interests, and as such bind a purchaser for value only if he has notice, actual or constructive, of them.

THE FEE SIMPLE ABSOLUTE IN POSSESSION

All land in England and Wales is now held on the one universal tenure known as freehold, so called because it is a holding free from all servile conditions, in which the only legal estate now obtainable is the fee simple absolute in possession. This, therefore, is the greatest estate in land a person can possess, being absolute ownership in all but name, or if one disregards the historical shadow of tenure it is absolute ownership as most people think of it. Each word in the name of this estate has particular significance, which may be elaborated as follows:

The word "fee" denotes the inheritability of the land, for it descends for ever to the heirs of the estate owner, unless that owner alienates (i.e. parts with) the land to someone else, as on a sale, or devises the land by will to someone else.

"Simple" denotes that the land may be inherited by the general heirs of the estate owner. These heirs include lineal relatives, i.e. descendants (children of the deceased owner and their descendants) and ascendants (parents and grandparents), and also collateral relatives (brothers and sisters, uncles and aunts). Thus, the land will pass to the one who can prove that according to the legal canons of descent he is the nearest heir to the deceased owner. Should the estate owner die intestate, leaving no next of kin as designated by the Administration of Estates Act 1925, then the land will pass as *bona vacantia* ("ownerless property") to the Crown, Duchy of Lancaster or Duke of Cornwall. The use of the word "simple" distinguishes this estate from one in which the land is limited to descend to a particular class of heirs, known as a "fee tail" or "entail", which is now an equitable entitled interest, for since 1926 there can be only the one legal estate in freehold land. The line of descent specified by the entail can be either in tail male, i.e. the estate descends only to males or only in the male line (and, theoretically at least, in tail female), or special tail, i.e. inheritable only by the issue by a certain wife or husband. Since 1926 a tenant in tail in possession has been able to dispose of his interest by will, and both before and after 1926 such a tenant could in his lifetime, and still can, bar the entail by a deed.

"Absolute" denotes that the estate must not be conditional or determinable in any way, in contrast, for example, to life interests (or "mere freeholds"). Life interests, which since 1926 are necessarily equitable, are the smallest freehold, being either for the life of the holder, or for the life of some other person or persons (*"pur autre vie"*). At the death of the person by whose life the duration of the interest is measured, the interest comes to an end, and nothing passes from the holder.

"In possession" is wider than actual physical possession, because it also includes receipt of rents and profits or the right to receive the same: s. 205 (1) (xix) of the Law of Property Act 1925.

THE TERM OF YEARS ABSOLUTE

Out of the freehold of unlimited duration may be carved a lesser or limited period holding, known as a leasehold, or in legal language a chattel real. The person granting a lease is called the lessor (or, more familiarly, the landlord) and the person to whom the lease is granted is called the lessee (or, the tenant). Since 1926 the only legal estate in leaseholds is the term of years absolute. Whilst "absolute" has the same meaning here as in the case of a fee simple, the words "term of years" are further elaborated by s. 205 (1) (xxvii) of the Law of Property Act 1925 as follows:

> "a term of years (taking effect either in possession or in reversion whether or not at a rent) with or without impeachment for waste, subject or not to another legal estate, and either certain or liable to determination by notice, re-entry, operation of law, or by a provision for cesser on redemption, or in any other event (other than the dropping of a life or the determination of a determinable life interest); but does not include any term of years

determinable with life or lives or with the cesser of a determinable life interest, nor, if created after the commencement of the Act, a term of years which is not expressed to take effect in possession within twenty-one years after the creation thereof where required by the Act to take effect within that period; and in this definition the expression 'term of years' includes a term for less than a year, or for a year or years and a fraction of year, or from year to year''.

Thus, the expression is more flexible than it appears at first sight, and covers not only the obvious cases of leases for twenty-one, ninety-nine or 999 years or even longer periods of years, but also the cases of fractions of a year, and tenancies from year to year which are so common in agricultural leases. On the other hand, leases determinable with lives, and leases determinable at the will of the landlord ("tenancy at will") do not come within the definition, and so are equitable interests, not legal estates. A lease may be "in possession", i.e. commencing at or before the date of the lease, or "reversionary", i.e. commencing at a future date, which must take effect in possession within twenty-one years to come within the statutory definition. The "provision for cesser on redemption" refers to the usual feature of the long lease created by a legal mortgage that the lease will come to an end if and when the moneys secured by a mortgage are repaid by the mortgagor: such a lease is a legal estate notwithstanding the uncertainty of its duration.

A freeholder may grant a lease of any duration, retaining the freehold reversion. As s. 1 (5) of the Act permits concurrent legal estates, a leaseholder, unless prohibited by his own lease, can himself grant a sub-lease (also known as an under lease) for any term less than that which he holds, so that there may exist in the same property the legal estate in fee simple with a legal term of years carved out of it and a legal sub-term carved out of that, and so on. The possession granted to the lessee (tenant) must be exclusive, and if a simultaneous right of possession remains in another, or if the intention is that the lessor should remain in substantial control, the lease is no more than a licence: *Cory* v. *Bristow* (1877). Thus, an hotel guest is a licensee.

A lease may be periodic (one that automatically repeats, such as year to year, or week to week), so that when the term is up the lease will be automatically repeated for another term of the same length unless either party gives notice of determination. By s. 5 of the Protection from Evictment Act 1977 this notice must be at least 4 weeks in the case of premises let as a dwelling.

The question of leasehold enfranchisement, that is to say, whether a leaseholder should be given a statutory right compulsorily to buy out his lessor and thereby convert his leasehold into a freehold, was long the subject of debate, which culminated in the passing of the Leasehold Reform Act 1967. This Act gives a leaseholder of a house originally let for twenty-one years or more, who has held it for at least five years, the right to enforce a sale to him of the freehold reversion on payment of the value of the freehold interest in the site, or, alternatively, to ask for a fifty year extension of the lease. The rateable value of the house had to be within certain limits, which are now contained in s. 118 of the Housing Act 1974, viz where the tenancy was created before 18 February 1966: £750 (and £1500 in Greater London); where the tenancy was created after 18 February 1966: £500 (and £1000 in Greater London). Although the Act initiates a decline in the number of leaseholds, this form of property will materially continue because houses in excess of the rateable value limit and flats are not affected by the Act, nor are short-term leases: even those houses within the Act's provisions will not all become freehold, as there are always some people who prefer to lease than to buy outright.

STATUTORY RESTRICTIONS ON THE DEVELOPMENT OF LAND

In the past century enormous inroads have been made on the traditional idea that "the Englishman's home is his castle". Apart from legislation relating to public health, to housing, and to compulsory purchase of property, there are the Town and Country Planning Acts 1971 and 1972 (which have replaced earlier Acts), supplemented by a mass of statutory rules, orders and instruments. The notable Town and Country Planning Act 1947 had a two-fold objective— to control the future planning and development of land, and to cut down the financial enjoyment of land by channelling into the state coffers some of the profit made out of the more gainful use of land, e.g. by using agricultural land for building.

So far as the control element is concerned, any development of land requires the permission of the local planning authority (which, ordinarily, is the county council or the new district council), unless it is a "permitted development" under the Town and Country Planning General Development Order 1977 (S.I. 1977 No. 289). By s. 22 (1) of the Act of 1971: "'Development' means the carrying out of building, engineering, mining and other operations in, on, over or under land or the making of any material change in the use of any buildings or other land". However, the Order of 1977 allows, *inter alia*, minor alterations to dwelling-houses without obtaining planning permission, so that in this way houses may be enlarged or improved or a garage erected so long as the cubic content of the original dwelling-house is not exceeded by more than 50 cubic metres or one-tenth, whichever is the greater, subject to a maximum of 115 cubic metres, and provided the alteration does not raise the height of the building or project beyond its forwardmost part. Similarly, a house owner may erect within his premises a building (other than another dwelling-house or a garage) for any purpose incidental to the enjoyment of his house, provided that the height does not exceed 4 metres in the case of building with a ridged roof, or 3 metres in any other case; examples are a shed or a green-house. He may also erect a tank holding not more than 3500 litres for the storage of oil for domestic heating as long as no part of it is more than 3 metres above the level of the ground. Where planning permission is required for the erection of a new building, the developer often makes an "outline application", supported by a site plan only, and permission may be granted on this basis, though it is customary for planning authorities to attach a condition requiring that detailed plans of the development be submitted within a given period, e.g. three years. In respect of any application, the planning authority must normally deal with it within two months, and grant or refuse permission, or grant it subject to conditions. Machinery exists for appeals from its decision.

The other aim of the Act of 1947—the attempt to cream off to the state by the imposition of a development charge part of the "betterment" or enhanced value of land arising from its development—failed, for the Act's financial provisions proved highly complicated and not very successful, and were repealed by the Town and Country Planning Act 1953. A change in the political shade of the Government brought about a second bite at the "betterment" cherry, this time the complex Land Commission Act 1967, but the Commission's activities were on a very small scale and were ended by the Land Commission (Dissolution) Act 1971. The next attempt was the Community Land Act 1975, which, with the swing back of the political pendulum in the general election of 1979, will no doubt meet the same fate that its predecessor received after the 1970 election.

METHOD OF TRANSFER

For the purposes of transfer of title (and use as security) all land may be classified as (A) Unregistered land; and (B) Registered land.

As deeds bearing the registry stamp of the former East, North or West Riding Registries will be seen in circulation for some years to come, a brief mention to the curious may be made that unregistered land in those now defunct administrative areas was subject to an old system of registration of *deeds*, but this was ended pursuant to the provisions of s. 16 of the Law of Property Act 1969 and the three registries have been completely closed. A similar system operated in the former county of Middlesex before 1937.

A. Unregistered land

(i) *Freehold.*— As land is not transferable by delivery because of its nature, ownership is established and transferred by documentary evidence which varies according to whether the land is unregistered or registered, and to the type of legal estate concerned. Title to unregistered freehold land is evidenced by a collection of deeds and documents known as title deeds, and, as s. 52 (1) of the Law of Property Act 1925 provides that: "All conveyances of land or of any interest therein are void for the purpose of conveying or creating a legal estate unless made by deed", transfer is effected by a deed known as a conveyance. Most transfers of land are the result of a sale, but if made without valuable consideration, they are called "voluntary conveyances" and are voidable if made with intent to defraud creditors.

Contracts for the sale of land may be "open", i.e. those which merely satisfy the requirements of s. 40 of the Law of Property Act 1925 (see Chapter 1, page 3), leaving all other terms to be implied by law; or they may be "formal", i.e. covering all the points in detail, as the vendor usually desires to exclude or modify the terms otherwise implied by law. Under an open contract for the sale of freehold land the purchaser is entitled, by s. 44 (1) of the Law of Property Act 1925 as amended by s. 23 of the Law of Property Act 1969, to have produced to him and to investigate the deeds recording previous transaction in that land for at least fifteen years (prior to the Act of 1969 the period was thirty years), i.e. the vendor must deliver to the purchaser an abstract of title, or epitome of the documents (commencing with a good root of title at least fifteen years old) and facts which constitute the vendor's title. In the case of a formal contract, it is possible for this period to be increased by agreement, or even reduced, but such a shortening throws a risk on the purchaser in that he is not only bound by all legal interests in the land which actually exist whether he discovers them or not, but also by all equitable interests which he would have discovered if he had insisted on an investigation for the statutory period of fifteen years.

When the purchaser is satisfied with the title, he prepares at his own expense a conveyance which is then submitted to the vendor. A conveyance is generally in the following pattern—it opens with a Commencement ("THIS CONVEYANCE") and Date; then come the Parties ("BETWEEN" . . .); the Recitals ("WHEREAS" . . .); the *Testatum* ("NOW THIS DEED WITNESSETH"); the Consideration; the Receipt therefor; the Operative Words ("The Vendor as Beneficial Owner hereby conveys"); the Parcels (i.e. description of the property, often with a plan); Exceptions and Reservations, if any (e.g. mineral rights may not be included); the *Habendum* ("TO HOLD unto the Purchaser in fee simple"); Covenants, Acknowledgments and Undertakings, if required; and finally the *Testimonium* (the sealing clause—"IN WITNESS WHEREOF the Parties hereto have hereunto set their hands and seals the day and year first above written").

At the date fixed for completion the vendor hands over the conveyance duly executed on his part together with the title deeds against payment by the purchaser of the balance of the consideration, the contract having usually provided for the payment of a deposit of ten per cent. by the purchaser when the contract was signed. Normally, completion is effected by the parties' solicitors and the payment is made by means of a bank draft. By this procedure the legal estate in the freehold land is transferred from vendor to purchaser, and the new conveyance is added to the bundle of title deeds, along with any discharged mortgage. Thus, the title deeds increase with each transaction, and the whole process has to be gone through again the next time the property changes hands.

Under the Stamp Act 1891, as amended by various Finance Acts up to that of 1974, the stamp duty on conveyances is £2 per cent., levied in multiples of £1 for each £50 of the consideration, but conveyances where the consideration does not exceed £15,000 and which are certified at that amount are free of stamp duty, and on those where the consideration is between £15,000 and £30,000 and which are similarly certified the rate of duty increases in steps of $\frac{1}{2}$ per cent. for each successive £5,000 until the full rate of £2 per cent. is reached on transfers exceeding £30,000. The necessary certificate is that the transaction does not form part of a larger transaction or a series of transactions in respect of which the amount or value, or the aggregate amount or value of the consideration exceeds the amount at which the instrument is certified.

(ii) *Leasehold*.—Unless prohibited by the terms of his lease, a leaseholder (or lessee) can dispose of his estate by assigning to someone else the whole of the residue or remaining period of his lease. Alternatively, unless prohibited, he can grant a sub-lease (or underlease) to someone else for any term less than that which he himself holds. In practice, leases usually impose a restriction on the lessee's right to assign, sub-let or underlet the premises or any part of them, because although the lessor knows the lessee to whom he granted the lease, he may not want the premises to pass to unknown third parties. This restriction may be absolute; or, more frequently, it may be qualified in that the lessee may not assign, sub-let etc. without the written consent of the lessor. Where the restriction is qualified, by s. 19 (1) of the Landlord and Tenant Act 1927 consent is not to be unreasonably withheld. This means that consent cannot be capriciously withheld, or granted subject to some unreasonable condition, but it can be justifiably withheld because of the character of the assignee or sub-lessee, or the use to which he proposes to put the premises.

By s. 52 (1) of the Law of Property Act 1925 a lease creating a legal estate must be under seal, but s. 52 (2) provides an exception where leases or tenancies are not required by law to be in writing, and s. 54 (2) allows the creation by parol of leases taking effect in possession for a term not exceeding three years at the best rent which can be reasonably obtained. The effect of ss. 52–54 is that every assignment of a lease must be under seal, whether the term exceeds three years or not. Thus, except in the case of an oral lease not exceeding three years, the title to unregistered leasehold property is evidenced by a lease, which may be an agreement under hand or a deed when it is for three years or less, but which must be a deed when it is for more than three years.

The foregoing, however, is subject to the doctrine in *Walsh* v. *Lonsdale* (1882) that an agreement for a lease may be as efficacious as a lease, for where a tenant holds under an agreement for a lease of which equity will decree specific performance he is deemed to occupy the same position *vis-à-vis* the landlord as he would occupy if a formal lease under seal had been executed. Thus, by the operation of the doctrine, a written (not sealed) lease for more than three years will confer an equitable term on the tenant, provided there is a sufficient memorandum in writing to satisfy the Law of Property Act 1925. Similarly, a verbal lease for more than three years will confer an equitable term on the tenant if there is a sufficient act of part performance by him, e.g. entry into possession of a house, or spending money in decorating it; in the absence of such an act, the contract is unenforceable but the verbal lease will create a yearly tenancy where the tenant is already in possession and pays rent on a yearly basis.

A lease under seal is generally in the following pattern—it opens with a Commencement ("THIS LEASE") and Date; then come the Parties; the *Testatum*; the Demise ("The Lessor doth thereby demise unto the Lessee"); the Parcels (description etc.); the *Habendum* ("To HOLD the premises unto the Lessee for a term of . . . years from the date hereof"); the *Redendum* ("YIELDING AND PAYING therefor the yearly rent of £ . . . . clear of all deductions on . . . ."); Lessee's Covenants (he usually covenants to pay the rent, rates, taxes etc., to keep the premises insured against fire, and in a good state of repair; not to carry on certain trades, and not to assign, sub-let etc. without the lessor's consent); Proviso for Re-entry (i.e. if the lessee breaks any of his covenants, the lessor may re-enter the premises and the lease is ended); Lessor's Covenants (for quiet enjoyment of the premises by the lessee, and often to keep the external parts of the premises in repair); and finally the *Testimonium* (the sealing clause).

A sub-lease follows a similar layout, with the addition of a Recital of the head lease out of which the further lease is being carved. An Assignment is also similar, with the variations of a Recital of the lease which is being assigned, and of a Covenant whereby the purchaser covenants with the vendor that he and his successors in title will observe the lessee's covenants contained in the lease being assigned. As both a sub-lease and an assignment often arise on sale, they may also contain a clause stating a lump sum consideration, together with a receipt therefor by the vendor.

Under an open contract for the grant or sale of leases and sub-leases, by s. 44 (2) of the Law of Property Act 1925 (as amended), an intending lessee cannot demand any proof whatsoever of the freehold title; while an intending sub-lessee, sub-sub-lessee etc. can call for his immediate landlord's title and nothing more, i.e. the production of the lease, or sub-lease etc. under which his immediate landlord is himself the tenant and for the dealings with such lease, or sub-lease etc. for at least 15 years if it is so old.

Under an open contract to assign an existing lease or sub-lease, the assignee is entitled to production of the actual lease or sub-lease being assigned, however old it may be, and to see the title under which it has been held for at least 15 years if it is so old, otherwise since its commencement. But he cannot demand any proof of the freehold reversion or any leasehold reversion: s. 44 (2), (3).

In the case of a formal contract it is possible to increase, or even reduce these requirements by agreement.

At the date fixed for completion, the lessor (or his solicitors) will hand over the lease duly completed by him to the lessee (or his solicitors), and usually receives a counterpart of the lease completed by the lessee, so that he can place it with his title deeds. A similar course is followed in the case of a sub-lease. When the sale is by way of assignment, the vendor will hand over to the purchaser the duly completed assignment, together with any other relevant deeds and documents, e.g. the consent of the original lessor to the assignment. Whenever there is a lump sum consideration (as distinct from rent) then at completion there will be payment by the purchaser of that consideration, or the balance thereof. Stamp duty on leases is a complicated topic, but, in brief, a lease must generally be stamped *ad valorem* on the rent and any other consideration or premium.

B.   Registered land

This is land the title to which has been officially examined and the holding, which must be a legal estate, then registered at the Land Registry under a title number. The registered proprietor is given a land certificate, which is equivalent to the title deeds of unregistered land in so far as it is his evidence of ownership, and better than them in so far as it is state-guaranteed title. Subsequent transfers of registered land are effected by the execution of a short and simple form of transfer, in place of the cumbersome conveyancing procedure with title deeds. This system of registered conveyancing, or registration of title, must be distinguished from the registration of charges, which relates only to unregistered land and will be discussed later.

Land registration was first introduced by the Land Transfer Acts 1875 and 1897, and is now governed by the Land Registration Act 1925, as amended in 1936, 1966 and 1971, and the Rules made thereunder. It is compulsory in certain areas of England, and voluntary in the rest of England and Wales. The compulsory areas were for a long time comparatively small but during the last two decades they have been considerably extended, and various District Land Registries have been established in the provinces, under the administrative supervision of the principal Land Registry, Lincoln's Inn Fields, London, WC2A 3PH. The Land Registration (District Registries) Order 1979 (S.I. 1979 No. 1019) sets out the areas of the country allotted to the various District Land Registries. The aim of covering all built-up areas by the mid-1970s has been very largely achieved, and the actual areas of compulsory registration as from 1 February 1978 are set out in the Registration of Title Order 1977 (S.I. 1977 No. 828).

Because of the rapid increase in the compulsory areas and the consequent volume of work at the Registries, the Land Registration Act 1966 provides that voluntary registration can now only be effected where the Registrar permits, and he may require the applicant to show there are special reasons making it expedient to grant the application. Special considerations justifying registration would be some cases of lost title deeds and the creation of a new town, or other large building development.

The Land Registration and Land Charges Act 1971 confers rule-making powers on the Lord Chancellor for enabling transactions in small "souvenir" plots of land to be made legally effective without registration of title where registrations would ordinarily be required, and this was done by S.I. 1972 No. 985.

Even in a compulsory area, certain land may remain unregistered for some time, since by s. 123 of the Land Registration Act 1925 registration is made compulsory only:

(a) On a sale of freeholds, when the title must be registered within two months of a sale.

(b) On a grant of a lease for a term of forty years or more, when the leasehold title must be registered within two months of the grant of the lease.

(c) On a sale of an existing lease, when the title must be registered within two months of the assignment, if at the time of the assignment the lease has forty or more years unexpired.

In the foregoing cases, failure to register within the two months (or within such longer time as the Registrar or the Court permits) will make the transaction void as regards passing the legal estate, and it will operate to give to the grantee a minor interest only.

It should be noted that by s. 8 of the Act certain leaseholds cannot be registered. These are:

(i) Leaseholds held under a lease with twenty-one years or less unexpired.

(ii) Leaseholds held under a lease containing an absolute prohibition against assignments *inter vivos*.

(iii) Leaseholds held under a lease created for mortgage purposes so long as there is a subsisting right of redemption.

If a lease has more than twenty-one years but less than forty years unexpired, the leasehold may be registered whether in a compulsory area or not, but registration is not compulsory except where the lessor's title is registered.

De-registration of Registered Land

Once land in a compulsory area has been brought within the registered land system, it cannot be "unscrambled" and necessarily continues on the Register. If, however, the land is situated in a non-compulsory area and has been voluntarily registered, then the registered proprietor may, with the consent of other interested parties (if any), get the land de-registered by surrendering the land certificate, and charge certificate (if any): s. 81 (1) of the Land Registration Act 1925.

The Register consists of three parts, which, with certain small exceptions, are strictly private, and inspection or searching requires the written authority of the registered proprietor of the land or a charge, or that of his solicitors. These parts are:

(a) *The Property Register.*— This contains the description of the land and estate comprised in the title, with a reference to the general map kept at the Registry, or to the filed plan of the land and such notes as have to be entered, e.g. the ownership of mines and minerals.

(b) *The Proprietorship Register.*— This gives (a) the class of title (Absolute, Possessory, Qualified or Good Leasehold); (b) the name, address and description of the registered proprietor; and (c) any cautions, inhibitions and restrictions affecting his right of disposing thereof, entered, for example, because of bankruptcy proceedings.

(c) *The Charges Register.*— This contains mortgages, charges, leases and other incumbrances affecting the land. There are, however, two varieties of interests which do not appear in this part of the register, and these are "minor interests" and "overriding interests".

Minor interests, as defined in s. 3 of the Land Registration Act 1925, are a miscellaneous collection of interests in registered land comprising all interests other than estates capable of subsisting as legal estates in respect of which a proprietor can be registered and overriding interests. Thus, minor interests consist of equitable interests which, though capable of registration, are not registered or protected, and equitable interests arising under a trust for sale or settlement. An agreement giving first refusal to purchase land does not constitute a minor interest (or indeed any interest in land): *Murray* v. *Two Strokes* (1973). However, this case was not followed in another first instance case, *Pritchard* v. *Briggs* (1978), where it was held that an interest in land was created by a mere right of pre-emption (i.e. a right of "first refusal"), so the effect of such a right is uncertain pending clarification by a higher court.

Minor interests are overriden by a subsequent registered disposition for value, unless protected by an entry on the register. Some minor interests may be entered in the Minor Interests Index, but this does not form part of the register itself, and persons dealing with the land are not concerned with this index, which regulates the priority of assignees of such interests.

Overriding interests are certain rights which are always binding on any person who acquires any interest in registered land, even though there is no reference whatever to them in any part of the register. These interests can be ascertained by enquiry of the occupier. A full list of overriding interests is given in s. 70 of the Land Registration Act 1925, but the most common ones are leases not exceeding twenty-one years, profits *à prendre*, and legal easements. The necessity for a purchaser or mortgagee to enquire as to rights of occupation is shown by *Hodgson* v. *Marks* (1971), where the plaintiff, whilst still in occupation, transferred her house into the name of her lodger, E, to prevent her nephew turning E out of the house. E subsequently sold the house to the defendant who mortgaged it to a building society. The Court of Appeal held that even where a vendor was or appeared to be in occupation another person might in certain circumstances be in "actual occupation" within s. 70 (1) (g) of the Land Registration Act 1925, so that a purchaser must pay heed to anyone occupying the premises; the plaintiff was in actual physical occupation of the house to which she was entitled in equity, for the resulting trust to her was excepted by s. 53 (2) of the Law of Property Act 1925 from the general requirement of writing under s. 53 (1), and E could not transfer the house free from her overriding interest. This point is re-emphasised by the creation of a new equity in *Williams and Glyn's Bank Ltd.* v. *Boland* (1979) where a husband and wife bought a house with their joint earnings, but the house was conveyed to the husband alone, and he mortgaged it to the bank under a registered charge without telling his wife. The bank made no enquiry as to whether the wife had any interest in the property and, when the husband was unable to pay, sought possession. The Court of Appeal rescinded the order for possession on the ground that since the wife was physically present and living in the matrimonial home she was in actual possession of it and therefore her equitable rights in it were an overriding interest within s. 70 (1) (g) which entitled her to remain in possession as against the Bank. The Court saw no reason why this new equity should not exist in unregistered land as well, so long as it came to the knowledge of the mortgagee or would have come to his knowledge if such enquiries and inspections had been made as ought reasonably to have been made, and stressed that anyone who lends money on the security of a matrimonial house nowadays ought to realise that the wife may have a share in it and ought to make sure that the wife agrees to the transaction or go to the house and make enquiries of her. Whether the House of Lords will uphold this protection of a wife's share remains to be seen.

The relevant entries are those on the register at the time of the purchase: *Freer* v. *Unwins, Ltd.* (1976), where it was held that the defendant, an assignee of a lessor, was not bound by a restrictive covenant which had been omitted from the register when the freehold was registered and the register was subsequently rectified under s. 82 of the Land Registration Act 1925.

The decision of the House of Lords in *National Provincial Bank Ltd.* v. *Ainsworth* (1965) has been largely reversed by the Matrimonial Homes Act 1967. Section 1 of this Act gives a statutory right of occupation to the spouse other than the one entitled by virtue of any estate or interest or contract or enactment to occupy the matrimonial home; thus, if the house is held by the husband in his sole name, his wife cannot be evicted or excluded by him except with the leave of the Court, nor can a husband where the house is held by his wife. During the continuance of the marriage this statutory right of occupation is stated by s. 2 to be an equitable charge on the estate or interest of the other spouse, and any order made under s. 1 will also take effect against persons deriving title under the other spouse (e.g. purchasers and mortgagees) who are affected by the charge. This will occur where before the purchase or mortgage takes place the charge has been registered, in the case of unregistered land as a land charge in an additional category designated Class F, and in the case of registered land by lodging a notice or caution, the Act providing that a spouse's rights of occupation shall not be an overriding interest within the meaning of the Land Registration Act 1925.

In practice, if such a charge is already registered at the time a mortgage is sought, the mortgagee will doubtless insist on its withdrawal as a condition precedent to granting the mortgage, or take a written postponement of priority from the spouse entitled to the charge.

In *Tarr* v. *Tarr* (1973) the House of Lords held that it had no jurisdiction under the Act to order the husband (the tenant of a council house) to vacate the house, since the power of "regulating the exercise" of the right to occupy conferred on the Court by s. 1 (2) did not include the power to prohibit a spouse from exercising those rights altogether.

A non-occupying spouse is given by s. 1 (1) (b) a right with the leave of the Court to enter into and occupy the dwelling-house. In *Watts* v. *Waller* (1973), where the wife, who had left the husband, saw a "sold" notice on the house and registered a charge under s. 2 before she applied for leave of the Court to enter and occupy, the Court of Appeal upheld the wife's registration on the ground that the right given by the Act to a non-occupying spouse was a continuous right of occupation, dependent on the Court granting leave, rather than a right which throughout the matrimonial history could repeatedly arise and be extinguished, for then the non-occupying spouse would be deprived of protection when he or she most needed it.

A mortgagee, if proceeding against the mortgagor, does not have to join the registering spouse as a defendant in the action because that spouse is not by virtue of the interest under s. 1 (5) of the Act in any better position than the mortgagor who could not resist an order for possession except by redeeming the mortgage, and on the facts there was no evidence of the spouse's ability to do this: *Hastings and Thanet Building Society* v. *Goddard* (1970).

TITLES AVAILABLE

On registration one of four types of land certificate may be issued:

(a) *A certificate of Absolute Title.*—This gives the registered proprietor an absolute right to the property, a state-guaranteed title, subject only to the incumbrances and other entries (if any) appearing on the register; to overriding interests (if any); and to minor interests of which he has notice. Freeholds may be registered with this title, and also leaseholds where the freehold out of which the lease is carved is itself registered with absolute title.

(b) *A certificate of Possessory Title.*—This is granted where the title has not been investigated thoroughly but the proprietor has produced *prima facie* evidence of his title. Here, the State gives no guarantee as regards any matters adverse to the title and capable of arising at the time of first registration. Although the proprietor does not immediately get an indefeasible right against all the world after fifteen years a freeholder may obtain a certificate of absolute title, and after ten years a leaseholder may obtain a certificate of good leasehold title.

(c) *A certificate of Qualified Title.*—This is granted where title can be established only for a limited period, or subject to certain reservations. Qualified title is very rare, because it cannot be applied for, the application in the first instance being for absolute or good leasehold title.

(d) *A certificate of Good Leasehold Title.*—Whereas the three previous titles are applicable to freehold and leasehold land, this title applies only to leaseholds. It is evidence that the leaseholder's title is good (the equivalent of the usual title deeds in perfect order of an unregistered leasehold), but it does not guarantee the title of the freehold. After ten years in which the proprietor or successive proprietors have been in possession an absolute title may be granted.

Thus, the aim of the Act of 1925 has been to enable the Registrar to grant Absolute and Good Leasehold Titles whenever possible, and to facilitate the conversion of the other, lesser titles into these two titles, because it is only in respect of these two titles that the full benefit of the system of land registration is obtained.

The objects of the land registration system are: (i) to facilitate and cheapen the investigation of title (an involved and oft-repeated process in unregistered land); (ii) to facilitate dealings in land subject to equities; (iii) to simplify and cheapen the transfer of land (by assimilating it as far as practicable to the transfer of shares in a company) and also charges or mortgages on land; and (iv) provide a state-guaranteed title, backed by a fund from which persons injured by such matters as errors or omissions in the register may, with certain exceptions, be indemnified.

Thus, on a sale of registered land, whether freehold or leasehold, the purchaser or his solicitor easily ascertains the title of the vendor by getting from him a letter of authority to search the Register, and doing so. At completion, the vendor or his solicitor hands over against the appropriate payment the land certificate plus the requisite instrument of transfer in the form prescribed by the Land Registration Rules 1925. This instrument states the title number and description of the land, the date, the consideration (with receipt clause) and that "the transferor as beneficial owner hereby transfers" to the transferee the land comprised in the title or title referred to (or part of a title with plan annexed etc.). It is executed as a deed in the presence of an attesting witness, impressed with the usual *ad valorem* stamp duty where applicable, and is then lodged at the District Land Registry appropriate to the area, with the land registry fee (the scales of which are set out below). By s. 64 the application must be accompanied by the land certificate, unless that is already deposited in the Registry— which may be the case where a title covering a large piece of land is being split up into various new titles. The Registrar retains the instrument of transfer, completes the transaction by entering in the Register the name of the transferee as proprietor of the land transferred, in place of the previous proprietor, officially indorses the land certificate to show the change of ownership, and then returns the amended certificate to the party lodging it.

As regards leaseholds, the foregoing applies where there is a transfer on assignment of the whole of the residue of a term granted by a registered lease. If the purchaser takes not an assignment but a sub-lease or underlease, then if that lease is registrable, he will have to submit such original deeds and documents as he has to the Registry for the granting of a new title. Different title numbers will exist as to the freehold and leasehold estates in the same land, but the leasehold title may at some time come to an end, as when it expires, or the leaseholder acquires the freehold reversion and merges his title with the freehold title.

Finally, it may be noted that an unregistered disposition of registered land is not wholly inoperative, for s. 101 provides that registered land may be dealt with by an unregistered assurance, just as if it were unregistered land, but such assurance will not be effective to transfer a legal estate, but will confer upon the grantee a minor interest only. As already mentioned, minor interests of any kind will be overriden by a subsequent registered transfer for value, but may be protected by notice, caution or inhibition in accordance with the provisions of the Land Registration Act 1925.

Land Registry fees

These fees are calculated on a sliding scale basis according to the value of the land, or the amount of the charge or mortgage. They are now prescribed by the Land Registration Fee Order 1976 (S.I. 1976 No. 1333). The current scale of fees for a transfer on sale, or for registration of a charge (Scale No. 4) is:—

Value of land or amount of charge	*Fee*
Not exceeding £20,000	£2.50 for every £1,000 or part of £1,000.
Exceeding £20,000, but not exceeding £100,000	£50 for the first £20,000 and £2.40 for every £1,000 or part of £1,000 over £20,000.
Exceeding £100,000	£242 for the first £100,000 and £0.50 for every £1,000 or part of £1,000 over £100,000 with a maximum fee of £567.

Where a charge by the transferee under a transfer for value is delivered with the application to register the transfer, the fee on the charge is waived.

Because of the abolition by the Finance Act 1971 of *ad valorem* stamp duty on mortgages and charges, it is now provided that a charge securing unlimited further advances is to be treated as a charge to secure an amount equal to the value of the registered land comprised in the charge, after deducting the amount secured on it by any prior registered charge.

Fees on the first registration of land

Where land is being initially placed on the register, a lower scale (Scale No. 1) applies:—

Value	Fee
Not exceeding £10,000	£1.70 for every £1,000 or part of £1,000.
Exceeding £10,000 but not exceeding £100,000	£17 for the first £10,000 and £1.50 for every £1,000 or part of £1,000 over £10,000.
Exceeding £100,000	£152 for the first £100,000 and £0.25 for every £1,000 or part of £1,000 over £100,000 with a maximum fee of £314.50.

Where, on an application for first registration, a charge by the applicant, or by a predecessor in title of the applicant, is delivered either with the application or before it is completed, no fee is payable in respect of the charge.

LAND AS SECURITY

Because of its indestructibility land is the basic form of wealth and for much of history has been the principal source of wealth. Just as ordinary shares have long been used as a "hedge" against inflation or the continuing erosion of the purchasing power of money, so land may be used in the same way. A person who invested £1,000 in a reasonably well-built freehold or long leasehold house 30 years ago is in a much superior financial position to one who invested the same sum in $3\frac{1}{2}$ per cent. War Stock, and is better off than one who kept it in a bank or building society. Subject only to intermittent set-backs due to "credit-squeezes", land and buildings have been steadily moving up in price since the Second World War ended, so that they are normally a sound and reliable security, provided the buildings are adequately insured. Whilst banks do not generally lend long-term for house purchases (though some banks will so lend for very large mortgages)—long-term lending being the function of building societies —banks frequently take land as security, either for short-term advances, e.g. to enable a person to buy a property before he sells his own property (a "bridging" loan), or as part of general security given by a company, firm or person. It may be lodged in support of a guarantee, or charged for specific projects, such as building schemes, or the conversion of big houses into flats, or property development in general. The actual way in which land is taken as security for bank advances depends on whether the bank's mortgage is a legal or an equitable one, and whether the land is unregistered or registered. The following broad principles apply to either type of land (the differences being elaborated later):

Legal Mortgage

By s. 85 of the Law of Property Act 1925 a legal mortgage is now effected in one of two ways:

1. By a lease of land for a term of years, subject to a proviso for cesser of the term on redemption, i.e. on repayment of the loan the lease will be extinguished. A term of 3,000 years is suggested by the Act; one bank, at least, uses a term of 4,000 years. Where the mortgagor has not a freehold but a leasehold estate, then there must be a sub-lease for a term less by one or more days (usually ten days, to allow for subsequent mortgages which will each be one day longer than the previous one) than the unexpired period of the lease; or

2. A charge by deed expressed to be by way of legal mortgage. The effect of this is to give the mortgagee the same protection and remedies as if a lease, as in (1), for 3,000 years had been created in his favour: s. 87. This type of legal mortgage has the advantage that it can be used for both freeholds and leaseholds. As regards leaseholds, it is not a breach of covenant by a leaseholder who cannot sub-let etc. without the landlord's consent if he gives such a charge without consent, whereas consent would be required for a mortgage by sub-lease.

Equitable Mortgage

Unlike a legal mortgage, an equitable mortgage does not convey a legal estate to the mortgagee, but it is a charge in favour of a person applicable to both freeholds and leaseholds and created in any of the following ways:—

(a) *An agreement to create a legal mortgage.*— An agreement by A to grant a legal mortgage to B in consideration of money advanced is an equitable mortgage, and if A defaults on his promise, B can bring an action for specific performance to compel A to execute such a legal mortgage.

(b) *Deposit of title deeds (or land certificate).*—This is the way equitable mortgages most frequently arise. A mere deposit of title deeds, or land certificate in the case of registered land, is sufficient, but though there need not be a written agreement, in practice, to put the transaction beyond argument, the mortgagee usually takes a memorandum of deposit from the mortgagor under hand (or sometimes, under seal) contemporaneously with the actual deposit in which the mortgagor undertakes to execute a legal mortgage as and when called upon to do so.

(c) *Equitable charge.*—This is created by any written memorandum, however, informal, by which a person agrees that his property shall be a security for money advanced. Such a charge is termed a General Equitable Charge.

A covenant by a leaseholder not to sub-let etc. without consent is not broken by an equitable mortgage accompanied by a deposit of the title deeds or land certificate.

It may be mentioned here that if a judgment creditor finds that his debtor has land or an interest in land he may obtain a charging order on that land or interest in land by an application to the Court under s. 35 of the Administration of Justice Act 1956 and such an order when obtained has the same effect as an equitable charge created by the debtor under hand. Where joint tenants of a house holding on trust for sale and jointly entitled to the beneficial interest in the house are jointly liable on a judgment debt, a charging order will be made on their legal interest in the house: *National Westminster Bank Ltd.* v. *Allen* (1971).

The Mortgagor's Equity of Redemption

So long as a mortgage remains outstanding the mortgagor has a right to redeem his property by paying off the principal, interest and costs, notwithstanding that any contractual date to redeem stated in the mortgage itself (often six months after the date of the mortgage) has passed, and this right is known as the equity of redemption. It was developed by equity, which has always insisted that a mortgage is no more than a form of security, and is not a right personal to the mortgagor, but may be conveyed, devised or entailed, and will pass on death with the rest of his property. It can be extinguished only in four ways: (1) when released by the mortgagor; (2) by lapse of time, when the mortgagee has been in possession of the land for twelve years: s. 12 of the Limitation Act 1939; (3) when the land is sold by the mortgagee under his statutory power of sale; or (4) when the mortgagee obtains a decree of foreclosure which is made absolute.

This equity of redemption is inviolable, and can only be "clogged", i.e. fettered or restricted, to the limited extent that it may be postponed by agreement for a reasonable time if it is mutual, as where the mortgagee may not call in his money during that period. But any provision postponing the contractual right to redeem unduly, so that redemption becomes illusory or the provision becomes oppressive, will be void as a "clog on the equity of redemption", a facet of law sometimes expressed as "Once a mortgage, always a mortgage". Whether or not the Court will uphold a particular postponement on the right to redeem depends on the facts, but the tendency is not lightly to interfere with transactions entered into at arm's length by commercial men. Thus, in *Knightsbridge Estates Trust, Ltd.* v. *Byrne* (1939) the company mortgaged a large block of property to the Royal Liver Friendly Society (whose trustees were Byrne and others) for £310,000 at $5\frac{1}{4}$ per cent. and at the suggestion of the mortgagor it was agreed that the loan be repaid by half-yearly instalments spread over forty years. When the mortgagor sought to repay the advance after a few years, the Court of Appeal upheld the restriction as being reasonable for a long-term investment of that size in the absence of any oppression; this decision was affirmed by the House of Lords on an entirely different ground, namely, that the mortgage was a debenture issued by a company, and as, under the Companies Act 1929, debentures could be perpetual, the doctrine of clogging the equity did not apply. (The point about debentures being perpetual is now carried by s. 89 of the Companies Act 1948).

BANK FORMS OF MORTGAGE

With legal mortgages, some banks prefer the first method offered by s. 85 of the Law of Property Act 1925 (see p. 222); others the second way. Some banks have separate forms for both unregistered and registered land, whereas one bank at least has a dual-purpose type with sufficient blanks for completion so that it can easily serve equally for either type of land. All forms are necessarily by deed.

The forms contain the usual undertaking to pay and discharge to the bank on demand all moneys and liabilities now or at any time hereafter due and owing to the bank on any account whatsoever, including interest, commission, etc., and any expenses incurred by the bank in taking or enforcing the security (making it a continuing security). The bank's power of sale in default of repayment of the advance will normally be exercisable at a much shorter period than the three months prescribed by s. 103 of the Law of Property Act 1925.

This also applies to the bank's power to appoint a receiver which, by s. 109, is exercisable after three months (though some bank forms omit any reference to receivers). The mortgagor will covenant, *inter alia*, to keep the property in good repair, insured against fire in such insurance office and for such amount as the bank shall require, and in the case of a leasehold to observe all the terms and conditions of the lease. The bank, as mortgagee, will sometimes take power to consolidate by excluding s. 93 of the Act of 1925 (though this power is of little practical value where the charge is an "all moneys" security). Consolidation occurs when several mortgages are made by the same person to the same mortgagee and is the name given to the option of the mortgagee to refuse to redeem one mortgage until all the mortgages are redeemed, thus preventing a valuable mortgage being redeemed whilst unsatisfactory ones are left. The mortgagor will also contract out of his power under s. 99 to grant leases and that under s. 100 to accept surrender of leases.

Where the land is held by two or more persons (known as joint tenants) all must join in the charge. If a mortgage is taken from one of several joint owners, then it is ineffective as a mortgage of the legal estate and in *Cedar Holdings, Ltd.* v. *Green* (1979), where a mortgage on the matrimonial home had been executed by the husband and a person impersonating his wife (the property being vested in husband and wife) the Court of Appeal held that it did not even amount to an effective charge over the equitable interest of the husband in the proceeds of sale.

Sometimes variations of the general form are used in special circumstances, such as agricultural land or licensed property. Thus, in the first example the mortgagor will undertake to make good, upon request by the bank, any defects etc., through inadequate cultivation or management; he cannot, however, exclude or abridge his leasing powers under s. 99 of the Act of 1925 because the Agricultural Holdings Act 1948, Schedule 7, para. 2 provides that such contracting out shall not have effect in a mortgage of agricultural land; but if a lease is made and then avoided by the mortgagee as a fraudulent conveyance, it does not give to the tenant any rights to relief under s. 66 of the 1948 Act: *Lloyds Bank Ltd.* v. *Marcan* (1973). In the second, the mortgagee will assign to the bank all trade and other fixtures and the goodwill, with full benefit of licences present and future, and in addition to its usual rights and remedies the bank will be empowered to appoint a manager for the business.

For equitable mortgages, banks have a more or less standard form of Memorandum of Deposit, signed under hand, which is taken in order to avoid disputes over the transaction. Its contents will make the deposit a continuing security, provide an undertaking by the mortgagor to execute a legal mortgage over the property when so requested by the bank, and cover the points of insurance, consolidation, contracting out of the statutory powers to grant leases, etc. Sometimes, particularly in the case of merchant banks, a Memorandum of Deposit under seal is used, which contains an irrevocable power of attorney or a declaration of trust, and power to appoint a receiver.

Both a legal mortgage and a memorandum of deposit may be worded to cover a fixed amount, e.g., "the total amount recoverable hereunder shall not exceed £3,000 in addition to interest, etc.", and if advances beyond that sum are made, another mortgage or memorandum must be taken. Numerous banks use the other alternative, unlimited forms. Legal and equitable mortgages or charges are now free of stamp duty, the former *ad valorem* duty on them, originally imposed under Schedule 1 of the Stamp Act 1891, having been abolished by the Finance Act 1971, and this has meant that banks now tend to insist on a legal mortgage.

SECOND MORTGAGES

As it is possible to have any number of mortgages, whether legal or equitable, in the same land, banks sometimes take second mortgages as security. They are not generally looked upon with great favour, because the second mortgagee is very much in the hands of the first mortgagee, who may sell the property without considering the interests of any later mortgagees. Such a sale extinguishes any subsequent incumbrances: s. 104 (2); though these later mortgagees are entitled to the surplus proceeds of sale, if any, up to the amount of their security. Nevertheless, banks will certainly take second mortgages where, as is often the case nowadays due to rising property prices, there is a reasonable equity, e.g. a house mortgaged to a building society where its current value is well in excess of the outstanding mortgage or sometimes as support for a shaky advance, even though the equity may be dubious. In the last resort, however, the second mortgagee may have to pay off the first mortgagee in order to obtain control over the security.

A second legal mortgage of freehold property may be granted by way of a lease for a term longer by one day than the term vested in the first mortgagee, or by a charge by way of legal mortgage. In the case of leasehold property the second legal mortgage will be a sub-lease for a term longer by one day than that granted to the first mortgagee, or a charge by way of legal mortgage. In the absence of the title deeds or land certificate a second equitable mortgage is effected by a general equitable charge, or by an agreement to create a legal mortgage. As the first mortgagee normally holds the title deeds or land certificate, the second mortgagee must protect himself by registering his mortgage as a land charge in the case of unregistered land (as a puisne mortgage, if legal; as a general equitable charge, if equitable), unless it is a floating charge by a company, when registration with the Registrar of Companies will suffice. In the case of registered land, a second mortgage, if legal, may be registered or alternatively protected by lodging a caution; if equitable, it cannot be registered but may be protected by a caution.

As soon as he takes his charge a second mortgagee should give direct notice to the first mortgagee, requesting an acknowledgment of the notice, together with a statement of the amount then outstanding under the first mortgage and whether the first mortgagee is under any obligation to make further advances. This last point arises because of the procedure known as "tacking" available under s. 94 of the Law of Property Act 1925 in certain circumstances. Thus, if the first mortgagee (or any other mortgagee) is under an obligation to make further advances, he is entitled to "tack" these further advances on to his original mortgage and so squeeze out a second (or subsequent) mortgagee by claiming priority for all his advances over him.

This obligation must be a term of the mortgage; the mere fact that the mortgage is expressed to be a continuing security for further or future advances (as bank mortgages invariably are) does not constitute an obligation to make such advances. If the first mortgagee is not under such an obligation, tacking is not available to him, except with the consent of a subsequent mortgagee (which may be given in a letter or deed of postponement) or if he has no notice of the subsequent mortgage at the time he makes the further advance. Tacking cannot be used in the reverse direction, i.e. a third mortgagee cannot by taking a transfer of the first mortgage add his own advances on to the first mortgage.

If a bank's customer, who has given a first mortgage to the bank, later gives a second mortgage elsewhere, then the bank on receiving notice of this second mortgage must, if lending on current account, immediately break the account to prevent the operation of the Rule in *Clayton's Case* (1816) to the bank's detriment. All transactions will thereafter go through a new account, which should be kept in credit, for any overdraft on it cannot be charged against the security in priority to the second mortgage. Failure to break a current account will mean that credits subsequently paid in will reduce and may ultimately extinguish the amount secured by the mortgage (which has been determined as a continuing security by the receipt of the notice) and any payments out will be a fresh advance which will rank after the second mortgagee's claim. This situation actually occurred in *Deeley* v. *Lloyds Bank Ltd.* (1912), so that when the bank eventually sold the property, which realised just enough to repay the bank's advance, Deeley as second mortgagee successfully claimed the proceeds of sale.

Section 2 (8) of the Matrimonial Homes Act 1967 provides that if, after the creation of a mortgage by the other spouse on his or her estate or interest in the matrimonial home, a spouse's rights of occupation are registered as a Class F land charge, that charge shall, for the purposes of s. 94 of the Law of Property Act 1925 be deemed to be a mortgage subsequent in date to the first-mentioned mortgage. Thus, if a bank as mortgagee receives notice of such a charge, it must treat it as notice of a second mortgage and act accordingly.

SEARCHES

Searches and the next topic, the protecting of mortgages, require different action according to the type of land concerned. When taking land as security, banks have to make various searches to be sure that their title as mortgagee is clear. These searches may be personal, i.e. undertaken by a member of the bank's staff, or possibly its solicitors or some organisation specialising in searches, or they may be official, i.e. by applying to the appropriate Registry, which will do the search and issue an official certificate. The method usually adopted is to make official searches, for the responsibility for any error does not rest with the bank, and generally speaking personal searches are uneconomic in the sense that time is money, though they are useful in urgent cases or when really detailed information is required. The searches to be made may be analysed as follows:

A.   Unregistered land

1.   *The Land Charges Register* (now kept at the Land Charges Department, Burrington Way, Plymouth, PL5 3LP).

This contains the six classes, A, B, C, D, E, and F, of land charges required to be registered under the Land Charges Act 1972, which replaced some earlier provisions in the 1925 Act as amended by the Matrimonial Homes Act 1967. By s. 198 of the Law of Property Act 1925 registration is notice to the whole world but as regards a contract of sale or other disposition of land this has now been amended by s. 24

of the Law of Property Act 1969 which provides that a purchaser under such a contract or disposition is affected only by actual knowledge of any such charge. An unregistered charge is void against a purchaser for value, and for this purpose "purchaser" includes a mortgagee.

The most important charges registrable comprise Class C—(i) puisne mortgages, i.e. legal mortgages not protected by a deposit of title deeds; (ii) limited owner's charges, i.e. equitable charges on settled property conferred by statute on a tenant for life of such property who has discharged some liability out of income which should have been discharged out of capital; (iii) general equitable charges, which include equitable mortgages not protected by a deposit of title deeds; and (iv) estate contracts, i.e. contracts to convey or create a legal estate, including an option to purchase or a right of pre-emption. Examples are: contracts for the sale of land, or to grant or assign a lease, and in *First National Securities, Ltd.* v. *Chiltern District Council* (1975) it was held that a sale of a house by a local authority under the Housing Act 1957 with a condition that the purchaser or his successor in title shall first offer to resell the house to the local authority came within this category. Class D charges consist of: (i) death duty charges; (ii) restrictive covenants; and (iii) equitable erasements. Class F consists of any charge affecting any land by virtue of the Matrimonial Homes Act 1967 i.e. where a spouse's rights of occupation are a charge on an estate of interest in a dwelling house held by the other spouse. The other classes are of little significance, but it may be noted that besides the land charges register there are four other registers: (1) the Register of Pending Actions, which includes petitions in bankruptcy; (2) the Register of Writs and Orders Affecting Land, which includes receiving orders in bankruptcy; (3) the Register of Deeds of Arrangement; and (4) the Register of Annuities. Within the provisions of the Act of 1972 the Court has discretionary power to vacate registration as regards pending actions.

In *Whittingham* v. *Whittingham (National Westminster Bank Ltd. Intervening)* (1978) the husband was the owner of a house which was not the matrimonial home. After a divorce in 1971 the wife applied in divorce proceedings under s. 24 of the Matrimonial Causes Act 1973 for a transfer of property order in respect of this house in which she and the children were living, but did not register the application as a pending land action. In 1974 the husband executed a legal charge over the house in favour of the bank. The trial judge held that as the wife's application was not registered pursuant to ss. 5 and 17 of the Land Charges Act 1972 it was not binding on the bank; and subsequently the Court of Appeal dismissed the wife's appeal.

The Land Charges Rules 1974 (S.I. 1974 No. 1286) prescribe the procedure and forms for registration and searches in the Land Charges Department taking account of the new facilities associated with computerisation of the index. The Land Charges Fees Order 1975 (S.I. 1975 No. 1315) similarly deals with the fees aspect, including credit accounts maintained at the Registry to which fees may be debited as required. For these searches no authority is required from the owner of the land, and the search is against the proprietor and not against the property. An official search is made on Form K15 and a certificate of search will be issued on Form K17 (no subsisting entries) or on Form K18 (details of the entries) as appropriate; the fee is 50p per name, or 70p for one by teleprinter; 80p for one by telephone; and 80p for a visual display.

2. *The Local Land Charges Registers*

These are kept at the office of the registering authority in whose area the land is situated, being the council of any district or of any London borough or the Common Council of the City of London, and are now regulated by the Local Land Charges Act 1975. Local land charges comprise charges acquired by statute by any local authority and other matters set out in s. 1 and not excluded by s. 2. Failure to register a local land charge or to disclose it on an official search will not affect its enforceability, but will entitle the purchaser to compensation for any resulting loss: s. 10.

The Local Land Charges Rules 1977 (S.I. 1977 No. 985) (as amended by S.I. 1978 No. 1638 which provides for the temporary use of facsimile forms and S.I. 1979 No. 1404) deal with the registration of local land charges and other matters registrable in local land charges registers. The Register is divided into 12 parts and search here is against properties, not proprietors. A personal search in the Register costs 65p; an official search is made on Form C, the normal fee being £1.60 for a search in the whole Register, or 65p for a search in any one part. If an office copy of an entry is required the fee is 45p; if a copy of a plan or other document is required then there will be a reasonable additional fee depending on the work involved.

An interesting case on liability for loss due to an inaccurate local land charges search certificate is *Ministry of Housing and Local Government* v. *Sharp* (1970). S had issued the certificate as Registrar, the inaccuracy being caused by the negligence of an employee of the local authority who prepared it. The Court of Appeal held that the employee was liable in negligence and the local authority was vicariously liable for him (the *Hedley Byrne* principle—see p. 35—was applied);

and also, by a majority, that S, the Registrar, was not liable under s. 17 (2) of the Land Charges Act 1925 [now s. 10 (3) of the Act of 1972] for the Ministry's loss, because s. 17 (2) did not impose an absolute duty on the Registrar to make an effective search and issue a complete certificate. The position has now been modified by s. 10 (6) of the Land Charges Act 1972, which provides a specific exemption from liability in tort for discrepancies between details of the requisition and the final certificate (i.e. responsibility rests with the applicant for checking that the two sets of particulars are the same).

3. *The Registrar of Companies' Register of Charges*

This register is kept at the back of the file held by the Registrar as a life history of each company, and includes land it has charged. By s. 95 of the Companies Act 1948 a charge on land, wherever situate, by a company must be registered with the Registrar of Companies within twenty-one days of its creation, otherwise the charge is void as against a liquidator or creditor of the company. The search procedure here is described at p. 121, *ante*.

B. **Registered land**

1. The relevant District Land Registry: A personal search will be permitted only on the written authority of the proprietor or his solicitors, or upon production of the land certificate in which event it will be written up to date with all charges standing against the land on the register. The date when the certificate was last compared with the register will be stamped on the certificate.

Under r. 3 of the Land Registration (Official Searches) Rules 1978 (S.I. 1978 No. 1600) a purchaser (which includes a lessee or chargee) may apply on Form 94A in respect of the whole of the land in a title, or on Form 94B in respect of part of the land in a title, for an official search of a register which he has authority to inspect. No fee is payable. An official search certificate is then issued on Form 94D. If such a certificate shows a clear title and application for registration of a charge is made within 20 working days of the date of the search, the mortgagee will obtain priority. Any one unable to make his registration application within the 20 day period may apply on Form 95 (fee £1) for an extension of the priority period. Any person other than a purchaser who has authority to inspect a register may apply on Form 94C for an official search (fee 50p) but this does not confer on him any priority for the registration of any dealing. For an official search of the

register by telephone or teleprinter under r. 9 the fee is £1.50. The fee
for a personal search is 50p.

In *Smith* v. *Morrison* (1974) the plaintiff had lodged a caution but the
application did not specify any of the six titles comprising the defendant's farm. Whilst the Land Registry was still trying to identify the
farm, a company obtained a clear search and completed its purchase
of the farm within the 15 day period [before it was increased to 20]: it
was held that the company had priority because the plaintiff's caution
had never been entered on the register.

Under the Land Registry Rules 1976 (S.I. 1976 No. 1332) an
application for an official search in the index of proprietors' names
may be made on Form 104 (fee £1 per name) by any person who can
satisfy the Registrar that he is interested generally (e.g. a trustee in
bankruptcy or a personal representative). It is also provided that the
consideration paid for the property will only appear if the registered
proprietor has made a special request to that effect.

2. The Local Land Charges Register, as in the case of unregistered
land.

3. Where land is charged by a company, the Registrar of Companies' Register of Charges with respect to that company.

REGISTRATION AND PROTECTING OF MORTGAGES

Having taken a mortgage of land, to ensure priority, banks have to
register or protect their mortgage in various circumstances, analysed
again as follows:

A.   Unregistered land

A legal or equitable mortgage accompanied by a deposit of the title
deeds is incapable of registration, except where the mortgage is
created by a company, when it must be registered at the Companies
Registry within twenty-one days of its creation, otherwise it is void as
against a liquidator or creditor of the company: s. 95 of the Companies Act 1948.

A legal or equitable mortgage unaccompanied by a deposit of title
deeds, normally the case with a second or subsequent mortgage, must
be registered at the Land Charges Registry as a puisne mortgage (if
legal), or as a general equitable charge (if equitable). Application for
registration is made on Form K1 and the fee is 50p. The same fee is
payable in respect of rectification of an entry, for which application is

made on Form K9. Except where the application for registration or rectification is made by a practising solicitor or relates to a land charge Class F, it must be supported by a statutory declaration on Form K14.

Priority notice

By s. 10 of the Land Charges Act 1972, a priority notice may be given (on Form K6: fee 50p) to the Land Charges Registrar by a prospective mortgagee who intends to register a charge at least fifteen days before that registration is to take effect. If the application to register the charge is presented within thirty days of the lodging of the priority notice and refers to that notice, registration shall take effect as if it had been made at the time when the charge was created, which time shall be deemed to be the date of registration. This method of obtaining retrospective priority is seldom used by banks.

Effect of non-registration

Puisne mortgages and general equitable charges are among the Class C land charges, and by s. 4 of the Land Charges Act 1972 a Class B, C, D or F charge is void against a purchaser of the land charged or of any interest therein, unless it is registered before completion of the purchase, though in the case of a Class D charge and an estate contract such purchaser must be a purchaser of a legal estate for money or money's worth. By s. 17 of the same Act a "purchaser" means "any person (including a mortgagee or lessee) who, for valuable consideration, takes any interest in land or in a charge on land". Mortgages unsupported by deposit of title deeds (other than floating charges) when made by companies after 1st January 1970 require registration as land charges, because the provision of s. 10 (5) of the Land Charges Act 1925 that registration with the Registrar of Companies was equivalent to registration at the Land Charges Registry was repealed by s. 26 of the Law of Property Act 1969.

In *McCarthy and Stone, Ltd.* v. *Julian S. Hodge & Co., Ltd.* (1971) the plaintiff builders' estate contract, although unregistered, was held to prevail over the defendant bank's subsequent equitable mortgage because the bank was not a purchaser of the legal estate and even though the bank later took a legal mortgage this did not give the bank priority because on the facts it must be taken to have had constructive notice of the builders' position under their agreement.

B. Registered land

(i) *Legal mortgage*

A legal mortgage of registered land is effected by registering the charge at the Land Registry, priority of charges being determined by the date of registration. For registration there must be submitted to the Land Registry, i.e. District Land Registry as appropriate, the following: an application form (this is Form A4 if the charge affects the whole of the land in the title or titles; and Form A5 if it affects part of the land in a title); the legal charge, in duplicate; the land certificate; and payment of the requisite land registry fee (see p. 220). The Registrar will register the charge, enter up the details inside the certificate and bind therein the original of the charge, after removing the ornate cover of the land certificate (a design embodying the coats-of-arms of the various Lord Chancellors who took part in the development of the land registration system). This cover is retained in the Registry, and replaced by a plain Charge Certificate cover, which can be readily distinguished at first sight from a land certificate cover. The Charge Certificate, with the various items sewn inside it, is then issued to the party who applied for registration of the charge. Only legal estates can be registered in this way, and second or subsequent legal mortgages are similarly treated, except that details of the earlier charge will appear in the second charge certificate, and so on.

Where the legal charge is created by a company, the usual registration with the Registrar of Companies must be effected, and in view of the twenty-one days period allowed for registration there, this registration will be done first, and thereafter the charge will be submitted to the Land Registry, the accompanying documents now including the Registrar of Companies' Certificate of Registration of that charge, for exhibition to the Land Registry and return.

If a company gives a debenture to a bank in the usual form, i.e. including a fixed first charge by way of legal mortgage on the freehold and leasehold property of the company, and the company already owns registered land, then after the debenture has been registered with the Registrar of Companies, some action must be taken in relation to the Land Registry. The easiest way is to get the land certificates deposited with the bank (the debenture always contains an undertaking by the company to do this) and then give Notice of Deposit of a Land Certificate. If the bank wishes to register its fixed charge at the Land Registry, then the debenture when taken must state specifically and by title number(s) the property affected, because without this the property would not be sufficiently identified. For land registry purposes, a registered charge must be specific, and a floating charge cannot be registered. The bank's title to land covered only by a floating charge, which will include after-acquired land, is equitable, and can be protected by lodging a Notice of Deposit, or a caution (see next heading). Alternatively, the bank can take a separate legal charge on after-acquired property picked up by the debenture and register this in the ordinary way described above.

(ii) *Equitable mortgage*

(a) *When supported by a deposit of the land certificate.* — An equitable mortgage of registered land may be created by deposit of the land certificate with or without a memorandum of deposit. The deposit of the land certificate creates a lien which takes effect subject to overriding interests, registered interests and any entries then upon the register: s. 66 of the Land Registration Act 1925. This lien is equivalent to that created in the case of unregistered land by a deposit of title deeds. Protection is attained by sending in duplicate to the Land Registry a Notice of Deposit of a Land Certificate (Form 85A), which is signed by the depositee or his solicitors. There is now no fee payable. The Registry will acknowledge receipt by rubber-stamping and returning the duplicate. The relative land certificate is normally forwarded as well, and this will then be indorsed as to its deposit with the mortgagee and returned to the depositee. If the Notice is not accompanied by the land certificate, e.g. because the proprietor does not want the deposit recorded in the certificate, then prudence demands that the land certificate be sent for writing up at the Registry and immediately it is received back showing a clear title, the Notice must be lodged; alternatively, it can be lodged immediately after the result of a search is known.

The Notice operates as a caution and the Registrar is then required to give the equitable mortgagee fourteen days' notice of any proposed dealing with the land, which thus enables the mortgagee to take steps to protect his interest, such as taking a legal mortgage and registering it. In *Re White Rose Cottage* (1965) the Court of Appeal held that a notice of deposit had priority over subsequent charging orders obtained by judgment creditors. This method of giving notice of deposit, whilst it has its limitations, is useful because possession of the land certificate is at least *de facto* protection against a registration of another party as proprietor or a subsequent mortgagee whose charge is registered or perhaps has been protected by a caution. It is also employed by banks which hold a legal mortgage form but which, to save the customer the land registry fees payable on registering a charge, are content with the status of an equitable mortgagee for the

Chap. 6 *Land*

time being. Thus, instead of registering its charge immediately it is taken and so making it a legal one, the bank lodges a Notice of Deposit of a Land Certificate, and as it already holds a legal mortgage form it can register this at any subsequent time, but it must do so within fourteen days of receiving notice from the Registrar of a subsequent charge in order to retain its priority. The efficacy of this procedure was upheld by the Court of Appeal in *Barclays Bank Ltd.* v. *Taylor* (1973) which, to the relief of banks, reversed the trial judge's decision, and s. 106 of the Land Registration Act 1925 which caused the difficulty in that case has been replaced by a new s. 106 set out in s. 26 of the Administration of Justice Act 1977, which provides for protection by this Notice, or any other such Notice as may be prescribed, or (see (c) below) by a caution.

A Notice of Deposit of a Land Certificate cannot be entered on the register while another such notice is already on the register, nor can it be given for part only of a title.

(b) *When the land certificate is not available, but will be deposited later.*—Sometimes a customer cannot produce the land certificate because either the title is in process of being registered for the first time, or a transfer to him has not yet been registered. In these circumstances registered land offers the bank a distinct advantage over unregistered land, because the bank can get the customer (or depositor) to sign a Notice of Intended Deposit of a Land Certificate, being Form 85B in the case of unregistered land, or Form 85C in the case of land already registered which is in course of being transferred. Such Notice is lodged at the Land Registry, and operates as a caution in the same way as a Notice of Deposit, and the land certificate when prepared will be sent direct to the bank named in the Notice. Unless the bank then wishes to register its charge, it need take no further action, because the original Notice of Intended Deposit continues to operate as though it were a Notice of Deposit.

(c) *When unsupported by a deposit of the land certificate.*—The most likely instance of this is where the equitable mortgage is a second or subsequent mortgage, and as notice of deposit cannot be used, the mortgage must be protected in some other way. It can be protected by lodging at the Land Registry a caution, Form 63, supported by a statutory declaration on Form 14 (the registration fee being 50p). The other type of caution in a specially prescribed form, the mortgage caution was abolished by the Administration of Justice Act 1977, which authorised the Chief Land Registrar to arrange for the conversion into a registered charge, in such circumstances and subject to such conditions as he might direct, of mortgages then protected by such mortgage cautions.

Under the new s. 106 (2) unless and until the mortgage becomes a registered charge it takes effect only in equity and is capable of being overriden as a minor interest, unless protected by a caution under s. 54 (or, see (a) above, by a Notice under s. 49 or such other Notice as may be prescribed).

It may be added here that if a legal mortgage is subsequently taken when an earlier mortgage (whether legal or equitable) has not been registered but has been protected by a notice or by a caution, the second mortgagee can protect his mortgage by lodging a caution, but if he wishes to register his mortgage he can do so only if and when the prior mortgagee has registered his charge.

Any equitable mortgage of land by a company must, of course, be registered in the usual way with the Registrar of Companies

As a postscript to registered land, it may be mentioned that s. 22 (1) of the Solicitors' Act 1974 (repeating earlier provisions) provides that any unqualified person who either directly or indirectly draws or prepares any instrument of transfer or charge for the purposes of the Land Registration Act 1925 or makes any application or lodges any document for registration under that Act at the registry is liable to a fine not exceeding £50, unless the act was not done for any fee, gain or reward. Thus, anyone not a member of the legal profession can do such work but cannot charge for it, so a bank which itself prepares and registers a charge or other documents at the Land Registry should not take any payment for itself from the customer for that service, though actual disbursements can be recovered.

REPORT ON TITLE, VALUATION AND INSURANCE

Some banks send all deeds relating to unregistered land to solicitors for a report on title, which is particularly important where there may be complications of a "Town and Country Planning" nature. Others take this course only where the title is complicated, for many abstracts of title are straightforward, the deeds and documents are all present, properly stamped and show the history of the property clearly, any deaths of owners being evidenced by a death certificate and/or Probate or Letters of Administration and followed up by a written assent signed by the personal representatives and naming the person to whom the property is being transferred.

So far as registered land is concerned, this system makes it much easier for banks when taking security, because the land certificate itself sets out the title. Absolute and Good Leasehold Titles speak for themselves, and no solicitors' report on title is necessary unless the planning position requires elucidation. Where the title is Possessory or Qualified, then a bank will normally seek a solicitors' report on such a title, coupled with one on the planning aspect if applicable.

On the question of valuation, banks will usually be content in mortgages of houses with an inspection and valuation by the manager or other senior branch official, but clearly with industrial and commercial premises or others that present difficulty it will be necessary to obtain a professional valuation. Property well situated, easily let, marketable and in a good state of repair is naturally to be preferred, and wherever possible the valuation should show a reasonable margin over the advance. The amount at which the property last changed hands has some relevance as a rough guide to its present value. Property prices have progressed on a steady upward course since the end of the Second World War, with a very large increase over the period 1970–73, though there are intermittent set-backs due to difficulties in obtaining mortgages and so on. If the bank relies on a professional valuation made for the customer, the *Hedley Byrne* principle (see p. 35) may be invoked, as in *Singer and Friedlander, Ltd.* v. *John D. Wood & Co.* (1977), where the plaintiff merchant bank made an advance to a third party on the security of a farm valued by the defendants for the third party. The third party having defaulted on the loan, it was found that the farm had been considered over-valued. Held, the defendants owed a duty of care to the plaintiff, and as they were in breach of that duty they were liable to the plaintiff in damages.

Freehold and long leasehold properties present few difficulties in valuation normally, but short-term leases and in particular leases at a rack-rent (i.e. the full annual value) will usually be rejected by banks as undesirable security, for they are full of pitfalls. With medium and short-term leases the property decreases in value year by year as the unexpired portion of the lease diminishes. At the end of a lease the property reverts to the lessor and often heavy claims for dilapidations are involved, though there may be valuable options to renew. In the result, short leases are seldom very saleable. Leases at a rack-rent, e.g. houses in London divided up into flats, are of little value because there is little or no margin between the ground rent which the lessee pays to his lessor and what the lessee himself receives from his sub-tenants, so that there is no realisable market value for a bank as mortgagee. All leases must be carefully examined as to the lessee's covenants, for these are sometimes onerous and restrictive (subleasing may not always be allowed) and non-performance of the covenants may entail forfeiture of the lease and consequent loss of the security.

Buildings on the land must be adequately insured against fire and the usual perils, and the cover increased as and when necessary to keep pace with inflation. Notice of the bank's interest as mortgagee is given to the insurers and acknowledged by them, or indorsed on the policy, or if a new policy is taken out this can be in the joint names of the mortgagor and the bank. The bank generally keeps the fire policy with the deeds of the property, and must ensure that future premiums are paid on the due date, a diary card system being essential here. It must be emphasised that fire insurance is a contract of indemnity, and subject to any maximum amount laid down in the policy, the insured may not recover more than his actual loss: *Castellain* v. *Preston* (1883). A recent illustration of this is *Leppard* v. *Excess Insurance Co., Ltd.* (1979) where a cottage insured for £14,000 was totally destroyed by fire. The Court of Appeal held that the plaintiff could recover only £3000 (being the market value at the date of the fire less the site value), and not the cost of re-instatement. A reminder of the "utmost good faith" nature of contracts of insurance occurred in *Woolcott* v. *Sun Alliance and London Insurance, Ltd.* (1978), where the defendant had issued a block insurance policy against fire and other risks to a Building Society. The names of the insured were expressed to be the Society as mortgagees and the mortgagors mentioned in the records annexed to the policy. The plaintiff, as a prospective purchaser, applied to the Society for a mortgage advance. The application form contained no question relating to an applicant's moral character, but one question read: "Are there any other matters which you wish to be taken into account?" to which the plaintiff replied in the negative. In fact, he had several convictions including one for robbery for which he had been sentenced to 12 years' imprisonment. When the house was destroyed by fire, the defendant satisfied the Building Society's claim to the extent of their interest as mortgagee, but repudiated the plaintiff's claim for the excess. It was held that the plaintiff's claim failed because it was his duty to disclose his criminal record, and the absence of a separate insurance proposal form did not in any way modify the duty to disclose such facts as a reasonable or prudent insurer might have treated as material.

RIGHTS AND REMEDIES OF MORTGAGEES

A. The Legal Mortgage

A legal mortgage is a right *in rem*, i.e. it gives to the mortgagee a legal estate in the land, so that he has rights against the property itself as well as his right of personal action against the borrower. It is, therefore, a stronger form of security than an equitable mortgage which is a right in *personam*, i.e. a personal right against the borrower or owner—a right to participate in the proceeds of sale of the property and to enforce a claim by invoking the aid of the Court—giving no rights against the property.

Being a "purchaser" of a legal estate in the land, a legal mortgagee takes free from existing equitable interests of which he has no express or constructive notice (the maxim being "where the equities are equal, the law prevails").

By the Law of Property Act 1925 the following rights are given to a legal mortgagee, subject to any provisions to the contrary expressed in the mortgage deed, which must be carefully followed when exercising remedies against the security:

(a) *Suing on the Personal Covenant to Repay.*—This right is a personal remedy only. The mortgagee may issue a writ in an ordinary action of debt for the loan and interest due to him within twelve years of the date of the loan, or the date of part payment of principal or interest, or from a written acknowledgment of the debt, whichever is the latest. This remedy can be used to advantage when the mortgagee does not wish to take action against the property itself, and the debtor has sufficient other assets on which, if necessary, execution can be levied after judgment has been obtained. Some modern bank forms do not contain this covenant.

(b) *Sale of the Property.*—By s. 101 (1) the sale of the mortgaged property may be either subject to prior charges or not, and either together or in lots, by public auction or by private contract, and subject to such conditions respecting title, or evidence of title, or other matter as the mortgagee thinks fit. Once a mortgagee has entered into a contract for sale in exercise of his statutory power, the mortgagor cannot prevent the sale from proceeding by tendering the mortgage money to the mortgagee: *Waring* v. *London and Manchester Assurance Co.* (1935), approved by the Court of Appeal in *Property and Bloodstock, Ltd.* v. *Emerton* (1967), which held that so long as an unconditional, or even a conditional, contract of sale subsists, the mortgagor's right of redemption is barred. When selling, a mortgagee must act honestly and equitably, e.g. he cannot sell to himself. He is not a trustee of the power of sale; re-affirmed by the Court of Appeal in *Cuckmere Brick Co. Ltd.* v. *Mutual Finance Ltd.* (1971), which also held that the mortgagee was not merely under a duty to act in good faith but also to take reasonable care to obtain the true market price at the time he chose to sell. However, in *Barclays Bank Ltd.* v. *Thienel* (1978) it was held that where a bank exercised a power of sale over a property charged to it by a customer as security for the customer's overdraft it did not owe to the guarantors of the overdraft a duty to take reasonable care and skill to obtain the best price obtainable for the property, for this was excluded by a clause in the bank's standard form of guarantee to the effect that it had power to realise any securities in such manner as it might think expedient. The efficacy of such a clause in a guarantee taken subsequent to the coming into force of the Unfair Contract Terms Act 1977 (discussed in Chapter 1) remains to be seen.

The right of pre-emption conferred on a local authority by the Housing Act 1957 where it sells a council house to a tenant and accepts a mortgage in satisfaction of nearly the whole purchase price does not confer on the authority any powers in addition to those in s. 101 (1). On this basis, in *Williams* v. *Wellingborough Borough Council* (1975) the Court of Appeal held that a transfer by the local authority of the mortgaged property to itself when its mortgagor defaulted was a nullity.

Under s. 103 the power of sale does not become exercisable until (a) a demand for repayment has been made and has been the subject of default by the mortgagor for three months; or (b) interest is in arrears for two months; or (c) there has been a breach of some other covenant in the mortgage deed than that relating to the payment of the mortgage money and interest. This position is greatly modified by bank mortgages, which provide for repayment on demand—the nature of banking makes this quick recall of advances a *sine qua non* in every type of security taken—and, on default, for the sale of the property with a minimum of formality. When a sale is made in professed exercise of the power of sale, s. 104 (2) provides that the title of a purchaser (who acts in good faith) shall not be impeachable on the ground that the sale was not authorised or that the power of sale was improperly or irregularly exercised.

If the property is in the actual occupation of the mortgagor or someone else, who refuses to leave voluntarily, difficulties may arise in obtaining vacant possession of the property, so that it can fetch the higher price commanded by a sale in such condition, as well as being more quickly marketable. In these circumstances a Court order for possession will be necessary, which may well involve the bank in adverse publicity, and in any event will be not obtainable where the property is let to tenants who are statutorily protected by the Rent Act 1977 (which consolidated earlier legislation). Similar protection is afforded to business premises under the Landlord and Tenant Act 1954, Part 2, and to agricultural land under the Rent (Agriculture) Act 1976. As already discussed, difficulties can arise over the wife's equity in the matrimonial home. A County Court has jurisdiction under s. 48 (1) of the County Courts Act 1959 in an action for possession where the net annual value for rating of the land in question does not exceed £400. In *West Penwith Rural District Council* v. *Gunnell* (1968) the Court of Appeal held that such an action lay where the amount due on the mortgage was £2742, notwithstanding that the jurisdiction in equity under s. 56 (1) (c) of the County Courts Act 1959 for enforcing any charge or lien was limited to £500.

Furthermore, under s. 36 of the Administration of Justice Act 1970 the court may adjourn, stay, suspend or postpone an action by the mortgagee for possession of a dwelling-house where it appears that within a reasonable time the mortgagor can make good his default. This has been extended by s. 8 of the Administration of Justice Act 1973 to cases where there is a reasonable prospect of paying instalments and to foreclosure actions. These sections were considered by the Court of Appeal in *Royal Trust Co. of Canada* v. *Markham* (1975) and it was held that any stay or suspension had to be for a definite or ascertainable period. In *Western Bank Ltd.* v. *Schindler* (1976) the Court of Appeal upheld a judge's refusal to exercise his discretion in favour of the mortgagor where although there had been no default under the terms of the mortgage there had been a failure of collateral security (the lapsing of a life policy) so that the debt was inadequately secured.

Even with owner-occupied property there may be difficulties where a deserted wife, or husband, remains in occupation. This is because of the protection conferred by the Matrimonial Homes Act 1967, though, as already explained, a mortgagee will normally arrange that a spouse entitled to rights of occupation releases them, or postpones them to the mortgage.

Where the property is occupied by the mortgagor, the mortgage deed, may contain an "attornment" clause whereby the mortgagor attorns (i.e. declares himself) tenant to the mortgagee of the mortgaged premises at a yearly rent, which is usually nominal, e.g. a peppercorn. The idea of the clause is to enable the mortgagee, if he wishes to recover possession, to do so summarily by proceedings before the justices under s. 1 of the Small Tenements Recovery Act 1838. However, mortgagees rarely avail themselves of this procedure, because summary judgment in claims arising out of mortgage transactions is now available independently of attornment under Order 14, r. 3 of the Rules of the Supreme Court 1965; and in fact the clause has now disappeared from some banks' mortgage forms. The attornment clause does, however, enable a mortgagee to enforce a covenant by the

mortgagor which touches and concerns the land against the successors in title of that mortgagor: *Regent Oil Co., Ltd.* v. *J. A. Gregory (Hatch
End), Ltd.* (1965).

When a sale does take place, the proceeds, after discharging or
providing for any prior incumbrances to which the sale is not made
subject, or after payment into Court of a sum to meet any prior
incumbrances, must be applied by the mortgagee to: (i) the costs of
the sale; (ii) discharge of the mortgage debt and interest; (iii) the
residue to the person entitled thereto (i.e the person formerly entitled
to the mortgaged property, or any subsequent incumbrancers). A sale
by a mortgagee in exercise of the powers conferred on him will
extinguish subsequent incumbrances: s. 104 (1); but it was held in *Re
White Rose Cottage* (1965) that where the sale is made by the mortgagor
as beneficial owner with the concurrence of the bank as mortgagee
(i.e. with a release by the bank of its rights under the mortgage), a
purchaser will take subject to any subsequent incumbrances, for he is
then in no better position than the mortgagor. A subsequent incumbrancer is still entitled to the surplus proceeds of sale up to the
amount properly due under the mortgage, notwithstanding that the
mortgagor is counterclaiming against him for unliquidated damages
that may possibly exceed the amount of the mortgage: *Samuel Keller
(Holdings), Ltd.* v. *Martins Bank Ltd.* (1970).

(c) *Appointment of a Receiver.* — By s. 101 (1) (iii) the mortgagee has
power, when he has become entitled to exercise his power of sale, to
appoint a receiver of the income of the mortgaged property or any
part thereof, by writing under his hand.

Banks rarely take this course but it may be expedient where the
property is let (e.g. a block of flats), or where it is desirable to wait
before selling but to keep the interest on foot in the meantime. The
receiver is deemed to be the agent for the mortgagor, who alone is to
be responsible for his acts and defaults, unless the mortgage deed
otherwise provides. The receiver must apply the income received by
him as follows: (i) in discharge of rents, rates, taxes, and other outgoings; (ii) in payment of his own commission and of fire, life or other
insurance premiums payable under the mortgage deed or the Act,
and the cost of repairs directed in writing by the mortgagee; (iii) in
payment of interest on the mortgage; and (iv) any surplus in or
towards the discharge of the principal money if so directed in writing
by the mortgagee. Thus, by appointing a receiver to manage the
property, the mortgagee obtains all the advantages but none of the
risks of entry into possession (see (e) below). If the property is
mortgaged by a company, and the mortgagee exercises his power of
appointing a receiver in respect of that property, then by s. 102 of the

Companies Act 1948 notice of that fact must be filed with the Registrar of Companies within seven days of the appointment.

By s. 110 of the Law of Property Act 1925, where the statutory or express power of a mortgagee to sell or appoint a receiver is exercisable only by reason of the mortgagor committing an act of bankruptcy or being adjudged a bankrupt, then in the case of mortgages created after 1925 such power cannot be exercised without the leave of the Court.

(d) *Foreclosure.*—A mortgage is said to be foreclosed when the mortgagor is deprived of his right to redeem the property, which thereupon becomes owned by the mortgagee. The consent of the Court is always required for this remedy, which is seldom used by mortgagees; instead of granting it, the Court generally orders a sale. The actual mechanics of foreclosure are that the mortgagee sues in the Chancery Division, praying that the mortgagor shall either pay what is due or be deprived altogether of his equity of redemption; if the mortgagor fails to pay, the Court issues an order for foreclosure nisi, directing that if he does not pay at the end of a specified period (usually six months) he shall be foreclosed absolutely. The effect of the order becoming absolute is that the property vests in the mortgagee (who can thereafter sell and retain the whole of the proceeds), and the rights in the land of the mortgagor and any subsequent incumbrancers are extinguished.

(e) *Entry into Possession.*—This remedy is seldom pursued by banks, for if a mortgagee takes this course, he must collect all rents at his own expense and undertake many onerous duties and liabilities. Equity holds a mortgagee in possession accountable not only for the profits that he actually receives, but also for what he might have received but for his own wilful default and neglect. Thus, in *White* v. *City of London Brewery Co.* (1889) the defendants, as mortgagees, entered into possession of the mortgaged property and leased it to a tenant, subject to a restriction that he should take his supply of beer entirely from them; the Court of Appeal held that they must account for the additional rent they would have received if they had let the property as a "free" house, instead of a "tied" house.

Should a mortgagee enter into possession of the property and remain in possession for twelve years without acknowledging the title of the mortgagor he may by deed enlarge his mortgage term into a fee simple, i.e. become the freeholder. A mortgagee in possession has power to grant leases or, if a receiver has been appointed, the mortgagee can delegate to him the power of leasing.

Finally, it may be noted that the rights and remedies of a legal mortgagee of leasehold property are virtually the same as those in the case of freehold property, except that the original lease may contain restrictive covenants and that the mortgagee's rights apply to the term held by the mortgagor and not to a fee simple.

B. The Equitable Mortgagee

The rights and remedies of an equitable mortgagee are generally set out in detail in the memorandum of deposit or charge form, but apart from those he has power:

(1) To sue for payment of principal and interest.

(2) To bring an action to compel the mortgagor to execute a legal mortgage if he has so undertaken or where title deeds have been deposited. Once he has a legal mortgage, he can then resort to the rights and remedies of a legal mortgagee.

(3) To bring an action for sale.

(4) To apply to the Court for the appointment of a receiver.

(5) To bring an action for foreclosure.

As an equitable mortgagee has no legal estate, he is not entitled to enter into possession unless such power is expressly reserved by the mortgage.

If the equitable mortgage is under seal, then such a deed gives the equitable mortgagee similar powers to those of a legal mortgagee to sell or appoint a receiver, but in order that he can convey a legal title to a purchaser without recourse to the Court his equitable mortgage under seal must contain an irrevocable power of attorney whereby he is made attorney for the sale of the land, or a declaration by the mortgagor that he holds the land in trust for the mortgagee, who is empowered to remove the mortgagor from that position and appoint new trustees in his place. The power of an equitable mortgagee under a sealed memorandum of deposit containing a power of attorney to convey the legal estate when selling as mortgagee was confirmed by the Court of Appeal in *Re White Rose Cottage* (1965), and HARMAN, L.J. further commented that the equitable mortgagee under a deed can convey to a purchaser the legal estate in the mortgaged property without first going through the form of calling for the execution by the mortgagor of a legal mortgage.

With leasehold property, the position of an equitable mortgagee as regards his rights and remedies is similar to that in the case of freehold property, subject to the differences already noted when discussing legal mortgages.

It must be remembered that equitable mortgages, whether under seal or not, are always subject to prior equities, for the maxim here is "where the equities are equal, the first in time prevails".

Finally, as regards any mortgage of land securing a consumer credit agreement or a consumer hire agreement other than an exempt agreement the mortgagee's rights are restricted by s. 126 of the Consumer Credit Act 1974 which makes such a mortgage enforceable on an order of the Court only.

TRANSFER AND DISCHARGE OF MORTGAGES

Mortgages, whether legal or equitable, may be transferred by the mortgagee to someone else. This is rare, for in the vast majority of cases the mortgage moneys are eventually repaid, and the security discharged. A transfer may be indorsed on the original mortgage, or a supplemental deed of transfer may be executed. It is not essential for the mortgagor to be a party to the transfer, as the mortgagee has power to assign the mortgage debt and interest and the security therefor without the concurrence of the mortgagor. It is, however, advisable to make the mortgagor a party to the transfer because by joining in it he becomes bound by the recital in the transfer deed as to the state of the debt. If he is not a party to the transfer, then notice of it must be given to him. A transfer for value of a non-marketable security attracts *ad valorem* stamp duty at the rate of 5p per £200 or part thereof on the amount of the debt transferred.

The transferability of bank mortgages is not in doubt, because it is usually expressed in them that "the Bank" shall include the Bank's successors and assigns (or persons deriving title under the Bank). Sometimes a bank will take a transfer of a mortgage from another bank when a customer changes banks, but normally each bank prefers to take its own form of charge (because these forms vary from bank to bank) and to have the original mortgage discharged.

With registered land, the prescribed instrument of transfer of a registered charge is Form 54 and the transfer must be completed by registration at the Land Registry, i.e. the entry on the register of the name of the new proprietor of the charge. This is achieved by submitting the charge certificate and the instrument of transfer, together with a registry fee which in the case of a transfer for value is Scale 4 (see p. 220). In the event of a transfer of a charge which is not registered but protected by a notice of deposit or by a caution, the existing notice or caution should be withdrawn and replaced by the appropriate new one.

Discharge of a Legal Mortgage

This is effected as follows:

(i) *Unregistered land*

Here, in most cases the mortgagee signs a simple form of receipt for the mortgage moneys which is indorsed on, written at the foot of or annexed to the mortgage deed. Bank mortgage forms usually have a vacating receipt printed on the back of them for completion by the bank as and when occasion demands. This is on the lines of: ". . . Bank Limited hereby acknowledge this . . . day of . . . 19 . . . to have received all moneys (including interest and costs) secured by the within-written Mortgage, the payment having been made by the within-named . . . In Witness whereof . . . Bank Limited have caused their Common Seal to be hereunto affixed the day and year first above written". It is followed by the usual sealing clause, i.e. that the Common Seal of the Bank was affixed in the presence of . . . (though it is not necessary for the receipt to be under seal). If the receipt shows that the money has been paid by some other person than the mortgagor, then the receipt will operate to transfer the mortgage to that person unless it is expressly provided therein that the receipt shall not operate as a transfer.

By s. 115 of the Law of Property Act 1925 such a form of receipt is sufficient to vacate the mortgage without any reconveyance, surrender or release, but the section allows mortgagors who prefer a more elaborate discharge to require a reconveyance, surrender, release or transfer to be executed in lieu of a receipt. Such elaborate methods are appropriate where the whole amount secured by the mortgage is not being repaid, but otherwise they are seldom used in practice.

A legal mortgage unsupported by a deposit of title deeds should have been registered as a puisne mortgage at the Land Charges Registry, and such entry will need discharging by filing at the Registry the appropriate form (fee 50p). This is Form K11, which applies to all land charges except Class F, where the form for cancellation is Form K13.

Where the mortgagor has repaid the advance it is not necessary for the bank to search for subsequent incumbrancers, and in the absence of any knowledge of them, the bank can hand back the title deeds, together with the discharged mortgage which now forms a link in the chain of title, to the original mortgagor. along with any surplus proceeds. If, however, the bank has sold the property, it must effect a "surplus proceeds search" before handing over any surplus.

(ii) *Registered land*

Discharge of a legal mortgage may be done by the usual form of receipt in the nature of a reconveyance, or, which is the standard practice, by a special form of discharge, Form 53, which can also be modified to release part only of the land by adding at the end of it "as to the land shown and edged with red on the accompanying plan, signed by me, being part of the land comprised in the said Charge". Where the mortgagor has sold the property, a useful alternative is Form 55, because this is a combined form of transfer and discharge, and when executed by the mortgagor as proprietor of the land and by the mortgagee as proprietor of the charge it passes the land to the purchaser free from the charge. A discharge by a company must be executed under seal, except that in the case of joint-stock banks the Chief Land Registrar will accept a discharge signed by a general manager, an assistant general manager, a departmental manager, a branch manager or someone of comparable standing.

The charge certificate and the discharge are submitted by the registered proprietor of the charge to the Land Registry, which will note the discharge on the register (thereupon, by s. 35 of the Land Registration Act 1925, the charge shall be deemed to have ceased). The Registrar will cancel the charge certificate and re-issue the land certificate, written up to date, in its place.

No surplus proceeds search is necessary, because the Registrar would have notified the bank of any subsequent charge, even if the mortgagee failed to do so.

Discharge of an Equitable Mortgage

This can be done by a simple receipt, but often the bank will merely cancel the memorandum of deposit (and retain it, for it does not form part of the abstract of title), returning the title deeds to the depositor. However, if the equitable mortgage has been registered or protected in some way that entry will have to be reversed, as follows:

(i) *Unregistered land*

An equitable mortgage without a deposit of title deeds should have been registered as a general equitable charge at the Land Charges Registry, and this entry will need discharging in the manner described above in connection with puisne mortgages.

(ii) *Registered land*

If a notice of deposit, or a notice of intended deposit, has been given, this is withdrawn by the person entitled to the lien created by the deposit of the land certificate simply completing the withdrawal form on the reverse side of his copy of the notice, and lodging it without fee at the Land Registry, together with the land certificate, if the notice has been recorded therein, for the necessary entries to be made. If a caution has been lodged at the Land Registry to protect the mortgage, then this should be cancelled, application for cancellation being made on Form 71, signed by the cautioner or his personal representative or solicitor. No fee is payable.

Unless notice of a subsequent charge has been received, the land certificate and any surplus proceeds may be returned to the mortgagor after repayment of the loan.

Finally, as any mortgage of land by a company must be registered at the Companies Registry, on the mortgage being discharged, the company concerned should file there a memorandum of satisfaction (which has to be supported by a statutory declaration by a director and the secretary). By s. 100 of the Companies Act 1948 such action is permissive, not obligatory; and some companies take a surprisingly long time to do it.

SUB-MORTGAGES

A sub-mortgage is a mortgage of a mortgage, and must be distinguished from second or subsequent mortgages of the same land. Sometimes a bank's customer who is seeking an advance may himself hold a mortgage on someone else's land which he may be unable or unwilling to call in. He can create a sub-mortgage, either legal or equitable, except that where his own mortgage is equitable, the sub-mortgage must necessarily be equitable. Such a security, though seldom encountered in practice, can be a very good one because of its double strength—to the liability of the original mortgagor is added that of the sub-mortgagor. For example, if a bank makes advances to a building society and feels that security is necessary, it can take a sub-mortgage on the mortgages received by the society from its own borrowers. Notice of any sub-mortgage should be given to the original mortgagor, and his acknowledgment requested together with his confirmation of the amount outstanding, and his undertaking to forward all repayments direct to the sub-mortgagee. The value of the security will, of course, diminish progressively as repayments are made.

A legal sub-mortgage recites the original or head mortgage and assigns the mortgage debt, and where the head mortgage is by demise, the property will be demised to the sub-mortgagee for a term less by at least one day than the term held by the original mortgagee.

Where the head mortgage is a charge by way of legal mortgage, the sub-mortgage is effected by a transfer of the benefit of the head mortgage. The legal sub-mortgagee can exercise both the power of sale in the original mortgage and also that in the sub-mortgage, subject to the two equities of redemption.

With registered land a legal sub-mortgage is effected by lodging the form of sub-charge in duplicate at the Land Registry together with the requisite land registry scale fee and the charge certificate, which will be retained at the Registry. The sub-charge having been registered, a Certificate of Sub-Charge will be issued. As an alternative to registration it is possible to protect the sub-charge by lodging a caution, for the caution machinery also applies, with some modifications, to sub-charges. If the head mortgage is not registered but protected by a notice of deposit or a caution, then the sub-mortgage cannot be registered so long as the head mortgage remains unregistered, and in the meantime a caution must be used.

An equitable sub-mortgage can be created by a deposit of the head mortgage with or without a memorandum of deposit; or by any general equitable charge. In the case of registered land, where the charge certificate is deposited, the sub-mortgagee can lodge at the Land Registry a Notice of Deposit of a Charge Certificate (a similar procedure to that in the case of equitable mortgages already described). Alternatively, it may be protected by a caution.

BUILDING SCHEMES

Sometimes banks finance building development schemes for houses, flats or factories; here a legal mortgage of the land is taken, which increases in value as the buildings go up. Advances are made on each building at certain progressive stages of construction, preferably against production to the bank of architects' certificates. In *Sutcliffe* v. *Thackrah* (1974) the House of Lords (overruling earlier case law) held that the defendant architects when giving certificates were not deciding a dispute between the plaintiff and the builder and as there was no agreement to abide by the defendants' decision, the defendants were not placed in the position of arbitrators and so owed the plaintiff a duty to exercise care and skill in the giving of certificates; they were therefore liable for their negligent over-certification of work done.

The bank should also arrange for periodic inspection of sites by its own staff and make sure that adequate insurance cover is taken out in respect of the building work and that the bank's interest is advised to the insurers.

Finally, the bank can ensure it receives payment as and when each completed unit is sold, because in the case of unregistered land it will have to join in the conveyance, and in the case of registered land it will have to release the land from its charge so that the Land Registry can create a new title for the part sold. In either instance, the instrument will only be handed over by the bank against payment of the net proceeds of sale, or the solicitors' undertaking in this behalf.

CONCLUSION

Real property figures prominently in the mixed array of securities taken by banks. Individual items of land and buildings come in all areas and sizes, in towns and the countryside, in industrial premises and agricultural land, and in dwellinghouses which may be anywhere. Land and buildings may form part of a larger security, as when they are included in the overall security conferred in a debenture created by a company. Basically, real property is very good security, because apart from the possibility of third party rights against the land which will diminish its value, land is indestructible and never wholly loses its intrinsic value, whereas stocks and shares, for example, even in well-known companies, can occasionally become completely worthless scraps of paper. From the legal point of view, land is a more intricate type of security than most, although in many cases it proves reasonably straight-forward, and the legal profession is at hand to sort out the complexities.

Given due care and attention to legal and practical points, land is a good, sound and much used banking security, especially as the banks' collection of mortgages is invariably of a mixed nature, both as to type and geographical location of property. Whilst lacking the immediate realisability of some securities, notably quoted stocks and shares and life policies with a surrender value, nevertheless land is reasonably marketable, and indeed usually has not merely an enduring but also an increasing value, because the same amount of land in this country has to cope with a gradually increasing population, not to mention persistent economic inflation.

Chapter 7

Life Policies

INTRODUCTION

A life policy is a document containing a contract whereby the assurer, in consideration of one or more premiums, undertakes to pay to the person to whom the policy is granted a certain sum of money or sometimes an annuity on the death of the person whose life is assured or on his or her attaining a certain age.

Although in common speech the terms "assurance" and "insurance", "assurer" and "insurer", and "assured" and "insured" are used interchangeably, the technically correct description so far as life cover is concerned is assurance, the life assured and so on. This is because the payment of a certain sum of money or periodical sums under a life policy is assured—once a policy is taken out payment is fixed. Thus, life assurance is not a contract of indemnity, in contrast to the other forms of insurance such as fire and marine insurance, which are agreements to compensate the insured for such damage to property as he may suffer on any occasion through the perils against which he is insured, and if no such loss occurs then he never has any claim.

To prevent gambling in life policies (e.g. by taking out policies on complete strangers) the Life Assurance Act 1774 was passed, which enacts as follows:

Section 1. No insurance shall be made by any person or persons, bodies politic or corporate, on the life or lives of any other person or persons, wherein the person or persons for whose use, benefit, or on whose account such policies shall be made shall have no interest or by way of gaming or wagering; and every insurance made contrary to this provision shall be null and void to all intent and purposes. [It was held in *Halford* v. *Kymer* (1830) that "interest" here means pecuniary interest.]

Section 2. The name of the person so interested, or for whose benefit the policy is made, shall be inserted in the policy.

Section 3. In all cases where the insured has such an interest, no greater sum shall be recovered than the value of the interest at the date of the policy.

INSURABLE INTEREST

Whilst in the general sense life assurance is taking a bet with death, what distinguishes it legally from gaming or wagering (where a person has no interest in the matter other than his bet) is the insurable interest required by s. 1 of the Act of 1774 set out above. This question of who has an insurable interest requires some elaboration. A person is deemed to have an insurable interest in his or her own life; a husband may insure his wife—*Griffiths* v. *Fleming* (1909), and a wife may insure her husband: *Reed* v. *Royal Exchange Assurance Co.* (1795): in these various circumstances there is no limit to the amount of assurance, because they are really exceptions to the general identification of insurable interest with pecuniary interest, for a person is clearly prejudiced by the loss of his or her own life or that of his or her spouse. In other circumstances the interest must be pecuniary, so that:

   (i) A creditor may take out a policy on the life of his debtor to the amount of the debt: *Anderson* v. *Edie* (1795).

  (ii) A surety or guarantor may take out a policy on the life of the principal debtor to the amount of his guarantee.

 (iii) An employer may take out a policy on the life of his employee, and *vice versa*: *Hebdon* v. *West* (1863).

 (iv) A trustee may insure in respect of the interest of which he is a trustee: *Tidswell* v. *Ankerstein* (1792).

  (v) A father has not necessarily an insurable interest in the life of his child merely by virtue of his being a parent: *Halford* v. *Kymer* (1830), but if he can show some independent pecuniary interest he can take out a policy in his own name and for his own benefit on the child's life. He may, however, effect a policy in the child's name and for the child's benefit. A child has no insurable interest in the life of the parent unless the parent is supporting the child: *Howard* v. *Refuge Friendly Society* (1886). Sisters have no insurable interest in each other's lives: *Evanson* v. *Crooks* (1911). This would also be the position as between other relatives.

 (vi) A litigant may insure the life of his judge. This is usually done in a very long and complex trial, which would mean immense additional costs if the judge were to die during the trial, and the case had to start again before another judge.

(vii) Contracts of life assurance are assignable, and an assignee of a valid policy need not have any insurable interest: *Ashley* v. *Ashley* (1829).

The essential time for the existence of the insurable interest is the date of the policy. Such interest does not have to continue down to the date of death, so that if it was originally present but has ceased in the meantime, the policy moneys are still recoverable at death: *Dalby* v. *India and London Life Assurance Co.* (1854). This can easily occur where the policy has been taken out by a creditor or a surety or an employer, and the debt has been repaid by the debtor in his lifetime, or the relationship of master and servant has been terminated.

It was held in *Harse* v. *Pearl Life Assurance Co.* (1904) that a person who has effected a policy on the life of another which is void for lack of insurable interest cannot repudiate the policy and recover the premiums paid. This is under the general rule that money paid under an illegal contract is irrecoverable (*ex turpe causa non oritur actio*, i.e. no action arises out of a base cause). An exception to this rule is where the policyholder has been induced by the fraud of the insurers or their agent to believe that the policy being effected was valid and legal: here, the premiums paid can be recovered because the parties are not *in pari delicto* (in equal fault): *Hughes* v. *Liverpool Victoria Legal Friendly Society* (1916).

UBERRIMAE FIDEI

Life policies, like other forms of insurance, are contracts *uberrimae fidei* (of the utmost good faith), so that non-disclosure of material facts by either party however innocently occurring makes these contracts voidable at the option of the other party. In ordinary contracts there is no duty of disclosure on a contracting party, but the law has always placed contracts of insurance in the category of contracts *uberrimae fidei* in order to redress the bias in favour of the insured, as the full facts relating to the subject-matter of the insurance are generally within the knowledge of the insured alone.

The definition of what is material for the purpose of disclosure contained in s. 18 (2) of the Marine Insurance Act 1906 is applicable to all classes of insurance: *Locker and Woolfe* v. *Western Australian Insurance Co.* (1936). It is as follows: "a representation is material which would influence the judgment of a prudent insurer in fixing the premium, or determining whether he will take the risk" and s. 18 (7) further provides that "whether a particular representation be material or not is, in each case, a question of fact".

In practice, a life policy is usually preceded by a proposal form in which the applicant answers a series of questions. This form is usually stated to be the basis of the contract and limits the duty to disclose to the answers to the questions set out therein. If, however, no such limitation is agreed, then the applicant must disclose every circumstance which would influence the assured's decision on whether to accept the risk or not, even though he has not been specifically asked about them. Nowadays, depending generally on the amount of the policy and the age and occupation of the life assured, medical examination is often waived, the life assured being asked various questions of a medical nature in the proposal form. The duty of disclosure continues up to the conclusion of the contract and covers any material alteration in the risk which may occur between proposal and acceptance: *Canning* v. *Farquhar* (1886).

The actual effect of non-disclosure may be varied at the agreement of the parties to the contract. Thus, where the assurers by express stipulation make the validity of the policy conditional upon an accurate answer to a question, it is of no importance whether the fact inquired into is or is not material to the risk: *Dawsons, Ltd.* v. *Bonnin* (1922). At the other extreme, some policies allow for non-forfeitability in the event of non-disclosure provided this is not of a wilful or fraudulent nature.

CRIME AND SUICIDE

A cardinal principle of all insurance is that it does not cover a loss deliberately brought about by the insured, and there is a parallel rule, based on public policy, that the policyholder cannot recover for a loss due to his intentional criminal act. Thus, it was held in *Amicable Society* v. *Bolland* (1830) that where the life assured had been executed for a criminal offence, his personal representatives could not recover the policy moneys. Again, in *Cleaver* v. *Mutual Reserve Fund Life Association* (1892), where a man had taken out a policy for the benefit of his wife, and was later poisoned by her, it was held that where the beneficiary murdered the life assured the policy moneys were payable, but neither the murderer nor the murderer's estate could benefit.

A more likely possibility than murder, or manslaughter, or any other crime causing death, is suicide, which, before the Suicide Act 1961 was itself a crime, a fact which gave rise to the rather artificial distinction between sane suicide and insane suicide. In *Beresford* v. *Royal Insurance Co.* (1938) it was held by the House of Lords that where the assured committed suicide whilst sane, the policy moneys could not be recovered by the personal representatives, even though the policy expressly so provided, because such a provision was contrary to public policy and therefore unenforceable, whereas insane suicide did not affect the right of recovery unless excluded by the provisions of the policy. By s. 1. of the Suicide Act 1961 suicide is no longer a crime, so that the public policy aspect does not now obtain. However, if a life policy does not contain any suicide clause, then the principle of the wilful act of the assured vitiating the policy may still be invoked. In practice, most life policies contain suicide provisions which will govern the position free now from any restrictions of public policy. Often, suicide is stated not to affect recovery of the policy moneys, except where it occurs within a specified period, e.g. one, two or three years from the commencement of the policy, in which event the policy may be avoided, or perhaps only the premiums paid may be recovered. Sometimes it is provided that suicide cannot constitute a claim except to the extent of any interest held by an assignee for value.

ALIEN ENEMIES

It was held in *Seligman* v. *Eagle Insurance Co.* (1917) that a policy effected on the life of a person who subsequently becomes an alien enemy does not become void and the continued payment and receipt of premiums do not involve unlawful transactions with an alien enemy, but in the event of the death of the assured the right of his personal representatives to demand payment of the policy moneys is suspended during the war.

ASSIGNMENT OF LIFE POLICIES

By s. 1 of the Policies of Assurance Act 1867 an assignee can sue in his own name, and by s. 5 the assignment may be made on the policy itself or by a separate instrument. Assignment is subject to the following two conditions:

(i) By s. 2 the assignee takes subject to equities, i.e. he is liable to be defeated by any defences which the issuer of the policy could have set up against the assignor.

(ii) By s. 3 notice in writing of the date and purport of the assignment must be given to the company, for in the event of a second or subsequent assignment the priorities of the various assignees will depend upon the date of their respective notices, and also if, before any notice is received, the company in good faith pays money to the assignor, the assignee loses his claim against the company.

The company must specify on the policy the place of business at which notices of assignment are to be given, and upon receiving notice it must, upon a written request and payment of a fee not exceeding 5s (25p), acknowledge the receipt of it in writing: ss. 4, 6. In practice, some companies waive this statutory fee. The Act also contains a schedule giving a brief specimen form of assignment, from which it would appear that the assignment need not be a deed though it must be attested. In practice, a deed is almost always used.

TYPES OF LIFE POLICIES

There can be infinite variations in the exact provisions of life policies, but there are two main categories of policies:

(i)   Whole life policies

The policy moneys here are payable only on death, so that in "own life" policies of this type the life assured never personally receives any moneys, which go to his or her estate (or assignees, if any). Because it may be a long time before such policies become claims, they represent the cheapest form of life assurance in terms of premiums.

(ii)   Endowment policies

In contrast to the unknown duration of whole life policies, the moneys under endowment policies are payable at the end of a specified period, but the liability of the assurer must be altered by death of the life assured during the currency of the policy. In other words, these policies are payable at a fixed future date or on previous death. In "own life" endowment policies the life assured will personally receive the moneys on survival to the maturity date of the policy, but if death occurs before that date the moneys will go to his or her estate (or, in either case, assignee, if any).

Both these types of policies may be "with profits" or "without profits", meaning that they do, or do not, participate in the profits of the issuing Life Office. Thus, a without profits policy for £1,000 will never yield more than this sum, whereas a with profits policy for £1,000 may amount to considerably more than this sum, say to £1,500 over the duration of the policy, due to additions to the capital sum by way of bonus usually declared every three years (since 1969 the maximum intervals between the actuarial valuations statutorily required to be done by the companies have been reduced from five years to three years). Whilst the premiums for with profits policies are naturally higher than for those which do not participate in profits, these with profits policies are popular because to some extent they help to mitigate the long-term loss due to continuing inflation of the national currency.

Sometimes policies provide for payment of the capital sum assured by instalments, so as to provide a pension or annuity, and these are particularly appropriate to persons whose occupation is not covered by any group pension or superannuation scheme.

One type of policy periodically encountered is that authorised by s. 11 of the Married Women's Property Act 1882, namely, a policy taken out by a husband on his own life for the benefit of his wife and/or children which creates a trust in favour of the beneficiaries. The insured may by the policy or by any memorandum under his or her hand appoint trustee(s) and from time to time appoint new trustee(s). In default of any appointment, such policy immediately on its being effected shall vest in the insured or his or her legal personal representatives in trust for the purposes of the section. So long as any object of this trust remains unperformed, the trust shall not form part of the insured's estate nor be subject to the insured's debts. However, the use of these policies as a means of avoiding estate duty was somewhat curtailed by the Finance Act 1968 and estate duty has now been replaced by capital transfer tax. The section also applies to policies taken out by a wife on her own life for the benefit of her husband and/or children, and to policies taken out by the spouses on each other's life for the benefit of the other and/or children, but these varieties are less frequent. As regards policies effected on or after 1st January 1970 the term "children" includes illegitimate children: s. 19 of the Family Law Reform Act 1969.

Difficulties have arisen in s. 11 policies taken out by a husband because the wife and/or children may, or may not, be specifically named therein. If the wife is designated as the beneficiary by name, e.g. "my wife A", then she acquires an immediate vested interest, which is not divested *ipso facto* on divorce (though the Family Court has power to vary the trust). If this wife pre-deceases her husband, the policy will pass to her personal representatives as part of her estate: *Cousins* v. *Sun Life Assurance Society* (1933). The husband is entitled in these circumstances to a lien on the policy moneys to the extent of the premiums paid by him since his wife's death, as being money expended by a trustee to preserve the property of a certain given trust: *Re Smith's Estate* (1937). Similar considerations apply where the children are designated, e.g. "my sons B and C, and my daughter D".

The case of *Re Browne's Policy* (1903) illustrates the opposite situation where a policy is taken out for the benefit of "my wife and children" without naming any of them. In these circumstances it was held that the trust is presumed to be in favour of those members of the class who are alive when the policy moneys become payable and that they take in equal shares; consequently, in the case in question the second wife and her children shared the policy moneys with the children of the first marriage to the exclusion of the executors of the first wife. In this type of policy the effect of a subsequent divorce is to destroy the contingent interest of the spouse because that person will no longer be the wife (or husband) of the life assured when the policy moneys become payable, and in the absence of any other beneficiaries the moneys will revert to the life assured or his (or her) estate.

Other types of life policies which may be noted are:

(i) *Mortgage protection policies*, which usually decrease in amount over the years as the mortgage moneys which they cover are gradually reduced.

(ii) *Personal accident policies*, which provide for the payment of the policy moneys only upon death by accident (as opposed to natural causes).

(iii) *Industrial policies*, which are the familiar small life policies involving frequent payment of small premiums, e.g. weekly, to a collector who records the payment in a passbook. In the days before the advent of the welfare state they were often taken out in order to cover funeral expenses, and they are usually subject to various restrictions on assignment.

(iv) *Family protection policies*, providing annuities to widows and children.

(v) *Equity linked policies*, issued in conjunction with a unit trust. These are very similar to endowment policies, but their surrender value usually fluctuates with the price of the underlying units. Generally, at maturity the capital sum or the number of units purchased during the currency of the policy (whichever is the greater) can be claimed.

(vi) *Policies covering possible tax liability*, if a person gave away property and died within 7 years of making the gift, estate duty (popularly but incorrectly called death duty) on the gift might have had to be paid by the recipient, who could insure against the donor dying during the 7 year period. Estate duty has now been replaced by capital transfer tax, but similar possibilities for insurance exist.

Occasionally a bank may insist on a life policy being taken out to cover a special situation, e.g. where a beneficiary under a trust who has a contingent not an absolute reversion, offers his reversion as security. In this event life cover will be needed to guard against the possible loss of the reversion because the reversioner may fail to survive the life tenant or to reach the age at which his interest will vest in him.

PREMIUMS

With most policies the premium is payable throughout the existence of the policy, either yearly, quarterly or monthly, or even—as in the case of industrial policies—weekly. The premiums remain the same over the full period of the assurance, being based on the average risk of death (not on the natural risk, which rises as each year passes, and so would give premiums starting quite low but climbing progressively higher and higher). Life assurance premiums have for a long time been a source of some relief from income tax, but the system has been changed by the Finance Act 1976 with effect from 6 April 1979, so that now an eligible holder of a qualifying policy is entitled to deduct the relief due before paying the premium (the current level of relief being $17\frac{1}{2}$ per cent) instead of the old method of having to pay the premium gross and then claiming relief from the Inland Revenue. Self-employed persons or those employed in non-pensionable employment may take out retirement annuity policies, and the premiums are allowable deductions for tax purposes within certain limitations laid down by the Inland Revenue under the Finance Act 1971.

Whereas with other types of policies the insurers are not bound to accept a renewal premium, with life policies the assured is usually given an absolute right to renew so that his renewal premium must be accepted when tendered in accordance with the policy's conditions. Alternatively, a life policy may take the form of a continuing assurance, subject to forfeiture on non-payment of a premium. A period of grace is normally allowed after expiration of the period of insurance for a renewal premium to be paid; life policies usually contain an express provision, which is commonly 30 days of grace for premiums payable less frequently than monthly. If death occurs before renewal but within the days of grace, then in the case of a life policy giving a right to renew on payment of a premium within the days of grace the position is not clear, but in practice the policy will usually expressly provide that in this event the policy moneys will be paid under deduction of the overdue premium. In the case of a life policy that is a continuing contract subject to forfeiture on non-payment of a premium it was held in *Stuart* v. *Freeman* (1903) that the policy was prevented from lapsing by a premium paid after death but within the days of grace and the plaintiff was entitled to recover the policy moneys.

Some policies are fully paid up, in which event no further premiums are repayable. Paid up policies may be taken out with a substantial once-for-all premium, or they may be issued in exchange for an ordinary policy of larger amount whose terms provide *inter alia*, that failure at some stage to keep paying the premiums results in exchange for a paid up policy of an appropriately smaller amount, instead of complete loss of the policy which would otherwise occur.

"COOLING-OFF" PERIOD

Under the Insurance Companies (Notice of Long-Term Policy) Regulations 1978 (S.I. 1978 No. 1304) persons taking out life policies have a right to a statutory 10 day "cooling-off" period. The companies are required to send to the proposer a notice drawing attention to the obligations being entered into and advising him of the "cooling-off" period. A "notice of cancellation" which can be used to terminate the contract must be attached to the statutory notice. These regulations cover most whole-life and endowment policies and regular premium linked life assurance business, together with term assurance effective for more than 7 years and regular premium deferred annuities (other than approved pension business).

LIFE POLICIES AS SECURITY

Within the limits imposed by each individual's financial position life assurance is both necessary and advantageous—a form of saving as well as a safeguard in the gamble of life—and one of the uses of life policies is as security for a loan, either from the Life Office issuing the policy or, more usually, from a bank, as the collection of life policies in any branch bank testifies. From a bank's point of view life cover may be vital as a buttress to other security or as a shield in the case of an unsecured advance, e.g. to a professional man, who may have a good income from which he can pay off the advance in the ordinary course of events, but little capital, and the income would cease if he were to die suddenly.

A bank or any other lender is not concerned so much with the capital sum assured (except in the special situations just mentioned), as with the surrender value, which is the amount that the Life Office issuing the policy will pay at any given time against surrender to it of the policy, i.e. the price it is prepared to pay in cancellation of its liability on the policy. A policy will have a surrender value generally after three year's premiums have been paid, and although initially it will be very small in relation to the premiums paid, it will increase as further premiums are paid and its ratio to the premiums paid also increases progressively. A new snag, the "tax clawback", was introduced by ss. 7–9 of the Finance Act 1975 whereby if a policy or its benefits, e.g. bonuses, be surrendered or converted into a paid-up policy within 4 years of its issue then the body by whom the policy is issued must deduct from the surrender proceeds or the paid-up proceeds and pay to the Inland Revenue a sum representing a part or whole of the tax relief already given on the premiums paid. Generally, if the policy is surrendered (i) within its first 2 years, all previous tax relief is lost; (ii) in its 3rd year, one half of previous tax relief is lost; (iii) in its 4th year, one third of previous tax relief is lost. In effect, this means a bank or other lender is unable to place much reliance on a life policy during its first four years, unless the policy becomes a claim by the death of the life assured.

The current surrender value may be found at any time by enquiring of the Life Office issuing the policy, although some policies, especially those issued by Canadian companies, contain a schedule setting out the surrender values throughout the duration of the policy.

Most Life Offices will themselves make loans on their policies within the surrender value. There are circumstances in which a bank may prefer the policy holder to take this course, since it makes for some reduction in an overdraft whilst at the same time preserving the valuable life cover, whereas a surrender or a sale of the policy means the loss of all rights by the policyholder.

So far as a bank is concerned, when offered a life policy as security, it must first obtain and examine the policy, which must be stamped, the present rate of duty under the Finance Act 1970 being 5p per £100 or part thereof on life policies from £50 to £1,000 and 50p per £1,000 or part thereof on policies over £1,000. Some customers' ideas of their policies are vague—instead of the policy being a straightforward own life endowment or whole life policy, it may turn out to be one for the benefit of wife and/or children, or even an accident policy which, having no surrender value, will be useless as security. Retirement annuity policies taken out under favourable tax concessions in the Finance Act 1971 cannot be surrendered or assigned, and therefore cannot be used as security for a loan. In respect of those life policies which are available as security, the following points should be noted:

(1)　The issuing Life Office

Normally this will be a first-class British Company, so that the bank need have no doubts about its financial standing. The same applies where the policy has been issued by the London office of a foreign or commonwealth company of repute, such as a leading Canadian company. Otherwise, the possibility of non-payment of a policy by an obscure or recently formed company must be borne in mind, and also the possibility of difficulties in obtaining payment of policies issued by companies domiciled abroad with no office in England. Policy moneys are recoverable at the place fixed by the policy or, if none has been fixed, at the office at which the contract was made: *New York Life Insurance Co.* v. *Public Trustee* (1924). Policies which may involve a foreign country's exchange control regulations or suing in a foreign court would not be looked upon with favour by British banks.

If legal difficulties arise over a policy not issued in England or expressed to be governed by English law, then resort must be had to that branch of English law known as Conflict of Laws, or Private International Law, which determines whether our Courts have jurisdiction over a case containing a foreign element, and if so what system of law is to be applied. For this purpose Scots law is regarded as a foreign law but this does not cause much practical difficulty, for in any event the House of Lords is the ultimate court of appeal for the United Kingdom. Conflict of laws will be referred to again later on when the mechanics of assignment are discussed.

(2) The financial provisions

These are the amount of the capital sum, and when and how it is to be paid, and also the amount and frequency of the premiums. Whilst a lender's main concern is the surrender value, as regards types of policies, banks prefer endowment policies to whole life policies because the former have a fixed maturity date. There is a difference between quarterly etc. premiums and annual premiums payable by quarterly etc. instalments—with the former a receipt is issued for each premium paid, but with the latter it is issued only when all instalments have been paid and, moreover, any instalments unpaid will be deducted from the sum assured if the policy becomes a claim.

(3) The beneficiaries

If the policy is for the benefit of parties other than or in addition to the mortgagor (e.g. his wife and/or children, under s. 11 of the Married Women's Property Act 1882 mentioned earlier), then all persons interested as beneficiaries must be of full age and join in the charge. If any of them are infants no charge will be effective. Furthermore, they must be named with reasonable certainty, because otherwise the charge, though effective when it is taken, may later be avoided if other beneficial interests are acquired, for instance, by a second wife and her children—see *Re Browne's Policy* (1903) on p. 258, *ante*. In particular circumstances a bank may require the signatory to have independent legal advice or at least to add a "free will" clause. If "children", though over eighteen years of age, have to join in a charge securing a parent's account, then a "free will" clause should again be used.

Occasionally the foregoing will not apply, because the policy contains a clause which permits the proposer being also the life assured to charge the policy by way of assignment to the exclusion of the beneficiary.

(4) Any special restrictions

These may relate to suicide, to foreign travel or residence, to occupation or to some particular mode of life. As far as possible the bank's knowledge of its customer should be used to check whether or not any restriction is being, or is likely to be, breached. It should, of course, be checked that there is no restriction on assignment; there normally is none, except in the case of industrial policies. Even with these the industrial life office will generally agree to an assignment to a bank, but due to their small amount and the difficulty of checking frequently-paid premiums banks are not keen to take them as security.

(5) Admission of age

The policy will state whether or not the age of the life assured has been admitted by production of a birth certificate to the Life Office. This must be done at some stage before it will pay out any moneys in respect of the policy because the age at which a policy is taken out determines the amount of the premium. Hence, a misrepresentation of age, though it will not void the policy, may mean an increase in premiums or an alteration in the amount recoverable under the policy. Thus, if age has not been admitted, the bank should request the customer to produce a copy of his birth certificate for submission to the Life Office. This is best done when the policy is charged, and, ideally, before any advance is made to the customer against the policy, for then he has an incentive to produce the birth certificate.

Apart from the policy itself, there are two other points, one legal and one practical, to be observed. First, the bank should note whether any previous assignment accompanies the policy, e.g. if an account is being taken over from another bank, the policy may have been assigned to that bank, and if so the document of charge, duly re-assigned, must be obtained and kept with the policy, as it forms part of the title. In any event, the Life Office should be asked whether there are any prior encumbrances oustanding. Secondly, the vital practical point is to ascertain that the current premium has been paid so as to keep the policy in force, for it will lapse if premiums are not paid as required. Hence, the current premium receipt must be obtained, as well as the subsequent ones from time to time whilst the policy is being relied on as security. A diary card system provides a check on this, but the best course is to get the customer to sign a standing order form so that premiums are not overlooked and are paid direct by the bank to the debit of the customer's account.

If the bank is satisfied with the policy and on the foregoing points, it can proceed to take a mortgage or assignment of the policy and this charge will be either legal or equitable:

(A) LEGAL MORTGAGE

The form of legal charge used by banks is an assignment under seal, and is a considerable elaboration on the brief specimen form set out in the schedule to the Policies of Assurance Act 1867. Some bank forms are fixed sum mortgages, but most are unlimited forms. The main features of the standard type of legal charge used by banks will now be considered in more detail. The operative clause of an assignment by a customer of a life policy to secure his own account is in terms similar to the following:

"The Assignor as Beneficial Owner hereby assigns unto the Bank ALL the Policy of Assurance mentioned in the Schedule hereto and all moneys (including bonuses) that may become payable thereunder or under any Policy that may be substituted therefor to HOLD unto the Bank absolutely but subject nevertheless to redemption upon payment to the Bank of all moneys and liabilities hereby convenanted to be paid."

Where there are other beneficiaries instead of, or in addition to, the grantee of the policy, then this clause must be varied so that the grantee and all the beneficiaries assign the policy to the extent of their respective rights and interests.

The Assignor covenants to pay and discharge to the Bank on demand all moneys and liabilities now or at any time hereafter due and owing to the Bank on any account whatsoever, including interest, commission etc. (making it a continuing security).

If the account being secured is not that of the mortgagor but that of someone else, then a "Third Party" charge can be taken, and this will state whose account(s) are being secured. It will also contain the usual power to the bank to vary arrangements with the customer without prejudicing the security, and to place any money received under the charge to a suspense account.

In any charge the assignor will further covenant to pay all premiums when due and not to do anything to render the policy void or voidable, or make increased premiums payable, and in the event of the policy becoming void to provide a substitute policy of at least equivalent capital sum and surrender value. However, if the policy holder becomes bankrupt, the bank cannot prove for the future premiums despite the covenant to pay them: *Deering* v. *Bank of Ireland* (1886). For its part, the bank will be empowered to keep the policy in force at the customer's expense, and in the event of the customer failing to meet his obligations on demand, to surrender the policy for cash or for a fully paid policy, to exercise any rights conferred by it, or to sell it in any way. The bank will also be authorised to give an effective receipt for any moneys payable under the policy, and sometimes the bank's power to consolidate (see p. 225, *ante*) will be preserved by excluding s. 93 of the Law of Property Act 1925.

Although a charge form may cover more than one policy, it is better to take a separate charge for each policy, as this avoids difficulties which may arise if only one form is used for a number of policies and it becomes necessary to realise part of the security.

Having taken its legal charge, the bank will give notice in duplicate to the Life Office concerned, together with the statutory fee of 25p where required. One copy of the notice will be returned as an acknowledgment for filing with the policy, and at the same time the bank will obtain final confirmation that there is no prior charge. It has already been noted that under the Policies of Assurance Act 1867 priorities of assignees are regulated by the date of receipt of notice by the company and not by the date of the assignment. However, priority will be lost if it can be proved that the assignee claiming it has notice, actual or constructive, of a prior charge. It was held in *Spencer* v. *Clarke* (1878) that non-production of the policy constituted constructive notice of a prior charge, so that an equitable assignee who had taken an agreement to assign and given notice of his charge could not obtain priority over an earlier equitable assignee who had not given notice. In this case the assured explained the non-production of the policy by falsely stating he had left it at home.

Careful inquiries are therefore needed if a bank is offered a duplicate policy as security. Some Life Offices make it clear that in no circumstances can duplicate policies be issued, and although those which do issue duplicates will check up before doing so, the bank's difficulty is that the original policy may be with an equitable mortgagee who is not obliged to give notice. It may be that the original is charged by a legal assignment of which the legal assignee has not given notice, and if in these circumstances the bank took a legal charge on the duplicate policy and gave notice, it might be able to avoid being fixed with constructive notice, if it had not been negligent when taking the charge. For example, the customer may have an apparently reasonable explanation, such as the policy was destroyed in a fire at his house, and the bank may find that there actually was a fire there, and as the first legal assignee has not given notice under the provisions of s. 3 of the Act of 1867 the bank, which has given notice, will take precedence over him.

If and when the legal charge is released, the bank will re-assign the policy to the mortgagor, by completing under seal the form of discharge endorsed on the charge form. Notice of the re-assignment should be given by the bank to the Life Office.

(B) EQUITABLE MORTGAGE

This is effected by deposit of the policy, with or without a Memorandum of Deposit, although in practice a bank nearly always takes such a memorandum to establish the nature of the transaction, to make the security a continuing security and to empower the bank to pay premiums if necessary. If the memorandum contains a written undertaking to assign it should, to give the mortgagee an immediate power of sale, be under seal.

Notice should be given to the Life Office because by the Rule in *Dearle* v. *Hall* (1828) the priority of equitable assignments is governed by the order in which notice is given. Life Offices need not recognise equitable interests, but in practice they often do so. Whether notice is given or not, an equitable mortgagee who holds the policy will, in the event of the mortgagor being adjudicated bankrupt, have priority over the bankrupt's trustee. If the mortgagor still holds the policy, then notice of assignment will be necessary in order to take the policy out of the bankrupt's order and disposition.

No re-assignment of an equitable charge is necessary, but where notice of the charge has been given and accepted, notice of withdrawal should be given when the security is released.

Banks seldom take equitable charges over life policies, because of the superior advantages of a legal charge. As the legal title to the property vests in the legal mortgagee or assignee, he can surrender or sell the policy without reference to the mortgagor or the Court, and if the policy becomes a claim, either as maturity or on death of the life assured, he can give a valid discharge for the proceeds without having to get the assured or his personal representatives to join in the discharge. Unlike a legal mortgagee, an equitable mortgagee cannot sue on the policy in his own name, and if the mortgagor is unco-operative he cannot realise the policy without the consent of the Court, even though the equitable mortgage contains an undertaking to create a legal assignment if and when called upon to do so. Again, the equitable mortgagee requires the concurrence of the mortgagor or his personal representatives in giving a discharge for the policy moneys.

Finally, the following two special points which relate to either type of mortgage should be noted:

(a) *Conflict of Laws.*— A conflict of laws may arise when a life policy is assigned in a different country to that whose law governs the original contract. In these circumstances the validity and effect of the assignment as between assignor and assignee or between competing assignees will be determined by the proper law of the assignment, i.e. the law which the parties have chosen to govern the assignment, or if none is chosen, then it is *prima facie* the law of the place where the assignment is made. Thus, if an English bank takes as security a policy the assignment of which is executed outside England and Wales, the assignment should contain a clause stating that it is to be construed and take effect according to the law of England, thereby preventing the local law of the place of execution from applying. If the assignment is executed in England but the policy is governed by a foreign system of law (which includes Scots law), in order to clarify the position the assignment should be expressed to be governed by English law, or alternatively the attestation clause should include a recital of the place where the assignment is executed.

(b) *Companies.*— Although a company itself cannot die, it may sometimes take out a life policy on its managing director or other key executive who can. When such a policy is charged as security, the charge does not require registration under s. 95 of the Companies Act 1948, as it is one of the few exceptions thereto. By s. 104 it must be recorded in the company's own register of charges, but failure by the company to do this does not invalidate the charge.

CONCLUSION

In the normal way life policies issued by a first-class Life Office and having a surrender value are a very good banking security. They possess the great advantages of being easily charged, easily valued and easily realised, for the surrender value is quickly ascertainable and is not liable to drastic depreciation though some companies cut surrender values in the mid 1970s because of a slump in the stock and share market and in property values. Normally, the surrender value steadily and progressively increases in amount as further premiums are paid. A legal mortgagee can obtain the cash surrender value with a minimum of formalities, and where the amount of the policy is sufficiently substantial to justify a sale of it, this can be done by public auction by a firm specialising in this field, and such a sale will generally yield a reasonable margin over the surrender value. Sometimes a relative of the policy holder may be prepared to buy the policy.

The only snags are the legal ones of insurable interest and *uberrima fides*, and the practical one of keeping up with the premiums. It might just occur that a grantee is subsequently discovered to have no insurable interest in the life assured, but Life Offices make careful inquiries on this point where necessary before issuing a policy, and are not likely afterwards to avoid the policy as against an innocent assignee for value. Non-disclosure of material fact is also a possibility, but fortunately it is a rather remote one. The real weakness is inability on the part of the customer to keep paying the premiums as and when they fall due, but even in this event the bank can, if it chooses (particularly where there is only a short period left before maturity), keep the policy in force at the customer's expense, or it may be able to convert the policy into a fully paid one.

Chapter 8

Stocks and Shares

INTRODUCTION

In legal classification, stocks and shares fall within the category of "choses in action", explained in Chapter 1 on Contract. In practice, they comprise a wide range of securities in two broad divisions—(a) the public sector, i.e. national and local government borrowing; and (b) the private sector, i.e. non-government borrowing, consisting mainly of capital and loans raised by companies, and also, in England, by building societies. Otherwise, in either division the body responsible for the indebtedness may be British, Commonwealth or Foreign. Cutting across these various securities are different methods of transfer, according to whether the securities are registered (and the vast majority are), or bearer, or inscribed. This range of stocks and shares, the methods of transferring them, and their use as security for bank advances will now be considered in detail.

TYPES OF STOCKS AND SHARES

GOVERNMENT AND MUNICIPAL STOCKS

The National Debt of the United Kingdom, or the money owed by the State in its corporate capacity, is an enormous amount, the bulk of which consists of stocks issued or guaranteed by the Government (sometimes called "the funds"). Most of these are redeemable at a fixed date, and are described according to their time scale as "short" or "long", an example of the last being $11\frac{3}{4}$ per cent Treasury Stock, 2003–7, known colloquially as the "James Bond" (007) Stock; but there are still some £3,500 million of undated stock, that is, stock with no fixed date for redemption, e.g. $3\frac{1}{2}$ per cent. War Stock.

In addition to the above stocks, which are handled by the Bank of England on behalf of the Government, there is a vast amount of National Savings handled by the Department for National Savings, consisting of various issues of (i) British Savings Bonds, and (ii) National Savings Certificates (including similar issues in Ulster), and (iii) Premium Bonds. The current statute under which the Department of National Savings is authorised to deal with securities is the National Debt Act 1958, as amended by the Post Office Act 1969, whereby the Director of Savings replaced the Postmaster General in this respect.

There are also various issues of local government stocks by county councils and municipalities. The Greater London Council, for example, has a larger annual budget than many of the world's independent states. These stocks are usually quoted on the Stock Exchange like the Government issues, but there are also unquoted municipal investments, whereby particular sums can be lent to councils of any size for specified periods of time and at specified interest rates, the loans being evidenced by mortgage documents.

The term "gilt-edged" is still used to denote Government stocks. It arose from the physical appearance of the stock certificates at one time, and is used generally to mark the superior status of Government stocks compared with private capitalist stocks where individual companies may fail. However, many years of progressive inflation in the present century, coupled with recurring balance of payments crises, have generally undermined the "gilt-edged" image.

COMMERCIAL AND INDUSTRIAL STOCKS AND SHARES

These exceed even the great volume of Government stocks, and consist of the share and loan capital of commercial and industrial undertakings, ranging from such giants as Imperial Chemical Industries Limited to a host of very small companies. Most of these undertakings are companies incorporated under the various Companies Acts, though there are still a few companies incorporated by Royal Charter, or by special Act of Parliament. Quite apart from companies, there are two other types of undertakings which are of considerable size and importance, and these are unit trusts, and building societies.

(i) Companies

The capital of any company can consist of a variety of stocks and shares, and there may also be loans in the nature of debentures or debenture stock or unsecured loan stock and so on. By s. 61 (1) (c) of the Companies Act 1948 all or any shares that are fully paid may be converted into stock, and *vice versa*. There are some technical differences between shares and stock, e.g. the price of shares is related to their denomination, whereas stock can be bought in fractions of any amount, subject to any provisions as to the minimum unit or multiple. In general, stock possesses the characteristics of shares, so that the following analysis of types of shares applies similarly to stock:

(a) *Ordinary Shares.*—The dividend on ordinary shares, or "equities" or "equity share capital" as they are called sometimes, is not fixed but normally fluctuates with the amount of profit made by the company concerned. It is a cardinal principle of company law that dividends can only be paid out of profits. As ordinary shareholders assume the biggest risk, they often have the sole voting rights in a company whose capital consists of more than one class of shares. If a company also has preference share capital, then the ordinary shareholders receive dividends only after the fixed dividends on the preference shares have been paid. In reasonable or prosperous times ordinary shares fare better than preference shares both as regards dividends and appreciation in value, but in hard times the position is reversed and preference shares come into their own.

Sometimes ordinary shares are divided into (i) Preferred Ordinary Shares, which have a right to a fixed dividend after the claims of the preference shareholders have been met; and (ii) Deferred Ordinary Shares, which are entitled to any profits that remain. Sometimes a company's capital may be divided into Ordinary and "A" Ordinary Shares, or into "A" Ordinary and "B" Ordinary Shares, or some similar "separation of the sheep from the goats", because the former have voting rights, whereas the latter have not. This is often done to keep control of a company within a family or small group, whilst allowing the general public to acquire non-voting shares. There are arguments for and against this system of a voting tail wagging a vote-less dog; in practice, the dividend will be the same on both sorts of share, but the voteless ones will be lower in value because they are unattractive to take-over bidders.

(b) *Preference Shares.*—The holders of these shares receive a preference or priority in respect of the payment of dividends and/or the return of capital in the event of the company being wound up. As regards dividends, entitlement is a fixed annual dividend, say seven per cent., before any dividend can be paid on the ordinary shares, but no more than the stipulated rate of dividend can be received, however great the profits may be. Preference shares may be "cumulative", so that if the profits in any one year are insufficient to pay the fixed dividend, the arrears are carried forward to the next year and thereafter until they are paid off. On the other hand, they may be "Non-cumulative", so that one year's deficiency is not carried forward, the unpaid dividend being irretrievably lost. They are "cumulative" unless they are expressly made "non-cumulative", or where provisions of Articles of Association or of the resolution of the company at the time of issue lead to that conclusion, e.g. they would not be cumulative if articles provided that "preference shareholders shall be entitled to a preference dividend at the rate of seven per cent. per annum out of the net profits of each year", the operative word being "each". Sometimes preference shares may be allowed to have a share of the profits in addition to their fixed dividend, and then they are described as "Participating Preference Shares".

Unless preference shares are made preferential as to capital, they rank equally with ordinary shares in the event of the company being wound up. Where they are preferential as to capital, any surplus capital after payment of all outside liabilities will be applied first in paying off the preference share capital, and then in repaying the ordinary shares; any remaining balance may, according to the Articles, belong entirely to the ordinary shares, or be divided rateably between the two classes, or be dealt with in some other way.

Preference shares may have full or restricted voting rights, or none at all, a frequent provision in Articles being that their holders can only vote if their dividend is in arrears for a specified period, e.g. six months, or one year, or if the resolution in question is one varying their class rights as shareholders, or winding up the company.

Redeemable Preference Shares.—A special feature confined to preference shares is that, within the provisions of s. 58 of the Companies Act 1948, they may be made redeemable. The statutory conditions are that the issue of such shares must be authorised by the company's Articles, the shares must be fully paid, and they may be redeemed either out of profits which would otherwise be available for dividend, or out of the proceeds of a new issue of shares made for the purposes of the redemption. Where the shares are redeemed out of profits, an equivalent amount must be transferred to a "Capital Redemption Reserve Fund" which is not available for distribution as a dividend, since it has no revenue character, but may be used to pay up unissued shares of the company to be issued to members as fully paid bonus shares. If the shares are redeemed at a premium, the premium must in every case be provided for out of profits or out of the share premium account. The company's balance sheet must show what part of the capital consists of redeemable preference shares and the date of redemption. (N.B. If a company does issue fully paid bonus shares as mentioned above, the practical effect on its balance sheet is that the capital redemption reserve fund will disappear as a separate item, being merged with the issued share capital.)

Very little use is made nowadays by companies of preference shares as a method of fund raising, loan stock or debentures (see below) being used instead.

(c) *Deferred Shares* (Founders' or Management Shares).—These are much less frequent than the previous classes, being usually taken by the promoters or founders of a company, though they are sometimes issued to persons who subscribe for ordinary shares. The holders of these shares are usually entitled to a proportion of the profits if the dividend on the ordinary shares exceeds a fixed amount, so they act as a spur to management to push up profits. Sometimes they may be given "weighted" voting rights so that the promoters or founders can retain control of the company, e.g. 5p Deferred Shares and £1 Ordinary Shares may be endowed with one vote per share.

Loans to Companies

Quite apart from issuing its shares, a company may raise funds by way of loan. This may be done by a general issue of Debentures or Debenture Stock, normally secured by a fixed and/or floating charge on the company's assets (see Chapter 4 on Companies), though they may be "naked" or unsecured, in which event the title of Unsecured Loan Stock is often used. Funds raised in these ways are loosely called Loan Capital, but strictly they are not part of a company's capital, for the lenders are not members but loan creditors of the company, and they are entitled to their fixed rate of interest whether the company makes a profit or not, and to the return of their loans in priority to all shareholders.

Sometimes, Convertible Debentures or Debenture Stock, or Convertible Unsecured Loan Stock may be issued, which gives a holder an option to convert his loan into ordinary shares of the company at specified future dates and prices. In this way, the holder gets the best of both worlds, for if the company prospers and its ordinary shares thereby rise in value beyond the option price, he can switch his loan into ordinary shares, but if the company languishes he can remain a loan creditor with the advantages already recited.

(ii) Unit Trusts

These organisations, which have had a spectacular growth since the Second World War, are governed by a trust deed and operated by managers. They act as a vehicle whereby the small, and not-so-small, investor can indirectly hold a share in a wide portfolio of quoted stocks and shares (usually held by a leading bank as trustee) thereby obtaining some degree of safety in numbers and spreading the risk of individual companies doing badly or failing. The investor subscribes for a number of units in the trust and receives a certificate for that amount. The moneys subscribed are invested by the trust managers in a variety of securities as authorised by the trust deed, the names of the trusts often indicating their scope, e.g. "High Income Trust", "Bank and Insurance Trust", "Mining Trust" and so on. The income on its investments received by the trust is paid out at so much per unit to the unit holders, usually in half-yearly distributions. The value of the units depends on the number of them outstanding in relation to the underlying securities of the trust as valued at any time. The price of many units are published daily by the trust managers under two headings "Bid" and "Offered", being the respective prices at which the managers will buy and sell the units, and they can be seen in numerous newspapers.

(iii)   Building Societies

The building society movement is a peculiarly English institution, and consists of some 300 individual societies spread over the country and ranging from very large organisations to quite small ones. Over more than a 100 years the movement has grown to financial magnitude, as evidenced by the size of the Halifax Building Society, the largest of the societies, whose 1979 balance sheet shows assets totalling £7,602 million. Building societies are currently regulated by the Building Societies Act 1962 and they receive funds from investing shareholders and depositors which in turn are lent on mortgages of real property, mainly dwelling houses. Shares may be paid up, or may be subscription shares, which are acquired by instalments over a period of time. The shareholder's title is nearly always evidenced by a passbook, in which transactions are recorded from time to time, though occasionally a society may issue certificates for paid up shares in round amounts, say, £50. Similarly, depositors have passbooks, and both shareholders and depositors receive a fixed rate of interest on their money, though the former receive a slightly higher rate, because the latter as loan creditors have priority over members if the society gets into financial difficulties and therefore are less at risk. The interest is paid free of income tax at the basic rate, because of special tax arrangements between the societies and the Inland Revenue.

METHODS OF TRANSFER

1.   REGISTERED STOCKS AND SHARES

The vast majority of securities are registered, that is to say the issuing body keeps a register of stockholders or shareholders, who receive as evidence of their ownership a certificate in their names. Provided that they are transferable by nature (e.g. National Development Bonds and National Savings Certificates are not transferable), the legal title to these securities is transferred by a signed transfer being lodged together with the relative certificate with the Registrar, who deletes the old owner from the register, or reduces his holding therein as the case may be, and makes corresponding entries in the register in respect of the new owner; he will also cancel the old certificate and issue a new one to the transferee, with a balance certificate to the transferor where requisite. The Register for the great majority of Government Stocks is kept by the Bank of England, though there are some stocks where the National Savings Stock Register may be used. With companies transfer work is handled by the Secretary or by the Registrar, the latter often being some outside organisation specialising in registration work, such as a bank department, or a firm of secretaries or accountants.

The form of transfer used may be either a deed, or what is called the common form of transfer (a transfer under hand, although in appearance it is identical with a deed), or the simplified form called a stock transfer introduced by the Stock Transfer Act 1963, which is now widely used, though occasionally the older types may still be encountered. The main features of a stock transfer form are a statement of the consideration money, the full name of the undertaking (i.e. the company or other corporation), full description of the security, the number or amount of the shares, stock etc. in words and figures, and details of the registered holder(s). Then comes the operative clause reading: "I/We hereby transfer the above security out of the name(s) aforesaid to the person(s) named below . . ." followed by details of the transferee(s). The form is signed under hand by the transferor(s), or under seal where the transferor is a body corporate; unlike the older forms, it is not signed by the transferee(s), the purpose of the Act being to save time and clerical work as far as possible. The Act further provides that the Treasury may, by statutory instrument, alter, replace or add to the transfer forms set out in the Act. This has been done as regards some minor amendments by the Stock Transfer (Amendment of Forms) Order 1974 (S.I. 1974 No. 1214).

Under the Stamp Act 1891, as amended by various Finance Acts up to that of 1974, the stamp duty exigible on transfers of stocks, shares or marketable securities is *ad valorem* duty at the rate of £2 per cent., the duty being levied in the following stages:

Where the consideration in the case of a sale (or the value in the case of a voluntary transfer or gift) does not exceed £5 . . . 10p;

Where the consideration etc. is between £5 and £100 . . . 20p per multiple of £10 or fraction thereof;

Where the consideration etc. is between £100 and £300 . . . 40p per multiple of £20 or fraction thereof; and

Where it exceeds £300 it is £1 for every £50 and for any fraction thereof.

Stamp duty on transfers of registered debentures (defined as comprising all capital raised by a company which has the character of borrowed money) was abolished by s. 126 of the Finance Act 1976, except where the debentures are convertible into shares or contain certain special terms, when the duty is the same as on the transfer of stocks and shares.

Certain features concerning transfer that apply specially to companies, or to unit trusts, or to building societies require more detailed treatment:

(i) Companies

As regards companies incorporated under the various Companies Acts, the following provisions of the Companies Act 1948 apply:

73.—The shares or other interest of any member in a company shall be personal estate, transferable in manner provided by the articles of the company, and shall not be of the nature of real estate.

A company may, of course, by its articles restrict the rights of its members to transfer their shares and a private company must do so, as this is one of the requisites under s. 28 of the Act for that type of company.

74.—Each share in a company having a share capital shall be distinguished by its appropriate number:

Provided that, if at any time all the issued shares in a company or all the issued shares therein of a particular class, are fully paid up and rank *pari passu* for all purposes, none of those shares need thereafter have a distinguishing number so long as it remains fully paid up and ranks *pari passu* for all purposes with all shares of the same class for the time being issued and fully paid up.

This section has enabled companies to do away with a lot of detailed clerical work which the numbering of shares involved. As previously noted, by s. 61 (1) (c) of the Act fully paid up shares may be converted into stock, which does not require distinguishing numbers.

75.—Notwithstanding anything in the articles of a company, it shall not be lawful for the company to register a transfer of shares in or debentures of the company unless a proper instrument of transfer has been delivered to the company.

Provided that nothing in this section shall prejudice any power of the company to register as shareholder or debenture holder any person to whom the right to any shares in or debentures of the company has been transmitted by operation of law.

Thus, oral transfers are prohibited. In *Re Greene* (1949) it was held that this section was contravened by articles which provided that upon the death of any director, his shares should be deemed to have passed to his widow, for no proper instrument of transfer had to be delivered, nor had the right to the shares been transmitted to the widow by operation of law; consequently, the registration of the widow, which has been authorised by the directors, was wrong and the register ought to be rectified by registering the shares in the joint names of the personal representatives. The Stock Transfer Act 1963 has interfered with the freedom of articles to stipulate what sort of instrument of transfer is required by introducing a new and simplified document known as a stock transfer and providing that such stock transfer is to be effective notwithstanding any contrary provisions in any enactment or instrument relating to the transfer of securities (s. 2).

76.—A transfer of the share or other interest of a deceased member of a company made by his personal representative shall, although the personal representative is not himself a member of the company, be as valid as if he had been such a member at the time of the execution of the instrument of transfer.

The personal representatives of a deceased member do not become members unless they get themselves so registered.

77.—On the application of the transferor of any share or interest in a company, the company shall enter in its register of members the name of the transferee in the same manner and subject to the same conditions as if the application for the entry were made by the transferee.

78.—(1) If a company refuses to register a transfer of any shares or debentures, the company shall, within two months after the date on which the transfer was lodged with the company, send to the transferee notice of the refusal.

(2) If default is made in complying with this section, the company and every officer of the company who is in default shall be liable to a default fine.

These two sections are self-explanatory. It may be added that a company is under no obligation to send a notice of refusal to the transferor: *Gustard's Case* (1869).

Section 79 deals with the procedure known as certification of transfers whereby, when a holding is divided, the transferor's certificate is lodged with the company which certifies on the transfer "Certificate lodged", or some similar wording. The section provides that certification is a representation by the company that documents showing a *prima facie* title have been lodged, but not a representation that the transferor has any title to the shares or debentures, and it makes the company liable for the fraudulent or negligent certification by any officer or servant of the company or other person authorised to certificate transfers. Under the Rules and Regulations of the Stock Exchange, the Share and Loan Department of the Stock Exchange undertakes certification of transfers as an alternative to certification by the company, but no liability is incurred by the Council of the Stock Exchange in respect of such certification.

Section 80 provides that the company must issue to the shareholder or debenture holder the appropriate certificate for shares, debentures or debenture stock within two months after their allotment or the lodgment of a duly stamped and valid transfer relating to them. This does not apply to transfers which the company is entitled to refuse to register and does not register. A default fine is again imposed, and it is also provided that the person entitled to the certificate may apply to the Court for an order enforcing the issue of the certificate, the costs of the application being borne by the company or by any officer of the company responsible for the default.

> **81.**—A certificate, under the common seal of the company [or the seal kept by the company by virtue of section 2 of the Stock Exchange (Completion of Bargains) Act 1976], specifying any shares held by any member, shall be prima facie evidence of the title of the member to the shares.

How the common seal is affixed is determined by the articles: for example, clause 113 of Table A of the Act of 1948 provides that every instrument to which the seal shall be affixed shall be signed by a director and shall be countersigned by the secretary or by a second director or by some other person appointed by the directors for the purpose. The articles of large companies often provide that facsimile or autographical signatures are sufficient or even that no attesting signatures to the common seal are required. The words in square brackets were inserted by the Stock Exchange (Completion of Bargains) Act 1976, passed to enable the Stock Exchange to operate effectively a new computerised settlement system. This new system is known as "Talisman", which is a contraction of Transfer Accounting, Lodgement for Investors and Stock Management for Jobbers, and involves a company formed by the Stock Exchange, Sepon

Limited (a contraction for Stock Exchange Pool Nominees) acting as a depository for securities in the course of settlement of bargains. Section 2 allows a company to have for use for sealing securities issued by the company an official seal which is a facsimile of the common seal of the company with the addition on its face of the word "Securities" and documents sealed with this seal do not require to be signed.

The certificate is the only documentary evidence the shareholder possesses. It is evidence of the legal title, but not of the equitable title: *Shropshire Union Railways and Canal Co.* v. *R.* (1875). Share certificates and transfers are not negotiable: *Swan* v. *North British Australasian Co.* (1863). The issuing company is estopped from disputing the truth of any statement in a share certificate against any person who, without knowledge that the statement is untrue, has acted on the faith of it and thereby suffered loss, and the measure of damages is the value of the shares at the relevant date together with interest therefrom: *Balkis Consolidated Co.* v. *Tomkinson* (1893).

Finally, mention must be made of a statute "more honour'd in the breach, than the observance"—the Banking Companies' (Shares) Act 1867 (commonly known as Leeman's Act). This renders void the sale of shares in a joint stock banking company, unless the contract sets forth in writing the numbers of the shares as stated in the register of the company; but the Stock Exchange custom is to disregard this requirement.

(ii) Unit Trusts

Units issued by unit trusts are generally transferable by deed or any usual or common form of transfer or such other form as the trustees may approve. However, a holder of units wishing to realise them will normally sell them back to the Managers of the trust at the current price for buying-back, and this is done by completing the Form of Renunciation on the back of the certificate, whereby the holder declares he is no longer interested in all or some of the units comprised in the certificate, and returning the certificate to the Managers. This is in contrast to the position of a company, which is forbidden to purchase its own shares, though it may reduce its capital in the circumstances and manner prescribed by s. 66 of the Companies Act 1948.

(iii) Building Societies

Building society shares are subject to restrictions on transfer, and realisation is effected by withdrawing the moneys, subject to any specified period of notice of withdrawal that may be required by individual societies.

2. BEARER SECURITIES

The title to bearer bonds, shares or debentures passes by mere delivery. Bearer securities are negotiable, and the essence of negotiability is that a person taking such securities in good faith and for value acquires an indefeasible title to them (an aspect discussed already in Chapter 1 on Contract, pages 53–55). Bearer bonds may be issued by British, Commonwealth or Foreign Governments, and s. 83 of the Companies Act 1948 allows a (public) company, if authorised by its articles, to issue warrants to bearer in respect of fully paid-up shares. Companies can also issue bearer debentures. By analogy, unit trusts could issue units to bearer; on the other hand, building societies are not concerned with bearer shares at all.

In practice, however, restrictions on the issue and circulation of bearer securities were imposed at the outbreak of war in 1939, with the object of preventing drains on the country's foreign currency reserves through private dealings in foreign or bearer securities. These restrictions were continued by the Exchange Control Act 1947, and regulations made thereunder by the Bank of England, until the regulations were dismantled in 1979, so that, among other consequences, the depositing of bearer securities and foreign currency securities with authorised depositaries like banks and stockbrokers was abolished. However, whilst s. 10 of the Act remains in force the issue of share warrants to bearer requires Treasury permission, but this restriction could be lifted by the Treasury issuing a general consent or by the Act being repealed, in which event it will be interesting to see whether there is a surge in the volume of bearer securities in circulation.

The initial stamp duty on bearer securities is £6 per cent. (i.e. three times heavier than the rate applicable to a transfer of registered securities), for once they are put into circulation the Inland Revenue gains no further duty on any subsequent transfers, as it does in the case of registered securities. No stamp duty is now payable on the issue of bearer debentures and debenture stock certificates to bearer, unless they fall within the exceptions set out in s. 126 of the Finance Act 1976.

Lastly, mention must be made of two particular types of bearer securities:

(a) *American and Canadian Share Certificates.*— These, although indorsed in blank, are only "quasi-negotiable". They generally have a combined transfer form and power of attorney on the back. When this has been signed by the registered holder (usually well-known London Stockbrokers or a trust company, hence the shares are said to be in "good marking [or, market] names" as listed in the Stock Exchange Year Book), the certificates thereafter pass as if they were bearer securities negotiable by delivery, though the position has not yet been settled in the Courts. The current owner must periodically claim the dividends from the registered holder, whereas normal bearer securities have interest coupons attached for this purpose.

(b) *Scrip.*—Scrip is the provisional certificate received by a holder of Government stock or company shares or debentures. It is issued whilst instalments are being paid, and when all instalments have been duly paid, it is exchanged for the definitive stock or share or debenture certificate. Nowadays, companies instead of issuing scrip certificates use Letters of Allotment to serve the same purpose. Since the Finance Act 1949 letters of allotment, letters of renunciation, scrip certificates and scrip have been free of stamp duty. A scrip certificate is normally negotiable by delivery, but in order to pass the title to shares or debentures represented by a Letter of Allotment, the allottee must complete the Form of Renunciation indorsed on the Letter and deliver it to the person who is to take the securities so that he can complete the Form of Application and lodge the renounced allotment letter with the company within the specified period. Once the period for renunciation and stamp duty-free registration by the renouncee has passed, then the usual transfer form for a registered security must be executed, the Letter of Allotment then merely acting as a substitute for the actual certificate still to be issued.

3. INSCRIBED SECURITIES

This method of title to Government stocks is now largely disused, having been abolished for British Government stocks in January, 1943, though it survived in relation to some Commonwealth stocks. The Local and Other Authorities (Transfer of Stock) Regulations 1949 (S.I. 1949 No. 1562, since replaced by S. I. 1974 No. 519), converted all inscribed stocks of local authorities into registered stocks. Inscribed holdings are not evidenced by certificates but by book entries, the stock receipt being of no value. Transfer is effected by attendance of the holder or his attorney at the office where the register is kept, though in the case of inscribed stocks domiciled at the Bank of England the common form of transfer may be used instead of a power of attorney.

Stocks on the National Savings Stock Register (formerly the Post

Office Register) are sometimes referred to as "Inscribed Stocks", but they are distinctive in that their transfer is effected by lodging the certificate and a special form of transfer with the National Savings Bank, Bonds and Stock Office, Blackpool, Lancs. FY3 9YP. In any event, these stocks can easily become registered stocks by being transferred to the Bank of England Register.

STOCKS AND SHARES AS SECURITY

1. REGISTERED STOCKS AND SHARES

As they comprise the great majority of stocks and shares, registered ones are those normally offered to a bank as security for advances. When registered stocks and shares are deposited in this way, the bank can take either a legal or an equitable charge, but in either event the bank usually gets the customer to execute a Memorandum (or Letter) of Deposit. This document is taken in order to establish the nature of the transaction, and so prevent a customer from subsequently alleging that he entrusted the securities to the bank in a bailor-bailee relationship, so that the bank would not have either an equitable charge by deposit or even a lien on them. The memorandum (no longer stamped, as the former 6d duty was abolished by the Finance Act 1970) may be an "omnibus" one, covering all stocks, shares, bonds, debentures etc. deposited at the time of signing or to be deposited thereafter whether for security, safe custody, collection or for any specific purpose and including dividends, interest, rights, bonuses, options etc. on such securities. Alternatively, it may contain a schedule to be filled in with the securities actually deposited, so that the memorandum then covers only the securities scheduled, and any substituted securities, for which written evidence should be obtained.

Either type of memorandum charges the stocks and shares to the bank as a continuing security for all moneys now or at any time hereafter due and owing to the bank on any account whatsoever. A "Third Party" Memorandum may be taken when the securities are being deposited by someone other than the customer, and this will further state whose account(s) are being secured and will empower the bank to vary arrangements with the customer without prejudicing the security and to place any moneys received under the charge to a Suspense Account. All memoranda confer on the bank a power of sale on default by the customer to pay and discharge to the bank on demand all moneys and liabilities secured by the charge, and the depositor of the securities undertakes to complete any documents necessary to perfect the bank's title. He also agrees to accept a return of the equivalent type and number of shares or debentures deposited, i.e. not necessarily the exact ones which he deposited, because this might be difficult technically to arrange where the securities have been transferred to a nominee company which handles a large volume of those particular securities. Another clause which may appear is an undertaking by the depositor to maintain a margin in the value of the securities over the amount of the indebtedness they secure. Sometimes merchant banks include in their memoranda a re-pledge clause, whereby they are authorised to lodge the securities elsewhere for their own account, e.g. they can then use parts of a large holding charged to them as security for re-finance obtained from any other source.

A deposit of certificates in joint names presents some technical points, principally, a clear possibility that the securities are being held in trust, and the need to make certain that the memorandum taken fits the circumstances. The trust angle will be explored a little later, but as regards the form of the memorandum, a memorandum signed jointly by A and B does not cover securities in the sole name of either A or B but only their joint holdings, so that additional memoranda, signed by A and B separately, are necessary to pick up any sole holdings for the joint liability. Moreover, a memorandum signed jointly by A and B does not cover the separate liabilities of A and B but only the joint liabilities of A and B, or their liabilities jointly with others.

Having obtained the securities and taken the appropriate memorandum, the bank can then decide whether to proceed to acquire a legal title, or whether to remain content with an equitable title.

(i)   Legal Title

The further step necessary to give the bank a legal title is to get the securities actually transferred into the name of the bank, or, in practice, into its nominees' name, by taking a transfer from the depositor and registering it. In past times banks used to use two members of their staff as nominees, but the modern practice is to incorporate a separate limited company as a subsidiary of the bank, usually with a £100 capital and the word "Nominees" as part of its name. The large banks, indeed, have an array of such companies, related to specific branches or on a geographical basis. This use of nominee companies ensures perpetual succession and so avoids the trouble of re-transfer that the death of a personal nominee would involve, and also permits a devolution of duties so that the main bank board of directors does not have to seal thousands of transfer forms.

A transfer as security for an advance, or a re-transfer to the original transferor when the security is no longer required, will state a nominal consideration, usually 50p. In order that the stamp duty on the transfer may be a fixed duty of 50p instead of the normal *ad valorem* duty of £2 per cent., the transfer must be indorsed with a certificate setting forth the facts of the transaction. This certificate should be signed by both transferor and transferee, or by a member of a Stock Exchange or a solicitor acting for one or other of them, or by an accredited representative of a bank. Where the bank or its official nominee is a party to the transfer, the certificate, instead of setting forth the facts, may be to the effect that "the transfer is excepted from Section 74 of the Finance (1909–10) Act 1910." The certificate on the transfer having been duly completed, the transfer will be passed by the Inland Revenue for stamping at the fixed duty of 50p. Transfers exempt from stamp duty in any event, as are those in respect of Governmental stocks, remain free. The transfer and relative certificate(s) for the stock or shares etc. are then lodged for registration, and in due course a certificate in the name of the nominee company will be issued. A similar procedure takes place in the reverse direction when the securities are re-transferred to the original transferor on repayment of the advance, or on the release of the security by the bank. Companies may charge a registration fee, but not if their stock or shares are quoted on the Stock Exchange, as the Rules of the Stock Exchange do not permit registration fees.

There are two possible snags that may arise as a result of a bank acquiring a legal title; first, the shares may not be fully paid, or they may even be shares in unlimited companies, carrying unlimited liability on the part of the shareholder. Partly-paid shares are rare now, as banks and insurance companies whose own share capital was often of this nature have largely re-organised their capital into fully paid shares; and unlimited companies are very rare indeed. Needless to say, banks are extremely careful before they allow their nominee companies to hold partly paid shares involving liability for calls, including that amount unpaid on the shares which cannot be recovered from the bank's transferee if the company goes into liquidation within a year of the bank ceasing to be a member: s. 212 of the Companies Act 1948. If a call is made on partly paid shares, the bank will be obliged to pay it, because apart from the likelihood of the shares being forfeited for non-payment, the company can sue the bank for the amount due. Any amount paid by the bank is, of course, added to the customer's indebtedness, though this may not be very attractive, since partly paid shares are not so much in demand as the normal, fully paid shares and may be more difficult to realise. Banks would fight very shy of shares in unlimited companies, because of the enormous obligations they may entail.

The second snag applies to all stocks and shares, but it is happily rare—forgery. Occasionally, certificates have been forged, but this would come to light if a transfer to the bank's nominee company is lodged for registration. It is more likely to be the transfer that is forged. The best way to eliminate this risk is to have all transfers signed at the bank, but if a bank does unwittingly accept a forged transfer, the document is a nullity and by sending it in for registration the bank warrants that it is genuine and is bound to indemnify the company or other body concerned against any loss resulting therefrom: *Sheffield Corporation* v. *Barclay* (1905). The bank has no claim to the shares under a forged transfer, for in these circumstances the transferee cannot compel the company to acknowledge him as the holder of the shares: *Simm* v. *Anglo-American Telegraph Co.* (1879). The name of the original holder will have to be restored to the register and the bank will be liable for any dividends paid to it. The same applies even if the securities have been subsequently sold to innocent third parties who have been registered and received certificates in their names. Restoring the name of the original holder would make the bank liable to the company or other body concerned for the full amount of the securities at the market price, if they had to be purchased for the innocent third parties, as well as for all back dividends. The claim to be indemnified by the bank only arises when the loss has occurred, i.e. when the company or other body concerned has to restore the original holder to the register, so that the bank may be held liable many years after the transaction seemed closed. At one time, secretaries or registrars used to write to transferors, advising them that the transfer had been lodged and would be dealt with unless they objected by return of post, but this practice has fallen into desuetude, and in any event the transferor is not bound to reply. The Forged Transfer Acts 1891 and 1892 allow companies to set up a fund for compensation for loss arising under a forged transfer.

Finally, it may be noted that under s. 27 of the Companies Act 1976 a company whose shares are listed as a recognised stock exchange may by notice in writing require disclosure of beneficial interests in its voting shares, and failure to comply with the notice is a criminal offence. Thus, a bank nominee company may be called upon to disclose for whom it holds the shares.

(ii)   Equitable Title

Mere deposit of registered stocks and shares as security gives the bank an equitable title, though, in practice, a memorandum of deposit is usually taken in order to put the nature of the transaction beyond ambiguity or argument. However, even with a memorandum containing an undertaking to perfect the bank's title upon request, if the person depositing the securities refuses to execute a transfer, the bank is unable to make an effective sale of the securities without a Court order. To overcome this difficulty, the bank, when taking an equitable charge, will often take in addition to the memorandum a "blank" transfer in respect of each security lodged (though some banks consider the practice undesirable and do not take them). A blank transfer is one signed by the depositor as transferor but otherwise incomplete, and so the bank is able at any future date to complete the transfer in favour of (i) its nominee company, so that, on registration of the transfer, the bank's title will be changed from an equitable one into a legal one, or (ii) a third party into whose name the security is transferred direct when the bank has had to realise it.

The reason for leaving the transfer undated is that once a transfer has been dated it must be stamped within thirty days of that date: s. 15 of the Stamp Act 1891. It is not invalidated as a written document if the date is filled in subsequently when the bank decides to utilise the transfer, but difficulties have arisen in the occasional instance where the articles of a company, or the relevant regulations governing other securities, require a transfer by "deed". This is because a transfer to be valid as a deed must be completed at the time of delivery, and blanks cannot be filled in at a later date except when authorised by a power of attorney or a Court order, whereas with the transfer under hand or written or common form transfer (even though it looks like a deed) a bank has implied authority to fill in the blanks, though in practice express authority can be conferred in the memorandum. This technical difficulty is even less likely to arise now, because stock transfer forms will normally be used, and they are effective nowithstanding any contrary provisions in articles or other relevant regulations, but a stock transfer form will still not apply to partly-paid shares because s. 1 of the Stock Transfer Act 1963 limits their use to fully-paid registered securities issued by companies (limited by shares), bodies incorporated under a statute or Royal Charter, the United Kingdom Government or local authorities and unit trusts.

Thus, it is only in the very rare combination of articles requiring a deed of transfer and the shares being partly-paid that a bank would have to take a complete, not a blank, transfer, and then stamp it within thirty days of its date. It can thereafter be held by the bank until it decides to register the transfer, though until such registration the bank's title is merely equitable. If a bank takes a blank transfer in circumstances where a deed is still essential, subsequently fills in the blanks and submits it for registration, the company will not know from looking at the transfer that it is invalid as a deed and will register it, but the bank's apparent legal title will crumble when the facts come to light. The bank will have only an equitable title (for the transfer will not be invalidated as a written instrument) but such title will be postponed to any prior equitable title, e.g. that of the beneficiaries under a trust. These circumstances actually occurred in *Powell* v. *London and Provincial Bank* (1893), but nowadays if a stock transfer form can be and is used, this will be effective to give the bank a legal title which ordinarily will take precedence over an equitable one.

As the bank gets a good equitable title from a deposit of certificates alone, if the depositor becomes bankrupt, it will have priority over his trustee, who cannot claim the certificates unless he pays off the indebtedness they secure. Not having blank transfers, the bank cannot make an effective sale without a Court order, or the execution of transfers by the trustee, who is able to do so under the general provisions of s. 53 of the Bankruptcy Act 1914. In practice the trustee will normally co-operate with the bank to enable the security to be realised, for he is entitled to any surplus proceeds.

Protection of an Equitable Title

This may be effected in the following two ways, though these are not greatly used in practice, because a bank which had the slightest doubt about the mortgagor's integrity would not be content with anything less than a legal title, and might decline the transaction altogether:

(a) *Notice of Lien.*— The bank can send a notice of lien to the company, which may ignore the notice, acknowledge it, or reply stating that by s. 117 of the Companies Act 1948 and/or its Articles of Association the company can take no notice of any trust, express, implied of constructive (which is at least an acknowledgment). The purposes for which this notice is given are:

(i) Where a company whose fully paid shares are not quoted on the Stock Exchange is given by its Articles a first and paramount lien on its shares for moneys owed to it by the shareholder, e.g. a brewery company whose members include its own licensees, the giving of notice of lien by a bank cannot be ignored by the company as a trading concern. Consequently, after receipt of the notice the company cannot claim its lien in respect of any subsequent debts incurred to it by the shareholder: *Bradford Banking Co., Ltd.* v. *Henry Briggs, Son & Co., Ltd.* (1886). By the Rules of the Stock Exchange, a company which obtains an official quotation for its fully paid shares cannot have an Article giving it a first and paramount lien on its shares; as the vast majority of stocks and shares deposited with banks are quoted securities, this point about lien will not arise in respect of them. However, deposits of shares in unquoted companies, or deposits of partly-paid shares, should be protected by notice of lien, although in small, "family" companies the customer may be reluctant to let the bank give such a notice because it will make known to the company that he is borrowing against the shares.

(ii) If the company is prepared to note in its records that a shareholder's certificate(s) is lodged with a bank, this protects the bank against the possibility that a dishonest shareholder may obtain a duplicate certificate from the company by pretending the original has been lost or destroyed and then sell his holding.

When a notice of lien has been given, it should be withdrawn when the bank ceases to be interested in the shares in question.

(b) *Stop Notice* (which has replaced the Notice in lieu of Distringas).—This rather cumbersome and expensive procedure under Order 50, Rules 11 to 15, of the Rules of the Supreme Court 1965 is little used.

The legal procedure is that the bank by application to the Court obtains a notice which is served on the company in respect of the shares in question, and then the company must give the bank eight clear days' warning of its intention to pass a transfer of the shares; if the bank takes no action via the Court within this time, the transfer can be registered. The notice may also include an intended payment of dividend.

Contrast between Legal and Equitable Titles

In general, legal rights prevail over equitable rights of which the legal mortgagee has no notice, and as regards purely equitable rights priority goes to the earliest created. Thus, where a bank takes a legal mortgage over stocks and shares before receiving notice of equitable interests (usually those of the beneficiaries under a trust), the bank will have priority. But if the bank has been content to take only an equitable title, then once notice of a prior equitable interest is received by the bank, it is too late for the bank to turn its equitable title into a legal one by registering a transfer, and even if it apparently succeeds in getting a transfer registered, this will be set aside by the Court at the instance of the party entitled to the prior equity, because between the two competing equitable titles, the first in time prevails: *Coleman* v. *London County and Westminster Bank Ltd.* (1916).

The other principal advantages of a legal title are that once the power of sale has come into effect by the bank's demand for repayment being unsatisfied, the bank can sell the securities and vest the legal title in the purchaser without any recourse to the mortgagor or to the Court; and that at all times the bank has full control over the security. Its nominee company has the legal title to the shares (subject to the equity of redemption of the beneficial owner) and as the registered holder it will receive direct all dividends, or interest payments, and other communications, of which in the case of companies any rights issues or bonus issues are particularly important.

The disadvantages of taking a legal title have already been noted so far as they concern partly-paid shares and forged transfers. To these may be added the practical points that considerable clerical work devolves on the nominee company; the customers may object to paying the nominal stamp duty of 50p per transfer, and any registration fees (where charged they are usually 12½p) on taking and on releasing the securities; and that some do not like the idea of their securities being taken out of their name and put into that of a bank nominee company. This last point is a real difficulty where a customer is a director of the company whose shares he is offering as security and those shares represent his director's qualification shares, i.e. the minimum number which articles may require a director to have registered in his name. If Clause 77 of Table A, the First Schedule to the Companies Act 1948, applies, no shareholding qualification for directors is required unless and until so fixed by the company in general meeting. If the company does so fix a share qualification for directors, and whenever articles specify such a qualification, then a director who ceases at any time to hold his qualification *ipso facto* vacates his office of director: s. 182 of the Companies Act 1948. Of course, if articles require a director to hold, say, 100 shares, and the director actually has 1,000 shares in his own name, then he can safely transfer 900 to the bank or its nominee company by way of legal mortgage.

The advantages of an equitable title are that it is acquired easily and cheaply, that there are no difficulties about a director's qualification shares, and that it does not involve the bank in any legal liability for calls on partly-paid shares. Its disadvantages are such that in practice some banks regard equitable charges over shares merely as evidence of means. These disadvantages may be summarised as: (1) the possibility of the bank's title being lost by forfeiture for non-payment of calls on partly-paid shares, or by postponement to a prior equitable title that may come to light, or by the mortgagor fraudulently getting a duplicate certificate and selling his holding to an innocent third party who would acquire a legal title on registration; (2) difficulties in realisation if blank transfers are not taken; (3) the not very satisfactory methods of protecting an equitable title; and (4) as the securities remain in the mortgagor's name all dividends or interest payments (unless mandated to the bank) will go to him, and what is of more consequence, so will any rights issues or bonus issues made by companies. Some further explanation of these issues is now called for.

Rights Issues

A rights issue is when a company offers shares, debentures or unsecured loan stock to its existing members for subscription by them, usually on favourable terms. If, however, a member does not wish to take up his rights, he can normally sell these on the market in the same way as any other quoted securities. As they are rights, he is not legally bound to take them up and pay for them. S. 22 of the Companies Act 1948 provides that alterations in the memorandum or articles of a company increasing liability to contribute to share capital do not bind existing members without their consent.

If, as is often the case, the new securities are payable by instalments, then after payment of the first instalment they become partly-paid securities and may be forfeited for non-payment of subsequent instalments. Where a nominee company holds shares and a rights issue is made, it will ask the beneficial owner if he wishes to take up the shares (this may depend on whether the bank will increase its advance), or to sell them, provided there is sufficient value in the rights, because funds are not available for them or they are not required in any event. Suppose a company's £1 Ordinary Shares stand at 300p and a 1 for 1 rights issue is made at par. This means, ignoring minor price movements, that after the issue the shares will be quoted at 200p (i.e. 300p per each original share plus 100p paid for each new share, divided by two, as the holder of one share now has two). Thus, if a member does not take up a new share, he can sell it nil-paid for 100p, which corresponds with the decrease in value of his existing share because of the rights issue. If the bank has only an equitable title, the rights issue documents will go to the mortgagor, and some shareholders lose money simply by doing nothing about them until it is too late. Shares not taken up will be sold by the company either on the market or to applicants for them. Hence, rights issue documents usually state: "This document is valuable. If you do not understand its purport, consult your stockbroker, accountant, bank manager or solicitor".

Bonus Issues

A bonus issue is when shares are issued fully-paid to existing ordinary members of a company. No cash is paid for them, because they are paid up by a capitalisation of reserves. Some flourishing companies issue bonus shares almost annually. It is quite wrong to call bonus shares "free shares" or "free issues", for they represent a portion of the company's reserves to which ordinary members are already entitled. Suppose a company's £1 Ordinary Shares stand at 300p and the company has sufficient capital reserves to make a 1 for 1 bonus issue. Each holder now has two shares instead of one, so the price will fall to 150p. If the existing shares are held by a bank nominee company, it will receive the bonus shares, nowadays often issued as actual certificates renounceable within a given period, instead of letters of allotment followed by definitive certificates. Where the bank has an equitable title, the bonus issue will go to the mortgagor. It will be charged to the bank by the memorandum of deposit, but it must be obtained by the bank for until it is, the security is diminished. Hence, banks must keep abreast with company affairs, and watch for danger signals such as shares going "ex bonus", or "ex rights" as the case may be.

Unquoted Shares

Lastly, mention must be made of unquoted shares, which have problems of their own, and consequently are seldom taken as security by banks, even though the company in question may be a very prosperous one. They are normally shares in private companies, which by their articles restrict the right to transfer their shares, though sometimes they are shares in public companies which have no stock exchange quotation. In either case the absence of a quotation makes these shares difficult to value and difficult to realise. Valuation has to depend on balance sheet analysis or possibly on the directors' own valuation, which will tend to be rather conservative, especially if they are thinking in terms of taking over the shares later should the bank wish to realise them. Sometimes articles provide a method, e.g. valuation by the company's auditors. The company secretary may be asked the price at which the shares last changed hands, or were valued for probate purposes.

In the absence of special circumstances (such as, in the near future the company may be obtaining a stock exchange quotation or be the subject of a take-over bid by another company), there is no ready market for unquoted shares, so realisation may take time, and in the case of private companies articles often provide that the shares must first of all be offered to existing members. This again may result in the bank having to accept less than the true value. If the articles require that notice must be given by the shareholder of his desire to sell, then a bank with only an equitable title will have to get the depositor of the shares to give this notice, unless the bank has obtained from him a power of attorney to enable the bank to act on his behalf in this matter. Similar drawbacks as to valuation and sale also arise in the case of unquoted debentures.

2. BEARER SECURITIES

As already observed, title to bearer securities passes by mere delivery, so that deposit of the bearer bond or certificate, preferably evidenced by a memorandum of deposit, gives the bank a good legal title, provided the securities are taken in good faith, for value (e.g. the giving of time to repay an existing debt is sufficient), and without notice of any defect in the title of the depositor.

For example, in *London Joint Stock Bank* v. *Simmons* (1892) a stock-broker had pledged certain Argentine bearer bonds belonging to clients with his bank as security for his own indebtedness. When the true owner sued the bank for their return, the House of Lords, treating the bonds as fully negotiable, held that the bank had an indefeasible title to the bonds. The owner's claim that having regard to the nature of its customer's business, the bank should have made enquiries as to the actual ownership of the bonds before accepting them as security was rejected; Lord Herschell remarking on this point: "I should be very sorry to see the doctrine of constructive notice introduced into the law of negotiable instruments". Thus, if no facts are actually present which ought to put a bank on enquiry, the bank is under no duty to probe into the pledgor's title.

This aspect of negotiability is further illustrated by *Lloyds Bank Ltd.* v. *Swiss Bankverein* (1913), in which the plaintiff bank had lent money on bearer bonds to bill brokers. When it called in the loan, the brokers came and paid the loan by cheque, receiving the bonds, which they thereupon pledged with the defendant bank. The cheque, which was drawn on a third bank, was dishonoured. When the plaintiff bank sued the defendant bank, which had received the bonds from the brokers in good faith, the Court of Appeal held that the defendants were entitled to the bonds; the plaintiffs received the cheque as conditional payment and had no claim to the bonds which had been released, for negotiable instruments could not be impressed with vendor's lien, implied trust or constructive notice.

To sum up, the advantages of bearer securities are the lack of expense in charging them, the automatic acquisition of a legal title in the normal course of events, and the ease of realisation. Being fully negotiable, they become security by way of pledge. Lien may arise by implication, but not by contract. In any event, bankers' lien includes, in the case of negotiable securities, a power of sale after reasonable notice. When taking bearer securities, a bank will, of course, examine them carefully, checking that they are properly stamped and numbered, not defaced in any way, and that all unpaid coupons are attached. By s. 38 (2) of the Banking Act 1979 bearer bonds join pledges of documents of title in being expressly excluded from the Consumer Credit Act 1974.

3.   INSCRIBED SECURITIES

So far as this very small category is concerned, a legal title is obtained by transfer to the bank or its nominee company. In order to get an equitable title, the bank can persuade the customer to transfer his holding, where possible, into registered form, and then the charge can be created in the normal way by deposit of the certificate with or without a memorandum of deposit and/or blank transfer. Whilst the holding remains inscribed, the stock receipt is of no value and its deposit does not give the bank an equitable charge. However, to a customer of the highest integrity a bank might make an advance against inscribed stock in his name on the strength of an instrument of charge including an undertaking not to deal with the stock without the bank's permission, and a power of attorney in the bank's favour in case of need. This would be a mere equitable charge, unsupported by any document of title.

4.   NATIONAL SAVINGS SECURITIES

These are dealt with separately because as security they are subject to various defects inherent in their nature. In the case of National Savings Certificates; British Savings Bonds; and Premium Bonds, they are not transferable (they are excepted from the Stock Transfer Act 1963), no charge can be registered, and the certificates and bond books are not documents of title, being of no value except to the registered holders. Consequently, any dishonest owner, having deposited the certificates or bond books with a bank, could get duplicates and obtain repayment. Once again, however, from customers whose integrity is undoubted banks will accept these securities, despite their inability to get an effective charge over them, by taking the certificates and bond books with a memorandum of deposit and the appropriate National Savings repayment form completed in the bank's favour, but undated.

Section 4 (1) of the National Debt Act 1958 provides that a dispute as to a holding shall be referred to the Chief Registrar of Friendly Societies. An interesting example of this is *R. v. Chief Registrar of Friendly Societies ex parte Mills* (1970) where Mrs Mills had deposited £500 of National Development Bonds with a bank as security together with an undated encashment form. When the bank sought to realise the security by sending up the bond book and form to the Director of Savings, she wrote to the Director countermanding the encashment form. The bank referred the matter to the Chief Registrar of Friendly Societies who ordered that the bonds should be encashed and paid to the bank. Her application to the Queen's Bench Divisional Court to have the registrar's decision quashed on the ground of lack of jurisdiction was rejected, because his jurisdiction was not confined to claims at law but included claims to be entitled to the bonds in equity

As regards Government stocks on the National Savings Stock Register, a legal title is obtained by transfer to the bank or its nominee company on a special form. An equitable title is obtained by taking a memorandum of deposit and an undated sale form, but this procedure is again subject to the disadvantages that no charge can be registered and that there is nothing to stop a dishonest owner from obtaining a duplicate certificate and selling the security behind the bank's back. Alternatively, these securities can be transferred to the Bank of England Register, and thereafter dealt with as registered securities.

5. BUILDING SOCIETY SHARES AND DEPOSIT ACCOUNTS

Provided the rules of the building society concerned permit, transfer into the name of the bank or its nominee company will give a legal title. Otherwise, an equitable title is obtained by taking the passbook (or possibly certificate) with a memorandum of deposit and the appropriate repayment form completed in the bank's favour, but undated. (Building Society securities are excepted from the Stock Transfer Act 1963).

TAKE-OVER BIDS

Take-over bids are where a company or a group of individuals or a syndicate attempts to buy up all or a majority of the equity share capital of some company so as to obtain control of that company. Bank lending in these circumstances requires care, for although there may be an additional "carrot" to the bank in the form of a promise of the bank account of the company if and when taken over, often the advances to the bidders are to be secured by the shares in the company the subject of the bid as and when they are acquired under the terms of the offer to the existing members. Consequently, the bank may end up with a large number of shares which it will not be easy to unload on the stock market, if for any reason difficulties arise and the bank wants to recall the loan. Realisation in these circumstances will be made more difficult because the take-over price offered is usually considerably above the current market quotation.

In the last resort the bank may have to appoint its own representative(s) to the board of the company and superintend the running of it until the indebtedness to the bank in respect of the shares is repaid. The normal memorandum of deposit also charges to the bank the voting rights attached to the stocks and shares deposited, and this provision becomes important if and when the bank has to intervene in the company's affairs. In practice, the financing and the tactical operation of take-over bids fall more within the sphere of merchant banking. Rules of practice and procedure for the conduct of take-over bids are contained in the City Code on Take-overs and Mergers which has no legal force but is nevertheless observed voluntarily and, like the Rules of the Stock Exchange, backed by disciplinary sanctions.

One hazard for the ordinary branch bank, unfamiliar with the tangled web that take-over bids may weave, is shown by *Selangor United Rubber Estates, Ltd.* v. *Cradock (No. 3)* (1968), discussed in Chapter 13.

CONCLUSION

Charges on stocks and shares are relatively easy and cheap to take, and, except in the now very rare instances of partly-paid shares, do not involve any future financial outlay. Their efficacy as security depends, from a banking point of view, on their stability of value and quickness of realisation. The vast majority of stocks and shares charged to banks are quoted on a stock exchange; their value can be ascertained at any time from a stockbroker, from the Stock Exchange Daily List, and in most cases from ordinary newspapers. A bank holding a legal charge on quoted securities can demand repayment from the customer and on non-compliance with this demand within the prescribed time it can forthwith sell the securities simply by telephoning or writing to a stockbroker.

The only drawback is the fluctuation in the market value, so that if, as is often the case, when the bank wishes to realise the stocks and shares, the stock market is depressed because of a "credit-squeeze" or hard times generally, the securities will yield less than they might once have done, and this will not please either the bank or the depositor of the securities. Sales on a falling market send prices plunging further down. Although stock market prices are sensitive to a wide range of events, both international and domestic, on a broad front since the end of the Second World War the prices of ordinary stocks and shares (equities) have advanced, those of preference shares and other fixed interest stocks have fallen as interest rates in general have risen, and those of low-interest, long-dated and undated gilt-edged securities have steadily declined. However, the "cult of the equity"—the vogue enjoyed by ordinary stocks and shares for so long—lost is supporters between May 1972 and January 1975 when the Financial Times share index fell from 543 to 146, though it reached a new peak of 558 the day after the General Election of 1979, receding considerably thereafter.

The only safeguard against such sudden drops in value that a bank can take is to insist on a margin in the market value of the securities over the amount of the indebtedness, and periodically to re-value the securities. This margin may be higher if the securities are of a type such as commodity shares (e.g. metals, rubber, tea and the like) where the quantity of the produce and the world prices for it can and do have wide swings, with consequent repercussions in the share prices. A mixed portfolio of securities is much safer than having all the proverbial eggs in one basket, or even one type of baskets. The spectacular collapse of an individual company is not unknown even nowadays; and there are fashions in shares which can run counter to the general trend—for example, property shares, bank shares or insurance shares may be in vogue and outpace the rest of the market, whereas at other times they may languish, whilst other types of shares enjoy the limelight. On the Stock Exchange the most reliable shares are known as "blue-chips", but at times even their virtues may be more false than true. A further disadvantage that may sometimes occur is that if the directors of a company offer that company's shares to its bank as security for personal advances to themselves, any setback in the company's fortunes causes the bank a headache not merely *vis-à-vis* the company where it is indebted to the bank, but *vis-à-vis* the directors as well.

The drawbacks of unquoted shares have already been mentioned; as regards other non-quoted securities, such as National Savings and building society shares and deposits, these at least do not fluctuate in value and apart from any requisite period of notice they are easily turned into cash.

On the whole, however, stocks and shares are an extensive and useful type of banking security. Ownership of ordinary stocks and shares, and unit trust units, is steadily widening, because, apart from intermittent setbacks in price, they offer some hedge against inflation so far as savings are concerned. Consequently, stocks and shares are increasingly likely to be offered as security, though a bank will naturally be happier to have them as a mixture with other securities, or if on their own, then in a mixed portfolio. This avoids over-reliance on one or two securities, for there is safety in diversity except for the sudden breaks in stock market prices as a whole.

Chapter 9

Guarantees

INTRODUCTION

When a bank is confronted by a would-be borrower who has no assets or no unencumbered assets, and it does not wish to grant him an unsecured advance, the last resort is that a relative or friend of the customer may be prepared to guarantee his account. In other words, some third party, preferably of substance, acts as surety in that he stands behind the debtor and underwrites his undebtedness to the bank. The same underlying principles are applicable to all forms of suretyship where third party securities are involved whether or not the surety is personally liable: *Re Conley* (1938). Thus, if X deposits stocks and shares with a bank as security for an advance made by the bank to Y, then X becomes a surety for the debt even though the bank's only recourse is against the security, since X has not given any personal covenant for the payment of any sum to the bank.

Accordingly, where a guarantee arrangement is being supported by other security, the bank can take either (1) a third party form of mortgage appropriate to the property being offered, or (2) a guarantee together with the usual, i.e. direct, form of mortgage. This latter alternative is possible because these direct bank forms invariably cover all the liabilities of the mortgagor to the bank "whether as principal or surety", and so are preferable where the guarantor is already a customer of the bank. Of course, many guarantees are unsupported, reliance being placed solely on the name of the guarantor, normally due to a satisfactory bank reference on him or to the bank's own knowledge of his financial standing and general reputation.

The nature of guarantees in general, and of bank forms of guarantee in particular, will now be considered. These forms are those taken as security in which a bank is the recipient of the guarantee and gets the benefit of it, though it may be noted in passing that sometimes the reverse situation occurs, i.e. the bank may itself give a guarantee, or an indemnity, on behalf of its customer, thereby assuming a burden in reliance on a counter-indemnity from the customer.

THE GENERAL LAW

A guarantee is an engagement to be collaterally answerable for the debt, default or miscarriage of another person. It must be distinguished from an indemnity, which is a promise to be primarily liable. A contract of guarantee involves the existence of another, prior contract, one party being common to each contract: the principal debtor is liable on the first contract, the guarantor or surety is only liable on the second contract, whereas the creditor is a party to both contracts. In an indemnity there are only two parties to the contract, and the person giving the indemnity assumes primary liability for the debt. The standard illustration of the difference between subsidiary and sole liability is that appearing in *Birkmyr* v. *Darnell* (1704): if two come to a shop and one buys, and the other says to the seller: "Let him have the goods; if he does not pay you, I will", this is a guarantee. But if he says: "Let him have the goods, I will be your paymaster", or "I will see you paid", this is an undertaking as for himself where the words show that he intends to pay for the goods in any event, and not merely if another party fails to pay (i.e. this is an indemnity).

This distinction is important because by s. 4 of the Statute of Frauds 1677 a guarantee is not enforceable by action unless it is evidenced by a written memorandum of the agreement signed by the party sought to be made liable under it. An indemnity need not be in writing, although in practice a bank is unlikely to accept an indemnity unless it is in writing. It is clearly dangerous for a bank to be content with an oral arrangement involving the provision of outside security, because the person providing it, if he is reluctant to pay when called upon, may argue that the circumstances are tantamount to a guarantee, and if this is so the security will be unenforceable. The bank would have to show that what he gave was an indemnity, but it would depend on the facts as established by the evidence whether the Court would uphold the bank's contention or not.

The use of the words "guarantee" or "indemnity" in a document is not, of course, conclusive, for the document and the transaction in which it arises must be looked at as a whole. In recent years this question of guarantee or indemnity has been much canvassed in the Court of Appeal in connection with hire-purchase documents, particularly the one known as a recourse agreement, whereby a car dealer backs in favour of a finance company the hire-purchase agreement made between the latter and the hirer of the car. Depending on the document's exact wording and the relevant circumstances, the answer has varied in different cases and this can have material consequences. Thus, in *Goulston Discount Co., Ltd.* v. *Clark* (1966) the plaintiff finance company could only sue the hirer for the arrears of the instalments, and as they could not recover these from him, they came down on the dealer, the defendant, under his recourse agreement; if this was a guarantee, the defendant had no more liability than the hirer, i.e. to pay the arrears, but if it was an indemnity, he would be liable to pay the whole of the hire-purchase price. The Court of Appeal, reversing the decision of the County Court Judge, held that that particular document was an indemnity.

In *Edward Owen Engineering, Ltd.* v. *Barclays Bank International Ltd.* (1978) the Court of Appeal dealt with what LORD DENNING, M.R., described as "a new business transaction called a 'performance guarantee' or 'performance bond'", and found that it had many similarities to a confirmed letter of credit. The bank was required to honour the guarantee according to its terms and was not concerned whether either party to the contract which underlay the guarantee was in default, the only exception being where fraud by one of the parties to the underlying contract had been established and the bank had notice of the fraud.

Unless under seal, a guarantee must be supported by consideration, but by s. 3 of the Mercantile Law Amendment Act 1856 a statement of the consideration need not be set out in the memorandum. Although the recipient of the consideration is the debtor, not the guarantor, the consideration moves from the promisee, e.g. a seller hands over the goods to the debtor, or a bank grants time or credit to its customer, on the strength of the guarantee, and this is sufficient to support the guarantor's promise. Where a guarantee under hand is given in respect of indebtedness incurred contemporaneously or to be incurred in the future—as where a bank takes a guarantee to secure an advance then being made or to be made subsequently—there is no difficulty as to the consideration. If, however, a guarantee under hand is taken for a past debt, e.g. by a bank to secure a dormant debit account, then to avoid the snag that a past consideration is not sufficient to support a simple contract (see page 13), there must be an express or implied promise to forbear as consideration. This is achieved by the bank demanding repayment of the dormant debt, or threatening to do so, in a letter to the customer and then, after receipt of a letter from the proposed guarantor offering a guarantee if the bank will grant time to its customer, agreeing to do so on completion and delivery of the guarantee. Alternatively, in these circumstances, the guarantee may be executed under seal, though in practice little use is made by banks of this type of guarantee.

Section 5 of the Mercantile Law Amendment Act 1856 provides that any surety who has paid his debt or performed his duty is entitled to any security held by the creditor in respect of such debt or duty, and to stand in the place of the creditor as regards all remedies.

A surety who has properly paid off the principal debtor's liabilities is entitled to be indemnified by him, and this indemnity may be expressly contained in the guarantee, or it may be implied. When the guarantee has been undertaken at the request, actual or implied, of the debtor, then an implied right of indemnity arises, but this is not so if the guarantor is a mere volunteer, officious or benevolent. An interesting illustration of this last point arose in *Owen* v. *Tate* (1975), where the defendants' overdraft with a bank had been guaranteed by a Miss Lightfoot, who charged her property by way of legal mortgage in support. Some years later she became concerned that her deeds were being held by the bank in this way and consulted the plaintiff, who offered to help her get her deeds back and did so by guaranteeing the debt himself and lodging cash in support. He did not consult the defendants before doing this and he was not asked to do so by them. Subsequently, the bank applied the cash supporting the plaintiff's guarantee in repayment of the defendants' overdraft. The plaintiff sought reimbursement from the defendants but the Court of Appeal held that if without an antecedent request a person assumed an obligation or made a payment for the benefit of another, the law would as a general rule refuse him the right of indemnity. If there was some necessity which had led him to assume the obligation, the law would grant him a right of reimbursement. Since the plaintiff had acted initially behind the backs of the defendants in order to oblige another and despite the protests of the defendants it would not be just and equitable to grant him the right of reimbursement.

As regards interest, it was held in *Re Hawkins* (1972) that any sum that a guarantor paid in respect of interest due from the principal debtor ranked as interest and not payment of a sum in lieu of interest, for a difference in the obligation to pay did not necessarily make a difference in the thing paid; in particular this was so where the guarantor had in terms guaranteed the "payment of . . . interest"; what mattered was the nature and quality of the thing paid and not the source of the obligation to pay it.

An innovation made by s. 49 of the Finance Act 1978 is that a guarantor of money lent to a borrower for trade purposes resident in the United Kingdom, who has made a payment under the guarantee which is irrecoverable from the borrower can treat such payment as a loss in respect of any capital gains tax liability. The claim will be reduced by any contribution payable by a co-guarantor and the guarantee must be made after 11 April 1978 (which may have spurred guarantors to ask banks to replace guarantees dated before 11 April

1978 with new guarantees created after that date).

Guarantees and indemnities are now free of stamp duty, as a result of the Finance Acts 1970 and 1971.

CAPACITY

Any person with full contractual capacity can give a guarantee. Thus, an infant is unable to do so, and certain other specific instances require more detailed analysis:

(1) Partnerships

Whether the partnership is a trading one or a non-trading one, a partner has no ostensible authority to give a guarantee in the firm's name, unless a trade custom be proved: *Brettel* v. *Williams* (1849). In the absence of such usage, the partner must be specially authorised by his co-partner(s) to bind the firm, and in view of the difficulties of proving usage or authorities, all partners should sign a guarantee given by the firm.

(2) Companies

Power to give a guarantee must be expressly provided in the memorandum of association. A trading company has implied power to borrow, but there is no implied power to give guarantees. Anyone taking a guarantee from a company must examine that company's memorandum of association to see that it includes a clause amongst its "objects" which will cover that particular type of guarantee, whether to a bank or anyone else. It all depends on the wording of any clause. Most companies incorporated under the Companies Act 1948 have a wide power covering guarantees and indemnities of all kinds, so that no ambiguity arises, but older companies are sometimes restricted to guarantees of a particular type, e.g. guarantees may be given in respect of "persons trading with the company". If a bank or anyone else taking a guarantee is in doubt about the company's power, then the company should first be asked to alter its memorandum of association by special resolution as laid down in the Companies Act 1948, which simplified the procedure (see Chapter 4 at page 119); otherwise there is always the possibility that, unless s. 9 (1) of the European Communities Act 1972 can be relied on, the guarantee may be held to be *ultra vires* the company and void. The articles of the company must then be consulted to ascertain the extent to which the power to give guarantees has been delegated to the directors, and whether there is any express provision as to the manner in which a guarantee has to be executed, e.g. under the common seal of the company, or under hand on behalf of the company.

The *ultra vires* doctrine in relation to an inter-company guarantee within a group of companies was considered in *Charterbridge Corporation, Ltd.* v. *Lloyds Bank Ltd.* (1969). The plaintiff alleged that a guarantee and a subsequent legal charge given to the bank by P (C) Ltd. (which had power to do so under its Memorandum) to secure the indebtedness of P. Ltd. were invalid as being *ultra vires* because P, a director of both companies, had failed to consider separately the interests of P (C) Ltd. when on its behalf he effected the security. This contention was rejected, the judge holding that on the proper test of whether an intelligent and honest man in the position of a director of the company concerned could, in the whole of the existing circumstances, have reasonably believed that the transaction was for the benefit of the company, the answer as regards P was in the affirmative. In short, it was commerically justifiable.

The contract of guarantee must be between the company (not its directors) and the creditor, so that a certified copy of the resolution of the board of directors authorising the creation and sealing or, more usually, signing of the guarantee should be obtained. This resolution should refer to the particular form of guarantee to be taken, for a bare resolution to give a guarantee for a specific sum or purpose might not cover the execution of the standard form of bank guarantee. Banks often provide the company with a draft resolution covering all the points, and they will require a certified copy of the resolution when passed to be annexed to, or indorsed on, the guarantee when returned after completion. It should be recorded on the guarantee that it is executed "pursuant to a resolution of the Board dated . . .", thereby linking it with the certified copy of that resolution.

The hazards of a short-cut or a centralised arrangement are shown in *Ford and Carter, Ltd.* v. *Midland Bank Ltd.* (1979) which concerned mutual guarantees that companies enter into when a bank lends to a group. The arrangement that was made was also intended to be extended to additional companies which subsequently joined the group. The plaintiff company was one of the "new joiners" and the finance director of the parent company committed it to a guarantee of the group borrowing supported by a floating charge. All the guarantors were called upon to pay and a receiver of the plaintiff company was appointed under the floating charge. When the plaintiff company went into liquidation, the liquidator challenged the validity of the guarantee and the appointment of the receiver and his claim was upheld by the House of Lords on the ground that when creditors become involved, the separate legal existence of the constituent companies of the group has to be respected, and in the absence of some contractual act or document the plaintiff company could not be bound to the bank; it was not committed through the actions of the finance director.

If the directors are personally interested in the giving of the guarantee, e.g. with inter-company guarantees where there are interlocking directorates, then the implications of *Victors, Ltd.* v. *Lingard* (1927)—already mentioned in connection with debentures in Chapter 4—must be borne in mind. Thus, unless the articles of the company giving the guarantee specifically authorise directors to vote in these circumstances notwithstanding their interest, the authorising resolution must be passed by an independent quorum of directors, and if this is not obtainable, then the resolution must be passed by the company in general meeting, or else the articles must be altered by special resolution to enable interested directors to vote.

Finally, any restrictions imposed by the Companies Act 1948 must be observed; e.g. s. 190 prohibits, with certain exceptions, a company from making loans to a director or to a director of its holding company, and from providing a guarantee or other security to cover an advance made to such a director by any other person. Section 54 also prohibits, again with certain exceptions, a company from providing direct or indirect assistance, whether by means of a loan, guarantee or other security, to enable any person to purchase or subscribe for its own, or its holding company's, shares. If the company's articles incorporate Clause 79 of Table A, 1948, the amount of the guarantee may have to be related to the directors' borrowing powers to ensure that they are not exceeded.

(3) Guarantees by two or more parties

If the undertaking to sign a guarantee is entered into on the strength of another or others also signing, and any of them refuses, or for any other reason fails, to join in the guarantee, those who have already executed it are entitled to consider their liability at an end: *Ward* v. *National Bank of New Zealand* (1883). Similarly, an unauthorised material alteration will sabotage a joint and several guarantee, as illustrated by *Ellesmere Brewery Co.* v. *Cooper* (1896). In this case four sureties executed a joint and several bond by which the liability of two of them was limited to £50 each, and that of the other two to £25 each. One of those whose liability was to be £50 signed the bond after the other three had signed, but added the words "£25 only". It was held that the words added made a material alteration in the bond so that the first three signatories were thereby discharged, and as the last signatory only executed the bond as a joint and several bond, he was also discharged.

Consequently, where two or more parties have undertaken to sign a guarantee for bank borrowing not yet taken up, the bank must not make the advance until all have actually and properly signed. In *National Provincial Bank of England Ltd.* v. *Brackenbury* (1906) four parties had agreed to sign a joint and several guarantee; three signed and the bank made the advance in anticipation of the completion of the guarantee, but the fourth party died before his signature could be obtained: it was held that the three signatories were discharged, in the absence of any consent by them that the fourth signature should be dispensed with. Probably the same may apply if the guarantees to be taken are individual ones, provided they are not wholly independent of each other but are connected together in such a way that it might be said that the taking of the other guarantees was a condition precedent to each guarantee becoming effective, i.e. each party knew the other parties were also to guarantee and relied on this fact as a basis of his own contract. Once taken, the terms of a guarantee by joint parties should not be varied without the consent of all parties.

The nature of guarantees by two or more parties may be joint, or several, or joint and several (this last being the form used by banks). In a joint guarantee, i.e. one given by all the guarantors, each of the various guarantors is liable but prior to the Civil Liability (Contribution) Act 1978 all had to be sued in a joint action for if some only were sued, even though any judgment obtained was unsatisfied, the rest were discharged. Now, under the Act, a judgment obtained against one person jointly liable shall be no bar to an action against others jointly liable "in respect of the same debt or damage". In a several guarantee, i.e. one given by each of the guarantors, each may be sued separately and judgment obtained against one does not discharge the others, subject only to the limit, if any, imposed by the guarantee on the amount recoverable thereunder. A joint and several guarantee combines the two methods in that it is a guarantee given by each and all of the guarantors, so that the parties may be sued in any way the creditor thinks fit, subject to any limitation as to amount. It is, therefore, the most flexible type and as such favoured by banks, for in a joint and several guarantee the financially strong guarantor(s) carry the weak one(s), which is to the creditor's advantage, though not to that of a guarantor who has to pay more than his mathematical proportion and whose right of contribution from his co-sureties may be of little practical worth.

Furthermore, if a party to a joint guarantee dies, his estate is free from liability, which now falls only on the survivor(s), so that the "several" element is necessary to make the estate of a deceased guarantor liable. The remedy against joint and several guarantors is cumulative until the whole amount guaranteed is recovered. As the release of one or more sureties out of a number of co-sureties discharges the other sureties at common law, bank forms of guarantee and of third party security take away this right by conferring on the bank complete freedom of action to release any surety without prejudice to the liability of the others. It must be remembered that with both single and joint and several guarantees, unless the guarantor has bound his personal representatives, his liability will be determined by notice, actual or constructive, of his death, so that to preserve the liability of his estate a current account must be broken by the bank to prevent the operation of the Rule in *Clayton's Case* (1816). A similar situation arises when liability is determined by any other event.

THE DEBTOR'S CAPACITY

Lastly, the question of capacity has to be considered from the point of view of its applicability to the principal debtor. There must be a valid debt in respect of which legal proceedings can be brought against the principal debtor, because it is a fundamental ingredient of suretyship that a guarantor who has paid off the creditor stands in the shoes of that creditor and can exercise the rights of such creditor both against the principal debtor and against any security held. If the principal debtor is under no legal liability to discharge the indebtedness, because, for instance, of infancy or of its unincorporated nature such as an association or club, then in the absence of any express provision in the guarantee, the guarantor is discharged. Banks overcome this difficulty by inserting an *ultra vires* clause in the guarantee, in effect making it an indemnity, so that the guarantor agrees to be liable as sole or principal debtor notwithstanding the invalidity of the original debt. However, the clause must be sufficiently clear and comprehensive to cover all eventualities, for in *Coutts & Co.* v. *Browne-Lecky* (1947) a clause designed to cover *ultra vires* borrowing by limited companies, firms and the impersonal customers was held not to be effective in the case of a loan to an infant, so that as the bank could not recover against the infant principal debtor, neither could it do so against the guarantor. The judge quoted Lord Brougham, who said in a 19th century Scottish appeal to the House of Lords: "If there is nothing due, no balance, the obligation to make that nothing good amounts itself to nothing"

Even though a guarantee does not contain an appropriate *ultra vires* clause, a surety for money borrowed by a company *ultra vires* will be liable on his guarantee if the transaction was entered into in good faith and in the honest belief that it was *intra vires* and legal: *Garrard* v. *James* (1925).

REALITY OF CONSENT

Difficulties over undue influence (see Chapter 1, page 29) as between the principal debtor and the guarantor may sometimes occur. Apart from those relationships in which it is presumed, undue influence may still be proved as a fact, as in *Bank of Montreal* v. *Stuart* (1911), where the wife was a confirmed invalid and guaranteed her husband's account, the guarantee was set aside on the grounds of undue influence. This will also apply where she guarantees a firm or company in which her husband is involved. It is essential in any situation where undue influence may arise that a "free will" clause be added to the guarantee, wherein the guarantor states that he or she signs the guarantee of his or her own free will and with full knowledge of the nature of the obligation being undertaken. Banks usually insist that the signature to this clause and to the guarantee be witnessed by the guarantor's own, i.e. independent, solicitor, who confirms in the attestation clause that he has explained the nature and contents of the document to the guarantor.

Although a woman can legally give a guarantee or other security just as easily as a man does, banks have preferred her to be separately advised before she signs by her own solicitor who attests the document accordingly, even though the situation is not one in which undue influence appears likely, lest she plead lack of business knowledge or failure to understand its nature and scope. However, such a plea is now less likely to succeed since the House of Lords reviewed the situation of *"non est factum"* in *Saunders* v. *Anglia Building Society* (1970)—see p. 21, and henceforth in view of the Sex Discrimination Act 1975 such an approach must not be based on sex but simply on possible inability to understand the transaction. An alternative, though lesser, precaution is for the guarantor to write in a clause such as: "At my own request I have not been legally advised, but I sign this document of my own free will and with full knowledge of the nature of my obligations hereunder", which will be done in the presence of a bank official, preferably at the bank.

The danger that arises because of the conflict of interest between the bank and the guarantor where the bank is seeking to obtain a benefit is illustrated by *Lloyds Bank Ltd.* v. *Bundy* (1975). A father, who had already guaranteed the indebtedness of his son's company to the bank and in support had charged half his assets (his farm), signed a further guarantee and charge which mortgaged his farm up to the hilt without being given an opportunity of taking independent advice (which he had had on a previous occasion) where the situation "cried aloud the defendant's need for careful independent advice". The Court of Appeal set aside the security, for in the circumstances there was a confidential relationship which imposed on the bank a duty of fiduciary care, i.e. a duty to ensure that the defendant formed an independent and informed judgment on the proposed transaction before committing himself; as the bank was in breach of this duty it could not therefore be allowed to retain the benefit of the transaction. Whilst this case will doubtless prompt some guarantors to try to escape their obligations, it really appears to be one decided on its own very special facts.

CONFLICT OF LAWS

This branch of English law is relevant to guarantees executed outside England and Wales either by British citizens or foreign nationals, or executed in England and Wales by foreign nationals. In these circumstances it is advisable to add a clause stating that the guarantee shall be construed and take effect according to the law of England. This clause makes English law the proper law of the contract, and it will cover the question of the formalities of execution, even though these may not comply with the requirements of the local law of the place of execution. However, it will not necessarily be fully effective, especially as concerns capacity, which is governed by the law of the domicile, so that before taking a guarantee from a foreign company or person a bank would require to be satisfied on this legal point. So long as the guarantee is governed by English law, an action in respect of it can be brought in the English Courts, but it must be remembered that if the guarantor has little or no assets in this country enforcement of any judgement obtained may be difficult. In the last resort action may be necessary in a foreign court, with all the hazards and expense such proceedings may involve.

DISCLOSURE OF INFORMATION

A contract of suretyship is not in the general sense a contract *uberrimae fidei* (of the utmost good faith) wherein mere non-disclosure without fraud of a material fact will automatically make the contract voidable. Nevertheless, it may do so depending on the circumstances, for guarantees are closely construed in favour of the surety. For example, in a guarantee for the fidelity of a servant an innocent omission by the employer to inform the surety of the servant's previous dishonesty whilst in his employment was held in *London General Omnibus Co.* v. *Holloway* (1912) to bar the employer from enforcing any claim in respect of the servant's subsequent dishonesty. On the other hand, as regards bank guarantees it was held in *Hamilton* v. *Watson* (1845) that the bank, if not asked for the information, need not volunteer to the surety information as to how the debtor's account has been conducted, whether the debtor is already overdrawn or whether he has been punctual and honourable in his dealings. Again, in *Cooper* v. *National Provincial Bank Ltd.* (1945) it was held that no disclosure need be made when the husband of a woman whose account is guaranteed is an undischarged bankrupt having authority to sign on her account; it was, however, suggested that there might be a duty to disclose voluntarily in the case of an undischarged bankrupt cloaking his trading activities by operating a bank account in his wife's name, so that the account was in effect his own, not that of his wife.

Although a bank is entitled to assume that the guarantor has made himself acquainted with the debtor's reputation and financial position, the bank must exercise care to avoid any possible charge of misrepresentation. If any information is given, it must be full and fair, and if the guarantor asks questions, the bank must make unequivocal replies. If the guarantor is under any misapprehension regarding the debtor, it is the bank's duty to correct it: *Royal Bank of Scotland* v. *Greenshields* (1914). So far as disclosure is concerned, the bank may feel constrained by its duty of secrecy owed to its customer, and so it is probably better to arrange for a tri-partite meeting of bank, customer and proposed guarantor to discuss the matter, or else to get the customer's authority for disclosure of the information sought by the guarantor.

A bank should not suggest the name of a possible guarantor to a customer, lest the guarantor should subsequently argue that the bank had made the customer its agent, so that any misrepresentation by him might enable the guarantor to avoid liability. There is a duty not to mislead a prospective guarantor, and very little said which ought not to have been said, or very little omitted which ought to have been said, will avoid the contract: *Davies* v. *London and Provincial Marine Insurance Co.* (1878).

Once the guarantee is signed, the guarantor is entitled to have particulars of his liability at any time, but not to inspect, or have copies of, the debtor's account. He usually agrees in the form of guarantee to accept the bank's statement of the amount due from him as conclusive evidence of that amount. Upon request, the bank should disclose only the limit of the guarantor's liability, i.e. if the debit balance on the account(s) guaranteed is below the limit fixed in the guarantee, he can be told the exact amount; but if the balance exceeds the limit, e.g. where his guarantee is limited to £750, and the balance is DR £1,000, he should be informed that his guarantee is being fully relied on, the excess not being disclosed without the principal debtor's approval. The validity of a conclusive evidence clause was upheld by the Court of Appeal in *Bache & Co. (London), Ltd.* v. *Banque Vernes et Commerciale de Paris S.A.* (1973). LORD DENNING, M.R. commented that this commercial practice of inserting conclusive evidence clauses was only acceptable because the bankers and brokers who inserted them were known to be honest and reliable men of business who were most unlikely to make a mistake. Their standing was so high that their word was to be trusted. So much so that a notice of default given by a bank or broker must be honoured.

The bank is under no legal duty to advise the guarantor of any change in the circumstances of the principal debtor: *National Provincial Bank of England Ltd.* v. *Glanusk* (1913). Thus, if the bank finds that the debtor is not using the account for the purposes contemplated when the guarantee was given, e.g. he is using the funds for gambling or speculating instead of for ordinary trading, legally the bank need take no action. However, if the debtor's position is deteriorating in consequence, there is a moral duty on the bank to try to protect the guarantor's interests, and this can best be done by arranging a tripartite meeting, so that the guarantor can be put in possession of the fresh facts and then decide what he wishes to do. If the debtor is unco-operative in these circumstances, the bank can assert itself by threatening to call in the advance.

CHIEF FEATURES OF BANK GUARANTEES

Forms of guarantee can be quite short and simple, but bank forms of guarantee are usually prolix, for banks wish to cover every eventuality and to cut down the surety's common law rights, because the surety, as a person undertaking responsibility for someone else's debt, is much favoured at common law. Occasionally a Court case will reveal some unforeseen loophole in the guarantee form, so thereafter a new clause will be added by the banks to close that gap, and so the form grows to a formidable and complicated aspect. The distinguishing features of bank forms of guarantee will now be examined in more detail:

(a) Consideration

The consideration for the contract is usually expressed in bank guarantee forms, and it is generally described as "affording banking accommodation", "making advances or otherwise giving credit", "continuing the account", or "granting (or giving) time and/or credit" to the customer for repayment. The consideration is never stated to be the lending of a definite sum, because the condition would have to be exactly fulfilled, otherwise the guarantee would be inoperative: *Burton* v. *Gray* (1873). Instead, flexibility is achieved by using the statements of consideration just mentioned. As the usual bank printed forms of guarantee are under hand, the difficulty that a past consideration is insufficient to support a simple contract sometimes arises, an aspect which was explained under the earlier heading of "The General Law" at page 301.

That the consideration must be correctly stated is shown by *United Dominions Trust, Ltd.* v. *Beech* (1972) where the defendants "in consideration of your extending certain banking facilities . . . by means of advances of cash or negotiable instruments and/or any other form of security or by any other means" guaranteed a block discounting of hire-purchase agreements done with the plaintiffs by the company of which they were directors. It was held that as the plaintiffs had failed to bring the transaction within the terms of their guarantee, since its form was that of a sale of hire-purchase agreements and not a loan, the basis of the guarantee disappeared and so the defendants were not liable.

(b) The "whole debt" clause

The surety will guarantee the whole debt on any account or in any manner whatsoever due from the principal debtor, either alone or jointly, together with all interest thereon and other banking charges including legal costs and expenses. This is normally followed by a proviso that the amount recoverable shall in no case exceed the sum of £ . . . in addition to such further sum for interest etc. Sometimes banks take unlimited guarantees, in which case the limitation clause will be deleted, this amendment being signed or initialled by the guarantor. To avoid arguments that the debt ceases to be due from the principal debtor on his death or bankruptcy and instead becomes due from his estate, the guarantee will provide that it shall be deemed to continue "due and owing" notwithstanding death or bankruptcy of the principal debtor. It is also customary for the guarantor to bind his legal personal representatives, so that if the guarantor dies during the currency of the guarantee, the bank need not break the debtor's account to avoid the Rule in *Clayton's Case* operating to the bank's detriment, for the guarantee remains in force.

It is much more advantageous to use the "whole debt" clause, i.e. to cover all moneys at any time owing by the principal debtor with a limitation on the amount, rather than merely mentioning a specific sum for two reasons. One has already been mentioned—the need to keep strictly to the sum specifically stated. The other relates to proof in bankruptcy when the principal debtor has been adjudicated bankrupt. If the guarantor were to guarantee a part of the debt, i.e. a fixed sum, say £500, or a proportion of the advance, say, half the amount advanced which is not to exceed £1,000, then on the principal debtor becoming bankrupt, the guarantor could pay the specified sum and prove for it against the bankrupt's estate, the bank having to reduce its own claim to that extent. Were the advance £1,000 and the guarantee for part of it, namely £500, then the guarantor would pay the bank the £500, and each would prove against the bankrupt's estate for £500, so that if a dividend of 50p in the £ was paid, each would receive £250 and consequently both the bank and guarantor would lose £250 apiece. An additional complication is that the guarantor is entitled to a proportionate share of any other securities which have been deposited in respect of the advance.

When the "whole debt" clause is used, it is normally coupled with a clause whereby the guarantor agrees not to prove in competition with the bank in the event of the principal debtor's bankruptcy, and also in any event not to take any steps against the principal debtor in respect of sums paid in discharge of his guarantee liability, until the whole of the bank's claim (i.e. not his guarantee limit only) has been satisfied. This means that any payment of part of the debt made by the guarantor can be placed to a suspense account and the bank can ignore this in its proof and claim for the full amount of its debt against the estate. Furthermore, the guarantor cannot claim the benefit of any securities held by the bank in respect of the advance until all the indebtedness has been repaid. Thus, in the same financial circumstances outlined in the previous paragraph, the bank with its "whole debt" clause etc. will prove for the whole advance of £1,000 and after receiving a dividend of 50p in the £, the residue of £500 can be recovered from the guarantor, or taken from the suspense account if he has already paid it. In this way, the bank receives payment in full, but whilst the bank suffers no loss, this time the guarantor loses £500, as he cannot prove here because the bank has already proved in respect of the whole debt and got the dividend.

(c)   Guarantees may be either specific or continuing

A specific guarantee is a promise to be collaterally answerable for a particular transaction only, e.g. a specific purchase at a shop. A continuing guarantee is a promise to be collaterally answerable for the fluctuating debit balance of an account. Whether a guarantee is or is not continuing is a question of construction, to be decided on the language of the document and the presumed intention of the parties. Because of the nature of banking business, bank guarantees are invariably made to be continuing, that is, they secure the general balance due or that may be due from time to time and at any time from the principal debtor. Sometimes the words "continuing security" actually appear, but whatever style or expression is used the effect is to prevent the operation of the Rule in *Clayton's Case* to the bank's detriment and to make the guarantor liable for the ultimate balance due to the bank, subject to any limitation of amount. Without a continuing security clause a guarantee, or any other security, would be of little use in respect of an overdraft on current account, for as soon as sufficient credits were paid in to discharge the amount of the indebtedness at the time the security was taken, the security would then be exhausted and any subsequent debit balances would be fresh, unsecured advances. The bank must have a type of security which is unaffected by the account in question swinging from debit to credit and back again or by, in ordinary circumstances, the turnover on the account, otherwise its managers—and its security clerks—would find life intolerable.

(d)   Time limits in guarantees

It is not usual for banks to accept guarantees containing a definite time limit, i.e. expiring at a fixed date, but it does occasionally happen. Subject to any special provisions about notice, a guarantee for a specified period of time can probably be withdrawn as to future advances within the period specified. The bank would not then be justified in making further advances after receipt of the notice, though it would be justified in paying cheques drawn before it had reasonable time to communicate with the customer. On similar equitable principles the bank ought to be covered in respect of bills of exchange accepted or discounted by it for the customer prior to the revocation and maturing between that date and the expiration date of the guarantee, provided acceptance and discount of bills are within the liabilities secured by the guarantee (which they normally are). A guarantee for a specified period may still be a continuing security, if expressed as such, covering the ultimate balance due at the date of expiry. Thus, in *Westminster Bank Ltd.* v. *Sassoon* (1926) the guarantee concluded with the line: "This guarantee will expire on June 30th 1925", and the guarantor was called upon to pay in October 1925; it was held that the guarantee was a continuing one.

(e) Notice of determination

So far as the bank is concerned, the question of notice of determination of the guarantee by the bank is simple—no period is required, for the guarantor undertakes to pay the amount due under the guarantee on demand in writing being made by the bank. In protection of its own interests, the bank does not usually allow such peremptory termination on the part of the guarantor, who will be required to give to the bank notice in writing of his intention to terminate the guarantee at the expiration of the period stated in the guarantee, which may be, say, one month or perhaps three months or even six months. This period allows the bank, on receipt of the notice, an opportunity of clarifying the position *vis-à-vis* the principal debtor and/or the guarantor before the expiry date arrives. In acknowledging receipt of the notice to the guarantor the bank will state that the amount of his liability under the guarantee will be advised to him on the expiration of the notice. In practice, a tri-partite meeting may be sought by the bank, so that the question of what arrangements the guarantor and/or customer intend to make for repayment or whether the customer can provide alternative security may be discussed between the three interested parties. The bank may, of course, use the receipt of notice of determination as reason for making upon the guarantor its own demand for immediate repayment, but there is no need to do this unless the bank has cause to prefer the indebtedness to be discharged sooner than later. Sometimes a bank's guarantee form may allow the guarantor to determine his guarantee immediately, thereby crystallising the customer's position subject to the payment of oustanding cheques dated on or before the date of receipt by the bank of the guarantor's notice of determination.

It has already been noted that when a guarantor who has bound his legal personal representatives dies during the currency of the guarantee, the effectiveness of the guarantee is unchanged. The bank will advise the legal personal representatives of the deceased guarantor of the existence of the guarantee and that it can be determined by them on whatever period of notice is specified in it. Again, there is no need for the bank itself to demand immediate repayment when it learns of the guarantor's death, unless there are special circumstances which make it wiser to take this course: these might be (a) if the principal debtor is also the sole personal representative, when there may be a conflict of interest, for he may deliberately not give notice of determination in order that further advances can be made to him personally; or (b) if it should come to the bank's knowledge that the whole of the guarantor's estate was devised on trust: *Harriss* v. *Fawcett* (1873), where the bank continued the advance knowing that there was no personal estate to answer the guarantee and it was held that the advances subsequent to the death were not covered.

(f)   Surrender of the guarantor's common law rights

The bank strengthens its own position by the insertion in the guarantee of various clauses whereby the guarantor renounces his common law rights. Some of these have already been discussed, e.g. postponement of the surety's right of proof in the bankruptcy of the principal debtor and his right to any security held by the bank until the bank has been paid in full, and his acceptance of the bank's statement of the extent of his liability as conclusive evidence thereof. At common law, if the creditor alters the terms of the contract guaranteed without the surety's consent, the surety will be discharged: *Holme* v. *Brunskill* (1878). This case was applied by the Judicial Committee of the Privy Council in *National Bank of Nigeria, Ltd.* v. *Oba M.S. Awolesi* (1964), where it was held that on its true construction the guarantee taken by the bank was of the account as it existed at the date the guarantee was made and that by permitting the opening of a second account, the bank had substantially varied the terms of the contract without the respondent guarantor's knowledge and to his detriment, and this unauthorised variation discharged the guarantor. Thus, it is most important that a clause is included whereby the bank takes power to release or modify securities, renew bills, grant time, discharge or vary arrangements etc. with the principal debtor without the consent of the guarantor and without in any way prejudicing or diminishing the validity of the guarantee. The validity of such a clause was upheld by the Court of Appeal in *Perry* v. *National Provincial Bank of England Ltd.* (1910), but it must be emphasised that the wording must be appropriate to the circumstances which the bank wishes the clause to cover. In the absence of such power, if the bank, for instance, gave time to the principal debtor by a binding contract, the position of the guarantor would be prejudicially affected, for if he paid up under the guarantee his remedy against the principal debtor would be delayed. Similar considerations would apply if the bank were to accept a composition under a deed of arrangement executed by the principal debtor.

In *Moschi* v. *Lep Air Services, Ltd.* (1973) the House of Lords held that no fresh agreement or variation of the terms of the original contract was involved when the party not in default elected to exercise his right to treat the contract as rescinded because of a repudiatory breach of contract by the other party; he was exercising a right conferred on him by law of which the sole source was the original contract. In the absence of any agreement to the contrary, the guarantor's obligation to the creditor did not thereby come to an end; it continued to exist although transmuted by operation of law into an obligation to compensate the creditor by way of damages for the loss he had suffered by reason of the debtor's breach.

In the case of a joint and several guarantee, a surety who has himself paid the full amount of the indebtedness secured by the guarantee is entitled to contribution from his co-surety or co-sureties, and securities which fall into their hands must be divided equally. Consequently, with this type of guarantee the bank must take in addition power to release or vary the securities it holds and to discharge any surety at its discretion without in any way prejudicing the bank's position or affecting the liabilities of any other co-surety. A case here in which the bank's claim failed because the wording of the protective clause on which it sought to rely was held to be inappropriate is *Barclays Bank Ltd.* v. *Trevanion* (1933). In the absence of such power, if the bank were to release any security given by either the principal debtor or any third party, or to discharge any surety, then the one or more remaining sureties would clearly be prejudiced and could avoid liability.

Another clause will state that the guarantee shall be in addition to and shall not be in any way prejudiced or affected by any collateral or other security of any kind now or hereafter held (and that such other security etc. shall not in turn be prejudiced or affected by the guarantee). This provision is necessary lest it be argued that other securities were taken in substitution for the security afforded by the guarantee, or, by merging or suspending the debt, have affected the liability of the guarantor, because a guarantor who pays off the customer's indebtedness is entitled by subrogation to a transfer of the debt and any other securities held by the creditor in respect of that indebtedness, whether the securities were already held when the guarantee was signed or were acquired subsequently, and whether the guarantor was aware of them or not. Sometimes, in bank guarantee forms the guarantor(s) will also agree not to take security from the principal debtor, and that if he should do so, then he will hold such security as trustee for the bank.

(g)　Guarantee supported by a cash deposit

Whenever possible a bank tries to get some support for a guarantee, and occasionally a guarantor with funds to spare may be persuaded to lodge these with the bank, usually on a deposit account so that he will receive interest, in whole or partial support of his liability. In this event, a clause will be added to the guarantee form in which the guarantor agrees to deposit the sum in question in an account in the name of the bank re the guarantor and not withdraw any of the money while there is any outstanding liability under his guarantee; he also gives the bank an immediate right of recourse against the money without further reference to him in the event of the guarantee being determined in any manner.

(h)　Retention of the guarantee after discharge

Some bank forms provide that the bank has the right to retain the guarantee itself either permanently or for at least six months after it has apparently been discharged because all the moneys secured by it have been repaid. This is really aimed at the situation which might arise in the event of a fraudulent preference, which was discussed in Chapter 5 at pages 184–7. If by virtue of a fraudulent preference being established the bank had to refund credits to the trustee, an apparent credit account might very likely become considerably in debit, and if any guarantee securing the indebtedness had already been given up to the guarantor or cancelled, legal proceedings against him would be complicated, though they are now possible under ss. 92 and 115 of the Companies Act 1947 in the case of bankruptcy, and under s. 321 of the Companies Act 1948 in the case of companies' winding up. It is simpler and easier for the bank to take action if the actual guarantee is retained uncancelled. Whilst it is normal banking practice to do this in any event, arguments between the guarantor and the bank are avoided where there is such a retention clause in the guarantee.

(i)　Change in the constitution of the parties

Bank guarantees (and other security forms) are usually expressed to be in favour of the bank, its successors and assigns, so that they are unaffected by any change in the constitution of the bank or by its merger or amalgamation with any other bank or banks.

Where the principal debtor is a partnership, then the guarantee, or third party charge, should provide that it shall not be affected by any change in the constitution of that partnership. Otherwise, such a change would revoke the guarantee or third party security as to future advances. This provision will continue the liability of the guarantor despite such a change, even though it will be necessary to break the account to preserve the liability of the estate of a deceased or bankrupt partner. In practice, the bank usually advises the guarantor of the change so that he can decide whether or not to give notice determining his guarantee. Sometimes such a clause purports also to cover changes in the constitution of a partnership which is giving the guarantee, but where the change is the entry of a new partner, who cannot be bound unless he expressly undertakes liability for the old debts, then a fresh guarantee should be taken.

(j) Miscellaneous

Two clauses which have already been dealt with are: the *ultra vires* clause designed to turn the guarantee into an indemnity where the borrowing it secures is void or irregular, and the "free will" clause for use where there is a possibility of undue influence or of a plea of ignorance as to contents. One other can now be mentioned—the attestation clause. Although legally a guarantee need not be witnessed, most bank guarantee forms do contain an attestation clause, and to ensure that the guarantor's signature is genuine banks normally require the guarantee to be executed on their own premises and/or in the presence of one of their officials. Handing a guarantee form to the principal debtor so he can obtain the signature thereon of the proposed guarantor may lead to his misrepresenting its contents, but this risk to the bank has been reduced by the overruling of *Carlisle and Cumberland Banking Co.* v. *Bragg* (1911) (see Chapter 1 at page 21). However, in so handing the form there is the possibility of another danger, namely, forgery, in which event there will, of course, be no guarantee at all.

In conclusion, to the extent that banks use separate forms for sole guarantees, joint and several guarantees, and guarantees in respect of, or by, a company, the clauses considered under the foregoing headings will be modified as occasion demands to fit the exact circumstances, e.g. death or bankruptcy does not arise in the case of companies, but winding up does, though the basic framework of the guarantee remains the same.

DETERMINATION OF A GUARANTEE

The various ways in which a guarantee may be put to an end will now be examined, although a number of them have already been mentioned briefly. A guarantee may be determined:

(i) By the guarantor

The guarantor can give whatever notice of determination is prescribed in the guarantee, e.g. three months, and at the end of this period discharge his liability under the guarantee by paying the appropriate amount. During the currency of the period of notice it is a moot point whether banks can make additional advances—in other words, if the guarantee is for £1,000 and three months' notice is given when the debt is £600, can the bank validly let the debt rise by up to £400 during the period of notice? It is argued on the one side that the debtor can continue to draw freely until expiration of the notice, and on the other side that only cheques or bills actually oustanding should be met. Whilst the former course would appear to be justified and is the one mostly followed, as discretion is the better part of valour, banks sometimes try to arrange a tri-partite meeting at which this question can be sorted out by the three parties involved. A sudden cessation of the security may seriously prejudice the customer in that he may have entered into obligations relying on the security; on the other hand, if the bank sees that the customer is taking advantage of the situation by rushing up his indebtedness, then, as bank advances are repayable on demand, the bank can itself demand immediate repayment from the customer, thus fixing the guarantor's liability.

When a guarantee is determined, the account must be broken to prevent the operation of the Rule in *Clayton's Case* to the bank's detriment, and any new account subsequently opened and kept in credit can be ignored when calculating the liability of the guarantor: *Re Sherry* (1884). However, if the guarantee secures the "ultimate balance", an account opened before determination must be combined in such calculation. Some bank forms contain an additional clause devised to protect the bank if it inadvertently fails to break the account on determination, and in *Westminster Bank Ltd.* v. *Cond* (1940) such a clause was held to be effective.

If the consideration for a guarantee has been given once and for all, e.g. where a lump sum is advanced at once on the security of the guarantee, that guarantee is irrevocable save by mutual consent: *Lloyd's* v. *Harper* (1880). For example, where in these circumstances £500 has been placed to a customer's credit, but only £300 has been withdrawn, the bank cannot dishonour cheques drawn against the remaining £200 if the guarantor wishes to withdraw.

If one or some of a number of co-sureties should give notice of determination or withdrawal, the procedure outlined above would again be followed. Provided the retiring guarantor(s) pay his or their share of the indebtedness secured and the other guarantor(s) sign a new guarantee, the account can be contined, Of course, the bank is under no obligation to apportion the liability between the co-sureties, for as bank forms are invariably joint and several each guarantor is liable to the extent of the entire amount covered by the guarantee. Probably notice by one or some of the co-sureties does not affect the liability of the remaining co-sureties for future advances, but it is better to take a new guarantee. In *Egbert* v. *National Crown Bank* (1918) the guarantee provided that it should be a continuing guarantee until the undersigned or the executor or administrator of the undersigned shall have given the bank notice in writing to make no further advances on the security of the guarantee: the Judicial Committee of the Privy Council held that the guarantee remained in force against all guarantors until each and all of them or their respective executors or administrators gave notice to determine it. Bank forms usually allow the bank to discharge a co-surety without prejudice to the liability of the other co-sureties, but even so a fresh guarantee from the latter is preferable. In the absence of such power in the guarantee form and where the remaining co-sureties decline to sign a new guarantee, the bank must demand repayment of the advance.

Should the guarantor make a part payment to the bank before the bankruptcy of the principal debtor, then if he intends this payment to be in support of his guarantee and not in reduction of his liability, it should be placed on a separate (usually a deposit) account. If the debtor eventually becomes bankrupt, the bank can prove against his estate for the full amount of the debt. Should the guarantor intend the payment to be in reduction of his liability, then it would be credited to the debtor's account (thus reducing the amount provable in a subsequent bankruptcy) except that to overcome this snag, bank forms generally provide for all such payments to be held in reserve on a suspense account as well as prohibiting the guarantor from proving in competition with the bank until the bank is paid in full. The bank being so protected can ignore any funds on suspense account, claim the full amount from the customer and in his subsequent bankruptcy prove for it against his estate. After the receipt of any dividend, the bank can use the funds on suspense account in whole or partial reduction of the shortfall. Similar considerations apply to part payment by one or some of a number of co-sureties; the guarantee is then discharged as to the amount paid but one or all are still liable for the balance of the indebtedness covered by the guarantee.

In *Thomas* v. *Nottingham Incorporated Football Club, Ltd.* (1972), where the plaintiff gave notice of determination of his guarantee to a bank, which thereupon closed the defendants' old account for which he was liable, it was held that the plaintiff was entitled to be discharged from all liability under his guarantee by cailing on the debtor to pay off the amount due, and it was immaterial that the bank was bound to make a demand on the guarantor before it could proceed against him and that no such demand had in fact been made.

(ii)   By the bank

The bank can at any time make a demand for immediate repayment. Such a demand made on the guarantor will determine the guarantee as a continuing security (unless it is expressly provided therein to the contrary) and as usual the account must be broken to prevent the operation of the Rule in *Clayton's Case* to the bank's detriment. The bank need not sue the debtor before resorting to the guarantor.

As regards limitation of actions, if the guarantor promises to pay on demand, as is customary in bank guarantees, no right of action accrues against him until a demand for payment has been made: *Bradford Old Bank* v. *Sutcliffe* (1918). Consequently, until such a demand has been made of him, or until expiration of the period of notice of determination given by him, time does not begin to run in favour of the guarantor. Once it starts to run, by s. 2 of the Limitation Act 1939 the claim against the guarantor will become statute-barred after six years in the case of a guarantee under hand, and after twelve years in the case of a guarantee under seal. Similar considerations apply to third party securities. If, therefore, the guarantee or third party security such as a mortgage of land is under seal, the claim against the surety will not be statute-barred for twelve years, but the claim against the principal debtor will be statute-barred six years after the right of action arose, unless he had been made a party to the deed and has therein given his personal covenant to repay on demand, when he also will be subject to the twelve year period applicable to his surety.

If a demand is not a condition precedent to payment, time begins to run from the day of each advance made, i.e. from the time each cheque is honoured in reliance on the guarantee. In these circumstances it is necessary to get the guarantor's acknowledgment of liability at intervals of less than six years in the case of a guarantee under hand, or less than twelve years in the rare instance of a guarantee under seal.

A payment, but not an acknowledgment, made within six years by the principal debtor whilst time is running in favour of the guarantor will revive the right against the guarantor. But a payment made after the period prescribed for the bringing of an action to recover the debt, although binding the principal debtor, will not bind the guarantor.

(iii) By change in the constitution of parties

Although such a change would normally determine a guarantee, in practice (as already discussed) the position is safeguarded as far as possible by a clause providing for its continuance notwithstanding changes in the constitution of the bank and by a similar provision as regards any partnership to which the guarantee relates. A change of name by a company is immaterial, for it is still the same legal entity, as it is not its constitution which is changed: in any event, s. 18 (4) of the Companies Act 1948 provides that such a change shall not affect any rights or obligations of the company or any legal proceedings by or against the company.

(iv) By death, unsoundness of mind, or bankruptcy

The implications of these events have to be considered in relation to the guarantor and also the principal debtor. Where a guarantee is given in respect of, or by, a company, then although a company cannot die or be made bankrupt, it can be wound up (see Chapter 4), in which event the guarantee will be determined at the commencement of the winding up.

(a) *Death.*— The death of a guarantor of which the creditor has no notice does not determine the guarantee: *Bradbury* v. *Morgan* (1862). Whether or not notice, actual or constructive, of the death of the guarantor determines the guarantee depends on if he has bound his personal representatives to continue the guarantee. Where he has done so, the guarantee continues in full force and effect until either the bank determines it or the personal representatives give the same notice of determination that the guarantor could have given. In the absence of express agreement to bind personal representatives, the guarantee is determined and, as usual, the account must be broken to prevent the operation of the Rule in *Clayton's Case* and so preserve the liability of the personal representatives for the amount owing at the date of notice of death of the guarantor. A new and distinct account must be opened for subsequent receipts and payments, and as it will not be covered by the guarantee, it must be kept in credit unless the bank holds other security or agrees to an unsecured overdraft. If the Rule is allowed to operate, then credits lodged after notice of death will reduce and eventually discharge the secured debt, whilst any withdrawals will constitute a fresh and unsecured debt.

In the case of a joint and several continuing guarantee, the death of one surety does not by itself release the co-sureties: *Beckett* v. *Addyman* (1882). If the consideration for the guarantee has been given once and for all, e.g. where a bank advances a lump sum at once on the security of the guarantee, the death of the guarantor does not release his estate from future liability under the guarantee: *Lloyd's* v. *Harper* (1880).

Needless to say, the death of the principal debtor will determine the guarantee, the debtor's account will be stopped and the extent of the guarantor's liability will thereupon be fixed.

(b) *Unsoundness of Mind.*— Immediately a bank learns from a reliable source that a guarantor has become mentally disordered, the principal debtor's account must be stopped, for the mentally disordered persons estate is liable only for the balance then due. The guarantee is terminated as to future advances, and the validity of any clause in the guarantee purporting to make it effective as a continuing security pending notice from the Receiver of the mentally disordered person does not appear to have been tested in the Courts. However, in *Bradford Old Bank* v. *Sutcliffe* (1918) it was held that a clause requiring notice of determination by the personal representatives on the death of the guarantor would not be applicable in the event of his lunacy.

The mental disorder of the principal debtor will also determine the guarantee, for immediately it comes to the bank's knowledge the debtor's account must be stopped and the liability of the guarantor will thereupon be fixed.

(c) *Bankruptcy.*— If the bank receives notice of a receiving order having been made against the guarantor, it must stop the principal debtor's account and demand repayment of the indebtedness from the principal debtor and, assuming this is not forthcoming, from the guarantor. On the guarantor being adjudicated bankrupt, the bank can prove against his estate for his contingent liability under the guarantee, as this type of debt is provable in bankruptcy. Any part payment of the indebtedness before proof must be deducted from the proof, but payments made after proof do not necessitate the submission of an amended proof.

The bankruptcy of the debtor and his subsequent discharge do not release a guarantor for him: ss. 16 and 28 of the Bankruptcy Act 1914. If the bank receives notice of a receiving order having been made against the principal debtor, his account must be stopped completely, and the usual formal demand made on the guarantor for payment under the guarantee. This is also necessary to ensure that interest runs against the guarantor. By virtue of the "whole debt" and other protective clauses in bank guarantee forms any moneys received from the guarantor as a result of this demand which are less than the entire indebtedness of the customer to the bank will be placed to a suspense account and ignored for the purposes of proof, so that the bank can claim for the maximum possible amount against the bankrupt's estate.

CONCLUSION

Guarantees figure prominently in any bank's security registers, for they certainly have their uses, though they are subject to some inherent defects not found in other securities. To illustrate their usefulness, a guarantee by a relative or friend or a joint and several guarantee from two or more of them may mean that a bank can support a small business with at that time little or no free assets, but with an ambitious and enterprising proprietor who can thereby develop the business over the years into a considerable one whose account, and goodwill, the bank will be pleased to have. Again, banks often take the personal guarantee of directors in respect of their company's account, for in addition to providing some security this also gives the directors an incentive to use their best endeavours to ensure the continued prosperity of the company.

The defects of guarantees as security centre round (1) the legal complications of the guarantee form and the rights of the guarantor; and (2) the guarantor's financial ability to honour his guarantee as and when called upon to do so. To meet the first point bank guarantee forms are drafted with the utmost care to protect the bank as much as possible and likewise to cut down the surety's common law rights. Even so, the tricky situations that may unexpectedly arise over guarantees must be handled carefully and correctly by the bank. In particular the bank must avoid any suggestion of misrepresentation or that it has either orally or by letter varied or waived any of the terms of its printed guarantee and thereby weakened its position. Any material alteration in the contract without the guarantor's consent, unless covered by an express stipulation, will enable the guarantor to avoid the contract.

The second point is a highly practical one. If a guarantee is fully supported by other security, then its value is that of the supporting security, whether cash, land, stocks and shares, life policies and so on.

But if the guarantee is only partially supported, or, as in perhaps a majority of cases, unsupported, then the absence of assets actually charged to the bank makes the guarantee a less dependable security than the other types of security just mentioned. Of course, even at worst an unsupported guarantee makes the bank an unsecured creditor of two or more persons instead of one, but if neither guarantor(s) nor customer has any assets, nothing can be obtained, and there is often little point in obtaining judgment against them and even less in instituting bankruptcy proceedings. Banks try to avoid taking guarantees from men of straw, and usually make status enquiries on guarantors, at, say, six monthly intervals. Nevertheless, the position of a guarantor apparently sound when he entered into the guarantee may change abruptly or gradually without the bank's knowledge. Giving a guarantee on behalf of someone who is indebted to his bank, and the parallel situation of going bail for a person, are onerous obligations often blithely entered into by sureties who never expect that one day they may be called upon to pay up. Ideally, the surety should regard an equivalent part of his assets as "frozen" or untouchable during the currency of his liability.

In numerous instances both the guarantor and the principal debtor are customers of the same bank, and the bank is in a better position to keep the guarantor and his affairs under surveillance. Generally, however, reliance has to be placed on the report of another bank, and as these reports are invariably unsigned and contain a clear disclaimer of responsibility clause (see Chapter 1) there is no legal liability on the bank supplying it; furthermore, the stilted phraseology of bank references must be carefully interpreted and noted by the recipient. "Undoubted", "quite good", and "good" are satisfactory, but more nebulous answers are not. If a renewal enquiry shows a deterioration in the guarantor's position, prompt action should be taken, with a view to reducing the indebtedness or obtaining additional security, or in the last resort calling in the debt.

The difficulty of keeping in touch with the financial position of the guarantor from time to time contrasts with the ease with which some other securities can be daily valued, e.g. quoted stocks and shares, and with the stability in value of such securities as land and life policies. In the case of these other securities the bank has actual control over them, for it normally possesses the appropriate instruments of title, but it has no similar control over a guarantor. Quoted stocks and shares and life policies with a surrender value can be quickly converted into cash, and land can be sold though it may take a little longer, but getting a guarantor to hand over cash is less certain and not always successful. Even wealthy guarantors are sometimes not keen to pay up, and though in case of need banks can and do institute proceedings against reluctant guarantors, such legal action may occasionally prove abortive and in any event lead to bad feeling and ill-will between all concerned. To show the contrary aspect to this gloomy side, one must add that there are numerous guarantors who meet their obligations promptly and courteously when called upon to do so, without in any way jeopardizing their own financial position.

Guarantees have both attractions and disadvantages; by nature they are as idiosyncratic as the persons giving them, for they cover a wide gamut from fully supported and first class ones to wholly unsupported ones by persons of doubtful standing taken more in hope than anything else. Thus, by and large, guarantees are not so reliable as other securities which posess an intrinsic value; they can be something of a gamble, and the degree of reliance which can be placed on them may not be easy to estimate, varying as it does from guarantor to guarantor.

Chapter 10

Bills of Exchange—Interpretation, Parties, Consideration and Negotiation

INTRODUCTION

This chapter and the remaining four chapters will deal with bills of exchange and cheques by taking the relevant Acts section by section, interspersed with comment which will vary in length as circumstances require. The Acts in question are the Bills of Exchange Act 1882 (as amended by the Bills of Exchange (Time of Noting) Act 1917) and the Cheques Act 1957. The codifying principal Act of 1882 was the work of a distinguished draftsman, Sir Mackenzie Chalmers, and is outstanding for its clarity. That of 1917 is a very minor amending Act; whereas the Act of 1957 is an important supplement on the topic of cheques, which are a particular type of bill of exchange but which since the original Act was passed have gradually come far to outnumber all other bills. A few amendments to the Act of 1882 have been made by the Banking and Financial Dealings Act 1971.

BILLS OF EXCHANGE ACT 1882
(45 & 46 Vict. c. 61)

An Act to codify the law relating to Bills of Exchange, Cheques, and Promissory Notes.   (18th August 1882)

PART I

PRELIMINARY

Short title

1.—This Act may be cited as the Bills of Exchange Act 1882.

It has also now to be construed with the Bills of Exchange (Time of Noting) Act 1917 and the Cheques Act 1957.

The Act applies to the whole of the United Kingdom (that is, Great Britain and Northern Ireland) and certain sections, as will be seen later, apply also to the Isle of Man and the Channel Islands. When the Act was passed, the United Kingdom included the whole of Ireland, but Southern Ireland became the Irish Free State under the Government of Ireland Act 1920, was re-styled as Eire at the end of 1937, and became the Republic of Ireland in 1949.

The provisions of the Act relate only to bills of exchange, cheques and promissory notes, so that any other negotiable instruments, e.g. bearer debentures, are dealt with by the general law.

Interpretation of terms

2.— In this Act, unless the context otherwise requires:

"Acceptance" means an acceptance completed by delivery or notification.

"Action" includes counter-claim and set off.

"Banker" includes a body of persons, whether incorporated or not, who carry on the business of banking.

"Bankrupt" includes any person whose estate is vested in a trustee or assignee under the law for the time being in force relating to bankruptcy.

"Bearer" means the person in possession of a bill or note which is payable to bearer.

"Bill" means bill of exchange, and "note" means promissory note.

"Delivery" means transfer of possession, actual or constructive, from one person to another.

"Holder" means the payee or indorsee of a bill or note who is in possession of it, or the bearer thereof.

"Indorsement" means an indorsement completed by delivery.

"Issue" means the first delivery of a bill or note, complete in form, to a person who takes it as a holder.

"Person" includes a body of persons whether incorporated or not.

"Value" means valuable consideration.

"Written" includes printed, and "writing" includes print.

This is the customary interpretation section in a statute (though it more often appears at the end) which shows the context in which certain words and phrases are used, and thereby saves repetition or elaboration on other sections. Generally, s. 2 is straightforward, but one point is worthy of comment, and that is the definition of "banker", which is vague in the sense that it begs the question. It is reminiscent of the witty but uninstructive definition of an archdeacon as a person who performs archidiaconal functions. In fact, the absence in any statute of a clear definition of banking has long caused difficulty. The man in the street will say he knows a bank when he sees one, but the real question is exactly what sort of business must therein be transacted. Though banking services have widened considerably in recent years, the basic features of banking remain the operation of current and deposit accounts, the payment of cheques drawn by customers, and the collection of cheques. The Post Office now has power to provide banking services without being restricted to the giro system: Post Office (Banking Services) Act 1976.

Upon this confused scene there has appeared the Banking Act 1979, which provides a system of recognition and licensing of banks and deposit takers by the Bank of England and sets up a Deposit Protection System. However, s. 36 of the Act continues the conundrum of "When is a bank not a bank?" as although sub-s. (1) provides that no person carrying on a business of any description in the United Kingdom other than (a) the Bank [of England]; (b) the central bank of a member state [of the EEC] other than the United Kingdom; (c) a recognised bank; (d) a trustee savings bank; (e) the Central Trustee Savings Bank Limited; and (f) the Post Office, in the exercise of its powers to provide banking services, may use any name or in any other way so describe himself or hold himself out as to indicate that he is a bank or banker or is carrying on a banking business, sub-s. (2) provides that nothing in (1) shall prevent a person who is not a recognised bank from using the expression "bank" or "banker" with reference to himself in any case where (a) he wishes to comply with or take advantage of any relevant provision of law or custom, or (b) it is necessary for him to use that expression in order to be able to assert that he is complying with or entitled to take advantage of such provision. There are certain minor exceptions from sub-s. (1) for savings and municipal banks under sub-s. (5). In other words, the Act does not affect the determination of any question whether a person, licensed institution or not, is a bank or banker for purposes other than those of the Act, for example, as regards the Bills of Exchange Act 1882. The resolving of this legal paradox should prove both difficult and interesting.

The new Act updates the definition of "bank" and "banker" in various statutes (though not as regards the Bills of Exchange Act 1882). For example, in s. 9 of the Bankers' Books Evidence Act 1879, the expressions "bank" and "banker" now mean:—

(a) a recognised bank, licensed institution or a municipal bank within the meaning of the Banking Act 1979;

(b) a trustee savings bank within the meaning of s. 3 of the Trustee Savings Banks Act 1969;

(c) the National Savings Bank; and

(d) the Post Office, in the exercise of its powers to provide banking services.

In s. 5 (7) of the Agricultural Credits Act 1928, "bank" now means the Bank of England, plus (a), (b) and (d) as set out above.

PART II

BILLS OF EXCHANGE

FORM AND INTERPRETATION

Bill of exchange defined

3.—(1) A bill of exchange is an unconditional order in writing, addressed by one person to another, signed by the person giving it, requiring the person to whom it is addressed to pay on demand or at a fixed or determinable future time a sum certain in money to or to the order of a specified person, or to bearer.

(2) An instrument which does not comply with these conditions, or which orders any act to be done in addition to the payment of money, is not a bill of exchange.

(3) An order to pay out of a particular fund is not unconditional within the meaning of this section; but an unqualified order to pay, coupled with (*a*) an indication of a particular fund out of which the drawee is to reimburse himself or a particular account to be debited with the amount, or (*b*) a statement of the transaction which gives rise to the bill, is unconditional.

(4) A bill is not invalid by reason—
    (a) That it is not dated;
    (b) That it does not comply with the value given, or that any value has been given therefor;
    (c) That it does not specify the place where it is drawn or the place where it is payable.

It will be seen that a cheque is a particular type of bill of exchange, because it must be drawn on a banker and it must be payable on demand (see s. 73 where the position will be more fully discussed). It is not perhaps stating the obvious to give the following illustrations of bills of exchange, because outside the export trade and the City of London, where acceptance credits give rise to them and discount houses are in business to discount them, ordinary bills of exchange are a vanishing race.

Example of a demand bill between two parties only.

                                                    1001, King Street,
                                                    London
£1,000-00.   1st April 1980

    Pay to my order on demand the sum of One thousand pounds
only, value received.

                                                    Arthur Brown

To: Charles Dawson,
        999, Queen Street,
            Manchester.

Here, Arthur Brown is called the drawer, because he draws (i.e. writes out, or initiates) the bill, and his is also the payee, the person to whom the money is to be paid. Charles Dawson, to whom the instruction to pay the money is addressed, is known as the drawee, the person on whom the bill is drawn. Under the Finance Act 1970 all bills of exchange, cheques and promissory notes have been free of stamp duty as from 1st February 1971. As variations, this example may read "Pay Bearer on demand", and instead of the words "on demand", the phrase "at sight" may be used, meaning that payment is to be made when the drawee first sees the bill, i.e. when it is first presented to him. A bill is also payable on demand where no time for payment is expressed: s. 10.

Example of a determinable future time bill between three parties.

                                                    1001, King Street,
                                                    London
£997-50.   1st April 1980

    Four months after date pay to Eric Freeman or order the sum of
Nine hundred and ninety-seven pounds 50, value received.

                                                    Arthur Brown

To: Charles Dawson,
        999, Queen Street,
            Manchester.

Now, Arthur Brown remains the drawer, but there is a separate person as payee, Eric Freeman, Charles Dawson is still the drawee, and if and when he agrees or assents to the order addressed to him, he will be known as the acceptor.

The first type of bill illustrated is now little used, because in practice the transaction will normally be settled by CD sending to AB his cheque for £1,000. The second type shows the bill of exchange at its best—a negotiable instrument which settles two debts—that between AB and CD and also that between EF and AB—and possibly more than two because EF may pass the bill on to his creditor GH and so on. In addition, the time lag before the bill has to be paid allows the drawee to dispose of goods etc. in respect of which the bill has been drawn on him by his supplier, thereby raising funds with which to pay the bill at maturity, whilst after it has been accepted and during its currency EF or any subsequent holder may discount the bill with his bank, so raising funds immediately, provided the bank is satisfied with the creditworthiness of the parties.

To look more closely at the definition, the bill must be unconditional, so that the type of document which runs "Pay AB the sum of £100 on condition that the receipt below is duly signed and dated" or "provided the receipt form at foot hereof is duly signed and dated" is not a bill of exchange, despite any outward similarity: *Bavins* v. *London and South Western Bank* (1900). It is usually called a conditional order to pay. On the other hand, in *Nathan* v. *Ogdens, Ltd.* (1905), where the document contained the words "the receipt at the back must be signed," it was held that these words were addressed to the payee, not to the drawee, and so the order on the drawee was unconditional and therefore was a valid bill of exchange. Another type of conditional order sometimes encountered is the pension warrant whereby the pensioner is authorised to receive an amount from the agent or bank of the authority or body paying the pension, provided that a certificate is completed to the effect that the pensioner is still alive.

The bill must be an order, and a mere request is not sufficient for this purpose: *Hamilton* v. *Spottiswoode* (1849), where it was held that a document reading "We hereby authorise you to pay on our account to the order of G £6,000" was not a bill of exchange.

The bill must be in writing, which by s. 2 includes print, but the section does not say on what material the writing must be. This has provided humorists, notably the late Sir Alan Herbert, with amusing ventures such as the drawing of cheques on eggs, and even on the side of a cow, the "negotiable cow" offered in the story to the Inland Revenue in settlement of a tax demand.

The parties and the phrase "on demand" have already been mentioned. It is necessary, however, to distinguish fixed future time from determinable future time. The Act does not define fixed future time, but it is a time so definitely fixed as to exclude the three days of grace which would have been added prior to their abolition by the Banking and Financial Dealings Act 1971 (see s. 14). A determinable future time is a fixed period, e.g. three months, after date or sight of the bill, or after the occurrence of a specified event which is certain to happen although the precise time of its happening is unknown, e.g. the death of a person—see s. 11.

In *Korea Exchange Bank* v. *Debenhams (Central Buying), Ltd.* (1979) an instrument read "at 90 days sight D/A of this first bill of exchange . . . pay . . ." but the word "sight" which was part of the printed form had been deleted by overtyping. In commercial usage "D/A" means "documents against acceptance", and so the instrument really read "at 90 days documents against acceptance . . . pay . . ." which was gibberish. The Court of Appeal therefore held that the instrument was not expressed to be payable at a fixed or determinable future time.

There must be a sum certain in money, i.e. legal tender, so that a document ordering the delivery of stocks and shares or goods is not a bill, whatever other resemblances it may have. By s. 2. of the Decimal Currency Act 1969 bills of exchange (and promissory notes) drawn in shillings and pence after 15th February 1971 are invalid.

The effect of s. 3 (3) is that a document which runs, say, "Pay £100 out of moneys to be received by you from X" is not a bill of exchange, though it may well operate as an assignment; whereas if the instruction runs "Pay £100 and charge the same to the proceeds of the sale of 100 bales of cotton shipped per SS. Peerless" then it will be a bill of exchange (given that the other requisites are satisfied). When the drawer has two or more accounts, then he will need to indicate which is to be debited, e.g. Private a/c, or No. 2 a/c, and this indication is permissible under the subsection.

Section 3 (4) allows the date, the words "value received" and the place of drawing or the place of paying to be omitted, without prejudicing the validity of the bill. Thus, the second illustration which has been given could be reduced simply to:

"Four months after date pay Eric Freeman the sum of Nine hundred and ninety-seven pounds 50.

Arthur Brown.

To: Charles Dawson."

Inland and foreign bills

4.—(1) An inland bill is a bill which is or on the face of it purports to be (*a*) both drawn and payable within the British Islands, or (*b*) drawn within the British Islands upon some person resident therein. Any other bill is a foreign bill.

For the purposes of this Act "British Islands" mean any part of the United Kingdom of Great Britain and Ireland, the islands of Man,

Guernsey, Jersey, Alderney, and Sark, and the islands adjacent to any of them being part of the dominions of Her Majesty.

(2) Unless the contrary appears on the face of the bill the holder may treat it as an island bill.

As a result of the constitutional changes already stated in connection with s. 1, "Ireland" is now limited to "Northern Ireland", so that bills which on their face are drawn or payable in or on a party in the Republic of Ireland are foreign bills (mutual arrangements as to stamp duty operate between the United Kingdom and the Republic but they are not now relevant to bills and notes).

If a London exporter draws a bill on his Paris importer payable in London, then it is an inland bill, but if payable outside the United Kingdom it will be a foreign bill. If the drawer and drawee are resident in the United Kingdom, it is an inland bill, even though payable abroad. If it looks like an inland bill, though in fact it is a foreign bill, the holder may treat it as either at his option. A bill which was not a foreign bill within the definition was held to be a valid inland bill notwithstanding it was written in French: *Re Marseilles Extension Rail and Land Co.* (1885).

It will be seen later, under s. 51, that a foreign bill, if dishonoured, must be protested, but this is not obligatory in the case of an inland bill.

In *Koch* v. *Dicks* (1933) the Court of Appeal held that alteration of a completed bill of exchange without the knowledge or consent of the acceptor by changing the place of drawing from London to Deisslingen (in Germany), so that the bill became a foreign bill instead of an inland bill, was a material alteration under s. 64 and the bill was thereby avoided.

Effect where different parties to bill are the same person

5.—(1) A bill may be drawn payable to , or to the order of, the drawer; or it may be drawn payable to, or to the order of, the drawee.

(2) Where in a bill drawer and drawee are the same person, or where the drawee is a fictitious person or a person not having capacity to contract, the holder may treat the instrument, at his option, either as a bill of exchange or as a promissory note.

It was held in *Chamberlain* v. *Young* (1893) that a bill drawn "Pay to . . . . . . order" and indorsed by the drawer was payable to the drawer's order, as if it had been made "Pay to my order". Where the drawee is also the payee, it follows that before it can be enforced the bill must be indorsed over to a third party. Sometimes a customer may make his cheques payable to his own bank, e.g. "Pay Yourselves a/c National Savings Certificates", or "Pay South Bank Ltd. a/c Arthur Brown".

Drawer and drawee will be the same person where one branch of an organisation draws on another branch. The holder may treat the instrument as a promissory note. An example of a fictitious drawee that often used to be given was a bill drawn on "the Man in the Moon", but scientific progress has now made this particular illustration inappropriate.

Address to drawee

6.—(1) The drawee must be named or otherwise indicated in a bill with reasonable certainty.

(2) A bill may be addressed to two or more drawees whether they are partners or not, but an order addressed to two drawees in the alternative or to two or more drawees in succession is not a bill of exchange.

A bill must be addressed to someone, reasonably identified, or expressed to be payable at a stated address and then accepted by a person who lives there—which will indicate the drawee with reasonable certainty.

If an instrument is addressed "To AB, CD and EF", it will be a valid bill, but not if it is addressed to alternative drawees, e.g. "To either AB or CD", or to a series of drawees, e.g. "To AB, or failing him CD, or failing him EF".

Certainty required as to payee

7.—(1) Where a bill is not payable to bearer, the payee must be named or otherwise indicated therein with reasonable certainty.

(2) A bill may be payable to two or more payees jointly, or it may be made payable in the alternative to one of two, or one or some of several payees. A bill may also be made payable to the holder of an office for the time being.

(3) Where the payee is a fictitious or non-existing person the bill may be treated as payable to bearer.

Whilst some cheques and a few bills are made payable to bearer, the great bulk of them are payable to order and in them the payee must be reasonably identified. It was held in *North and South Insurance Corporation.* v. *National Provincial Bank Ltd.* (1936) that a cheque form made out "Pay Cash or Order" was not a bill of exchange for "cash" is an impersonal payee (not a specified person) and therefore no payee had been named or otherwise indicated: it was, however, a good direction to the bank to pay £250 to bearer and, the bank having done so, the plaintiffs' claim failed.

Payees may be joint, as often occurs when dividends are paid on stocks and shares registered in joint names. Payees may be alternative as well, which contrasts with the position as regards drawees laid down in the preceding section, but then the question of who receives payment is not so vitally specific as is the question of who is to pay. The point about the holder of an office for the time being covers such cases as cheques made payable to, for example, "The Treasurer of the Loamshire County Council", so that the cheque will not be affected by the fact that the office may happen to be vacant at the particular moment when it is drawn.

The meaning of the word "fictitious" has given rise to a certain amount of litigation, not in the obvious case of a cheque made payable to a legendary character in song or story, but in borderline instances of fraud, as shown by the following cases:

In *Bank of England* v. *Vagliano Brothers* (1891) V. Bros. were in the habit of accepting bills of exchange drawn by a foreign correspondent, Vucina, in favour of P. & Co. of Constantinople. A fraudulent clerk of V. Bros. forged bills as regards the drawer's signature, inserted P. & Co. as payee, then got the bills genuinely accepted by V. Bros., and subsequently forged the payee's indorsement and cashed the bills at the Bank of England. The Bank's right to debit V. Bros'. account with the bills turned on whether the bills were payable to bearer or not. The House of Lords held that they were bearer bills (and hence the forged indorsements were immaterial) because the drawer (i.e. the clerk) never intended P. & Co. to receive payment, so that the payee was fictitious, even though that name was actually borne by someone.

Similarly, in *Clutton* v. *Attenborough* (1897), where a fraudulent clerk made out a cheque to a person whose name he had invented and persuaded his employer to sign it by falsely representing that he was a creditor in respect of work done, the House of Lords held that the payee was non-existent and the cheque therefore payable to bearer, even though the drawer had believed it was in favour of a real person.

These two cases were distinguished in *Vinden* v. *Hughes* (1905), where a fraudulent clerk made out cheques to certain well-known customers and persuaded his employer to sign them when no money was in fact owing to them. He then forged the indorsements and negotiated the cheques to the defendant. It was held that the payees were not fictitious, because the drawer believed he owed money to the payees who were known to him and intended those payees to receive payment.

This last case was followed in *North and South Wales Bank* v. *Macbeth*

(1908), where the respondent was induced by fraud of one White to draw a cheque for £11,250 to the order of T. A. Kerr, an existing person whom he intended to be the payee. W forged K's indorsement and paid the cheque into his account with the appellant bank (which admitted it could not rely on the protection of s. 82 of the Bills of Exchange Act 1882). The House of Lords held that the drawer could recover the amount of the cheque from the bank.

What bills are negotiable

8.—(1) When a bill contains words prohibiting transfer, or indicating an intention that it should not be transferable, it is valid as between the parties thereto, but is not negotiable.

(2) A negotiable bill may be payable either to order or to bearer.

(3) A bill is payable to bearer which is expressed to be so payable, or on which the only or last indorsement is an indorsement in blank.

(4) A bill is payable to order which is expressed to be so payable, or which is expressed to be payable to a particular person, and does not contain words prohibiting transfer or indicating an intention that it should not be transferable.

(5) Where a bill, either originally or by indorsement, is expressed to be payable to the order of a specified person, and not to him or his order, it is nevertheless payable to him or his order at his option.

The Court of Appeal held in *Hibernian Bank Ltd.* v. *Gysin and Hanson* (1939) that when the words "not negotiable" appear on a bill they do not have the special meaning given to them by s. 81 of the Bills of Exchange Act 1882 in the case of cheques, but they restrict the transferability of the bill. That is, they are in terms of s. 8 (1) above: "words prohibiting transfer or indicating an intention that the bill should not be transferable".

By virtue of s. 8 (4) a bill made out "Pay EF One hundred pounds" is payable to EF or order. Section 8 (5) cuts out any possible argument that a bill made out "Pay One hundred pounds to the order of EF" cannot be paid to EF himself but only to someone designated by him, by putting such a bill on the same footing as if it were payable to EF or order.

Sum payable

9.—(1) The sum payable by a bill is a sum certain within the meaning of this Act, although it is required to be paid—

    (a) With interest.

    (b) By stated instalments.

    (c) By stated instalments, with a provision that upon default in payment of any instalment the whole shall become due.

(d) According to an indicated rate of exchange or according to a rate of exchange to be ascertained as directed by the bill of exchange.

(2) Where the sum payable is expressed in words and also in figures, and there is a discrepancy between the two, the sum denoted by the words is the amount payable.

(3) Where a bill is expressed to be payable with interest, unless the instrument otherwise provides, interest runs from the date of the bill, and if a bill is undated, from the issue thereof.

The amount of a bill is still a "sum certain" even though interest requires to be calculated. If interest is included in the bill, but no rate is specified, then it will be five per cent per annum: *Re Commercial Bank of South Australia* (1887). However, the high commercial rates of the last decade have made this rate unrealistic, and it would seem reasonable that it could be increased in these circumstances. In the case of a bill payable by instalments, the date and amount of the instalments must be given, e.g. "Pay EF Four hundred pounds in four equal instalments due January 1st, April 1st, July 1st and October 1st 1981". A bill may include an exchange clause giving an actual rate of exchange for a foreign currency, or a method for its ascertainment, e.g. a bill drawn in London on a foreign drawee may instruct that it is "payable at the collecting banker's selling rate for sight drafts on London".

Section 9 (2) provides that where the words and figures differ, the words have priority. Normally, in these circumstances, the paying bank will return the cheque or other instrument unpaid marked "Words and figures differ", but if the error is spotted by the collecting bank and the payee is content to take the smaller of the two different amounts, the cheque will be marked "We claim smaller amount" by the collecting bank, and will be dealt with in the ordinary way on this basis. Doubtful cases depend on their particular facts as regards interpretation, e.g. a bill made out as "Pay to my order fifty two, ten pence" would be taken as one for £52.10. With present day mechanisation as regards their drawing, many dividends and even cheques often have no amount in words (or no exact amount in words), the bank taking an indemnity from the customer to cover the situation.

Bill payable on demand

10.—(1) A bill is payable on demand—
    (a) Which is expressed to be payable on demand, or at sight, or on presentation; or
    (b) In which no time for payment is expressed.

(2) Where a bill is accepted or indorsed when it is overdue, it shall, as regards the acceptor, or any indorser who so indorses it, be deemed a bill payable on demand.

This is a summary of circumstances in which a bill is payable on demand, and it will be seen that where a bill has already run its course and become overdue, it is deemed to be a demand bill as regards the subsequent acceptor or any subsequent indorser.

Bill payable at a future time

11.— A bill is payable at a determinable future time within the meaning of this Act which is expressed to be payable—
(1) At a fixed period after date or sight.
(2) On or at a fixed period after the occurrence of a specified event which is certain to happen, though the time of happening may be uncertain.
An instrument expressed to be payable on a contingency is not a bill, and the happening of the event does not cure the defect.

It was held in *Williamson* v. *Rider* (1963) that a document payable "on or before December 31, 1956" was not a bill of exchange because of uncertainty and contingency in the time of payment. This case has not been followed in Ireland, where a promissory note payable "on or before the 1st day of November 1970" was held to be payable at a future time and to be a valid promissory note: *Creative Press, Ltd.* v. *Harman and Harman* (1973).

Bills in the first category laid down in this section present no difficulties, e.g. "Three months after date (or sight) pay EF . . ." However, an instrument payable "at 90 days after acceptance" does not satisfy s. 11 because "after acceptance" is a different expression from "after sight"—there can be sight without acceptance: *Korea Exchange Bank* v. *Debenhams (Central Buying), Ltd.* (1979). The standard example of the second category is a bill payable on or at a fixed period after the death of someone, for death is a specified event which is certain to happen, though the time when it will befall a particular individual is uncertain. Examples of a contingency are when the money is payable, say, three months after the marriage of a person, or upon the arrival of a specified ship at Liverpool; these events, though they may be extremely likely, are not certain and documents so drawn are not bills, notwithstanding that in fact the person does subsequently marry or the ship does arrive.

Omission of date in bill payable after date

12.— Where a bill expressed to be payable at a fixed period after date is issued undated, or where the acceptance of a bill payable at a fixed period after sight is undated, any holder may insert therein the true date of issue or acceptance, and the bill shall be payable accordingly.

Provided that (1) where the holder in good faith and by mistake inserts a wrong date, and (2) in every case where a wrong date is inserted, if the bill subsequently comes into the hands of a holder in due course the bill shall not be avoided thereby, but shall operate and be payable as if the date so inserted had been the true date.

This allows undated bills to be dated and thereby regularised, except as between immediate parties where the wrong date is inserted.

Ante-dating and post-dating

13.— (1) Where a bill or an acceptance or any indorsement on a bill is dated, the date shall, unless the contrary be proved, be deemed to be the true date of the drawing, acceptance, or indorsement, as the case may be.

(2) A bill is not invalid by reason only that it is ante-dated or post-dated, or that it bears date on a Sunday.

The date, wherever it appears on a bill, is presumed to be the true date unless and until the contrary is proved. Ante-dating a bill does not by itself invalidate a bill, e.g. a bill may be dated yesterday in error for today; a bill may be ante-dated so much that it will appear to be a "stale" bill (see. s. 36) until the date is corrected. Post-dating a bill does not by itself invalidate a bill, nor does dating it on a Sunday; Saturday is also now a non-business day: see s. 92.

Difficulties over dates tend to centre round the post-dating of cheques. A post-dated cheque is in many ways equivalent to a bill payable after date. The difficulty in which a bank may find itself if it pays a post-dated cheque (instead of returning it marked "Post-dated", or getting the customer to alter the date) is that this is a breach by the bank of its customer's mandate. Consequently, in these circumstances the bank will have to bear the loss if the customer dies, becomes bankrupt or stops payment of the cheque before its due date arrives, and damages will be increased where the bank has dishonoured other cheques because available funds were exhausted in paying the post-dated cheque. Customers sometimes get in the habit of post-dating cheques deliberately in order to play for time financially, but this is a practice on which banks naturally look with disfavour.

By way of postscript it may be noted that s. 1 of the Forgery Act 1913 provides that the time or place of making where either is material may make a document false for the purposes of the crime of forgery.

Computation of time of payment

14.—Where a bill is not payable on demand the day on which it falls due is determined as follows:

(1) [The bill is due and payable in all cases on the last day of the time of payment as fixed by the bill or, if that is a non-business day, on the succeeding business day.]

(2) Where a bill is payable at a fixed period after date, after sight, or after the happening of a specified event, the time of payment is determined by excluding the day from which the time is to begin to run and by including the date of payment.

(3) Where a bill is payable at a fixed period after sight, the time begins to run from the date of the acceptance if the bill be accepted, and from the date of noting or protest if the bill be noted or protested for non-acceptance, or for non-delivery.

(4) The term "month" in a bill means calendar month.

The new subsection (1) was inserted by s. 3 (2) of the Banking and Financial Dealings Act 1971 in replacement of the original provision of the Act of 1882 that three days of grace were added to the time of payment of bills payable at a determinable future time and that payment was advanced or postponed if the last day of grace was a non-business day. For non-business days, see s. 92.

The Banking and Financial Dealings Act 1971 has repealed and replaced the Bank Holidays Act 1871 and the Holidays Extension Act 1875. Section 1 of the Act of 1971 provides that the days specified in Schedule I of the Act shall be bank holidays and also that Her Majesty may by proclamation declare that a day specified in Schedule I shall not in any particular year be a bank holiday and appoint another day in place of it as a bank holiday in that year, and may from time to time by proclamation appoint a special day to be, either throughout the United Kingdom or in any place or locality in the United Kingdom, a bank holiday. The section further provides that no person shall be compellable to make any payment or to do any act on a bank holiday which he would not be compellable to make or do on Christmas Day or Good Friday [which are *common law* holidays] and where such obligation would have fallen on a bank holiday it shall be deemed to be complied with if made or done on the next following day. Schedule I provides:—

1. The following are to be bank holidays in England and Wales:—
   [New Year's Day—added by Royal Proclamation on 26th October 1973], Easter Monday, [the first Monday in May—added by Royal Proclamation each year from 1978], the last Monday in May, the last Monday in August, 26th December, if it be not a Sunday, 27th December in a year in which 25th or 26th December is a Sunday.

2. The following are to be bank holidays in Scotland:—

> New Year's Day, if it be not a Sunday or, if it be a Sunday, 3rd January. 2nd January, if it be not a Sunday or, if it be a Sunday, 3rd January. Good Friday, the first Monday in May, the first Monday in August, Christmas Day, if it be not a Sunday or, if it be a Sunday, 26th December.

(The bank holidays in Northern Ireland are the same as those in England and Wales with the addition of 17th March, if it be not a Sunday or, if it be a Sunday, 18th March.)

Where a bill is payable at a fixed period "after sight", then there must be some act beyond merely showing the bill to the drawee, i.e. there must be an acceptance, or failing that noting or protesting. To illustrate the time factor: a bill payable three months after 14th February will be payable on 14th May.

Case of need

15.— The drawer of a bill and any indorser may insert therein the name of a person to whom the holder may resort in case of need, that is to say, in case the bill is dishonoured by non-acceptance or non-payment. Such a person is called the referee in case of need. It is in the option of the holder to resort to the referee in case of need or not as he may think fit.

This accounts for the phrase sometimes seen on bills: "In need with Messrs X. & Co." or "First and in need with Messrs X. & Co." The referee in case of need acts as a stand-by in the event of the bill being dishonoured by the drawee/acceptor, but, as will be seen later, a bill must be protested before it can be presented to such a referee.

Optional stipulations by drawer or indorser

16.— The drawer of a bill, and any indorser, may insert therein an express stipulation—

> (1) Negativing or limiting his own liability to the holder:
> (2) Waiving as regards himself some or all of the holder's duties.

Various phrases may be used in this connection, e.g. liability is negatived by "*sans recours*" or without recourse; it is limited by "*sans frais*" (without dishonour expenses).

Definition and requisites of acceptance

17.— (1) The acceptance of a bill is the signification by the drawee of his assent to the order of the drawer.

(2) An acceptance is invalid unless it complies with the following conditions, namely:

    (a) It must be written on the bill and be signed by the drawee. The mere signature of the drawee without additional words is sufficient.

    (b) It must not express that the drawee will perform his promise by any other means than the payment of money.

By assenting to the order of the drawer, the person to whom the order to pay the sum of money is addressed (the drawee) is said to "accept" the bill, and thereafter he is known as the acceptor. Until the bill is accepted, the primary liability on it rests with the drawer, but the effect of acceptance is to make the acceptor the party who is primarily liable on the bill. Acceptance may be by signature alone, but the word "Accepted" written by the drawee without his signature is not enough. It is normally effected on the face of the bill, though it could be done on the back of it, but it must be a promise to pay money, so that any phrase such as "Accepted payable in goods" does not constitute a valid acceptance.

Time for acceptance

18.— A bill may be accepted:

(1) Before it has been signed by the drawer, or while otherwise incomplete:

(2) When it is overdue, or after it has been dishonoured by a previous refusal to accept, or by non-payment:

(3) When a bill payable after sight is dishonoured by non-acceptance, and the drawee subsequently accepts it, the holder, in the absence of any different agreement, is entitled to have the bill accepted as of the date of first presentment to the drawee for acceptance.

Sometimes a person will make out and accept a bill for a sum of money owing by him to his creditor and then send it to that creditor for him to sign as drawer, thereby completing the bill: this procedure is valid. Sometimes the drawee may have refused to accept the bill when it is first presented to him; if it is re-presented to him a week later and he then changes his mind and accepts it, this acceptance is valid.

General and qualified acceptances

19.— (1) An acceptance is (a) general or (b) qualified.

(2) A general acceptance assents without qualification to the order of the drawer. A qualified acceptance in express terms varies the effect of the bill as drawn.

In particular an acceptance is qualified which is:

(a) conditional, that is to say, which makes payment by the acceptor dependent on the fulfilment of a condition therein stated:

(b) partial, that is to say, an acceptance to pay part only of the amount for which the bill is drawn:

(c) local, that is to say, an acceptance to pay only at a particular specified place:

>An acceptance to pay at a particular place is a general acceptance, unless it expressly states that the bill is to be paid there only and not elsewhere:

(d) qualified as to time:

(e) the acceptance of some one or more of the drawees, but not of all.

A general acceptance must be unqualified. Section 19 sets out five particular instances in which there will be a qualified acceptance, and examples of these qualified acceptances are:

(a) *conditional.*—"Accepted payable on delivery of Land Certificate Title No. . . . ."

(b) *partial.*—When a bill for £500 is "Accepted payable for £250 only".

(c) *local.*—"Accepted payable at South Bank Ltd., Mudtown and there only" (or ". . . and not elsewhere"). If this last restrictive phrase is omitted, then it will be a general acceptance, even though a bank and branch is specified. As far as the bank is concerned, it does not require any independent advice to pay the bill, the fact that the bill is accepted payable at the acceptor's branch bank being sufficient authority for the bank to debit his account with it. On the other hand, the fact that the bill has been accepted payable at a bank does not create any privity of contract between the drawer or a holder and the acceptor's bank: *Auchteroni & Co.* v. *Midland Bank Ltd.* (1928).

It may be mentioned here that as the Act does not define "place" the holder of a bill would be bound to take a general acceptance even if payable abroad, and could not treat it as a qualified acceptance. This would necessitate presentment at maturity at the place abroad where accepted payable, otherwise (as will be seen later) the drawer and indorsers would be discharged.

(d) *qualified as to time.*—A bill payable three months after date, which is "Accepted payable six months after date". Alternatively the qualified acceptance may be for a shorter period than that stated in the bill.

(e) *qualified as to parties.*—When a bill is drawn on AB, CD and EF, but only AB and EF accept, CD refusing to accept.

Inchoate instruments

20.—(1) Where a simple signature on a blank . . . paper is delivered by the signer in order that it may be converted into a bill, it operates as a prima facie authority to fill it up as a complete bill, for any amount . . . using the signature for that of the drawer, or the acceptor, or an indorser; and, in like manner, when a bill is wanting in any material particular, the person in possession of it has a prima facie authority to fill up the omission in any way he thinks fit.

(2) In order that any such instrument when completed may be enforceable against any person who became a party thereto prior to its completion, it must be filled up within a reasonable time, and strictly in accordance with the authority given. Reasonable time for this purpose is a question of fact.

Provided that if any such instrument after completion is negotiated to a holder in due course it shall be valid and effectual for all purposes in his hands, and he may enforce it as if it had been filled up within a reasonable time and strictly in accordance with the authority given.

Inchoate means incomplete, and like the adjective "disgruntled" it is a negative word to which there is no corresponding positive, i.e. there is no word "choate" in our language. The words deleted in s. 20 (1) referred to stamping and were repealed by the Finance Act 1970 because as the Act abolished stamp duty on bills of exchange and promissory notes the words had ceased to have any relevance.

Inchoate instruments are really an authority to create a bill of exchange, and though they are sometimes used, they have the same inherent risks as are involved in giving blank (but signed) cheques. If someone fills up the blanks for more than the amount intended, then in the hands of a holder in due course it will be good for that amount. In any event, apart from negotiation, the common law doctrine of estoppel may operate so as to prevent a defendant from denying the validity of the document as against the plaintiff, as it did in *Lloyds Bank Ltd.* v. *Cooke*, (1907) where the defendant had given a blank stamped paper to a customer of the bank to fill in as a promissory note and hand to the bank as security, and the customer fraudulently completed it for a larger amount than agreed.

As a question of fact, "reasonable time" varies with the particular circumstances of the case. In *Griffiths* v. *Dalton* (1940) an undated cheque had been given in August 1931 and had been completed in February 1933: it was held that reasonable time had long ago elapsed.

In the case of an incomplete "not negotiable" cheque which is wilfully and wrongfully filled in, the drawer can deny the authority of his servant or agent. This is shown by *Wilson and Meeson* v. *Pickering* (1946), where a partner in the plaintiff firm signed a blank cheque crossed in print "not negotiable" and delivered it to his secretary to fill in for the sum of £2 in favour of the Commissioners of Inland Revenue. She fraudulently filled it in for £54 in favour of the defendant to whom she owed money and for whom it was collected by a bank. The Court of Appeal held that the defendant must refund the money to the plaintiffs, because the instrument was not negotiable, the payee being a person within the meaning of s. 81 of the Bills of Exchange Act 1882.

Delivery

21.—(1) Every contract on a bill, whether it be the drawer's, acceptor's, or an indorser's, is incomplete and revocable, until delivery of the instrument in order to give effect thereto.

Provided that where an acceptance is written on a bill, and the drawee gives notice to or according to the directions of the person entitled to the bill that he has accepted it, the acceptance then becomes complete and irrevocable.

(2) As between immediate parties, and as regards a remote party other than a holder in due course, the delivery:

(a) in order to be effectual must be made either by or under the authority of the party drawing, accepting, or indorsing, as the case may be;

(b) may be shown to have been conditional or for a special purpose only, and not for the purpose of transferring the property in the bill.

But if the bill be in the hands of a holder in due course a valid delivery of the bill by all parties prior to him so as to make them liable to him is conclusively presumed.

(3) Where a bill is no longer in the possession of a party who has signed it as drawer, acceptor, or indorser, a valid and unconditional delivery by him is presumed until the contrary is proved.

Delivery (defined in s. 2 as the "transfer of possession, actual or constructive, from one person to another") is necessary to constitute a contract, save that the acceptance will be complete if the acceptor gives notice of his acceptance once he has done so, though he retains the bill. Otherwise, until delivery the person in possession of the bill may change his mind in respect of what he has done in relation to the bill, for he still has control over it.

In *Ex Parte Cote* (1873) MELLISH, L.J. said: "In order to make the property in bills pass, it is not sufficient to indorse them; they must be delivered to the indorsee or to the agent of the indorsee. If the indorser delivers them to his own agent, he can recover them; if to the agent of the indorsee, he cannot recover them". The case concerned the effect of the French postal regulations—in France a letter may be reclaimed by the sender as long as it has not left the office at which he posted it, whereas in England our postal regulations prevent any letter being reclaimed once it has been posted.

Immediate parties are those between whom there is a direct

relationship, e.g. drawer and acceptor; or drawer and payee; or first indorsee and second indorsee.

A bill may be delivered conditionally or for a special purpose only: this is similar to the conditional delivery of a deed which is then known as an escrow, i.e. it is delivered subject to a condition or until a certain time has elapsed, and so does not take effect until the condition has been fulfilled or the time has elapsed. The relationship between a party who delivers a bill conditionally and the one who receives it is generally that of principal and agent, or bailor and bailee.

CAPACITY AND AUTHORITY OF PARTIES

Capacity of parties

22.—(1) Capacity to incur liability as a party to a bill is co-extensive with capacity to contract.

Provided that nothing in this section shall enable a corporation to make itself liable as drawer, acceptor, or indorser of a bill unless it is competent to it so to do under the law for the time being in force relating to corporations.

(2) Where a bill is drawn or indorsed by an infant, minor, or corporation having no capacity or power to incur liability on a bill, the drawing or indorsement entitles the holder to receive payment of the bill, and to enforce it against any other party thereto.

Capacity to contract has been discussed in Chapter 1 on Contract, and that of companies in particular in Chapter 4 on Companies. It may be noted here that under the Bank Charter Act 1844 no banker or banking company other than the Bank of England may issue in England or Wales any bill of exchange or promissory note which is expressed to be, or in legal effect is, payable to bearer on demand.

The effect of s. 22 (2) is that the acceptor and any indorser who have capacity to contract are liable to pay the bill and cannot shelter behind the legal incapacity of the drawer or any indorser.

By s. 12 of the Family Law Reform Act 1969 "minor" (a Scots law term) may be used instead of the traditional English law term "infant" to describe a person under 18 years of age. Whilst an infant cannot be sued on a bill of exchange, whether for necessaries or not, if the bill is given to the supplier of necessaries his right to sue on the original contract is not prejudicially affected: *Re Soltykoff, Ex parte Margrett* (1891).

Signature essential to liability

23.— No person is liable as drawer, indorser, or acceptor of a bill who has not signed it as such: Provided that

(1) Where a person signs a bill in a trade or assumed name, he is liable thereon as if he had signed it in his own name.

(2) The signature of the name of a firm is equivalent to the signature by the person so signing of the names of all persons liable as partners in that firm.

Signature is the means of authenticating a bill or note by writing a person's name thereon. By s. 91 it is not necessary that the person sign it with his own hand, but it is sufficient if his signature is written by his authority.

Though signature is a necessary pre-requisite to liability on a bill of exchange, a party who has signed may be able to avoid liability by pleading *non est factum* (mistake as to the nature of the document— see Chapter 1, page 21) though this defence will be lost if he has been careless when signing the instrument: *Foster* v. *Mackinnon* (1869), a point which will be looked at again in relation to s. 88 concerning promissory notes. Another illustration is *Credit Lyonnais* v. *P. T. Barnard and Associates, Ltd.* (1976), where the defendants' managing director (a businessman educated at a public school with 7 'O' levels but not one in French) accepted on their behalf two bills of exchange drawn in French, a language of which he was completely ignorant, which moreover had been folded when he was asked to sign them: the plea of *non est factum* was rejected, because the signatory had failed to show he had acted carefully. Some foreign systems of law safeguard certain categories of persons who sign bills of exchange, e.g. on the grounds of age, or sex, or infirmity, but there are no special provisions of this nature in English law. Unsoundness of mind or drunkenness cannot be set up against a holder in due course: *Imperial Loan Co.* v. *Stone* (1892).

The various aspects of partnership have been considered in Chapter 3, but it is relevant to re-state here that a partner in a trading partnership has implied authority to bind the firm by drawing, accepting or indorsing bills in the firm's name, but a partner in a non-trading partnership has no such implied authority.

Forged or unauthorised signature

24.— Subject to the provisions of this Act, where a signature on a bill is forged or placed thereon without the authority of the person whose signature it purports to be, the forged or unauthorised signature is wholly inoperative, and no right to retain the bill or to give a discharge therefor or to enforce payment thereof against any party thereto can be acquired through or under that signature, unless the party against whom it is sought to retain or enforce payment of the bill is precluded from setting up the forgery for want of authority.

Provided that nothing in this section shall affect the ratification of an unauthorised signature not amounting to forgery.

A forged signature, and an unauthorised signature except where ratified, are no signature at all and so cannot pass any title to a bill, save that a holder of a bill on which a prior indorsement is a forgery can enforce payment against any party who has indorsed the bill subsequently to the forged indorsement.

It was held in *Alexander Stewart & Co., of Dundee, Ltd.* v. *Westminister Bank* (1926) that the unauthorised use of a signature is the same as an unauthorised signature, and that although a director of the plaintiff company had ostensible authority to indorse cheques on its behalf it could only be exercised for the benefit of the company and his misuse of that authority precluded the bank, as holder for value, from setting up as a holder in due course under s. 29.

If a bank pays a cheque on which the customer's signature as drawer has been forged, it cannot debit the customer's account therewith, as there is clearly no mandate, unless the customer is estopped from setting up the forgery against the bank. Thus, estoppel may arise where the customer knows of the forgery and unreasonably delays notification to the bank so that it thereby suffers loss, or where he has induced the bank to rely on a forgery.

In *Greenwood* v. *Martins Bank Ltd.* (1933) a wife repeatedly forged her husband's signature to cheques: he learned of the forgeries but was persuaded to keep silent. Some months later, although there had been no further forgeries, the husband, because of a matrimonial disagreement, threatened to inform the bank of the forgeries, whereupon the wife committed suicide. The House of Lords held that the husband was estopped from setting up the forgeries against the bank, not because his silence induced the bank to pay the cheques, for this had occurred before he became aware of the forgeries, but because his failure to inform the bank until the forger was dead prevented the bank from suing the forger. (Under the law as it then stood, i.e. prior to the Law Reform (Miscellaneous Provisions) Act 1934, the right to sue in tort died with the tortfeasor.)

In *Brown* v. *Westminister Bank Ltd.* (1964) estoppel enabled the bank to succeed in a claim against it where it was admitted that the plaintiff's signature as drawer on 100 cheques was forged, for successive branch managers had queried certain of the cheques and were assured by the plaintiff, a widow aged 86, that they were genuine, so that she was debarred from setting up true facts as to cheques already forged and as to future cheques.

The question whether a bank which has honoured an apparently genuine cheque on which the signature of its customer was in fact skilfully forged could recover the money from the payee of the cheque after he had acted to his detriment in direct reliance on the cheque having been honoured fell to be considered in *National Westminister Bank Ltd.* v. *Barclays Bank International Ltd.* (1974). It was held that the mere fact that a bank had honoured a cheque on which its customer's signature had been undetectably forged did not carry with it an implied representation by the bank to the payee that the signature was genuine. Furthermore, it was immaterial that the cheque had been specially presented. Accordingly, the paying bank was not estopped from pursuing its claim to recover the money as having been paid under a mistake of fact. As it happened, the defendant bank had not parted with the proceeds to its customer. However, the judge added that if the defendant bank had parted with the money in reliance on the cheque being honoured, it would have had a good defence on the basis that, as the collecting bank, it was in the same position as agents who had parted with the money to their principal; that is, it was no longer recoverable from them.

There are certain circumstances in which a bank paying or collecting instruments bearing forged or unauthorised signatures is given statutory protection, and these will be considered under ss. 60 and 80 of the Act of 1882, and also under the Cheques Act 1957.

Procuration signatures

25.—A signature by procuration operates as notice that the agent has but a limited authority to sign, and the principal is only bound by such signature if the agent in so signing was acting within the actual limits of his authority.

A *"per procurationem"* (per pro. or p.p.) signature on a bill shows that the actual signatory has only a limited authority, and operates as notice of this to parties who take the bill whenever it is negotiated or delivered. In *West London Commercial Bank Ltd.* v. *Kitson* (1884) a bill of exchange payable to order and addressed to a tramway company which had no power to accept bills was accepted for and on behalf of the company by K and others and was discounted by the drawer with the bank. The Court of Appeal held that the defendants were personally liable to the bank for a false representation of fact, namely, that they had authority to accept on behalf of the company. In this connection, the Rule in *Turquand's Case*, discussed in Chapter 4 on Companies, may assist the holder of a bill.

Persons signing as agent or in representative capacity

26.—(1) Where a person signs a bill as drawer, indorser, or acceptor, and adds words to his signature, indicating that he signs for and on behalf of a principal, or in a representative character, he is not personally liable thereon; but the mere addition to his signature of words describing him as an agent, or as filling a representative character, does not exempt him from personal liability.

(2) In determining whether a signature on a bill is that of the principal or that of the agent by whose hand it is written, the construction most favourable to the validity of the instrument shall be adopted.

It is a question of fact whether the words added to the signature indicate signature in a representative capacity so that the agent excludes his own liability but binds his principal, or are merely descriptive, as "agent", "manager" etc., in which event the attachment will leave the signatory personally liable and will not bind any principal. In *Chapman* v. *Smethurst* (1909) a promissory note for £300 lent to a limited company was signed: "J. H. Smethurst's Laundry and Dye Works, Limited, J. H. Smethurst, Managing Director.", the words other than the actual signature being made by rubber stamps. The Court of Appeal held that the note was that of the company, and Mr. Smethurst was not personally liable.

The operation of s. 26 (2) is shown by *Elliott* v. *Bax-Ironside* (1925), where a bill of exchange drawn on a company was "accepted payable at the W. Bank, A.B. and C.D., directors, F. Ltd." The drawer had informed the company that he required the bill to be indorsed by the directors as well as accepted by the company, and the same two directors indorsed the bill by signing it: "F. Ltd. A.B. and C.D., Directors". The Court of Appeal held that the directors were personally liable on the indorsement, because if it was treated as the indorsement of the company it was superfluous, and therefore by s. 26 (2) the most favourable construction, that it was the personal indorsement of the defendants, was to be adopted.

In *Rolfe Lubell & Co.* v. *Keith* (1979) the defendant accepted two bills of exchange drawn by the plaintiffs on the company of which he was managing director, and it was arranged orally that the bills be indorsed by the defendant personally. Each bill was accepted "For and on behalf of . . . (signed) Director" but the indorsement consisted of a rubber stamp and signature and so was the same as the acceptance. The bills having been dishonoured, the defendant claimed that under s. 26 (1) he was not personally liable. HELD, where there was a dispute as to the capacity in which an indorser had indorsed a bill, evidence was admissible to resolve any ambiguity, and on the evidence that the defendant had agreed to indorse the bills personally,

the words "For and on behalf of . . . Director" in the indorsements
were to be ignored as being contrary to that clear agreement, and so
the defendant was personally liable. It was observed that where a bill
is indorsed by the acceptor in the same capacity in which he accepts
the bill the indorsement is meaningless because it purports to transfer
liability from the acceptor to himself.

THE CONSIDERATION FOR A BILL

Value and holder for value

27.—(1) Valuable consdieration for a bill may be constituted by:

(a) Any consideration sufficient to support a simple contract;
(b) An antecedent debt or liability. Such a debt or liability is
deemed valuable consideration whether the bill is payable on
demand or at a future time.

(2) Where value has at any time been given for a bill the holder is
deemed to be a holder for value as regards the acceptor and all parties to
the bill who became parties prior to such time.

(3) Where the holder of a bill has a lien on it arising either from
contract or by implication of law, he is deemed to be a holder for value to
the extent of the sum for which he has a lien.

What is consideration has been examined in Chapter 1 on Contract, and it will be recalled that in making an antecedent debt or
liability sufficient consideration, the Act creates a statutory exception
to the common law rule that a past consideration is no consideration.
This is necessary because many cheques are drawn, or bills accepted,
in settlement of past debts: thus, in *M'Lean* v. *Clydesdale Banking Co.*
(1883) an overdrawn customer of C. Bank obtained a cheque from M.
(drawn on another bank) in order to reduce his indebtedness; the
House of Lords held that C. Bank were holders of the cheque for
value and could recover its amount from M. when he stopped it. In
Hasan v. *Willson* (1977) it was held that the "antecedent debt" under s.
27 (1) (b) had to be that of the drawer of the instrument, and that
consideration must move from the payee to the drawer, and not from
a stranger to the bill.

As will be seen under s. 29, the holder for value may or may not also
be a holder in due course.

In *Diamond* v. *Graham* (1968), which concerned a dishonoured
cheque, the defendant argued that the requirement of s. 27 (2) that
value should have been given for the bill was subject to a qualification

that valuable consideration should have passed directly between the parties (plaintiff and defendant). The Court of Appeal rejected this argument, holding that there was nothing in s. 27 (2) which required that value for the bill should have been given directly by the holder to another party to the bill, so long as value had been given for it.

A bank will have a lien on a bill where it is deposited as security, banker's lien in the case of a negotiable instrument being in effect an implied pledge, as the bank can realise the security after reasonable notice. This use of a bill as collateral security must be distinguished from the discounting of a bill by a bank—in the latter instance, the bank buys the bill, i.e. it gives full value for it and normally becomes a holder in due course.

Accommodation bill or party

28.—(1) An accommodation party to a bill is a person who has signed a bill as a drawer, acceptor, or indorser, without receiving value therefor, and for the purpose of lending his name to some other person.

(2) An accommodation party is liable on the bill to a holder for value; and it is immaterial whether, when such holder took the bill, he knew such party to be an accommodation party or not.

The party signing a bill without receiving value in return is the accommodation party, and he is in effect a surety for the party accommodated. Whilst an accommodation bill looks like an ordinary bill, it does not in fact arise out of a trading or commercial transaction, i.e. there is no consideration or element of exchange behind it, for it is drawn purely to raise funds. Thus, a drawer may arrange with someone to accept bills for his accommodation; after acceptance, the drawer has a bill which he may be able to discount or otherwise pay away, the idea being that he will put the acceptor in funds just before the due date so that he can meet the bill at maturity, or possibly that he will arrange to retire the bill just before maturity. The above example, in which the acceptor is the accommodation party, is the correct illustration of an accommodation bill, although the phrase is frequently, but incorrectly, used where the accommodation party is the drawer or indorser, an instance of the latter being where a person of substance "backs " the bill, i.e. lends his name to it by indorsing it. This distinction is important in relation to various aspects of discharge of a bill, to be considered later.

The lack of consideration is not a defence available to an accommodation party against a holder for value, although it is available against any one who has not given value.

Holder in due course

29.— (1) A holder in due course is a holder who has taken a bill, complete and regular on the face of it, under the following conditions; namely,

   (a) That he became the holder of it before it was overdue, and without notice that it had been previously dishonoured, if such was the fact;

   (b) That he took the bill in good faith and for value, and that at the time the bill was negotiated to him he had no notice of any defect in the title of the person who negotiated it.

(2) In particular the title of a person who negotiates a bill is defective within the meaning of this Act when he obtained the bill or the acceptance thereof, by fraud, duress or force and fear, or other unlawful means, or for an illegal consideration or when he negotiates it in breach of faith, or under circumstances as amount to a fraud.

(3) A holder (whether for value or not), who derives his title to a bill through a holder in due course, and who is not himself a party to any fraud or illegality affecting it, has all the rights of that holder in due course as regards the acceptor and all parties to the bill prior to that holder.

This is an important section because it goes to the root of negotiability, the full benefits of which are the prerogative of a holder in due course. By s. 2 the term "holder" includes the payee, the indorsee and the bearer of a bill. (A person holding under a forgery or one who has stolen a bill payable to the order of another is not a holder, but a wrongful possessor.) By s. 27 a "holder for value" is one who holds a bill for which value has at any time been given, that is, by he himself or some other person. The definition of a "holder in due course" goes beyond these two earlier ones, for to qualify as a holder in due course a person must satisfy all the requisites of s. 29— completeness and regularity of the bill; not overdue and without notice of previous dishonour; good faith and for value; and without notice of any defective title of the transferor.

A bill of exchange does not require acceptance to make it "complete and regular on the face of it": *National Park Bank of New York* v. *Berggren & Co.* (1914). However, it is not complete if the signature of the drawer is absent: *Ayres* v. *Moore* (1939). In *Arab Bank Ltd.* v. *Ross* (1952), where DENNING, L.J. (as he then was) aptly commented that "a bill of exchange is like currency. It should be above suspicion", it was held that "the face" includes the back, and also that an indorsement is irregular if it raises any doubt whether it is the indorsement of the named payee.

Consequently, a holder cannot be a holder in due course if he has been guilty of lack of good faith, e.g. when he is aware of some fraud or illegality in connection with the bill, or if he has actual or constructive notice of a defect in the title on the part of his transferor. Constructive notice arises where circumstances are suspicious or doubtful, combined with wilful disregard of the means of knowledge. A holder's knowledge that the negotiation of the bill to him takes place in such circumstances as amount to a fraudulent preference (see Chapter 5 on Bankruptcy) will prevent that person from being a holder in due course: *Banca Popolare di Novara* v. *John Livanos & Sons, Ltd.* (1965).

In *R. E. Jones, Ltd.* v. *Waring and Gillow, Ltd.* (1926) the House of Lords held that the original delivery of a bill to the payee was not negotiation, and the payee could not therefore be a holder in due course.

In *Barclays Bank Ltd.* v. *Astley Industrial Trust, Ltd.* (1970) the bank paid cheques drawn by a customer after being assured that five cheques payable to the customer and drawn by the defendants would be lodged. The cheques were paid in, but the defendants stopped payment of them. Held, a banker could be at the same time an agent for collection of a cheque and a holder of that cheque for value; there was no distinction to be drawn between the expressions holder for value and holder who had given or taken for value as used in the Act of 1882; accordingly, the bank had a lien on the five cheques and by virtue of s. 27 (3) was deemed to have taken the cheques for value within s. 29 (1) to the extent of that lien, and since on the facts it was a holder in due course it was entitled to recover in respect of the cheques from the defendants.

Section 29 (2) gives various illustrations of defects in title. The phrase "force and fear" covers the position in Scotland that corresponds with "duress" in English law, the latter term being unknown in Scots law. A defective title must be distinguished from no title at all; thus, a person holding under a forgery has no title of any kind and thereafter no one can become a holder in due course. The intervening forgery prevents subsequent parties suing those who were parties before the forgery occurred.

The rights of a holder in due course are that he can sue in his own name all or any of the other parties to the bill or note, free from any defences, whether due to defects of title or to mere personal reasons, available to prior parties amongst themselves. For example, if A draws a bill on B payable to C, and after B has accepted it and C has indorsed it, C loses it in the street, whereupon D finds it and transfers it for value to E, then as there is no forgery and provided E can establish himself as a holder in due course, E has a perfect title to the bill and can sue all or any of A, B, C and D. The instrument being negotiable, the defect in title as regards D is overcome when E takes it in good faith and for value etc. and thereby gets a better title than his transferor had. If the instrument in question had been "not negotiable", e.g. a cheque so crossed, then once the defect in title arose, the chain of title would thereafter, be permanently defective.

To take the above illustration one step further, suppose E gives the bill as a present to F, then F, as he did not give value, is not a holder in due course, but he is a holder for value, as value has already been given for the bill, so he can sue all or any of the parties except E.

Another example of this nature is where A gives his son B a cheque as a birthday present; if he stops this cheque B cannot enforce it against him because of the absence of consideration between them as immediate parties, but if B has already indorsed the cheque over to a shopkeeper, C, in settlement for goods purchased, C as holder in due course can sue either A or B on the cheque, being unaffected by the personal position between them.

The strong position of a holder in due course is illustrated by the decision of the Court of Appeal in *Jade International Steel Stahl und Eisen G.m.b.H. & Co. K.G.* v. *Robert Nicholas (Steels), Ltd.* (1978) where the plaintiff had sold to the defendant a quantity of steel to be delivered in two equal instalments, and had drawn a bill of exchange on the defendant for the price. On delivery the defendant claimed that the first consignment was sub-standard, and refused to accept the second. When the bill (which had been discounted by the plaintiff with a bank) was presented for payment, it was dishonoured; the bank duly debited the plaintiff's account and handed back the bill to the plaintiff. HELD, the plaintiff was entitled to immediate judgment for the amount of the bill. Where a bill is discounted through a bank by the drawer, he ceases to be an immediate party to the bill, and does not regain that capacity when the bill is subsequently returned to him after dishonour, but can sue on the bill with all the rights of a holder in due course by virtue of s. 29 (3) of the Bills of Exchange Act 1882 since he derives his title through a holder in due course (the discounting bank) and is entitled to immediate judgment for the full amount of the bill, notwithstanding that if he had sued as drawer there would have been a discretion to grant leave to defend because of a counterclaim by the acceptor. (It must be added that this discretion under RSC Ord. 14, r. 3 (a) when the action is between immediate parties to the bill of exchange is rarely exercised save in exceptional cases.)

Consumer Credit Act 1974

Although s. 125 (4) provides that nothing in this Act affects the rights of a holder in due course of any negotiable instrument, nevertheless ss. 123–125 do contain some wide-ranging modifications as regards the use of negotiable instruments in relation to regulated agreements, which are defined in s. 189 (1) as consumer credit agreements or consumer hire agreements (other than exempt agreements).

Under s. 123 (1) a creditor or owner shall not take a negotiable instrument, other than a bank note or cheque, in discharge of any sum payable by a debtor or hirer or surety under or in relation to a regulated agreement. Thus, bills of exchange and promissory notes cannot be taken in payment, which was often the practice. Subsection (2) restricts the negotiation of any cheque taken under (1) to a banker (within the meaning of the Bills of Exchange Act 1882, i.e. in s. 2). Subsections (3) and (4) prohibit the creditor or owner from taking a negotiable instrument as security, though (5) does provide that the section does not not apply where the regulated agreement is a non-commercial agreement.

By s. 124 the consequences of contravening s. 123 are that the sums payable under the agreement or by the sureties are enforceable on an order of the Court only.

Section 125 (1) provides that a person who takes a negotiable instrument in contravention of s. 123 (1) and (3) is not a holder in due course and is not entitled to enforce the instrument. In any event, as already noted on page 356, the payee cannot be a holder in due course. Under subsection (2), where a person negotiates a cheque in contravention of s. 123 (2) his doing so constitutes a defect in his title within the meaning of the Bills of Exchange Act 1882, and subsection (3) provides that if a person mentioned in s. 123 (1) (a) or (b) ("the protected person") becomes liable to a holder in due course of an instrument taken from the protected person in contravention of s. 123 (1) or (3) or taken from the protected person and negotiated in contravention of s. 123 (2) the creditor or owner shall indemnify the protected person in respect of that liability.

Presumption of value and good faith

30.— (1) Every party whose signature appears on a bill is prima facie deemed to have become a party thereto for value.

(2) Every holder of a bill is prima facie deemed to be a holder in due course; but if in an action on a bill it is admitted or proved that the acceptance, issue or subsequent negotiation of the bill is affected with fraud, duress, or force and fear, or illegality, the burden of proof is shifted, unless and until the holder proves that, subsequent to the alleged fraud or illegality, value has in good faith been given for the bill.

This section settles the question of the burden of proof by providing that a holder is presumed to be a holder in due course until a defect in title comes to light, and thereafter the onus shifts to the holder to prove that after the alleged fraud etc. which constitutes the defect he gave value in good faith for the bill. The various flaws which may arise in a contract have been examined in Chapter 1.

Whilst cross-claims based on fraud, duress etc. or on a failure of consideration when the amount is ascertained and liquidated can be relied on, it is settled law that the Courts will not allow a defendent in an action on a bill of exchange to set up a case for unliquidated damages by reason of the breach by the plaintiff of some other contract or the commission of some tort. This was re-affirmed by the House of Lords in *Nova (Jersey) Knit, Ltd.* v. *Kammgarn Spinnerei G.m.b.H.* (1977), where it was held that a claim for unliquidated damages could not be raised by way of defence, set-off or counter-claim to an action on dishonoured bills of exchange. A vendor and purchaser who agree to payment by acceptance of a bill of exchange enter into a contract separate from the contract of sale, and LORD WILBERFORCE commented that bills of exchange payable at future dates were "equivalent to deferred instalments of cash". The unliquidated claims must be the subject of a cross-action and cannot be used to create a "dispute" on a bill of exchange within s. 1 (1) of the Arbitration Act 1975.

NEGOTIATION OF BILLS

Negotiation of bills

31.— (1) A bill is negotiated when it is transferred from one person to another in such a manner as to constitute the transferee the holder of the bill.

(2) A bill payable to bearer is negotiated by delivery.

(3) A bill payable to order is negotiated by the indorsement of the holder completed by delivery.

(4) Where the holder of a bill payable to his order transfers it for value without indorsing it, the transfer gives the transferee such title as the transferor had in the bill, and the transferee in addition acquires the right to have the indorsement of the transferor.

(5) Where any person is under obligation to indorse a bill in a representative capacity, he may indorse the bill in such terms as to negative personal liability.

Negotiation is a much more elaborate concept than transfer: a negotiable instrument must not only be transferable, but be so transferable as to convey a perfect title to the transferee who takes it in good faith and for value, regardless of any defects in the title of his transferor. Bearer bills are negotiated by mere delivery; order bills require indorsement to pass the property in them, followed by delivery. If the transferee has to get the bill indorsed subsequently, in accordance with his right conferred by s. 31 (4), then the transfer will operate as a negotiation from the time the indorsement is made.

Section 31 (5) would, for instance, be relevant where personal representatives are obliged to indorse a bill which the deceased should have indorsed but failed to do so. For example, the transferee for value of an unindorsed order bill can call for its indorsement under s. 31 (4), and when indorsing it in lieu of the deceased transferor the personal representatives may add a phrase such as "so far as assets only" which restricts liability to the assets of the estate and negatives their personal liability.

Requisites of a valid indorsement

32.—An indorsement in order to operate as a negotiation must comply with the following conditions, namely:

(1) It must be written on the bill itself and be signed by the indorser. The simple signature of the indorser on the bill, without additional words, is sufficient.

An indorsement written on an allonge, or on a "copy" of a bill issued or negotiated in a country where "copies" are recognised, is deemed to be written on the bill itself.

(2) It must be an indorsement of the entire bill. A partial indorsement, that is to say, an indorsement which purports to transfer to the indorsee a part only of the amount payable, or which purports to transfer the bill to two or more indorsees severally, does not operate as a negotiation of the bill.

(3) Where a bill is payable to the order of two or more payees or indorsees who are not partners all must indorse, unless the one indorsing has authority to indorse for the others.

(4) Where, in a bill payable to order, the payee or indorsee is wrongly designated, or his name is mis-spelt, he may indorse the bill as therein described, adding, if he thinks fit, his proper signature.

(5) Where there are two or more indorsements on a bill, each indorsement is deemed to have been made in the order in which it appears on the bill, until the contrary is proved.

(6) An indorsement may be made in blank or special. It may also contain terms making it restrictive.

Indorsement is still important as regards bills of exchange (other than cheques) and promissory notes, but it has been largely dispensed with so far as cheques are concerned by the Cheques Act 1957, as will be seen later when that Act is discussed. It may be done by writing the word "Indorsed" (or "Endorsed") on the bill and signing it, but in practice it is always done, as s. 32 permits, by simple signature without additional words. Indorsement is normally effected on the back of the instrument (hence the derivation of the word), but it can be done on the face of the instrument.

An order bill or note must be indorsed by the payee or indorsee as the first stage in making over the instrument to someone else, the second and last stage being delivery. An allonge is an extension or annexe attached to the bill when there is not sufficient space available on the bill itself for the indorsement. For the purposes of negotiation, there cannot be a split indorsement, e.g. if a bill for £100 is payable to AB or order, AB cannot indorse it "Pay £50 to CD or order" (retaining the balance for himself), or "Pay £50 to CD or order; and pay £50 to EF or order". This is because there is only one negotiable instrument, the bill for £100, and it cannot be divided into two, or more; though if AB did make such a partial transfer it could operate as an equitable assignment.

Whilst there cannot be several, or separate, indorsees (e.g. CD and EF in the example above), there can be joint indorsees, e.g. a bill may be indorsed "Pay CD and EF or order". Where there are several payees or indorsees who are not partners, all must indorse, unless the one indorsing has authority to indorse for the others: but this does not apply to dividend warrants because s. 97 (3) (d) expressly saves the usages in respect of such warrants (and these include paying on only one indorsement warrants payable to the order of two or more persons).

As to what is a correct indorsement, the signature must match the name of the payee, though some latitude in minor details is permitted. Thus, a bill payable to J. Smith or order may be indorsed John Smith, or any other Christian name beginning with a J followed by Smith, and *vice versa*, but if such a bill was indorsed simply Tom Smith, it would be irregular. Where the payee's name really is Tom Smith, by s. 32 it is permissible for him to indorse the bill as he was therein described, i.e. J. Smith, the custom normally being to add his proper signature thereafter. The same applies to misdescription or misspellings of names. In short, the indorsement must be such as not to cast doubt on whether the indorser is the party intended to receive payment.

Certain categories of indorsements involve special features. As regards executors, the signature of one is accepted for all but the indorsement should show on the face of it for whom he is executor, e.g. "For self and co-executors of GH deceased, IJ, Executor". In contrast, all trustees must indorse, unless the trust deed otherwise provides. In the case of partnerships, the simple signature of the firm name only will suffice, or alternatively it may be effected by a "per pro." signature. In the case of companies, the indorsement is usually "For (or 'For and on behalf of') KL Ltd., MN, Director (or Secretary, or General Manager)", or alternatively it may be effected by a "per pro." signature. As it is quite common for a company's name to be misdescribed or mis-spelt, the company will often have a multiple rubber stamp setting out likely variations, but care must be taken to ensure that the particular style of the payee's name is covered by the permutations on the rubber stamp.

Under s. 32 a series of indorsements are deemed to be made in the order in which they appear on the bill—this is descending order—until it is shown that any one of them has been placed on out of order or in the wrong chronological order. There have been various cases in which the contrary has been proved, often because the indorser has not signed as such in the course of negotiation but in order to back the bill or note, i.e. to give it additional financial strength by his signature. A person playing such a role is often called a "quasi-indorser" and his position will be looked at under s. 56.

Conditional indorsement

33.—Where a bill purports to be indorsed conditionally the condition may be disregarded by the payer, and payment to the indorsee is valid whether the condition has been fulfilled, or not.

This section is of great value to a bank in that when paying any bill or note bearing a conditional indorsement the bank can safely disregard the condition. However, the use of the word "may" allows the payer, if he so desires, to insist on reasonable proof that the condition has been fulfilled before payment. Examples of a conditional indorsement would be: "Pay EF or order on his marriage to GH", or "Pay EF or order on arrival of SS. Peerless at London".

Indorsement in blank and special indorsement

34.—(1) An indorsement in blank specifies no indorsee, and a bill so indorsed becomes payable to bearer.

(2) A special indorsement specifies the person to whom, or to whose order, the bill is to be payable.

(3) The provisions of this Act relating to a payee apply with the necessary modifications to an indorsee under a special indorsement.

(4) When a bill has been indorsed in blank, any holder may convert the blank indorsement into a special indorsement by writing above the

indorser's signature a direction to pay the bill to or to the order of himself or some other person.

An indorsement in blank is one which does not specify any indorsee, that is, a further party to whom the instrument is being transferred. It normally consists simply of the indorser's signature (see s. 32), e.g. a cheque payable to A. Brown or order, and indorsed A. Brown. When followed by delivery, this transfers the property to the recipient, now the bearer.

In contrast to the above, a special indorsement designates the person to whom the bill is being transferred, e.g. a cheque payable to A. Brown or order, and indorsed "Pay C. Dawson or order, A. Brown". Such a specially indorsed cheque is payable to the indorsee, and can only be further negotiated by his signature. Section 34 (4) allows the holder of a bill indorsed in blank, say, by A. Brown, to write over that signature his own name; "Pay C. Dawson", or alternatively the name of some other person, say: "E. Freeman or order". In the latter event, the holder, C. Dawson, is not liable as indorser, not having signed the bill, but the procedure takes effect as a special indorsement from AB to EF.

Restrictive indorsement

35.—(1) An indorsement is restrictive which prohibits the further negotiation of the bill, or which expresses that it is a mere authority to deal with the bill as thereby directed and not a transfer of the ownership thereof, as, for example, if a bill be indorsed "Pay D only", or "Pay D for the account of X", or "Pay D or order for collection".

(2) A restrictive indorsement gives the indorsee the right to receive payment of the bill and to sue any party thereto that the indorser could have sued, but gives him no power to transfer his rights as indorsee unless it expressly authorises him to do so.

(3) Where a restrictive indorsement authorises further transfer, all subsequent indorsees take the bill with the same rights and subject to the same liabilities as the first indorsee under the restrictive indorsement.

A restrictive indorsement has exactly the same effect as words in the body of the bill prohibiting or restricting transfer, e.g. an indorsement: "Pay AB only, CD". Examples where a restrictive indorsement is a mere authority to deal with the bill as directed are: "Pay South Bank Ltd. for account of AB"; or, as where a person sends cheques by post to his bank for credit to his account, "Pay South Bank Ltd. for collection" (or "for credit of my account" or "for my use"). The relationship between indorser and restrictive indorsee is in essence that of principal and agent, and any transfer of the bill confers only the rights and liabilities of the restrictive indorsee.

Negotiation of overdue or dishonoured bill

36.—(1) Where a bill is negotiable in its origin it continues to be negotiable until it has been (a) restrictively indorsed or (b) discharged by payment or otherwise.

(2) When an overdue bill is negotiated, it can only be negotiated subject to any defect of title affecting it at its maturity, and thenceforward no person who takes it can acquire or give a better title than that which the person from whom he took it had.

(3) A bill payable on demand is deemed to be overdue within the meaning and for the purposes of this section, when it appears on the face of it to have been in circulation for an unreasonable length of time. What is an unreasonable length of time for this purpose is a question of fact.

(4) Except where an indorsement bears date after maturity of the bill, every negotiation is prima facie deemed to have been effected before the bill was overdue.

(5) Where a bill which is not overdue has been dishonoured, any person who takes it with notice of the dishonour takes it subject to any defect of title attaching thereto at the time of dishonour, but nothing in this subsection shall affect the rights of a holder in due course.

This section deals with the duration of negotiability. Basically, a bill continues to be negotiable until it has been restrictively indorsed or discharged by payment or otherwise. If neither of these events occurs, the bill will cease to be negotiable when it becomes overdue, which in the case of bills payable otherwise than on demand is after the date of payment, and for those payable on demand is when it appears that the bill has been in circulation for an unreasonably long time, which is a question of fact. In *London and County Banking Co.* v. *Groome* (1881) it was held that a cheque which was negotiated eight days after date was not overdue. On the other hand, in *Serrel* v. *Derbyshire Railway* (1850) it was held that a cheque taken two months after date was stale. So far as the payment of cheques is concerned, the usual practice of banks is not to pay cheques dated more than six months previously, but to return them marked "Out of date" or "Stale" (unless the customer confirms that payment is in order) though there is no direct authority for this six month period.

By s. 36 (4) indorsements which are not dated after maturity of the bill are presumed to have been effected at some time before the bill was overdue (the exact time is not presumed), but it is always possible to rebut the presumption. Where a person takes a bill which is not overdue but which, to his knowledge, has been dishonoured, then by

s. 36 (5) he takes it subject to defects of title at the time of dishonour; this does not affect a holder in due course, because amongst the requisites for that status laid down in s. 29 is that he must take the instrument without notice of any previous dishonour.

Negotiation of bill to party already liable thereon

37.— Where a bill is negotiated back to the drawer, or to a prior indorser, or to the acceptor, such party may, subject to the provisions of this Act, re-issue and further negotiate the bill, but he is not entitled to enforce payment of the bill against any intervening party to whom he was previously liable.

This is to prevent circuity of action. Thus, if B draws a bill payable to C or order on A, which the latter accepts, and the bill thereafter passes via C, D, and E and back to B, then B can put it into circulation again, but he cannot enforce payment against C, D and E for although they are prior parties they in turn could claim against B.

Rights of the holder

38.— The rights and powers of the holder of a bill are as follows:
(1) He may sue on the bill in his own name;
(2) Where he is a holder in due course, he holds the bill free from any defect of title of prior parties, as well as from mere personal defences available to prior parties among themselves, and may enforce payment against all parties liable on the bill;
(3) Where his title is defective (a) if he negotiates the bill to a holder in due course, that holder obtains a good and complete title to the bill, and (b) if he obtains payment of the bill the person who pays him in due course gets a valid discharge for the bill.

This section sets out the rights of the holder as acquired by negotiation. These rights—suing in one's own name all or any parties liable on the bill; taking as a holder in due course free from prior defects of title, and, where his title is defective, passing to a holder in due course a perfect title—are the essence of negotiability. Once again, however, a defective title must be distinguished from no title at all. Whilst a good title to a negotiable instrument may be acquired through a thief by a subsequent holder in due course, if there is a forgery in the chain of title the person claiming under that forgery has no title and cannot pass on any title to anyone else.

When the holder of a bill sues as agent for someone else, or when he sues wholly or partly as trustee for someone else, his right of action is qualified to the extent that any defence or set-off which would have

been available against that other person is available *pro tanto* against
the holder. In *Thornton* v. *Maynard* (1875), an action by a holder
against the acceptor of several bills of exchange, the defendant was
held to be entitled to set off the sum of £425 which the holder had
already received as a dividend in respect of the bills from the estate of
the bankrupt drawers, on the ground that as to that sum the plaintiff
was suing only as trustee for the drawers. This principle was applied
by the Court of Appeal in *Barclays Bank Ltd.* v. *Aschaffenburger Zell-
stoffwerke A. G.* (1967) where the bank was suing as holder in due
course in respect of two dishonoured bills (in which its beneficial
interest was some 73 per cent) accepted by the German defendants,
who pleaded a set-off, and this was allowed against the proportion of
the claim which the bank held as trustee, and not beneficially.

Chapter 11

Bills of Exchange—Duties of the Holder

BILLS OF EXCHANGE ACT 1882, SECTIONS 39–52

GENERAL DUTIES OF THE HOLDER

When presentment for acceptance is necessary

39.—(1) Where a bill is payable after sight, presentment for acceptance is necessary in order to fix the maturity of the instrument.

(2) Where a bill expressly stipulates that it shall be presented for acceptance, or where a bill is drawn payable elsewhere than at the residence or place of business of the drawee, it must be presented for acceptance before it can be presented for payment.

(3) In no other case is presentment for acceptance necessary in order to render liable any party to the bill.

(4) Where the holder of a bill, drawn payable elsewhere than at the place of business or residence of the drawee, has not time, with the exercise of reasonable diligence, to present the bill for acceptance before presenting it for payment on the day that it falls due, the delay caused by presenting the bill for acceptance before presenting it for payment is excused, and does not discharge the drawer and indorsers.

This section prescribes the three cases in which presentment for acceptance is legally necessary. The purpose of presenting a bill for acceptance is two-fold: (a) to secure the liability of the drawee as a party to the bill—once he becomes the acceptor, he incurs the primary liability on the bill; and (b) to obtain an immediate right of recourse against the antecedent parties should the bill be dishonoured by non-acceptance—these prior parties are the drawer, who is primarily liable on the bill until it is accepted, and any indorsers. Presentment for acceptance is of a personal nature in that so long as the bill is presented to the drawee, wherever he may be, it will be good.

Section 39 (4) protects the holder in respect of a bill required to be presented for acceptance by s. 39 (2) where he is not to blame because the time factor makes it impossible to present for acceptance before maturity. For example, a bill may be drawn abroad on say, a Plymouth merchant, but payable at a London bank, and due to postal delays it may only reach the English holder on the day it matures. As he must present the bill for acceptance to the drawee in Plymouth, the Act provides that in doing so he is not prejudiced *vis-à-vis* the drawer and indorsers.

Time for presenting bill payable after sight

40.— (1) Subject to the provisions of this Act, when a bill payable after sight is negotiated, the holder must either present it for acceptance or negotiate it within a reasonable time.

(2) If he does not do so, the drawer and all indorsers prior to that holder are discharged.

(3) In determining what is a reasonable time within the meaning of this section, regard shall be had to the nature of the bill, the usage of trade with respect to similar bills, and the facts of the particular case.

What is a reasonable time, within which a sight bill must be presented for acceptance or negotiated, depends on all the circumstances, regard being had to the interests of the drawee as well as to those of the drawer and indorsers, and to the nature of the bill and trade usage applicable to similar bills.

Rules as to presentment for acceptance, and excuses for non-presentment

41.— (1) A bill is duly presented for acceptance which is presented in accordance with the following rules:

(a) The presentment must be made by or on behalf of the holder to the drawee or to some person authorised to accept or refuse acceptance on his behalf at a reasonable hour on a business day and before the bill is overdue:

(b) Where a bill is addressed to two or more drawees, who are not partners, presentment must be made to them all, unless one has authority to accept for all, then presentment may be made to him only:

(c) Where the drawee is dead presentment may be made to his personal representative:

(d) Where the drawee is bankrupt, presentment may be made to him or to his trustee:

(e) Where authorised by agreement or usage, a presentment through the post office is sufficient.

(2) Presentment in accordance with these rules is excused, and a bill may be treated as dishonoured by non-acceptance:

(a) Where the drawee is dead or bankrupt, or is a fictitious person or a person not having capacity to contract by bill:

    (b) Where, after the exercise of reasonable diligence, such pre-
sentment cannot be effected:

    (c) Where, although the presentment has been irregular, accep-
tance has been refused on some other ground.

    (3) The fact that the holder has reason to believe that the bill, on
presentment, will be dishonoured does not excuse presentment.

This section details the mechanics of presentment for acceptance.
Thus, it must be done by the holder or his servant or agent to the
drawee or his servant or agent within business hours in the case of a
trader, and within banking hours in the case of a bank, and before the
bill is overdue. For example, presentment at 4 a.m. on a weekday, or
at any time on a Sunday, would not be good. Where there are two or
more drawees, other than partners, presentment must be made to all,
unless one has authority to accept for the others, but it will be recalled
from s. 19 (2) (e) that if one or more out of a number of drawees refuse
to accept, this is a qualified acceptance (i.e. qualified as to parties).

Where the drawee is dead or bankrupt, the holder has the alternatives of presenting the bill to the personal representative in the former
case and to the bankrupt or his trustee in the latter case, or of waiving
presentment and treating the bill as dishonoured by non-acceptance.
An example of s. 41 (2) (c) would be where presentment was made
outside business hours, but acceptance was refused not for that reason
but for some other reason, e.g. lack of funds. By s. 41 (3) a bill
requiring presentment for acceptance msut be so presented even
though the holder anticipates that acceptance will be refused; this
prevents argument by a holder over the likelihood of presentment
proving an empty formality. After all, his fears may be unfounded.

Non-acceptance

    42.— When a bill is duly presented for acceptance, and is not accepted
within the customary time, the person presenting it must treat it as
dishonoured by non-acceptance. If he do not, the holder shall lose his
right of recourse against the drawer and indorsers.

The usual procedure is to present the bill for acceptance during
business hours one day, and if not accepted then and there (which
may not be possible because signatories are absent) the bill will be left
with the drawee and called for on the following business day. Before
the close of business on that day, the drawee must re-deliver it
accepted or unaccepted, and if the latter is the case, the bill must be
noted for non-acceptance or otherwise treated as dishonoured. If the
drawee destroys the bill, this does not amount to an acceptance.

Dishonour by non-acceptance and its consequences

43.— (1) A bill is dishonoured by non-acceptance:
  (a) when it is duly presented for acceptance, and such an accep-
       tance as is prescribed by this Act is refused or cannot be
       obtained; or
  (b) when presentment for acceptance is excused and the bill is not
       accepted.
(2) Subject to the provisions of this Act when a bill is dishonoured by
non-acceptance, an immediate right of recourse against the drawer and
indorsers accrues to the holder, and no presentment for payment is
necessary.

Once a bill is dishonoured by non-acceptance, in whichever way
this occurs, the holder has an immediate right of recourse, i.e. he can
fall back on the drawer and any indorsers, though his right of action
against them is subject to his having first carried out the appropriate
requirements regarding the giving to them of notice of dishonour and,
when necessary, the protesting of the bill. As the bill has already been
dishonoured by non-acceptance, presentment for payment would be
superfluous and, therefore, is not required.

Duties as to qualified acceptances

44.— (1) The holder of a bill may refuse to take a qualified acceptance,
and if he does not obtain an unqualified acceptance may treat the bill as
dishonoured by non-acceptance.
(2) Where a qualified acceptance is taken, and the drawer or an
indorser has not expressly or impliedly authorised the holder to take a
qualified acceptance, or does not subsequently assent thereto, such
drawer or indorser is discharged from his liability on the bill.
  The provisions of this subsection do not apply to a partial acceptance,
whereof due notice has been given. Where a foreign bill has been
accepted as to part, it must be protested as to the balance.
(3) When the drawer or indorser of a bill receives notice of a qualified
acceptance, and does not within a reasonable time express his dissent to
the holder he shall be deemed to have assented thereto.

For example, if a clerk calls for a bill which his bank has presented
for acceptance, unless otherwise instructed by the customer for whom
the bank is acting, he should refuse to take a qualified acceptance (five
varieties of which are set out in s. 19) and insist on a general acceptance. If the latter is not forthcoming, the bill should be treated as
dishonoured by non-acceptance. If a qualified acceptance other than
a partial one is taken without the authority of the drawer and
indorsers, they are discharged from liability on the bill, unless they

fail to notify their objection within a reasonable time. In the case of a partial acceptance, they will be bound provided due notice of it has been given to them; that is, the holder's rights against them are reduced during the currency of the bill to the amount for which it was accepted, but in the event of the bill being dishonoured by a failure to pay the partial acceptance then their liability reverts to the full, original amount. As will be seen later, s. 51 (2) requires a foreign bill to be protested for non-acceptance, and where there is a partial acceptance s. 44 (2) makes such protest necessary in respect of the balance not accepted.

Rules as to presentment for payment

45.—Subject to the provisions of this Act a bill must be duly presented for payment. If it be not so presented the drawer and indorsers shall be discharged.

A bill is duly presented for payment which is presented in accordance with the following rules:

(1) Where the bill is not payable on demand, presentment must be made on the day that it falls due.

(2) Where the bill is payable on demand, then, subject to the provisions of this Act, presentment must be made within a reasonable time after its issue in order to render the drawer liable, and within a reasonable time after its indorsement, in order to render the indorser liable.

In determining what is a reasonable time, regard shall be had to the nature of the bill, the usage of trade with regard to similar bills, and the facts of the particular case.

(3) Presentment must be made by the holder or by some person authorised to receive payment on his behalf at a reasonable hour on a business day, at the proper place as hereinafter defined, either to the person designated by the bill as payer, or to some person authorised to pay or refuse payment on his behalf if with the exercise of reasonable diligence such a person can there be found.

(4) A bill is presented at the proper place:

　(a) Where a place of payment is specified in the bill and the bill is there presented.

　(b) Where no place of payment is specified, but the address of the drawee or acceptor is given in the bill, and the bill is there presented.

　(c) Where no place of payment is specified, and no address given, and the bill is presented at the drawee's or acceptor's place of business if known, and if not, at his ordinary residence if known.

　(d) In any other case, if presented to the drawee or acceptor wherever he can be found, or if presented at his last known place of business or residence.

(5) Where a bill is presented at the proper place, and after the exercise of reasonable diligence no person authorised to pay or refuse payment can be found there, no further presentment to the drawee or acceptor is required.

(6) Where a bill is drawn upon or accepted by two or more persons who are not partners, and no place of payment is specified, presentment must be made to them all.

(7) Where the drawee or acceptor of a bill is dead, and no place of payment is specified, presentment must be made to a personal representative, if such there be, and with the exercise of reasonable diligence he can be found.

(8) Where authorised by agreement or usage a presentment through the post office is sufficient.

This long section deals with the vital question of presentment for payment, for with a bill or note the whole object of the procedure is to obtain the money which the instrument represents. It will be observed that in presentment for payment the accent is on locality, that is, presentment at the proper place (whereas presentment for acceptance should be personal). The section sets out eight rules showing whys and wherefores of a proper presentment for payment. A bill must be presented for payment on the due date—or if a demand bill within a reasonable time *vis-à-vis* issue and indorsement—and in any case at a reasonable hour on a business day, i.e. if payable at a bank, within banking hours; if at a trader's place of business, then within normal business hours; and if at a private residence, then probably up to bedtime.

Failure to present for payment will discharge the drawer and indorsers unless the delay is excused, but it does not discharge the acceptor (s. 52 (1) refers), though it is most unlikely that a holder would start suing for payment before having applied for it in the ordinary way. The acceptor may, however, be able to mitigate any loss due in consequence of the delay, e.g. if a bill domiciled at a bank or other agent is not presented on the due date without any just cause or excuse and the bank or other agent fails, the holder's claim against the acceptor is subject to any loss the latter has suffered by the failure of the payer.

The bill should be presented at the appropriate time at the designated place, even though the acceptor has already stated that he will not pay it, or has failed or is dead. If alternative places of payment are designated, presentment at either one will suffice. Presentment to any person apparently authorised to give an answer is sufficient. A bill presented at the wrong address is not a good presentment though it will be good if the bill is presented at the address given, even though the acceptor has removed. Where the bill is payable at an address, and the acceptor has died, presentment there is sufficient, without seeking out the personal representative. Where a bill is accepted payable at a bank, then it must be presented to that bank and branch, and presentment to the acceptor personally would be sufficient.

That one day's delay in presenting for payment can discharge a party to the bill is shown by *Yeoman Credit, Ltd.* v. *Gregory* (1963), where the plaintiff finance company held a bill due on December 9th, 1959 accepted by E. C. Ltd. payable at the N. P. Bank and personally indorsed (as arranged, by way of guarantee) by the defendant, who was managing director of E. C. Ltd. The plaintiffs were told by another director shortly before the time for presentment that there were no funds at the N. P. Bank and that the bill should be presented to the M. Bank. Without obtaining the consent of the defendant and other indorsers to the alteration, the plaintiffs presented the bill to the M. Bank on the due date and when it was dishonoured presented it to the N. P. Bank on the following day (December 10th) when it was again dishonoured. It was held that the defendant was discharged under s. 45 (1) because the presentment was bad.

A further illustration of the necessity of adhering rigidly to the provisions of s. 45 is *Hamilton Finance Co., Ltd.* v. *Coverley Westray Walbaum and Tosetti, Ltd.* (1969) in which the following presentments for payment were considered to be bad: (a) where a bill due on Saturday 1st January 1966 was sent for collection the previous day but not received until 4th January and on the evidence the delay could not be explained away by assumed New Year postal delays; and (b) where another bill also due the same day was presented one day before the due date, returned dishonoured the same day, and never presented on the due date.

Banks are frequently concerned in presenting bills for payment because they act as agents for collection on behalf of their customers. As agents they must use all reasonable care to secure acceptance (where necessary) and due payment of bills lodged with them for collection, and must also take the appropriate proceedings in the case of dishonour. Failure to do so renders an agent liable to his principal, and the agent is also in general liable for the default of his sub-agent. A pledgee or person who holds a bill as security is similarly liable to his pledgor. If the bank is presenting for payment directly at the appropriate place and an immediate answer is not forthcoming, the bill should not be left there (unless that place is a bank), but a notice should be left stating that the bill may be taken up at the bank before the close of business on that day. Many bills are domiciled at a bank, and then all that the presenting bank need do is to put the bill into the appropriate clearing in sufficient time to reach the bank at which it is payable on the due date, except where it is necessary to employ a sub-agent for collection when the calculation of the time factor must be adjusted accordingly.

Excuses for delay or non-presentment for payment

46.—(1) Delay in making presentment for payment is excused when the delay is caused by circumstances beyond the control of the holder, and not imputable to his default, misconduct, or negligence. When the cause of delay ceases to operate presentment must be made with reasonable diligence.

(2) Presentment for payment is dispensed with:

   (a) Where, after the exercise of reasonable diligence presentment, as required by this Act, cannot be effected.
   The fact that the holder has reason to believe that the bill will, on presentment, be dishonoured, does not dispense with the necessity for presentment.

   (b) Where the drawee is a fictitious person.

   (c) As regards the drawer, where the drawee or acceptor is not bound, as between himself and the drawer, to accept or pay the bill, and the drawer has no reason to believe that the bill would be paid if presented.

   (d) As regards an indorser, where the bill was accepted or made for the accommodation of that indorser, and he has no reason to expect that the bill would be paid if presented.

   (e) By waiver of presentment, express or implied.

For example, delay in making presentment for payment or complete absence of presentment will be excused where it is due to such outside factors as the outbreak of war, or perhaps a sudden and unforeseeable postal or transport strike (during the seven weeks' postal strike in 1971 the banks made their own very effective arrangements to keep the clearing system in being). On the other hand, anticipation that the bill will not be paid if presented, as where the drawee or acceptor has become bankrupt in the meantime, does not excuse presentment for payment; nor is it excused because the drawee is a person having no capacity to contract, unless he is a fictitious person (in the case of presentment for acceptance, the holder may treat bankruptcy, lack of capacity to contract, and fictitious personality as excusing presentment and constituting dishonour by non-acceptance: s. 41 (2) (a) ante). Section 46 (2) (c) and (d) excuse respectively presentment for payment at the hands of an accommodation drawer, or of an accommodation indorser, where neither has any reason to believe the bill would be paid (because neither has furnished consideration for it). As regards s. 46 (2) (e), to waive is to relinquish or abandon, and so in this context waiver is any agreement to dispense with presentment for payment, and may be express or implied, as well as made before or after the time for presentment.

Dishonour by non-payment

47.—(1) A bill is dishonoured by non-payment (a) when it is duly presented for payment and payment is refused or cannot be obtained, or (b) when presentment is excused and the bill is overdue and unpaid.

(2) Subject to the provisions of this Act, when a bill is dishonoured by non-payment, an immediate right of recourse against the drawer and indorsers accrues to the holder.

Once a drawee accepts a bill, he becomes the party primarily liable to pay the bill at maturity, whether he has received consideration or not. If he does not accept the bill, he is not liable on it, the liability to any outside party remaining primarily with the drawer. So far as the holder of an accepted bill is concerned, the drawer and prior indorsers, if any, are secondarily liable on the bill, rather as though it were a multiple guarantee, the security increasing with every additional signature. On the bill being dishonoured by non-payment, which is explained in s. 47 (1), the holder can at once give notice to the drawer and indorsers, though he cannot commence an action against the acceptor till the next day: *Kennedy* v. *Thomas* (1894). Any party who has to pay the holder may recover from prior parties, for they in turn are liable to him, and so on down the line, until the drawer is reached and his only claim is against the acceptor, without even that right if the bill was accepted for the drawer's accommodation.

Notice of dishonour and effect of non-notice

48.— Subject to the provisions of this Act, when a bill has been dishonoured by non-acceptance or by non-payment, notice of dishonour must be given to the drawer and each indorser, and any drawer or indorser to whom such notice is not given is discharged; Provided that:

(1) Where a bill is dishonoured by non-acceptance, and notice of dishonour is not given, the rights of a holder in due course subsequent to the omission, shall not be prejudiced by the omission.

(2) Where a bill is dishonoured by non-acceptance and due notice of dishonour is given, it shall not be necessary to give notice of a subsequent dishonour by non-payment unless the bill shall in the meantime have been accepted.

If the drawer and any indorser do not receive notice of dishonour when necessary, they are freed from liability, not only on the bill or note, but also on the consideration for which it was given. Notice is still necessary even though the drawer or indorser may know *aliunde* ("from another source") that the instrument has been dishonoured.

Rules as to notice of dishonour

49.— Notice of dishonour in order to be valid and effectual must be given in accordance with the following rules:

(1) The notice must be given by or on behalf of the holder, or by or on behalf of an indorser who, at the time of giving it, is himself liable on the bill.

(2) Notice of dishonour may be given by an agent, either in his own name or in the name of any party entitled to give notice, whether that party be his principal or not.

(3) Where the notice is given by or on behalf of the holder, it enures for the benefit of all subsequent holders, and all prior indorsers who have a right of recourse against the party to whom it is given.

(4) Where notice is given by or on behalf of an indorser entitled to give notice as hereinbefore provided, it enures for the benefit of the holder and all indorsers subsequent to the party to whom notice is given.

(5) The notice may be given in writing or by personal communication, and may be given in any terms which sufficiently identify the bill, and intimate that the bill has been dishonoured by non-acceptance or non-payment.

(6) The return of a dishonoured bill to the drawer or an indorser is, in point of form, deemed a sufficient notice of dishonour.

(7) A written notice need not be signed, and an insufficient written notice may be supplemented and validated by verbal communication. A misdescription of the bill shall not vitiate the notice unless the party to whom the notice is given is in fact misled thereby.

(8) Where notice of dishonour is required to be given to any person, it may be given either to the party himself, or to his agent in that behalf.

(9) Where the drawer or indorser is dead, and the party giving notice knows it, the notice must be given to a personal representative if such there be, and with the exercise of reasonable diligence he can be found.

(10) Where the drawer or indorser is bankrupt, notice may be given either to the party himself or to the trustee.

(11) Where there are two or more drawers or indorsers who are not partners, notice must be given to each of them, unless one of them has authority to receive such notice for the others.

(12) The notice may be given as soon as the bill is dishonoured, and must be given within a reasonable time thereafter. In the absence of special circumstances, notice is not deemed to have been given within a reasonable time, unless:

    (a) where the person giving and the person to receive notice reside in the same place, the notice is given or sent off in time to reach the latter on the day after the dishonour of the bill.

    (b) where the person giving and the person to receive notice reside in different places, the notice is sent off on the day after the dishonour of the bill, if there be a post at a convenient hour on that day, and if there be no such post on that day then by the next post thereafter.

(13) Where a bill when dishonoured is in the hands of an agent, he may either himself give notice to the party liable on the bill or he may give notice to his principal. If he give notice to his principal, he must do so within the same time as if he were the holder, and the principal upon receipt of such notice has himself the same time for giving notice as if the agent had been an independent holder.

(14) Where a party to a bill receives due notice of dishonour, he has after the receipt of such notice the same period of time for giving notice to antecedent parties that the holder has after the dishonour.

(15) Where a notice of dishonour is duly addressed and posted, the sender is deemed to have given due notice of dishonour, notwithstanding any miscarriage by the post office.

This long section prescribes the rules regarding notices of dishonour, and it will be seen that considerable latitude is given as regards the form of notice, so long as it sufficiently identifies the bill and states whether it was dishonoured by non-acceptance or non-payment. The mere return of a dishonoured bill to the drawer or an indorser is adequate notice of dishonour, though in practice when doing this collecting banks normally send a printed letter, with the relevant details typed in, advising the position. On the other hand, if a dishonoured bill payable to bearer, either originally or because of a subsequent indorsement bill payable to bearer, either originally or because of a subsequent indorsement in blank, is returned to a person (other than the drawer or any indorser) then this alone is not sufficient, and actual notice is required. If a bank has given value for, or has a lien on, a bill or cheque and intends to sue on it, then it must retain the instrument when giving notice of dishonour (see p. 428).

There is also the possibility, according to the rules, of giving notice to some other person on behalf of the party concerned, e.g. notice to the clerk or servant of a tradesman, or to the wife of a non-tradesman. Though rule 9 does not specifically so provide, it seems reasonable to assume that a notice given to a party who, unknown to the giver, is dead would be sufficient. It was held in *Golfarb* v. *Bartlett* (1920) that where a bill drawn before the dissolution of a partnership was dishonoured after dissolution, notice to the continuing partner was also effective as against the retiring partner.

With reference to the important question of time, notice may be given as soon as the bill is dishonoured, and must be given within a reasonable time, which is a mixed question of law (in so far as rule 12 lays down certain conditions) and of fact. Except in the case of personal notice, the vital factor is the time when the notice is sent, not when it is received, because delays in the post are excused, though it is important to have evidence showing actual posting on the proper day, usually the registered letter receipt. The exact meaning of "place" in rule 12 is not clear; however, MOCATTA, J., in *Hamilton Finance Co., Ltd.* v. *Coverley Westray Walbaum and Tosetti, Ltd.* (1969) took the view that Upper Brook St., W.1. (the West End of London) was the same "place" as Seething Lane, E.C.3. (the City of London), for "they were a modest bus or tube journey apart, both in the central area". Thus, it would appear that if the parties reside in the same postal area (all the postal sub-divisions of a city or town being treated as the same), the one giving the notice can either post it on the day of dishonour or even the next day if there is a reasonable chance that it will be delivered the same day, or he can take or send it round by hand on either day. When they reside in different postal districts, the notice will normally be posted, which has to be done not later than the day after the dishonour of the bill if there is a convenient post, and if not then by the next post thereafter.

Rule 13, regarding agents, is relevant in banking when one bank is acting as collecting or clearing agent for another bank, or where one branch of a bank is acting for another branch in such a way that they will be treated as distinct parties. For example, the clearing agent may present a cheque for payment and have it dishonoured; it will then notify the non-clearing bank for whom it is acting, and then that bank will notify its own customer on whose behalf the cheque has been received. If each bank gives notice within the designated time, the notice to the ultimate party to the instrument will be good. The same applies where one branch of a bank acts as agent for another branch, as in a special presentation outside the normal clearing. It was said in *Yeomen Credit, Ltd.* v. *Gregory* (1963) that there is nothing in rules 12 and 13 read together which enables a principal to add on to his own time the time saved in the agent's notice to him (i.e. delay by one cannot be set-off against expedition by the other).

Normally, the holder will give notice to the immediate party from whom he received the instrument, e.g. the previous indorser, and not to the remote parties, being any other, prior indorsers and the drawer, because he may not know their addresses. If he gives notice to a remote party, he must do so within the same time limits as are available in the case of an immediate party. If no notice is given to a remote party, or if it is not given within the prescribed time, the holder can only claim against such party when he has given notice to his immediate party, who in turn has given notice within the same time (rule 14) to the remote party, for then the holder gets the benefit of the second notice.

In *Eaglehill, Ltd.* v. *J. Needham Builders, Ltd.* (1972) the defendants drew a bill which fell due on 31 December. Before the due date arrived, the acceptor, F. Ltd., went into liquidation and so both the defendants, and the plaintiffs who had discounted the bill, knew the bill would be dishonoured. The plaintiffs drew up a notice of dishonour dated 1 January but through inadvertence it was posted on 30 December, and arrived in the first post on 31 December. The House of Lords held that the notice was valid and effectual because (i) there was nothing in s. 49 to indicate that a notice which was sent by post and delivered in the ordinary course of post had been "given" when it was posted; the notice had not therefore been "given" until it was received on 31 December: since there was nothing in the wording of the notice to lead the defendants to think that it was referring to anything other than a dishonour which had already occurred on 31 December, the notice was good unless it had been received by the defendants before the bill was in fact dishonoured; (ii) where, in the case of commercial documents, two acts had been done, one of which ought to have been done after the other to be valid, in the absence of evidence to the contrary, they would be presumed to have been done in the proper order, i.e. the notice of dishonour would be presumed to have been received after the bill had been dishonoured.

Excuses for non-notice and delay

50.— (1) Delay in giving notice of dishonour is excused where the delay is caused by circumstances beyond the control of the party giving notice, and not imputable to his default, misconduct, or negligence. When the cause of delay ceases to operate the notice must be given with reasonable diligence.

(2) Notice of dishonour is dispensed with:

(a) When, after the exercise of reasonable diligence, notice as required by this Act cannot be given or does not reach the drawer or indorser sought to be charged:

(b) By waiver express or implied. Notice of dishonour may be waived before the time of giving notice has arrived, or after the omission to give due notice:

(c) As regards the drawer in the following cases, namely:

(1) where drawer and drawee are the same person, (2) where the drawee is a fictitious person or a person not having capacity to contract, (3) where the drawer is the person to whom the bill is presented for payment, (4) where the drawee or acceptor is as between himself and the drawer under

no obligation to accept or pay the bill, (5) where the drawer has countermanded payment:

(d) As regards the indorser in the following cases, namely:

(1) where the drawee is a fictitious person or a person not having capacity to contract, and the indorser was aware of the fact at the time he indorsed the bill, (2) where the indorser is the person to whom the bill is presented for payment, (3) where the bill was accepted or made for his accommodation.

If the wording of s. 50 (1) seems familiar this is because it is couched in similar phraseology to s. 46 (1), which deals with excuses for delay in presenting for payment. A case in which delay in giving notice was excused under s. 49 (12) and s. 50 (1) is *The Elmville* (1904), in which the master of the ship of that name had drawn a bill on its owners in favour of the plaintiffs in respect of supplies. The bill was accepted in London, but dishonoured on presentment for payment on a Saturday. The plaintiffs were informed of this by their bank on the Monday, and after ascertaining that the ship was in the Tyne gave notice of dishonour to the master at Newcastle-upon-Tyne on the following Thursday—this notice was held to be good.

Notice must still be given to the drawer or indorsers even though all or any of them had no belief that the bill would be paid on presentment, or knew that the acceptor was dead or bankrupt. The type of circumstances in which notice may be excused because of impossibility would be if the holder visits the drawer's place of business during business hours to give him notice of dishonour, and finds the premises closed and deserted with no forwarding address; or if letters posted to the correct address are returned by the post office marked "Gone away" or some similar phrase. It really comes down to a question of fact whether or not the holder has done all that can reasonably be expected of him in endeavouring to give notice; for example, if he discovers a new address, he must give notice there. On the other hand, if a notice properly addressed is lost in the post, it will be a good notice, though as a matter of evidence it is preferable to send notice by registered post or recorded delivery.

Section 50 (2) (c) sets out certain instances in which notice of dishonour need not be given to the drawer. For example, in the case of a cheque which is returned unpaid by the drawee bank because of the drawer's lack of funds, the bank need not advise the customer that his cheque has been dishonoured, though it usually does so, by way of remonstration in general or by a request for funds in particular where it has marked the cheque "Refer to Drawer; please re-present". Again, if a bank returns a cheque because payment of it has been stopped by the drawer, there is no need to give him notice. Section 50 (2) (d) makes parallel provisions on when notice need not be given to an indorser.

Noting or protest of bill

51.—(1) Where an inland bill has been dishonoured it may, if the holder thinks fit, be noted for non-acceptance or non-payment, as the case may be; but it shall not be necessary to note or protest any such bill in order to preserve the recourse against the drawer or indorser.

(2) Where a foreign bill, appearing on the face of it to be such, has been dishonoured by non-acceptance, it must be duly protested for non-acceptance, and where such a bill, which has not been previously dishonoured by non-acceptance is dishonoured by non-payment, it must be duly protested for non-payment. If it be not so protested the drawer and indorsers are discharged. Where a bill does not appear on the face of it to be a foreign bill protest thereof in case of dishonour is unnecessary.

(3) A bill which has been protested for non-acceptance may be subsequently protested for non-payment.

(4) Subject to the provisions of this Act, when a bill is noted or protested [it may be noted on the day of its dishonour, and must be noted not later than the next succeeding business day]. When a bill has been duly noted, the protest may be subsequently extended as of the date of the noting.

(5) Where the acceptor of a bill becomes bankrupt or insolvent or suspends payment before it matures, the holder may cause the bill to be protested for better security against the drawer and indorsers.

(6) A bill must be protested at the place where it is dishonoured; Provided that:

(a) When a bill is presented through the post office, and returned by post dishonoured, it may be protested at the place at which it is returned and on the day of its return if received during business hours, and if not received during business hours, then not later than the next business day:

(b) When a bill drawn payable at the place of business or residence of some person other than the drawee, has been dishonoured by non-acceptance, it must be protested for non-payment at the place where it is expressed to be payable, and no further presentment for payment to, or demand on, the drawee is necessary.

(7) A protest must contain a copy of the bill, and must be signed by the notary making it, and must specify:

(a) The person at whose request the bill is protested:

(b) The place and date of protest, the cause or reason for protesting the bill, the demand made, and the answer given, if any, or the fact that the drawee or acceptor could not be found.

(8) Where a bill is lost or destroyed, or is wrongly detained from the person entitled to hold it, protest may be made on a copy or written particulars thereof.

(9) Protest is dispensed with by any circumstances which would dispense with notice of dishonour. Delay in noting or protesting is excused when the delay is caused by circumstances beyond the control of the holder, and not imputable to his default, misconduct or negligence. When the cause of a delay ceases to operate the bill must be noted or protested with reasonable diligence.

This lengthy section deals with the twin topics of noting and protesting. Once a bill has been dishonoured the holder may hand it to a notary public (i.e. a person publicly authorised to act in this capacity) who re-presents the bill, and in the event of it being again dishonoured "notes" the bill. Noting is the brief record made by a notary public on a bill at the time of its dishonour, the annotation consisting of the notary's initials, date, noting charges and a reference to the notary's register in which a copy of the bill will have been entered. A ticket is also attached to the bill stating the answer given to the notary's clerk when he makes the notarial presentment, e.g. "no advice", "no funds", or "premises closed". The protest is the formal notarial declaration or certificate attesting that the bill has been duly presented and dishonoured, and its form is prescribed by s. 51 (7). In the case of an inland bill noting and protesting is optional, except where acceptance or payment for honour is sought (a topic covered by ss. 65–68). On the other hand, a foreign bill that appears on the face of it to be such must be protested for non-acceptance or non-payment (if not previously dishonoured by non-acceptance) in order to preserve recourse against the drawer and indorsers: this brings the English legal position into line with numerous foreign systems which make protesting essential. Protest is not necessary where the bill does not appear on the face of it to be a foreign bill—s. 51 (2), or in the case of foreign promissory notes—s. 89 (4).

As the protest is really an extension of the original noting, provided the noting is effected within the stipulated period, the protest may be done subsequently at leisure. As regards the time factor, the words in square brackets in s. 51 (4), making the period available either the day of dishonour or the next succeeding business day, are an amendment made by s. 1 of the Bills of Exchange (Time of Noting) Act 1917. The subsection had originally provided that "it must be noted on the day of its dishonour", but this was sometimes difficult to do in practice, and as the difficulties were accentuated by personnel shortages during the Great War, the time was extended to include the next business day by the short Act of 1917 (it contains only one other section, s. 2, which is merely declaratory as to the title and construction of the Act).

Subject to the two exceptions mentioned in s. 51 (6), protesting is done at the place where the bill is dishonoured; s. 51 (8) allows a protest to be made notwithstanding the non-availability of the original bill; and s. 51 (9) excuses protest in circumstances similar to those which excuse notice of dishonour.

Duties of holder as regards drawee or acceptor

52.—(1) When a bill is accepted generally presentment for payment is not necessary in order to render the acceptor liable.

(2) When by the terms of a qualified acceptance presentment for payment is required, the acceptor, in the absence of an express stipulation to that effect, is not discharged by the omission to present the bill for payment on the day that it matures.

(3) In order to render the acceptor of a bill liable it is not necessary to protest it, or that notice of dishonour should be given to him.

(4) Where the holder of a bill presents it for payment, he shall exhibit the bill to the person from whom he demands payment, and when a bill is paid the holder shall forthwith deliver it up to the party paying it.

As the general rule at common law is that the debtor must seek out his creditor in order to pay him, a general acceptance is sufficient to make the acceptor liable on the bill, and as regards him presentment for payment is unnecessary to establish liability. By s. 89 the maker of a promissory note is in a similar position as regards his liability. In practice, a holder normally presents for payment (after all, he wants to turn the instrument into cash) but if he did sue without first trying to obtain payment he would usually be mulcted in costs and deprived of interest.

If by a qualified acceptance the acceptor makes presentment for payment a condition precedent to his liability, e.g. a bill "accepted payable at South Bank Ltd., Mudtown and there only", then the holder must first present it for payment at that branch before he can proceed against the acceptor, but in the absence of an express stipulation to that effect, the acceptor cannot avoid liability merely because of the omission to present the bill for payment on the proper date. The position is similar in the case of a promissory note made payable at a particular place.

Notice of dishonour to the acceptor is not necessary in order to render him liable, e.g. he may have accepted a bill payable at a bank in another town; if the bank refuses to pay it on presentment, no notice of dishonour need be given to the acceptor, or, in similar circumstances, to the maker of a promissory note. Even with a foreign bill protest is not necessary as against the acceptor.

Surrendering the actual bill is a concurrent condition at the time of payment. The party liable on the bill, or his paying agent (often a bank), is entitled to have the bill exhibited to him when payment is demanded, and having discharged his obligation, he is entitled to acquire the bill for his own protection and as a voucher evidencing payment of the money due thereunder.

Chapter 12

Bills of Exchange—Liability of Parties, Discharge of Bills, etc.

BILLS OF EXCHANGE ACT 1882, SECTIONS 53–72

LIABILITY OF PARTIES

Funds in hands of drawee

53.—(1) A bill, of itself, does not operate as an assignment of funds in the hands of the drawee available for payment thereof, and the drawee of a bill who does not accept as required by this Act is not liable on the instrument. This subsection shall not extend to Scotland.

(2) In Scotland, where the drawee of a bill has in his hands funds available for the payment thereof, the bill operates as an assignment of the sum for which it is drawn in favour of the holder, from the time when the bill is presented to the drawee.

Except in Scotland, a drawee of a bill who does not accept it incurs no liability on it. For this reason, if a bank on which a customer draws a cheque in favour of a third party dishonours the cheque when presented for payment, the payee or holder has no remedy against the bank. Similarly, if an acceptor's bank dishonours a bill accepted payable at the bank, the holder or payee or drawer cannot sue the bank. Failure to pay the cheque or bill may be a breach of contract as between the bank and its customer, but there is no privity of contract as between the bank and other parties to the instrument. Furthermore, except in Scotland, a cheque or bill does not operate as an assignment of funds in the hands of a drawee. For example, if a customer with a credit balance of £20 (and no arrangement to overdraw) draws a cheque for £100, this will be returned unpaid by the bank when presented for repayment, but this fact does not "freeze" the credit balance or inhibit the bank in any way, so that if subsequently the customer draws cheques for £10 and £5 respectively, these two, in the normal course of events, may be safely paid by the bank on presentation.

All the foregoing is otherwise in Scotland, where the instrument operates as an assignment of funds from the time when it is presented to the drawee, even though, in the case of a bill, the drawee does not accept it. Thus, in the example in the preceding paragraph about the presentation of cheques, if that situation occurred in Scotland, the credit balance of £20 could not be used to pay the cheques for £10 and £5 because it would already have been impressed with an assignment in favour of the holder of the dishonoured cheque for £100.

Liability of acceptor

54.— The acceptor of a bill, by accepting it:

(1) Engages that he will pay it according to the tenor of his acceptance:

(2) Is precluded from denying to a holder in due course:

  (a) The existence of the drawer, the genuineness of his signature, and his capacity and authority to draw the bill;

  (b) In the case of a bill payable to drawer's order, the then capacity of the drawer to indorse, but not the genuineness, or validity of his indorsement;

  (c) In the case of a bill payable to the order of a third person, the existence of the payee and his then capacity to indorse, but not the genuineness or validity of his indorsement.

Once he accepts the bill, the acceptor becomes liable to the drawer for so long as the bill remains in the drawer's hands, and is always the party primarily liable on the bill to any subsequent holder. So far as estoppel is concerned, there are certain designated circumstances which the acceptor cannot deny as against a holder in due course, e.g. if an acceptor has accepted a bill on which the drawer's signature has been forged, he cannot set up the forgery against a holder in due course. If it is the payee's signature that has been forged, then the acceptor may decline to pay on that ground. Thus, with a bill payable to the drawer's order, the acceptor can set up a forgery of the drawer's indorsement against a holder in due course, who therefore cannot recover. The reason for this distinction is that in the normal course of events the drawer will have signed the bill as such before the drawee accepts it, but will not indorse it until he receives it back duly accepted.

In so far as the drawee has any doubts about the drawer or the bill, he should make inquiries and receive a satisfactory explanation before accepting, otherwise he will be caught by the estoppel set out in s. 54 (2).

Liability of drawer or indorser

55.— (1) The drawer of a bill by drawing it:

(a) Engages that on due presentment it shall be accepted and paid according to its tenor, and that if it be dishonoured he will compensate the holder or any indorser who is compelled to pay it, provided that the requisite proceedings on dishonour be duly taken;

(b) Is precluded from denying to a holder in due course the existence of the payee and his then capacity to indorse.

(2) The indorser of a bill, by indorsing it:

(a) Engages that on due presentment it shall be accepted and paid according to its tenor, and that if it be dishonoured he will compensate the holder or a subsequent indorser who is compelled to pay it, provided that the requisite proceedings on dishonour be duly taken;

(b) Is precluded from denying to a holder in due course the genuineness and regularity in all respects of the drawer's signature and all previous indorsements;

(c) Is precluded from denying to his immediate or subsequent indorsee that the bill was at the time of his indorsement a valid and subsisting bill, and that he had a good title thereto.

It has already been mentioned that the relationship of acceptor to drawer and indorsers (the latter, in effect, acting as new drawers) is largely that of principal and surety. The drawer and indorsers are jointly and severally liable to the holder for the due acceptance of the bill, where required, and once it is accepted they are then similarly liable to the holder if the acceptor fails to pay it, in which event the holder may sue the acceptor, the drawer or indorsers, or all or any of them, as he chooses. Estoppel again operates in appropriate circumstances—against the drawer in s. 55 (1) (b), and against an indorser in s. 55 (2) (b) and (c). For example, if a holder in due course sues an indorser it is no defence to the latter to show that the signature of the drawer or of the acceptor has been forged, or that the amount of the bill was altered after issue but before his indorsement.

Stranger signing bill liable as indorser

56.—Where a person signs a bill otherwise than as drawer or acceptor, he thereby incurs the liabilities of an indorser to a holder in due course.

An indorsement in the strict sense is made by the holder, but sometimes a person who is not the holder of a bill or note signs it on the back, usually in order to give the instrument greater financial standing or credit worthiness by lending his name to it. Such a person, by s. 56, incurs the liability of an indorser to a holder in due course. Hence, he is sometimes called a "quasi-indorser". For example, a bank may require that a bill to which a company is a party be personally indorsed by the directors of the company for extra security as a condition precedent to discounting the bill. Alternatively, the party backing the instrument could write out a guarantee on it, but this course is seldom adopted. Such a backing indorsement or guarantee is known abroad as an "aval".

The question arose in *Gerald McDonald & Co.* v. *Nash & Co.* (1924) whether the drawer could sue such a quasi-indorser; this is rather like swimming against the stream, in that a prior party is claiming against an apparently later party, the process normally taking place in the opposite direction. The facts of the case were that M. & Co. sold goods to A. & Co., and N. & Co. undertook to guarantee payment for them. M. & Co. drew a series of bills on A. & Co. payable to their own order, but did not indorse them. A. & Co. accepted them, and thereafter N. & Co., before the goods were supplied, backed the bills with their signature and handed them to M. & Co. The House of Lords held that (1) on the facts N. & Co. must be taken to have intended to make themselves liable to M. & Co. on the bills; (2) the bills, when handed to M. & Co., were wanting in a material particular (the absence of M. & Co.'s indorsement above the signature of N. & Co.), but by virtue of s. 20 of the Bills of Exchange Act 1882 M. & Co. had implied authority to sign the bills over the signature of N. & Co., and that when so filled up, the bills became retrospectively enforceable.

A similar situation has arisen on later occasions; for example, in two hire purchase instances as follows:

(i) *Lombard Banking Ltd.* v. *Central Garage and Engineering Co., Ltd.* (1962), where it was held that the plaintiffs, as drawers of bills payable to their order accepted by the defendant company and indorsed by the defendant individuals as directors of the company (i.e. backing the bills as part of the arrangement), could sue the indorsers even though the payee's subsequent indorsements to complete the bills were in the wrong chronological order and in the wrong place (being put below the directors' indorsements).

Although the judge described the plaintiffs (payees) as holders in due course, this is incorrect in view of the House of Lords decision in *R. E. Jones, Ltd* v. *Waring and Gillow, Ltd.* (1926)—see the comment on s. 29 in Chapter 10. However, this does not appear to be material, because s. 56 was not referred to in the judgement, and the case really rests on the finding that the indorsers had intended to make themselves liable to the plaintiffs.

(ii) *Yeoman Credit Ltd.* v. *Gregory* (1963), where the point about the order and signatures again came up, and *Gerald McDonald & Co.* v. *Nash & Co.* was again followed. This time a different judge described the plaintiffs (payees) as holders in due course within s. 56, for the

1926 case was again overlooked. Consequently, this part of the decision must be taken as wrongly decided, but this decision can similarly be supported on the general grounds of upholding the intentions of the parties, for here also the defendant director who indorsed the bills and was held liable on one bill was found to have intended at all times to make himself liable if his company defaulted as acceptor of the bills. The defendant avoided liability on another bill because of the delay in presentment for payment—a point explained in the comment on s. 45—and on a further 12 bills because of the delay in giving notice of dishonour.

Measure of damages against parties to dishonoured bill

57.— Where a bill is dishonoured, the measure of damages, which shall be deemed to be liquidated damages, shall be as follows:

(1) The holder may recover from any party liable on the bill and the drawer who has been compelled to pay the bill may recover from the acceptor, and an indorser who has been compelled to pay the bill may recover from the acceptor or from the drawer, or from a prior indorser:

(a) The amount of the bill:

(b) Interest thereon from the time of presentment for payment if the bill is payable on demand, and from the maturity of the bill in any other case:

(c) The expenses of noting, or, when protest is necessary, and the protest has been extended, the expenses of protest.

(2) [Repealed by the Administration of Justice Act 1977.]

(3) Where by this Act interest may be recovered as damages, such interest may, if justice require it, be withheld wholly or in part, and where a bill is expressed to be payable with interest at a given rate, interest as damages may or may not be given at the same rate as interest proper.

Because the measure of damages in respect of a dishonoured bill can be calculated, the damages are deemed to be liquidated, i.e. a genuine pre-estimate of the probable loss or damage in the event of breach, and s. 57 sets out the factors to be taken into the calculation. Subsection (2), which dealt with the measure of damages for bills dishonoured abroad, was repealed in order to enable judgment on a bill of exchange dishonoured abroad to be given in the relevant foreign currency (see *Miliangos* v. *George Frank (Textiles), Ltd.* (1975) discussed in the comment on s. 72).

To reduce his liability a party will sometimes add to the bill the phrase *"sans frais"* (without dishonour expense)—see s. 16. The dishonour expenses are the expenses of protest, postage, customary commission and brokerage.

On the question of interest, it was seen that s. 9 (1) provides that the bill itself may provide for the payment of interest, this being known as interest proper and being recoverable as of right. S. 57 (3) provides that interest by way of damages is in the discretion of the Court and may be disallowed or reduced if the circumstances are considered to justify this course; the rate of interest will normally be five per cent. per annum—*Re Commercial Bank of South Australia* (1887). A case in which the Court exercised its discretion as to interest is *N. V. Ledeboter* v. *Hibbert* (1947), where interest was disallowed on a bill payable in 1940 and not paid until 1945, because the holder was in enemy-occupied territory (Holland) and to have paid the bill would have been illegal under the Trading with the Enemy Act 1939.

Transferor by delivery and transferee

58.—(1) Where the holder of a bill payable to bearer negotiates it by delivery without indorsing it, he is called a "transferor by delivery".

(2) A transferor by delivery is not liable on the instrument.

(3) A transferor by delivery who negotiates a bill thereby warrants to his immediate transferee being a holder for value that the bill is what it purports to be, that he has a right to transfer it, and that at the time of transfer he is not aware of any fact which renders it valueless.

A holder of a bill payable to bearer (i.e. expressly made so payable or with the only or last indorsement made in blank) can pass it on without indorsing it himself; as he does not sign it, he does not incur liability on the bill itself. such a person is known as a "transferor by delivery" and although incurring liability to his immediate transferee who has given value for the bill in respect of any breach of the warranties set out in s. 58 (3) he does not guarantee the acceptance or payment of the bill, and cannot be sued by remoter transferees.

For example, if the bill is subsequently found to be a forgery, then the immediate transferee can sue his transferor by delivery, not on the bill but on the consideration and the breach of warranty. Consideration may be either an antecedent debt or a cash transaction at the time, as where the transferee cashes a cheque or discounts a bill for the transferor. The latter circumstances imply an indemnity on the part of the seller of the instrument against loss incurred on it by the buyer, but in practice banks always require a customer to indorse a bill before they will discount it for him. To the limited extent to which banks cash third-party cheques for customers, they usually take an "exchange slip" giving authority to debit unpaid items to their customer's account.

DISCHARGE OF BILL

Payment in due course

59.—(1) A bill is discharged by payment in due course by or on behalf of the drawee or acceptor.

"Payment in due course" means payment made at or after the maturity of the bill to the holder thereof in good faith and without notice that his title to the bill is defective.

(2) Subject to the provisions hereinafter contained, when a bill is paid by the drawer or an indorser it is not discharged; but

   (a) Where a bill payable to, or to the order of, a third party is paid by the drawer, the drawer may enforce payment thereof against the acceptor, but may not re-issue the bill.

   (b) Where a bill is paid by an indorser, or where a bill payable to drawer's order is paid by the drawer, the party paying it is remitted to his former rights as regards the acceptor or antecedent parties, and he may, if he thinks fit, strike out his own and subsequent indorsements, and again negotiate the bill.

(3) Where an accommodation bill is paid in due course by the party accommodated the bill is discharged.

This section and succeeding ones up to and including s. 64 deal with the ways in which a bill may be discharged (to be distinguished from the discharge of some parties to a bill, dealt with in other sections e.g. certain persons may be discharged by failure to give them notice of dishonour, or by failure to present for payment, or by taking a qualified acceptance and so on). Discharge of the bill may be effected by: (1) payment in due course to the proper person; (2) the acceptor becoming the holder of the bill in his own right at or after maturity; (3) waiver; (4) cancellation; (5) material alteration. The Act does not specifically define "maturity", but s. 14 sets out the time of payment for all bills other than those payable on demand, and s. 36 (3) provides that demand bills become overdue when they have been in circulation for an unreasonable length of time, i.e. they are never immature, unless post-dated, but are mature until they become overdue.

Discharge of the instrument itself is the last stage in the life-cycle of the bill; it is performance or payment or fulfilment of the bill, and when it takes place all rights of action on the bill are extinguished and all parties to it are discharged. At least, this is the position where the party paying the instrument takes the customary course of cancelling it, but difficulties may arise if an instrument which has been paid but shows no sign of this fact is put back into circulation whilst it is still current and gets into the hands of a holder in due course. The legal position here is doubtful—Chalmers considered that on discharge the instrument ceased to be negotiable and a subsequent holder in due course would acquire no rights of action on the instrument. However, in *Glassock* v. *Balls* (1889) LORD ESHER, M.R. remarked that in those circumstances the holder in due course could sue. From a practical point of view, it may be difficult to establish a position of holder in due course here, but if a person succeeds in doing so and sues the party apparently liable, the latter may find himself estopped from relying on the discharge through his earlier payment because he failed to cancel or obtain or retain the instrument.

Payment in due course

The effect of s. 59 is that payment in due course by, or on behalf of, the acceptor discharges the bill. Such payment, however, must be at or after maturity; payment before the bill is due does not operate as a discharge, but only as a mere purchase of the instrument which may, if its form permits, be re-issued and further negotiated. Payment by the drawer or an indorser does not discharge the bill, except where it is an accommodation bill and the drawer or indorser who pays it is the party accommodated: often such a party will "take up" the bill from a bank with whom he has discounted it (or from some other holder) a few days before it is due for presentment for payment to avoid it being presented to the acceptor.

In *Auchteroni & Co.* v. *Midland Bank Ltd.* (1928) the plaintiffs drew a bill for £876 9s. 0d. in their own favour and this was accepted payable at the defendant bank. At maturity, the bill was correctly indorsed and handed to a clerk with instructions to pay it into the plaintiffs' bank account, but the clerk presented the bill direct to the defendant bank, obtained cash for it and absconded. WRIGHT, J. held that cashing an ordinary bill of exchange over the counter though infrequent and unusual was not sufficiently out of the ordinary as to deprive the paying bank of its statutory protection under s.59, and therefore the plaintiffs' claim failed. His Lordship commented, however, that presentation for payment over the counter by a tramp, or a postman or an office boy would be very special circumstances of suspicion.

If the holder of a bill takes a smaller sum from the acceptor in full discharge, but expressly reserves his rights against the drawer and indorsers, they are not discharged because their own rights against the acceptor have thereby been preserved. If the holder takes a composition under the Bankruptcy Act 1914 from the acceptor, he can still claim for the balance against the drawer and indorsers, because the acceptor has been discharged by operation of law.

It may be added here that it is settled law that if a bank honours a cheque or bill in the mistaken belief that it has sufficient funds from its customer to do so, then the money cannot be recovered from the recipient, because a mistake of this nature only operates between the bank and its own customer and not between the bank and the recipient.

Renewal bills

Sometimes, in lieu of cash payment, the holder of a bill may take from the acceptor another bill payable at a later date. Unless the drawer and indorsers of the old bill are parties to the renewal bill they will be discharged. Similarly, if the holder of an instrument gives time to the acceptor of a bill or the maker of a note (i.e. to the principal debtor) by renewing the bill or note itself, such an extension of the time for payment will discharge all other parties liable thereon (as sureties) unless they consent to the renewal.

Banker paying demand draft whereon indorsement is forged

60.— When a bill payable to order on demand is drawn on a banker, and the banker on whom it is drawn pays the bill in good faith and in the ordinary course of business, it is not incumbent on the banker to show that the indorsement of the payee or any subsequent indorsement was made by or under the authority of the person whose indorsement it purports to be, and the banker is deemed to have paid the bill in due course, although such indorsement has been forged or made without authority.

This section protects the paying banker in the case of forged indorsements on cheques drawn upon him (it does not protect him when paying any other bill of exchange accepted by his customer). The protection was necessary because of the difficulties of ascertaining whether or not an indorsement was genuine in the case of cheques presented through the clearing or open cheques presented over the counter for cash. Hence, if the paying banker pays a cheque in good faith and the ordinary course he receives statutory protection if the indorsement on an order cheque turns out to be forged. The protection is against an action for the tort of conversion brought by the true owner of the cheque who has been deprived of his money by the payment of the cheque to someone not entitled to it. In practice, s. 60 has lost much of its scope, because the Cheques Act 1957 (to be discussed later) has largely dispensed with the need for indorsing cheques, but the section remains important and operative wherever indorsement of a cheque is still necessary.

As regards the constituent element of good faith, this is unlikely to be questioned in practice, since fortunately banks seldom act in bad faith. Instances of lack of good faith which would cost a bank its s. 60 protection would be if the bank knew that an indorsement had been forged, or had been notified that a cheque payable to order had been lost or stolen whilst still unindorsed by the payee, but nevertheless paid the cheque when presented.

The other prerequisite for protection, payment in the ordinary course of business, is more likely to be overlooked by a bank. Thus, a bank would not pay in the ordinary course of business in the following circumstances:

(1) If it pays before or after banking hours, except that some latitude is allowed in paying after hours: *Baines* v. *National Provincial Bank Ltd.* (1927), where a cheque was presented and paid at 3.5 p.m. (when closing time was 3 p.m.) a countermand of payment by the drawer coming too late: Lord HEWART, C. J. held that the bank was justified in paying within a reasonable time after the advertised closing time. Thus, a bank may safely deal with customers already in the branch when the doors are closed, but if a customer was admitted into the branch more than a few minutes after the doors had been closed and conducted a transaction, the position would be less certain, and would really depend on the particular circumstances. This ruling could also assist a bank where a sub-branch closes at the same time as the parent branch, and the sub-branch work is subsequently incorporated into that of the parent branch after the close of banking hours each day. Otherwise, if a customer wishes to stop payment of a cheque as soon as the bank opens, then the bank could not debit the customer's account with that cheque if it had already been paid outside hours.

(2) If the bank pays a crossed cheque contrary to the crossing.

(3) If the bank pays an open cheque presented through the post by a stranger who asks for cash to be sent to him in payment. This would be an unusual method of paying a cheque, whereas if it was a customer who sent his own open cheque by post requesting that cash be remitted to him therefor, this would be payment in the ordinary course.

(4) Having regard to the judicial remarks made in *Auchteroni & Co.* v. *Midland Bank Ltd.* (1928), discussed under s. 59, payment of an open cheque over the counter to a tramp, or a postman or an office boy might not be a good payment, particularly if the cheque was for a

large amount, in that the bank should have been put on notice by these circumstances and should have checked up on the title of the presenter. However, in *Carpenters' Company* v. *The British Mutual Banking Company* (1937) two judges of the Court of Appeal were of opinion that a bank might act negligently but still be acting in the ordinary course of business. Nevertheless, although s. 60 does not mention negligence, it will be preferable for a bank not to have acted negligently if it seeks to rely on the section. In any event, a prudent banker will act with caution in any doubtful circumstances though care must be taken not to cast any adverse reflections on the honesty of the presenter, until the contrary is proved.

So far as the payment of cheques under advice, or open credit arrangements, is concerned, it is thought that this practice is sufficiently widespread and well-known to constitute payment in the ordinary course of business. Where the paying office is another branch of the bank which sends the advice or opens the credit at its customer's behest, payment would be covered by s. 60 (which refers simply to "banker") in so far as a bank and its branches are deemed to be one entity in law. Where the paying office is another bank, then it will not be protected by s. 60 because it is not the bank on which the cheque is drawn. Similar considerations would appear to apply to the modern practice of cashing cheques at other branches or banks for a person producing a cheque card or a credit card.

Analogous instruments

Section 60 does not protect a bank when paying analogous instruments, i.e. documents commonly treated as cheques, but which in fact do not come within the definition of a cheque, e.g. bank drafts, though when crossed they are now within the "crossed cheques sections" (ss. 76–81) of the Act of 1882 by virtue of s. 5 of the Cheques Act 1957. However, the paying bank may be able to claim protection in respect of open analogous instruments under s. 19 of the Stamp Act 1853 which provides that: "Any draft or order drawn upon a banker for a sum of money payable to order on demand which shall, when presented for payment, purport to be indorsed by the person to whom the same shall be drawn payable, shall be a sufficient authority to such banker to pay the amount of such draft or order to the bearer thereof; and it shall not be incumbent on such banker to prove that such indorsement, or any subsequent indorsement, was made by or under the direction or authority of the person to whom the said draft or order was or is made payable either by the drawer or any indorser thereof". It would appear, however, that this s. 19 does not apply to conditional orders to pay, since they are not payable to order—indeed, they are not negotiable and not legally transferable. In addition, there is now protection to bankers paying unindorsed or irregularly indorsed cheques and analogous instruments under s. 1 of the Cheques Act 1957 (set out on page 424).

Acceptor the holder at maturity

61.— When the acceptor of a bill is or becomes the holder of it at or after its maturity, in his own right, the bill is discharged.

This is based on the succinct principle that a man cannot sue himself. If the bill comes back again to the acceptor at or after its maturity, in his own right, then the bill is discharged, but, as will be recalled from s. 37, if it comes back to him before maturity he may, if the bill's form so permits, put it back into circulation though he cannot enforce payment against any intermediate parties to whom he himself was previously liable.

Express waiver

62.— (1) When the holder of a bill at or after its maturity absolutely and unconditionally renounces his rights against the acceptor the bill is discharged.

The renunciation must be in writing, unless the bill is delivered up to the acceptor.

(2) The liabilities of any party to a bill may in like manner be renounced by the holder before, at, or after its maturity; but nothing in this section shall affect the rights of a holder in due course without notice of the renunciation.

If the holder of a bill at or after maturity unconditionally gives up in writing his rights against the acceptor or other party to be charged, then the bill is discharged, but if the bill is allowed to continue in circulation the waiver is no defence against a holder in due course who is unaware of it.

Cancellation

63.— (1) Where a bill is intentionally cancelled by the holder or his agent, and the cancellation is apparent thereon, the bill is discharged.

(2) In like manner any party liable on a bill may be discharged by the intentional cancellation of his signature by the holder or his agent. In such case any indorser who would have had a right of recourse against the party whose signature is cancelled, is also discharged.

(3) A cancellation made unintentionally, or under a mistake, or without the authority of the holder, is inoperative; but where a bill or any signature thereon appears to have been cancelled the burden of proof lies on the party who alleges that the cancellation was made unintentionally, or under a mistake, or without authority.

Any apparent cancellation of a bill by the holder or his agent discharges that bill, or, if such cancellation is not general but applies to a particular party to the bill, it will discharge that party, together with any indorser who would have had a right of recourse against him. The cancellation must be intentional, otherwise it will be inoperative. Thus, where a paying bank receives through the clearing a cheque drawn on it by a customer and cancels the cheque in the usual way, but then within the time available for returning the cheque unpaid finds it necessary to do so, the cancellation will be revoked by marking the cheque "Cancelled in error", or some similar phrase, duly initialled.

Sometimes cancellation of the bill or cheque is effected by physical destruction—tearing it up—provided this act is intentional. On the other hand, if, for example, a holder accidentally tears or cuts a cheque into two or more pieces, as when opening an envelope containing it, he can stick the pieces together, but where it is an open cheque which he intends to cash at the drawee bank, he will have to get the drawer's confirmation before the bank will pay the cheque. Where he is passing the cheque through his own account, he can either get the drawer's confirmation or write on the cheque "Accidentally torn by me" (or some similar narrative) sign this statement and get his own bank, as collecting bank, to add its confirmation or guarantee. Failure to take such action will mean that the drawee bank will return the cheque unpaid, marked "Mutilated cheque", for if it paid such a cheque without explanation etc., where the drawer had intended to cancel it but some unscrupulous person had retrieved the pieces and put them together again, it would have to stand the loss. A cheque torn but not in two may be paid unless the paying bank is in any doubt about the matter, when it would be advisable to return it.

Alteration of bill

64.—(1) Where a bill or acceptance is materially altered without the assent of all parties liable on the bill, the bill is avoided except as against a party who has himself made authorised or assented to the alteration, and subsequent indorsers.

> Provided that, where a bill has been materially altered, but the alteration is not apparent, and the bill is in the hands of a holder in due course, such holder may avail himself of the bill as if it had not

been altered, and may enforce payment of it according to its original tenor.

(2) In particular the following alterations are material, namely, any alteration of the date, the sum payable, the time of payment, the place of payment, and, where a bill has been accepted generally, the addition of a place of payment without the acceptor's assent.

A material alteration is one which changes the operation or business effect of the instrument and the liability of the parties, whether the change be for better or worse. Where made, such an alteration will discharge all parties who did not make it or consent to it, though it will bind subsequent indorsers. An alteration is apparent when it is one that would be noticed by an intending holder scrutinising the document with reasonable care: *Woollatt* v. *Stanley* (1928). If the alteration is not apparent, a holder in due course may sue on the bill as it was before the alteration: *Scholfield* v. *Earl of Londesborough* (1896).

Furthermore, the holder of a bill which has been avoided by a material alteration cannot sue on the consideration for which it was negotiated to him unless:

(i) the bill was negotiated to him subsequently to the alteration, and he was not aware of the alteration, or

(ii) the bill was altered by mistake whilst in his possession, provided the party sued has not been deprived of his remedy on the bill against prior parties by virtue of the alteration.

Whether or not a particular alteration is material is a question of law, s. 64 (2) giving guidance on the main points, with s. 78 providing that altering the crossing of a cheque is material. Needless to say, there has been considerable case law, from which the following examples are culled:

Material alterations:

(1) Changing an inland bill into a foreign one.

(2) Varying the rate of interest.

(3) Indorsing a particular rate of exchange where not authorised by the bill.

(4) Converting a joint note into a joint and several note, or adding a new maker.

(5) Substituting a particular consideration for the words "value received".

(6) Altering the number on a Bank of England note.

Immaterial alterations:

(1) Converting a bill to X or bearer into one payable to X or order.

(2) Converting an indorsement in blank into a special indorsement.

(3) Adding the words "on demand" to a note wherein no time for payment is stated.

(4) Adding an incorrect due date to a bill.

(5) Where the acceptor strikes out the words "or order" on a bill payable to X or order.

(6) Where the number on a bank note is missing (the note was one issued by the Hong Kong and Shanghai Banking Corporation and had been patched together from fragments after its accidental partial destruction during the laundering of a garment).

ACCEPTANCE AND PAYMENT FOR HONOUR

Acceptance for honour supra protest

65.—(1) Where a bill of exchange has been protested for dishonour by non-acceptance, or protested for better security, and is not overdue, any person, not being a party already liable thereon, may, with the consent of the holder, intervene and accept the bill supra protest, for the honour of any party liable thereon, or for the honour of the person for whose account the bill is drawn.

(2) A bill may be accepted for honour for part only of the sum for which it is drawn.

(3) An acceptance for honour supra protest in order to be valid must
  (a) be written on the bill, and indicate that it is an acceptance for honour;
  (b) be signed by the acceptor for honour.

(4) Where an acceptance for honour does not expressly state for whose honour it is made, it is deemed to be an acceptance for the honour of the drawer.

(5) Where a bill payable after sight is accepted for honour, its maturity is calculated from the date of the noting for non-acceptance, and not from the date of the acceptance for honour.

If the drawee of a bill chooses not to accept it when it is presented to him for acceptance, the holder may thereupon immediately exercise his right of recourse against the drawer and any indorsers, or he may decided to note and protest the bill for dishonour by non-acceptance. If the bill is not overdue and has been protested or noted (in the latter event, by s. 93, the protest may be extended later), and if the holder consents, any person not already liable on the bill may accept the bill supra (i.e. after) protest. It would seem from the wording of s. 65 (1) that the drawee, as well as a stranger to the bill, could accept it for honour. An acceptance for honour may be for part only of the bill, and whilst it must be written on the bill and state that it is an acceptance for honour, it can be done simply by writing "Accepted S.P." on the bill and signing it, though it may also state for whose honour the acceptance is made. If this latter statement does not appear, the acceptance is presumed to have been made for the honour of the drawer. Normally, an acceptance for honour will be attested by a "notarial act of honour", that is, the intervener declares before a notary public that he accepts the protested bill for the honour of a specified party and this declaration is recorded by the notary at the foot of the protest; this procedure is not obligatory, but is certainly prudent where there are foreign parties to the bill.

Liability of acceptor for honour

66.—(1) The acceptor for honour of a bill by accepting it engages that he will, on due presentment, pay the bill according to the tenor of his acceptance, if it is not paid by the drawee, provided it has been duly presented for payment, and protested for non-payment, and that he receives notice of these facts.

(2) The acceptor for honour is liable to the holder and to all parties to the bill subsequent to the party for whose honour he has accepted.

Even though acceptance has been refused by the drawee in the first instance, the bill must still be presented to him for payment, before resort can be made to the acceptor for honour—after all, the drawee's financial position may have improved between the two dates. The effect of s. 66 (2) can be illustrated by a situation in which the acceptor for honour, H does so for the honour of E in respect of a bill indorsed by C, D, E, F and G. Here, H will be liable to F and G, but not to E, D and C and any prior parties, and if H pays the bill for honour he can recover from E, for whose honour he intervened, and from the prior parties, but the parties after E (i.e. F and G) are discharged.

Presentment to acceptor for honour

67.—(1) Where a dishonoured bill has been accepted for honour supra protest, or contains a reference in case of need, it must be protested for non-payment before it is presented for payment to the acceptor for honour, or referee in case of need.

(2) Where the address of the acceptor for honour is in the same place where the bill is protested for non-payment, the bill must be presented to him not later than the day following its maturity; and where the address of the acceptor for honour is in some place other than the place where it was protested for non-payment, the bill must be forwarded not later than the day following its maturity for presentment to him.

(3) Delay in presentment or non-presentment is excused by any circumstance which would excuse delay in presentment for payment or non-presentment for payment.

(4) When a bill of exchange is dishonoured by the acceptor for honour it must be protested for non-payment by him.

The liability of the acceptor for honour depends on the following sequence of events taking place: presentment for payment to the original drawee or acceptor; protest for non-payment by him; notice of these facts to the acceptor for honour; and then presentment to the acceptor for honour within the time prescribed by s. 67. Should the acceptor for honour decline to pay the bill, it must again be protested for non-payment by him. In contrast to the foregoing, an ordinary acceptor is liable even though there has been no presentment for payment, no protest and no notice of dishonour.

Payment for honour supra protest

68.—(1) Where a bill has been protested for non-payment, any person may intervene and pay it supra protest for the honour of any party liable thereon, or for the honour of the person for whose account the bill is drawn.

(2) Where two or more persons offer to pay a bill for the honour of different parties, the person whose payment will discharge most parties to the bill shall have the preference.

(3) Payment for honour supra protest, in order to operate as such and not as a mere voluntary payment, must be attested by a notarial act of honour which may be appended to the protest or form an extension of it.

(4) The notarial act of honour must be founded on a declaration made by the payer for honour, or his agent in that behalf, declaring his intention to pay the bill for honour, and for whose honour he pays.

(5) Where a bill has been paid for honour, all parties subsequent to the party for whose honour it is paid are discharged, but the payer for honour is subrogated for, and succeeds to both the rights and duties of, the holder as regards the party for whose honour he pays, and all parties liable to that party.

(6) The payer for honour on paying to the holder the amount of the bill and the notarial expenses incidental to its dishonour is entitled to receive both the bill itself and the protest. If the holder do not on demand deliver them up he shall be liable to the payer for honour in damages.

(7) Where the holder of a bill refuses to receive payment supra protest he shall lose his right of recourse against any party who would have been discharged by such payment.

Payment for honour differs in certain respects from acceptance for honour, discussed under s. 65. Once a bill has been dishonoured by non-payment and protested, any person whether liable on the bill or not may pay it for honour. The consent of the holder of the bill is not necessary in payment for honour, and the bill may be overdue, but the payment for honour must be attested by a "notarial act of honour" (in the case of acceptance for honour, such notarial act is not essential, though normally effected).

The person paying the bill for honour stands in the shoes of the party for whose honour he has intervened as regards rights and duties, so that he can proceed against all parties liable to that party, but all parties subsequent to the one for whom he has intervened are discharged. If there are competing interveners offering payment for honour, the one whose payment will discharge most parties is preferred, e.g. where a dishonoured bill has been drawn by A accepted by B, and indorsed by C, D and E, if F wishes to pay the bill for the honour of D, but G wishes to pay it for the honour of A, G will have the preference because his payment would discharge C, D and E, whereas F's action would discharge only E. Having paid the holder in this way, G can recover from A and B. Dealing with bills for honour supra protest is not very frequent, and so the holder of a dishonoured bill is usually only too pleased if someone will pay it for honour; however, if for any reason he refuses such payment, he loses his right of recourse against those parties who would have been discharged by that particular intervening payment for honour.

LOST INSTRUMENTS

Holder's right to duplicate of lost bill

69.— Where a bill has been lost before it is overdue, the person who was the holder of it may apply to the drawer to give him another bill of the same tenor, giving security to the drawer if required to indemnify him against all persons whatever in case the bill alleged to have been lost shall be found again.

If the drawer on request as aforesaid refuses to give such duplicate bill he may be compelled to do so.

Any one losing a current bill should immediately advise all parties to it and get payment stopped. Section 69 enables the loser to get a duplicate bill from the drawer, subject to giving him an indemnity if required, but there is no provision for obtaining a second time the acceptance and any indorsements. A drawer will normally insist on a full indemnity before giving a duplicate bill, because in the absence of any forgery he would have to pay the lost bill if it subsequently reached the hands of a holder in due course and was dishonoured by the drawee or acceptor.

Action on lost bill

70.— In any action or proceeding upon a bill, the court or a judge may order that the loss of the instrument shall not be set up, provided an indemnity be given to the satisfaction of the court or judge against the claims of any other person upon the instrument in question.

This modifies the common law rule that if a negotiable instrument was lost no action could be brought on the instrument or on the consideration for it, by allowing the action to proceed despite the loss, subject to an appropriate indemnity being given.

BILL IN A SET

Rules as to sets

71.— (1) Where a bill is drawn in a set, each part of the set being numbered, and containing a reference to the other parts, the whole of the parts constitute one bill.

(2) Where the holder of a set indorses two or more parts to different persons, he is liable on every such part, and every indorser subsequent to him is liable on the part he has himself indorsed as if the said parts were separate bills.

(3) Where two or more parts of a set are negotiated to different holders in due course, the holder whose title first accrues is as between such holders, deemed to be the true owner of the bill; but nothing in this subsection shall affect the rights of a person who in due course accepts or pays the part first presented to him.

(4) The acceptance may be written on any part, and it must be written on one part only.

If the drawee accepts more than one part, and such accepted parts get into the hands of different holders in due course, he is liable on every such part as if it were a separate bill.

(5) When the acceptor of a bill drawn in a set pays it without requiring the part bearing his acceptance to be delivered up to him, and that part at maturity is outstanding in the hands of a holder in due course, he is liable to the holder thereof.

(6) Subject to the preceding rules, where any one part of a bill drawn in a set is discharged by payment or otherwise, the whole bill is discharged.

Whilst the vast majority of bills are "sola" or single bills, it is possible to draw a bill in a set (usually a set of three parts), though in practice this is confined to drawing bills on persons abroad, generally with the idea of forwarding the various parts by different mails or routes. Such a bill is drawn on several pieces of paper, each identical with the others except for its numbering— "First", Second", "Third" of a set of three, and so on. The whole of the parts constitute one bill, so that if one part is paid, the others are of no value (a point which is usually recited on the various parts), but s. 71 has to deal with the situations which may arise when the various parts, instead of following each other through the same hands, diverge and get into different hands.

If one part of the set does not refer to the other, that part will become, in the hands of a *bona fide* holder, a separate bill. Any part can be accepted, but only one part should be accepted or indorsed, though acceptance and indorsements need not necessarily be on the same part. Any multiple acceptance will make the acceptor liable on the various accepted parts to different holders in due course as though the parts were separate bills, and the same applies to an indorser who indorses more than one part. The reason for sending the various parts by different routes or posts is to achieve the quickest transit, but an acceptor must be sure that he pays against delivery of the accepted part, otherwise he will have subsequently to pay a holder in due course of the accepted part.

A person may sometimes send the first part of a set to his foreign correspondent who will be instructed to get that part of the bill accepted and retain it until the holder of the second part claims it. This fact will be indicated on the second part of the bill, which may in consequence be negotiated more easily by the sender, by a phrase such as "First with Messrs. X & Co."—showing that the first part lies accepted with X & Co. and can be claimed by presenting to them the other part (or parts if the set consists of more than two). This indication may also be coupled with an additional intimation that Messrs. X & Co. will act as referee in case of need (see s. 15), i.e. will accept or pay the bill supra protest for honour of the party concerned, the combined phrase usually reading "First and in need with Messrs. X & Co." or, in French, "Premiere acceptee et au besoin chez . . .", or, in German "Prima und falls bei . . ."

CONFLICT OF LAWS

Rules where laws conflict

72.— Where a bill drawn in one country is negotiated, accepted or payable in another, the rights, duties and liabilities of the parties thereto are determined as follows:

(1) The validity of a bill as regards requisites in form is determined by the law of the place of issue, and the validity as regards requisites in form of the supervening contracts, such as acceptance, or indorsement, or

acceptance supra protest, is determined by the law of the place where such contract was made.

Provided that:

(a) Where a bill is issued out of the United Kingdom, it is not invalid by reason only that it is not stamped in accordance with the law of the place of issue:

(b) Where a bill, issued out of the United Kingdom, conforms as regards requisites in form, to the law of the United Kingdom, it may, for the purpose of enforcing payment thereof, be treated as valid as between all persons who negotiate, hold or become parties to it in the United Kingdom.

(2) Subject to the provisions of this Act, the interpretation of the drawing, indorsement, acceptance or acceptance supra protest of a bill, is determined by the law of the place where such contract is made.

Provided that where an inland bill is indorsed in a foreign country the indorsement shall as regards the payer be interpreted according to the law of the United Kingdom.

(3) The duties of the holder with respect to presentment for acceptance or payment and the necessity for or sufficiency of a protest or notice of dishonour, or otherwise, are determined by the law of the place where the act is done or the bill is dishonoured.

(4) [Repealed by the Administration of Justice Act 1977.]

(5) Where a bill is drawn in one country and is payable in another, the due date thereof is determined according to the law of the place where it is payable.

Conflict of laws, or that branch of English law which comes into operation whenever a matter contains a foreign element, has already been noted in connection with securities that may have an international flavour, e.g. life policies, and it is of particular concern in relation to bills of exchange, which are often the means whereby international commercial transactions are settled and can represent a series of transactions spread over various countries. Section 4 having defined inland foreign bills, s. 72 makes rules as to which country's law governs bills of exchange involving more than one country's law. Broadly speaking the law of the place where the act is done regulates that act, and according to general principles an act is not done until it is completely done.

An illustration of formal validity under s. 72 (1) is *Koechlin et Cie* v. *Kestenbaum Bros*. (1927) where a foreign bill drawn on an English acceptor payable to the order of a named payee was indorsed in France with the payee's authority by an agent in his own name *simpliciter*. Though it would have been invalid as an indorsement of an inland bill, that indorsement, being valid by French law, was held to be sufficient to entitle the indorsee to sue the English acceptor.

An example of interpretation under s. 72 (2) is *Embiricos* v.

Anglo-Austrian Bank (1905): a cheque drawn in Roumania on a London bank in favour of the plaintiffs was stolen and the signature of the special indorsee was forged; a bank in Vienna cashed the cheque and according to Austrian law obtained a good title thereto; it forwarded the cheque to the defendant bank, its London agent, who collected the money from the drawee bank. The Court of Appeal held that Austrian law must prevail, the transfer of the cheque having been made in that country, and therefore the plaintiffs' claim failed.

Subsection (4), which dealt with the rate of exchange, was repealed in order to enable judgment on a bill of exchange dishonoured abroad to be given in the relevant foreign currency. This was because in *Miliangos* v. *George Frank (Textiles), Ltd.* (1975) the House of Lords abrogated a long-standing rule that English Courts could only give judgment in sterling, by holding that where a plaintiff brought an action for a sum of money due under contract he was entitled to claim and obtain judgment for the amount of the debt expressed in the currency of a foreign country if the proper law of the contract was the law of that country and the money of account and payment was that of the same country. If it was necessary to enforce the judgment that amount was to be converted into sterling at the date when leave was given to enforce the judgment. As the proper law of the contract was Swiss law, and the money of account and payment was Swiss francs, judgment was given in Swiss francs. This, of course, was greatly to the plaintiff's benefit because of the continuing fall in the value of sterling since 1971 when the contract was made. It must be added that three of the Law Lords doubted the view of the Court of Appeal that there was jurisdiction to give judgment in the currency of a member state of the E.E.C. under art. 106 of the E.E.C. Treaty (incorporated into our law by the European Communities Act 1972), and considered that any other Court where such issues arose would be well advised to refer them under art. 177 of the E.E.C. Treaty to the European Court for clarification.

Payment may be affected by exchange control regulations of other countries, those of the United Kingdom having been dismantled in 1979.

By s. 72 (5) ascertainment of maturity is governed by the law of the place of payment, i.e. by the *lex loci solutionis* ("the law of the place of performance"); for example, the question of whether or not days of grace are allowed.

The validity and effect of any discharge are governed by the law of the place where the contract was made, i.e. by the *lex loci contractus.*

The measure of damages is governed by the law of the place at which the party has undertaken to pay the instrument, i.e. by the *lex loci solutionis.*

Chapter 13

Cheques

INTRODUCTION

This chapter will deal with the sections of the Act of 1882 relating to cheques (ss. 73–82) followed, for the sake of continuity, by the provisions of the Cheques Act 1957. The remaining provisions of the Act of 1882, relating to promissory notes and miscellaneous supplementary matters, will then be discussed in the next and last chapter.

BILLS OF EXCHANGE ACT 1882, SECTIONS 73–82

PART III

CHEQUES ON A BANKER

Cheque defined

73.— A cheque is a bill of exchange drawn on a banker payable on demand.
　　Except as otherwise provided in this Part, the provisions of this Act applicable to a bill of exchange payable on demand apply to a cheque.

The relation of a cheque to a bill of exchange is that of the part (albeit a very large part) to the whole. All cheques are bills of exchange, but not all bills of exchange are cheques, in the same way that companies registered under the various Companies Acts are corporations, but all corporations are not companies. A cheque must be drawn on a bank and be payable on demand; its form is too well known to require a diagram, though the various banks have their own ideas of design and colour as to the printed crossed or open cheque books which they issue. The general law regarding bills of exchange payable on demand applies to cheques, except in so far as the Act makes special provisions for cheques, which are now supplemented by the Cheques Act 1957. Certain features of cheques, however, require some elaboration:

(1) A cheque must be unconditional. Any document addressed to a bank requiring the payment on demand of a sum of money provided that some condition, normally the completion of a receipt form on the document, is compiled with is not a cheque, and is usually described as a "conditional order to pay" (see p. 333). The popular "travellers' cheques" are seldom legally classifiable as cheques, because usually they are drawn subject to a condition that they are countersigned by the holder in the presence of the paying agent.

(2) A cheque must be addressed by one person to another. Thus, as a cheque must be drawn on a bank, any document drawn by a branch of a bank on its head office or on another branch, or drawn by the head office on a branch is not a cheque, in as much as a bank and its branches are deemed to be one entity in law. Such documents are described as bankers' drafts or bank drafts, particularly when drawn on a bank's head office, and in other circumstances they are often called bankers' cheques or bank cheques.

(3) A cheque must be for a sum certain in money, and be signed by or on behalf of the drawer.

Cheque forms have been free of stamp duty since 1st February 1971 under the Finance Act 1970. Computerisation of the sorting of cheques has added to the left hand bottom margin of cheque forms three sets of figures in magnetic ink, viz the individual number of the cheque, the branch's national number, and the drawer's account number. Cheque books now contain a page at the back, for bank use only, in connection with the cashing of cheques through other banks or branches with a cheque guarantee card up to the prescribed limit; the page must be stamped to indicate the date of withdrawal, and where there has been one withdrawal that day already at any bank or branch, confirmation of the issuing bank, e.g. by telephone, is required before a second payment is made.

If the words and figures are in conflict as to the sum payable, then, as already noted under s. 9 (2) the words have priority. Where the sum payable is stated only in figures the cheque can be returned "Incomplete" or "Requires amount in words" unless the customer confirms payment notwithstanding the blank. Where the sum payable is stated only in words the cheque must be paid, though in practice the figures will have been added somewhere if the cheque requires collection through the clearing.

Any alteration of the sum payable must be signed or initialled by all the signatories who have drawn the cheque. Where the sum payable has been fraudulently raised, this is a material alteration (s. 64 (2) refers) and the bank cannot normally debit the increase to the customer's account because there is no mandate in respect of it. However, it was decided in *Young* v. *Grote* (1827) that where a customer carelessly drew a cheque for £50 so that it was easy for the holder to change both words and figures to £150, which sum was paid by the bank, then the bank could charge the customer with the full amount paid. This principle was reaffirmed by the House of Lords in *London Joint Stock Bank Ltd.* v. *Macmillan and Arthur* (1918) where a partner in a firm drew a cheque without any amount in words, but with £ 2 0s. 0d. in the space for figures. A clerk subsequently wrote in the words "One hundred and twenty pounds" and put a figure 1 before, and a figure 0 after, the existing figure 2, and obtained £120 from the bank. It was held that the bank could debit the customer's account with £120 and the legal position was elaborated as follows:

(a) A customer owes a duty to his bank to use reasonable care in the drawing and signing of cheques so as not to facilitate additions or alterations.

(b) If the customer fails to use such care and loss ensues, the customer and not the bank must stand the loss, but if the bank is negligent e.g. where the alteration is obvious, then the loss will fall on the bank. (It will also rest with the bank if the customer has used due care and the alteration is not obvious.)

(c) It does not matter whether it is by forgery or other crime that the loss occurs.

(d) The bank is justified in refusing payment of a cheque if there are reasonable grounds for suspecting it has been tampered with or if its form is unusual or irregular, but the answer placed upon the cheques should be such as not to cast doubt on the customer's credit.

In *Slingsby* v. *District Bank Ltd.* (1932) where the words "per Cumberbirch and Potts" were added after the payee's name in a cheque the Court of Appeal declined to hold that there was a duty on the drawer to leave no space after the payee's name, as it was not a usual precaution to draw lines before and after this name.

(4) The date of a cheque is not essential in that it can be antedated, post-dated or dated on a non-business day; if dated on a Saturday or Sunday and presented on the preceding Friday the cheque should be returned "post-dated". If the cheque is undated, the bank can refuse to pay it, though in practice the holder will usually write the date in. Any alteration of the date is material and must be signed or initialled by all the signatories who have drawn the cheque. As mentioned under s. 36, the normal practice of banks is to treat cheques as stale or out-of-date after six months from their date. In the case of dividend warrants, it is often pointed out in a footnote that

after six months have passed the warrant must be returned for verification by the Secretary or Registrar, and sometimes the period for
presentment by the payee is shortened, e.g. to three months.

(5) The payee. A cheque must be payable to or to the order of a
specified person or to bearer. The difficulties of a fictitious payee have
been discussed under s. 7, but it may be mentioned here again that the
problem as regards cheques concerns those payable to "cash" or
"wages". In a case after the Cheques Act 1957, *Orbit Mining and
Trading Co., Ltd.* v. *Westminster Bank Ltd* (1963) it was again held that a
document expressed to be payable to "Cash or order" was not a bill of
exchange and therefore not a cheque, though the Court of Appeal
added that when issued by a customer it might enable a bank to claim
the statutory protection of s. 17 of the Revenue Act 1883 and s. 4 (2)
(b) of the Cheques Act 1957.

The drawer may change the word "order" printed on a cheque to
the word "bearer" but should sign or initial the alteration. If a cheque
printed with the words "or order" is filled in with the word "bearer",
the written "bearer" will override the printed "or order". If a cheque
is drawn payable to bearer, it cannot be converted by indorsement
into an order cheque, and any indorsements can be disregarded. By s.
34 an order cheque becomes payable to bearer when the only or last
indorsement is in blank; but it is possible by a subsequent indorsement to make it again payable to order. However, in practice the large
scale abolition of indorsements by the Cheques Act 1957 has robbed
the distinction between "bearer" and "order" cheques of much of its
old significance.

(6) Finally, it may be noted that in *Director of Public Prosecutions* v.
Turner (1973) the House of Lords held that the accused, who had paid
a debt by cheque which he knew would be dishonoured, was properly
convicted of dishonestly obtaining for himself a pecuniary advantage,
i.e. the evasion of a debt for which he was then liable, by deception,
contrary to s. 16 (2) (a) of the Theft Act 1968. However, the effect of
this decision has now been narrowed in that s. 16 (2) (a) has been
repealed by the Theft Act 1978, which makes other provisions against
fraudulent conduct, so that a debtor who by deception gains more time
to pay a debt does not commit an offence unless he intends never to pay.

In *Metropolitan Police Commissioner* v. *Charles* (1976) the House of
Lords held that the offence of obtaining a pecuniary advantage by
deception contrary to s. 16 (1) of the Theft Act 1968 was committed
by the holder of a cheque card who, in the course of one evening at a
gaming club, drew 25 cheques each for £30 and backed by the cheque
card, which, when presented, put his bank account into debit far
beyond the limit of his authorised overdraft.

Presentment of cheque for payment

74.—Subject to the provisions of this Act:

(1) Where a cheque is not presented for payment within a reasonable time of its issue, and the drawer or the person on whose account it is drawn had the right at the time of such presentment as between him and the banker to have the cheque paid and suffers actual damage through the delay, he is discharged to the extent of such damage, that is to say, to the extent to which such drawer or person is a creditor of such banker to a larger amount than he would have been had such cheque been paid.

(2) In determining what is a reasonable time regard shall be had to the nature of the instrument, the usage of trade and of bankers, and the facts of the particular case.

(3) The holder of such cheque as to which such drawer or person is discharged shall be a creditor, in lieu of such drawer or person, of such banker to the extent of such discharge, and entitled to recover the amount from him.

The effect of this section is to protect the drawer of a cheque who suffers loss because of the holder's failure to present the cheque for payment within a reasonable time when his bank becomes insolvent. Bank failures amongst the small local banks were frequent in hard times during the 19th century, but the growth of great joint stock banks eliminated this situation by spreading the risks of lending over the whole country and the whole range of industry, commerce and agriculture. However, even today there is the odd occasion when a bank collapses financially, though fortunately those that do are in general small and little-known. Suppose a customer draws a cheque for £200 on a bank where his credit balance is £300, the cheque is not presented within a reasonable time as prescribed by s. 74 (2) and the bank fails when his credit balance is still £300. The customer has now lost £300 (less any dividend to the creditors that may ultimately be paid to the liquidation or bankruptcy as the case may be) whereas if the holder had presented the cheque in the normal course of time, the customer's balance would have been reduced to £100 (thereby reducing his loss). The effect of s. 74 (1) and (2) is to put the customer in the same position as he would have been in if the cheque had been paid, i.e. he is discharged from paying the £200 a second time to the holder, and the holder has to prove for his £200 against the bank. It is not clear what the position would be if the circumstances were the same except that instead of having a credit balance the customer was allowed to overdraw and the cheque would have been paid on that basis: it would seem that the customer would still be liable to the holder because he would not have suffered loss through the failure to present for payment—he would owe the bank £200 less than he would have if the cheque had been paid, and as the holder could not prove against the bank on the cheque when the account was overdrawn he ought on equitable grounds to be paid again by his debtor.

Revocation of banker's authority

75.— The duty and authority of a banker to pay a cheque drawn on him by his customer are determined by:
   (1) Countermand of payment:
   (2) Notice of the customer's death.

The liability of a bank to pay a cheque drawn on it is a contractual one owed to its customer, and not to any holder of the cheque because the bank, although the drawee of the cheque, does not sign it. Such a paying bank is under a duty to honour its customer's cheques if presented at the branch where the account is kept in proper form and within a reasonable time provided the customer has sufficient available funds to his credit to cover the cheques, or they are within the limit of an agreed overdraft. This duty is, however, determined if the customer stops payment of the cheque or if the bank receives notice in any way that the customer has died.

Countermand of payment is the cancellation by the customer of his mandate to the bank represented by the cheque, but to be effective the countermand must actually come to the bank's notice. Constructive countermand e.g. that the bank is in a position to learn of it, is not enough: *Curtice* v. *London City and Midland Bank Ltd.* (1908). In this case, C drew a cheque on the bank in payment for three horses which were not delivered, so at about 5.30 p.m. he telegraphed his branch of the bank to stop payment. As the bank was closed the messenger boy put the telegram in the letter box at 6.15 p.m. but the next day the telegram, by an oversight, was not taken out of the letter-box, and by the time it was found on the second day the cheque had already been paid. The Court of Appeal held that the cheque was not counter-manded within the meaning of s. 75, although there might have been negligence on the part of the bank's officials, and therefore the plain-tiff's claim failed. Some doubt was expressed whether in any event a bank could accept an unauthenticated telegram as sufficient author-ity to stop a cheque, though this might depend on the course of dealing between the parties in any particular case. In these circum-stances it would be preferable for the bank to return the cheque with an answer explaining the state of affairs (so as not to damage the customer's credit) and requesting re-presentation; in the meantime confirmation would be sought from the customer.

It is more likely nowadays that initially payment will be stopped by telephone, and although the position will depend on exactly what was said, unless the bank is satisfied that it actually was the customer who telephoned, similar tactics to those outlined above in the case of an unauthenticated telegram would appear necessary.

Needless to say, the details of the "stop" furnished by the drawer to his bank must be accurate. In *Westminster Bank Ltd.* v. *Hilton* (1926) H drew a cheque No. 117285 post-dated August 2, and on August 1, he telegraphed the bank to stop payment of cheque 117283 mentioning the payee and the amount (but not that the cheque was post-dated). When cheque No. 117285 was presented on August 6, the bank paid it, assuming it was a duplicate for that which had been stopped, whereas in fact it was the cheque the drawer intended to stop. The House of Lords held that as the one certain item of identification was the number the bank was not negligent and the plaintiff's claim failed.

It was held in *London Provincial and South Western Bank Ltd.* v. *Buszard* (1918) that for the purposes of countermand of payment, the branches of a bank are to be treated as separate parties, the "stop" being effective only at the branch to which it is sent, so that notice of the "stop" given to one branch did not prevent another branch which had become holder for value of the cheque from recovering the amount of the cheque from the drawer.

This question of different branches came up in another form due to the introduction of computer mechanisation in *Burnett* v. *Westminster Bank Ltd.* (1965). B had for some years accounts at both the Borough and the Bromley branches of the bank, and eventually because the Borough branch had introduced computer accounting his cheque book on that branch for the first time included a notice that "the cheques in this book will be applied to the account for which they have been prepared". B drew a Borough branch cheque for £2,300 but altered the branch in ink to Bromley, and later instructed Bromley branch to stop payment, but the cheque, as the computer could not read the ink alteration, was sent to Borough branch where no action was taken on the alteration and the cheque was paid, because no "stop" had been received at that branch. It was held that the cheque book cover fell within a class of documents which recipients would reasonably assume did not contain conditions varying existing contractual arrangements between themselves and their bank, and as the plaintiff had long had accounts with the bank he was not bound by the notice on the cheque book cover as to the restricted use of the cheque forms for only one account, and could recover the £2,300 from the bank.

If a bank inadvertently pays a "stopped" cheque it commits a breach of its customer's mandate and can incur a dual liability—

(i) for paying the "stopped" cheque, and possibly (ii) for wrongfully dishonouring other cheques which could have been paid had not the available funds of the customer been utilised in the wrong payment. Whilst the bank will have to refund the amount of the cheque to the customer it has hitherto been generally considered that it obtained no right of subrogation against the payee, but where the cheque was given in respect of goods, the bank could mitigate its loss by claiming the actual goods, if identifiable. However, the bank's position has recently been much improved by a decision at first instance in *Barclays Bank Ltd.* v. *W. J. Simms Son and Cooke (Southern), Ltd.* (1979) that where the bank had paid a stopped cheque for £24,000 drawn by its customer, the Royal British Legion Housing Association, Ltd., in favour of the defendant company in respect of work done under a building contract the bank could recover the money from the payee as money paid under mistake of fact. Near the end of his long, reserved judgment, ROBERT GOFF, J. said: "I must confess that I am happy to be able to reach the conclusion that the money is recoverable by the plaintiff bank. If the bank had not failed to overlook its customer's instructions, the cheque would have been returned by it marked 'Orders not to pay', and there would have followed a perfectly *bona fide* dispute between the Association and the Receiver [of the defendant company] on the question arising on the terms of building contract, whether the Association was entitled to stop the cheque—which ought to be the real dispute in the case. If the plaintiff bank had been unable to recover the money, not only would that dispute not have been ventilated and resolved on its merits but, in the absence of ratification by the Association, the plaintiff bank would have had no recourse to the Association. Indeed, if under the terms of the building contract the money had not been due to the defendant company, non-recovery by the plaintiff bank would have meant quite simply a windfall for the preferred creditors of the defendant company at the plaintiff bank's expense." If his Lordship's innovation finds general acceptance, banks will be happy too.

The customer's power to countermand payment may be restricted by agreement with the bank, e.g. under the modern system of cheque guarantee cards, whereby the issuing bank undertakes that payment of the drawer's personal cheques will be made if certain conditions are observed, items so drawn cannot be stopped by the drawer. These conditions are: (a) settlement is in respect of one transaction which must not exceed the prescribed limit (at present £50); (b) the signature on the cheque agrees with the specimen on the card and is written in the presence of the payee; (c) the payee records the card number on the reverse of the cheque; and (d) the expiry date shown on the card has not been reached. If a bank has reason to believe that a cheque has not been issued and accepted in accordance with the regulations, (for example, where it appears to have been sent by post, because it has been folded and the card number on the reverse seems to have been written by the customer) it could return the cheque, and would be likely to do so where the customer's account is insufficiently in credit or he has reached his overdraft limit.

Finally, although the drawer is the only person who can instruct his bank not to pay a particular cheque which he has issued, sometimes the holder of a cheque may inform the bank that the cheque has been mislaid or stolen, in which event the bank should seek the instructions of the drawer, its customer. If the cheque is presented in the meantime the bank should exercise caution and make inquiries appropriate to the circumstances, otherwise it may jeopardise its statutory protection under ss. 60 and 80.

On the other point under s. 75, as the death of a customer cancels his mandate to the bank, any cheques subsequently presented should be returned marked "Drawer deceased", the payee having then to settle the matter with the deceased's personal representatives. What the bank requires is notice of the death, mere rumour not being sufficient. The notice need not be direct, e.g. from relatives, but may be seen in a newspaper, or acquired in some other way, though in any case the bank customarily confirms any report and seeks to have a sight of a copy of the death certificate for noting in its records.

As a company is a separate legal person, notice of the death of an official who has signed cheques on behalf of his company does not revoke the company's mandate to the bank to pay its cheques.

In addition to the two instances set out in s. 75, a bank will have to decline to pay a customer's cheques in the following circumstances:

(a) On receipt of notice that the customer has become of unsound mind.

(b) On receipt of any Court order affecting the account. The one most likely to be encountered is a garnishee order i.e. a notice to any party holding funds or property of another that they are attached at the behest of a third person who has a charge on them. Although, because a garnishee order attaches or "freezes" the whole of the customer's credit balance, a bank should not strictly speaking pay any cheques at all even if the balance of the account greatly exceeds the amount where this is stated in the order, normally cheques will be paid against the excess where ascertainable, i.e. after deducting from the balance the amount of the garnishee order and all possible expenses relating thereto.

(c) On receipt of notice of an available act of bankruptcy, in which event cheques will be returned unless presented by the drawer or his assignee. If the bank at any time receives notice of the presentation of a bankruptcy petition no cheques can be paid at all; the same applies after a Receiving Order has been made, whether the bank has notice of it or not. The effect of bankruptcy proceedings (the subject of Chapter 5) is to take the bankrupt's property out of his control and place it in that of the Official Receiver or Trustee in bankruptcy so that it may be dealt with for the benefit of the creditors as a whole.

(d) On receipt of notice of the commencement of winding up proceedings in respect of a company incorporated under any of the various Companies Acts (see Chapter 4 on Companies).

(e) Knowledge of any defect in the title of the presenter (this would deprive the bank of its statutory protection under ss. 60 and 80).

(f) Where the bank knows or ought to know that the cheque is a misapplication of funds.

Even though a cheque is correctly drawn in accordance with the mandate, the paying bank will be liable to its customer if it pays a cheque when it knows or ought to know from the facts that the person(s) signing the cheque are misapplying the customer's funds or using them for an unlawful purpose. An example of this is the purchase of its own shares by a company (unlawful under s. 54 of the Companies Act 1948—see p. 151, *ante*) and it arose in a lengthy and involved case *Selangor United Rubber Estates, Ltd.* v. *Cradock* (*No. 3*) (1968), where the plaintiff company now in compulsory liquidation was the subject of a take-over bid by the first defendant, now bankrupt and out of the country, by a series of complicated and virtually simultaneous transactions which included the D. Bank taking a transfer of the company's account from another bank and innocently paying a cheque on it which in effect had been used to buy the company's shares. It was held, *inter alia*, that on the facts a reasonable banker would have concluded that the payment of £232,500 out of the company's account was to finance the purchase by Cradock of shares in the company and so the bank was liable as constructive trustee to replace so much of that money as had been misapplied; and also that the bank was liable to the company in contract for failure to exercise reasonable care and skill in paying the cheque for £232,500 without making enquiry of that company's directors as to the purpose for which it was being applied. This case was followed at first instance in *Karak Rubber Co., Ltd.* v. *Burden* (No. 2) (1972) where, in virtually identical circumstances, another bank was held liable.

Wrongful dishonour of a cheque

The opening of a current account implies a contract that the bank will pay at the branch concerned cheques drawn by the customer in correct form and with funds available, whether consisting of a credit balance or an authorised overdraft limit. If the bank dishonours a cheque wrongfully i.e. where funds are available and no legal impediment to payment exists, then this is a breach of contract for which the customer can sue for damages, and the measure of the damages is not the amount of the cheque but such sum as is reasonable compensation for the injury to his credit. In the case of a non-trader, unless special damage can be proved, damages will be merely nominal—they reflect the infringement of the plaintiff's legal rights but no more—for example, in *Gibbons* v. *Westminster Bank Ltd.* (1939) a woman who was not a trader received £2 damages. However, in the case of a tradesman, and by analogy in that of a professional man or a commercial agent, reasonable compensation can be recovered without proof of special damage; *Fleming* v. *Bank of New Zealand* (1900). In an Irish case, *Kinlan* v. *Ulster Bank Ltd.* (1928), the damages were nominal because the cheque wrongfully dishonoured was one payable to "self" and presented by the customer. In that case there was no libel aspect because one of the necessary elements in the tort of defamation is that the defamatory statement must be published to someone other than the plaintiff, and that element was lacking.

In the great majority of cases the cheque will have been returned unpaid to a third party, and difficulties may arise over whether the answer placed on the returned cheque (in accordance with Clearing House rule) is libellous or not. If a libel is committed, then the drawer of the cheque can sue his bank in tort for defamation, as well as in contract. In *Frost* v. *London Joint Stock Bank Ltd.* (1906) the Court of Appeal held that the words "Reason assigned—not stated" on a returned cheque were not libellous. On the other hand in *Davidson* v. *Barclays Bank Ltd.* (1940) where a cheque for £2 15s. 8d. drawn by the plaintiff, a bookmaker, was wrongfully dishonoured with the words "Not sufficient" (because the bank had exhausted the balance by paying a stopped cheque), it was held that the words were libellous and the plaintiff obtained £250 damages. In *Baker* v. *Australia and New Zealand Bank Ltd.* (1958) a New Zealand Court held that the phrase "present again" was libellous.

The main argument has centred round the phrase "Refer to Drawer", traditionally placed on cheques by banks (or in the case of bills of exchange "Refer to Acceptor"). In *Flach* v. *London and South Western Bank Ltd.* (1915) SCRUTTON, J. held that "Refer to Drawer" was not libellous—the words, in his opinion, in their ordinary meaning, amounted to a statement by a bank, "we are not paying; go back to the drawer and ask why", or else "go back to the drawer and ask him to pay". This view was followed in *Plunkett* v. *Barclays Bank Ltd.* (1936). However, the phrase has come to mean to the man in the street "lack of funds". In *Jayson* v. *Midland Bank Ltd.* (1968) the Court of Appeal dismissed the plaintiff customer's appeal without considering this point; at first instance the jury had found that "Refer to Drawer" was libellous but that there had been no breach of contract by the bank. In 1972 the Post Office paid damages to settle a libel claim when it had wrongfully returned to payees five National Giro cheques marked "refer to drawer".

Where possible a bank will seek to use some alternative to "Refer to Drawer", either "Effects not cleared" (where the customer's balance is dependent on uncleared cheques, against which the bank is not prepared to pay), or, if applicable, technical irregularities, such as "Words and figures differ" or "Signature varies". If two or more cheques are presented contemporaneously the bank will decide which to pay and which to return (where some but not all are not covered by available funds) on the basis not only of the respective amounts but also of the payees of the cheques, e.g. a smaller cheque in settlement of rates or a trade debt would be paid in preference to a cheque for a larger amount for a personal or private debt where returning the cheque would involve less harm to the customer's credit. If the customer has an insufficient balance on current account, but ample funds on deposit account, the bank is not obliged to pay a cheque in excess of the current account but will normally do so because it would have a lien on the deposit balance to the extent of the overdraft created on the current account. Thus, banks take considerable care before returning cheques unpaid for shortage of funds.

PASSBOOKS AND STATEMENTS

The law relating to passbooks and the looseleaf statements which have now replaced them is distinctly unsatisfactory from a bank's point of view. If the customer returns a passbook to the bank without objection, entries therein to his debit are *prima facie* evidence against him and where a balance has been struck this is evidence of a stated and settled account: *Blackburn Building Society* v. *Cunliffe, Brooks & Co.* (1882), but even so it appears that the customer owes his bank no duty to examine his passbook or statement and, even if he does, is not estopped from subsequently disputing entries: *Chatterton* v. *London and*

County Banking Co., Ltd. (1891). The periodical statements of accounts now supplied by banks are retained and accumulated by the customer, not returned as passbooks used to be, and although they usually carry a legend to the effect that any discrepancies therein are to be notified to the bank forthwith, the general legal view remains that there is no duty on the customer to examine his statement (or passbook) and paid cheques if returned to him. The point is one on which there are conflicting opinions, but certainly the banks' position here contrasts unfavourably with that in the U.S.A. where the Courts have placed the onus of verifying his account on the customer.

Credits entered in error may be rectified within a reasonable time: *British and North European Bank Ltd.* v. *Zalzstein* (1927), for a customer cannot accept the credit without regarding also the debit. But if the customer is unaware of being over-credited and genuinely alters his position to his detriment in reliance on the incorrect balance the bank cannot successfully reclaim the excess credit: *Lloyds Bank Ltd.* v. *Brooks* (1951), where this state of affairs happened in relation to dividends over credited to the account of the Hon. Cecily Brooks and the bank had to stand the loss. On the other hand, in *United Overseas Bank* v. *Jiwani* (1977) the defendant's claim that the bank was estopped from seeking restitution of the sum mistakenly credited to his account was rejected, because he failed to show that he had altered his mode of living in a way which he would not have done but for his reliance on the mistake.

CROSSED CHEQUES

General and special crossings defined

76.—(1) Where a cheque bears across its face an addition of:
   (a) The words "and company" or any abbreviation thereof between two parallel transverse lines, either with or without the words "not negotiable"; or
   (b) Two parallel transverse lines simply, either with or without the words "not negotiable";
that addition constitutes a crossing, and the cheque is crossed generally.

   (2) Where a cheque bears across its face an addition of the name of a banker, either with or without the words "not negotiable", that addition constitutes a crossing, and the cheque is crossed specially and to that banker.

Crossing a cheque is writing across its face either type of general crossing or the special crossing as set out in s. 76. If the name of a bank is written between two parallel transverse lines, the name of the bank constitutes the special crossing and the lines are purely ornamental. Other documents which can be effectively crossed are dividend warrants, by virtue of s. 95; and under s. 5 of the Cheques Act 1957 the analogous instruments set out in s. 4 (2) (b) (c) and (d) of that Act. Under r. 22 (2) of the National Savings Stock Register Regulations 1976 (S.I. 1976 No. 2012) the crossed cheques sections 76–81 apply to any crossed warrants issued under the Regulations as if the warrant were a cheque drawn on the Director of Savings by the officer issuing the warrant but nothing in the Regulations shall make any such warrant negotiable. Although money orders and postal orders may be crossed generally or specially, this not by virtue of s. 76 but by Post Office schemes made under s. 28 of the Post Office Act 1969, namely: the Post Office (Money Order) Scheme 1973; and the Post Office (Postal Order) Scheme 1971.

Crossing by drawer or after issue

77.—(1) A cheque may be crossed generally or specially by the drawer.

(2) Where a cheque is uncrossed, the holder may cross it generally or specially.

(3) Where a cheque is crossed generally the holder may cross it specially.

(4) Where a cheque is crossed generally or specially, the holder may add the words "not negotiable".

(5) Where a cheque is crossed specially, the banker to whom it is crossed may again cross it specially to another banker for collection.

(6) Where an uncrossed cheque, or a cheque crossed generally, is sent to a banker for collection he may cross it specially to himself.

These rules show who may cross a cheque and the limits within which a crossing may be varied.

Crossing a material part of cheque

78.—A crossing authorised by this Act is a material part of the cheque; it shall not be lawful for any person to obliterate or, except as authorised by this Act, to add to or alter the crossing.

This is a logical sequence to the previous section. The main point to note is that the Act does not provide any way in which crossings may be cancelled. As the object of crossing a cheque is to prevent it being cashed by a person who has no title to it, and the majority of cheques used are crossed ones, customers who have printed crossed cheque books, on the occasions when they require cash, are in the habit of writing "Please pay cash" or "Crossing cancelled" or some similar phrase over the crossing and signing it. Although there is no statutory provision for this practice, banks will cash such cheques for the drawer or his known agent, e.g. his wife—after all, the drawer is the only person who could complain about it and he himself is the perpetrator of the cancellation. It may also be mentioned that the Act is silent on the words "Account payee" or "Account payee only" which are sometimes added to cheques. These words do not affect a paying bank but they have significance for a collecting bank, and will be discussed later under s. 4 of the Cheques Act 1957.

Duties of banker as to crossed cheque

79.—(1) Where a cheque is crossed specially to more than one banker, except when it is crossed to an agent for collection being a banker, the banker on whom it is drawn shall refuse payment thereof.

(2) Where the banker on whom a cheque is drawn which is so crossed nevertheless pays the same, or pays a cheque crossed generally otherwise than to a banker, or if crossed specially otherwise than to the banker to whom it is crossed, or his agent for collection being a banker, he is liable to the true owner of the cheque for any loss he may sustain owing to the cheque having been so paid.

Provided that where a cheque is presented for payment which does not at the time of presentment appear to be crossed, or to have had a crossing which has been obliterated, or to have been added or altered otherwise than as authorised by this Act, the banker paying the cheque in good faith and without negligence shall not be responsible or incur any liability, nor shall the payment be questioned by reason of the cheque having been crossed, or of the crossing having been obliterated or having been added to or altered otherwise than as authorised by this Act, and of payment having been made otherwise than to a banker or to the banker to whom the cheque is or was crossed, or to his agent for collection being a banker, as the case may be.

If the paying bank pays a cheque which is crossed specially to more than one bank (except where one acts as collecting agent for the other, e.g. where a Scottish bank sends cheques to its London clearing agent for collection) then it incurs statutory liability to the true owner for any loss sustained thereby, unless it can bring the situation within the proviso to s. 79 (2). Normally, a collecting bank will refuse to take a cheque already crossed by some other bank but if it should do so, the collecting bank will indorse the cheque with an indemnity to the paying bank covering the latter in respect of paying a cheque crossed by two banks. This might occur, for example, where a customer of bank A has paid in a cheque for his credit at bank B using the credit transfer system, and the cheque having been returned dishonoured he subsequently seeks to re–present it through his own bank A so that the cheque acquires the crossings of two different and unconnected banks. A cheque crossed by two branches of the same bank is in order, as it is not crossed by two banks, and therefore not within s. 79.

Protection to banker and drawer where cheque is crossed

80.— Where the banker on whom a crossed cheque is drawn, in good faith, and without negligence pays it, if crossed generally, to a banker, and if crossed specially, to the banker to whom it is crossed, or his agent for collection being a banker, the banker paying the cheque, and, if the cheque has come into the hands of the payee, the drawer, shall respec- tively be entitled to the same rights and be placed in the same position as if payment of the cheque had been made to the true owner thereof.

This important section gives statutory protection against the claims of the true owner, both to a paying bank which pays a crossed cheque in good faith and without negligence in accordance with its crossing, and to the drawer if the cheque has actually or construc- tively reached the payee. Clearly, if a bank cashes over the counter a crossed cheque drawn upon it, the protection of s. 80 will be lost as payment will have been made in contravention of the crossing; even if the crossed cheque is presented by another customer of the same branch (when it is often called a "house debit") it should be placed to that customer's credit and not cashed. The only payment of a crossed cheque over the counter which would be within s. 80 would be a payment of a cheque specially presented by another bank. As far as the drawer of the cheque is concerned, once the crossed cheque has reached the payee then the drawer is discharged from liability to the true owner if the bank on which the cheque is drawn pays it within the conditions of s. 80.

Effect of crossing on holder

81.— Where a person takes a crossed cheque which bears on it the words "not negotiable", he shall not have and shall not be capable of giving a better title to the cheque than that which the person from whom he took it had.

This section points out that the negotiability of a crossed cheque is destroyed by adding the words "not negotiable" to the crossing, which is permissible under s. 76. As explained in Chapter 1, these words do not affect the transferability of the cheque, but prevent a transferee from acquiring a better title to the cheque than that of his transferor. A "not negotiable" crossed cheque can circulate just as freely as an ordinary, negotiable cheque and so long as no defect of title arises in the circulation of the former the position is exactly the same as with the latter. But once a defect of title occurs in relation to a "not negotiable" cheque, then all subsequent holders take subject to that defect. Hence, the use of "not negotiable" on a crossed cheque is beneficial to the drawer of the cheque, which is why some drawers always add the words when making out cheques, and the cheque books specially printed at the request of company customers often include them. The reason is that a subsequent holder for value after a defect of title has arisen cannot set himself up as a holder in due course, so that, if, for example, the drawer has already stopped payment of the cheque, he cannot be successfully sued by the holder, however innocent the latter may be. The benefits of a "not negotiable" crossing are also available to dividend and interest warrants (see s. 95) and to certain documents analogous to cheques (see ss. 4 and 5 of the Cheques Act 1957).

It has already been noted that money orders and postal orders are not negotiable by origin; and, in discussing s. 8, that when placed on a bill "not negotiable" are words prohibiting transfer: *Hibernian Bank Ltd.* v. *Gysin and Hanson* (1939). Thus, on a bill they have a similar effect to a restrictive indorsement on a cheque. If used alone on an open cheque, the words "not negotiable" have no significance for they must be used in conjunction with either a general or a special crossing.

Protection to collecting banker

82.—(This well-known section, which has been the subject of more litigation than any other section of the Act, was repealed by the Cheques Act 1957 and re-enacted therein but in a wider context.)

CHEQUES ACT 1957

The remainder of this chapter will now deal section by section with:

CHEQUES ACT 1957

(5 & 6 Eliz. 2, c. 36)

An Act to amend the law relating to cheques and certain other instruments.   [17th July, 1957]

Protection of bankers paying unindorsed or irregularly indorsed cheques

1.—(1) Where a banker in good faith and in the ordinary course of business pays a cheque drawn on him which is not indorsed or is irregularly indorsed, he does not, in doing so, incur any liability by reason only of the absence of, or irregularity in, indorsement, and he is deemed to have paid it in due course.

(2) Where a banker in good faith and in the ordinary course of business pays any such instrument as the following, namely:

(a) a document issued by a customer of his which, though not a bill of exchange, is intended to enable a person to obtain payment from him of the sum mentioned in the document;

(b) a draft payable on demand drawn by him upon himself, whether payable at the head office or some other office of his bank;

he does not, in doing so, incur any liability by reason only of the absence of, or irregularity in, indorsement, and the payment discharges the instrument.

This Act emanated from the findings of the Mocatta Committee on Cheque Endorsement set up in April 1955 to see whether it was possible to cut down the laborious task of indorsing many millions of order cheques each year, involving the subsequent labours of both collecting and paying banks in checking these indorsements and getting irregular ones confirmed, and how this could be effected in relation to the framework of the Act of 1882 as then amended. The question had in fact been raised occasionally in earlier years because of the continual increase in the number of cheques used, but it was really brought into the limelight by the appointment of the Mocatta Committee, whose recommendations were largely but (as is so often the case) not exactly followed in the drafting of the Act.

The method adopted was not to abolish indorsements altogether, but as far as practicable to make them redundant by giving protection to banks paying unindorsed or irregularly indorsed cheques, whether crossed or open. As far as the paying bank is concerned, this is achieved by s. 1 of the Act, which applies to cheques, analogous documents (e.g. conditional orders to pay) and internal bank drafts. As will be seen under s. 4 a similar situation obtains in relation to a collecting bank. Parties other than banks are still required to obtain indorsements of cheques which are negotiated. Thus, if A receives a cheque of which he is the payee, he can pay it into his own bank account unindorsed (the great majority of cheques being dealt with in this way). But if he has no bank account and so cashes it with a local tradesman, the latter should insist on the payee's indorsement, both to complete his title under the Act of 1882 and to enable him to pay the cheque into his own account, because in any event collecting banks are still insisting on the indorsement of third party cheques. Where indorsement of a cheque is still necessary, then s. 60 of the Act of 1882 remains of significance to a paying bank where an indorsement has been forged or made without authority. Whilst the position is not clear, it would seem that s. 1 does not cover the case of a forged indorsement, because in such circumstances payment would not be in the ordinary course of business of a paying banker.

As the Act of 1957 introduced a fundamental change in the practice followed by banks for more than a century of insisting on the payee's indorsement on an order cheque, the Committee of London Clearing Bankers, in a memorandum dated September 23rd, 1957, laid down certain rules of practice which they deemed expedient for their own protection. In so far as the banks are voluntarily cutting-down the very widespread protection of the Act this may ultimately redound to their disadvantage, for as these practice rules appear to have become the standard for the ordinary course of banking business any deviation from them could be perilous in that the bank concerned might be held to have thereby forfeited its statutory protection. The rules may be summarised as follows:

(1) Paying banks. Cheques and other instruments presented in the clearings or specially presented, and "house debits" will not be examined for indorsement except when they are combined cheque and receipt forms marked "R"; travellers' cheques; bills of exchange (other than cheques); and promissory notes. Cheques and other instruments cashed at the counter (including those cashed under open credits) still require indorsement or receipt.

(2) Collecting banks. Cheques and other instruments collected for the ostensible payee's account will not be examined for indorsement, or dividend and interest warrants for discharge, with certain exceptions (being those set out in the previous paragraph, and some others). Similarly, cheques and other instruments payable to a bank for credit of a customer's account will not require indorsement or discharge by the payee bank. Where the payee's name is mis-spelt or he is incorrectly designated, no indorsement or discharge will be required unless there are circumstances to suggest that the customer is not the person to whom payment is intended to be made.

Indorsement or discharge will still be required where the cheque or other instrument is being collected for some other account than that of the ostensible payee or of the special indorsee; where the instrument is within the exceptions already mentioned (e.g. a bill of exchange other than a cheque); and where it is payable to joint payees but tendered for credit of an account to which all are not parties (in the reverse situation, i.e. instrument payable to one or more of joint account holders and lodged for credit of the joint account, no indorsement or discharge is required).

(3) Clearing banks which act as collecting agents for non-clearing banks, the Post Office, or Trustee Savings Banks need not examine instruments lodged by such customers for indorsement or discharge, and it may be assumed this will already have been seen to by the customer against whom the collecting agent will have recourse.

(4) Cheques and other instruments exchanged at the counter will require indorsement or discharge, as previously.

(5) All markings in connection with the Exchange Control must in future be placed upon the face of the instrument.

(6) Collecting and paying banks will not accept responsibility for examining receipts on cheques and other instruments incorporating receipt forms unless they bear a bold outline letter "R" on the face of them.

Rights of bankers collecting cheques not indorsed by holders

2.— A banker who gives value for, or has a lien on, a cheque payable to order which the holder delivers to him for collection without indorsing it, has such (if any) rights as he would have had if, upon delivery, the holder had indorsed it in blank.

Where a bank is not merely collecting a cheque for a customer but has some personal financial interest in the cheque, i.e. it has given value for it, or circumstances give the bank a lien on it, so that it is a holder for value to the extent of the sum for which it has that lien, then the bank, if a holder in due course, takes the cheque free from any defect of title of prior parties and can sue in its own name all parties liable on the cheque. Section 2 is designed to preserve this position if the cheque in question bears no indorsement, but it must be noted that it does not apply to cheques irregularly indorsed or to any of the analogous instruments which are not cheques though they figure in ss. 1 (2) and 4 (2) of the Act.

There are four cases where a bank handles a cheque as holder for value (and, where the other conditions in s. 29 (1) are satisfied, as holder in due course): (1) Where a bank has cashed or exchanged a cheque for a customer or any other holder. No difficulties arise here because the bank has bought the cheque and when it collects the cheque it is doing so on its own behalf, not for a customer; (2) If a cheque is paid in for the express purpose of reducing the customer's overdraft: *M'Lean* v. *Clydesdale Banking Co*. (1883) discussed under s.

27; (3) If there is a definite authority or agreement between the bank and its customer that the customer may draw against uncleared items: *Capital and Counties Bank Ltd.* v. *Gordon* (1903); (4) Where the bank has paid cheques against uncleared items as a regular practice. But merely crediting a cheque to an overdrawn account in the ordinary way or allowing a customer to draw against uncleared items as opposed to agreeing with him to do so, thus making the bank bound to pay cheques so drawn, is not enough to constitute a bank a holder in due course or for value. In any event, some banks' paying-in books expressly reserve to the bank the right to refuse to pay against uncleared items. Borderline cases will depend on the circumstances of each particular case. Thus, in *Midland Bank Ltd.* v. *R. V. Harris, Ltd* (1963) there was an agreement between the bank and its customer that the latter could draw against uncleared cheques, including in particular and specifically the two cheques drawn by the defendant (and subsequently "stopped") which were the subject of the action so that the bank was a holder in due course and its claim succeeded.

The point was again considered by the House of Lords in relation to s. 2 in *Westminster Bank Ltd.* v. *Zang* (1966), where a cheque payable to a director named Tilley personally had been paid in by him unindorsed to his company's account, which was overdrawn, and been subsequently dishonoured by the drawer, Zang. The company's bank therefore sued Zang as holders in due course or for value of the cheque. Whilst the case was being heard in the Court of Appeal, Lord DENNING, M.R. succinctly commented that the cashier "ought to have got Tilley to indorse the cheque before paying it to the credit of the company. But he did not do so. Hence all the trouble." It will be seen that this failure to get the indorsement was contrary to the practice rules formulated in 1957, discussed above. The House of Lords held that the cheque was delivered to the bank and received by it "for collection" within the meaning of s. 2 of the Cheques Act 1957, in which the expression was not confined to collection for the payee's own account, but the bank had failed on the evidence to establish that it gave value for the cheque since it had charged interest on the uncleared cheque for four days pending its clearance, and it had not shown either that an agreement on its part to allow the company to draw against uncleared effects should be implied or that it had in fact allowed the company to draw against the cheque; accordingly, the bank had no rights under s. 2 of the Cheques Act 1957: and having received the cheque unindorsed the bank was not "the holder" of it within s. 2 of the Bills of Exchange Act 1882. The bank's claim therefore failed.

Even if the bank did have any rights under s. 2, the Court of Appeal held that it had lost them by returning the cheque to Tilley's solicitors (at their request, for his action against Zang, which proved abortive) but the House of Lords did not consider it necessary to express any opinion on this point. Thus, where a cheque is dishonoured in circumstances in which the bank has given value for, or has a lien on it, then it must not be returned to the customer with, or as, notice of dishonour. The bank should give such notice but retain the cheque and sue the drawer.

It can be advantageous to a bank to claim as holder in due course where there is a possibility that it has been negligent. In *Lloyds Bank Ltd.* v. *Hornby* (1933) a new account was opened with a cheque for £250 against which the customer was allowed to draw before clearance and when the drawer stopped payment of the cheque the bank as holder in due course sued him for the amount advanced against it. He endeavoured to bring in s. 82 [now replaced by s. 4 of the Cheques Act 1957], alleging that the bank had been negligent in opening the account without a proper introduction. It was held that as the bank was a holder in due course, s. 82 was not relevant, and even if the bank had been negligent (which on the facts it was not) it would still succeed provided the negligence was not tantamount to bad faith, for acting without negligence is not a condition of being a holder in due course. Another advantage is that being a holder in due course may assist the bank in the event of the person paying in the cheque becoming bankrupt—see *Re Keever* (1966), discussed in Chapter 5 at page 188.

Unindorsed cheques as evidence of payment

3.— An unindorsed cheque which appears to have been paid by the banker on whom it is drawn is evidence of the receipt by the payee of the sum payable by the cheque.

This section is designed to make a paid unindorsed cheque evidence of receipt by the payee in the same way that a paid indorsed cheque is. The receipt forms on cheques often favoured by companies and local authorities have thus become superfluous, and banks have accordingly sought to cut down their use, but where they still remain they are designated on their face by a denoting letter "R". Like the previous section, s. 3 does not apply to any of the analogous instruments which are not cheques. It does, however, apply to crossed warrants issued under the National Savings Stock Register Regulations 1976 (S.I. 1976 No. 2012) by virtue of r. 22 (2) thereof.

Protection of bankers collecting payment of cheques, etc.

4.—(1) Where a banker, in good faith and without negligence:

    (a) receives payment for a customer of an instrument to which this section applies; or

    (b) having credited a customer's account with the amount of such an instrument, receives payment thereof for himself;

and the customer has no title, or a defective title to the instrument, the banker does not incur any liability to the true owner of the instrument by reason only of having received payment thereof.

(2) This section applies to the following instruments, namely,

    (a) cheques;

    (b) any document issued by a customer of a banker which, though not a bill of exchange, is intended to enable a person to obtain payment from that banker of the sum mentioned in the document;

    (c) any document issued by a public officer which is intended to enable a person to obtain payment from the Paymaster General or the Queen's and Lord Treasurer's Remembrancer of the sum mentioned in the document but is not a bill of exchange;

    (d) any draft payable on demand drawn by a banker upon himself, whether payable at the head office or some other office of his bank.

(3) A banker is not to be treated for the purposes of this section as having been negligent by reason only of his failure to concern himself with the absence of, or irregularity in, indorsement of an instrument.

This important section has replaced with certain extensions the statutory protection conferred on collecting banks by s. 82 of the Act of 1882. That old section was the subject of much litigation, particularly on the phrase "without negligence" and in so far as the wording in s. 82 is repeated in s. 4 that case law is still relevant. However, before examining the section and the cases in detail it is necessary to understand the why and wherefore of this statutory protection. If there were no such protection then every time a bank collected a cheque for a person who was not entitled to it the bank would be liable to the true owner for the tort of conversion, i.e. that the defendant has converted to his own use the property of the plaintiff. Conversion was somewhat modified by the Torts (Interference with Goods) Act 1977, which now subsumes this tort and the various other torts affecting goods under the comprehensive description of "wrongful interference with goods". Conversion is an act of wilful interference, without lawful justification, with any chattel in a manner inconsistent with the right of another, whereby that other is deprived of the use and possession of it. It is thus an attack upon or interference with the plaintiff's right to possess his property, or an assertion by the defendant of a right which is inconsistent with the owner's title. In short, the defendant comes between the plaintiff and his property. Conversion is done in relation to chattels or goods, but for this purpose in the case of cheques the chattel is the piece of paper, the cheque under which the money was collected, but its value is the money received under it. As conversion may be done by an innocent party acting without negligence, i.e. one who genuinely does not know that he is interfering with the true owner's title, such as when an auctioneer or broker unwittingly sells goods for a rogue and is subsequently obliged to make restitution to the true owner, banks would be liable in conversion whenever the collection of cheques had the effect of depriving the true owner of his property. Because of the many millions of cheques collected by banks each year for their customers banks would be in an intolerable situation, were it not for the statutory protection conferred originally by s. 82. There has never been any statutory protection for a bank collecting either bills of exchange other than cheques or promissory notes.

The old protection under s. 82 applied only where a bank collected in good faith and without negligence crossed cheques for a customer, and the protection was extended to analogous instruments which were not cheques by s. 17 of the Revenue Act 1883, supplemented by s. 1 of the Bills of Exchange Act (1882) Amendment Act 1932 as regards bank drafts. In addition, to overcome the decision in *Capital and Counties Bank Ltd.* v. *Gordon* (1903) that the normal banking practice of crediting the customer's account on the day the cheques are paid in instead of waiting until the paying bank has paid them deprived the collecting bank of the protection of s. 82, the Bills of Exchange (Crossed Cheques) Act 1906 was passed. Section 82 and all the foregoing amendments have now been repealed and re-enacted in s. 4 of the Act of 1957 which has been extended to cover both crossed and open cheques and analogous instruments. Section 4 (1) repeats the points that the items must be collected in good faith and without negligence for a customer, with s. 4 (1) (b) carrying the point formerly in the Act of 1906, whilst s. 4 (2) details the instruments in respect of which protection is available, and s. 4 (3) is necessary to preserve the protection in view of the general purpose of the Act, namely, to curtail the indorsement of cheques.

Section 4 is also applied by s. 22 (2) of the National Savings Stock Register Regulations 1976 (S.I. 1976 No. 2012) to any crossed warrant issued under the Regulations.

So far as the collecting bank's protection is concerned it is immaterial whether the words "not negotiable" appear on the cheque or not:

Crumplin v. *London Joint Stock Bank Ltd*. (1913), but, of course, if the bank is collecting for itself and not a customer, then a "not negotiable" crossing on the cheque may defeat the bank's claim where the title of a prior holder is defective.

In good faith

The requirement of good faith has already been noted in connection with s. 60 of the Act of 1882, and there is little likelihood of a lack of it arising in practice.

Without negligence

The great bulk of case law has centred round the words "without negligence", meaning in this sense that the bank has failed to act with reasonable care. In the law of tort "negligence" has two distinct meanings—in the general sense it denotes careless conduct or total or partial inadvertence to the consequences of one's actions, or as it is sometimes expressed "mental indifference to known risks" and this can be a feature in various torts, as here in conversion when its presence will deprive a collecting bank of the statutory protection against the true owner which it would otherwise have had. The other meaning of "negligence" is the specific tort of that name—the most widespread and frequently encountered tort—this requires a legal duty of care on the part of the defendant, a breach by him of that duty (i.e. negligence in the general sense) and non-remote damage arising from that breach. This specific tort of negligence is quite distinct from the tort of conversion to which s. 4 relates. The best known example of the tort of negligence is *M'Alister (or Donoghue)* v. *Stevenson* (1932), the celebrated "snail in the ginger-beer bottle" case, in which the House of Lords laid down that the manufacturer of products intended to reach the ultimate consumer in the form in which they left him with no reasonable possibility of intermediate examination owes a duty of care to that consumer.

From the great amount of case law on "negligence" within the old s. 82 and its successor s. 4 the following are typical examples of circumstances in which a bank forfeited its statutory protection because on the facts it was held to have acted negligently:

(a) *Negligence when opening the account.*—(i) Whilst it is possible for a collecting bank to claim the statutory protection in respect of the very cheque with which the account is opened, the protection will be lost by the bank's failure to take up references when opening the account: *Ladbroke & Co*. v. *Todd* (1914). In this case the plaintiffs posted a cheque crossed "A/c payee only" in payment of a betting win to one Jobson; the cheque was stolen in transit and the thief, posing as Jobson, opened an account at the defendant bank with the cheque, requested its clearance as soon as possible, and then withdrew his balance. Whilst it was held that the bank acted in good faith and that a person becomes a customer with the first transaction, the bank's failure to observe the common practice of obtaining references was held to be negligence, and so the defendant had to repay the proceeds of the cheque.

(ii) Even when references are taken then the bank must ensure that they are genuine, and failure to do so resulted in loss of the statutory protection in *Hampstead Guardians* v. *Barclays Bank Ltd.* (1923). Two orders (which were assumed to be cheques) drawn by the plaintiffs in favour of D. Stewart & Co. were stolen and later on a person posing as Donald Stewart opened an account with the defendant bank and gave as a reference a Mr. Woolf of whom the bank knew nothing, and who gave a satisfactory reference which was a forgery. The bank did not check the name and address of the customer in a directory etc. or check up on the referee, and had to repay the proceeds of the cheques.

Similarly, in *Lumsden & Co.* v. *London Trustee Savings Bank* (1971) where a stockbrokers' clerk had forged his employers' cheques made out to clients and paid them into his account with the defendant bank, it was held that the bank had lost its statutory protection under s. 4 by being negligent with regard to the clerk's references when opening his account; however, as the plaintiff stockbrokers had also been careless when drawing the cheques, the Law Reform (Contributory Negligence) Act 1945 was applied and the damages awarded to the plaintiffs were reduced by 10 per cent. because of their degree of contributory negligence. As regards this last point, although s. 11 of the Torts (Interference with Goods) Act 1977 provides that contributory negligence is no defence in proceedings founded on conversion or on intentional trespass to goods, a bank's right to plead contributory negligence in an action where proof of absence of negligence would be a defence under s. 4 of the Cheques Act 1957 has been reinstated by s. 47 of the Banking Act 1979.

But in *Marfani & Co., Ltd.* v. *Midland Bank Ltd.* (1968), where the plaintiff company's office manager, K, prepared a cheque for £3,000 payable to one E., had it duly signed and then opened an account with it at a branch of the defendant bank by posing as E and giving as a reference a man who knew him by that false name—thereafter he withdrew the proceeds and left for Pakistan—the Court of Appeal held that the bank had not been negligent. In particular, it decided that the following facts did not amount to negligence:—

(a) that the bank had not enquired any further about the referee (a customer of the bank for some six years) or had acted on only the one reference;

(b) that the bank had not asked for identification by production of a document (e.g. a passport) or had not enquired as to the new customer's employment in view of the reference concerning him;

(c) that the cheque had been cleared before the reference was received.

However, one of the judges, CAIRNS, J., (as he then was) ended on a note of caution: "It may be that competition between banks for customers tempts them to relax to some extent precautions taken on opening a new account. We have heard that former decisions of the courts adverse to banks have had the effect of causing them to tighten their rules about the inquiries to be made when an account is opened. I should be sorry if the effect of our decision in this case were to encourage any loosening of those rules. If the defendant bank here exercised sufficient care, it was in my view only just sufficient".

(iii) Failure to ascertain the occupation of the husband of a married woman customer: *Lloyds Bank Ltd.* v. *E. B. Savory & Co.* (1933); see below.

(b) *Negligence when collecting cheques.* — This is much more frequent, as it can occur at any time and with any sort of account. It may be negligence not to observe the account of a customer from time to time and consider whether it is a proper or a suspicious account. For example, such a scrutiny may reveal that a customer has changed his employer. Negligence has been constituted in this wide field by:

(i) Collecting without inquiry for the private account of an official of a company a cheque payable to the company and indorsed by that official: *A. L. Underwood, Ltd.* v. *Bank of Liverpool* (1924), where the official concerned was the sole director of what is popularly known as a "one-man" company (legally there is no such thing—see Chapter 4—and in any event the company is a separate legal person).

(ii) Collecting without inquiry for the private account of a partner a cheque payable to the firm. In *Baker* v. *Barclays Bank Ltd.* (1955) one partner had misappropriated some cheques payable to the firm, indorsed them in the firm's name and handed them to a third party whose bank, the defendant, had collected them. The bank manager saw the cheques and queried them but was content with a rather unsatisfactory explanation and did not make further inquiries. It was held that the other partner, the plaintiff, could sue in conversion for his wrongful exclusion from the joint property and the bank, having lost its statutory protection, was liable.

(iii) Collecting for the private account of an official cheques payable to him in his official capacity, e.g. a corporation rate or rent collector: *Ross* v. *London County Westminster and Parr's Bank* (1919), where the official concerned was the officer in charge of the administration of the estates of deceased Canadian soldiers. It will be in order if the official is specially authorised to act in this way. Similarly, in *Bute* v. *Barclays Bank Ltd.* (1954) it was held to be negligence on the bank's part to collect for the private account of an agent a warrant made payable to him in his capacity of agent, namely, "D. McGaw for Marquess of Bute".

(iv) Collecting without inquiry cheques drawn by a company or firm in favour of third parties and paid in for the credit of an employee, or of the wife of an employee, of the drawer: *Lloyds Bank Ltd.* v. *E. B. Savory & Co.* (1933) in which the inter-branch credit system was involved, as well as failure to ascertain the husband's occupation. In this case the bank collected without inquiry numerous cheques payable to bearer drawn by a firm of stockbrokers and intended to be applied in paying jobbers' account for the account of one employee of the firm or for that of the wife of another employee, both these accounts being at country branches which were ignorant of the facts because the cheques themselves were paid in at various City branches. The House of Lords, by a majority of 3 to 2, held that the bank was liable because the failure of the branches which received the cheques in the first instance to inform the crediting branches of the names of the drawers of the cheques and the failure of the managers of the crediting branches to make sufficient inquiries when opening the accounts amounted to negligence. A noteworthy feature of the case was the use of the failure of the bank's officials to observe the bank's own internal rules and regulations as evidence of negligence and there have been later occasions when a bank has been "hoist with its own petard". As a postscript, it is interesting to note that in the *Marfani* case in 1968 (see p. 432, *ante)*, DIPLOCK, L.J., (as he then was) said of *Savory's* case: "That case, as all other cases, depended on its own particular facts. The frauds had gone on for a very long time. There were many other matters caclulated to arouse suspicion in the social conditions of the 1920s. It was decided on expert evidence, not of what is now current banking practice, but of what it was nearly forty years ago. I find it no more than an illustration of the application of the general principle that a banker must exercise reasonable care in all the circumstances of the case."

In *Nu-Stilo Footwear, Ltd.* v. *Lloyds Bank Ltd.* (1956) the plaintiff company's secretary opened an account with the bank under an assumed name, giving his real name as referee. The first cheque paid in was for £172 in his own favour, but the second cheque was a third-party cheque for £550. It was held that in the circumstances the bank had not acted negligently when opening the account or in collecting the first cheque which was not so large as to arouse suspicion, but it had been negligent in failing to make proper inquiry before collecting the second cheque.

(v) Collecting without inquiry a cheque for the private account of an attorney or agent made payable to him but drawn by him on behalf of his principal: *Midland Bank Ltd* v. *Reckitt* (1933); in which Sir Harold Reckitt's fraudulent attorney drew a series of cheques on Sir Harold's account and paid them into his own account with the Midland Bank, with whom he had an overdraft. The House of Lords held that the bank had lost the protection of s. 82 by its negligence in failing to inquire as to the attorney's authority to make these payments into his own account, and that the ratification clause in the power whereby the principal agreed to ratify whatsoever the attorney should do did not affect the principal's right to maintain the action.

In an earlier case concerning an agent, *Morison* v. *London County and Westminster Bank Ltd.* (1914) the plaintiff's clerk, who had authority to sign *per pro*, drew a number of cheques payable to "Selves" or to himself and paid them into his private account with the defendant bank. The Court of Appeal held that, although the bank had been negligent in collecting the earlier cheques, the fact that such cheques had not been questioned over a period of more than two years was enough to negative negligence in the collection of later, similar cheques. The bank's appeal was therefore allowed because sufficient time had elapsed during which the plaintiff had received back his passbook and cheques and had not challenged the validity of the cheques that the bank was entitled to assume there was no cause for suspicion or inquiry. However, this "lulling to sleep" doctrine did not receive approval in subsequent cases and must now be considered doubtful.

(vi) Collecting without inquiry for the account of one company a cheque payable to another company: *London and Montrose Shipbuilding and Repairing Co.* v. *Barclays Bank Ltd.* (1926). This course will be in order if the cheque is specially indorsed by the payee company to another company, or if the bank holds general instructions from its customers on the matter, which it may do where both companies are part of the same group.

(vii) Collecting without inquiry cheques payable to the collecting bank for the private account of an employee of the drawer when that employee has signed the cheques: *Lloyds Bank Ltd.* v. *Chartered Bank of India, Australia and China* (1929). Here, the chief accountant of the plaintiff's Bombay branch (with authority to draw) drew cheques on his employers and paid them into his private account with the defendant bank, whence much of the money was soon paid out to stockbrokers. The defendant bank made no inquiries and the Court of Appeal held that it had lost its statutory protection through negligence. It is interesting to note that one of the judges, SANKEY L.J. commented, "In my view, a bank cannot be held to be liable for negligence merely because they have not subjected an account to a microscopic examination. It is not expected that officials of banks should also be amateur detectives".

(c) *"A/c payee" cheques.*—These words have no statutory significance because neither the Act of 1882 nor the Act of 1957 mentions them. They are not binding on the paying bank and do not affect the transferability or negotiability of the cheque: *National Bank Ltd.* v. *Silke* (1891), but their use has become fairly widespread (some payees ask for cheques to be crossed "a/c payee" e.g. cheques payable to the Post Office in settlement of telephone accounts). Consequently, the collecting bank will disregard them at its peril—after all, it is the collecting bank and not the paying bank which is in a position to see the direction is obeyed. Thus, in *Bevan* v. *National Bank Ltd.* (1906) it was said that collecting a cheque crossed "A/c payee" for someone other than the specified payee would be negligence (though on the facts relating to the two accounts the bank was held not negligent) and this was followed in *House Property Company of London* v. *London County and Westminster Bank* (1915) where the cheque was in fact payable to a specified payee "or bearer" and the bank was held liable. On the other hand, in *Importers Co.* v. *Westminster Bank Ltd.* (1927) the Court of Appeal held that it was not negligence for an English bank to collect cheques so crossed for a foreign bank, which was its customer, where the "A/c payee" originally referred to that foreign bank's customer.

Sometimes the phrase "account payee only" is used, and this was treated as the same as "account payee" by the Judicial Committee of the Privy Council in *Universal Guarantee Pty., Ltd.* v. *National Bank of Australasia, Ltd.* (1965). However, an argument not so far resolved is that a cheque crossed "account payee" could be credited to a joint account so long as the person named in the cheque is one of the parties to the account, whereas if crossed "account payee only" it ought not to be so credited.

(d) *Cheques collected and paid by the same bank.*—Where one bank both collects and pays a cheque then that bank must uphold its statutory protection in both capacities in order to avoid liability, i.e. it must act within s. 4 when collecting and within s. 60 of the Act of 1882 or s. 1 of the Act of 1957, as well as s. 80 of the Act of 1882 if the cheque is crossed, when paying. This was established in *Carpenters' Company* v. *The British Mutual Banking Company* (1937) where a dishonest clerk of the plaintiffs, a City of London livery company, stole cheques drawn by them on the defendant bank and paid them into his private account with that bank (which, in fact, had only one office). The Court of Appeal held that the bank was negligent in not inquiring why the clerk was paying his employer's cheques into his private account and was therefore liable as collecting bank, even though as paying bank it had paid the cheques "in the ordinary course of business" within s. 60. In view of the extensions to the old s. 82 now made by s. 4 it would seem that a similar situation arises in respect of open cheques and analogous instruments.

It will be seen that the connecting thread running through all the above cases is failure by the bank to make inquiries, or sometimes being too easily satisfied by the answers received and so not making further inquiries. In some of the cases it is obvious that the customer's transaction was not one he would normally be expected to make, and therefore the circumstances as a whole in which the transaction was done, set against the background of the bank's knowledge of its customer's affairs, ought to have alerted the bank. This point was expressed judicially in *Commissioners of Taxation* v. *English, Scottish and Australian Bank* (1920) as: "the test of negligence is whether the transaction of paying in any given cheque, coupled with the circumstances antecedent and present, was so out of the ordinary course that it ought to have aroused doubts in the bankers' mind, and caused them to make inquiry."

A case in which a bank was too easily satisfied with the reply and so was held to be negligent is *Motor Traders Guarantee Corporation, Ltd.* v. *Midland Bank Ltd.* (1937) where the past banking history of the customer who had induced the plaintiffs to make out a cheque was unsatisfactory and the bank's cashier was satisfied with the explanation given, whereas by an internal regulation of the bank the matter should have been referred to the manager. Whilst it was held that a customer is not entitled to require literal performance of such regulations, on the facts, had the matter been referred to the manager, he would no doubt not have been satisfied and would have made further inquiries.

Against this rather long list of cases in which banks have been unsuccessful, there are a number of cases in which inquiries having been made and a satisfactory answer having been given, banks have retained their statutory protection. For example:

(1) *Slingsby* v. *Westminster Bank Ltd.* (1931), in which the bank manager made inquiries of the solicitor paying in the item and

received answers which appeared to harmonize perfectly with information he had previously received from a man then in the highest repute, so s. 82 was successfully relied on. (The item was a warrant in respect of a half-year's interest on five per cent. War Stock— see s. 95.)

(2) *Smith and Baldwin* v. *Barclays Bank Ltd*. (1944), in which the bank collected for a private individual cheques payable to the Argus Press, under which name the plaintiffs were trading but had not been registered under the Registration of Business Names Act 1916. When the bank queried these cheques its customer stated he had bought the business and produced a certificate under the Act (he himself having registered the name of Argus Press), and it was held that this was a sufficient explanation to preserve the bank's statutory protection, and the true owners' claim failed.

(3) *Penmount Estates, Ltd*. v. *National Provincial Bank Ltd*. (1945), in which the bank collected a cheque from the War Damage Commission payable to the plaintiffs for a solicitor, who answered an inquiry by saying he had arranged for cheques from the Commission to be indorsed by his clients and paid into his clients' account and he would then send them his own cheque after deducting his fees. The judge commented that in the light of after events the solicitor's explanation might sound improbable to a suspicious person but in his opinion bank officials exercising their duties under s. 82 had not to be abnormally suspicious, and moneys must be paid out, among a multiplicity of transactions, with reasonable despatch: accordingly, the claim against the bank failed.

(4) A last, and slightly different example, in that the bank was held not to have been put on inquiry at all by the circumstances, is *Orbit Mining and Trading Co., Ltd*. v. *Westminster Bank Ltd*. (1963), where the plaintiff company had an account with Midland Bank Ltd. on which any two directors could sign. One director, W, was often abroad and at the request of E, another director, signed a few cheque forms in blank believing they would be used for the company's business. E completed the cheques to "Cash or order" and counter-signed them with his own illegible signature, similarly indorsed them and paid them into his private account with the defendant bank, which did not know of E's connection with the plaintiff. Having decided that the instruments as drawn were not cheques but were analogous documents in respect of which statutory protection was available, the Court of Appeal held that as the drawer's signature was illegible and indorsement was not needed there was nothing to connect the one signature with the other which required scrutiny by the cashier, and the plaintiff's claim failed.

In conclusion, although it may appear that on the whole the Courts have leant rather heavily on collecting banks as regards negligence, were it not for s. 4 (and its predecessor, s. 82) collecting banks would have no protection at all against the true owner when circumstances amounted to the tort of conversion. The statutory protection conferred by s. 4 takes away from a plaintiff who has been deprived of his property his right to a successful action in tort, and this deprivation is offset by the conditions upon which Parliament has made the protection depend. Whilst absolute protection might have been conferred, that would be to condone negligence; as this course has not been adopted, in the last resort, banks, like the rest of the community, must learn from their mistakes and sometimes pay for their learning.

For a customer

The other pre-requisite for the collecting bank's statutory protection is that it must act for a "customer" (though no statutory definition of the word is given). However, for the ordinary business of banking it is broadly possible to define a customer as a person who keeps an account with the bank, whether current, deposit or savings account. It has already been noted that if an account is opened, as it often is, by paying in a cheque which is accepted for collection, that first transaction creates the relationship of banker and customer, and the banker, in the absence of negligence as to references and so on, will be protected in respect of that cheque.

The distinction to be borne in mind in this connection is that if the bank cashes or exchanges the cheque, then it has bought it and will thereafter be collecting for itself, not for a customer, so that s. 4 does not apply. Consequently, the bank runs various risks, mainly that the cheque will not be paid, though provided the bank is a holder in due course (and here a "not negotiable" crossing may cause difficulty), it can enforce payment against all parties liable on the cheque. No device such as passing the transaction through an impersonal account styled "Sundry Customers", or "Sundry Persons" or similar nomenclature will bring the bank within the terms of s. 4.

In *Great Western Railway Co.* v. *London and County Banking Co. Ltd.* (1901) a rate collector by false pretences obtained a "not negotiable" crossed cheque from the railway payable to his order and took it to the bank, which at his request paid part of the amount of the cheque into the account of one of its customers and handed the balance in cash to the collector. It transpired that the bank had been cashing cheques for the collector in a similar manner for twenty years, but he had no account or pass-book there. The House of Lords held that the collector was not a customer of the bank, and as he had no title to the cheque, neither had the bank and it had to refund to the railway the amount of the cheque.

A bizarre case concerning whether or not the relationship of banker and customer had come into existence is *Robinson* v. *Midland Bank Ltd.* (1925). The plaintiff's wife was found in compromising circumstances with a man referred to in the case as Mr. A, due to a conspiracy by three people who thereby obtained a cheque for £150,000 from Mr. A. Neither the plaintiff nor his wife was a party to this blackmail plot. The cheque, which had been made payable to a firm of solicitors, was then specially indorsed by one of the conspirators without the authority of the firm in favour of the plaintiff and used to open an account in the plaintiff's name with the bank. Subsequently the person who had opened the account withdrew £130,000 and gave £25,000 to the plaintiff. When the plaintiff later discovered that £150,000 had originally been deposited in his name he sued the bank for the remaining £125,000. The Court of Appeal held that a man could not open an account at a bank unless he himself intended to become a customer or unless an agent opened the account on his behalf and he subsequently ratified the agent's act; the facts disclosed no evidence of any intention by the plaintiff to open an account and his claim was dismissed.

Finally, although it did not concern s. 4, *Rowlandson* v. *National Westminster Bank Ltd.* (1978) is an interesting case that highlights the risks of opening an account in circumstances that put the bank on notice that it is a trust account. A lady wished to give £500 to each of her 4 grandchildren, the plaintiffs, who were minors. She wrote out four cheques for £500 payable to them individually and, accompanied by her son, M, the plaintiffs' father, she took the four cheques to a branch of the defendant bank and instructed the bank to place the cheques on deposit for the plaintiffs. Neither she nor M nor any of the plaintiffs had an individual account at that branch but there were accounts held there by other members of the family, including another son, A. She did not specify in detail what she wanted done or how it was to be done. The bank opened an account, which it described as a "trust account" for the plaintiffs, in the name of A and a third son, G, and to which it credited the four cheques. A fraudulently withdrew all the money for his own purposes. HELD, once the bank opened what was clearly a trust account, it was under a fiduciary duty to the plaintiffs, the beneficiaries of the trust, and was liable to them if it knowingly assisted in a dishonest and fraudulent design on the part of the trustees. Since the bank failed to question or prevent the withdrawals which should have put it on enquiry, it was liable to the plaintiffs for the total sum of £2000.

Application of certain provisions of Bills of Exchange Act 1882 to instruments not being bills of exchange

5.— The provisions of the Bills of Exchange Act 1882 relating to crossed cheques shall, so far as applicable, have effect in relation to instruments (other than cheques) to which the last foregoing section applies as they have effect in relation to cheques.

This section is necessary to bring the analogous instruments mentioned in the Act within the crossed cheques sections (76–81) of the Bills of Exchange Act 1882, since the earlier enactments in 1882 and 1932 which had done this are repealed by s. 6 (3) of the present Act. The law is not changed, but merely tidied up: in short, a bank paying a crossed analogous instrument has the benefit of s. 80, but if it is an open one the bank does not have the benefit of s. 60 where it is paid over the counter though it may be protected by s. 19 of the Stamp Act, 1853; a bank collecting analogous instruments, whether crossed or open, is given protection by the preceding section, s. 4.

Post Office money orders and postal orders

Money orders and postal orders, the latter being money orders for small sums in a special form prescribed by the Post Office, are not negotiable, and though, under Post Office schemes, they may be crossed generally or specially (see comment on s. 76), they do not come within the crossed cheques sections of the Act of 1882 or within the Cheques Act 1957.

As regards money orders, collecting banks have no protection at all. The Post Office has the right to return money orders to the bank presenting them if they are irregular and to deduct their amount from sums due to the bank. For this reason the Institute of Bankers recommended a long time ago that collecting banks should advise their customers that payment and credit to their account in the case of money orders are provisional only. The bank has the right to debit the customer's account with the amount of refunds on money orders claimed by the Post Office: *London and Provincial Bank* v. *Golding* (1918); but there is always the risk that the account may have been closed or reduced to a small dormant balance and the customer will be untraceable.

As regards postal orders, when stamped and presented by a bank, the Post Office will pay them without formalities: the Post Office (Postal Order) Scheme 1971, para. 10. Collecting banks receive protection under the Post Office Act 1953 as follows:

Section 21 (3). Any person acting as a banker in the British postal area who, in collecting in that capacity for any principal, has received payment or been allowed by the Postmaster General [or the authority established by section 6 of the Post Office Act 1969] on account in respect of any postal order, or of any document purporting to be a postal order, shall not incur liability to anyone except that principal by reason of having received the payment or allowance or having held or presented the order or document for payment; but this subsection shall not relieve any principal for whom any such order or document has been so held or presented of any liability in respect his possession of the order or document or of the proceeds thereof.

The words in the brackets were added by the Post Office Act 1969 which replaced the old government office of Postmaster General with an independent public authority, the Post Office.

This section, however, does not overcome the operation of the decision in *Capital and Counties Bank Ltd.* v. *Gordon* (1903) which, as already discussed, has been statutorily excluded in the case of cheques and analogous instruments. In practice, banks credit their customer's account with the amount of postal orders before collecting them, and thereby appear to be collecting for themselves and not for a principal (the customer), so losing the protection of s. 21 (3). Thus, banks will be liable to the true owner if the customer has no title or a defective title to the postal order, whether crossed or open.

Construction, saving and repeal

6.—(1) This Act shall be construed as one with the Bills of Exchange Act 1882.

(2) The foregoing provisions of this Act do not make negotiable any instrument which, apart from them is not negotiable.

[(3) and the Schedule to which it referred were repealed by the Statute Law (Repeals) Act 1974 on the grounds that they were no longer of practical utility.]

This section deals with the position of the Cheques Act 1957, in relation to its background of the general law on negotiable instruments. The present Act has to be read in conjunction with the Bills of Exchange Act 1882, because although it is an important amending Act, in itself it is of a fragmentary nature and like a piece of a jig-saw puzzle it has to be put into the picture as a whole set out in the Act of 1882. Section 6 (2) merely repeats a provision in the repealed s. 17 of the Revenue Act 1883, and its aim is to show that the Act does not create new categories of negotiable instruments unintentionally.

Provisions as to Northern Ireland

7.—This Act extends to Northern Ireland but, for the purposes of section six of the Government of Ireland Act 1920, so much of the provisions of this Act as relates to, or affects, instruments other than negotiable instruments shall be deemed to be provisions of an Act passed before the appointed day within the meaning of that section.

Whilst the Act applies only to England, Wales, Scotland and Northern Ireland, similar legislation has been passed as follows in order to obtain uniformity:

(a) In the Isle of Man, The Bills of Exchange Act 1958.

(b) In the Channel Islands, The Cheques (Jersey) Law 1957, and The Bills of Exchange (Guernsey) Law 1958.

(c) In the Republic of Ireland, The Cheques Act 1959.

Short title and commencement

8.—(1) This Act may be cited as the Cheques Act 1957.

(2) This Act shall come into operation at the expiration of a period of three months beginning with the day on which it is passed.

The Act came into operation on October 17th, 1957.

Schedule

[This has been repealed—see comment on s. 6.]

Chapter 14

Promissory Notes and Supplementary Matters

BILLS OF EXCHANGE ACT 1882, SECTIONS 83–100

PART IV

PROMISSORY NOTES

Promissory note defined

83.—(1) A promissory note is an unconditional promise in writing made by one person to another signed by the maker, engaging to pay, on demand or at a fixed or determinable future time, a sum certain in money, to, or to the order of, a specified person or to bearer.

(2) An instrument in the form of a note payable to maker's order is not a note within the meaning of this section unless and until it is indorsed by the maker.

(3) A note is not invalid by reason only that it contains also a pledge of collateral security with authority to sell or dispose thereof.

(4) A note which is, or on the face of it purports to be, both made and payable within the British Islands is an inland note. Any other note is a foreign note.

Promissory notes other than bank notes are not very widely used in modern commercial life. The definition of a promissory note in s. 83 has much in common with that of a bill of exchange in s. 3, the principal difference being that a note is a promise to pay and has only two parties, the maker who is liable to pay the note, and the payee (or holder in the case of a bearer note) who is entitled to the money it represents; whereas a bill of exchange is an order to pay a specified person or bearer addressed by one person to another person. A promissory note is really a glorified I.O.U. The latter is not a negotiable instrument, carries no stamp duty, and is merely evidence of an account stated between the parties, but if it includes further words importing a promise to pay it may constitute a promissory note. Since 1st February 1971, under the Finance Act 1970 all promissory notes have been free of stamp duty.

The features in the definition, viz "unconditional", "writing", the time element, and the "sum certain in money" have already been discussed in connection with s. 3. Like a bill of exchange, a promissory note must not be tied to any other act than the payment of money, and this is illustrated by a recent Scottish case *Dickie* v. *Singh* (1974), where the document in question read: "I, . . ., do hereby agree to pay . . . the sum of £950 to be paid at the rate of £50 per month. First payment on the first day of every month commencing 1 February, 1969. Also the present staff to be employed and paid by myself for the next two weeks (from 20 January, 1969)." The document was duly signed and delivered by the maker. It was held that the document was not a promissory note. As regards s. 83 (2) a notice payable to the maker's order is not a promissory note unless and until it is converted into a note payable to bearer by the maker's indorsement, because otherwise the right and the liability of the maker correspond and cancel each other out (see s. 61 for this factor in relation to bills of exchange). The effect of s. 83 (3) is to allow greater flexibility in the use of notes, which can, for example, be accompanied by a deposit of stocks and shares or of title deeds. Sometimes a series of promissory notes payable at intervals may be taken as collateral security for a mortgage or charge, so that if necessary they can be sued on individually without calling in the entire mortgage or charge. In practice, however, payment of a debt by instalments is more likely to be effected by taking a series of appropriately post-dated cheques from the borrower. The distinction between inland and foreign notes in s. 83 (4) is paralleled in the case of bills of exchange by s. 4, which also defines "British Islands".

Example of a promissory note

> 1001, King Street,
> London
> 1st April 1980
>
> £1,000-00
> I promise to pay Charles Dawson on demand the sum of One thousand pounds only, value received.
>
> Arthur Brown

For another example of a promissory note, one can simply look at a Bank of England note. However, bank notes differ in some important respects from ordinary promissory notes, particularly in that they may be re-issued after payment, and in so far as the Bank of England is concerned its notes are part of the currency of the realm and are put on a special statutory basis. As a result of the Bank Charter Act 1844 the Bank of England came to have the sole right to issue banknotes in England or Wales. Some English banks issue their own notes in the Island of Man and the Channel Islands but the best known private bank notes in England are the decorative ones issued by the Scottish banks, to whom the Act of 1844 did not apply.

Delivery necessary

84.—A promissory note is inchoate and incomplete until delivery thereof to the payee or bearer.

Unless and until put into circulation, a promissory note is ineffectual, because there is no one in a position to sue the maker.

Joint and several notes

85.—(1) A promissory note may be made by two or more makers, and they may be liable thereon jointly, or jointly and severally, according to its tenor.

(2) Where a note runs "I promise to pay" and is signed by two or more persons it is deemed to be their joint and several note.

Section 85 (1) is in contrast to the position regarding acceptance of bills of exchange by two or more acceptors, who are liable jointly, but not jointly and severally. A promissory note may read "We jointly promise to pay", in which case there is only one debt, and before the Civil Liability (Contribution) Act 1978 (see p. 95, *ante*) an action against one party barred an action against the other(s); or it may read "We jointly and severally promise to pay", in which case all or any of the makers can be sued, and an unsatisfied judgment against one does not bar an action against the other(s). By s. 85 (2) a note reading "I promise to pay" but signed by two or more persons is a joint and several note. On the other hand, a note reading "We promise to pay" and signed by two or more persons is a joint note. Makers cannot be liable in the alternative, and adding a new maker to a joint and several note is a material alteration within s. 64. It was held by the Court of Appeal in *Wauthier* v. *Wilson* (1912) that where a father and his son, who was an infant, gave a joint and several promissory note in respect of a loan to the son, by virtue of the Infants Relief Act 1874 the son was not liable; but the father was liable as principal.

Note payable on demand

86.—(1) Where a note payable on demand has been indorsed, it must be presented for payment within a reasonable time of the indorsement. If it be not so presented the indorser is discharged.

(2) In determining what is a reasonable time, regard shall be had to the nature of the instrument, the usage of trade, and the facts of the particular case.

(3) Where a note payable on demand is negotiated, it is not deemed to be overdue, for the purpose of affecting the holder with defects of title of which he had no notice, by reason that it appears that a reasonable time for presenting it for payment has elapsed since its issue.

"Payable on demand" has here the same connotation as it has in relation to bills of exchange, by the combined effect of s. 10 and s. 89. It will be observed that s. 86 (1) and (2) are similar in content to s. 45 (2), which deals with bills payable on demand. Section 86 (3), however, makes a variation from the position laid down in s. 36 (2) and (3) as regards bills payable on demand, which cease to be negotiable when overdue, for such bills are intended to be paid immediately. In contrast, promissory notes payable on demand are often intended to be in the nature of a continuing security, and so the holder taking a note which has been in circulation an unreasonable length of time can still acquire a good title as against the maker, even though any indorsers may have been discharged by s. 86 (1).

Presentment of note for payment

87.— (1) Where a promissory note is in the body of it made payable at a particular place, it must be presented for payment at that place in order to render the maker liable. In any other case, presentment for payment is not necessary in order to render the maker liable.

(2) Presentment for payment is necessary in order to render the indorser of a note liable.

(3) Where a note is in body of it made payable at a particular place, presentment at that place is necessary in order to render an indorser liable; but when a place of payment is indicated by way of memorandum only, presentment at that place is sufficient to render the indorser liable, but a presentment to the maker elsewhere, if sufficient in other respects shall also suffice.

If a note is not made payable at a particular place, the holder of it can sue the maker without any prior presentment or demand. If the note is expressed in the body of it to be payable at a particular place, e.g. a bank (though in practice a cheque is far more likely to be issued than a note), then the note must be presented there to render the maker liable. In any event, presentment for payment is necessary to render an indorser liable.

Liability of maker

88.— The maker of a promissory note by making it:

(1) Engages that he will pay it according to its tenor;

(2) Is precluded from denying to a holder in due course the existence of the payee and his then capacity to indorse.

The maker of a promissory note is the person at all times primarily liable on the note, and thus in general is in a similar position to the acceptor of a bill of exchange. The payee of a note who indorses it, or the first indorser of it, is in a similar position to the drawer of an accepted bill of exchange. This is emphasised by the next section, s. 89.

As already mentioned in Chapter 1 under "mistake" (page 21), it may be possible to avoid liability on a bill or note by pleading "*non est factum*", provided the person signing has not been negligent. Thus, in *Foster* v. *Mackinnon* (1869) an old man of feeble sight was induced, without any negligence on his part, to sign his name on the back of a bill by a fraudulent statement that it was a railway guarantee which, in fact, he had undertaken to sign, and it was held that he was not liable on the bill.

A later case concerning a promissory note was decided the same way, in so far as nothing in the Bills of Exchange Act 1882 had changed the position since *Foster* v. *Mackinnon*. This case was *Lewis* v. *Clay* (1897), the facts of which were that Lord William Nevill produced to Clay, who had just come of age, some documents entirely covered with blotting paper except for four blank spaces cut in it, and explained that the hidden documents concerned a private family matter and that his own signature required witnessing, and so Clay signed his name in the blank spaces. In reality, the documents were promissory notes totalling £11,113 signed by Clay as joint maker with Lord William in favour of Lewis, on the strength of which Lord William obtained money from Lewis. It was held that the defendant was not negligent in placing confidence in the statement made to him and in signing his name as he did and so was not liable, for he had no contracting mind and his signature obtained by untrue statements fraudulently made to documents of whose existence he had no knowledge could not bind him.

Application of Part II to notes

89.— (1) Subject to the provisions in this part, and except as by this section provided, the provisions of this Act relating to bills of exchange apply, with the necessary modifications, to promissory notes.

(2) In applying these provisions the maker of a note shall be deemed

to correspond with the acceptor of a bill, and the first indorser of a note shall be deemed to correspond with the drawer of an accepted bill payable to the drawer's order.

(3) The following provisions as to bills do not apply to notes; namely, provisions relating to:

(a) Presentment for acceptance;

(b) Acceptance;

(c) Acceptance supra protest;

(d) Bills in a set.

(4) Where a foreign note is dishonoured, protest thereof is unnecessary.

Bills of exchange and promissory notes are intersecting circles, and so, apart from certain distinguishing features of notes, this section provides that in the area of common ground the Act's provisions in respect of bills apply also to notes, thereby saving the repetition in this part of the Act of earlier sections. Whilst it is not necessary to protest a dishonoured foreign note, it is prudent to do so as it may be that action has subsequently to be taken in a foreign country whose laws require protest in these circumstances.

PART V

SUPPLEMENTARY

Good faith

90.—A thing is deemed to be done in good faith within the meaning of this Act, where it is in fact done honestly, whether it is done negligently or not.

In other words, to upset good faith evidence is required of dishonesty or fraud, not merely of negligence or carelessness.

Signature

91.—(1) Where by this Act, any instrument or writing is required to be signed by any person, it is not necessary that he should sign it with his own hand, but it is sufficient if his signature is written thereon by some other person by or under his authority.

(2) In the case of a corporation where, by this Act, any instrument or writing is required to be signed, it is sufficient if the instrument or writing be sealed with the corporate seal.

But nothing in this section shall be construed as requiring the bill or note of a corporation to be under seal.

Signing of an instrument does not have to be done personally, but may be done on behalf of a party by an authorised agent, and in the case of corporation signatures may be either by such authorised signatories or by the affixing of the corporate seal in the prescribed manner.

Computation of time

92.— Where, by this Act, the time limited for doing any act or thing is less than three days, in reckoning time, non-business days are excluded.

"Non-business days" for the purposes of this Act mean:

(a) [Saturday] Sunday, Good Friday, Christmas Day;

(b) A bank holiday under [the Banking and Financial Dealings Act 1971];

(c) A day appointed by Royal proclamation as a public fast or thanksgiving day;

(d) a day declared by an order under section 2 of the Banking and Financial Dealings Act 1971 to be a non-business day.

Any other day is a business day.

This section is relevant, for example, in giving notice of dishonour under s. 49 (12), and in presentment to an acceptor for honour under s. 67 (2).

Saturday was made a non-business day and inserted in paragraph (a) of this section by s. 3 (1) of the Banking and Financial Dealings Act 1971 which thus gave statutory recognition to the five-day week already adopted by banks. The amendment in paragraph (b) and the new paragraph (d) were effected by s. 4 of the Act of 1971. As regards paragraph (b), see pages 342–3, *ante*. As regards paragraph (d), s. 2 (1) of the Act of 1971 gives the Treasury, when it appears necessary or expedient in the national interest, power to order by statutory instrument a suspension of financial dealings on a day specified in the order, and by s. 2 (4) contravention of such an order is made a criminal offence. Section 4 (3) provides: "An order under section 2 above may be made with respect to a bank holiday or other day which is a non-business day for the purposes of enactments relating to bills of exchange and promissory notes or with respect to a business day; but if a day specified under section 2 (1) is otherwise a business day for those purposes, the order may declare it a non-business day." Accordingly, s. 4 (4) adds the new paragraph (d) to s. 92 of the Act of 1882.

When noting equivalent to protest

93.— For the purposes of this Act, where a bill or note is required to be protested within a specified time or before some further proceeding is taken, it is sufficient that the bill has been noted for protest before the expiration of the specified time or the taking of the proceeding; and the formal protest may be extended at any time thereafter as of the date of the noting.

As noting is stage one in the procedure of protesting a bill or note, where noting is accomplished within a prescribed period, this is sufficient because the formal protest, being stage two, can be carried out at any subsequent time.

Protest when notary not accessible

94.— Where a dishonoured bill or note is authorised or required to be protested, and the services of a notary cannot be obtained at the place where the bill is dishonoured, any householder or substantial resident of the place may, in the presence of two witnesses, give a certificate, signed by them, attesting the dishonour of the bill, and the certificate shall in all respects operate as if it were a formal protest of the bill.

The form given in Schedule 1 to this Act may be used with necessary modifications, and if used shall be sufficient.

As notaries are far from numerous and may be difficult to find, particularly outside large cities, s. 94 allows a householder's protest to be used in lieu, a specimen being set out in Schedule 1.

Dividend warrants may be crossed

95.— The provisions of this Act as to crossed cheques shall apply to a warrant for the payment of dividend.

Dividend warrants are orders drawn by a company on its bank (often on a separate Dividend Account) for the payment of dividends declared on its stocks and shares as a means of distributing profits, and are normally in the form of cheques. Section 95 clearly envisages that dividend warrants are not merely a form of cheque (though in practice they almost invariably are; occasionally they may be conditional orders). It was designed to make it clear that dividend warrants are within the crossed cheques sections of the Act (now ss. 76–81), and a similar provision is made in s. 5 of the Cheques Act 1957. Thus, whether the warrants comply with the definition of a cheque or not, i.e. whether they are cheques or analogous documents, a bank collecting them is protected by s. 4 of the Cheques Act 1957, and a bank paying them when crossed is protected by s. 80 of the Act of 1882. It may be added here that in *Thairlwall* v. *G. N. Rly. Co.* (1910) it was held that a dividend warrant which ended with the words, "This warrant will not be honoured after three months from date unless specially indorsed by the secretary," was unconditional for the words merely denoted what the company thought was a reasonable time for presenting the warrant.

It was held in *Slingsby* v. *Westminster Bank Ltd.* (1931) that "dividend" includes sums payable as interest on Government Stock. The warrant in question was one for the payment of interest on War Stock (then five per cent, now $3\frac{1}{2}$ per cent) and the special statutory provisions relating to this Stock actually describe the half-yearly payments on it as "dividends". Secondly, although that warrant was drawn on the Bank of England by the Chief Accountant of that Bank it was held to be a cheque because the bank official, when signing it, was acting as the agent of the Government. This technicality would not arise in respect of interest warrants on corporation stocks or on company debentures or loan stock, but in any event interest warrants now appear to be covered by ss. 4 and 5 of the Cheques Act 1957, as well as s. 80 of the Act of 1882, whether they comply with the definition of a cheque or not.

Repeal

96.—(This section repealed certain enactments set out in Schedule 2, but the section and schedule were themselves repealed as spent or dead law by the Statute Law Revision Act 1898.)

Savings

97.—(1) The rules of bankruptcy relating to bills of exchange, promissory notes, and cheques shall continue to apply thereto, notwithstanding anything in this Act contained.

(2) The rules of common law, including the law merchant, save in so far as they are inconsistent with the express provisions of this Act, shall continue to apply to bills of exchange, promissory notes, and cheques.

(3) Nothing in this Act or in any repeal effected thereby shall affect:

(a) . . . any law or enactment for the time being in force relating to the revenue:

(b) The provisions of the Companies Act 1862, or Acts amending it, or any Act relating to joint stock banks or companies:

(c) The provisions of any Act relating to or confirming the privileges of the Bank of England or the Bank of Ireland respectively:

(d) The validity of any usage relating to dividend warrants, or the indorsements thereof.

The purpose of this savings section is to make it clear that other aspects of the general law which the Act might be thought to have affected remain unaltered. For example, the rules of bankruptcy relating to proof in respect of bills of exchange, promissory notes and cheques are preserved; they are now embodied in the Bankruptcy Act 1914—see Chapter 5 on Bankruptcy. The background of the common law, including the law merchant, is still relevant as regards negotiable instruments, except where it runs contrary to the Act's express provisions. The words omitted at the beginning of s. 97 (3) (a) were repealed by the Statute Law Revision Act 1898.

Saving of summary diligence in Scotland

98.— Nothing in this Act or in any repeal effected thereby shall extend or restrict, or in any way alter or affect the law and practice in Scotland in regard to summary diligence.

The Scots law procedure known as summary diligence, which is here expressly preserved, is founded on a protest for non-acceptance or non-payment which has to be registered within six months.

Construction with other acts, etc.

99.— Where any Act or document refers to any enactment repealed by this Act, the Act or document shall be construed, and shall operate, as if it referred to the corresponding provisions of this Act.

Parole evidence allowed in certain judicial proceedings in Scotland

100.— In any judicial proceedings in Scotland, any fact relating to a bill of exchange, bank cheque, or promissory note, which is relevant to any question of liability thereon, may be proved by parole evidence: Provided that this enactment shall not in any way affect the existing law and practice whereby the party who is, according to the tenor of any bill of exchange, bank cheque, or promissory note, debtor to the holder in the amount thereof, may be required, as a condition of obtaining a sist of diligence, or suspension of a charge, or threatened charge, to make such consignation, or to find such caution, as the court or judge before whom the cause is depending may require.

This section shall not apply to any case where the bill of exchange, bank cheque, or promissory note has undergone the sesennial prescription.

Proceedings in Scotland have been facilitated by allowing parole (oral) evidence to be given, though certain technicalities of Scots law and practice are expressed to be unaffected by this change in the law of evidence.

Schedules

Section 94.   FIRST SCHEDULE

Form of protest which may be used when the services of a notary cannot be obtained

Know all men that I, A. B. (householder), of   , in the county of   , in the United Kingdom, at the request of C. D., there being no notary public available, did on the   day of   , 188 , at   , demand payment (or acceptance) of the bill of exchange hereunder written, from E. F., to which demand he made answer (state answer, if any) wherefore I now, in the presence of G. H. and J. K., do protest the said bill of exchange.

(Signed) A. B. ⎫
        G. H. ⎬   Witnesses.
        J. K. ⎭

N.B.: The bill itself should be annexed, or a copy of the bill and all that is written thereon should be underwritten.

(The Second Schedule has been repealed—see the comment on s. 96.)

Index